THE BLUE GUIDES

Austria
Belgium and Luxembourg
Channel Islands
China*
Corsica
Crete
Cyprus
Egypt
England
France
Germany
Greece
Holland
Hungary*
Ireland
Northern Italy
Southern Italy
Morocco
Portugal
Scotland
Sicily
Spain
Switzerland
Turkey: Bursa to Antakya
Wales
Yugoslavia

Boston and Cambridge
Florence
Istanbul
Jerusalem
London
Moscow and Leningrad
New York
Oxford and Cambridge
Paris and Versailles
Rome and Environs
Venice

Cathedrals and Abbeys of England and Wales
Literary Britain and Ireland
Museums and Galleries of London
Victorian Architecture in Britain

*in preparation

Angel of the Resurrection: fresco in Mileševa Monastery, 1228

BLUE GUIDE

YUGOSLAVIA

Paul Blanchard

Maps and plans by John Flower

A & C Black
London

W W Norton
New York

First edition 1989

Published by A & C Black (Publishers) Limited
35 Bedford Row, London, WC1R 4JH

© A & C Black (Publishers) Limited

Published in the United States of America by
WW Norton & Company, Incorporated
500 Fifth Avenue, New York, NY 10110

Published simultaneously in Canada by
Penguin Book Canada Limited
2801 John Street, Markham, Ontario LR3 1B4

ISBN 0–7136–3034–5

A CIP catalogue record for this book
is available from the British Library.

ISBN 0–393–30485–X USA

Paul Blanchard has lived in Italy since 1975. He studied art history in
Florence and now works as editorial consultant to a Milan-based
journal of conemporary art as well as to numerous European art
publishers. He is also the author of Blue Guide Southern Italy.

Printed and bound in Great Britain by
Butler & Tanner Ltd, Frome and London

PREFACE

Yugoslavia has lately become one of the livelier holiday areas in Southern Europe, holding its own against Spain, Italy and Greece. And no wonder: with one of the lovelier coastlines on the Mediterranean and a great diversity of cultural assets, it's an ideal place to visit. But Yugoslavia offers far more than sun and sand, churches and paintings. It's a world of its own, a microcosm combining Eastern and Western, Turkish and European, Islamic and Christian influences. The art, language, customs, even the cuisine of Yugoslavia reflect this diversity, of which the Yugoslav people (or peoples: the modern nation counts about a dozen different ethnic groups) are rightly proud.

The present guide will, it is hoped, play a part in fostering an intelligent interest in this lovely region. Like other volumes in the *Blue Guide* series it is based on a series of routes by which the traveller by road or sea can explore not only the major places, but also the lesser-known areas in some depth. Even the most remote islands have been described in detail, and various inland routes have been laid out in the hope that sun-seekers may be encouraged to discover different beauties. The routes, while generally progressing from N to S, have been arranged also to reflect, as faithfully as possible, the personalities of Yugoslavia's six constituent republics (Slovenia, Croatia, Serbia, Bosnia-Hercegovina, Montenegro, and Macedonia) and two autonomous provinces (Vojvodina and Kosovo), with a view to helping the visitor to understand and appreciate their similarities and differences; for one of the more fascinating aspects of Yugoslavia consists precisely in the Yugoslavs themselves and in the subtle and complex system of sympathies and antipathies that, for historic, social, religious, or other reasons, bind them together or force them apart. Yugoslavia today is still a very delicate union, as the recent movements for self-determination in Slovenia and Kosovo testify; and the economic difficulties that the country has experienced in recent years have not been conducive to stability. Nevertheless there prevails a firm belief in the idea of a socialist republic of South Slavs that draws strength, and not weakness, from its internal contrasts.

The author is indebted to all those people who contributed in various ways to the making of the book—especially to cartographer John Flower, who has designed a full complement of attractive maps and plans; and to series editors Tom Neville and Gemma Davies, who have been most helpful in producing the guide. The chapters regarding the Adriatic coast are largely the work of the late Stuart Rossiter, who in 1969 edited *Blue Guide Yugoslavia: the Adriatic coast*, one of the first English-language publications devoted to this region. Acknowledgement is also due to the Turistički Savez Jugoslavije (Yugoslav Tourist Association) for their generous assistance, and particularly to Olga Kostić and her colleagues, whose co-operation was indispensable to the accurate preparation of the guide. Special thanks are owed to Guido Uni, who helped plan the author's travels; and to Predrag Djordjević, Suzana Znaor, Pave Brailo, and the many other friends who assisted in on-the-spot editing; to John Clark, who first awakened the author's interest in this fascinating land; and to Isabella Toraldo di Francia, who provided encouragement and support throughout the preparation of the book. The publishers would like to thank Flora Turner and Hrovje Šercar for providing a number of the illustrations.

As with other volumes in the *Blue Guide* series, suggestions for the correction or improvement of the guide will be gratefully welcomed.

A NOTE ON BLUE GUIDES

The Blue Guide series began in 1918 when Muirhead Guide-Books Limited published 'Blue Guide London and its Environs'. Finlay and James Muirhead already had extensive experience of guide-book publishing: before the First World War they had been the editors of the English editions of the German Baedekers, and by 1915 they had acquired the copyright of most of the famous 'Red' Handbooks from John Murray.

An agreement made with the French publishing house Hachette et Cie in 1917 led to the translation of Muirhead's London Guide, which became the first 'Guide Bleu'—Hachette had previously published the blue-covered 'Guides Joannes'. Subsequently, Hachette's 'Guide Bleu Paris et ses Environs' was adapted and published in London by Muirhead. The collaboration between the two publishing houses continued until 1933.

In 1931 Ernest Benn took over the Blue Guides, appointing Russell Muirhead, Finlay Muirhead's son, editor in 1934. The Muirhead's connection with the Blue Guides ended in 1963 when Stuart Rossiter, who had been working on the Guides since 1954, became house editor, revising and compiling several of the books himself.

The Blue Guides are now published by A & C Black, who acquired Ernest Benn in 1984, so continuing the tradition of guide-book publishing which began in 1826 with 'Black's Economical Tourist of Scotland'. The Blue Guide series continues to grow: there are now more than 30 titles in print with revised editions appearing regularly and many new Blue Guides in preparation.

'Blue Guides' is a registered trade mark.

EXPLANATIONS

Type. The main routes are described in large type. Smaller type is used for branch-routes and excursions, for historical and preliminary paragraphs, and (generally speaking) for descriptions of greater detail or minor importance.

Asterisks indicate points of special interest or excellence.

Distances are given from point to point throughout the route or subroute in kilometres. Mountain heights have been given in the text and on the atlas in metres.

Main Roads are designated in the text by the Yugoslav national (N) and European (E) numbers, as Yugoslavia is currently (1988) attempting a transition from the former to the latter system.

Populations have been given from the latest official figures (based on the census of 1981). They refer to the size of the administrative area, which is often much larger than the central urban area.

Abbreviations. In addition to generally accepted and self-explanatory abbreviations, the following occur in the guide:

Abp = archbishop
adm. = admission
Bp = bishop
C = century
c = circa
m. = nautical miles
min = minutes
R. = room(s)
Rte = route
Slov. = Slovene
Sv. = sveti (saint)
ul. = ulica (street)

CON FENTS

MAPS AND PLANS

GROUND PLANS

10 CONTENTS

INTRODUCTION

Geography. Yugoslavia is a federation of six republics: Slovenia, Croatia, Serbia, Bosnia-Hercegovina, Montenegro, and Macedonia. There are also two autonomous provinces—Kosovo and Vojvodina—which form part of Serbia.

The country covers an area of 255,804km² in SE Europe, between 40°51′ and 46°53′ latitude north, and 13°23′ and 23°2′ longitude east. It is bordered on the N by Austria and Hungary, on the E by Romania and Bulgaria, on the S by Greece and Albania, and on the W by Italy, with which it also shares the maritime frontier of the Adriatic Sea. With an area of 255,804km², it is ninth in size among the European nations.

About 70 per cent of Yugoslavia is hilly or mountainous. The lowland areas, which include the valley of the Danube and part of the great Pannonian Plain, are mainly concentrated in the NE part of the country. The highest mountains are, of course, the Alps, culminating in Mt Veliki Triglav, 2864m. Alpine Yugoslavia is limited to Slovenia, a green mountainous region traversed by the limestone-dolomitic chains of the Caravanche and Julian Alps (*Karavanke, Julijske Alpe*). To the S these give way to the Karst (*Kras*), which name indicates both a distinct geographical area and the phenomena of erosion and modelling of the calcareous rock which in this area are particularly common. This great limestone desert can be considered the N limit of the majestic Dinaric Alps (*Dinara Alpe*), which stretch some 700km along the W edge of the Balkan Peninsula, towering over the Adriatic. Occupying c 40 per cent of the territory of Yugoslavia, the Dinaric Alps form the backbone of W Croatia, Bosnia-Hercegovina, and Montenegro. In the S part of the country they extend eastward to join up with the Šar and Jablanica chains, the first spurs of the Rodope Massif, and the westernmost fringe of the Balkan Range.

In the W the Dinaric Alps plunge into the sea, forming the rocky coast and myriad islands for which Yugoslavia is justly famous. From the Bay of Trieste to Dubrovnik there are more than 1500 islands, with a cumulative coastline c 4000km long. Together with the deep, fjordlike bays that characterise the coast, they testify to the process of slow, constant submersion that has distinguished this part of the Adriatic littoral in recent geological times.

Climate. Climatic conditions in Yugoslavia are closely related to the country's geographic position and orographic structure; to the influence of the moist W winds which blow in from the Adriatic; and to that of the cold, dry continental winds which blow across the Pannonian Plain.

The climate of the Adriatic coast is tendentially Mediterranean, with rainfall generally less than 1000mm annually (but reaching peaks of over 3000mm in the hinterland). In winter the littoral is often swept by the *bura*, the cold, dry NE wind that blows down at high speeds off the Karst highlands. Considerable differences exist between the temperatures of the coast and those of the interior. The monthly averages in July remain around 24°C along the coast, whereas in the interior they waver between 18° and 20°. In January the differences become more marked: 6–9° on the coast, below zero in the interior. During the summer the coast is often swept by the *scirocco*, a hot, dry wind, the opposite of the winter bura. Slovenia is particularly rainy, the Julian Alps receiving over 3000mm of precipitation annually, with high points in summer and winter. In this alpine region temperature is usually related to altitude; at Ljubljana (293m) the mean monthly values range from 2° in January to 19° in July, with c1250mm of precipitation annually. Roughly the same conditions apply in the mountainous areas of Serbia and Macedonia, where the continental climate brings considerable differences between summer and winter temperatures. Precipitation is most intense between November and May, with abundant snows. In Macedonia the climate is mitigated by the influences of the Aegean Sea, which ride up the valley of the Vadar on the cold, dry winter wind called the *vadarac*. On the plains traversed by the Danube and its tributaries, finally, continental features again prevail, with precipitation (800–1000mm annually) prevalently in the spring and autumn, and temperatures, in Zagreb and Belgrade, ranging between 3° in January and 20–21° in July.

Flora and Fauna. The flora of Yugoslavia, where it has not been altered by agriculture, faithfully reflects the prevailing climatic conditions. On the Adriatic coast and in many valleys of the interior still affected by the sea, Mediterranean vegetation prevails, with evergreen maquis up to an altitude of c 400m and species more resistant to cold, such as *Juniperus oxycedrus*, *Phyllyrea*, *Quercus coccifera*, and *Quercus trojana*, above. In the mountainous areas of the interior thrive the combinations of deciduous and evergreen forests typical of Central Europe, distributed according to altitude. Below 600m, especially in Macedonia, *sibljak* (an association of bushy coppice with hornbeam, linden, oak, hazelnut, hawthorn, cornel, etc.) prevails, giving way at higher altitudes to *hrastalak* (maple, chestnut, and beech) which, higher still (1200–1500m), is replaced by conifers and firs, including the characteristic loricated pine (*Pinus leucodermis*). Above 2000m the arboreous vegetation yields to juniper, lily of the valley, and alpine pastures.

The fauna of Yugoslavia is, generally speaking, like that found elsewhere in Central Europe. The mountainous terrain (which is still largely covered by forests) and low demographic pressure, have favoured the preservation of a large number of wild species. These include deer, wolf, fox, wild boar, roe deer, ermine, chamois, bear, lynx, jackal, hare, squirrel, and marten; eagle, hawk, pheasant, and marsh fowl (heron, stork, wild duck, etc.); and numerous varieties of fresh- and salt-water fish (notably carp, perch, sturgeon, pike and trout; and sardine, mackerel, Spanish mackerel, tuna, sprat, grey mullet and dentex). The Dinaric mountains are inhabited by the dangerous horned viper or *poskik* (*Vipera ammodytes*); and in Bosnia and Hercegovina the red turtle (*Testudo graeca*) is quite common. Throughout Yugoslavia the areas of special natural interest are carefully protected.

Population. The latest census (1981) reports the population of Yugoslavia around 22,000,000. This figure includes 4,428,000 Croats, 1,340,000 Macedonians, 579,000 Montenegrins, 2,000,000 Muslims, 8,140,000 Serbs, 1,754,000 Slovenes, 1,219,000 persons who declare themselves as Yugoslavs; as well as 1,730,000 Albanians, 427,000 Hungarians, 101,000 Turks, 80,000 Slovaks, 168,000 Romanies, 36,000 Bulgarians, 55,000 Rumanians, 23,000 Ruthenians, 20,000 Czechs, 15,000 Italians, and 13,000 Ukrainians. The average population density is c 88 persons per square kilometre. The present trend is toward a decline in the birth and mortality rates, and an overall population increment.

Economy. Yugoslavia is a communist country, in which the means of production and distribution of goods are collectively owned. Unlike other communist peoples of E Europe, however, the Yugoslavs take an openly critical view of the centralised, authoritarian model of the Soviet Union. The cornerstone of the Yugoslav economic system is in fact the principle of self-management, by which workers play a direct role in managing the businesses in which they are employed. This principle makes it possible to eliminate a great deal of bureaucratic red tape, giving individual firms considerable leeway in gauging production, directing development, and planning investments. Today industrial activities account for just under 50 per cent of the GNP, although 40 per cent of the population is still employed in the primary sector. Growth, unfortunately, has not kept up with demand, and inflationary tendencies, accompanied by a considerable devaluation of the dinar, have driven prices sky high (with respect to domestic wages; for foreigners Yugoslavia is still a bargain), while the increased volume of consumption has added to the deficit in the balance of trade. With a view to curbing these tendencies, the Yugoslav government has recently opened the economy to private capital.

Political Order. The Constitution of 1974 defines Yugoslavia as a federative socialist republic (*socijalistička federativna republika*). The central legislative body, the Federal Assembly, is composed of 308 members elected for a term of four years. It is divided into two houses, the Federal Council and the Council of Republics and Provinces. The Federal Council has 220 members elected from among the delegates of the self-managed organisations and communities and the socio-political organisations, 30 representing each republic and 20 representing the autonomous provinces. The Council of Republics and Provinces counts 88 members elected by the various republics and autonomous provinces, 12 for each republic and eight for each province.

The Federal Assembly elects, for a term of five years, the nine members of the Collegial Presidency of the Republic, and the President of the League of Yugoslav Communists (the only legally recognised political party); the members of the Presidency in turn elect one of their number President of the Republic, for a five-year term. Executive power is entrusted to the Federal Executive Council, composed of at least three members for every republic and at least two for every province. The President of the Federal Executive Council is elected by the Federal Assembly on recommendation of the President of the Republic.

HISTORICAL INTRODUCTION: PAST AS PRESENT

By *Mark Wheeler*

'The land,' enthused the advertisement, 'is neither Greek nor Turkish, Renaissance nor Roman, Viennese nor Venetian, Alpine nor Adriatic, but a little bit of all of them.' Appearing in *The New Yorker* in 1988 under the heading 'Was it 1928 or was it last night?', the National Tourist Office's blurb goes on to acclaim Yugoslavia as 'a Grand Tour in a single country where the present is tangled with the past and the prices date from another age.' With a touch more whimsy and no loss of accuracy the copywriter might have continued to pile up alliterative pairings (neither Balkan nor Baroque, Capitalist nor Communist, *Mitteleuropa* nor Middle East, Peasant nor Proletarian, Fish nor Foul) before coming to the real selling point: Yugoslavia is 'Europe like it used to be' because all that history, variety, comfort and romance is going 'for a song'.

Making the best of economic enfeeblement demonstrates, no doubt, an admirable resourcefulness. What is interesting and apposite about the advertisement, however, is the effort it makes to sell a complicated set of historical images in a market which is thought to appreciate them. Yet history does count in Yugoslavia, and the visitor in search of more than sun and sea should at least be alive to it; not just to appreciate its visible artefacts, but sometimes to account for their absence; not simply to comprehend the country's kaleidoscopic ethnic, cultural and economic diversity, but also to have some inkling of its contemporary politics. (The style, obviously, is catching.) Yugoslavia is far from unique in these respects, and has, of course, no *more* history than other lands. Neither, though, does it have *less*, regardless of the likelihood that its past is either largely unknown to the Western tourist or is imagined to have begun only in 1918 or 1945. What distinguishes Yugoslavia from other countries is that its history is also the separate histories of the nations and national minorities inhabiting it, of the many overlords they have had through the centuries, and of the weight both these factors continue to exert on ordinary people's lives.

It would not, for example, be exceptional for the traveller, engaging other patrons in conversation at an open air café in one of Ljubljana's tidy baroque squares, to find himself the beneficiary of an impromptu lecture on the Slovenes' central European identity, their consequential commitment to a civil—and civilised—society in which the state affords the citizen as much space as possible for his or her private endeavours, and concluding with a self-congratulatory enumeration of those features of the Slovenes' character which set them apart from their neighbours to the south and east: industriousness, efficiency, levelheadedness and modesty.

In Zagreb, meantime, the local variation on the old Viennese quip about the East starting at the Ringstrasse can still be overheard in the elegant *Gradska kavana*, albeit with greater topographical exactitude: the Balkans obviously begin on the River Sava to the south of the stolid and quintessentially Habsburg 'new town'. Self-revealing jokes about slow-witted Bosnians or strident complaints about the brake on Croatian prosperity represented by so-called political factories in the south and an iniquitous regime for the retention by the federal government of Croatia's hard currency earnings will often follow. For a sense of having been exploited, whether by Vienna and Budapest in the last century or by Belgrade in this, is common currency in Croatian political discourse.

To portray the Croats as cultivating their grievances and the Slovenes as celebrating their virtues may be to indulge in stereotypes, but that in large measure is how people think of themselves and others. In both these cases the point is that the putative speaker feels different from and not a little superior to those Yugoslavs (decidedly *not* regarded as compatriots) on whom the stamp of history has been less benign, whose degree of enlightenment is thus low, and who yet possess the power adversely to affect the complainant's own circumstances. The visitor, observing the skull-capped Albanians who collect Ljubljana's rubbish and the tongue-tied incomprehension of the Bosnians who drive its buses, or admiring the colourful peasant bustle of Zagreb's large central market and its grandiose new mosque, or savouring the smell of roasting peppers that pervades the residential districts of both cities, may conclude, on the other hand, that a good bit of the Balkans has invaded central Europe.

In Belgrade, where older residents still occasionally refer to Zemun across the Sava as Austria (that is, 'Europe') and where—despite the newly pedestrianised shopping precincts, chic boutiques and crowded private enterprise restaurants—late trains, foul toilets and other lapses from modernity can be met with the explanatory question 'what do you expect after 500 years of the Turks?', historical imprecations are no less in evidence. (The Croat riposte, by the way, is to inquire why Turkey is still a backward country. The answer: 500 years of ruling over the Serbs.) Nowadays a prominent strain of Serb complaint relates to the sufferings of the Serb minority at the hands of the Albanian majority in the semi-detached province of Kosovo, a region Serbs regard as the cradle of their medieval greatness and the reconquest of which in 1912 was felt to avenge the national cataclysm at Kosovo Polje in 1389. It afflicts them mightily that Croats and Slovenes fail to evince an equivalent concern over Kosovo's ethnic alienation. What good is the Yugoslav state to them, they ask, if it cannot even guarantee a secure existence in their own land to the people who sacrificed so much in order to create it?

History in Yugoslavia, then, is no mere academic pursuit; nor is it a set of commonly held myths and legends, celebrated achievements and much mourned tragedies. All efforts to make it into such an instrument of socialisation, whether on behalf of the old royalist or the new socialist orders, have failed. It is, rather, an argument without end, and one in which virtually everyone consciously or unconsciously participates. Why this should be so will emerge below. First, however, it is necessary to deal with a few of the misconceptions which foreigners especially, in their quest for simplifying generalisations, have perpetrated.

What Yugoslavia is Not

Seventy years since its formation as the Kingdom of Serbs, Croats and Slovenes under the Serbian Karadjordjević dynasty, and 45 years after its re-formation as a socialist federation under the Communist Party, the Yugoslav (or South Slav) state is still widely viewed as a newcomer among independent countries, as a multinational anomaly in a world of nation-states, and as a happy exception to most of the rules that are meant to apply to Communist-ruled lands. Partaking simultaneously of the geographical, historical, cultural, religious, economic and political influences we term 'Eastern' and 'Western', the peoples of Yugoslavia have been variously perceived as a bridge between the two, as a bulwark against the one or the other, as a collective barometer offering timely warnings of impending international storms, and as tiresome malcontents whose obscure quarrels ought not to be allowed to get out of hand.

Latterly, the cleavage between the developed 'north' and the underdeveloped 'south', between the rich and the poor, has been superimposed upon the older, east-west divide. The inhabitants of Yugoslavia's north-western regions enjoy today a standard of living—and are animated by material and political expectations— akin to those of their Italian and Austrian neighbours; while many Yugoslavs to the south-east endure almost Third World conditions and the attendant psychological frustrations as they watch the glittering images of programmes like 'Dynasty' on their television screens. This gulf has contributed in recent years to the revival of yet another notion (referred to above) about the ostensible place of some of the Yugoslav peoples in a central European political and cultural community: a sort of Habsburg Empire without the tears. The southerners, meanwhile, are either consigned to the Oriental sloth and despotism to which they are heir, or suffered to migrate north to do the jobs the locals will not touch.

Although quite a few perhaps rash generalisations have already appeared here, the only generalisation about Yugoslavia which can be made without fear of contradiction or qualification is that it is a cause of despair to all who would generalise. Consider, for example, the three initial propositions set out above: Yugoslavia is a 'new' state; its multinational composition is exceptional; and its Communist regime is uniquely beneficent. The first and second are mostly false; while the third is no longer so true as once it was.

Yugoslavia is not an especially 'new' country. A political scientist calculated in the mid-1970s that the average lifespan of a polity in the 19C and 20C has been 32 years. By this measure Yugoslavia was already relatively elderly. Even on the European mainland several states have come and more have gone since the 'successor states' were born of the disintegration of the Romanov, Hohenzollern, Habsburg and Ottoman empires between 1912 and 1920. The two most important creations since 1945, the Federal Republic of Germany and the German Democratic Republic, illustrate a vital distinction which is also highly relevant to Yugoslavia: namely, the difference between 'nations' and 'states'. As the two (or three) German states show, young states can play host to old nations. But so too can old states (France, Spain and Britain, to name but three) find themselves facing challenges mounted by new or reviving nations.

The middle-aged Yugoslav state is, as it happens, home both to old and new nations, not to mention numerous national minorities whose presumptive motherlands are elsewhere. A good many of the men who helped found and give shape to the Yugoslav kingdom at the end of the Great War imagined they were creating a nation as well as a state. Not only were their efforts vain, but they called into question whether or not Yugoslavia had any future, even as the loose association of nations it has subsequently become. Although an inherently invidious exercise, and one much resented by nationalists straining against history to confer upon their nations the dignity of an ancient pedigree, the South Slav nations of Yugoslavia can be so divided. The old nations are the Serbs, Croats and Slovenes, honoured as such in the official title of the original kingdom and long possessed of separate national identities and ideologies based in part on real or mythical state traditions. The new nations are the Montenegrins (who had a state before 1918, but who usually regarded themselves as taller and fiercer Serbs), the Macedonians (Orthodox Slavs for whose allegiance Bulgarians, Greeks and Serbs have competed rancorously since the late 19C), and the Muslims of Bosnia-Hercegovina (Slav converts to Islam long claimed by both Serb and Croat nationalists as properly theirs, but whose distinctive identity, founded primarily and ironically on Islam's antinational ethos, has only been affirmed since the 1960s). The emergence of these new nations is, depending on one's politics and nationalism, either the result of communist manipulation or the culmination of long-stymied processes of 'ethnogenesis' which only a federal and socialist Yugoslavia had both the wit and wisdom to recognise.

Despite the formidable complexity of its multinational population, neither is Yugoslavia the anomaly it sometimes appears. Multi-national states in fact predominate in the contemporary world, notwithstanding the hold which the nation-state ideal has long exercised on the thinking of both Europeans and their former colonial subjects. The distinctiveness of Yugoslavia in Europe stems, rather, from the extent to which it is multinational: from the facts that one nation—the Serb—possesses a plurality but not a majority (giving rise to the oft-quoted conundrum that the country's curse is to have both too many and too few Serbs), that the six republics and two autonomous provinces of Serbia which make up the federation are themselves in most cases highly multinational, that the two largest national minorities—the Albanian and Hungarian—have their natural homelands across Yugoslavia's fron-tiers, and that an intricately consensual theory and practice of government has had to be elaborated to deal with these inescap-able realities.

That government is, of course, in the hands of the League of Communists, so named in 1952 to distinguish it and Yugoslavia from the Stalinist parties and regimes to the east which had expelled Tito and his comrades from the fold in 1948. It was this shock which impelled them soon afterwards to chart an indepen-dent course in both foreign and domestic affairs. The novel spectacle of Communists defying Stalin, then proclaiming workers' self-management and nonalignment between the superpowers, taming their secret police and expanding the purview of the rule of law, embracing market mechanisms in the economy, opening their borders to foreigners and Yugoslavs alike, and developing an ever more decentralised and genuinely federalised system of government—all these factors conferred upon Yugoslavia in the lifetime of its charismatic father figure, Josip Broz Tito, a status, importance and interest disproportionate to the state's power, size, wealth or strategic significance. Since Tito's death, not only has the much-vaunted Yugoslav experiment faltered in a morass of debt, inflation, strikes, financial scandals and governmental paralysis, but rather more exciting (if no more far-reaching) initiatives in Com-munist reform have been undertaken in the once immobile Soviet bloc. Yugoslavia has been relegated to the sidelines of academic and media attention, a veritable land that time forgot, if not quite in the comfortably prosperous and nostalgic sense implied by the ad agency copywriter quoted at the outset. The country may yet recover its star billing, but if it does so it could be for retrogression towards a primitive socialism of the Rumanian variety rather than for a resumption of liberating and mould-breaking innovation. At the time of writing no more can be hazarded.

The Yugoslavs before Yugoslavia

English-language introductions to Yugoslav history tend to treat the South Slav peoples' separate experiences before 1918 largely in terms of their preparation for the apotheosis of unification. While natural enough, especially in view of the still widespread belief that multi-national Yugoslavia is an anomaly, if not indeed an offence against nature, such an approach has its pitfalls. Two of these should be mentioned before an essentially similar interpretive framework is employed here.

In the first place, emphasising the Yugoslav theme relegates much of what contemporaries would have considered important to the margins. Thus the two great 19C proponents of the Yugoslav idea, the Croats Ljudevit Gaj and Bishop Josip Jurej Strossmayer, usually receive more—and more positive—attention than do the *Kaisertreu* Baron Josip Jelačić of 1848 fame and the fiery tribune of late 19C Croatian nationalism, Ante Starčević. This hierarchy of interest and approbation would have struck politically aware Croats as perverse, even on the eve of the First World War and the creation of the circumstances which finally made Yugoslav union a practical proposition. In analogous fashion, Serbia's 19C rulers, party leaders and men of letters have been ranked according to the contributions they made to forging closer links with the other South Slavs and re-casting the Serbian state in the mould of a Yugoslav Piedmont. That these were not necessarily the same thing has posed difficulties for historians intent on identifying the progenitors of Yugoslavia. For the Serbs most successful in projecting their state's unifying power often also possessed scant sympathy for the cultural, linguistic, religious and political equality and reciprocity which underlay the Yugoslav idea as understood by Croats and Slovenes. Just as the achievements of Bismarck and Cavour inspired mixed feelings among idealistic adherents of German and Italian unity, so too have Vuk Karadžić (author of the Serb doctrine which substituted language for religion as the principal criterion of nationality), Ilija Garašanin (would-be architect of a revived Serbian empire), and Nikola Pašić (premier at the time of Serbia's expansion into Yugoslavia) elicited as much dread as respect.

Another pitfall inherent in tracing backwards the origins of the Yugoslav state does even greater violence to historical realities. This is the practice of applying modern notions of nation, of national identity and of nationalism to ages and states in which they were either unknown or possessed an entirely different content. Just because 19C and 20C South Slav historians, writers and politicians professed to find relevant precedents in their early states' powers, glories and territorial extents does not mean, for instance, that Tomislav's 10C kingdom was *Croatian* or Stefan Dušan's 14C empire was *Serbian* in any modern sense. Nor does the fact that these and other medieval dynastic states which arose among the South Slavs were 'multinational' make them precursors of Yugoslavia. Finding themselves, centuries later, inhabiting other great multinational realms in which they were denied the status to which they had come to aspire, South Slav nationalists commonly invoked a romanticised past in which their 'nations' had ruled and their dynasties had been the equals of the Arpads or Habsburgs or Ottomans. Such visions of ie past gave nationalists the courage and the dubious constitutional arguments they needed to fight their contemporary battles, but they are a better guide to the uses to which history can be put than they are to early South Slav history.

Early Times

The visitor to Yugoslavia may, with lesser or greater effort, see abundant evidence of the country's habitation before the advent of the Slavs. Roman *fora* and *castra* are there aplenty, as are some of Europe's most famous archaeological sites of prehistoric provenance. Even more obvious are the artefacts of subsequent civilisations, whether Venetian campanili, Ottoman mosques, hans and bridges, Habsburg townscapes, or post-war Stalinist structures. Up until a few years ago it was possible also to point to the illogicality of the road and railway networks as a legacy both of an unhelpful geography (which denies the country any obvious centre) and of long centuries of partition by alien overlords. But for the sake of coherence and brevity it will be necessary here to focus on what Yugoslavs regard as their history, and not on that of their lands' many other occupiers.

The future South Slavs had reached the left bank of the Danube basin from their original homeland beyond the Carpathians by the late 4C AD. In the 6C and 7C they swarmed across, moving in advance of or in association with Asiatic hordes such as the Huns and the Avars. They overran and settled almost all of the Balkan peninsula. In the north and middle of the peninsula they either assimilated the indigenous Romanised and Hellenised populations or set them in flight to highland or west coast redoubts. In the south they were themselves Hellenised. Given that one aspect of the antagonism between Serbian and Albanian nationalism in this century has been the controversy over whether or not the Albanians are the lineal descendants of the autochthonous Illyrians, and hence have some sort of prior claim on the lands they occupy, it will be apparent that no history is too ancient or too obscure to become a political battleground. Inherently inconclusive debates have also raged over the origins and names of the peoples who became known as the Serbs and Croats. (The Slovenes simply retained the generic name for Slavs.) The Serbs and Croats were presumably leading tribes in the areas they settled: the former to the east and south of the River Neretva, the latter to the west and north. Because the border between the eastern and western halves of the former Roman Empire, and latterly between their Byzantine and Frankish successors and the 'true' churches they claimed to embody, also passed through this territory, the initially undifferentiated Slav settlers were to find themselves exposed to competing political, cultural and religious influences as they, in turn, imposed their dawning ethnicity upon it.

The ancestors of the Slovenes, who come to rest in the upper Sava valley between the eastern Alps and the Adriatic, and adjacent to lands lately occupied by the Germanic Lombards and Franks, fell relatively quickly under Western dominance. Conversion to Latin Christianity came from the Franks during the 8C and 9C, was followed by incorporation in the Holy Roman Empire in the 10C, and the piecemeal acquisition by the Habsburgs in the 13C and 14C of the feudal duchies, marches and counties into which the Slovene lands had come to be divided. Only their brief inclusion in Samo's 7C Slavonic empire and Ottokar's 13C Bohemian-based state permitted 19C Slovene nationalists to lay claim to the 'historic' status on which

that century set such store. Given the failure of a Slovene-speaking
nobility either to establish a state or to maintain itself, this was an
implausible claim, rendered more tenuous by the territorial attrition
suffered by the Slovenes at the hands of the Germans and Italians
over the intervening centuries.

More important in retrospect in preserving the Slovenes for their
19C national awakening was the impact of the Reformation. This was
both a testimony to the extent to which their fortunes had become
bound up with those of central Europe, and a reflection of the
challenge posed even there by the Ottoman Turks between the 15C
and 17C. Uniquely in the South Slav lands, Protestantism spread from
the thin stratum of German nobles and burghers intent upon resisting
the dynasty's militarising centralism to a rebellious Slovene peasantry
endeavouring to evade an ever more onerous enserfment. The
Habsburg-sponsored Counter-Reformation was destined to make
short shrift of this social and religious ferment, but the production in
the meantime of Bibles, catechisms and grammars in the Slovene
vernacular provided a basis for the creation of a Slovene national
consciousness 300 years later. In the absence of Slovene 'state's
rights', language rights were made to serve.

The Croat tribes, who accepted the Roman variant of Christianity
through the mediation of the still Latinate Dalmatian towns (and
despite vigorous Byzantine proselytization), possessed geopolitical
advantages denied the Slovenes when it came to making a bid for
statehood. The 9C confusion caused by the erruption of the Bulgars
into the eastern Balkans, the arrival of the Magyars on the Danubian
plain, and the rise of Venice in the Adriatic provided an opportunity.
A native feudal state, based on northern Dalmatia, emerged in the
interstices of Byzantine and Frankish power. Tomislav became the
first Croatian and South Slav king when he secured a crown from the
pope in 925. This independent kingdom endured inside fluctuating
frontiers until 1102, when the Croatian estates elected the Hungarian
King Koloman sovereign of the entire Triune Kingdom of Croatia,
Slavonia and Dalmatia following a decade of quarrels over the
succession.

The exact nature of Croatia's 800-year subordination to Hungary
was to become a matter of fierce dispute, particularly in the period of
Austrian enlightened despotism and the subsequent age of nationalism: was Croatia merely a conquered land, possessed of no special
constitutional rights, or was it, rather, a separate kingdom linked with
Hungary only by a dynastic compact, the terms and conditions of
which guaranteed its nobles 'nation' autonomy in their own realm? In
fact it was both, depending on the balance of power between king
and nobles, Christians and Turks. For when the Ottoman danger was
most pressing, and much of Slavonia, all of Bosnia and part of 'civil'
Croatia had been engulfed, quibbles about Croatian rights were
abjured. On the other hand, the Croatian diet's election of Ferdinand
of Habsburg as King of Croatia in 1527, in the wake of the Battle of
Mohács and the assumption by the Habsburgs of the territorially
denunded Crown of St. Stephen, did at least represent a marker for
better times to come.

During the next three centuries, however, Croatia's position was
unenviable. It was reduced to a 'relic of relics' as its locus shifted
northwards and westwards to the region around Zagreb. Dalmatia,
over which Hungary and Venice had warred repeatedly from the 12C
to the 15C, fell finally (with the exception of Ragusa/Dubrovnik) to
Venice in 1420. From then on the shifting Venetian-Ottoman border,

like its Habsburg-Ottoman counterpart, was the scene of recurrent wars, ritualised freebooting and a steady infusion of Slav refugees. The latter development meant that Latinate Dalmatia was thoroughly Slavicised. But the gradual retreat of the Ottoman Empire from its late 17C apogee benefitted the Croats' Venetian and (especially) Habsburg rulers rather than the Croatian nobility and its vestigial statehood. The despoiled and depopulated lands reclaimed in Hungary, Slavonia and Croatia were constituted as a Military Frontier under direct imperial control and resettled by soldier-colonists either in flight from Ottoman territory or recruited from the Habsburgs' far-flung dominions. Not only were former Croatian lands not reunited with 'civil' Croatia before 1881, but they became heavily Serb in population, a feature which was to complicate and envenom Croat efforts in that latter century to resuscitate an historically and territorially-based conception of nationhood. The commingling of peoples in whom discreet national consciousnesses were evident by the 18C turned out to be—and to remain—one of the principal arguments in favour of a Yugoslav state.

The people who were to become Serbs took their Christianity and their basic political and cultural conceptions from Byzantium. Disciples of Cyril and Methodius, 'the Apostles to the Slavs', brought them the Slavonic liturgy in the 9C. This was to prove a potent force in the Serbs' integration. Like the Slavicised Bulgars before them, having created a state and a church in the image of Byzantium and under its nominal suzerainty, the Serb rulers came to aspire to supplant their inspirator, and so to assume the mantle of ecumenical empire which could no longer fit the enfeebled second Rome. In its rise from the late 12C, however, when the several Serb proto-states in Hercegovina and Montenegro were united under the Nemanja dynasty of Raška (centred on the Ibar valley in southern Serbia), the Serbian kingdom was not oriented exclusively towards the East. Its links with the West—diplomatic, economic and artistic (as the surviving monasteries of the Raška school attest)—were strong. The first Serb king to bear the title obtained his crown from the pope in 1217, benefitting from the fall of Byzantium to the Crusaders in 1204. Two years later his brother, the monk and future Saint Sava, secured from Constantinople the coveted right to organise an independent (or autocephalous) Serbian church. Successive kings expanded the confines of the state at Byzantium's and Bulgaria's expense, enhanced its wealth by reactivating mines founded by the Romans and encouraging trade, and provided it with a codified legal system. What they failed to do, despite the symbiosis of church and state, was to subdue their nobles. This incomplete feudalisation was to prove the kingdom's undoing.

Medieval Serbia reached its zenith under Stefan Dušan in the mid 14C. His realm stretched from his capital at Skopje to the Danube and Sava in the north, to the Gulf of Corinth in the south, to the Adriatic in the west, and to the Struma and Mesta valleys in the east. In 1346 the archbishopric at Peć was raised to the status of patriarchate and Dušan assumed the style 'Emperor and Autocrat of the Serbs and Greeks, the Bulgarians and Albanians'. At his death in 1355 he appeared to be on the brink of achieving his twin ambitions of leading Europe's defence against the Ottomans and seizing the emperor's city (Tsarigrad, Constantinople) for himself. Ironically, it was the Serbian challenge which had moved the Byzantines to invite the Turks to establish themselves on the Thracian coast the year before. Now, with the partition of Dušan's empire among the great lords he had kept in check but whom his son was unable to control, a vacuum was created which the Ottomans from the south and the Hungarians and Venetians from the north hastened to fill.

The symbolic birth of Serbian statehood came with the Battle of Kosovo on *Vidovdan* (St. Vitus' Day, 28 June) 1389 when Sultan Murad I defeated Christian armies led by Prince Lazar Hrebeljanović, ruler of the principal Serb successor state. The battle, which was regarded as portentous both because of the long efforts to forge a Christian alliance that preceded it and for the carnage it produced, was in reality less significant for the fate of the Balkans than the 1371 Battle of Chirmen on the river Maritsa. It was Kosovo, however, which became the Serbian epic, and the deaths of Lazar and Murad on the field of battle the centre of a cycle of folk poetry which mourned the passing of Serb greatness, provided explanations both sacred and profane, and offered the consolations of martyrdom now and revenge later. In fact, several so-called despotates endured for nearly a century or more, either as vassals of the Ottomans or Hungarians or, in the case of Montenegro, as an inaccessible stronghold which it was not worth the Turks' while to subdue until 1499. The most important of the Serbian rump states, the capital and centre of which moved north along the Morava valley from Lazar's court at Kruševac to its final and massively fortified resting place at Smederevo on the Danube, had fallen to the Turks in 1459. It was in the century after Kosovo, and in an atmosphere of accelerating apocalypse, that much of medieval Serbia's cultural flowering took place.

The submission of the remnants of Dušan's empire to the Ottomans left only Bosnia and Ragusa as effectively independent South Slav states. The Bosnian kingdom, although nominally an Hungarian vassal, expanded as Serbia declined until it, too, fell to the Turks in 1463. It is remembered largely on account of its ecclesiastical heterodoxy. Bogomilism, a dualistic creed akin to the Cathar (or Albigensian) heresy of northern Italy and southern France, became Bosnia's state church, offering as it did an integrative principle in a border region subjected to conflicting political and religious pressures. The heresy, however, put Bosnia outside the pale of Catholic Europe's sympathies, and when the Bosnian king renounced it in 1440 in order to win help against the Turks, he was deserted by his nobles. They, in turn, were quick to embrace the faith of their Ottoman conquerors. Bosnia, like Albania, became a land of three religions. Unlike Albania, however, it also became a land of three nationalities, since notwithstanding their common Serbo-Croat speech, Bosnians adopted the Ottoman identification of religion and nation. The Catholics were Croats, the Orthodox were Serbs and the Muslims were Turks.

The city-state of Ragusa, known as Dubrovnik to the Slavs who had become its majority population by the end of the 13C, was founded in the 7C by Romanised colonists from today's Cavtat. It was already a maritime and overland trading power by the time it fell to Venice in 1205. Under Venetian dominion for the next century and a half, it evolved its distinctive institutions of oligarchic patrician rule. Thereafter a republic under nominal Hungarian suzerainty, it exchanged Hungarian for Turkish protection in 1397 and flourished as a commercial and cultural intermediary between the Ottoman Empire and the west. Embracing only 421 square miles of territory on the mainland and offshore islands, and supporting a population of just 30,000 at its height in the mid-15C, Dubrovnik was as famed for its artful diplomacy and Renaissance arts and sciences as it was for its banking and trading acumen. Devastated by an earthquake in 1667,

Dubrovnik afterwards declined along with its Ottoman suzerain until it was finally extinguished by Napoleon in 1806. Aside from its intrinsic interest, the importance of Dubrovnik's place in South Slav history is two-fold. First of all, its citizens' trading activities throughout the Ottoman Balkans kept a small window open to developments in the West. Perhaps more importantly, the discovery by both Serbs and Croats in the 19C that such an exemplar of Western high culture and high finance had existed in their midst during what had come to be viewed as the long night of Turkish slavery—and twilight of Habsburg oppression—was no small fillip to their self-esteem.

The 'Lost' Centuries

By the 16C, then, not only were nearly all South Slavs under foreign rule, but all were being affected in one way or another by the Ottomans' advance into Europe. Reduction to the status of a share-cropping peasantry was the lot of the vast majority of Orthodox Christians who found themselves inside an Islamic empire dedicated, above all else, to production of the sinews of war. Such of their nobles who had not perished or fled in the course of the Ottomans' long wars of conquest, or who had not apostatised (as in Bosnia) in order to retain their privileges, were replaced by Turkish feudatories. This certainly represented a boon to the mass of peasants chafing under native feudal regimes far harsher than that introduced by the Ottomans, but the effect of such a levelling down was to cut the Balkans off from those developments which were already transforming the western half of the continent. The fact that the one institution which remained, and indeed was accorded an enhanced administrative, judicial and social role in the Ottoman scheme of things—the Orthodox Church—was as profoundly hostile to the Latin West as were the Turks reinforced the parochial isolation that was to become the Balkan norm. It may not have mattered much that the Serb peasant, his priest and his priest's bishop knew little and cared less about the glories of the Renaissance or the ferment of the Reformation, but it was ultimately to make a vast difference to their national lives that they were excluded for so long from the west European population explosion, from the breakup of the feudal order and the emancipation and monetisation of agriculture, from the rise of cities, from the boom in commerce and overseas exploration and trade, and from the consolidation of centralised, bureaucratic and interventionist monarchies. If the Mediterranan, generally, was relegated in these years to a position secondary to that of north-western Europe, the rank of the Ottoman south-east was tertiary at best.

Although the Sultan's Orthodox South Slav flock appeared peculiarly disadvantaged as the tide of history turned against the Ottomans almost at the moment of their greatest achievement, the fate of the Catholic Croats and Slovenes under their Habsburg sovereigns was not that much better. Their inheritance was relative—if not absolute—backwardness as the pace of change accelerated in western Europe. They were, moreover, at greater risk of denationalisation than were their brethren under Ottoman rule as their lands were settled and governed by more powerful or numerous neighbours. For the inherent geographical and human obstacles to modernisation in east central Europe were compounded by political ones, and particularly by the Habsburgs' decision to organise their diverse realm as a military machine, both for defence against the Turks and for the exaltation of their own power. Far from disappearing, feudalism was given a new lease on life. Towns, in any case places of alien habitation, atrophied; commerce was inhibited; the population slumped. The Slovenes, already a peasant people, became more firmly bound to the soil they tilled for foreign lords implanted by the dynasty. The Croats, their nobility decimated and impoverished by the almost constant warfare along the Ottoman frontier, also assumed an overwhelmingly peasant guise. The territories which began to be reclaimed from the Turks by the end of the 16C either became the fiefs of German and Hungarian magnates or were added to the Military Frontier.

This portion of 'central Europe' was scarcely distinguishable from the 'Balkan barbarism' to the south-east. Each new war or raid across a highly permeable frontier set large numbers of people in motion. As we have seen, in the South Slav lands this was mainly a northward flow of Orthodox Serbs: from southern highlands to depopulated valleys inside the Ottoman realm, and then, with the next war or incursion, across the shifting border into the Military Frontier in Croatia and southern Hungary (known as Vojvodina by the 18C). But all over the peninsula others, too, were on the move. Albanians, for example, although no doubt always present, arrived in force to replace Serbs on the plains of Kosovo. Besides its wholly positive impact on Balkan cuisine and wholly negative effect on the region's level of development, the principal legacy of the Ottoman conquest and of the protracted struggle to roll it back was an ethnic mosaic of phenomenal intricacy, even by east European standards. This, combined with the animosity of Christian for Muslim (and vice versa) and of Catholic for Orthodox (and vice versa), would give Balkan nationalism its special intensity, even when all concerned spoke the same language and 'enjoyed' the same standard of living.

National Revivals

Nationalism is both a political idea and a response to economic and social change. The fact that it arrived in south-eastern Europe so soon after its appearance in the West during the French Revolution belies the conventional image of a region sunk in medieval stupor and adrift from the continent of which it had once formed an integral part. The explanation that Napoleon brought it directly—and in its Yugoslav incarnation to boot—when he carved out the short-lived Illyrian Provinces (1809–14) from former Venetian and Habsburg territories in Istria, the Slovene lands, north-west Croatia, and Dalmatia is far too simple. On the other hand, the alacrity with which nationalism spread among South Slavs on either side of the Ottoman-Habsburg divide is testimony to the extent to which conditions in both empires were coming to seem insupportable. Nationalism provided the corpus of beliefs and assumptions which persuaded first a handful of people, and then whole peoples, not only that things were bad, but, more importantly, that there was an alternative.

The agents of nationalism were not, of course, always or even often conscious of their role. The efforts of Selim III and Joseph II to reform, revitalise and rationalise their respective realms were (like Napoleon's imperialism) designed, among much else, to preclude challenges from below, not to stimulate them. The *uskoks* (pirates) of Senj on the Croatian littoral, the *hajduks* (brigands) of the Ottoman interior, and the rebellious clans of Montenegro were naturally innocent of any thought that their primitive depredations might

:ovide patriotic inspiration to their contemporaries or their posterity. Nor, for that matter, did the Serb churchmen, Croat nobles, Slovene poets, and 'new men' of commerce and the professions among all three peoples necessarily know what they were doing, despite the fact that they are rightly credited with presiding over the Yugoslavs' re-entry into European history.

Among Serbs and Croats national consciousness had never disappeared. It and the memories of statehood with which it was associated had been nourished with varying degrees of effectiveness by the Serbian Orthodox Church and the Croatian nobility throughout their years of 'Babylonian captivity'. By the late 18C, however, both these traditional institutions were coming to the end of their periods of exclusive guardianship. Croatia's nobles were too weak to withstand either the centralising reforms of the dynasty's enlightened despotism or the countervailing and expansive pretensions of the gentry nationalism to which it had given rise among their would-be Hungarian masters. The Croatian nobility needed allies, and found them in the nascent middle class of journalists, lawyers, scholars and merchants which was coming into existence in the early 19C, even in a relatively backward Habsburg borderland. These men (and a few women) added the ideas of romantic nationalism, based on the proposition that each nation displayed its unique genius through its language, to the defence of Croatia's state's rights. Although in some cases barely capable of speaking or writing their native tongue themselves, their success by the end of the 1830s in fostering the use of the dialect predominant among both Croats *and* Serbs revivified and extended to the whole people the Croatian concept of nationhood, gave birth to an explicitly political programme of Croatian territorial unity, and laid the foundations for a Yugoslav movement.

This national revival was known by its principal begetter, Ljudevit Gaj, as the 'Illyrian Movement'. The name demonstrated his all-embracing, pan-South Slav intent, as well as his rudimentary historical knowledge, since it was based on the erroneous belief that the Yugoslavs were both the descendants of the ancient Illyrians and the original Slavs. The Illyrian Movement was destined to expire in the 1848 revolutions, when Croats confronted most starkly the irresolv-able dilemma that was now their lot inside the Habsburg Empire: should they remain true to the emperor in Vienna in the hope of crumbs from the table of victorious reaction, or side with the Hungarian revolution in spite of the likelihood that it would deny to Croatia what it demanded for itself. In 1848 their Ban (or viceroy), Jelačić, chose the emperor, and Croatia afterwards received as its reward what Hungary got as punishment. Divided by territorial and social boundaries both old and new, and lacking a foreign patron, the Croats were simply not numerous, cohesive or important enough to serve as anything more than a cat's-paw in the long duel between Vienna and Budapest that was the bane and foundation of the monarchy's politics to the very end.

When the empire was reconstituted as Austria-Hungary in 1867, Croatia-Slavonia was left to work out its own terms with Budapest. The resulting compact, although promising a certain autonomy, actually exposed Croats to increased Magyarisation, economic penetration, and political frustration. Istria and Dalmatia were retained by Vienna. The 'Balkanisation' of Croatia was completed in 1878 when, following the Congress of Berlin, Austria-Hungary took Bosnia and Hercegovina from the Turks. Despite Croat hopes to the contrary, these provinces were not added to Croatia-Slavonia. Instead, and in

order to maintain the precarious Austro-Hungarian balance and g.
no encouragement to Croats or Serbs, a special yet typically Hab
burg solution was found: the region would be governed by the join
imperial finance ministry in Vienna. In such a situation it was not
surprising that Croats (and Serbs too) found it necessary to re-invent
Yugoslavism, although opinions varied as to whether a future Yugoslavia should be a third force inside the Habsburg realm or an
independent state anchored in the Balkans. The great ecumenist and
promoter of cultural Yugoslavism, Bishop Strossmayer, opted for the
latter. But while the empire endured as a great power—and as a
German-Hungarian duopoly—neither option was available. A larger
proportion of Croatia's tiny enfranchised class gave itself over to a
more classically egocentric variant of nationalism, and demanded an
independent 'greater Croatia' in which 'mountain Croats' (i.e.
Slovenes) and 'apostate Croats' (i.e. Serbs) would join to swell the
ranks required to overawe both Vienna and Budapest and reclaim
Croatia's historical-territorial patrimony. This too was a non-starter,
not least because the lesser breeds refused to play.

Napoleon created the first 'Slovenia', but its tenure was brief and its
legacy small. Inhabiting a half-dozen Habsburg provinces in only one
of which they formed an overwhelming majority (Carniola), the
Slovenes had benefited materially from being at one remove from the
centuries' of confrontation with the Turks and were to benefit more
from living astride one of the main axes of industrialisation in 19C
central Europe. The other side of this particular coin, however, was
that their small numbers, lowly status, and territorial-political subdivi-
sion in units dominated by Germans and Italians made political action
on a national basis difficult even after all feudal inhibitions had been
removed. Their national revivalists therefore saw their task as to save
their people by saving and elevating their language, and then to fight
for the right to use it in schools, courts and provincial administrations.
They were determined to break the equation between illiterate
peasant and Slovene, and so for many years the printing of primers and
poems was given a higher priority than the production of political
programmes. The predominantly clerical politicians who emerged
after the extension of the franchise in the 1860s would have liked to see
a united and autonomous Slovenia inside the monarchy. In practice,
they settled for smaller concessions. Yugoslavism was only a vague
attraction, outweighed by fears of being gobbled up by Italians—or
Croats—should they find themselves cut loose from Vienna.

The dilemmas which confronted Croats and Slovenes in the 19C
were not unknown to the Serbs, naturally enough since so many of
them lived in the same Habsburg realm. But there was one crucial
difference: the Serbs also had a state. In fact, they had two states and
three homegrown dynasties. Serbia and Montenegro, in common
with the other national states which emerged from the Ottoman
Empire before 1914, were not all their leaders or peoples desired.
Indeed, they were regarded as mere beginnings on the path to glory;
and a sense of incompleteness dominated their politics. This quest for
territorial aggrandisement, either in the cause of 'liberating' their
unredeemed brethren or re-creating their medieval empires (no
matter who might now inhabit the lands concerned) was not just the
risible small power imperialism it frequently seemed to condescend-
ing west Europeans. It was also based on the entirely accurate
perception that they were too small and too poor otherwise to catch up
with the Western nations to which and on which they compared and
modelled themselves. (The setting of such standards for imitation

s, of course, Europe's principal gift to the wider world.) Meanwhile, e existence of two Serb states, each with its own dynastic and reign policy interests, was bound to complicate as well as to sustain efforts to provide a Yugoslav answer to the Habsburg monarchy's increasingly ominous 'South Slav question'.

By the beginning of the 19C the Ottoman Empire had been in decline for three centuries. While the battles and territorial losses which registered its descent had been far away, and while the integrity of the 'Pax Ottomanica' had been maintained in the areas inhabited by them, the Serbs were little affected. The wars and attendant migrations of the 17C and 18C changed all that. After their last desperate assault on Vienna in 1683, the Turks were no longer able to strike deep into Europe. But Habsburg armies began regularly to penetrate what had heretofore been the core of the Ottoman Balkans, and to call upon the resident Christians to rise up in their support when they arrived. The war ended by the Treaty of Karlowitz (Sremski Karlovci) in 1699 not only restored most of Hungary and Slavonia to Vienna's control, and so made Serbia a frontier province, but resulted in a mass exodus of Serbs (with their patriarch at their head) when the Austrians abandoned their campaign far to the south. In 1718 the Habsburgs actually took northern Serbia (Šumadija) into their realm. Its retrocession in 1739 precipitated another great Serb migration into Vojvodina under the patriarchal banner. In the meantime, wars on the Venetian frontier had permitted the mountaineers of south-central Montenegro, bound together by their Orthodox metropolitans of the Petrović-Njegoš clan, to defy their distant sovereign and to cultivate the myth that they had never in fact submitted to Ottoman power. The defection of the Montenegrins was symptomatic of what was happening generally on the empire's fringes in the 18C. The provinces furthest from Istanbul were in revolt, most seriously so when led by malcontented members of what was meant to be the Ottoman fighting and ruling caste. The transfer to the rural Balkans of the mayhem and disorder which had long been endemic in the capital was to provide the spur to Christian rebellion.

However inspiring the legend of Montenegrin freedom, the growth of the Serb colony in southern Hungary was far more important to the emergence of a semi-modern Serb elite possessed of a fully modern doctrine of national rebirth. When in 1767, the sultan abolished the Peć Patriarchate in reprisal for its incumbents' manifest disloyalty, the centre of Serb gravity shifted decisively to the north: to the metropolitanate at Sremski Karlovci in Vojvodina. It was not long, however, before the church, having preserved and then led its flock out of the wilderness, surrendered national leadership to the men of commerce, arms and enlightenment who flourished in the new environment. The Serbs owed their opportunities for cultural emancipation to the Habsburgs, as they did their possession of an increasing body of military expertise; but the wealth which sustained the creation and consumption of the products of the Serb renaissance was derived in large measure from the growing trade across the Habsburg-Ottoman frontier.

The relegation of the Ottoman state to an exporter of agricultural produce made the Serbs' position athwart its northern border increasingly significant. And it was more through commerce than by participation in their co-nationals' cultural revival that the Serbs of the Belgrade pashalik learned about the outside world and their own comparative deprivation. The livestock traders, freight forwarders and consignment agents who emerged from the peasant villages t

make marks and modest fortunes for themselves comprised
potential secular leadership every bit as important as the or
developing among the more sophisticated Habsburg Serbs
Moreover, their rise excited the envy and enmity of the unemployed
Muslim soldiery which roamed the countryside in search of the status
and booty that were no longer to be had from foreign wars. The
struggle for control of the rural economy set the Serbs and their
traditional Muslim feudatories against the rampaging janissaries. In
the early 1790s the reforming sultan, Selim III, authorised the Serbs of
the Belgrade pashalik to take the defence of law and order into their
own hands and to expel the janissaries. The Serbs developed a taste
for self-rule as quickly as they had taken to making money. By the end
of the decade, however, war with France and Muslim outrage at the
arming of Christians compelled the sultan to renege. The janissaries
returned and set about having their vengeance. It was against the
janissaries, and their plans to decapitate—literally—several hundred
of the Serbs' new men of substance, that the populace rose in 1804.

The Serbian National State

The first Serbian uprising quickly became the first Balkan national
revolution. Its elected leader, Djordje Petrović (known as Karadjordje,
eponym of the dynasty and epitome—as a former *hajduk*, Habsburg
NCO and pig merchant—of Serbia's new class of notables), decided
by 1807 to abandon all pretence that Serbs were fighting in defence of
the sultan's prerogatives, and to declare for full independence. The
learned Habsburg Serbs were at hand to provide the essential
statecraft, money for arms, and nationalist ideology. Although the
rebels held out for nine years, defeating several Ottoman offensives
and expelling or killing all the pashalik's Turks, the complexities of
European diplomacy during the Napoleonic wars denied them the
foreign patron they required if they were to make good their victory.
Their most likely supporter, Russia, was otherwise engaged against
Napoleon when the crunch came. The rebel state disintegrated in
1813 as Ottoman armies approached and Karadjordje fled to Habsburg territory. The reign of terror which followed disposed Serbs to try
again in 1815. This time they elected as their leader one of the
notables, Miloš Obrenović, whom the Turks had entrusted with
pacifying the province. Unlike Karadjordje, whom he later had
murdered lest his strategy and authority be undermined, Miloš was
prepared to settle for an autonomous regime in which he was
recognised as supreme prince. With Europe now at peace, he also had
the inestimable advantage of Russian diplomatic backing in his
negotiations with the Porte.

The Serbian state's progress—from *de facto* autonomy in 1817, to
full-fledged autonomy under the hereditary rule of the Obrenović
family in 1830, to internationally recognised autonomy under a
Karadjordjević prince in 1856, to independent principality (again
under the Obrenović dynasty) in 1878, to kingdom in 1882, to
democratic Karadjordjević monarchy in 1903—was obviously gradual, and depended in large measure on the varying answers offered
by the great powers to the perennial 'Eastern Question'. It was also, as
the alternation in dynasties hints, fraught with internal conflict. Of
greater long term significance than the dynastic struggle, however,
were the concomitant struggles for territory and modernity. The
ambition to gather together all Serbs and all 'Serb lands' was part and
parcel of the Serbs' national ideology; but territorial growth seemed,

too, a vital prerequisite to attaining the European level of development to which educated Serbs had come to aspire. A liberal and constitutional regime appeared to be another essential attribute of modernity.

Prince Miloš, who never learned to read or sleep in a bed, and whose political values were Christian analogues of the Ottoman despotism, guile, ruthlessness, and lust for personal enrichment with which he had grown up, was not the ideal philosopher-prince some Serbs thought they required. On the other hand, his identification of his own interests with those of his tiny realm (38,000 sq. miles in 1830) did make him a zealous promoter of its autonomy and a paternalistic guardian of the peasant proprietors who had formed the vast majority of its population (700,000 in the same year) since the enforced departure of the Turks. Yet even the would-be pasha Miloš was obliged to call some sort of state machine into existence and occasionally to take the counsel of his more enlightened subjects. By forming an army and administration, initially staffed largely by Habsburg Serbs, Miloš both launched Serbia on the road to political modernisation and created a rival locus of power and self-interest which would render him and his capricious tyranny redundant by the end of the 1830s.

Before the age of popular politics dawned in the 1880s, Serbia was ruled or misruled either by its prince or by its bureaucracy. The peasant masses were involved only to the extent that they were periodically called upon to sanction some momentous change or themselves rose up in rebellion against their masters. Dynasty and bureaucracy were equally intent upon subduing the localistic and anarchistic tendencies which the final phase of Ottoman decay had bequeathed and the national revolution enhanced. Their efforts went under the names of absolutism or constitutionalism, conservatism or liberalism, but always implied the imposition of a centralistic order by the forces of light in the capital upon the forces of darkness in the countryside. Such an understanding of politics was to cause trouble when the Serbian state expanded its embrace to include peoples with different historical experiences.

Miloš's bureaucratic successors, the so-called Defenders of the Constitution, ruled under the titular authority of Karadjordje's son, Prince Alexander, during the 1840s and '50s. Their regime was notable for its modernising zeal and the charting of an expansionist programme which was to preoccupy Serb statesmen for years to come. No progress was made, however, between 1833 (when Miloš secured the cession of six districts which had formed part of the revolutionary state) and 1878 (when the Congress of Berlin awarded Serbia the Niš region in order to help quash ideas of a big Bulgaria and in spite of the Serbs' poor showing in the preceding wars). In the meantime, during the 1860s, a more substantial gain had been won by the country's most successful 19C prince, Michael Obrenović, when he manoeuvred the Turks out of their remaining—and symbolic— fortresses. Prince Michael's larger project—the formation of a Balkan-wide alliance to expel the Ottomans from Europe—came to naught before the window of opportunity opened by the Habsburg wars in Italy and with Prussia was closed and Michael himself fell victim to an assassin.

Like Italy and the other revived Balkan states, Serbia had a big appetite but weak teeth. (None yet had cause to doubt their digestive systems.) Moreover, and in common with the Rumanians, the Serbs laboured under the disadvantage of hungering as much for lands in

the possession of a great power—Austria-Hungary—as for those i
the palsied hands of the Turks. The triple humiliation of defeat by the
Ottomans, desertion by Russia for the sake of the Bulgarians, and the
distraint of Bosnia and Hercegovina by Vienna between 1876 and
1878 were by no means assuaged by the acquisition of the Niš-Pirot
region or the formal abolition of Ottoman suzerainty. Prince Milan
Obrenović was well aware of his dynasty's precarious position. Many
people thought the now secularised Petrović-Njegoš dynasty of
Montenegro would cut a more dashing figure, including Prince
Nikola himself. In addition, there was the Karadjordjević pretender,
Peter, who had fought with distinction in the Bosnian uprising that
had precipitated the whole 1875–78 crisis. Most worrying of all, Milan
faced a new sort of domestic opposition in the Radical Party, which
was actually seeking the support of the abused peasantry with the
promise of local self-government.

Milan endeavoured to strengthen his grip by entering a secret
alliance with Vienna which both made Serbia a Habsburg satellite
and permitted him to proclaim himself king. Having taken the
precaution of securing the right to garrison the Sandžak of Novi Pazar
(which separated Serbia from Montenegro) when they occupied
Bosnia and Hercegovina, the Austrians advised Milan to concentrate
his territorial ambitions on Macedonia. His first venture out was to
make war on Bulgaria when, in 1885, it united with Eastern Rumelia.
The war was a disaster; and only Vienna's intercession saved Milan
and Serbia. Nonetheless, it was from this time that Serbia and Greece
began seriously to contest the Bulgarians' ecclesiastical and educational head start in the race to win the hearts and minds of the
people inhabiting the last great chunk of territory belonging to the
Turks in Europe. Medieval precedent gave each state the 'right' to the
area; and the knowledge that its acquisition would make the winner
the dominant Balkan power provided the incentive. Terrorist bands
soon followed the priests and teachers.

Tired of crushing rebellions, subverting conspiracies and imprison-
ing his opponents, Milan abdicated in favour of his under-age son,
Alexander, in 1889 after one last *jeu*: a liberal constitution. The young
king was not long restrained either by his regents or by his father's
constitution. Nor was he as solicitous towards Vienna and public
opinion as he ought to have been. His marriage to his mistress, a
widow who could not bear children, was regarded with repugnance:
not only because of the offence it offered to patriarchal values, but
also because it and Alexander's subsequent efforts to redeem himself
and ingratiate his queen made Serbia a laughing-stock. The last
Obrenović and his consort met a gruesome end in a military plot in
1903. Although the conspirators had aimed to rid Serbia of ignominy,
and had secured the sanction of Vienna, St. Petersburg and Peter
Karadjordjević before they acted, newspaper accounts of the gore of
the regicide and the popular gloating with which it was met repelled
and titillated Europe. Serbia's woes appeared endless.

The South Slavs and the Coming of the Great War

Yet the Karadjordjević restoration and the installation thereafter of a
genuinely democratic regime under Radical auspices launched
Serbia on its most dynamic period of development. For the first time
since the 1860s the country exerted a potent attraction on the
Habsburg Yugoslavs. King Peter may have trembled at the thought of
crossing or disciplining the conspirators to whom he owed his throne,

but the Radicals (who had put their early social radicalism behind them and joined the establishment) proved self-confident managers of domestic and foreign affairs. Their nationalism was so ardent, in fact, as to alarm Vienna, which soon signalled its disquiet by imposing a customs embargo on Serbia's vital livestock exports. Instead of bringing the Serbs to heel—or, as the Viennese press had it, causing them to suffocate in their own swine fat—the 'Pig War' led to Serbia's partial economic emancipation and the first stirrings of industrialisation. A more complex process of socio-economic differentiation was taking place in a society which had been divided principally between capital and countryside, governors and governed. Nationalism, however, continued to provide a powerful cement.

The re-emergence of Serbia as the Yugoslav Piedmont would not have worried Vienna so much had it not been for a simultaneous revival in pro-Yugoslav sentiment and practical Serbo-Croat political co-operation in the monarchy itself. In Croatia and Dalmatia the Habsburg policy of setting Croats against Serbs (by favouring the Serb minority) came unstuck when Croat and Serb politicians combined in 1905 to offer their support to the Hungarians' latest challenge to Vienna. In return they aimed to get the reunification of the Triune Kingdom and democratic reforms. Their attempt to exert leverage failed, but the Croato-Serb coalition endured and won a majority in the subsequent elections to the Sabor (diet). It was solidified further by the Zagreb 'treason trials' of 1908 in which prominent Serb and Dalmatian politicians faced trumped-up charges of plotting on behalf of Serbia. The monarchy's reputation for at least maintaining the rule of law took a severe knock, while the prestige of Serbia was enhanced.

It was as a consequence of events in Bosnia and Hercegovina, however, that the Balkan and Yugoslav logjams were broken. Since their occupation of the provinces the Habsburg authorities had conciliated the Muslim element at the expense of the Christian majority. A near-feudal regime had been perpetuated on the land, though a certain measure of colonial-style economic development had taken place. The resulting social and national fissures were deep. But as in the monarchy proper, divide and rule was now breaking down; pro-Serb and pro-Yugoslav feelings (which could seem the same thing) were in the ascendant, abetted by secret societies of both local and Serbian origin. Among half-educated young nationalists faith in the liberating power of the individual act of violence was also growing. Confronted with such an opposition, alarmed by its transcendence of religious and national differences, and keen to deal a devastating blow to Serbia's pretensions, Vienna took advantage of the Young Turk Revolution and Russian diplomatic ineptitude formally to annex the two provinces in 1908.

The annexation crisis set much in train. Forced to accept this *fait accompli* by the Austrians and their German allies, the Serbs and their Russian allies determined never again to back down and to work to have their revenge. The Russians attempted to get the Balkan states (including Turkey) to combine against Austria. The Balkan governments, more than ever convinced that the time had come to eject the Turks from Macedonia, forged instead a series of offensive alliances against the Porte. The result was the First Balkan War, which Montenegro was given the honour of starting in 1912. The powers were shocked that states they regarded as mere playthings should be so bold as to dispose of Turkey-in-Europe. The Austrians, moreover, were nearly apoplectic at the hydra-headed Serbian challenge. The

Serbs had been content in the pre-war negotiations to concede the bulk of Macedonia to Bulgaria, expecting that they and the Greeks would be left to partition the Albanian lands. Austria now forbade this arrangement and—ironically for a multinational empire—sponsored with Italy the formation of an independent Albania.

Denied the access to the sea they had come to cherish since the Pig War, the Serbs demanded 'compensation' in the Macedonian areas they already occupied. This Bulgaria refused, attacking its former Serb and Greek allies in 1913. The victory of the latter in the Second Balkan War (in which Romania and Turkey also joined) left Serbia and Greece to engorge themselves on Macedonian territory. Serbia doubled in size and acquired a common border with a much-enlarged Montenegro. Serbian prestige and self-confidence reached new heights. Having despatched Turkey and fulfilled their destiny in the south, Serbs spoke openly of the coming contest with the colossus to the north for its unredeemed Serbs.

This was mostly bravado, despite the presence of secret societies like the army-based Unification or Death (better known as the Black Hand) which took such ideas seriously. The government, aware of the cost which the Balkan Wars had already exacted and locked in struggle with the military over the governance of the new territories, was in no mood to provoke the Dual Monarchy. In Vienna matters appeared differently. The Ottomans' demise seemed to portend a similar fate for the Habsburgs if decisive action were not taken to put an end to the Serbian and Yugoslav threats. The assassination in Sarajevo on 28 June 1914 (*Vidovdan!*) of the heir apparent, Archduke Franz Ferdinand, by a Bosnian Serb with presumed links to Belgrade provided the pretext Vienna needed. Yet the Austrians did not behave with the ruthless urgency required if they were to eradicate Serbia before Europe's system of alliances transformed a small war in the Balkans into a world war. For Serbia and for Yugoslavia, on the other hand, only a great war would do.

The Making and Unmaking of the First Yugoslavia

The Great War made Yugoslavia a possibility, but only if the Entente (or Allied) Powers won and Austria-Hungary disintegrated. Neither event looked likely until well into 1917. In the meantime both the Serbian government and the political leaders of the Habsburg South Slavs were required to keep their options open and to pursue their own interests as best they could while their peoples fought on opposing sides. This was not a situation conducive to the elaboration of well thought-out blueprints or the maintenance of perfect harmony. Nobody knew—though many claimed to intuit—what it was the people themselves wanted. Just because pro-Yugoslav sentiment had been so vague, so replete with mutually contradictory notions held simultaneously, and so totally devoid of practicality before war began, the process of creating a Yugoslav state was bound to be a leap in the dark.

The Yugoslav Committee, composed of self-appointed representatives of the Habsburg Yugoslavs, established itself in France and Britain soon after the war began with the objects of promoting the cause of a Yugoslav state and bridging the gap created by the presence of Yugoslavs in both belligerent camps. Its relations with the Serbian government, which also found itself in exile after the success in 1915 of the third Austro-German attempt to crush Serbia, were not smooth. Although the government had declared the creation of a

Yugoslav state *its* war aim before Serbia was overrun, its allies' indifference or hostility to the idea, coupled with their refusal before 1918 to consider making the destruction of Austria-Hungary *their* war aim, compelled Pašić and his colleagues to consider what other offers came their way. The leaders of the Yugoslav Committee rightly concluded that Pašić's government was far more interested in liberating Serbs and acquiring an outlet to the Adriatic than it was in uniting on terms of equality with Croats and Slovenes. The Serb leaders, for their part, harboured equally well-founded suspicions about the extent to which the Yugoslav Committeemen could really claim to speak on behalf of their people. Serbia's practical politicians were happy for the more polished Habsburg Yugoslavs to conduct their propaganda activities abroad, but refused either to accord them a status equal to themselves or to subscribe to their idealistic vision of 'one people with three names'—unless that meant the others were willing to be Serbs in all but name.

The force of events, not the force of idealism, made the Yugoslav state. The Treaty of London, by which the Entente purchased Italian co-belligerency in 1915, contained secret provisions promising Italy Yugoslav-inhabited regions on and at the head of the Adriatic. When these leaked out the Habsburg South Slavs in uniform fought with renewed vigour for their emperor, but those in western exile redoubled their efforts to reach an agreement with Serbia which would save their lands and exempt them from the fate of the vanquished. Only in the summer of 1917, following the Serbs' loss of their tsarist Russian mentor and their acquisition of a new and more pro-Yugoslav American ally, did they summon the Yugoslav Committee to their Corfu headquarters to draw up a provisional contract of marriage. The Corfu Declaration hailed the forthcoming union of Serbs, Croats and Slovenes in a constitutional, democratic and parliamentary monarchy under the house of Karadjordjević, but offered no hints about the future state's internal ordering beyond promises of universal manhood suffrage and full equality for the three Yugoslav names, flags and religions, and for the two languages and alphabets.

The momentum accelerated when, early in 1918, the Allies abandoned hope of a separate peace with Austria-Hungary and began, instead, to encourage its captive peoples to revolt in the name of national self-determination. By the autumn, hungry and full of revolutionaries animated as much by Bolshevism as by nationalism, the monarchy duly fell apart. Talks and arguments continued among the exiles, but the centre of action shifted to the Yugoslav lands. A National Council was formed in Zagreb by the politicians who had lately represented their peoples in the disintegrating empire's various diets. They both declared their independence of the Habsburgs and signalled their desire to unite with Serbia and Montenegro. They also begged the Serbs to send their army to protect them from the advancing Italians and the jacquerie and land seizures which appeared to constitute the peasant masses' vision of national liberation. Having broken through with its allies on the Salonika Front during the autumn, the Serbian government was in a position to comply, but also to drive a hard bargain. Delegates of the National Council journeyed to newly-liberated Belgrade and, on 1 December 1918, affiliated themselves with the Prince Regent Alexander's proclamation of the Kingdom of Serbs, Croats and Slovenes. The Montenegrins had already deposed their dynasty and joined Serbia.

A Yugoslav state, created by Yugoslavs, thus existed well before Allied statesmen gathered in Paris to make the peace. The conventional depiction of it and the other 'successor states' as the handiwork of the Treaty of Versailles is quite simply wrong. Its abiding usage reflects the fact that none of these states was to be quite the brilliant success its promoters promised, as well as the retrospective regret of Hitler's and Mussolini's Western appeasers in the 1930s that they should have got mixed up at all in such an intractable region. What the Paris Peace Conference did do was give the new Kingdom some of its frontiers, while washing its collective hands of the impossible task of sorting out the Italo-Yugoslav territorial quarrel in the north Adriatic. Given the balance of power, this was bad for the Yugoslavs, who were forced to yield several hundred thousand Croats and Slovenes to Italian rule.

The absence of recognised frontiers was, however, only one of many lacunae. The new state had no common laws, tariffs, railways, currency, administration, or army. Nor, it was soon apparent, did it possess a common purpose. Its formation was a geopolitical necessity, but too many of its citizens were unhappy either at their presence inside it (mainly the national minorities, but also a good many Macedonians) or at the form it was taking (a grievance of most Croats and many Slovenes and Montenegrins). It was natural that the Serbs, stirred both by their horrific losses to war and disease and by their superhuman triumphs since 1912, should have been determined to make the new state in their own image and for their own recompense, but it was also unwise. It rubbed Croats especially the wrong way, and seemed to demote them to the same second class status they had occupied under the Habsburgs. Their discontent with the state's evolution into the centralistic and Serb-dominated realm it became with the adoption of the *Vidovdan* constitution in 1921 was not all the fault of the Serbs. For the Croats were, in effect, trying to change the rules of the game after it had started. Failing that, they refused to play, boycotting, for instance, the constituent assembly which debated and enacted the constitution. Such a tactic merely made it easier for the Serbs—allying themselves with the ex-Habsburg advocates of a single Yugoslav nation and buying the votes of the ex-elite of Bosnian Muslims with offers of compensation for their expropriated estates—to get the result they wanted.

The upsurge in dissent in the kingdom's early years not only reflected conditions which were objectively awful in a devastated, disorganised and poverty-stricken land, but also the fact that people who had never before taken part in political life, let alone done so together, found themselves invited to cast their votes. Women, of course, were still excluded, but the participation of all men changed the basis of politics. Among the exiguous industrial working class, and in regions where no other national or religious vehicle of protest was available, it meant the rise of a large Communist Party, which was soon to be banned. In Croatia it transformed the Republican Peasant Party into the almost monolithic voice of the nation, and rendered politically irrelevant those middle class parties which had been most keen on Yugoslavia and most prepared to sacrifice the Croatian national-historical identity on the altar of Yugoslavism. Thus, no matter what the Serbs argued initially, the rules of the game *had* changed. Always respectful of political realities, a good many Serb politicians came to appreciate this fact, and were ready during the mid-1920s to engage with the Croatian Peasant Party in the sort of horse-trading and deal-making they practiced successfully with the Slovenes. But the Croats' eccentric tribune, Stjepan Radić, either asked the impossible (a Croat republic) or sabotaged such temporary coalitions as he joined.

By 1928, when Radić and several other Croatian deputies were shot on the floor of parliament, the pretence of democratic government could be maintained no longer. The absence of any consensus about the state's constitutional order—centralism or federalism, monarchy or republic—had rendered government by consent impossible. Little had been accomplished by way of integrating the diverse parts of the state or implementing the long-promised land reform. The Serb parties were splitting and re-splitting. The Croats withdrew to form their own counter-parliament in Zagreb. The international situation was no longer friendly to successor states. The mundane but vital routine of administration ground to a halt. King Alexander took to constructing and deconstructing cabinets within the palace walls. Then, in January 1929, he declared a personal dictatorship.

Despite the predictable appearance to the contrary, produced by stifling dissent and smashing heads, this was no solution either. The king's principal innovations—changing the state's name to Yugoslavia, banning all narrowly national parties, abolishing the old historical provinces, and insisting that Yugoslavs were really one people—succeeded only in giving Yugoslavia and Yugoslavism a bad name. For, as soon became obvious, the king's vision of Yugoslavia was merely that of a monarcho-militarist Great Serbia. The new leader of the Croatian Peasant Party, Vladko Maček, had, like many others sickened by the parliamentary charade, initially expected great things of the king. He would give Croatia the autonomy parliament refused. Although disappointed—and in gaol—for much of the dictatorship, Maček's faith in the Karadjordjević dynasty proved better placed than had the Croats' 19C trust in the Habsburgs.

The rigours of the dictatorship were ameliorated somewhat in 1931 by the king's decision to grant a new constitution and to permit a sham parliamentary life. They were mitigated further after his death at the hands of assassins in Marseilles in 1934. The plot to kill Alexander was a paradigm of the ills which beset Yugoslavia. It was hatched by the Croatian *Ustaše* (or Rebels, a separatist and terrorist band with fascist pretensions founded in 1929 by Ante Pavelić). The trigger was pulled by a hit-man on loan from the Bulgarian-backed IMRO (Internal Macedonian Revolutionary Organisation). The cash came from fascist Italy. And facilities and training were provided by Hungary. The hopes of all of them that Yugoslavia would fracture proved vain. The regency which the late king's testament provided should rule during the minority of his son, King Peter II, was duly established under the effective control of his cousin, Prince Paul.

Prince Paul, an aesthete out of sympathy with the Serbian military ethos of Alexander's regime, nonetheless professed to regard the 1931 constitution as immutable. Not until the eve of the Second World War would he consider Croatian devolution. He refused throughout to countenance the restoration of democratic government, though the political parties (except the Communists) were permitted to operate and, indeed, to combine in a united opposition bloc to contest the rigged elections called by the variously named government parties. The united opposition linked Serbs, Croats and Slovenes (as the electoral law requiring nationwide lists effectively ensured) and was generally perceived as the moral victor in the 1935 and 1938 elections; but its component parties were never able to resolve the question of whether the reinstatement of democracy should precede Croatian autonomy or vice versa. This gave Prince Paul his opening when, in 1939, he ditched his strongman premier and signed a separate peace with Maček establishing an autonomous Croatia. The Serbs and Slovenes were left high and dry.

Yugoslavia's diplomatic and economic weaknesses proved mutually reinforcing in the 1930s. Approximately 70 per cent of the population was dependent upon farming. Yet Yugoslav agriculture was mostly backward technically, unproductive, undercapitalised, and overmanned. Perhaps as many as half the people who attempted to eke out a living from the land were surplus to requirements and a drag on the rest. Industrialisation, urbanisation and immigration were all theoretical solutions, but none was possible once the great depression hit. Prices of the foodstuffs and raw materials on the export of which Yugoslavia depended tumbled further and faster than the prices of the manufactured goods it imported or produced behind high tariff barriers. Peasant debts soared and privation became general. This was bad enough, but it was rendered even worse by the facts that Yugoslavia's best customer, Italy, was also its worst enemy, and that Nazi Germany, gearing up for war, stepped into the breach created by the evaporation of the country's other markets. Britain and France were far away countries which cared to know less and less about the fate of their onetime ally. As Hitler intended, political leverage followed economic dominance.

When war broke out Yugoslavia declared its neutrality. A year later, however, Mussolini invaded Greece and so brought the war to the Balkans. The Italians' failure quickly to subdue the Greeks, and the consequent British decision to send troops to Greece's aid, compelled Hitler to make plans to come to his ally's rescue, particularly as he did not dare to launch his invasion of the Soviet Union while there were British forces on his southern flank. Needing now to make sure of Yugoslavia, Hitler pressed Prince Paul to join the Axis. The prince played for time, unaware that it was running out. The British, meanwhile, were doing everything in their power both to stiffen Paul's resolve and to identify an alternative and determinedly anti-Nazi government should he cave in. This he did on 25 March 1941; but within 36 hours he was overthrown in a military coup d'état which in fact owed little to British intrigue. The officers responsible declared King Peter of age and called upon representatives of the country's political parties to join a government led by one of their number. Serbs took to the streets in celebration of their regained honour and the prospect of a just war; while Croats sulked at home over such folly and expected the worst. Hitler naturally was furious, and immediately ordered that Yugoslavia be obliterated as soon as the attack on Greece was ready. The efforts of the new government in Belgrade to stave off German retribution were thus unavailing.

The German invasion came on 6 April. Ill-prepared, ill-equipped, ill-led, and ill-motivated, the Yugoslav army put up little resistance. The king and his government promptly fled, leaving it to subordinate officers to conclude an armistice on 17 April. Hitler had already sketched out the country's partition. Italy, Hungary, Bulgaria, Albania (an Italian satellite), and Germany itself all got shares. A so-called Independent State of Croatia (which also embraced Bosnia, Hercegovina and such parts of the coast not taken by Italy) was set up under the Ustaše with Pavelić as *Poglavnik* (i.e. Leader). A rump Serbia was left under German occupation. This was not just a military defeat. It was the destruction of an entire ruling order and of the political and national conceptions which underlay it. That a united Yugoslav state was to re-emerge during and after the Second World War was nothing short of miraculous—or would have been so regarded had it not been for the fact that the agents through which this miracle was accomplished were Marxist-Leninists.

The Making and Re-Making of the Second Yugoslavia

Resistance to the newly imposed Axis order was to be expected in a land where the tradition of fighting alien domination was a strong and still-living part of most people's national identity. Elements of the army took to the hills as the magnitude of their defeat became obvious. There they intended to reorganise and await developments. The Communists too were organising, though in their case it was for the revolutionary seizure of power they trusted Hitler's invasion of the USSR would unleash. That both royalist officers (soon to be known as Četniks) and Communist revolutionaries (soon to be known as Partisans) were impelled to rise in the summer of 1941 and, for a time, to co-operate was the result of the quick degeneration of Hitler's solution to the South Slav problem. This happened for a variety of reasons, but the most important was the initiation by the Ustaše in May of a campaign of terror and genocide against greater Croatia's two million Serbs. Both the Communists (under the leadership of their Croatian-born party secretary, Josip Broz Tito) and the predominantly Serb officers (who gradually recognised the command of Colonel Draža Mihailović) sought to take control and advantage of the spontaneous and inchoate Serb uprisings which the Ustaše massacres and Axis reprisals were provoking. Not wanting to be left out, and encouraged by the Soviets' entry into the war and the Communists' subsequent call to arms, Montenegrins and the Serbs of rump Serbia rose in July and August.

Such unity as the various uprisings possessed was not destined to endure. In the first place, the Communists and the Serb officers were fighting for different ends. These, in turn, implied different strategies. The Četniks sought the restoration of Yugoslavia as a Serb-dominated monarchy under King Peter. Their potential appeal to non-Serbs was thus small. As professional soldiers they were dubious of the benefits to be derived from armed struggle against an enemy so formidable as the Germans, and believed instead that their movement's proper role was to build an underground army which would only spring into action when the western Allies appeared on the scene. As Serbs they were obsessed by fears of their nation's extinction, and so regarded it as their duty to conserve and protect Serb lives as best they could until the day came for the final rising and the settling of accounts with Serbdom's foreign and domestic enemies. The grisly mass reprisals against civilians which had become the German answer to rebellion by the autumn confirmed Mihailović in his opinion that the uprising was premature and that the Communists were no better than criminals for seeking to prosecute it. In this assessment lay the seeds of Četnik collaboration with the Axis and a long civil war.

The Communists, on the other hand, were fighting for a revolutionary transfer of power. Although this, their ultimate objective, was more or less effectively obscured from the bulk of their followers, they evolved a potent mix of radical and traditional slogans and promises in their effort to appeal to all Yugoslavs. Militarily, they differed from the Četniks by emphasising unremitting war on the Axis and its domestic helpmates: at first in order to lend aid and comfort to an embattled USSR, but later because to do otherwise was to serve the enemy and betray one's own people. By their readiness to brand their domestic rivals as traitors the Partisans also took up the gauntlet of civil war. Sectarian zeal and overconfidence led Tito and his comrades to make many military and political blunders during their first six months in the field; but these were overcome with experience and the advice of the Comintern. Experience dictated that they must not try to hold static fronts against inherently superior Axis forces as they had done in the autumn. Moscow meanwhile set them straight on the need to construct the widest possible patriotic front and to dispense with overtly Communist symbols and rhetoric. They complied not only by emphasising that it was national freedom and 'brotherhood and unity' for which they were fighting (which came to mean the recreation of Yugoslavia on federal lines, the recognition of Macedonians and Montenegrins as separate peoples, and the acquisition of Croat-, Slovene- and Macedonian-speaking land), but also by offering social liberation and a political role to women, young people and peasants: all groups that had been largely ignored in the old Yugoslavia. Although they had initially depended for recruits on their own clandestine cadres and on those people (such as the Serbs of the Ustaše state) who had no alternative but to fight for their lives, their establishment of people's liberation committees and other organs of popular self-government gradually made manifest the new beginning for which they stood.

By the autumn of 1941 the dismembered lands of Yugoslavia had become the scene of Europe's greatest resistance struggle and one of its bloodiest civil wars. Partisans and Četniks fought the occupiers, their servants and each other in order to win anti-Axis leadership and the right to organise the post-war state. The several quisling movements fought the resisters and sometimes one another under the benevolent gaze of their rival Axis patrons. Catholics, Orthodox and Muslims massacred each other in the name of religion. Brother fought brother in the name of politics. It was the Partisans, however, who gave primacy to the struggle against the invaders, even if they too spent themselves profligately in the multifaceted civil war.

The Mihailović movement was in the ascendant during most of 1942, owing to the natural appeal it had to Serbs, the propaganda backing it received from the exile government and the Allies, its cosy arrangement with the Italians for joint anti-Communist operations, and its rivals' previous errors. The tide, however, was turning in favour of the Partisans. Their 'long march' from south-east to north-west Bosnia in the second half of 1942 translated them from an area in which they had worn out their welcome to one sympathetic to their now less ferocious-looking mien. When they convoked the first meeting of their political front (the Anti-Fascist Council of National Liberation, known by the acronym AVNOJ) in Bihać in November 1942 they gave it a moderate and strictly patriotic cast. In the first half of 1943 they survived—just— two great Axis offensives against them, inflicted crippling defeats on the Četniks outside Serbia, extricated themselves from negotiations with the Germans for an anti-Četnik *modus vivendi* without being found out, and welcomed their first British liaison officers. In the second half of the year they won the lion's share of the spoils from the Italians' surrender, summoned in Jajce a second session of AVNOJ which stated forthrightly their claim to post-war power, and acquired bountiful Allied moral and material support. By the end of 1943 they claimed to have upwards of 200,000 men and women at arms.

With their strength waxing as those who had chosen the wrong side or previously kept aloof rallied to them (especially Croats), the Communists devoted much of their attention during 1944 to winning international recognition. This they did with the help of Churchill, who bludgeoned King Peter and his government to face facts and come to such terms as they could with the country's future masters. An agreement envisaging the eventual establishment of a joint AVNOJ-royal government was signed in June. Tito was also concerned to liquidate Mihailović; for although the Partisans could now expect to take control in most Yugoslav lands when the Germans withdrew, the Četniks still seemed to command near-total support in Serbia. It was with this in mind he appealed to Stalin to divert the Red Army from its route into central Europe and to help the Partisans secure the Serbian heartland. Stalin graciously complied; the Četnik movement crumbled; and Belgrade was liberated in October. The Red Army then departed for Hungary, leaving the Partisans to finish the job as the Germans and their Yugoslav followers gradually withdrew. Full liberation came only with the end of the European war in May 1945. An internationally recognised coalition government had been formed under Communist domination in March.

The Yugoslavs' claims to have liberated their own country and to have played a notable part in the defeat of Hitler were perhaps exaggerated, but basically true. The war cost them some 1.2 million dead (i.e., roughly ten per cent of the pre-war population). A frighteningly large proportion of these, however, had perished at the hands of other Yugoslavs. The toll in material devastation was almost as bad, its impact attenuated only by the fact that an underdeveloped country had less to lose in the first place. Hunger, grief and fear were thus concomitants of the pride, joy and relief with which Yugoslavs greeted the peace. The Communists among them were dizzy with success, and keen to get on with the jobs of redeeming their pledges of social and economic transformation, punishing their enemies and enjoying the fruits of victory.

Over the next three years the Communists consolidated their power and began to remake their land in the image of the only other authentically revolutionary Marxist-Leninist state. Having shunted aside the non-Communist ministers and would-be leaders of a democratic opposition, they abolished the monarchy and declared Yugoslavia a Federal People's Republic before the end of 1945. Early the next year they adopted a constitution modelled on Stalin's 1936 document. Such industry as survived, the savings of the urban middle class and richer peasants, and 'excess' agricultural land and residential property had already been nationalised or expropriated on grounds of wartime collaboration. They paid the Soviet Union the compliment of slavish immitation heedless of the fact that Stalin himself was irked by their boastful self-confidence, revolutionary adventurism and autonomous power base. Viewed in the west as the dreadful shape of things to come in the new Soviet empire, the brutal fervour with which the Yugoslavs set about building socialism came to be regarded by Stalin as inimical to his wider interests. Unable to tolerate a Communist regime which he did not control and which arrogantly pressed its claim to a legitimacy every bit as genuine as that of the Bolsheviks, Stalin decided by 1948 to overturn Tito and his colleagues and to replace them with pliant tools.

Stalin's offensive (which he ineptly chose to make public on *Vidovdan*, 28 June 1948) set the scene for the Yugoslav Communists' second defence and recreation of their country. In resisting the Soviet threat to Yugoslav independence they were, of course, defending their own skins; but they and their countrymen soon also came to perceive their defiance of Stalin's anathemas as a logical and necessary continuation of their wartime resistance and revolution. This was what their struggle had always been about, if only they had realised it. Their survival, on the other hand, they owed to Stalin's initial overestimation of his power to command their obedience and his subsequent exaggeration of the likelihood of American retaliation should he intervene militarily. Once the shock of their excommunication had worn off—and those who sided with Stalin had been disposed of—Tito and his colleagues began a fundamental reconsideration of their principles and practices. Obviously they had no intention of giving up their exclusive hold on power, although this too was debated. (And cost Milovan Djilas his place in the leadership.) But they did resolve to jettison as much of the heretofore sacrosanct Soviet model as they could, and to look to the pre-Stalinist sacred texts for socialist inspiration. As we have seen, nonalignment and workers' self-management were the most highly touted innovations after 1950. For the bulk of the population, however, the de-collectivisation of agriculture, the curbing of the secret police, and the promise of the good life to come when industrialisation was completed were probably just as satisfying as real and spiritual independence.

A decade of stability followed the ideological transformation of Yugoslav Communism in the early 1950s. The party's claim to have solved the national question with a federalism which was 'national in form but socialist in content' seemed justified. Extensive economic development took place in a system which wedded local initiative, symbolic workers' control and highly centralised resource allocation. Commanding and receiving the credit for having twice saved the country, Tito and the party basked luxuriantly in the exercise of their power.

This golden age lasted until about 1963, when accumulating economic difficulties ushered in a new bout of reform. But attempts to enlist the magic of the market and otherwise to liberate the economy from residual central government controls—and to pass from extensive to intensive economic development—led to political crisis. The reforms met with resistance, not just from a federal bureaucracy reluctant to give up its economic prerogatives, but also in debates over the party's own competence which took up where those of the early 1950s had left off. Most ominously, the national question re-emerged: first tacitly in arguments for economic devolution which aimed to energise and reward the most successful firms clustered in the north and west of the country, but soon in overt, separatist and even violent form. The nationalism of republics which increasingly regarded themselves as nation-states was proving a double-edged sword. It provided the motive force behind the liberalising and decentralising coalition that developed to wrest leadership from the old guard centred around the former secret police chief, Aleksander Ranković, in 1966; but it also led to the chauvinism and party turmoil which later brought the country to what many feared—and Tito averred—was the brink of another civil war. Prophetically, it was Kosovo which errupted in 1968. Croatia followed in 1970–71.

By the beginning of the 1970s, the challenge of the Croatian 'mass movement' appeared to have overwhelmed that republic's party leadership. Moreover, the newly-won powers of the bankers, managers and technocrats looked likely to render the workers and their party irrelevant, whilst simultaneously evading both the stimulants and the disciplines that the market had been expected to provide. Finally, 'rotten liberalism' seemed set to consolidate its hold on the leaderships of the Serbian, Slovene and other republican and provincial parties. Tito, seeing his life's work in peril, called a halt, threatening use of the army and reasserting—in the political vocabulary of the Stalinist era—the need for 'democratic centralism' in the party and eternal vigilance against the mechinations of the 'class enemy' in society. The purge that followed, starting in the Croatian party, but later extending across several republics, would be bewailed 20 years later for having deprived the party of talent and delivered it into the hands of mediocrities. At the time, however, it appeared that Tito's unique ability to hold the country and party together had been demonstrated yet again, even if the price was destined to be descent into neo-Stalinism. The alternative, in any case, looked worse, both to a populace and to a community of informed foreign opinion for years inclined to regard Tito as the sole guarantor of Yugoslavia's statehood.

What happened in the remainder of the 1970s confounded expectations. In the first place, these were again years of stability. Not coincidentally, they were a time too of giddy prosperity: long pent-up urges to consume were gratified, funds were borrowed abroad at a prodigal rate and in an uncontrolled manner, and the party's leading role went all the while unchallenged. But instead of a re-centralisation of state and economic power equivalent to that which was supposed to have taken place in the party, the search for viable, institutionalised and decentralised instruments of decision-making and resource allocation continued. The twilight of Titoism led not to the grooming of a new Tito, but to the total confederalisation of the state and the partial confederalisation of the party as power bases shifted along with control over investment to the republican and provincial capitals.

With both euphoric nationalism and dissentient party factions laid low, the 1974 constitution and the 1976 Law on Associated Labour sought to complete the creation of a self-managing society and economy. The aim was to maintain a balance between competing national, regional, social, and economic interests by establishing mechanisms for issue aggregation, conflict regulation, consensus-building, and policy implementation that would neither require nor permit the emergence of another Tito. Rather, the integrity, unity and permanence of the socialist order would be guaranteed by the party, operating in and through every level of the whole atomised yet theoretically interlocking system.

It did not work out that way. Or at least the costs of an incredibly complicated system founded on endless meetings, intricate bargaining, republican and ethnic personnel quotas, annual rotation of offices, elaborate trade-offs, a *liberum veto* for each republic and province, bureaucratic mazes, the politicisation of the economies of the increasingly autarkic federal units, and the toleration of inefficiency, corruption, drift, stalemate, and a mind-deadening political discourse came to seem unreasonable to more and more Yugoslavs once the music of prosperity stopped and the old man was no longer directing the band. By the late 1980s one Belgrade wag was quoted as observing that Yugoslavia's paralysis was so far advanced that it was no longer capable even of collapsing.

However deep and mutually reinforcing the country's current economic and political crises, the necessity which gave birth to the Yugoslav idea in the 19C and to the birth and re-birth of the Yugoslav state in this century remains undiminished. As the foregoing pages have shown, crises have been Yugoslavs' companions for centuries. Even if the second Yugoslavia should go the way of the first, it is more than likely there will be a third.

INTRODUCTION TO THE ART AND ARCHITECTURE OF YUGOSLAVIA

By *Flora and Eric Turner*

> '...since that time till this day I have been employed in considering the antiquities of this place which I hope will prove a work very acceptable to the public as it is different from all other things yet published....The people vastly polite, everything vastly cheap, a most wholesome air & glorious situation....'

Letter from Robert Adam to his brother, James, Split, 6th August, 1757.

The visitor to Yugoslavia today, like Robert Adam on the Grand Tour, will be impressed by the climate, the natural beauty, and the extent and variety of the cultural heritage. The present article provides a brief survey of the important art historical developments. Not every major monument can be mentioned; space alone prevents this, and those works that are mentioned do not always fall easily into one continuous artistic tradition. Because of its geographical position, Yugoslavia has been subject to various migrations and foreign conquests, and it has formed a demarcation zone between different civilisations and cultures. Consequently, while Yugoslav cultural achievements have significantly contributed to the mainstream development of European art, they have also absorbed external influences which have merged to create a genuinely original tradition of their own.

Prehistoric. Paeolithic remains found in the north-west region of the Balkans date from as early as 35,000 BC. However, artefacts of cultural consequence emerge only much later: between 13,000 and 12,000 BC in the Badanj region of Hercegovina, where stones and animal bones, with crudely scratched designs, as well as fragments of shell jewellery have been discovered.

The most important prehistoric archaeological site is generally recognised to be the *Lepenski Vir settlement*, discovered in 1965 on the bank of the River Danube near Djerdap. By 1985, 15 superimposed levels of this Mesolithic settlement had been uncovered, dating from 7000 to 6000 BC. At first the Lepenski Vir settlement was considered to be an isolated find, but as the excavation has progressed over the last twenty years archaeologists have been persuaded that Mesolithic culture in the Balkans was rather more substantial and widespread than was initially realised.

The preservation of the Djerdap site is probably a result of its unusual location, and because it has remained relatively undisturbed the evidence it offers is exceptionally rich. The grave sites have revealed a range of stone sculptures representing both human and animal forms. The impressive detail gives the sculpture tremendous vitality and an overall monumental quality; the finds now form part of the collections of the National Museum in Belgrade.

With the coming of the Bronze Age (c 1200 BC) the decorative treatment of the metal at first differed little from the Neolithic tradition. Stylized spiral patterns were imitated by embossing on to the surface of the metal, and the naturalistic features of a Neolithic ceramic sculpture, exemplified by the Vučedol dove, were perpetuated through the use of cast anthropomorphic and zoomorphic details.

Initially the work was very crude. Metal jewellery made in the early Bronze Age consists of simple spiral loops; and although every

Stone sculpture from the Lepenski Vir settlement, 7000–6000 BC

attempt was made to formulate a decorative language for metalwork, the standard of pottery declined. In the later Bronze Age artistic standards improved considerably. Rich geometric patterns appear on bronze vessels and armour. One of the best surviving illustrations of this development is the *Japodian bronze cap* (c 500 BC), decorated with repoussé work, in the Archaeological Museum of Zagreb. The jewellery, both in its increasing complexity and in its use of exotic materials, reflects a steady development of the skills of artisans and of the cultural expectations of the society for which it was made.

The production of weaponry was supremely important and supported the entire metalworking industry during this period. Every burial site contains swords, daggers, and spear- and arrow-heads. Military considerations even determined the form of settlements, particularly along the Istrian and Dalmatian coasts, where a series of hill forts followed a standard pattern consisting of dry stone walls built in concentric circles following the configuration of the terrain. Dwellings duplicated this circular plan and were capped by conical slate roofs. Today this form of simple shelter persists in the rural regions of Dalmatia, where it is used as a storm refuge or food store.

The Iron Age represents the end of this prehistoric period in the Balkans. During this age contact developed increasingly with other nations, particularly Greece and later Rome. The Celtic migrations (from the middle of the 5C BC) were the first to have any decisive impact on the cultural history of the region; their influence was felt especially in the Panonic region (northern Bosnia and Serbia), and one of their most important contributions was the introduction of the potter's wheel. The *Glasinac site* has provided an enormous wealth of evidence, including votive objects, richly ornamented jewellery and ceramic cult objects, as well a wide range of domestic cooking implements and weaponry. Much of this material is preserved in the National Museum of Sarajevo.

Greek and Roman. The spread of Greek culture along the Eastern Adriatic began as early as the 8C BC and superimposed its influence on those of the Illyrian (Celtic) culture of the late Iron Age already established there. The Greek culture was comparatively sophisticated. For example, the walls of the Greek fortified settlements were constructed of regular stone building blocks and ran continuously, the streets followed a geometric pattern, intersecting at right angles, and public buildings and spaces were given a distinctive architectural character; whereas the Illyrian fortified settlements, as we have seen, were encircled by walls of dry stone, following the contours of the hill, within which simple dwellings again of dry stone construction and restricted plan were arbitrarily placed.

The most important Greek settlements include *Issa* on Vis, *Pharos* (Starigrad) on the island of Hvar, the Doric colony of *Korkyra* on Korčula, and *Salona, Tragurion* (later Trogir) and *Epetion* on the mainland. The colonies of Issa and Pharos became independent city states c 390 BC after the collapse of the Syracusan empire, but these Greek communities remained isolated from their surroundings. They never gained sufficient military superiority to subjugate the native Illyrians, although warfare was frequent between the two groups. It is in fact a gravestone fragment from the tomb of a soldier which provides the earliest evidence of writing on Yugoslav territory. A Greek inscription on the face of the stone reads:

> From this town that needs your bravery so much,
> You hurled yourself upon the Illyrian boat,
> And there death overcame you...

The oldest written records of Greek colonisation date from the 4C BC. They are inscribed marble fragments of verse or of legal documents, such as the code of colonisation procedures for the island of Korčula now preserved in the Archaeological Museum, Zagreb. Little material evidence remains from this period, although it is obvious from what has been discovered so far that significant trading did occur. Large hoards of Greek coins have been excavated from the sites of inland Illyrian settlements, and at the coastal site of Salona large bronze and clay vessels decorated with frieze work and originally made in Corinth, have been found. Comparatively few examples of sculpture (perhaps the epitome of Greek art of this period) have been found, and those which have are often incomplete. None the less it is immediately apparent that their artistic quality is far superior to contemporary Illyrian work. The *marble relief of Kairos* (the divinity of the fleeting moment), discovered in Trogir, shows a realistic portrayal of the young boy's musculature, with correctly proportioned limbs, and, altogether, is a convincing representation of the subject, whereas the representation of the human figure by Illyrian sculptors was typically very schematic, ill-proportioned, and lacking in detail.

Marble relief of 'Kairos' (the divinity of the fleeting moment), Trogir

The Greek colonies were gradually usurped by the Romans, whose occupation of the Dalmation coast began as early as the 2C BC. Whereas the Greeks had never succeeded in completely conquering the Illyrians, the Romans were more ruthless, better organised and more successful. Roman civilisation gradually spread inland from the Adriatic coast and eventually covered most of present-day Yugoslavia. The Romans founded important administrative centres throughout the territory, creating provinces such as Illyricum (later divided into Dalmatia and Panonia) and Mezija. The occupation of the Eastern Alpine region caused new towns to be built; examples include *Emona* (Ljubljana) and *Poetovio* (Ptuj), the latter of which was to develop into an important economic centre. At the crossroads of East and West, the important settlements were *Singidunum* (now

Belgrade) and *Naissus* (Niš) which became an important centre for the production of metalwork, particularly arms and armour. Other towns of significance were Stobi, Scupi (now Skoplje), Lihnid (Ohrid) in Macedonia and Butua (Budva) in Montenegro, all of which have important Roman remains.

In most areas local, traditional values merged with Roman imperial culture to create a new provincial civilisation with greatly enhanced standards. All major centres were connected by a system of roads which is still visible in many parts of the country, and which some towns, like Poreč, retain to this day the rectangular street pattern they received from their Roman town planners. Water was supplied by numerous aqueducts; that built by Diocletian to supply his summer palace was 9km long. Spas were popular social centres; the most important was *Aquae Iasae*, now known as Varaždinske Toplice. It is believed that one of the reasons why the emperor Diocletian built his palace where he did was because of the local sulphur springs, which are still in use.

Town planning followed a typical Roman pattern. Public activities were concentrated round the forum or main square. Typical civic architecture included arcades, remains of which can still be seen at Zadar; theatres such as those at Salona, Epidaurus (Cavtat), Stobi, and Skoplje; and amphitheatres such as that at Pula. *Pula* has the largest concentration of Roman architectural remains. The monumental amphitheatre is the sixth largest to survive from the Roman Empire. The Temple of Augustus is preserved largely intact, whereas the Temple of Diana has become incorporated with later architectural developments and is substantially altered. The triumphal arch, built by the Sergii family in the early 1C AD, has inspired a remarkable number of artists from the Renaissance onwards, including Michelangelo and Robert Adam.

Sculpture adorned temples and other public spaces; much of it is now preserved in local museums. Mural paintings exist as fragments, and important mosaics have been found at all major sites, e.g. Pula, Salona, Risan, Emona, Stobi and Gamzigrad. They match the high quality achieved by the best imperial workshops. The very rich discoveries of decorative objects and small sculptures reveal that the standard of living generally enjoyed within the Roman townships was high and that local demand for ceramic, glass and metal objects was met by local workshops as well as by imports.

An interesting architectural development was the country estate or 'villa rustica' found outside urban areas. One of the more luxurious examples is on the island of *Brioni*, in Verige Bay. But it is *Diocletian's Palace* which was the grandest and most complex structure ever built outside an urban centre during the Roman Empire. Substantial sections of the palace still remain. From the 7C it became the town centre of Split, which it still is today. When it was originally built in the early 4C AD it served both as a palace and as a military garrison, and it remains as one of the more comprehensive and ambitious examples of Roman architecture.

Early Christian and Pre-Romanesque. From the end of the 6C until the beginning of the 12C, the standard of cultural achievement fluctuated considerably. The decline of the Roman Empire made its territories increasingly vulnerable to invasion by Barbaric tribes. Nevertheless, Roman civilisation continued to survive in the coastal regions of the Eastern Adriatic. The emperor Justinian I (527–565 AD) sought to restore the glory of the Roman Empire by regaining some of

Roman mosaic at Stobi

the western territories, uniting them with the eastern, and making the new western capital Ravenna. He established several important centres between Ravenna and the capital of the Eastern Empire, Constantinople. Caričin Grad (near Leskovac), assumed to be Justiniana Prima, was an important religious and administrative centre but did not survive the Avar-Slav invasions in 614–15. Neither did the basilicas built in Pula and Salona. However, the episcopal complex in Poreč, built by Bishop Euphrasius, does remain substantially intact. Its principal buildings consist of a basilica with a memorial chapel, a baptistery and the bishop's palace. It is the best preserved monument of this period in Yugoslavia. The splendid mosaics can be compared with the famous mosaics in Ravenna. The rare stucco decoration and sophisticated marble inlay, the innovative iconography of the Virgin Mary and the intricate sculptural decoration on the capitals, makes the *Basilica Euphrasiana* one of the more significant monuments of Byzantine art in the West.

In the period immediately following the collapse of the Roman Empire, a multitude of influences prevailed. Artistic production used elements from late antiquity, Carolingian and Byzantine ornament,

Diocletian's Palace, early fourth century, Split

Christian iconography and pagan myths. But at the same time an indigenous architectural and artistic tradition began to emerge which was independent and unique to Yugoslavia. Approximately 100 'early Croatian' churches from this pre-Romanesque period survive. Each is of modest proportions. The ground plan varies, following either the form of a basilica or a central, circular plan. In its simplicity it inspires an extraordinary sense of dignity. The location and positioning of the building in its relation to the landscape and its alignment with the sun have, in most cases, been worked out very carefully. Sometimes the building itself was built directly on a prehistoric site; e.g. 11C *St. Nicholas* near Nin. These churches illustrate a general tendency towards reduction in architectural scale. For example, in the medieval transformation of Diocletian's Palace, the outside walls became city ramparts, the internal corridors became city streets, and the original guard post over the north gate, initially intended for one man, was converted into the church of St. Martin. However the largest, and certainly the most striking example of pre-Romanesque architecture, comparable to San Vitale in Ravenna or to Charlemagne's chapel in Aachen, is *St. Donatus* (Sv. Donat) in Zadar, an impressive rotunda, which, in its present form, dates from the 9C and was originally built directly over the remains of a Roman forum.

All these churches have lost much of their original decoration, which consisted largely of carved stonework and fresco paintings.

Sv. Križa (St. Holy Cross), Nin

From the fragments that survive, we can gain a clear picture of the intense activity of the local stonemasons. Monumental sculpture entirely disappeared during the pre-Romanesque period. In its place, a more painterly approach was adopted, using shallow relief, highly stylized figures and geometric decoration. Ornamental plaitwork decorated the surfaces of ciboria, altar slabs and window frames. Sometimes the composition echoes the classical format of a Roman sarcophagus, as in the altar closure slabs from the church of Sv. Nedjeljica in Zadar, now in the Zadar Archaeological Museum. A fine collection of pre-Romanesque stonework can be seen in the Museum of Croatian Archaeological Monuments in Split. The appearance of the human figure on these reliefs marks the beginning of Romanesque art.

St. Donatus in Zadar, which dates from the ninth century

Romanesque. *Split Cathedral* includes some very important examples of Romanesque art. Diocletian's Mausoleum was gradually converted, from the 8C onwards, into a Christian church. The first Ecclesiastical Councils were held there, in the presence of King Tomislav, in 925 and 927–28, and the building's conversion was completed by the construction of its monumental bell tower during the 13C and 14C. (This was completely renovated between 1890 and 1908.)

The cathedral has one of the more important and certainly the best preserved pair of Romanesque wooden doors in the world. They are the work of the highly respected painter and sculptor, *Master Buvina of Split*. (He is mentioned in contemporary documents as 'pinctor de Spalato' by Toma Archidjakon, 1200–68). The door-frame is richly ornamented with foliage, birds, animals and human figures, and each of the 28 panels making up the doors is bordered by geometrical plaitwork. Each scene concisely illustrates a major event in Christ's life. Like an illustrated Bible, the doors enlighten the faithful and prepare them for the service within. The original effect must have been even more striking, as the panels were initially painted and gilded. Buvina's doors, finished in 1214, are a synthesis of the standard iconographic motifs of Western and Byzantine art, but his overriding concern for visual clarity rather than mere iconographic accuracy makes these doors a genuinely original contribution to European Romanesque art.

A panel from Master Buvina's wooden doors, completed in 1214 for Split Cathedral

The elaborately carved backs of the choir stalls, which have parellels with English misericords, can be dated to the mid 13C and anticipate the emergence of the Gothic style. But the most outstanding transitional work in Yugoslavia is *Trogir Cathedral*, begun in 1240. This date is carved above the doors of the main entrance along with the stonemason's signature, *Master Radovan*, and a declaration describing the latter as the 'the most distinguished in his art', which indeed he was. Classical precedents may have encouraged Radovan to break with the usual Christian reticence over the portrayal of the human body. Full-length nude sculptures of Adam and Eve, placed at the main entrance, were very unusual. Although the structure of the portal is Romanesque, the use of highly naturalistic motifs and complicated iconography, incorporating detailed biblical scenes with everyday imagery, is Gothic. The gradual liberation of sculpture from prescribed formulas, beginning with the altar slabs in Zadar, reached its zenith in the achievements of Radovan and his workshop.

The character of many Croatian towns was established during the Romanesque period. Rab, for example, has many surviving Romanesque buildings, and the layout of the city centre dates from this period. In particular, the townscape with distinctive bell towers is typical throughout the region and is very similar to the configuration of Tuscan hill towns of the same time.

Detail of the portal of Trogir Cathedral by Master Radovan, 1240

Byzantine. Important contributions were made by Serbian and Macedonian artists to the development of Byzantine art. Macedonia is one

˙ne richest areas in Europe for medieval wall-paintings. Some of the ˙rliest, dating from the beginning of the 13C, are the frescoes in the ˙˙urch of St. Sophie (Sv. Sofija) in Ohrid. Over ten artists can be ˙dentified by signed works dating from the second half of the 13C. These include *Mihajlo*, *Astrapa* and *Eutihije*, who were the leading figures in Balkan fresco-painting during this period. Astrapa's work in Ohrid and Prizren introduced several important innovations. He incorporated a realistic background in place of a neutral space. He also initiated new iconography with fresh allegorical content. Instead of being traditionally static and hieratic, his figures were represented in motion, and his use of bright colours created vivid contrasts.

Astrapa and Eutihije worked not only for the Macedonian nobility but also for King Milutin of Serbia, forging a connection between these two cultures which flourished until the Turkish invastion (1459).

The highest achievements of Serbian ecclesiastical art dates from the end of the 12C, coinciding with the formation of the Raška school of architecture, painting and sculpture. This was encouraged by the monk *Sava* (later St. Sava), who actively promoted the arts by directly commissioning artists to decorate churches in the Raška region. The Raška school represents a synthesis of Byzantine art with Western Romanesque and Gothic. The former is more apparent in the architectural structure, while the latter is more evident in the applied decoration. The same process of assimilation of the so-called 'Maniera Graeca' and the 'Maniera Latina' occurred equally in the applied arts and particularly in goldsmiths' work.

The *monastery* and *church of Studenica*, begun in 1190, became the model for subsequent buildings in the medieval period. The façades are faced with marble and the interior painted with frescoes. The most impressive is the scene of the Crucifixion covering the west wall. Later frescoes introduce the novelty of illustrating events from contemporary history and include portraits of various rulers. The inspiration for this development stems from contemporary literature, while illuminated manuscripts offer parallels with the richly decorated masonry of the window frames.

The splendid frescoes in *Mileševa Monastery* (1228) introduce simplified volumetric treatment and mark the beginning of a new style which reached its apotheosis in the artistic decoration for the *Monastery at Sopoćani*. These frescoes are among the more significant paintings of the 13C. They present an extraordinary vision of the ethereal and real worlds. Each figure is imbued with a warm humanity and classic elegance, regardless of whether it represents a saint or an angel, or is a naturalistic contemporary portrait. The subjects and stylistic themes of these frescoes reflect the cosmopolitan atmosphere of the Serbian court of this period, which, connected by marriage to Venice, France and Hungary, was well acquainted with both Western and Eastern cultural tendencies.

In the 14C, painters became more concerned with narrative themes. The church of *Dečani Monastery*, built by the Franciscan, Vito of Kotor, contains frescoes in the new narrative style. The only artist who has identified any of his work signed himself 'sinful Srdj'. The outside of this church is faced with alternate rows of yellow and dark red marble. The rich zoomorphic and floral decoration of the main entrance is essentially Romanesque, but some details, such as the pointed arches of the windows, anticipate the arrival of the Gothic style.

Finally, mention must be made of the Morava School of painting. This was a regional development which arose out of two massive

The Dormition of the Virgin, detail of the thirteenth-century frescoes in the monastery at Sopoćani

military defeats: the battle of the River Marica in 1371, and the battle of Kosovo in 1389, in which the greater part of southern Serbia was lost to the Turks. As a consequence of these events, the political and cultural focus moved northwards to the region of the River Morava and its tributaries. Moravan painting, dependent as it was on the court and its entourage, was aristocratic in character, reflecting the luxury and wealth of its patrons. Its style indicates a renewed interest in monumental form, although now treated rather more decoratively. The drawing is accomplished, the colouring lavish (gold was freely mixed with other costly pigments), but never vulgar, and the composition of figures against an architectural or landscape background was more naturally achieved.

The art of the tombstone: Stećak. Stećaks are tombstones, wholly indigenous to medieval Bosnia, made between the 12C and the 16C. Nearly 70,000 have survived on over 3000 sites in an area which now covers Bosnia, Hercegovina, and parts of Croatia, Serbia and Montenegro. Although it seems that the majority can be associated with the Bogomil cult, stećaks were also adopted in the burial customs for the Orthodox and Catholic populations. The 'Bogomils' believed in a God of Light who created virtue and all spiritual values and a God of Darkness who created the world and all corporeal evils. They did not build churches, acknowledge the pope, or recognise the feudal system.

The largest site, with over 700 tombstones, is at the source of the River Cetina. The monuments vary from simple blocks to more elaborate architectonic forms incorporating pillars and crosses. Twenty-seven have relief decoration which varies from purely stylized ornament to more naturalistic and symbolic representations; the most interesting include hunting and tournament scenes. Some are signed by *Grubač*, distinguished stonemason in the Stolac area. The formal characteristics of this work, in particular its simplified stylization, is Romanesque in origin, but the content, chronicling the life of medieval knights, is Gothic in spirit.

Gothic. The Gothic style began to establish itself in the Yugoslav region from the mid 13C onwards. However the Romanesque tradition was so strong that a mixed Romanesque-Gothic vocabulary persisted in some regions right through to the late 14C. Similarly in the 15C a transitional style emerged when artists began to accept Renaissance ideas but still retained identifiable Gothic mannerisms. These gradual transitions in the art historical morphology of Yugoslavia are a recurrent feature, particularly during the Middle Ages, and produce an art which has very few parallels anywhere else in Europe.

The three works which symbolise the beginning of the Gothic period in western Yugoslavia are the portal of the cathedral in Trogir (1240), the cathedral in Zagreb (1275), and the Franciscan church in Pula (1285). Radovan's naturalistic carving for the doorway of what is essentially a Romanesque structure has already been discussed. *Zagreb Cathedral* is the only building which breaks convincingly with the Romanesque tradition. The original building was reduced to ashes by the invading Tartars in 1242 and rebuilding was slow. Only the sanctuary, with three polygonal apses covered by ribbed vaults, and the sacristy were completed by the end of the century. The ground plan is similar to that of Troyes Cathedral (probably because Bishop Timothy, who commissioned the rebuilding, saw Troyes when he stayed at the Court of Pope Urban II), but the use of closed wall masses and narrow windows with separate roundels is principally Germanic in origin. The interpolation of a round tower in the Romanesque style was an archaic retention which emphasised the architects' rather conservative approach to the introduction of the Gothic. The building proceeded very slowly. The plan was altered in the 14C according to late Gothic practice; the vaulting was completed only in the 15C. The cathedral remains the largest Gothic structure in northern Croatia, although it later acquired Renaissance, baroque and neo-classical features; these were largely removed during the restoration that followed after the major earthquake of 1880.

The religious orders were the agents responsible for introducing the Gothic style to Croatian and Slovenian architecture. The first purely Gothic building is the Cistercian church at Kostanjevica on the River Krka. It was begun in 1234 and closely followed French precedents. By the second half of the 14C, buildings as ambitious and as splendid as the Sainte Chapelle in Paris, for example the *chapel of the Virgin Mary in Celje* and the choir of *Maribor Cathedral*, were being constructed. The pilgrim church of St. Mary in Ptujska Gora (1398–1410) achieves, by the use of elaborate architectural features and rich sculptural and fresco decoration, the unity of the International Gothic style. This church contains an unusual relief of the Virgin, showing her sheltering 80 individually identifiable figures.

An important contribution to Gothic sculpture in northern Yugoslavia is the work of a group of artists known as the Ljubljana workshop. Many of their wooden and stone sculptures survive in churches in Slovenia and Istria and by the 15C their work was even reaching Trieste. A particularly important collection is on display in the National Gallery in Ljubljana. In Istria Gothic achievements were generally made on a smaller scale, although the church of St. Mary in

A contemporary relief in the pilgrim church of St. Mary
Ptujska Gora (1398–1410) with the Virgin giving
shelter to eighty individually identifiable figures

the cemetery near Beram contains one of the more interesting fresco paintings of this period. Painted by *Vincent of Kastav* in 1474, the composition is an extraordinary 'Danse Macabre' illustrating the equality of all before death. The same subject was repeated by *Ivan of Kastav* in 1490 for the church of the Holy Trinity in Hrastovlje.

An outstanding example of early Franciscan architecture is the Gothic church in Pula, begun in 1285. The Franciscan churches in

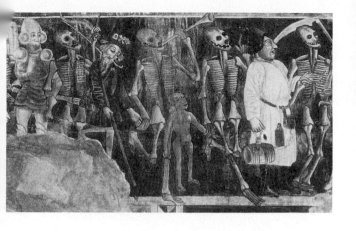

Detail of the 'Danse Macabre' by Vincent from Kastav, 1474, in the church of St. Mary near Beram

Koper, Piran and Poreč belong to the same hall type which is peculiar to the Franciscan order. During this period, Franciscan and Dominican churches were built also in Zadar and Split. Two of the more significant monastic complexes in Dubrovnik belong to the Franciscan (Little Brothers) and Dominican (White Friars) orders and are strategically placed by the western and the eastern city gates. The cloister of the Franciscan monastery is a fine example of the transitional Romanesque-Gothic style. It was built by *Mihoje Brajkov* of Bar, who died in Dubrovnik in 1335. The cloister of the Dominican monastery was built during the 14C and 15C, and the richly carved, late Gothic Windows are the work of the local stonemasons *Utišenović, Grubačević* and *Vlatković*.

In the 14C Dalmatian towns enjoyed a sustained period of prosperity, which is evident not only in the quality of their architecture but also in the numerous works of art which can be seen today in the collections of local church treasuries. The distinguished Italian painter of the late 14C, *Paolo Veneziano*, is represented in collections in Krk, Rab, Zadar, Trogir and Dubrovnik. The largest of all his recorded works is the painted Crucifix in the Dominican church in Dubrovnik. It was commissioned by a wealthy merchant, Šimun Restić, who bequeathed it to the church in 1348. It has hung in the same place, from one of the principal arched beams within the nave, since 1358, in accordance with a condition stipulated in the will. It is an interesting example of the rising power of an increasingly wealthy middle class and the pervasive and important influence of Italian culture on the Dalmatian coast. In 1358 a peace treaty between the Croato-Hungarian king, Louis of Anjou, and the Venetian Republic was signed in the sacristy of the Franciscan church in Zadar. Thenceforth to the end of the century Zadar remained a major economic and cultural centre. It also became an important place for goldsmiths' work, an outstanding example of which is *St. Simeon's shrine*, constructed of silver-gilt sheets over a wooden frame. On the sloping

The cloister of the fourteenth-century Franciscan monastery in Dubrovnik; one of the more significant architectural achievements in the transitional Romanesque-Gothic style

roof is a full-length recumbent figure of the saint; the texture and patterning of his shroud is exquisitely chased. The remainder of the surface is divided into panels, most of which contain scenes in relief connected with his life, the removal of his body and the preparation of his shrine. The figures are naturalistically treated and clothed in contemporary dress, and the architectural details in each scene are in the contemporary style. The panels are surrounded by conventional Gothic floral ornament. The religious scene shows the influence of contemporary Italian painting, particularly the work of Giotto and his followers. On the back is an elaborate inscription stating that the shrine was made by Francesco di Antonio of Milan in 1380 (a self-portrait along with the tools of his trade is included in one of the panels). The city archives disclose the names of all the local goldsmiths who assisted him. The piece was commissioned by Elizabeth, wife of King Louis and the daughter of the Bosnian ruler, Ban Kotromanić. In the 19C this shrine attracted much attention among European art historians, and apart from being the subject of numerous publications, an electrotype copy was made for the South Kensington Museum (later the Victoria and Albert) in London in 1894.

A recent discovery by Croatian art historians is the work of *Blaž Jurjev*, a painter of the Dalmatian school in the late medieval period. Archival records date his activity between 1412 and 1450 and indicate that he received commissions from most of the major Dalmatian towns. Fifteen works have so far been identified. Those of exceptional quality include the Crucifixion in Ston, and altarpieces for the Abbey Treasury in Korčula and the church of St. John the Baptist in Trogir. His work shows the influence of the International Gothic style but none the less retains links with the local Mediterranean tradition.

St. Simeon's shrine, by Francesco di Antonio of Milan, 1380, church of St. Simeon, Zadar

Throughout the 15C, architecture along the west coast was principally influenced by the Venetian Gothic aesthetic. But changes were already occurring. In 1441, the Šibenik council of nobles invited the master builder, Juraj, to leave Venice, where he was already well established, and sign a six-year contract with them to finish their Gothic cathedral. Juraj, a native of Zadar, in his work for the cathedral considerably extended the range of late Gothic ornamental sculpture, and his baptistery supplies the first evidence of the transitional Gothic-Renaissance style. His exceptional talent, encouraged through experience of the work of Donatello and Brunelleschi, introduced Renaissance ideals to Dalmatia.

Renaissance. *Juraj Dalmatinac* returned to his native Dalmatia at a propitious moment. Humanism was beginning to infiltrate intellectual society, which was therefore susceptible to new stylistic concepts. In *Šibenik Cathedral*, architectural and sculptural elements are perfectly integrated and the engineering is revolutionary. The walls and vaulted roof are composed entirely of stone slabs, tightly joined without bolts or mortar by a tongue-and-groove technique which the architect invented, achieving complete uniformity of material throughout the building. Juraj's sculptural ingenuity is particularly evident in the external frieze around the apse, composed of 72 heads, regularly spaced, each a portrait of a local citizen (a secular element unusual in the decoration of a cathedral). In Split Cathedral his work on the monument to St. Anastasius includes a carved panel in high relief, depicting the flagellation of Christ, which is one of the finer pieces of Early Renaissance sculpture in the whole of Dalmatia. The fortifications for Dubrovnik and the town

Polyptych by Blaž Jurjev (fl. 1412–50), Korčula

plan of Pag combine his engineering and artistic talents, exercising them to the full.

Juraj's colleagues and followers in Dalmatia increasingly incorporated Renaissance elements in their work. *Andrija Alexi* and *Nikola Firentinac* are his two most famous associates. They collaborated on the building of Šibenik Cathedral. Nikola, trained in Florence where he built some notable monuments, arrived in Trogir in 1466 and spent the next 40 years in Dalmatia. He was a major figure in the development of European Renaissance architecture. In 1467 he started work on his masterpiece, the *Orsini Chapel* in Trogir Cathedral. In this he was assisted by Alexi who, having used Gothic solutions for the baptistery, proved sufficiently flexible to adapt to the pure Renaissance ones generated by Nikola. A third collaborator on this project was the Trogir sculptor, *Ivan Duknović* (or Johannes Dalmata, as he signed his work). His sculpture of St. John for the Chapel was one of the few works he did for his native town. He received commissions from several popes and cardinals in Rome, and introduced the Renaissance to the Hungarian court of Matthias Korvin (1458–90), a famous art collector who gathered around him some of the more eminent artists of the day. Korvin rewarded Duknović for his artistic achievements with a title and a grant of land.

Like Duknović, the miniaturist *Julije Klović* (Georgius Croata, 1498–1578) worked for the senior Church hierarchy and was friends with some very illustrious contemporaries including Michelangelo, Vasari and Brueghel. He introduced the young El Greco to Cardinal Farnese, and El Greco painted two portraits of his sponsor. His work is represented in the collection of the Metropolitan Library, Zagreb Cathedral.

Šibenik Cathedral by Juraj Dalmatinac, 1441–47

Another Croatian artist of international importance is *Andrija Medulić* (Andrea Meldola, c 1500–63). He was one of the many Croatian artists who settled outside his native land. Medulić was a prominent painter of the Venetian school, a follower of Titian and Parmigianino and an influence on El Greco and the young Tintoretto. His work remains mostly in Italy but it is also represented in the collections of the Strossmayer Gallery in Zagreb, Hampton Court and the British Museum.

Several artists did return home after working in Venice. Among them is *Nikola Božidarević*, a gifted painter of the transitional period between the Early and High Renaissance. His most accomplished work is the Annunciation of 1513 for the Dominican church in Dubrovnik.

This city was a flourishing centre for the arts and sciences during the Renaissance. Unfortunately much of the original architecture from this period was lost in an earthquake in the 17C, although the summer

Sculpture by Nikola Firentinac, assisted by Andrija Alexi, in the Orsini Chapel, Trogir Cathedral; begun 1467

palaces of the nobility outside the city limits remain largely unaltered. That of the Sorkocević family, built at Lapad in 1521, combines Gothic and Renaissance features in a harmonious whole; moreover, the relationship between the interior and the exterior, the architecture and the landscape design, is perfectly realised. The villas built for the poets Hektorović and Lucić on the island of Hvar also illustrate, on a smaller scale, the attempt to achieve a unity of nature and architecture.

Detail from a polyptych (c 1500) by Nikola Božidarević showing the patron saint of Dubrovnik, St. Blaise (Sv. Vlaho), holding a model of the city; the Dominican church, Dubrovnik

Throughout the 16C the Balkans were constantly threatened with invasion by the Ottomans. At least two-thirds of Croatia was occupied, and inevitably building activity concentrated on military fortification. Developments in Italian military science provided the models for much of the construction that took place, even if in some instances the work was largely carried out by local architects. Sisak was reinforced by Italian and Croatian builders between 1544–50 and, as a consequence, successfully repelled the Turks in 1593. The construction of Karlovac, begun in 1579 by the Habsburg Archduke Charles, follows a rigid ground plan. The bastions and moat form a six-pointed star and the network of streets within follows an orthogonal pattern. Karlovac conforms in every respect to the Renaissance ideal of the citadel, and was completed 14 years before the Italian town of Palma Nuova, the best known fortress town of this shape in Europe. The fear of Ottoman invasion even extended to the Adriatic coast. Seven castles were built in the small area between Split and Trogir to protect the local inhabitants. Fortified churches, an architectural oddity, were built at Vrbovska on the island of Hvar and at Sudjuradj on Šipan.

Baroque and Rococo. Whereas the Renaissance built on an indigenous classical heritage, the baroque was a style which was wholly imported from Italy and Austria. It emerged gradually; first in the western province of Slovenia and later in Vojvodina, which formed the eastern boundary of its influence. The reasons for its protracted infiltration can be explained by historic circumstances. The Yugoslav region was divided between the Ottoman Empire, the Habsburgs and the Venetian Republic. Only the smaller republic of Dubrovnik managed to retain its independence, by very skilful diplomacy. The Turkish defeat at Sisak in 1593 stopped any further expansion westwards and the armistice at Sremski Karlovci in 1699 set the western borders of the Ottoman Empire at the rivers Sava and Una. There followed a period of relative peace and prosperity.

From the end of the 17C the baroque sensibility dominated Slovenian art. All artistic activity focussed on Ljubljana. The new style was promoted by the Jesuit order, which saw it as the language of a revived and increasingly influential Catholic Church, and by the newly established (1693) Academia Operosorum, a group of intellectuals who sought to make Ljubljana a cultural centre that would emulate Rome. Several distinguished Italian architects, painters and sculptors were invited to Ljubljana in order to achieve this goal. Plans for the new cathedral were commissioned in 1701 from *Andrea Pozzo* (1642–1709), one of the more eminent Roman architects and painters of the day. The cathedral was completed in 1706 under the supervision of a local architect, *G. Maček* (1682–1745), who later became one of the founders of the Ljubljana school of architecture. He built several churches in Slovenia which used rich spatial compositions and ingenious fenestration to create the dramatic theatrical effects so typical of baroque architecture.

The Italian *Francesco Robba* (1698–1757) was one of the many sculptors who undertook important commissions in Ljubljana. He introduced major innovations in sculptural composition and modelling. This is particularly evident in his treatment of drapery, where the play of light over the surface gives a flickering effect; the composition itself is very dynamic, characteristic of the work of such major baroque sculptors as Bernini. His work includes several altarpieces for the cathedral, sculpture for other baroque churches, and the fountain in the main square (Mestni Trg).

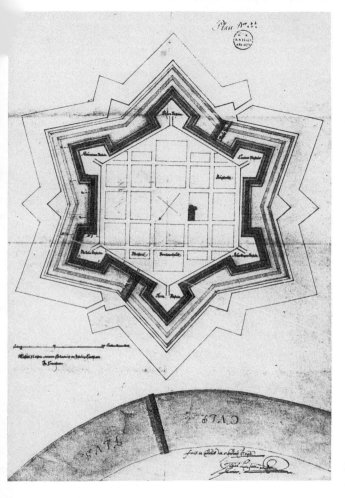

Ground plan of Karlovac, begun in 1579 by Habsburg Archduke Charles

The cathedral interior was decorated with trompe-l'oeil frescoes by Guilio Quaglio (1668–1751) who, trained in the tradition of the Bolognese School, was a major contributor to the development of baroque painting. He was an important influence on *Franc Jelovšek* (1700–64), a major Slovenian artist who painted numerous frescoes reflecting both Italian and Austrian influence, and whose later work incorporates genre elements and rococo details.

The tradition of richly sculpted and gilded altarpieces reached its apotheosis in the 17C. These works became particularly popular in

Northern Croatia through the workshop of *I. Komersteiner*. His sculptures for Zagreb cathedral were removed during the 19C restoration and are now in the collection of the Museum of Applied Arts.

A proper impression of the full glories of baroque architecture can only be gained by experience of interiors which have their original decoration intact. Among the best examples that have survived the effects of time and later restoration are the *church of Marija Snježna* at Belec, near Zlatar, and the pilgrim *church of St. Mary of Jerusalem* in Trški Vrh, which admirably demonstrates the baroque fusion of interior decoration and architecture.

Baroque decoration in the church of Marija Snježna, Belec

The *church of St. Catherine* in Zagreb is a simplified version of Vignola's church of Il Gesu in Rome. The outside gives a misleading impression of austerity. The church was originally built between 1620 and 1632, but a series of fires in the late 17C and early 18C gutted it, and the interior was rebuilt in the most lavish baroque manner. Much of the work was done by those who had built Ljubljana Cathedral. The elaborate stucco ceiling (1721) is by A. Quadrio and the frescoes by Quaglio and Jelovšek. Each of the six-sided chapels has two altars;

ne most distinguished (1728–29), by Robba, combines the elegance of late mannerism with the vitality of the mature baroque. The influence of Italian architects and artists was so strong during this period that contemporary critics described the style as 'imitationem gustus Italici' (imitation of the Italian taste).

Next to the church is a collegiate building in the late Renaissance manner which originally belonged to the Jesuits (it is now used as an exhibition space). The Jesuits made an enormous contribution to raising the level of education. Not only did they reform the school system, but it was their initiative which established the University of Zagreb in 1669. The same combination of church and college was duplicated in Rijeka and Dubrovnik.

Dubrovnik suffered a massive earthquake in 1667 and consequently a large part of the town had to be rebuilt. The major reconstruction work was undertaken by Italian architects. The church of St. Ignacije in Dubrovnik was designed by A. Pozzo and begun in 1669. The Jesuit complex was connected to the lower part of the town by a grand staircase designed by P. Passalaqua in 1735 and modelled on the Spanish steps in Rome. The new cathedral is a typical example of Roman baroque architecture. Several architects worked on it but it was finished by a local master, I. Katičić, in 1713. The main façade of the third baroque church, Sv. Vlaho (St. Blasius) was built between 1705 and 1715 by the Venetian architect and sculptor M. Gropelli (c 1664–1723) and gives a dramatic presence to the main square. Although churches were the primary focus of baroque town planning, many public buildings and private residences contributed to the central townscape.

The baroque style was chiefly confined to the Catholic regions of Slovenia and Croatia. In Serbia it met with strong opposition from the Orthodox Church because of its religious associations, whereas the Byzantine tradition, with its strict iconography, strongly resisted Western influences. Nevertheless the baroque aesthetic gradually became popular with the prosperous middle class, which initially adopted elements of the new style in architecture, and later in painting after a generation of painters had received their training in Vienna and Venice. The most famous Serbian painter in the baroque manner was *Teodor Kračun* (died 1781), who successfully introduced baroque forms to the Byzantine tradition, whereas the work of *Teodor Ilić Češljar* (1746–93) serves as a link between baroque, rococo and neo-classical tastes.

The rococo was an ornamental style which flourished in Europe in the mid 18C. It was a light and delicate form of the grotesque, its chief characteristics being its asymmetrical and curvilinear qualities. It was much more popular in France, Germany and Austria than it ever was in Italy or Yugoslavia, and therefore evidence of it in Yugoslav art and architecture is slight. There are fine rococo interiors in Miljana and Brezovica, and the style is evident in the delicate stucco decoration of the *Patačić Palace* in Varaždin.

From Neo-Classicism to the Twentieth Century. The reaction to the baroque and its more frivolous successor, the rococo, occurred in the latter part of the 18C. The neo-classical movement was a direct result of the increasing interest in classical antiquities that had been gathering momentum since the 1730s with the discovery of important archaeological sites, such as Herculaneum in Italy. The interest in such discoveries spread rapidly amongst the European aristocracy, which enjoyed a cultural homogeneity in the 18C, seldom

Rococo interior at Miljana

equalled before or since. The Grand Tour, which included obligatory stops in Paris and Rome, came to be regarded as an essential part of a gentleman's education. One of the more enterprising travellers doing this Grand Tour in the 1750s was the Scottish architect Robert Adam who was to have a profound influence in promoting this new fashion on his return to England. He in turn was enormously influenced by the Roman remains along the Adriatic coast, particularly those in Pula, such as the Sergii Arch and the Temple of Augustus and most of all, the remains of Diocletian's Palace in Split. His exhaustive studies of these monuments determined the development of the fashion he was later to promote so successfully. His publication, *Ruins of the Palace of the Emperor Diocletian at Spalato in Dalmatia* (1764) helped establish neo-classicism as the dominant fashion in England and gradually elsewhere in Europe. Thus, in one sense the western Adriatic region of Yugoslavia played a crucial role in the development of European neo-classicism, but the fashion itself had relatively little impact within Yugoslavia during the 18C.

In Slovenia, where the baroque style had been dominant, neo-classicism was particularly slow to emerge and first appeared as an architectural style for the nobility and the increasingly affluent middle class. An early and distinguished example is the complex of buildings at the spa of *Rogaška Slatina*, which was begun in 1819. The painter, F. Kavčić (1755–1828), born in Gorica, became an important neo-classical painter with an international reputation (he was a friend of Canova), but his career developed largely outside his native country. He was appointed head of the Vienna Academy in 1817 and retained this position for the rest of his life.

The principal representative of neo-classicism in Croatia was the Zagreb architect B. Felbinger (1785–1871). Many of his buildings remain and attest to his consummate handling of this style. There was a considerable amount of landscape rennovation undertaken throughout Croatia during the early 19C. The most ambitious project was the landscaping of the Maksimir Park, which incidentally was the first public park in South East Europe. Work began in 1812. The design followed French neo-classical prototypes at first, but by the time the park was completed, in 1843, it had changed to a more informal style in the English romantic tradition of landscape architecture.

In Serbia the baroque had never been a particularly strong influence, and so the introduction of neo-classicism met with little resistance. Neo-classicism also became identified with progressive intellectual trends, such as the emerging sense of nationalism and increasing religious tolerance. Again, it first emerged in architecture where it was readily adopted by the State, particularly for military buildings. It was not long before neo-classicism was also adopted by the nobility and the church.

From the end of the Napoleonic era in 1815, when the western territories of Yugoslavia were ceded to the Habsburgs by the Treaty of Vienna, until 1848, the year of revolution throughout Europe, a particular form of neo-classical interior became popular following a fashion which had been initiated and developed in Vienna itself. The Biedermeier style was a form of neo-classicism which was peculiarly suited to bourgeois needs and tastes. It had none of the monumentality of the French Empire style. The furniture was functional, comfortable and supplied to standard designs. It was on an altogether less pretentious scale than before, as it had to fit inside the relatively modest dimensions of a middle-class town house. A sentimental note was added by the frequent inclusion of family portraits in interior schemes. Reconstructed examples of Biedermeier interiors are to be found in the applied arts museums of Zagreb, Belgrade, Ljubljana, Osijek and Varaždin.

The revolutionary turmoil of 1848 prompted various national movements to flourish throught Europe. The Illyrian Movement, which fostered the idea of pan-Slav unification, was already established in Croatia before such ideas had become generally fashionable elsewhere. The movement provided a common theme throughout all the arts. Elsewhere, as in Slovenia and Serbia, it emerged mainly in the literature of the time. In Montenegro, encouraged by Prince Njegoš, who was himself an established poet, the local culture become strongly Westernised. The foundation of regional scientific foundations and cultural academies can also be attributed to this upsurge in nationalism.

In the latter part of the 19C, historicism dominated architecture and the decorative arts in Yugoslavia as throughout the rest of Western Europe. The work of the architect *Herman Bollé* (1845–1926) embodies most of the historical styles in fashion throughout Yugoslavia during this period. Born and trained in Cologne, he settled in Zagreb in 1878, where he designed an impressive number of public and private buildings. This included the renovation of the cathedral in a neo-Gothic style, and the Municipal Cemetery and Museum of Arts and Crafts in an Italianate style. Bollé was one of the first directors of the museum which was ultimately modelled on the South Kensington Museum in London. Like its English prototype it provided an educational centre for craftsmen as well as a public collection to stimulate a general interest in the arts and crafts. Bollé's influence on Croatian art education was enormous. He also assisted in the development of the town plan of Zagreb, although the sequence of tree-lined squares arranged in a U-shaped pattern, which gained recognition at the Budapest International Exhibition of 1896, was designed by Milan Lenuci. The baroque and rococo styles were also revived, chiefly by the Viennese firm of Helmer and Fellner which built the opera houses in Zagreb, Rijeka and Varaždin. In Serbia and indeed outside the western republics of Croatia and Slovenia, this historical eclecticism survived until well into this century. After Serbian independence was established in 1878, there emerged a local school of architecture which revived a Byzantine idiom in an attempt to create a Serbian national style. In Bosnia a typical example of this stylistic nationalism is the National Library, in a pseudo Moresque style, in Sarajevo.

The radical break with historicism was precipitated by a group of young artists who established 'The Society of Croatian Artists' in 1897. The leaders of this group, all of whom had trained in Paris and Vienna, were the painter *Vlaho Bukovac* and the sculpors, *Frangeš-Mihanovič* and *Valdec*. Their most influential exhibition was the 'Croatian Salon' of 1898, which showed the powerful influence of the Vienna Secession and caused a considerable stir. In Ljubljana, the first sign of activity was the 1900 exhibition organised by the Slovenian Art Society, which was more markedly influenced by the French Impressionists. Belgrade was host to 'The First Yugoslav Art Exhibition' in 1904, which was the first of a series of modern exhibitions. Despite continual controversy, these events were successful in establishing a new, contemporary art. The sculptor *Ivan Meštrović* (1883–1962) was one of the contributors to the Belgrade exhibition. He was to become one of the major European sculptors of the early 20C. In 1908 he exhibited at the Salon d'Automne in Paris. His work was much admired by Rodin who said: 'Meštrović is the greatest phenomenon amongst sculptors'. A typical example of his early work is the 'Well of Life' (1905), a sculptural fountain outside the Zagreb Opera House. His use of unconventional iconography, the dynamic arrangement of figures and impressionistic surface treatment, make this one of his finer works. Later this work was to become more ideologically committed and monumental.

The Ljubljiana earthquake of 1895 necessitated major reconstruction, and the city was the first to build in a Secessionist style. The two prinicpal architects who introduced the new idiom were *Maks Fabiani* and *Josip Plečnik*. Both had worked in Vienna in the office of Otto Wagner, who exerted a profound influence on their development. Fabiani was later to become internationally distinguished as a

The Well of Life by Ivan Meštrović, 1905, Zagreb

town planner. Plečnik, while still in Vienna, built the first reinforced concrete church in the Austro-Hungarian Empire. After returning to Yugoslavia he started an architectural school as well as a practise as an architect and town planner. He also designed and furnished most of the interiors of his buildings.

The Zagreb architect *Viktor Kovačić* also trained in the office of Otto Wagner, and, on his return, promoted the idea of a modern Croatian architectural style which was to be both novel and contemporary and yet practical and comfortable. These ideas were ultimately derived from the English Arts and Crafts Movement, which encouraged the development of individual craftsmanship and a stylistic simplicity dependent on the nature of the material rather than historical precedent. This radical approach influenced a whole generation of architects and produced some of the best Secessionist architecture in Yugoslavia. The most outstanding example is the *Zagreb University Library* designed by Rudolf Lubynski and completed in 1913. It perfectly illustrates the unified concept, characteristic of Secessionist architecture even in such details as the furnishings, which remain largely intact to this day.

Zagreb University Library, designed by Rudolf Lubynski and completed in 1913

Architecture between the wars reflected trends established elsewhere in Europe. The first graduates from the Zagreb School of Architecture in 1923 emphasised the functional and structural aspects of their buildings and eschewed all superficial ornament. The advent of the Great Depression in 1929 prompted several progressive architects and artists to form the coalition Zemlja (The Land), which sought to develop a socially committed art and architecture. It was officially suppressed in 1935 because of its political overtones. One of the founders of this group was the painter *Krsto Hegedušić* (born 1901), who established a school of painting in the Croatian village of Hlebine. Working alongside peasants, he revived the baroque technique of painting on glass in a naive style. This subsequently has become very popular while remaining indigenous to Yugoslavia. In 1952, a gallery exclusively devoted to naive painting was founded in Zagreb (Galerija Primitivne Umjetnosti).

The immediate post-war period saw a concentration on social realism in the visual arts, but this was soon abondoned. The experimental group EXAT 51, based in Zagreb, was the first to encourage the development of abstract art in the early 1950s, which in turn lead to experimentation with op art, minimalism, conceptual art and other avant-garde tendencies. Annual exhibitions of contemporary art are held in every major regional capital, and an important international biennial exhibition of graphics and industrial design is held in Ljublijana. Thus the post-war art and architecture of Yugoslavia, while fully integrated with European art, continues to undergo vigorous developments giving it an individual character of its own.

GLOSSARY OF ART TERMS

AGORA, public square or marketplace

AISLE, side of a church nave separated by piers from the nave proper

AMBO (pl. *ambones*), pulpit in a Christian basilica; two pulpits on opposite sides of a church from which the gospel and epistle were read

AMPHORA, antique vase, usually large, for oil and other liquids

AMPULLA, glass or earthenware flask with a globular body and two handles used to hold ointment, perfume, or wine

ANTIS, *in antis* describes the portico of a temple when the side walls are prolonged to end in a pilaster flush with the columns of the portico

APSE, a projecting part of a building, esp. a church, usually semicircular in plan and vaulted

ARCHITRAVE, lowest part of the entablature

ARCHIVOLT, moulded architrave

ATLANTES (or *Telamones*), male figures used as supporting columns

ATRIUM, forecourt, usually of a Byzantine church or a classical Roman house

BAPTISTERY, a part of a church or formerly a separate building used for baptism

BAROQUE (architecture), style prevalent esp. in the 17C, marked generally by elaborate ornamentation, dynamic opposition and the use of curved and plastic figures

BASILICA, originally a Roman building used for public administration; in Christian architecture, an aisled church with a clerestory and apse, and no transepts

BAS-RELIEF, sculptural relief in which the projection from the surrounding surface is slight and no part of the modelled form is undercut

BEMA, the part of an Eastern church containing the altar

BEZISTAN, covered market

CALDARIUM (or *Calidarium*), room for hot or vapour baths in a Roman bath

CAPITAL, the top of a column

CARAVANSERAI, an inn where caravans rest at night, usually a large bare building surrounding a court

CARDO, the main street of a Roman town, at right angles to the Decumanus

CARYATID, female figure used as a supporting column

CATHEDRA, official throne of a bishop

CAVEA, the part of a theatre or amphitheatre occupied by the rows of seats

CELLA, sanctuary of a temple, usually in the centre of the building

CHANCEL, the part of a church lying E of the nave and including choir and sanctuary

CHAPTER HOUSE, building or rooms where the canons of a cathedral or members of a religious house meet

CHASUBLE, the outer garment of the celebrant at the Eucharist

CHIAROSCURO, distribution of light and shade, apart from colour in a painting; rarely used as a synonym for grisaille

CIBORIUM, casket of tabernacle containing the Host

CIPPUS, sepulchral monument in the form of an altar

CHOIR, part of a church occupied by the singers or by the clergy

COLUMN, supporting pillar usually consisting of a round shaft, a capital, and a base

CORBEL, architectural member that projects from within a wall and supports a weight

CORINTHIAN, the lightest and most ornate of the three Greek orders of architecture characterised esp. by its bell-shaped capital enveloped with acanthuses

CORNICE, highest part of an entablature

CRYPT, vault under the main floor of a church

CUNEUS, wedge-shaped block of seats in an antique theatre

CUPOLA, dome

DADO, the lower part of an interior wall when specially decorated or faced; also, the decoration adorning this part of a wall

DECUMANUS, the main street of a Roman town running parallel to its longer axis

DIPTERAL, temple surrounded by a double peristyle

DIPTYCH, painting or ivory tablet in two sections

DORIC, the oldest and simplest Greek architectural order

DZAMIJA, mosque

ENTABLATURE, the part above the capital consisting of architrave, frieze, and cornice) of a classical building

EPHEBUS, Greek youth under training (military or unviersity)

EXEDRA, semicircular recess in a Byzantine church

EXULTET, an illuminated scroll

EX-VOTO, tablet or small painting expressing gratitude to a saint

FIBULA, clasp resembling a safety pin used by the ancient Greeks and Romans

FORUM, open space in a town serving as a market or meeting place

FRESCO, painting executed on freshly spread moist lime plaster with pigments suspended in a water vehicle

FRIEZE, part of an entablature between the architrave and the cornice

FRIGIDARIUM, room for cold baths in a Roman bath

GOTHIC (architecture), style developed in N France and current throughout W Europe from the middle of the 12C to the early 16C, characterised by the converging of weights and strains at isolated points upon slender vertical piers and counterbalancing buttresses, and by pointed arches and vaulting

GRAD, town

GRAFFITI, design on a wall made with an iron tool on a prepared surface, the design showing in white. Also used loosely to describe designs or words on walls

HAN, hotel or inn

HAMAN, public baths in a Moslem town

HERM (pl. *hermae*), quadrangular pillar decreasing in girth towards the ground, surmounted by a bust

HEXASTYLE, temple with a portico of six columns at the end

ICON, conventional religious image typically painted on a small wooden panel and venerated by Eastern Christians

ICONOSTASIS, screen or partition with doors and tiers of icons that separates the bema from the nave in Eastern churches.

INTARSIA, inlay of wood, marble, or metal

INTRADOS, the interior curve of an arch

IONIC, an order of Greek architecture characterised esp. by the spiral volutes of its capital

KASTEL, castle

KATEDRALA, cathedral

KRATER, antique mixing-bowl, conical in shape with rounded base

KULA, tower

KYLIX, wide shallow vase with two handles and short stem

LOGGIA, covered gallery or balcony, usually preceding a larger building

LOMBARDESQUE, or *Lombard Romanesque*, Romanesque substyle developed by the Lombards, a Teutonic people who invaded Italy in AD 568, settling in the Po valley

LOZA, see *Loggia*

LUNETTE, semicircular space in a vault or ceiling, often decorated with a painting or relief

MADRASA, Koran school, usually attached to a mosque

MATRONEUM, gallery reserved for women in early Christian churches

MAUSOLEUM, large tomb, esp. a stone building with places for entombment of the dead above the ground

METOPE, panel between two triglyphs on the frieze of a temple

MIHRAB, sanctuary niche for a mosque

MINARET, slender lofty towner attached to a mosque and surrounded by one or more projecting balconies from which the summons to prayer is cried

MINBAR, pulpit of a mosque

MISSAL, book containing all that is said or sung at Mass during the entire year

MONSTRANCE, vessel in which the consecrated Host is exposed for the adoration of the faithful

MOSAIC, surface decoration made by inlaying small pieces of variously coloured material to form pictures or patterns

MOSQUE, building used for public worship by Moslems

NAOS, main part of an Eastern church

NARTHEX, vestibule of a Christian basilica

NAUMACHIA, mock naval combat for which the arena of an amphitheatre was flooded

NAVE, the main part of the interior of a church; esp. the long narrow central hall in a cruciform church that rises higher than the aisles flanking it to form a clerestory

NECROPOLIS (pl. *necropoleis*), large elaborate cemetery of an ancient city

NYMPHAEUM, a sort of summer-house in the gardens of baths, palaces, etc., originally a temple of the Nymphs, and decorated with statues of those goddesses

ODEION, a concert hall, usually in the shape of a Greek theatre, but roofed

OINOCHOE, wine-jug usually of elongated shape for dipping wine out of a krater

PALACA, any dignified and important building

PANTOKRATOR, the Almighty

PATRIARCHATE, seat of a patriarch, or Orthodox bishop

PEDIMENT, gable above the portico of a classical building

PERIPTERAL, temple surrounded by a colonnade

PERISTYLE, court or garden surrounded by a columned portico

PIER, vertical support at the end of an arch or lintel

PILASTER, upright architectural member that is rectangular in plan and is structurally a pier but architecturally treated as a column and that usually projects a third of its width or less from the wall

PILLAR, square post or shaft standing alone, providing upright support for a superstructure

PIETÀ, group of the Virgin mourning the dead Christ

PISCINA, Roman tank; a basin for an officiating priest to wash his hands before Mass

PITHOS, large pottery vessel

PODIUM, a continuous base or plinth supporting columns, and the lowest row of seats in the cavea of a theatre or amphitheatre

POLYPTYCH, painting or tablet in more than three sections

PORTAL, the architectural composition surrounding and including the doorway of a church or palace

PORTCULLIS, grating of iron hung over the gateway of a fortress and lowered between grooves to prevent passage

PORTICUS, colonnade or covered ambulator esp. in classical architecture and often at the entrance of a building

PREDELLA, small painting attached below a large altarpiece

PRONAOS, porch in front of the cella of a temple

PROSTYLE, edifice with free-standing columns, as in a portico

RENAISSANCE (architecture), the neoclassic style prevailing in W Europe between the 14C and the 17C

REREDOS, ornamental wood or stone screen or partition wall behind an altar

ROMANESQUE (architecture), style developed in Italy and W Europe between the Roman and the Gothic styles and characterised in its development after 1000 by the use of the round arch and vault, substitution of piers for columns, decorative use of arcades, and profuse ornament

SACRISTY, room in a church where sacred utensils and vestments are kept

SAHAT-KULA, clock tower

SANCTUARY, the most sacred part of a religious building, as the part of a Christian church in which the altar is placed

SARCOPHAGUS, pl. *sarcophagi*, stone coffin

SEDILIA, seats on the S side of the chancel for the celebrant and his assistants

SOFFIT, the underside of an architectural structure, esp. the intrados of an arch

STALL, seat in the chancel of a church with back and sides wholly or partly enclosed

STELE, upright stone bearing a monumental inscription

STYLOBATE, basement of a columned temple or other building

SUDATORIUM, room for very hot vapour baths (to produce sweat) in a Roman bath

TELAMONES, see *Atlantes*

TEPIDARIUM, room for warm baths in a Roman bath

TESSERA, a small cube of marble, glass, etc., used in mosaic work

TETRASTYLE, having four columns at the end

THERMAE, originally simple baths, later elaborate buildings fitted with libraries, assembly rooms, gymnasia, circuses, etc.

TONDO, round painting or bas-relief

TRANSENNA, open grille or screen, usually of marble, in an early Christian church

TRANSEPT, the part of a cruciform church that crosses the nave at right angles

TRIGLYPH, blocks with vertical grooves on either side of a metope on the frieze of a temple

TRIPTYCH, painting or tablet in three sections

TURBEH, monumental tomb

VESTIBULUM, passage or room between the outer door and the interior of a building

VILLA, country-house with its garden

VRATA, town gate

PRACTICAL INFORMATION

Approaches to Yugoslavia

Direct *air services* operate between Britain, North America, Australia, and Yugoslavia throughout the year. There are also scheduled flights from most European and many Middle Eastern countries. The principal Yugoslav towns and resorts are linked with London by a variety of *rail* routes via Calais, Ostend, Dunkirk, and Boulogne. The most agreeable way to arrive is by *boat* from Venice: the international service calls at main ports between Rijeka and Bar. By *car*, entry can be made from Austria by several mountain passes, or having traversed the Alps into Italy, from Trieste without recourse to further mountain roads. The coast may be approached from several points farther S in Italy by car-ferry (details below).

Travel Information. General information may be obtained from the Yugoslav National Tourist Office, 143 Regent Street, London W1, tel. (01) 734–5243, 439–0399; or, in the USA, the Yugoslav National Tourist Office, 630 Fifth Avenue (Rockefeller Center), Suite 210, New York, NY, 10020, tel. (212) 757–2801. They issue free an invaluable booklet entitled *Travel Information* (revised every year).

Air Services between London and Yugoslavia are maintained by British Airways and JAT (Jugoslovenski aerotransport), as well as by Jugotours, a charter organisation. JAT also flies nonstop to Yugoslavia from the USA and Canada. The principal international airports are located at Belgrade and Zagreb; domestic flights connect to all major cities and the more important resorts. Considerable reductions for international travellers (up to 60 per cent) can be obtained for Apex, Pex, Superpex, and Excursion Fares. Children and students are entitled to a discount ranging from 25 to 60 per cent, depending on country of origin. Prices on domestic routes are well below the European average. The cost of transport between airports and town air terminals varies with the distance and must be paid in local currency.

Railway Services. The most direct international trains are the *Simplon Express* (Paris–Milan–Belgrade) and the *Tauern Express* (London–Ostend–Aachen–Cologne–Munich–Zagreb–Knin–Split); the *Akropolis* (Munich–Ljubljana–Belgrade–Kosovo Polje–Skopje–Athens); the *Jugoslavia Express* (Frankfurt–Munich–Ljubljana–Zagreb–Belgrade); the *Hellas Express* (Dortmund–Munich–Belgrade–Skopje–Athens); the *Istanbul Express* (Munich–Belgrade–Sofia–Istanbul); and the *Mostar-Dalmacija Express* (Stüttgart–Munich–Zagreb–Sarajevo–Kardeljevo and Zagreb–Knin–Split). These services have sleeping cars (1st class: single or double compartment; 2nd class: three-berth compartments) and couchettes (1st class, four; 2nd class, six), and connect with trains directed to other Yugoslav cities. Return fares for the journey from London are usually double the single fare; reductions are available for children and groups. Car-sleepers run from s'Hertogenbosch, Schaerbeck, and Düsseldorf to Ljubljana; and from Hamburg Altona to Koper. It is also possible to reach Milan or Rimini similarly if crossing by one of the Adriatic ferry routes. Information from the Yugoslav National Tourist Office, London.

Arrival by Car. British drivers taking their own cars by any of the many routes across France, Belgium, Luxembourg, Switzerland, Germany, Austria, and Italy need only the vehicle registration book, a valid national driving licence, and an International Insurance Certificate (the 'Green Card'). A nationality plate (GB) must be affixed to the rear of the vehicle so as to be illuminated by the tail lamps. Motorists who are not owners of the vehicle should possess the owner's permit for its use abroad. Remember that membership of the *Automobile Association*, the *Royal Automobile Club*, or the *Royal Scottish Automobile Club* entitles motorists to many of the facilities of affiliated societies on the continent and may save trouble and anxiety. In Yugoslavia membership of the neighbouring European organisations carries the same privileges. American drivers renting a car in Yugoslavia need only a valid national driving licence.

Car Ferries are operated by Sealink from Dover to Calais, Boulogne, and Dunkirk and from Newhaven to Dieppe; also by Townsend Thoresen Ferries from Dover to Calais; by British Rail and Zeeland Steamship Co. from Harwich to Hook of Holland; by Belgian State Marine from Harwich to Ostend and from both Dover and Folkestone to Ostend. A hovercraft service operates from Ramsgate to Calais, and from Dover to Boulogne and Calais. In London full particulars are available from the AA, RAC, or British Rail, all at the *Continental Car Ferry Centre*, 52 Grosvenor Gardens, SW1, and at Liverpool Street.

Drive-on car ferries connect the Adriatic ports of Italy and Greece with points on the Yugoslav coast. In summer many of these are supplemented by hydrofoils. The principal services operate from Ancona to Zadar; Bari to Dubrovnik or Bar; Ancona to Split, Stari Grad, and Vela Luka; Igoumenitsa and Corfù to Bar and Dubrovnik; Rijeka, Rab, Zadar, Split, Hvar, Korčula, and Dubrovnik to Corfù and Igoumenitsa; Venice to Dubrovnik; Venice to Split; Trieste to Zadar; Trieste to Split; Trieste to Dubrovnik; Rimini to Zadar; Rimini to Split; Rimini to Dubrovnik; Ancona to Zadar; Ancona to Split; Ancona to Dubrovnik; Pescara to Split; Bari to Split; and Bari to Dubrovnik.

Coaches. Regular long-distance bus services (more frequent in summer) connect Yugoslavia with Italy, Austria, West Germany, Hungary, Romania, Bulgaria, France, and Turkey. Domestic bus traffic is highly developed and reaches all the major resorts. Connections along the coast are especially frequent, and even the main tourist attractions of the interior are served by express buses. Many extra services are introduced in summer.

Passports are necessary for all British and American travellers entering Yugoslavia and must bear the photograph of the holder. No visa is required of citizens of the UK, the Republic of Ireland, and most European countries. Citizens of other countries, including the USA, Canada, Australia, and New Zealand, must possess an entrance visa issued at home by the Yugoslav consular authorities, or at the frontier crossings open for international traffic (including airports and seaports); or obtain a 30-day Tourist pass, also issued at the frontier. Visas and passes are issued with a minimum of formality.

Customs. Provided that dutiable articles are declared, travellers will find the Yugoslav customs authorities courteous and reasonable. The following are admitted without formality (beyond an oral declaration) for personal use, but may not be disposed of in Yugoslavia: personal jewellery, two cameras with 12 plates or five rolls of film each, a small movie-camera with two rolls of film, one pair of field glasses, one portable musical instrument, one portable record- or tape-player with ten records/tapes, one portable radio, one portable typewriter, one baby carriage, camping equipment, one bicycle or moped, one boat with or without motor, one set of sporting equipment (fishing rod and tackle, gun with 50 cartridges, pair of skis, skin- or scuba-diving equipment, tennis racket, etc.). Quantities beyond these may be admitted duty-free but must be declared in writing.

Travellers may also carry in 200 cigarettes, 50 cigars, or 250g of tobacco, one bottle of wine, 0.25 litre of whiskey, and small amounts (e.g., sufficient for personal use) of scent.

Dogs and cats must have a regular certificate of vaccination against rabies, issued no more than six months and no less than 15 days before entry.

Souvenirs bought in Yugoslavia may be exported free of duty, but special permits are necessary for original objects of cultural, artistic, archaeological, ethnographic, historical, or scientific value.

Currency Regulations. There are no restrictions on the amount of sterling the traveller may take out of Great Britain, or on the amount of dollars that can be taken out of the USA. However, there are frequent variations in the amount of Yugoslav notes which may be taken in or out of Yugoslavia. Since there are normally strict limitations, the latest regulations should be checked before departure.

Money. In Yugoslavia the monetary unit is the Dinar. On their first visit to Yugoslavia in a given calendar year, travellers may bring in and take out up to 2500 dinars per person in notes of 1000 dinars or less. On subsequent visits they may bring in and take out up to 500 dinars per person. Notes are issued for 10, 20, 50, 100, 500, and 1000 dinars. Coins are of 1, 2, 5, and 10 dinars.

When changing money travellers may request dinars or dinar cheques; the latter may be spent like dinars and may be changed back upon leaving the country, whereas cash may not. Dinar cheques also entitle the bearer to discounts in certain hotels, restaurants, etc.

Hotels and Restaurants

Hotels in Yugoslavia are classified into five categories: L (DeLuxe), A, B, C, and D. Pensions are classified into three categories: I, II, and III. In this guide hotels have not been indicated in the text since it can now be taken for granted that almost every small centre in the country will be provided with adequate accommodation. More detailed information about hotels and restaurants can be found in the Michelin Hotel and Restaurant 'Red Guide', revised annually. Generally speaking, hotels and pensions of every class will be found in the larger towns and along the coast. In major cities and resorts the Tourist Information Centre (*Turistički informativni centar*) has up-to-date information regarding hotel categories, prices, and facilities, and local tourist offices (*Turist biro*) help travellers to find accommodation on the spot.

The charges current in any particular year are listed annually in

Hotelske cene (Hotel Prices), a bulletin issued by the General Association of the Tourist Industry of Yugoslavia (*Opste Udrezenje turističke privrede Jugoslavije*), Belgrade, and are usually given in dollars or DM. Hoteliers are bound to conform to the prices given in this bulletin and are required to display the official cost of each room on a notice fixed to the inside of the door. A sliding scale operates in all cases, the higher rates being charged during the tourist season (July, August, and sometimes September), and low rates in the winter, with an intermediate rate for May, June, and October. Service charges are included, but not the visitors' tax, which ranges from 120 to 500 dinars per day according to the amenities of the town. Full board in Yugoslavia includes continental breakfast, lunch, and dinner, but is not available for stays under three days.

In addition to hotels there is now a growing number of *motels*, along major highways; and *tourist villages* (consisting of separate villas or bungalows with or without kitchen, and a central service pavilion) along the coast.

Consideration should be given while travelling in Yugoslavia to the widespread availability of *private rooms* (*privatne sobe*). These are graded like pensions and hotels, but are considerably cheaper, and thanks to the hospitality of the Yugoslavs and efficient supervision, offer excellent value for money. Meals, except breakfast, are not normally provided, but such accommodation offers an unrivalled opportunity of acquiring a more intimate knowledge of the country and the people. Private rooms can be booked either on the spot or in advance through the local Turist biro.

Camping in Yugoslavia is organised on normal European lines. The main sites are usually shown on standard tourist maps of the country. The minimum provisions are running water, electricity, and parking space, but the main sites offer all the amenities usually associated with this form of accommodation.

Youth Hostels and student accommodation are administered by the Office for International Youth and Student Exchange. This operates youth centres at Dubrovnik, Rovinj, Bečiči, and Kopaonik and organises visits to other cities as well as study-tours through Yugoslavia. Details may be obtained from Jugotours-Narom, 31 Djure Djakovica, Belgrade, tel. 763–729, or through their agencies in Belgrade, Zagreb, and Skopje.

Restaurants (*restorani*, Slov. *restavracije*). Yugoslav food is usually good and inexpensive. The least prententious restaurant often provides the best value, and the menu displayed outside the restaurant indicates the kind of charges the customer should expect. Fixed-price meals (*menu*, pronounced and sometimes spelled *meni*) are generally obtainable in hotel restaurants and are spreading rapidly to other establishments. The service charge is now almost automatically added at the end of the bill. Tipping is therefore not strictly necessary, but a few dinars may be given to show appreciation for exceptional service. There is rarely a cover charge.

A less expensive place to eat is the *gostoina* or *gostionica* (Slov. *gostilina*), where the dishes are traditionally chalked up on a board or else recited by the waiter, though menus are also appearing now. The food is simple' and the number of dishes limited, but the qualitt is often excellent. *Gostione* usually specialise in national dishes. Rather more impersonal are the modern self-service restaurants (*samopo-*

služni restoran, Slov. *samopostrežna restavracija*) that have sprung up in many places. Simple food may also be obtained in snack bars (*bife*), where it is often eaten standing up. Breakfast, consisting of rolls, butter, jam, doughnuts, and coffee, tea, or hot milk, is to be had cheaply in dairy restaurants known as a *mlječni restoran* (Slov. *mlečna restavracija*), some of which in the bigger towns are able to provide more ambitious menus.

Meals compare favourably in price with those in Britain or the USA and are usually of a higher standard, bearing in mind the Mediterranean preference for spices and an abundance of olive oil. A simple three-course lunch or dinner can generally be had in a restaurant for the equivalent of about £5.00 ($10.00), including wine. This may be reduced further in cheaper establishments. Breakfast in general follows the continental pattern, though cold meats, bacon, eggs, cheese, etc., may be ordered if desired. The main meal of the day is lunch (*ručak*, Slov. *kosilo*), consisting of soup, a main dish based on meat or fish, together with vegetables and usually a salad, and dessert. Dinner (*večera*, Slov. *večerja*) is similar, but usually substitutes an hors d'ouevre for soup and is generally lighter.

Red or white table wine (*črno* or *bijelo vino*, Slov. *črno* and *belo*) is the usual accompaniment to meals, the wine being strong and natural and able to stand dilution. Water is readily available, except on some of the smaller islands, and the Yugoslavs are very fond of mineral water (*mineralna voda*), of which some of the best-known varieties are *Radenska* and *Rogaška* in the N and *Bukovička* in the S. Beer (*pivo*) is also readily available, and is usually of the lager variety.

Food and Wine. Yugoslav cooking consists of a distinctive blend of Mediteranean and Austrian elements, together with a selection of Serbian, Bosnian, and Macedonian dishes of basically Greek and Turkish origin. Meat (*meso*) is invariably fresh and plentiful and first-rate, particularly the lamb (*janjetina*) and veal (*teletina*); salads (*salate*) and fruit (*voče*, Slov. *sadje*) are outstanding; the cooked vegetables (*variva*) are more variable and, like all food in Yugoslavia, depend heavily on the season; desserts are generally delicious; and the cheeses (*sirevi*) can offer some pleasant surprises (*Bohinjski, Paski sir; Kačkavalj* in Serbia). As is to be expected, seafood is plentiful and available in great variety. A tendency in recent years for Yugoslav restaurants to lean too heavily in the direction of featureless 'international' dishes and ignore their local cuisine, seems to be changing again in favour of national dishes.

Some Oriental dishes, such as *sarma* (stuffed cabbage or vine leaves), *djuveč* (a rich casserole with meat, rice paprikas, etc.), *kapama* (lamb stewed with spinach, shallots, and yoghourt) or *musaka* are highly recommended, while the Yugoslav predilection for grilling and spit-roasting finds expression in numerous kebabs (*ćevap*) and shashliks (*šašlik*) of which the best known are the ubiquitous *ćevapčići* (grilled balls of minced beef) and *ražnjići* (grilled slices of veal and pork), both served with chopped raw onion and cayenne pepper. Popular variations on this formula are *pljeskavice* (grilled balls of minced veal and pork) and *ćulbastija* (grilled pork cutlets). Finally a word should also be said for the fine *pršut* (smoked ham) of Istria and Dalmatia and the Gavrilović *salama* (salami) from Croatia.

The **Wines** in Yugoslavia are generally of good standard. Many of them are referred to in the text. In Slovenia and the northern part of Istria it is a good idea to try *teran* or the lighter *refoško*, both red, and the white wine *rebula*, while the sweet *malvazija* (Malmsey) is found all over Istria. Farther down the coast the red wines tend to predominate, the best being the *opoli* (almost a rosé) from mainland Dalmatia, the full-bodied *plavac* from the south Dalmatian islands and *dingač*, a very strong and fruity wine from the Pelješac peninsula. Among the best-known white wines are *pošip, vugava, grk*, and *maraština*. The ubiquitous *prošek*, made from dried fermented grapes, may be too sweet for many palates but varies considerably from place to place. Also available in many restaurants are some of the better known wines from other parts of Yugoslavia: *silvanac, traminac, rizling, žilavka, blatina, prokupac, Fruškogorski biser*, and *kavadarka*. Those with a taste for liqueurs and brandy should try the national specialities of *šljivovica* (plum brandy), the well-known *maraschino*, a sweet after-dinner liqueur made from morello cherries, and the cherry brandy.

The following MENU includes many dishes that are likely to be met with:

JELOVNIK (Slov. *Jedilnik*)—MENU

Doručak (Slov. *Zajtrk*)—**Breakfast**
Doručak komplet, Continental breakfast
Kruh, hleb, Bread
Pecivo, kifla, Roll
Maslac, puter, Butter
Džem, marmelada, Jam
Crna kava (or kafa), Black coffee
B(ij)ela kava, White coffee
Turska kava, Turkish coffee
Čaj sa ml(ij)ekom, Tea with milk
Čaj sa limunom, Tea with lemon
Čokolada, Drinking chocolate
Šunka sa jajem, (h)emendeks, Ham and eggs

Ručak i obed ili večera (Slov. *Kosilo i Večerja*)—**Lunch and dinner**
Hladna predjela (Slov. *Narezek*)—**Cold hors d'oeuvre**
Kavijar, ajvar, Caviar
Pašteta, Pâté
Hladni narezak, Cold cuts
Dalmatinski pršut sa sirom, Smoked Dalmatian ham with cheese
Ruska jaja, Hard-boiled eggs with Russian salad
Sardine u ulju, Sardines in oil
Masline, Olives

Topla predjela (Slov. *predjed*)—**Warm hors d'oeuvre**
Špageti na milanski, bolonjski način, Spaghetti all milanese, bolognese
Omlet sa šunkom, sirom, povrćem, Ham, cheese, 'Spanish' omelet
Srpska jaja, Omelet with tomatoes, paprikas and cucumber
Kajgana, Scrambled egg
Meko, tvrdo, kuvano jaja, Soft, hard, boiled egg
Špargle sa sirom, Asparagus with cheese
Kranjska kobasa, kobasica, Pork sausages from Kranj (Slovenia)

Juhe, supe, čorbe—**Soups**
Supa od povrća, Vegetable soup
Govedja juha, Consommé
Juha od rajčice, paradajza, Tomato soup
Supa od kokošijeg mesa s knedlama od džigerice, Chicken soup with liver dumplings
Riblja čorba, Čorba od morske ribe, Fish soup
Govedja juha sa graškom, Pea soup

Ribe—**Fish**
Brodet na Dalmatinski, Bokeljski način, Dalmatian, Boka Kotorska, fish stew
Bakalar na mornarski način, Smoked cod, sailor's style
Barbun, trlja u pergamentu, Striped mullet in waxed paper
Pečena kečiga, Baked sterlet
Orada s paradajzom, Bream baked with tomatoes

Rizoto od kalamara, Squid risotto
Pohovan file od smudja, Fried perch fillets
Smudj sa pečurkama, Perch fried and then baked with mushrooms.
Kuvane skuše, Boiled mackerel
Pržena pastrva, pastrmka, (postrv), Fried trout
Pijani šaran iz Skadarskog jezera, Baked Skadar carp
Jastog, Lobster
Kamenica, oštriga, Oyster
Školjka, kapica, Clam
Rak, rakovica, Crab
Bjelica, kesiga, Whiting
Oslić, Hake
Zubatac, Dentex
Cipalj, Mullet
Tuna, tunj, Tunny
Pic, špic, Sheepshead bream
Murina, Moray eel
Ugor, grunj, Conger eel
List, Sole
Sardele, Fresh sardines

Gotova jela (Slov. *jedi*)—**Plats du jour**
Punjeni plavi patlidžani, Baked stuffed aubergines (eggplants)
Pasulj sa suvim jezikom, Beans with smoked pork
Bosanski lonac, Bosnian casserole cooked in white wine
Teleći rizoto, Veal risotto
Pileči paprikaš sa noklicama, Chicken stew with dumplings
Pašta i fažol, Macaroni with beans
Kelerabe nadevene mozgom, Cabbage stuffed with brains
Pilav od ovčetine, Mutton pilaff
Svinjksi paprikaš s kiselim kupusom i pavlakom, Pork stew with sauerkraut and cream
Punjeni papadajz, Stuffed tomatoes
Punjene paprike, tikvice, Stuffed paprikas, courgettes
Kuhana govedina, Boiled beef
Teleće grudi punjene spančem, Breast of veal stuffed with spinach
Govedji gulaš, Beef goulash

Specijaliteti na ražnju i roštilju—Grills and Roasts
Pečeno pile, pečena patka, Roast chicken, roast duck
Svinjsko, teleće pečenje, Roast pork, veal
Pečena ćurka nadevena pečurkama, Roast turkey stuffed with mushrooms
Pečena guska sa limunom, Roast goose with lemon
Džigerica (jetra), bubrezi, srce na žaru, Grilled, liver, kidneys, heart
Jagnjeći šašlik, Lamb shashlik
Šiš-ćevap, Shish-kebab
Hajdučki ćevap, Kebab of mixed meats

Jela po narudžbi (Slov. *Jedi po naročilu*)—**Dishes to order**
Biftek sa jajem, Steak with a fried egg on top
Ramstek, Rump steak
Šatobrian, 'Chateaubriand'—double steak garnished with vegetables
Svinjski kotlet, Pork chop
Naravni odrezak, (zrezek), Escalope of veal
Zagrebački odrezak, Escalope of veal stuffed with ham and cheese
Bečki, (Dunajski) odrezak, šnicel, (zrezek), Veal fried in bread-crumbs (Wiener schnitzel)
Sprska plość; Mešano meso na žaru, Mixed grill
Prepelice na lovački način, Stewed quail, chasseur
Prepelice s pirinčem, rižom, Quail casserole with rice
Jarebic na žaru, Grilled partridges
Pečeni fazan, Roast pheasant

Povrće (Slov. *Zelenjava*)—**Vegetables**
Mrkva, šargarepa, Carrots
Grašask, Peas
Pasulj, Red or kidney beans
Boranija, French beans
Bobovi, Broad beans
Krompire (kuhani, pečeni), Potatoes (boiled, roast)
Prženi krompir, pomfrit, Fried potatoes, chips

Spanać, špinat, Spinach
Kupus, (zelje), Cabbage
Kiseli kupus, (kiselo zelje), Sauerkraut
Prokelji, Brussels sprouts
Cvetača, karfiol, Cauliflower
Pirinač, riž, Rice
Paprika, Paprika
Patlidžan, (melancan), Aubergine
Pečurka, Mushroom
Celer, Celery
Repa, Turnip
Luk, (čebula), Onions
Ren, Horseradish
Šparga, špargle, Asparagus
Tikva, (buča), Pumpkin, marrow
Tikvica, Courgette (Zucchini, squash)

Salate—Salads
M(ij)ešana salata, Mixed salad
Zelena salata, Green salad (lettuce)
Paradajz, rajčice, (paradižnik), Tomato
Krastavac (kiseo), (kumarica), Cucumber (gherkin)
Cikla, (pesa), Beetroot
Rotkva, Rotkvica, Radish

Poslastice, Kolači (Slov. *Slaščice*)—**Desserts**
Sladoled, Ice cream
Šerbet, Sherbet
Palačinka sa dzemom, čokoladom, Jam, chocolate pancake
Strudla, savijača od jabuka, (jabučni zavitek), Apple strudel
Torta, Gâteau
Medenjaci, Honey cakes
Istarske fritule, Istrian fritters, a form of crêpes suzettes made with Maraschino
Pita, A kind of paper-thin pastry that can be filled with fruits, nuts or cheese
Ratluk, Turkish delight
Kompot, Stewed fruit (generally cold)

Voće (Slov. *Sadje*)—**Fruit**
Voćna, (sadna) salata, Fruit salad
Smokve, Figs
Trešnje, (češnje), Cherries
Višnje, Sour cherries
Jabuke, (jabolke), Apples
Kruške, Pears
Šljive, Plums
Jagode, Strawberries
Breskve, Peaches
Marelice, kajsije, Apricots
Narandže, naranče, pomarandže, Oranges
Limuni, Lemons
Dinja, Melon
Lubenica, Watermelon

Sir(ev)i—Cheese
Paški, Krčki sir, Sheep's milk cheese from the islands of Pag and Krk
Primorski, granički sir, The same made near Rijeka
Trapist, 'Trappist', one of the best cow's milk cheeses in Yugoslavia. International varieties can also be found under their usual names (Bel paese, gorgonzola, edam, etc.)
Zdenka, Processed cheese
Kačkavalj, A hard cheese of sheep's or sheep's and cow's milk mixed
Gibanica, Cheese pie
Pogačice od sira 'kačkavalja', Kačkavalj cheese biscuits
Štruklji, Slovenian cheese pie

Miscellaneous
So, (Sol), Salt
Biber, (poper), Pepper
Ulje, Oil
Sirće, Vinegar
Senf, muštarda, (gorušica), Mustard
Beli luk, (česenj), Garlic

ećer, (sladkor), Sugar
Sendvič, Sandwich
Nož, Knife
Vilica, Fork
Kašika, (žlica), Spoon
Tanjir, (krožnik), Plate
Šalica, šolja, (skodelica), Cup
Tanjurić, Saucer
Čaša, (kozarec), Glass
Stolica, (sto), Chair
Sto, (miza), Table
Stolnjak, (prt), Table cloth
Ubrus, salvet, servijeta, Napkin
Konobar, Kelner, (natakar), Waiter
Račun, Bill
Plaćati!, May I pay the bill!
Napojnica, (napitnina), Tip

Transport

Railways. The Yugoslav National Railways (*Jugoslovenske železnice*) run four main categories of trains. (1) EX, long-distance express trains running between the main Yugoslav (and European) cities. (2) P, Business Trains (Inter City), running between main towns. (3) B, fast trains stopping only at major stations. (4) Trains with no special designation: slow trains stopping at all, or nearly all, stations. A special supplement is charged and seat reservation is obligatory on many trains in the EX, P, and B categories.

Trains in Yugoslavia are usually crowded, especially in summer; seats can be booked (though not for all trains) from the main cities at the station booking office or through a travel agent. Fares are still much lower than in England.

RESTAURANT CARS are attached to most international and international long-distance trains. Some trains now also have self-service restaurants. Also, snacks, hot coffee and drinks are sold throughout the journey from a trolley wheeled down the train. At every large station snacks are on sale from trolleys on the platform, and can be bought from the train window.

Tickets must be bought at the station before the journey. Reductions on the price of domestic travel are available for return tickets (20 per cent), for the elderly, age 60 and over (30 per cent), for children ages 4–12 (50 per cent; children under four ride free), and for groups of five or more persons (30 per cent). Inter-Rail passes give further discounts.

Coaches. Local buses abound between the main towns. In addition many of the principal Yugoslav coach companies operate regular long-distance coach services. Details from the Yugoslav National Tourist Office in London/New York, or from the local information bureau.

Air Services. Regular scheduled flights operate frequently between major cities and resorts. Prices for domestic air travel in Yugoslavia are considerably lower than the European average.

Boats and Ferries play a large part in Adriatic transport. The regular services are run by *Jadrolinija*, the principal Yugoslav passenger shipping line, with headquarters at Rijeka and agencies in every port where tickets may be booked in advance. In high summer cabins are well booked, but it is rarely that a deck passage cannot be obtained. Fares are comparatively cheap.

An express service serves main ports daily in summer (four times weekly in winter) on route Rijeka–Rab–Zadar–Split–Hvar–Korčula–Dubrovnik.

The main ports are connected by local services with their neighbouring islands. These services run all the year round. Being mail boats and market boats or school boats, they run at the times most convenient to the local users, often involving very early starts and late arrivals to the outlying ports. An indication of connected points and of frequency is given in the text, but inquiry should always be made at the local Jadrolinija office. Weather conditions permitting, the services are regular, punctual, and well organised, and printed timetables may be obtained.

Motoring

Highway Codes. The rule of the road in Yugoslavia, as elsewhere on the continent, is to drive on the right and overtake on the left. Road signs and markings follow international norms. Speed limits are posted and strictly enforced: the maximum is 120kmph on motorways, 100kmph on major highways, 80kmph on other roads, and 60kmph in built-up areas. Most large cities have a 'blue zone' where parking is prohibited; in some cities and resorts cars may be left only in designated paid parking areas. Motorists and their passengers must wear seat belts at all times. All vehicles must carry a red triangle in case of accident or breakdown. This serves as a warning to other traffic when placed on the road at a distance of 50m from the stationary car. In case of breakdown, the nearest office of the *Auto-Moto Savez Jugoslavije* (Yugoslav Automobile Club) can be contacted by telephone number 987. An emergency repair service operates seven days a week, from 8.00 to 20.00 (24hrs a day in the season). Yugoslav law requires that motorists stop to assist accident victims.

Tolls are charged on only a few roads, namely the motorways from Ljubljana to Razdrto, Hoce to Arja vas, Zagreb to Karlovac, Ivanja Reka (Zagreb) to Lipovljani, Pojate to Niš, Belgrade to Cuprija, and Belgrade to Novi Sad; the Učka tunnel, and the bridge between the Island of Krk and the mainland.

Petrol and Service. Most stations sell two grades of petrol, *premium* (86 octane) and *superior* (98 octane). Petrol stations are numerous, and some operate round the clock; nevertheless the tank should not be allowed to get too low, as the distance between one station and another may vary considerably. Petrol coupons, giving a discount, may be bought before departure (through the automobile clubs, for instance) or at the frontier.

Service is available throughout the country for most current European cars, though only those service centres located in major cities or resorts stock parts.

Roads. The road system in Yugoslavia has improved remarkably over the last few years. All major highways and most minor roads are now asphalted, the surface in most cases being smooth and new. Some gravel or tar roads still exist in less-travelled areas, and where city streets are paved with cobblestones the surface may be uneven or broken. Drivers using the *Adriatic Highway* should take particular care on blind curves, not only because the locals drive near the crown of the road, but because of the prevalence of rock falls. A dangerous hazard in certain seasons is posed by the 'Bura', a violent cross-wind. Some particularly susceptible areas of road are equipped with wind-socks on exposed curves. In sudden storms it may prove impossible to continue because of blinding rain, when at night it is too hazardous to drive off the road; a flashing red lamp, held in readiness in an easily accessible position inside the car, and placed in the rear window, affords a modicum of additional protection from accident.

Maps. The Auto Moto Zveza Slovenije publishes an excellent roadmap on a scale of 1:850,000, available through the Yugoslav National Tourist Office. Michelin also publishes a detailed, but somewhat less readable, map of the country.

General Information

Season. Generally speaking, July and August are the hottest months on the Adriatic coast and are to be preferred by those in search of sun, though southern Montenegro may be found rather too hot at this time of year. June and September are easier to bear everywhere and often provide periods of almost perfect weather, but it should be borne in mind that they also include the equinoxes, when unsettled spells of about 7–10 days are usually the rule. May and October may be relied upon as excellent months for travelling, while the sea is warm enough in both months, and sometimes even into November, for comfortable bathing to be possible. In the remaining months many hotels are closed and tourist facilities in the smaller places are reduced or nonexistent, but the larger resorts are encouraging winter visitors and a high proportion of warm sunny days makes this an excellent time for sightseeing and getting to know the local populace. The climate is in general not severe throughout the winter and snow and frost are both rare occurrences.

Language. English is fairly widely spoken in towns, but elsewhere is less well known than Italian or German, while French is a popular language in Montenegro. It cannot be expected that many people will take the trouble to master the Yugoslavs' own language, but the acquisition of a few basic phrases will do wonders to smooth the visitor's path and creates a favourable impression out of all proportion to the effort needed to acquire them. The official language of Yugoslavia is Serbo-Croatian, so named for the two closely related dialects of the Croats and Serbs. There are also several recognised minority languages, the most important of which, Slovenian, is spoken in the north. Serbo-Croatian has the great advantage of possessing a completely phonetic alphabet, so that once the sounds are mastered it may be pronounced, save for some stress difficulties, with impunity by beginners and foreigners alike. Some hints for pronunciation follow.

Consonants are roughly the same as in English, but with the following exceptions: c has the sound of ts as in Betsy; h is more guttural, as in German, than in English; j is like consonantal y as in yard. Certain additional consonants are denoted by letters with diacritical marks: č has the sound of ch as in church; ć has the sound of t as in vulture; d (also written as dj) has the sound of d as in verdure; š has the sound of sh as in shell; ž has the sound of s as in measure; dž has the sound of j as in jug.

Vowels are all open and pure in Serbo-Croatian as in Italian and have their full value; there are no diphthongs. In addition there is a vocalic r which need present no difficulties if approached with a cool head. Its sound is like the Scottish rolled r as in kirk.

Stress is not fixed, but generally speaking tends to be towards the beginning of words.

In Montenegro, Macedonia, and southern Serbia the Cyrillic alphabet is officially in use and although signposts, street names, and official signs are supposed to show Latin equivalents, this does not always occur in practice. It is desirable, therefore, when visiting those regions, to have a knowledge of the alphabet for reference purposes. A full list of letters follows, together with their Latin equivalents.

Cyrillic		Latin		Cyrillic		Latin	
А	а	A	a	Н	н	N	n
Б	б	B	b	Њ	њ	Nj	nj
В	в	V	v	О	о	O	o
Г	г	G	g	П	п	P	p
Д	д	D	d	Р	р	R	r
Ђ	ђ	Đ Dj	d, dj	С	с	S	s
Е	е	E	e	Т	т	T	t
Ж	ж	Ž	ž	Ћ	ћ	Ć	ć
З	з	Z	z	У	у	U	u
И	и	I	i	Ф	ф	F	f
Ј	ј	J	j	Х	х	H	h
К	к	K	k	Ц	ц	C	c
Л	л	L	l	Ч	ч	Č	č
Љ	љ	Lj	lj	П	п	Dž	dž
М	м	M	m	Ш	ш	Š	š

Manners and Customs. The manners of the Yugoslavs can be informal to the point of abruptness when dealing with one another, but usually take on a more formal character when foreigners are addressed. In shops and offices a certain amount of self-assertion is taken for granted, as queues are not the general rule and it is incumbent on the inquirer or customer to get himself a hearing. Nevertheless, requests for service, information or advice should normally be prefaced by *molim* or *molim Vas* (please)—or *prosim* in Slovenia—and it is appreciated (though not expected) if such transactions are concluded with *hvala* (thank you) or the more fulsome *hval Vam l(ij)epo*—in Slovenia *hvala lepa* (thank you very much). The almost universal response to thanks is again *molim* or *prosim* (don't mention it) and this is also used when asking someone to repeat a phrase that has not been properly heard. In buses or crowded places it is helpful to say *izvinite* (excuse me) when pushing past other people, while an apparent breach of manners is best apologised for by *oprostite* (forgive me). In Slovenia *oprostite* is used on both these occasions.

As in most parts of the continent, it is customary in Yugoslavia to shake hands with people not only on first meeting them but at each subsequent separate meeting, and in homes to shake hands on rising and before retiring. To this should be added the appropriate greeting of *dobar dan* (good day), *dobro veče* (good evening) or *laku noć*—Slovenia *dober dan*, *dober večer*, and *lahko noč*. General greetings are rendered by *zdravo* (hello) and this is frequently accompanied by the inquiry *kako ste* (how are you?), to which the normal reply is *dobro*, *hvala*, *kako ste Vi* (very well, thank you, and how are you?). The word for welcome is *dobrodošli*, for goodbye *do vidjenja* (Slovenian *na svidanje*); yes is *da* (Slovenian *ja*) and no *ne* (a difficult adjustment to make when crossing into Yugoslavia from Greece!).

The Yugoslavs are an intensely hospitable people and the code of hospitality is treated with some seriousness, particularly away from the big towns. On entering a private house one is invariably offered Turkish coffee together with a liqueur of some kind—usually *šljivovica* (plum brandy) or one of its cousins. One or the other of these may be refused, but not both, without giving offence. The cup or glass will then be replenished as soon as it is empty, so it is essential to leave some in until the end of the visit if one wishes not to continue drinking. In the South may also be experienced the Balkan custom of offering preserves with coffee and water; in such a case it is usual to take one spoon of preserves and sip or drink the water before drinking the coffee. A stranger is rarely permited to play host to a native and will experience some difficulty in repaying debts of hospitality. Needless to say, payment in kind is the only method acceptable and the best course is to offer small gifts for the household or children or to bring flowers. At meals one is usually wished *dobar* (Slovenian *dober*) *tek* beforehand, to which the reply, if one's companions are also eating, is *hvala*, *i Vam takodje* (thank you, and the same to you).

The '*corzo*' or evening walk is universal and takes place usually between about 6 and 8 pm in summer and slightly earlier in winter. It is usually confined to certain streets or a particular street in larger towns (often itself named the *corzo*) and traffic is barred for its duration.

Photography. There are few restrictions on photography in Yugoslavia, but permission is necessary to photograph the interiors of churches and museums and may sometimes be withheld. Care should also be taken before photographing individuals such as soldiers or policemen or peasants from the interior, some of whom may feel insulted and protest. Moslems in particular may not be photographed without their permission unless in groups and from afar. Photography is normally forbidden near military and naval installations and this is indicated by a sign consisting of a picture of a camera with a cross over it.

Churches are normally closed for a considerable period during the middle of the day (12 to 15, 16 or 17.00), whereas smaller churches and chapels open only for a few hours in the morning or perhaps only on saints' or feast days. In the case of the former the sacristan may usually be found by inquiring locally, but the keys of the smaller churches are frequently kept in episcopal or parish offices or by local conservationists or museum curators and sometimes take a considerable time to obtain, particularly in country districts. Once a church is open access can normally be had to sacristies, closed chapels and paintings without any difficulty and only the smallest gratuity is necessary (and even so may be rejected) to the person bringing the key. In the cities an entrance fee is becoming customary for admission to treasuries, bell towers, etc. In Catholic churches visitors may move about during services (except during high mass), provided they do not approach the altar(s) in use, but at all times are expected to cover their legs and women are expected to cover their heads. In Orthodox churches moving about during services is not encouraged and women are not allowed in the sanctuary.

Museums are usually open six days a week, the commonest closing day being Monday. Typical opening hours are from 10–17, though these may vary slightly from place to place and with the size of the museum. A few museums are open only in the morning, whereas in small places museums are often opened on request. Entrance fees are generally small.

Public Holidays. The main public holidays in Yugoslavia are as follows: 1 and 2 January (New Year), 1 and 2 May (Labour Day), 4 July (Veterans Day), 29 and 30 November (Day of the Republic). In addition each constituent republic has its own national day, for example: Slovenia (27 April, 22 July, 1 November); Croatia (27 July); Bosnia and Hercegovina (27 July; 25 November), and Montenegro (13 July). The observance of patron saints' days and major Christian festivals is ill-defined owing to the disestablished nature of the church in Yugoslavia, but most cities on the coast contrive at least an informal holiday to coincide with Christmas, Easter, the Assumption, and the patronal festival.

Amusements. The organised entertainment that most visitors are likely to patronise is the cinema, of which there is at least one in all places of any size and up to a dozen or more in the larger cities. A wide selection of up-to-date foreign and domestic films is shown, usually in the original versions with subtitles, and cinemas may be indoors or in the open air. Performances occur once, twice or sometimes thrice nightly and tickets may be purchased at the cinema box office between 10–12 during the day or one hour before the performance begins. Admission prices are modest.

Details of the annual international FESTIVALS held in Split, Dubrovnik, and Pula, are indicated in the text: their programmes are widely publicized in advance. EXHIBITIONS of folk dancing and local handicrafts are organised during the tourist season and locally publicised. Other local entertainments are indicated in the text.

Newpapers. Foreign newspapers and magazines, including English, are readily obtainable in the larger towns from kiosks or shops specialising in them, but rarely elsewhere. The principal national newspapers are *Borba* and *Politika* (published in Belgrade), *Vijesnik* (Zagreb), and *Delo* (Ljubljana).

Working Hours. Government and business offices usually work from 7.30–15.30 daily except Saturday and Sunday. School hours are either 8–1 or 2–7 (Monday–Friday). Banks and official exchange offices are open to the public from 7–19, Saturday 7–13, closed on Sundays and national holidays. Most restaurants are open from 7 am till midnight.

Weights and Measures. The metric system is used in Yugoslavia, with basically the same terminology as in other countries. The unit of length is the *metar*, of weight the *gram*, of land measurement the *ar*, and of capacity the *litar*. Greek-derived prefixes (deka, hekto, kilo) are used with these names to express multiples, Latin prefixes (deci, centi or santi, mili) to express fractions (dekogram = 10 grama, santimetar = 10 milimetara). In measures of weight 100 kilograma = 1 quintal and 10 quintala = 1 tona.

Topographical Glossary

Aerodrom, Airport
Banja, Spa
Bedem, Wall
Biskupija, Bishop's palace
Blato, Pond, swamp
Brdo, Hill, mountain
Cesta, Road, street
Crkva, Church
Dolina, Valley
Donj-i, a, e, Lower
Draga, Cove, inlet
Dvor, Dvorac, Palace
Fortica, Fortress
Gat, Pier, mole
Gledalište (Slov.), Theatre
Gora, Hill, mountain
Gornj-i, a, e, Upper
Grad, Town, city
Groblje, Graveyard
Istok, Istočni (adj.), East
Jadran, Jadransko, Adriatic
Jezero, Lake
Jug, Južni (adj.), South
Kamen, Stone
Kamenolom, Quarry
Kanal, Channel
Kapela, Chapel
Katedrala, Cathedral
Kazalište, Theatre
Kuča, House
Kula, Tower
Kupalište, Bathing place
Loža, Loggia
Luka, Harbour
Mal-i, a, e, Small
Manastir, Monastery
More, Sea
Most, Bridge
Muzej, Museum
Nov-i, a, o, New
Obala, Shore, quay
Opatija, Abbey
Otok, Island
Palača, Palata, Mansion, town house

Pjaca, Square
Placa, Square
Planina, Mountain
Plaža, Beach
Poljana, Square
Polje, Field, meadow
Poluotok, Peninsula
Pozorišt, Theatre
Pristanište, Jetty
Prolaz, Passage, cut
Put, Road, street, path
Rijeka, Reka, River
Rt, Rat, Headland, point
Rudnik, Mine
Samostan, Monastery, nunnery
Selo, Village
Sever, Seven-i, a, o, North
Slap, Waterfall
Spilja, Cave
Spomenik, Monument
Star-i, a, o., Old
Stolnica (Slov.), Cathedral
Svet-i, a, o., Saint, holy
Šetalište, Promenade
Tjesnac, Narrows
Toranj, Tower
Trg, Square
Trgovina, Shop
Tržnica, Market
Tvrdjava, Fortress
Ulica, street
Ušće, River mouth
Uvala, Small bay
Vel-, Velik-i, a, o., Big, large
Vijećnica, Town Hall
Vrata, Strait, gate
Vrh, Peak, summit
Zaljev, Bay
Zapad, Zapadn-i, a, o, West
Zgrada, Building
Zid, Zidina, Wall
Zvonik, Bell tower, belfry

I   SLOVENIA

Slovenia, occupying the northwestern part of Yugoslavia, borders on Italy, Austria, and Hungary. It covers an area of 20,251km^2, or 8 per cent of the nation's total area. The western and northern parts of the region are dominated by the Julian, Karawanken and Kamnik Alps, culminating in Mt Triglav, or Tricorno (2864m), near the Italian border. This lovely alpine region abounds in wooded plateaux and hills, deep fertile valleys, waterfalls, canyons, and glacial lakes (including Bled and Bohinj, once fashionable watering places of the Austrian aristocracy). In the S, beyond the broad Ljubljana and Celje valleys, the Alps give way to the Dinaric highlands and to the limestone region known as the *karst*, a desert land of porous white rock that absorbs rainwater so rapidly, only the most robust vegetation manages to survive. Many unusual and beautiful natural features distinguish the area, notably the spectacular Postojna and Škocjan caverns, Lake Cerkniško, which disappears into the ground periodically, and a variety of swift underground rivers that spring from the rock and vanish again.

The southernmost part of Slovenia extends to the Adriatic, forming a coastline 47km long embracing the port of Koper and the summer resorts of Piran, Portorož, Izola, and Ankaran. Rolling hills, covered mostly with vineyards, extend to the E and NW of the littoral, yielding gradually to the fertile lowlands of the Pannonian Plain.

Slovenia has a population of 1,892,000, which is composed of 91 per cent Slovenes, 3 per cent Croats, 2 per cent Serbs, 1 per cent 'Yugoslavs', 1 per cent Muslims, a fractional percentage of ethnic Hungarians and Italians, and 2 per cent other nationalities. The capital and largest city is Ljubljana; other major towns are Maribor, Celje, Kranj, Koper, Novo Mesto, Nova Gorica, Titovo Velenje, Jesenice, and Trbovlje.

Slovenia is the wealthiest region of Yugoslavia. Industry, mining, building, transportation, and tertiary activities employ 85 per cent of the labour force, and the per capita income is equal to that of countries which have attained a medium level of economic development. Slovenia's natural resources include timber (more than half the republic is forested), non-ferrous metals, and various types of building materials. Arable land makes up 32 per cent of the total area, and is exploited with remarkable efficiency: the rural population in 1981 was a mere 9 per cent. Half the arable land is used for growing grain crops, and one quarter for animal fodder. Considerable quantities of potatoes and other vegetables are raised.

Slovenia offers excellent winter sports (popular resorts are located at Kranjska Gora, Planica, Kanin, Velika Planina, Krvavec, Golte, and Pohorje), mountaineering, bathing, fishing (trout, grayling and pike), and hunting (bear, red deer, chamois, wild boar, row deer, hare, pheasant, partridge, etc.); and there are quite a few spas, mineral-water springs, and climatic resorts, set in beautiful and tranquil surroundings (Rogaška Slatina, Dobrna, Laško, Podčetrtek, Čateške Toplice, Šmarješke, and Dolenjske Toplice are among the more renowned). No less important, of course, are the numerous monuments of cultural and historical interest, including fine examples of Northern Gothic and baroque architecture. These are concentrated mainly in Ljubljana and in the larger towns.

Key to Route Maps

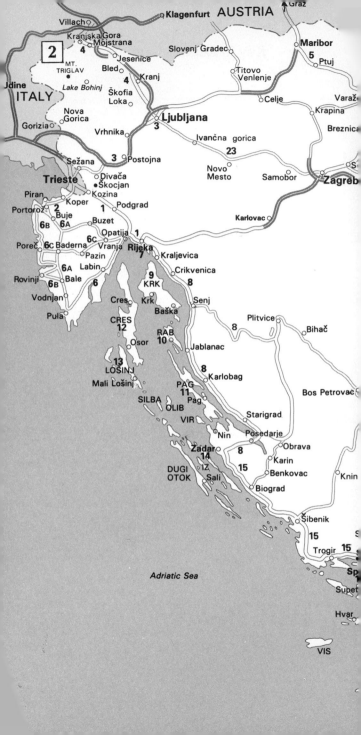

1   Trieste to Rijeka

ROAD, 77km—Highway N12/E63.—17km *Kozina*.—10km *Markovščina*.—10km *Podgrad*.—30km *Jušići*.—10km **Rijeka**. BUSES, c 4 times daily, usually via Opatija, in c 3 hours.

RAILWAY, in 3½ hours, via Poggioreale then after crossing the frontier via *Sežana*, *Divača*, *Pivka* (where a change is necessary) and *Ilirska Bistrica*.

Trieste (Slovene and Serbo-Croatian *Trst*), see *Blue Guide Northern Italy*.

The road runs via *Basovizza* to (14km) the frontier (customs, exchange, petrol coupons). The first Yugoslav village is (3km) *Kozina*, where N12 is crossed by a main road linking Postojna and Ljubljana with Koper and the Istrian coast. Beyond, the highway leads across typical karst countryside, characterised by green pastureland stretching away on either side to a bare rocky landscape of long ridges and deep ravines, with high mountains rising to the NE and SW. The limestone is honeycombed with underground rivers and caverns, and the turf forms only the thinnest of coverings on its surface.

10km **Markovščina**. Here a guide and key may be found to the cave of *Dimnice*, 1km N on the way to Slivje. The cave extends nearly 2km with stalagmites and stalactites.—At (25km) *Rupa* join the main Ljubljana–Rijeka road.—15km *Jušići*. Nearby, in the hamlet of Jurdani, are two small limestone caves, *Sparožna pečina* and *Crljenčina pečina*.

Kastav, a charming and historic small town, stands 3km from Jušići on the old Trieste–Rijeka highway (frequent buses from Rijeka), which also provides a good alternative route to the busier main road. As a Roman settlement (*Castra*, from which the present name derives) it was a strategic junction of the Roman roads from Tergeste (Trieste) and Pola (Pula) to Tarsatica (Rijeka) and the province of Liburnia. Later, as a border town between Austria-Hungary and Italy, it belonged to the Habsburg family. It is known for its barrel-making and for traditional vintage customs. The only remaining Roman traces are fragmentary walls near the cemetery, but six towers of the medieval fortifications still stand.

Kastav was the home of the 15C fresco painters Vincent and Ivan of Kastav, thought to have been father and son. Vladimir Nazor (1876–1949), the Croatian author, lived and taught here for many years, and Milan Marjanović, the critic, was born here. Their houses are marked by plaques.

At the entrance to the town a fine 16C *Loggia* faces Lončarija, a tree-shaded square where the colourful feast of Bela nedelja is celebrated each year (first week of October). The small Renaissance church of *Sv. Sebastijan* has an attractive painted ceiling. Inside the medieval *Town Gate*, bearing Jesuit arms, the narrow main street leads to the LOKVINA, or main square. In the centre a well bears a locally famous inscription describing how Morelli, an unpopular and repressive governor, was drowned here by the outraged citizens. In the disused 15C Gothic church of *Sv. Trojica* (Holy Trinity) frescoes have been discovered.

On the N side of the town the arcaded parish church of *Sv. Jelena*, in an 18C baroque style, has carved choir stalls. The view from the detached bell tower (381m) extends S over the Kvarner Gulf and islands and E to Mts Obruč (1353m) and Snježnik (1784m) and the Gorski Kotar. On the E side of the town rise the walls of an enormous church started by the Rijeka Jesuits in the 18C and never finished.

From Jušići the main road descends through Matulji and Zamet (Rte 6) to the shore of the Bay of Rijeka.—10km **Rijeka**, see Rte 7.

2   Trieste to Piran

ROAD, 43km. Highway N2/E751.—15km *Albaro Vescova/Škofije* (frontier).—10km **Koper**—7km *Izola.*—7km **Portorož.**—4km **Piran**. Frequent local buses.

Trieste, see *Blue Guide Northern Italy*. Thread the S suburbs of Trieste and, leaving the road to Muggia on the right, cross the frontier at (15km) *Albaro Vescova*, known to the Yugoslavs as Škofije.—4km Križišće Ankaran crossroads. To the right lies Ankaran (4km; see below); to the left the main road goes to Kozina, Postojna, and Ljubljana. Keep straight on and at the main gate of Koper bear left for the waterfront.

6km **KOPER**, a thriving town (24,000 inhab.) situated on a small peninsula that was formerly an island, is the principal town of Slovene Istria and the chief port of Slovenia. Still perhaps better known by its former name *Capodistria*, it combines the distinct personalities of a typical Venetian coastal settlement of narrow streets and old houses, and a bustling and rapidly growing modern seaport.

Post Office: Muzejski trg.

Information: Prištaniški trg and Kidričeva ulica.

Buses near the railway station. Frequent services to all parts of Istria and to Trieste; long distance to *Belgrade*, *Zagreb*, and *Ljubljana*, and in the season *Vienna* and *Venice*.

Ferries from Staro prištanište. Frequent connections with all places between Trieste and Pula.

Festival of National Folklore last week in July, tickets locally or in advance through Kompas travel agency.

History. Situated on or near the site of the Greek *Aegida*, mentioned by Pliny the Elder, Koper derives its present name from the later Roman *Capris*. During the 7C it was settled by the Slavs, in 788 became part of the Frankish empire, and from the 10C came under increasing Venetian influence, acknowledging Venetian sovereignty in 1279. The town then flourished under the name of *Capodistria* (from Caput Histriae), reaching the height of its prosperity in the 15–16C, when it was the chief town of Istria. Five of its podestà-captains became Doge of Venice. It was incorporated into Napoleon's Province of Illyria from 1809 to 1813, became Austrian after the Congress of Vienna, and from 1918 till the Second World War (in common with the rest of Istria) was occupied by Italy. After the war Koper was the chief town in the internationally administered Zone B of the Free Territory of Trieste and in 1954 was joined to Yugoslavia as a result of the London Agreement.

From UKMARJEV TRG on the waterfront, take KIDRIČEVA UL., to the E, passing (right) a former salt warehouse (15–16C) that now serves as a restaurant. Behind lies CARPACCIEV TRG where St. Justina's column, erected in 1571, commemorates the battle of Lepanto, to which Koper contributed a galley. In the far corner of the square the house in which Benedetto Carpaccio reputedly lived provides the entrance to a night club. The tradition that Benedetto (died 1560) and even his more famous father, Vittore, were natives of Capodistria is not proven. Continuing along Kidričeva ul. pass Sv. Trojica and Sv. Nikolaj, two small Renaissance churches both closed, and reach the 16C baroque *Palača Totto*, the ground floor of which has been converted into shops.

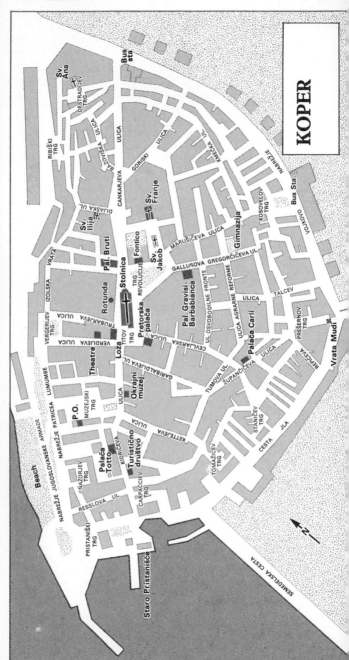

Inside a baroque staircase and portal have been preserved, and set in the outer wall is a winged lion of St. Mark, brought here from a former Venetian fortress that guarded the causeway. Opposite are medieval houses with protruding upper stories resting on exposed beams.

The large irregular Muzejski trg extends N on the site of a demolished Italian prison. On the right is the handsome baroque *Palača Belgramoni-Tacco*, built at the end of the 16C with fine balustrades. The main portal has an iron grille in the tympanum enshrining a medusa's head, and a bronze door-knocker in the form of Venus rising from the Waves, by Tiziano Aspetti. The palača houses the **Pokrajinski Muzej za zgodovino in umetnost** (Art and Historical Museum; adm. 9–12, 17–19).

VESTIBULE. Escutcheons of former Koper nobles and a 15C Gothic font, with a relief of the Madonna. A lapidary collection (left) includes Roman mosaics and two Romanesque columns from the first cathedral of Koper.—FIRST FLOOR. In the Banqueting Hall a good collection of 16–18C paintings includes a Nativity by *Correggio* and works by Padovanino, Fiamminghini, Romanino, and the schools of Benedetto Carpaccio and Iacopo Bassano. The ethnographical collection has recently been transfered to new quarters in Granscijev trg. Here may be seen Venetian icons, porcelain figurines, modern Slovene and Italian paintings, a reconstructed Istrian kitchen of the 18C, and the study of Angelo Calafati, governor of Istria under Napoleon; as well as historical memorials of Koper, a musician's gallery, and the armoury.

Kidričeva ul. ends at *TITOV TRG, a beautiful old square and Koper's principal attraction, recently closed to traffic. Immediately on the left is the fine **Loža** in Venetian Gothic, built in 1462–63 by Nikola of Piran and Tomaso da Venezia. It was restored in 1698 and now houses a pleasant kavarna. Set in its walls are a Madonna, a lion of St. Mark, and the arms of former mayors. Verdijeva ul., to the left of the loggia, leads to the summer theatre and cinema.

The **Stolnica**, or *Cathedral of Sv. Nazarij* (St. Nazarius), on the E side of the square, displays a mixture of styles. The lower story built at the beginning of the 15C, is in decorated Venetian Gothic, with a W door (no longer used) flanked by twin-canopied alcoves containing effigies of saints (attributed to Domenico da Capodistria) and blind arcading. A fresco of St. Nazarius fills the tympanum. The upper story was completed about a century later in Renaissance style, with Corinthian pilasters and a wheel-window filled with stained glass. At the SW corner the massive Romanesque *Campanile*, planned as a watch-tower at the beginning of the 13C, was completed when the present cathedral was built, and the belfry (view) added in 1660.

INTERIOR. The cathedral is entered through one of the doors on the S side, which were constructed of 15C materials garnered when the interior was reconstructed in the baroque style in 1714 by Giorgio Massari. Notable are the ceiling of the apse, the 16C sarcophagus of St. Nazarius behind the high altar, the walnut choir stalls, and the bishop's throne.

Above the throne are two paintings by Vittore Carpaccio. The Massacre of the Innocents appears to be only a half, while the Presentation at the Temple derives its shape from having been painted for an organ door; until 1959 both hung in a single frame. Other paintings include a Madonna with saints, also by Vittore Carpaccio (1516), and the same subject in less detail by Benedetto Carpaccio.

The *Treasury* (apply to sacristan) includes a fine Byzantine casket (12C), silver crucifixes and a silver monstrance (15C).

Just behind the cathedral, on the N side, is the *Rotunda Carmine*, a 13C Romanesque edifice with a baroque interior that serves as the baptistery.

Across the square the *Town Hall* occupies the 16C Venetian barracks, with a Renaissance doorway in the SW corner. The **Pretorska palača**, former residence of the mayor and of the Venetian podestà, fills the fourth side of the square and now houses the law courts. It is an impressive but cluttered building, half in Venetian Gothic, with a pleasing four-light window, and half in Renaissance style.

Koper, the Pretorska palača

Originally there were two separate mansions, erected in the 13C, with the town loggia between them. In the mid-15C the loggia was moved to the other end of the square (comp. above) and the two parts joined. Later in the same century the centre and W wing were given a Renaissance façade, and in 1664 the decorative battlements were added. The façade is incrusted with medallions, inscriptions, coats of arms and busts of successive governors, and a large lion of St. Mark. In the centre of the parapet a curious statue represents Justice: the body is Roman, the head Gothic, and the limbs Venetian baroque.

An arch in the E wing of the Pretorska palača leads into picturesque narrow ČEVLJARSKA UL., the town's main shopping street. Beneath the arch (right) the 'bocca del leone' for anonymous denunciations still bears its Venetian inscription. About thirty paces down on the right a narrower arch admits to the courtyard of the *Palača Orlandini* (1774) with a baroque staircase and balustrade and a painted ceiling at the head of the stairwell. Leave Čevljarska ul. by ŽUPANČIČEVA UL., passing (left) the 17C *Palača Carli*. In PREŠERNOV TRG an ornate Renaissance well, erected in 1423 and twice restored in the 17–18C, has a bridge-like superstructure modelled on the arms of the Podestà Lorenzo da Ponte. On the far side are the plain Renaissance church of Sv. Basso and the *Vrata Muda*, the former main gate of the town (1516). Outside begins the main road to Trieste and Ljubljana by which you approached the town.

Turning back, take TOMINČEVA UL. and, bearing left and right, reach Gimnazijski trg, dominated by the *Gimnazija*, a 17C school for the sons of Venetian noblemen (now the Italian grammar school).

ntinue down GALLUSOVA UL., where, on the left in UL. OSVOBO-
.LNE FRONTE, opposite the new Koper radio station, are the 17C
alača Tarsio and *Palača Gravisi-Buttorai*. In Gallusova ul., a little
farther on, the *Palača Gravisi-Barbabianca*, also 17C, has a good
baroque façade but suffered by use as barracks during the war. It
now houses a music school and entry is easily gained to the striking
banqueting hall, with trompe l'oeil murals and ceiling paintings.

The spacious TRG REVOLUCIJE, also known as the *Brolo*, lies at the
SE end of the cathedral. The E side of the square is dominated by the
Fontico, a former grain warehouse built in Venetian Gothic in 1392.
A fine classical pediment was added in 1529, and the façade bears
the coats of arms of various podestà of Koper. Flanking it are the
small 14C Gothic church of *Sv. Jakob*, now deconsecrated, and the
17C *Palača Vissch-Nardi*, while to the rear are the abandoned
monastery of Sv. Klara and 13C church of *Sv. Frančiško* with a Gothic
W door and apse and 17C painted ceiling. On the N side of the
square the heavy baroque *Palača Bruti*, by Massari, is occupied by
the public library.

Leaving the square by CANKARJEVA UL. pass the former Catholic Seminary, a
19C imitation of Venetian Gothic, and make for the oldest corner of the town.
The street and its side streets are lined with Renaissance houses, including the
late-15C *Palača de Belli*, and in Dijaška ul. is the Romanesque Rotunda of *Sv.
Elijo* (?9C) with 17C additions. A five-minute walk leads to DESTRADIJEV
TRG, with the former Franciscan monastery and church of *Sv. Ana* (apply to the
sacristan for admission). The monastery is used as a prison, but the church
includes in its small collection of paintings, a Madonna Enthroned with Saints
by Girolamo da Santacroce, a polyptych by G.B. Cima (1513) and pictures by
Palma Giovane. Behind Destradijev trg is the quaint old *Fishing Quarter*
centred on RIBIŠKI TRG, with a number of houses dating from the 14C and in
continuous occupation to this day.

Excursions. To Postojna, 62km. Frequent buses in the season. Leaving Koper
by LJUBLJANSKA CESTA, take the main road as far as (5km) *Križisce Ankaran*
and turn right towards Ljubljana, following the course of the river Rizana. In this
valley Charlemagne's emissaries called a popular assembly in 804 to settle
grievances between the Slavonic rural population of Istria and the Romanic
inhabitants of the towns. Shortly beyond (7km) *Rizana* a branch road (right)
leads to Rizana Park (3km) and Hrastovlje (6km) with its famous church.

Rizana Park, a pleasant oasis amid the karst, surrounds the second source of
the Rizana. Its true source is some 20km to the E, but for 15 of these the river
flows underground before re-emerging here. An experimental beaver farm was
once established in the park and some animals have been retained in an
enclosure. There is also a pheasant farm, a small aviary, and a collection of
native mammals including deer. The river is stocked with trout; fishing licences
may obtained at the inn (gostilna) in the village.

About 1km after the park branch left along a minor road (unsignposted) that
descends into the Dolina gradov (Valley of the Castles), so called from a legend
that nine castles stood here; the ruins of three remain on the far ridge. On a hill
beside the rustic village of **Hrastovlje**, the church of *Sv. Trojice* (Holy Trinity)
was constructed in a primitive Romanesque style on the basilican plan,
probably in the 13C. Its best feature is the plain Romanesque tower. The main
door dates from 1727. The fortifications built around 1500 to protect it from the
Turks still stand.

The Interior has the most complete and best-preserved *Frescoes of the
Istrian school extant. They are in a rustic Gothic style and were painted,
according to a Latin inscription, by Ivan of Kastav (Johannes de Kastua) in 1490.
Traces of earlier frescoes can be seen underneath in places, also Glagolitic
inscriptions. The frescoes illustrate the history of the world in terms of the Old
and New Testaments. Of particular interest are the 12 Apostles in the main
apse; the Life of Christ, on the W wall and the upper part of the S wall; the

monumental Genesis cycle on the roof of the nave; the months of the year medallions on the roofs of the aisles; the Journey of the Magi on the N wall and the Dance of Death on the lower part of the S wall, a fine example and one of the only two in Istria. In the sacristy, entered from the S apse, are preserved 15C and 17C reliquaries.

Continuing along the main Ljubljana road, climb a barren karst plateau and pass through (5km) *Črni Kal* and (2km) *Gornji Črni Kal*, which has a handsome leaning church tower, with views left across the Osp Valley and the city of Trieste to the sea.—At (3km) the next crossroads a minor road leads left to the village of *Kastelec* (1km) and the 14C castle of *Socerb* (2.5km) on the very border with Italy. Inside the castle (restaurant, open all the year) is a carved well-head. The terrace provides excellent views of the Julian Alps, the Dolomites, Trieste and its bay. About 100m from the castle is a limestone cave in which St. Socerb (2–3C) reputedly lived; a rude altar that stood here was destroyed during the Second World War.

Beyond (7km) *Kozina*, where the main Trieste–Rijeka road is crossed, lies (6km) **Divača**, whence to Postojna, see Rte 3.

Leave Koper by the causeway, passing through the suburb of *Semedele*. The road, close to the sea, traverses the Izola plain, flat fertile country noted for strawberries and Refoško wine.

7km **Izola** is a small coastal town (7500 inhab.) having, like Koper, a dual Venetian and modern character, but less historical interest. Founded by refugees from Aquileia, it passed to Venice, Austria, Italy, and with the rest of Zone B to Yugoslavia in 1954. In GREGORČIČEVA UL. the *Palača Besenghi degli Ughi*, a rococo mansion of 1775–81, with a lavish interior, is now the music school. Nearby are the *Palača Manzioli* (1470) in Venetian Gothic and the 16C *Palača Lovisato*. In *Sv. Mavro* (St. Maurus), the 16C parish church, hang Madonnas by Girolamo da Santacroce and Zorzi Ventura; an Entombment by Palma Giovane, and St. Lawrence Distributing Alms by Antonio Carneo. The sacristy contains a 15C monstrance, three illuminated antiphonaries, and eight large paintings by Peter of Koper (1473).

Climbing through pinewoods, pass the *Hotel Belvedere*, the terrace of which commands a superb view over the Bay of Trieste; then descend to the valley and village of *Strunjan*, where Tartini (comp. below) had a villa, surmount another ridge and descend by hairpin turns.

7km **Portorož**, a pleasant sophisticated resort (2000 inhab.) in riviera style, quadruples its population in summer. Set in an amphitheatre of olive-clad hills and fruit trees, and planted with exotic shrubs, the town still preserves a mildly Austrian atmosphere.

Buses (in the season) to *Piran* every 10 minutes; daily to towns in Istria and Slovenia. Excursions to Škocjan; Postojna; Hrastovlje.

Sculpture Exhibition ('Forma Viva'), annual competition in July–August.—The FESTIVAL OF FOLKLORE (see Koper) opens at Portorož.

Portorož dates from at least the 12C, though nothing remains of the old settlement where Doge Dandolo took refuge with his fleet in 1202, and where in 1380 Carlo Zeno, admiral of Venice, did the same. The Emperor Conrad IV stayed here in 1252. In the late 19C, under Austria, Portorož salt was discovered to have healing properties and a spa came into being.

A pleasant brief excursion may be made on foot past the bus station and SE along the shore to the hamlet of *Sečovlje*. The road runs through salt-flats where wind-pumps having two rectangular sails on a wooden frame raise sea-water into the beds for evaporation. Beyond is a cypress-shaded park with a permanent exhibition of sculpture comprising pieces donated after the annual competition.

18km **PIRAN**, just round the headland from Portorož on a narrow-jutting peninsula, is a small town (5500 inhab.) of Venetian type, one of the better preserved and more fully restored on the Adriatic coast. After a turbulent early history, it passed to Venice in 1283 and thereafter shared the fortunes of its neighbours. It is the most popular of the Slovene resorts and crowded in summer.

The focal point of the town is the spacious TARTINIJEV TRG, facing the harbour, which occupies the position of an older inner harbour (filled in 1893–94). In the centre stands a monument by Antonio dal Zotto (1896) to Giuseppe Tartini (1692–1770), the famous Piran violinist and composer after whom the square is named; his birthplace stands on the E side (plaque). Beside it stands the church of *Sv. Petar* (1818), with a Madonna by Polidoro da Lanciano (?), a pupil of Titian, and in the NE corner, a 15C mansion in Venetian Gothic, known as the *Beneška hiša*, or Benečanka, with lovely windows and balconies; the tourist office occupies the ground floor. Continuing round the W side of the square we come to the *Art Gallery*; the imposing *Town Hall* (Mestna hiša; 1879), with a lion of St. Mark built into its façade and incorporating the Post Office; and the *Law Courts* (Sodišče; 1874), in the Tuscan style, into which are incorporated two 17C baroque portals. Adjoining this on the harbour side is the former town gateway of *Sv. Nikola*, erected in 1663.

The two stone flagpoles standing in the SW corner of the square date from 1466 and were moved here in 1895 when the old town hall was destroyed. The city flagpole bears a relief of St. George on horseback, and the inscription 'By our prayers you remain safe, land of Piran'; the other, for the Venetian flag, bears the lion with the inscription 'Behold the winged lion who spans the earth, the seas and the stars', the arms of Piran, and various medieval measures of length.

From the corner of the main square CANKARJEVO NABREŽJE leads past the harbour to the yacht-club and an open-air cinema and thence along the shore to Portorož. At the near end, facing the harbour, is the **Pomorski muzej Sergej Masera** (Sergej Masera Maritime Museum; adm. Tues, Thurs, and Sat 9–12; Apr–Oct daily 9–12 and 16–17, closed Mon). The museum's collections include material illustrating the history of the Piran salt mines, archaeological remains from prehistoric to early Slavonic times, a minor survey of the development of marine weapons, records relating to the origins and development of Slovene shipbuilding, the Tartini room with some of the composer's relics (the displayed violin is a copy of his original Amati), a section on Slovene navy units in the War of National Liberation and the history of the Splosna plovba Piran shipping company.

A little behind Cankarjevo nabrežje and parallel to it, the narrow vaulted UL. SVOBODE leads from Tartinjev trg to the *Vrata Marciana* (1553), originally the main entrance to the town, with a lion of St. Mark set over it. Just outside is the small baroque chapel of *Sv. Rok* (1649). Of the **Walls**, erected in 1475–1534 to protect Piran on the landward side, about 300m remain. These can be reached by ascending the steps from Gortanova ul. (alternative routes lead from Tartinijev trg via Ul. IX korpusa or Rozmanova ul.). Seven handsome crenellated lookout towers extend from Vrata Rašpor to the top of the hill; the furthest one, standing on the highest part of the peninsula, can be climbed for excellent views of the town and bay of Piran and, to the NE of Koper, Trieste and the Julian Alps.

Descending by UL. IX KORPUSA, we turn left down the steps of BOLNIŠKA UL. to reach the **Franciscan Church and Monastery**. The

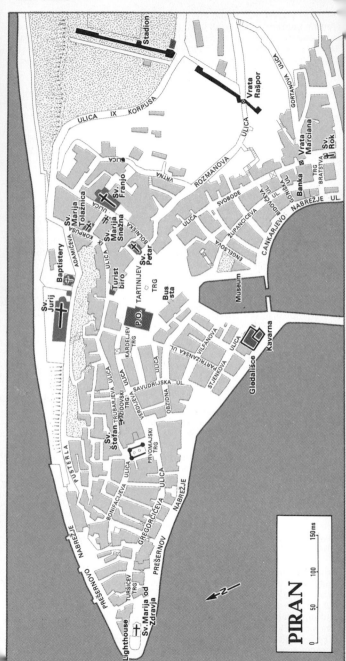

PIRAN

0   50   100   150ms

foundation was established by Bishop Manolesso of Koper at the beginning of the 14C, but the church was enlarged a century later and the adjoining cloister rebuilt in the Renaissance style in the 16C (restored 1951) when the bell tower was also constructed. The first of the three chapels added on the S side, in the shape of a baldacchino (1518), is outstanding. The 15C pulpit is carved and there is a painting of Mary Magdalene by Palma Giovane. The altarpiece by Carlo Caliari replaces a celebrated earlier one, by Vittore Carpaccio, removed to Italy during the war and not returned.

Opposite is the small church of *Sv. Marija Snežna*, originally Gothic (1404) but reconstructed in the baroque style in the 17C and restored in 1967. Inside are paintings attributed to the Piran artist Tomaso Gregolin (1660) and a recently discovered 15C Crucifixion by an unknown Italian artist. The narrow ISTRSKA UL. leads in a few paces to the attractive little baroque church of *Sv. Marija Tolažnica*, where the paintings include a 14C Venetian icon and four pictures either by Fontebasso or G. Angeli (18C). A little higher up Ul. IX korpusa, steps mount to **Sv. Jurij** (St. George) in an imposing position on a hill above the town. The church was founded in the 14C but the present baroque structure dates from 1637. Within, above the N door, is a curious equestrian figure of St. George. Adjoining are a detached *Campanile* (1607–08) by Giacomo de' Nodari, modelled on that of St. Mark's in Venice, and a hexagonal *Baptistery* (1637), with a font adapted from a 2C Roman sarcophagus (relief showing Cupid riding on a dolphin), a 14C Gothic painted crucifix in wood ('the tree of life'), and a small painted pietà in stone (c 1450). Set into the exterior wall is an early Croatian Romanesque transenna. In the treasury (apply to sacristan) are two 17C baroque statuettes of St. George in silver, and contemporary candlesticks, all the work of local smiths.

Lying to the W of Tartinijev trg is the picturesque and peninsular *Old Quarter of Piran, a maze of winding narrow streets crowded with houses painted in pastel colours and well supplied with cafés, inns, and bathing places. OBZIDNA UL, one of the older streets in Piran, leads W through the ancient gateway of *Vrata Delfin* (1483). Here part of the town's inner walls dating from the 15C are surmounted by overhanging houses of a slightly later period. The central PRVOMAJSKI TRG is almost entirely occupied by the great baroque *Cistern* (1776), which once supplied the town with water. Two female statues flanking the S staircase represent Law and Justice, and the upper stairs are flanked by cherubs holding fish. On the N side of the square a baroque mansion houses the town *Pharmacy*, established in 1682. On Kidričevo nabrežje beside the harbour are the *Gledališče* (theatre; guest performances in the summer), and the Kavarna Tartini. Beyond, the PREŠERNOVO NABREŽJE leads to the *Punta* at the tip of the peninsula. Here stands a lighthouse adjoined by the tiny 17C church of *Sv. Marija od Zdravja* (main altar by Gasper Albertini). The promenade leads back along the opposite waterfront past a small open-air summer theatre to the parish church (see above).

3   Trieste to Ljubljana

ROAD, 108km. Highways N10–6 and N10/E70–E63. 18km *Sežana.—* 22km *Razdrto.—*12km **Postojna.**—36km *Vrhnika.—*20km **Ljubljana**.

RAILWAY, via Villa Opicina, Sežana, Divača, and Postojna in c 4 hrs.

This route, which crosses the frontier, touches the white limestone desert known as the *karst*, described in the introduction to this section, then crosses the gently rolling farmland of western Slovenia. The area possesses many unusual and spectacular natural features, notably the Postojna and Škocjan Caves, among the largest and most impressive in the world.

Summer travellers should expect extenuating queues (two hours or more during peak season) at the Trieste–Fernetti border post, a situation which hopefully will be improved when the new motorway from the present exit to the frontier is completed. If the situation looks bleak, try the alternative crossings at Basovizza (Bazovic) or Lipizza (Lipica).

Trieste, see *Blue Guide Northern Italy*. Leave from the NE by Via Fabio Severo, then turn left on Highway N58 to (14km) *Fernetti* and the Yugoslav frontier.

At (4km) *Sežana* a road diverges E to (5km) **Lipica**, the original stud farm where the Lipizaner horses were bred for the Spanish riding school in Vienna. The farm was founded by Archduke Charles, son of the emperor Ferdinand, in 1580, and the Lipizaners were bred by crossing Andalusian thoroughbreds with the native ponies of the karst region. Owing to wars the Lipica stud has been moved and divided many times, so that there are now also studs for breeding Lipizaner horses in Austria, Hungary, Czechoslovakia, and Italy. Guided tours are given throughout the year, twice daily (10 and 15) between November and March, and five times daily (8, 10, 12, 15, and 17) in high season. There are also exhibitions of riding every Tuesday.

It is a short drive from Sežana (7km) or Lipica (8km) to *Divaca* and the **Škocjan Caves** (*Škocjanske jame*), which can be reached by car via the hamlet of Matavun or on foot (c 1hr) along a well-marked, shady path through *Dolnje Lezece*. Just beyond this village (left) a side path leads to Razgledišče (see below). The caves were discovered at the beginning of the 19C but, despite their wildness and grandeur, they are less well-known than those at Postojna (described below) and have at times been closed to the public. They owe their existence to erosion by the river Reka and extend for c 5km along its course, of which about two-thirds is accessible.

Adm.: Tours daily in Nov–March at 10; in Apr, May, and Oct at 10 and 15; in June, July, Aug and Sept at 10, 13, 15, and 17. Special visits by appointment.

The tour begins at Matavun, whence a steep footpath leads down and across the foaming river into *Mahorčičeva jama* (Mahorčič cave). Descend to a small lake and pass by rapids into the gloomy *Mariničeva jama*. Ahead, where the light glimmers, is a narrow passage by which you reach the *Naravni most* (Natural Bridge) and pass into the open *Mala dolina* (Little Swallow-hole), with breathtaking views at the end of it of the *Velika dolina* (Great Swallow-hole) and of the Reka, which plunges in a waterfall into the lake below. At periods of full flood this fall can raise metre-high waves in the lake. Recross the river by another bridge in the *Velika Dolina*, whose perpendicular cliffs rise 160m on either side. At the top of the cliffs, at the far end, can be seen Razgledišče, while all around is a rich and varied flora, including Karstic, Mediterranean, Illyrian, Pontic, Baltic, and Central European species. Following a footpath cut in the side of the rock, continue to *Tominčeva jama* (Tominc Cave), the first to be discovered and opened to the public (1823). Excavations here show the caves to have been inhabited in the Stone Age. Hence proceed to the majestic *Schmidlova dvorana* (Schmidl Chamber), with magnificent stalactites and stalagmites, the *Rudolfova dvorana*, even larger, and into the long water-filled cave known as *Jezero Haron* (Charon's Lake). At its narrowing far end is *Hankejev most* (Hanke Bridge),

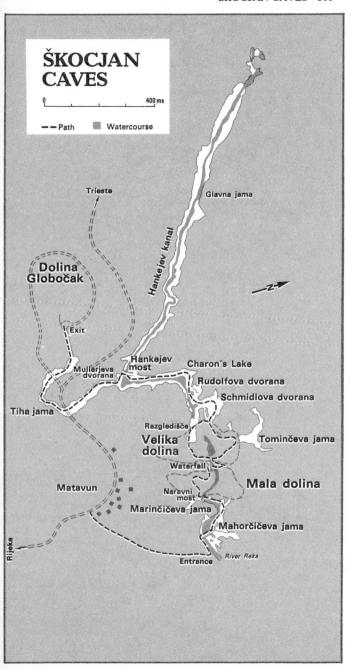

providing a view of the mysterious gorge leading to the 2km-long Hankejev kanal and further caves beyond; this section is open only to exerienced speleologists. After the bridge leave the course of the river and walk through *Müllerjeva dvorana* to the long, well-named *Tiha jama* (Peaceful Cave) and the swallow-hole *Globočak*, whence a road leads back to Matavun.

From the hamlet of *Škocjan* (400m) there are excellent views over the surrounding karst and of Mt Snežnik (1662m) to the E, as well as into the 92m-deep gorge of Okroglica. *Razgledišče*, a noted vantage point, commands similar views and a superb aerial view of the Velika and Mala dolina and the Reka waterfall.

Beyond Senožeće the road rises, sometimes through forest, then descends to Razdrto, where entrance is gained to the new *Slovenica* motorway (Highway N10/E70/E63).

34km **Postojna** is a thriving small town and an excellent centre from which to explore the whole karst region. In the main square an 18C mansion houses the *Notranjski muzej* (Regional Museum), containing ethnographical and archaeological exhibits, and, on the first floor, the *Institut za raziskovanje krasa* (Karst Exploration Institute), with an exhibition illustrating the peculiarities, history, and development of the region.

The ****Postojna Caves** (*Postojnska jama*; also known under the name POSTUMIA and the German ADELSBERG), one of the finer systems of limestone caves in Europe, lie about 1.5km from the town centre along the well-signposted road to Veliki otok (parking, restaurants, exchange and information offices). Discovered in 1818, the caves are estimated to be two million years old (beginning of Pleistocene age) and have been formed by the erosive action of the river Pivka. Recent explorations have shown them to be part of a unified system extending for some 21km; the Postojna section comprises 16.25km, while other sections have become known under different names (comp. map) and are visited separately (see below).

The part open to the public, comprising the largest and most spectacular chain of caverns, extends for c 4km. A further 3km of side passages are open only to speleologists. The main caves are open all the year. **Guided tours** (English commentary) daily in Nov–March 9.30 and 15; in Apr, May, and Oct 8.30, 10.30, 13.30, 16, and 18. The normal tour, partly effected by a small electric railway, takes 1¾ hours, and it is advisable to take advantage of the special clothing offered at the start. The average temperature of the caves is 8°C. Elderly or infirm visitors should also bear in mind that though the railway extends for 2km, a further 2km are covered on foot over quite difficult terrain.

The entrance gallery is completely denuded of stalagmites and stalactites and its walls are smoke-blackened, the result of guerrilla action during the Second World War when a German fuel and ammunition dump here was sabotaged by the Partisans. The first hall is in the *Velika dvorana* (Great Hall), 120m by 50m, whose walls have also suffered from wartime damage. Leading off this hall is the *Imenski rov* (Tunnel of Names) with names carved on its walls dating back to the 15C. The gallery then narrows. Pass a barred tunnel on the right where Postojna's first Biospeleological Institute was founded by Andrej Perko in 1910, then a stalactite formation known as the *Slonova glava* (Elephant's Head), and come to the caves *Zvrnjena ladja* (Capsized Boat) and *Gotska dvorana* (Gothic Hall). You now fork right along the gallery *Snežnik* (Snow Mountain) and enter the spacious *Plesna dvorana* (Ballroom), where dances and festivals have been held regularly since the first half of the 19C. At the entrance to the cave is a plaque dedicated to two of Postojna's leading explorers, Jeržinovič and Schmidl.

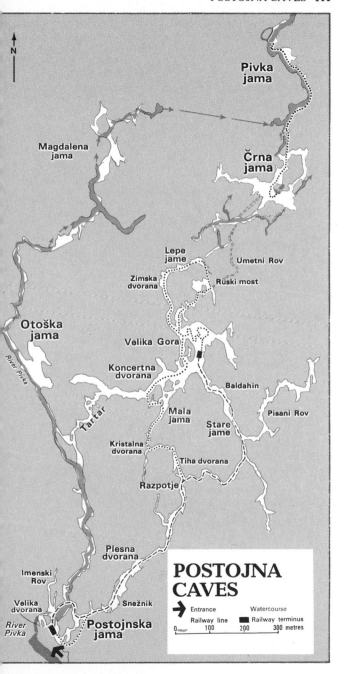

N

Pivka
jama

Magdalena
jama

Črna
jama

Lepe
jame

Umetni Rov

Zimska
dvorana

Ruski most

Otoška
jama

Velika Gora

River Pivka

Koncertna
dvorana

Baldahin

Tartar

Mala
jama

Stare
jame

Pisani Rov

Kristalna
dvorana

Tiha dvorana

Razpotje

Plesna
dvorana

Imenski
Rov

Velika
dvorana

Snežnik

River Pivka

Postojnska
jama

POSTOJNA
CAVES

→ Entrance   Watercourse

Railway line   ■ Railway terminus

0 _____ 100   200   300 metres

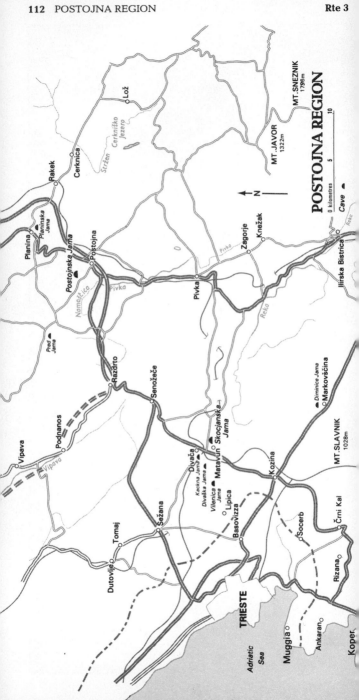

Next traverse a series of cleverly lit galleries and caves displaying outstandingly beautiful stalactite and stalagmite formations, including *Želvi* (The Tortoises), *Pralnica* (The Wash House), *Palmi* (The Palm Trees), *Oglarske kope* (The Charcoal Piles), *Mumije* (The Mummies), *Vodnjak* (The Well), *Senene Kopice* (The Haystacks) and arrive at a large hall called *Razpotje* (The Crossroads). The tour now forks right through the *Stare Jame* (Old Grottoes) and past the *Mali baldahin* (Little Canopy) and *Cipresa* (Cypress) to the *Baldahin* (Canopy), a marvellously delicate drapery formation. The railway ends by a forest of stalagmites and stalactites, many of them picturesquely named, upon an enormous rift formation, 45m high, known as *Velika gora* (Big Mountain) or *Kalvarija* (Mount Calvary), caused by the collapse of the roof of one of the largest chambers.

Continue on foot and cross the *Russian Bridge*, built by Russian prisoners of war during the First World War, to the *LEPE JAME (Beautiful Grottoes), so named for the delicate shapes of their stalagmites and stalactites and their extraordinary range of colour. You have now reached the farthest point of the Postojna Caves.

A man-made tunnel stretches right to *Črna jama* (Black Cave, see below); turn back to the *Zimska dvorana* (Winter Hall), pass the pillar called *Briljant* (The Brilliant) and come out once more by the railway terminus. Turn right here down yet another gallery, passing on the right the long gallery known as *Tartarus* that connects with Otoška jama (see below), and come to the prodigious *KONCERTNA DVORANA (Concert Hall), the largest cave in the system. Measuring 43 × 70 × 33m, this cave is said to accommodate over 10,000 people for concerts. In the season it contains a restaurant and a special post office accepting cards. Here a terrarium and two aquaria contain specimens of cave fauna, including the extraordinary Proteus Anguinus, or 'man fish' (named for the peculiar texture of its skin), thought to be a survivor from the Tertiary period.

After a pause for refreshment and card writing the guide now leads you through the beautiful *Mala jama* (Little Grotto), the *Kristalna dvorana* (Crystal Hall), and the *Tiha dvorana* (Hall of Silence) and back to the crossroads, from which the train returns to the entrance.

Near Postojna a number of smaller caves are linked with the Pivka river system. The nearest is *Otoška jama*, just outside the village of *Veliki otok* and c 30-minute walk away.—At 5km by asphalt and gravel road is *Pivka jama* (guided tours twice daily in 1½ hours), a well-lit cave reached by descending 256 steps. The cave is set in a pleasant wooded park with restaurant, shop, camp site, and chalet bungalows set among the trees. Fresh trout are usually available. Included in the entrance fee and 10 minutes walk away is *Črna jama* (Black Cave), the most beautiful of the smaller caves, with 3km of galleries.—At the village of *Planina*, 10km N of Postojna on the road to Ljubljana, is the *Paninska jama* (guide on request), at the underground confluence of the Pivka and the Rak. A subterranean lake and many underground streams necessitate the use of a boat for much of the tour (1½ hours).

From Postojna a good asphalt road (bus three times daily) leads to (9km) the cave and castle of *Predjama*. Strikingly situated in the mouth of a huge cavern in the hillside, the present Renaissance castle was built in 1570 by Johannes Cobenzl, later Austrian ambassador to Moscow and governor of Carniola. An earlier castle, built higher inside the cave, was reputedly the scene of a legendary siege of Erasmus Lueger, a 15C Robin Hood. The castle is interesting for its 'impossible' situation and the skilful way in which it is grafted on to the rock, rather than for any architectural nicety. Inside are exhibited archaeological finds, furniture, armour, and, in the small chapel, a

15C Gothic Pietà. The local parish church (1449) acquired its façade in the 17C.

Enthusiasts may inquire at Postojna about the caves at *Rakek* in the beautiful Rak valley and at *Lož*, also for the celebrated disappearing *Cerkniško jezero* (Cerknica Lake), which commonly dries up in summer.

36km **Vrhnika** (4000 inhab.) grew up around the Roman military camp of Nauportus, on the Ljubljanica. Just outside the town stands Bistra Monastery, dating from the 16C and now housing the *Tecniski Muzej Slovenije* (Technological Museum of Slovenia), dealing with regional arts, crafts, and industries.

20km **LJUBLJANA** (310,000 inhab.), the capital of Slovenia, is an elegant and refined city combining Viennese and Italian tastes. It played an important role in East-West and Italo-Germanic relations, especially during the 17–18C, its age of greatest splendour. Following an earthquake of 1895 it was restored and rebuilt by the architects J. Plecnik and M. Fabiani. It is the cultural as well as the administrative capital of Slovenia, and the seat of a university. In recent years it has also become a leading industrial and commercial centre, playing somewhat the same role for Yugoslavia that Milan plays for Italy. Its Biennial of Graphic Art is known throughout the world.

Post Office: Cigaletova ulica 15.

Information: *Turistični informacijski center*, Titova cesta 11, tel. 215412.

Airport: at Brnik, 27km NW; *JAT*, Miklošićeva 34, tel. 314340.

History. According to the legend Ljubljana (the name means 'well loved') was founded by Jason and the Argonauts, who sailed down the river Ljubljanica to the Adriatic. This is unlikely, if for no other reason, because the Ljubljanica disappears underground a few km downstream. Nevertheless the origins of Ljubljana are very ancient: the site was occupied by an Illyrian town, *Emona*, which was colonised by the Romans in the 1C BC and was enlarged and fortified by Augustus. Destroyed by Attila in the 5C, it was gradually rebuilt by the Slovenes in the 6C. In the 12C it flourished under the Spanheim dukes of CarintHia. In 1282 it passed to the Habsburgs, in whose possession it remained until 1918, except for a brief interval during the Napoleonic period (1809–13) during which it was named capital of the reconstituted Illyrian Provinces.

The River Ljubljanica divides the town into two unequal parts. The old quarter, on the right bank, is most conveniently reached by the **Tromostovje**, a triple bridge begun in 1832 and completed in 1931. From here STRITARJEVA ULICA leads past the marketplace (left) to MESTNI TRG, with a marble *Fountain* of 1751 symbolising the Sava, Krka, and Ljubljanica rivers. This is the work of Francesco Robba, an Italian artist who had a virtual monopoly on civil and religious commissions in the city in the 18C. Facing the fountain, with an arcade on the ground floor and a clock tower above, is the *Magistrat* (Town Hall), built in 1484 and remodelled in the baroque taste in 1718. In the courtyard, decorated with graffiti, is a *Fountain of Narcissus*, also by Robba. Behind the Fountain of the Rivers stands the oldest hotel in Ljubljana (the Wilderman), with a baroque façade.

From Mestni Trg it is a short walk to the **Stolnica** or *Cathedral of St. Nicholas*, an imposing baroque edifice built in 1701–08 to designs by the Italian Jesuit Andrea Pozzo, the same architect who designed the Jesuit church in Dubrovnik. The sumptuous interior contains large illusionistic frescoes by Giulio Il Quaglio (1703–06), frescoes in the dome by M. Langus (1843–44), and statues by Jacopo Contieri, Angelo Pozzo Padovani, and Francesco Robba. The **Bishop's Palace**, which faces the cathedral, has a façade of 1778 and an arcaded courtyard of 1695. On the N side is the former **Seminary**, built in

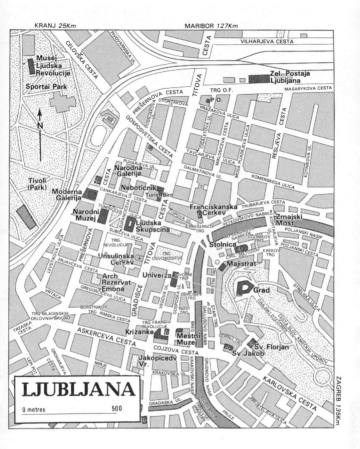

1708–60 by Carlo Martinuzzi, with a spectacular doorway called the
Portal of the Giants carved in 1714 by Angelo Pozzo. Within is a
baroque *Library*, with frescoes by Quaglio (1721) and furniture by J.
Wer (1725).

Just behind the cathedral is the broad VODNIKOV TRG, named after
the Slovene philologist and poet Valentin Vodnik (1785–1819), whose
statue (by A. Gangl, 1889) adorns it. The square hosts a lively herb
market. To the N is the **Zmajski most** (Bridge of Dragons) on the
Ljubljanica, which the people of Lujbljana consider the symbol of
their city; it was built in 1900 by J. Melan.

Across the river to the E, in HRVATSKI TRG, stands the oldest parish church in the
city, the **Zupna Cerkev Sv. Petra**. Founded in the 13C, it was destroyed by the
Turks and rebuilt in 1730. Within are ceiling frescoes by F. Jelovsek and oil
paintings by V. Metzinger, two well-known painters of the 18C. Other works by
these artists can be seen in the National Gallery (comp. below).

From the S side of Vodnikov Trg, almost opposite the statue, the
narrow STUDENTOVSKA ULICA ascends in a series of steep bends to

Fountain of the Kranj rivers by Francesco Robba, 1745–51, Mestni Trg, Ljubljana

the **Citadel**, originally a small fortified hill village of the 12C. Built, probably, on the site of the old Roman military camp, it commands the city from a position of obvious strategic importance. The present complex, which incorporates parts of the medieval buildings, was erected by the dukes of Carniola in the 16–17C. It was used for centuries as a prison, but restoration is gradually turning it into a musuem. The *View from the ramparts extends across the town to the Alps and the valley of the River Sava.

Leaving the citadel from the S and descending through the park, take ROZNA ULICA past the 18C church of *Sv. Florian* to LEVSTIKOV TRG, theatrically composed around a 17C *Column of the Virgin*. The large, elegant house on the W side of the square was designed in 1775 by Gabriel Gruber in *Zopfstil* (Louis XVI). Within are a spiral staircase with stucco decorations and a dome painted by A. Herrlein. The small private chapel, also in Zopfstil, has paintings of the Life of the Virgin ɔy J.M. Kremser-Schmidt. The E side of the square is occupied by the church of *Sv. Jakob, built by the Jesuits in 1613 and containing a showy high altar by Robba (1732) and side altars with statues by Contieri and Pozzo. The octagonal chapel of St. Francis Xavier was added in 1669; it contains an altar of 1720 by Contieri and elaborate stucco decorations.

STARI TRG, the Old Square, in reality a street flanked by handsome 17–18C houses, leads back to Mestni trg. From here the Tromostovje crosses the Ljubljanica to PREŠERNOV TRG, named after Slovenia's greatest poet, France Prešeren (died 1849), a lyricist, who is little known outside Yugoslavia. His statue, by Zajec and Fabiani (1905), is a popular meeting place. Overlooking the square is the handsome baroque **Franciskanska cerkev** (church of the Franciscans; 1640–60) with two bell towers and, within, a high altar by Robba (1756). The frescoes are by an artist named Langus.

Follow the river S to the little NOVI TRG (New Square), at the W end of which is GOSPOSKA ULICA, the Street of the Nobility. Along both sides are handsome palaces, notably No. 3, the *Bardi Palace*, dating from the mid 18C and now housing the Slovene Academy of Science and the Arts; Nos 2 and 4 (adjoining Novi trg) built in the 16C and remodelled in the following century; and No. 15, the 17C Turjak-Auersperg Palace, now the **Mestni Muzej** (Municipal Museum). Within (adm. Tues, Thurs 9–12, 16–18; Sun 9–12) are collections of archaeological material and furniture, including several interesting Biedermeier pieces.

The **Krizanke**, across the street, is a lovely complex founded in the 13C by the Knights of the Cross, a Teutonic order. Rebuilt and remodelled in the 16C and 17C, it consists of a palace (today a school; the arcaded courtyard hosts the annual Ljubljana Summer Festival) and a church of 1714, designed by the Venetian architect Domenico Rossi. The square in front of the complex, dedicated to the French Revolution, is adorned with an *Illyrian Column* by Plečnik (1930).

Return by Gosposka ulica or the parallel VEGOVA ULICA (the National Library, in the latter street, was designed by Plečnik) to TRG OSVOBO-DITIVE (Liberation Square), a public garden laid out in 1821 over a Roman necropolis. The underground **Galerija Emonska Vrata**, in the SE corner, was constructed on the site of a gate in the Augustan walls of Emona; the gallery is used for temporary exhibitions of art and archaeology. Facing the E side of the square is the Slovene Philharmonic Hall (1891); the Philharmonia dates from 1701, its honorary members include Ludwig von Beethoven. At the SW corner of the square stands the majestic *Ursulinska cerkev (Ursuline church), with a lofty façade. Built between 1718 and 1726, it has a high altar with statues of St. Ann and St. Catherine by Robba (1744) and altarpieces by Palma the Younger and Metzinger.

The area formerly occupied by the gardens of the Ursuline convent is today TRG REVOLUCIJE, a busy square dominated by the modern *Ljudska Skupscina* (Assembly of the Socialist Republic of Slovenia, 1955). On the S side (entrance at 15 Erjavceva cesta), lies the *Arheoloski Rezervat Emona, a small archaeological area with vestiges of a 5C baptistery and other structures built over an earlier bath complex.

Return to Trg Osvoboditive, from which TITOVA CESTA, high street of Ljubljana, runs in a straight line dividing the old town from the modern quarters. Halfway along, on the left, is the *Neboticnik*, a 13-floor 'skyscraper' built in 1933 by V. Šubić. In the neighbourhood (rebuilt after the earthquake of 1895) are several *Secession St.* buildings, including (Presernov trg at Miklosiceva), the *Urbanc House* of 1902–04; (1 Miklosiceva cesta), the *Hotel Union* of 1903; (4 Miklosiceva cesta) a house with sculptured pediment; (8 Miklosiceva cesta) the so-called *Déco House* of 1922, with a particularly colourful façade; (16 Miklosiceva) the *Bamberg House* by Max Fabiani (1907); (Taicarjeva Ulica at Miklosiceva cesta) the *Cuden House* by C.M. Koch (1901); and 1 Cigaltetova Ulica) the Pogacnik House (1901).

The gardens of TRG NARODNIH HEROJEV (National Heroes Square, named for the victims of the National Liberation struggle buried here) lie between the Skupscina building and the *Narodni Muzej (National Museum; adm 9–13, Wed and Fri 9–13 and 16–19; closed Mon). The latter is situated in a neo-Renaissance building of 1885 (architect W. Treo), preceded by a monument to the historian J.V. Valvasor (1903). Baroque sculptures by V. Königer (1760), from a house in Novo Celje, adorn the steps. Inside, the dome is frescoed with allegories by J. Šubic (1885). GROUND FLOOR. On the left: Egyptian and Roman antiquities. On the right: a Slovenian house, complete with furniture, tools and household items, and costumes. FIRST FLOOR. The central rooms are used for temporary exhibitions. On the right: palaeontology and natural history (including several interesting fossils and a mammoth skeleton). On the left, more fossils and Stone Age, Bronze Age, and Hallstatt Culture material (bronze situlae, arms, tools and personal items, jewellery, pottery); Illyrian and Celtic antiquities, notably a finely decorated situla from Vace (7C BC) and a 3C BC helmet; Roman antiquities, including glass, arms, mosaics, and bronze vases; and Slovene antiquities taken from 7–8C tombs.

Just across the Presernov Cesta lies the **Moderna Galerija** (Modern Gallery; adm 10–18, Sun 10–13, closed Mon) which, in addition to housing a permanent collection of modern Slovene art, hosts an internationally famous Biennial of Graphic Art.

The **Narodna Galerija** (National Gallery), one block further N (entrance at 20 Cankarjeva cesta; adm. 10–18, Sun 10–13), is devoted to Slovene art from the Middle Ages to the late 19C; it has an extensive baroque section with works by J. Holzinger, V. Köninnger, V. Metzinger, F. Jelovsek, and F. Bergant.

Tivoli, across Presernova cesta from the National Gallery, is one of the largest, most immaculately kept parks in Yugoslavia. Just beyond the entrance is the *Grad*, a fortification built by the Jesuits in 1703 and remodelled after the earthquake of 1895. Nearby are sports facilities and fairgrounds and, on a knoll, the 17C *Cekin Palace*, today seat of the **Muzej Ljudske Revolucije** (Museum of the Slovene Revolution). Also interesting is the **Jakopicev Vrt** (adm. May 1–Oct 31, 9–12, 16–18, closed Mon), a small garden containing remains of a Roman insula of the late 4C BC, with mosaic pavements and heating conduits. In the nearby *Mirje* is a tract of the Roman walls of Emona, restored and partially rebuilt in the 1930s.

EXCURSIONS. To **Maribor**, road, 126km through alpine countryside. From Ljubljana centre follow TITOVA CESTA N to Highway N10.

12km Trzin: turning for (11km) **Kamnik** (406m, 15,000 inhab.), a popular resort in lovely surroundings on the S slope of the Kamniske Alpe (2558m). In the old town are two castles: the 12C *Mali Grad*, now little more than a ruin, but preserving a Romanesque chapel with elevated sanctuary and interesting crypt; and the 18C *Chateau Zaprice*, seat of the Regional Museum (adm. Wed and Sat 9–16, Fri and Sun 9–12) containing locally made furniture. The area around the town is famous for walking, mountaineering, hunting, fishing, and skiing.—The

.oad continues E to the Logarska Dolina, a magnificent valley of glacial origin on the N side of the Kamniske Alpe, whence the return may be made to the main highway at (73km) *Celje*.

51km **Semeter** lies on the old Roman road between Emona (Ljubljana) and Celeia (Celje). An archaeological park contains reconstructed tombs from a Roman necropolis (Rimska nekropola, adm. Mar–Oct, 7–18) discovered beneath the village. The most interesting are the aediculae of the Prisciani (II), Ennio (III), and Secundiani (IV) families, all dating from the 2C BC.

4km Highway N10 joins the new motorway, Autocesta N1/E57.

A mountain road leads N to (127km) *Klagenfurt*, via (24km) *Velenje* (398m, 6000 inhab.) a modern town with an important medieval castle; and (26km) *Slovenjgradec* (409m, 3000 inhab.), where the Gothic church contains 13C frescoes.

5km **Celje**, the *Claudia celeia* of the Romans, is a small provincial town known for its chemical and textile industries. Until the 18C it was the capital of an autonomous county; today it is still an aristocratic place, its many fine buildings giving it an air of unusual elegance. On a hilltop overlooking the town centre are the ruins of the medieval *Citadel*. Also of interest is the *Opatijska cerkev*, or parish church of St. Daniel, in the central Slomskov trg. This is a Gothic edifice with 15C frescoes, a baroque high altar of Venetian workmanship, and a chapel (the 14C Chapel of the Seven Sorrows) with beautiful stained-glass windows. At 1 Muzejski trg stands the 16C *Grofija, the former palace of the counts of Celje, today a Regional Museum (*Pokranjinski Muzej*; adm. 9–13, Wed 9–13 and 14–16, closed Mon). Within are an archaeological section containing Celtic, Roman, and medieval material (notably a bronze Bacchus from Claudia Celeia); a decorative arts section displaying ceramics, glass, furniture, and clocks; an ethnographical section; and a gallery of paintings and sculptures from the 17–19C. The central room on the first floor has a fine wooden ceiling with trompe l'oeil paintings by the Polish artist M. Theofilowicz (1622–23).

In the environs are (33km) *Rogaška Slatina* (228m, 1500 inhab.), an elegant spa with alkaline waters used in the treatment of liver and kidney disorders; and (23km) *Zicki samostan*, a ruined Carthusian monastery in a romantic position on the edge of the Konjinska Gora.

50km **Maribor**, see Rte 5.

4   Villach to Ljubljana

ROAD, 109km. Highways N1/E70.—23km *Kranjska Gora*.—23km *Jesenice*.—38km *Kranj*.—25km **Ljubljana**.

RAILWAY, in c 2½ hours, crossing the Alps E of the highway and rejoining the latter at *Jesenice*.

The most direct approach to Yugoslavia from Northern Europe, this route connects with Austrian motorway A10 from Salzburg. The frontier is crossed at the *Wurzen/Koren Pass* (1073m), beyond which the road joins Highway 1 from Tarvisio, Italy, and proceeds across spectacular alpine countryside in northern Slovenia. Here are to be found the highest peaks of the Julian and Carnic Alps; the lovely lakes of Bled and Bohinj (frequented for their climate since the 18C); and numerous delightful villages, the distinctly Germanic air of which is a reminder that this region belonged to the Austrian duchy of Carinthia until 1918.

Villach (501m, 36,000 inhab.), see *Blue Guide Austria*.

23km **Kranjska Gora** (810m, 1000 inhab.), is a climatic resort in a lovely position at the head of Sava Dolinka Valley.

A road to the left winds through the Soča valley to *Trenta*, *Plezzo*, and *Tolmin*, three small villages in delightful surroundings ideal for walking and mountain climbing. At Trenta, the Trentarska Muzejska Zbirka (adm. 8–12 and 13–17) has collections illustrating local history and ethnography.

13km **Mojstrana** (541m, 1000 inhab.), at the intersection of three valleys, is a starting point for the ascent of **Mt Triglav** 2863m, the highest peak of the Julian Alps and before 1947 the international frontier between Yugoslavia and Italy. The ascent, recommended for expert climbers only, may be made from the Vrata Valley (5 hours), the Kot Valley (8 hours), or the Krma Valley (9 hours).

Mt Triglav ('the Three-Headed') is the Olympus of the Slavonic gods, and is regarded with a certain mystical reverence by the Slovenes. There are numerous legends attached to it. One of the better known concerns a white chamois with golden horns, which was reputed to have inhabited its slopes.

10km **Jesenice** (585m, 16,000 inhab.) is known for its steel mills (the surrounding area is rich in iron); nearby is *Vrba*, birthplace of poet France Preseren (1800–49). His house has been turned into a museum.

13km Turning for (5km) **Bled** (501m, 5000 inhab.). Situated on a delightful lake encircled by forest-shaded mountains, this famous resort has been frequented since the 18C. In high season it hosts numerous festivals, spectacles, and tournaments. High on a rocky cliff above the lake stands the *Castle*, which was given in 1004 by the emperor Henry II to the bishops of Brixen, under whose jurisdiction it remained until the mid 19C. The fortress is now a museum. It is surrounded by two sets of ramparts, between which is a lower court; an enormous cylindrical tower guards the entrance to the upper court, around which are edifices of various epochs (one with a restaurant), and from which there is a splendid *View. The keep houses a small Museum (adm. 8–18) with archaeological finds from the Bronze Age to the early Slavic period (8–9C), historical documents, weapons, antique furniture, and some Italian paintings mainly of the 17C. There is also a Gothic chapel, subsequently remodelled to suit baroque tastes, with frescoes representing the emperor Henry II and his wife Cunegonda. At the foot of the castle is a neo-Gothic parish church (1904) with modern frescoes.

The **Lake** (*Bledsko Jezero*), measuring 2.1 by 1.3km, is of glacial origin and is fed by warm water springs that bring the water temperature up to 25°C in summer. On a small island (Blejski Otok; boat service from Bled, 8–20), stands the baroque sanctuary of **Marjka Božja** (*Our Lady of the Lake*), built on the site of a pagan temple. The sanctuary, today a popular place of pilgrimage, was established in the 8C but rebuilt and enlarged several times in subsequent epochs (the Gothic bell tower, 52m high, has a baroque spire of 1669). The island was inhabited in prehistoric times, and a Slavic necropolis of the 9–11C has been localised around the church. Details of the archaeological excavations and of the history of the church itself (which shows six different building phases, from the primitive Carolingian chapel to the present baroque edifice) are displayed on panels beneath the portico. Within the church are some spectacular altars and fragments of 15C frescoes (in the presbytery).

EXCURSIONS. To **Mt Straža**, 646m, by chair-lift: *View of the town and lake.

To **Pokljuka Plateau**, 1250m (17km W). A magnificent pine forest on the S slope of Mt Triglav.

To **Bodešče** (3km E). At this small village, the Gothic church of St. Leonard contains several fine 15–16C frescoes, notably a Christ among the apostles (in the presbytery); Legend of St. Leonard; St. Christopher, St. Leonard and Christ; and St. George and St. Florian.

To ***Lake Bohinj**, 523m (31km SW along the magnificent narrow valley of the *Sava Bohinjka). This delightful lake, larger and more beautiful than Bled though not so frequented, lies amidst high wooded hills at the foot of Mt Triglav. On the E shore is the village of *Bohinj*, where the Gothic church of Sv. Janez has

Lake Bled with island sanctuary of Sv. Marika Božja

a 17C wooden altar and 14–16C frescoes. In the nave, Legend of St. John; in the presbytery, Apostles and St. George. On the outside figures of St. Christopher and Legend of St. John (c 1530). Late September, Kravlji Bal (literally 'Cow Dance'), a vivid and convivial festival which celebrates the return of the cattle from the mountains.

From the end of the lake a cableway ascends to 1888m (ski slopes), near the rocky summit of Mt Vogel, 1923m. The road ends at the Savice Refuge, 660m, starting point for ascent of Mt Krn (2245m) and Mt Triglav.

From the lake it is a short (15-minute) walk to the source of the Sava Bohinjka, which springs from a cascade 60m high. Here entrance is gained to the **Dolina Triglavski jezero Narodni Park** (Seven Lakes Valley National Park), in a dense forest of beech and fir. A footpath leads in 4 hours to the Dompri Triglavskih Jezerih refuge, 1683m, between the fifth and sixth lake; and in 2 hours more to the Zasavska Koča refuge, 2071m, between the two highest lakes of the park.

A few kms further on, on the right, is **Radovljica** (491m, 7500 inhab.), another small resort with a Gothic church, *Sv. Peter*, of 1495. In the baroque Château Thun (18C) is the *Cebelarski Muzej* (Beekeeping Museum: adm. May–Oct daily; Nov–Mar Wed, Sat, and Sun, 10–12 and 15–17). This curious museum, devoted to the history of beekeeping (the Slovenes are traditionally great apiarists, and their bees are exported all over the world), contains an interesting collection of painted *beehive fronts of the 18–19C, a typical local popular artform

Lake Bohinj, at the foot of Mt Triglav

Early beehives were decorated with stars and ornamental symbols. Later, the range widened to include illustrations of the Bible, seasonal events, and everyday village life. There are also pictures of Job, the patron of beekeepers, and numerous paintings of the fable genre, often involving a hunter with wild animals.

A secondary road winds S to *Kropa*, a village of smiths where the houses are decorated with wrought-iron objects. There was a tradition in Kropa that you couldn't become a master smith until you could forge a horseshoe that would fit an egg without cracking or burning it.—The road returns to the highway just N of Kranj.

28km Highway 1 is joined by (left) Highway N1A/E94 from (48km) Klagenfurt.

10km **Kranj** (385m, 24,000 inhab.), situated high above the left bank of the Sava, is the Roman *Carnium*; it gives its name to the central region of Slovenia, the Kranjska. Today it is an important industrial centre (electronics, textiles, leather). It has a Gothic church, an example of the 'hall churches' (hallenkirchen) of Slovenia, the vault of which is painted with a star pattern and decorated with reliefs; and a small museum (*Gorenjski Muzej*, 43 Tavcarjeva, adm. 10–12 and 17–19, closed Mon) with archaeological, historical, and ethnographical collections as well as a few paintings.

EXCURSIONS. To (36km) **Jezersko** and (36km) **Kamnik**, both important resorts.

To (11km) **Škofja Loka** (4000 inhab.), one of the older towns in Slovenia, a picturesque place well worth a visit. The Castle, on a green hill, has a good collection of wood carvings and folk art, notably paintings on glass (of biblical and rural subjects characteristic of peasant life in many parts of Central Europe) mostly done by peasant women.

The highway continues S, past the villages of *Medvode* and *Sentvid* to (25km) **Ljubljana**, Rte 3.

5   Graz to Zagreb

ROAD, 237km. Highways A9, 10, 3, and 12.—66km **Maribor**.—23km **Ptuj**.—43km *Varaždin*.—14km *Čakovec*.—91km **Zagreb**.

RAILWAY, via Celje in c 4½ hours.

Alpine scenery and charming old towns combine to make this one of the more rewarding itineraries in northern Yugoslavia.

Graz (365m, 352,000 inhab.), see *Blue Guide Austria*. Leave from the S, by Motorway A9, which follows the Mur Valley to the frontier.— 49km *Šentilj*, the motorway ends; Yugoslavia is entered and southbound traffic is channelled onto Highway 10.

17km **Maribor** (274m, 119,000 inhab.), the largest city in Slovenia after Ljubljana, lies along the River Drava at the foot of the Alps. It was founded in the 12C or 13C, and its early economic development was tied to the lumber trade and milling industry. Today it is a major industrial centre and the capital of the Podravlje and Pomurje regions. The old town, much of which is closed to automobile traffic, spreads out at the foot of the *Citadel, erected in the 12C but rebuilt in its present form in the 15–18C. The interior is largely occupied by the *Pokrajinski Muzej* (Provincial Museum, adm. 9–13, Sun 10–12, closed Mon), with interesting archaeological and ethnographical collections, some antique furniture, a collection of 16C portraits, and several examples of painting on glass, one of which is attributed to Dürer. The baronial hall and the staircase, in the rococo style, date from the 18C. The chapel is an imitation of the Sancuary of the Virgin at Loreto, Italy.

From the Citadel take SLOVENSKA ULICA W to TRUBARJEVA ULICA, then turn left to the *Cathedral of St. John the Baptist, a 12C Romanesque structure with a fine 16C flamboyant Gothic choir. Within are some Gothic sculptures, an interesting high altar, and 18C choir stalls by J. Holzinger. POSTNA ULICA, opposite the S flank of the church, leads in just one block to GLAVNI TRG, or municipal square. Here stand the 15C *Town Hall* (rebuilt in the 16–18C) and the baroque church of *St. Louis*. From the NE corner of the square VETRINJSKA ULICA winds back up to the Grad.

The **Slovenska Gorica**, the famous wine-producing area around Maribor, is dotted with picturesque villages and hamlets, neat farms, and water mills, some of which are still in working order. Also in the environs are two well-known resorts: *Mariborski Otok*, an island in the Drava, a national wildlife preserve which possesses a bathing beach and boating facilities; and *Pohorje*, a winter sports centre connected to the town by cable-car.

At Maribor Highway 10/E57 diverges SE to Celje and Ljubljana (Rte 3). Turn SW on Highway 3, which follows the valley of the Drava.

23km **Ptuj** (230m, 11,000 inhab.), a gay, colourful town, spreads out at the foot of a 12C castle.

Post Office:Trg Svobode.

Information: Turistički biro, 4 Trg Svobode, tel. 771569.

History. The ancient *Poetovium*, a wealthy residential town founded by Augustus, was destroyed by the Goths and Huns and only gradually rebuilt. In 1278 it was given in fee by the Habsburgs to the Archbishop of Salzburg, in whose possession it remained until the Napoleonic era, when it was annexed to the Austrian Empire. It passed to Slovenia in 1918.

The BEZJAKOVA ULICA, principal thoroughfare of the town, is lined
with handsome baroque houses, vestiges of a past affluence. To the
W, in the main square, is a parish church of the 13–14C (*Sv. Juri*) with
fine Gothic choir stalls and a free-standing bell tower, the lower part
of which incorporates Roman stonework, sculptural fragments, and
inscriptions. In the square is a large plinth bearing a relief of Orpheus,
erected by Septimus Severus in 194: here, during the Middle Ages,
debtors and other criminals were held up for public ridicule.

The **Castle**, now a museum (*Pokranjinski Muzej*; adm. 15 Apr–1
Dec, 8–16; closed Mon), contains Flemish and Gobelin tapestries,
baroque furniture, some portraits, and an ethnographical section with
some curious costumes and painted masks worn during the Kurenti
ritual, a rite of spring celebrated today as a historical pageant in
February. In the baronial hall hangs an unusual group of portraits of
Turkish men and women, in all likelihood business associates or
political allies of the Herberstein family, to whom the castle belonged.
In the middle of the hall is a four-sided ottoman sofa with a central
backrest large enough to conceal a small man, who presumably
would have listened in on the conversations of conspiring barons. The
adjoining chapel contains a painting of the martyrdom of St. Peter
ascribed to Tintoretto.

More Roman reliefs and inscriptions can be seen in the *Archaeological Museum* in the former **Benedictine Convent** (Muzejski trg, adm.
10–13, closed Mon). The convent itself has a profusely decorated
façade and a fine Gothic cloister with carved keystones and 16C
frescoes, now a repository for Gothic and baroque sculptures and
inscriptions removed from local churches. Less erudite but equally
interesting is the *Viniculture Museum*, housed in a round stone tower,
formerly a wine vault, near the bridge on the Drava. The wines of Ptuj
rightly enjoy an excellent reputation.

EXCURSIONS. To **Ptujska Gora**, on a wooded hill 13km W of Ptuj. This
picturesque village has a beautiful Gothic church, perhaps the finest in Slovenia,
erected in 1400 and surrounded by ramparts. The three-aisled interior contains
numerous excellent Gothic and baroque sculptures, and some fine frescoes by
followers of Giovanni da Brunico (c 1420).

To the **Mura Valley**, 30km N, a pretty farming district where willows and alders
grow along clear streams and storks roost on the roofs of cottages.

69km **Varaždin** (173m, 34,000 inhab.), the ancient capital of Croatia,
was founded by early Slav settlers. Like Ptuj, it is dominated by its
castle, the **Erdödy Grad**, erected in the 13C but rebuilt as a château in
the 18C. The rooms of the interior now house the *Gradski Muzej*
(adm. 8–14, Sat 8–13, Sun 10–13), with weapons, glass, a 17C
pharmacy, furniture, maps and a section devoted to local crafts. In the
same square (4 Trg Žrtava Fašističkog Terora) are the *Prethistorijski
Odjel* and the *Galerija Slika* (adm. daily 10–13 and 17–19), with finds
from local excavations, and 19–20C paintings, respectively. Also
interesting are the many distinctive baroque palaces and churches,
reminders that Varaždin was once an important place on the old
highway from Vienna to the Adriatic, which fell into disuse following
the construction, in 1857, of the Vienna–Trieste railway. The best of
these buildings include *Sv. Nikola* (1741–68), which retains the bell
tower of an earlier Gothic oratory (1494); the Franciscan church of *Sv.
Ivan Krštitelj* (St. John the Baptist, 1650–55), with a baroque interior of
1715; and the *Uznesenja Marijna* (1642–46) with a monumental
gilt-wood high altar of 1737 and stucco decorations by the Italian
artist Quadrio.—Across from the castle is the *cemetery*, with many

interesting baroque tombs. The inhabitants of Varaždin consider this
a fine place for evening promenades and summer socialising.

14km NE of Varaždin (reached by turning left on Highway 12) is
Čacovec (176m, 10,000 inhab.), described as 'a place of unusual
beauty' by the Turkish ambassador Evlia Čelebija (1660). The *Castle*,
built in 1562 to plans by the Italian architects Secco and Arconati, has
been turned into a museum. The Franciscan church of *Sv. Nikola*
(1707–67) has Gothic furnishings. Outside the town is the church of
Sv. Jelena, with fragmentary late-Gothic frescoes (15C).

At Varaždin turn right onto Highway 12, which bears SW.—At (32km)
Breznica, a road (left) winds up to (10km) *Kalnik*, a town with a 13C
castle and a 16C Gothic church, situated at the centre of the Kalničko
Gorje massif (643m).

34km *Sesvete*, turning (left) for (69km) **Bjelovar** (Rte 24B).

11km **ZAGREB**, see Rte 23.

II CROATIA

Of the six Yugoslav republics, Croatia (Serbo-Croatian *Hrvatska*) is second largest in territory and population. It covers an area of 56,538km^2 or 21 per cent of Yugoslavia's total area. Of its 4,601,000 inhabitants, 75 per cent are Croats, 12 per cent Serbs, 8 per cent 'Yugoslavs', and the remainder members of other nationalities. The capital of the republic is Zagreb, with a population of 856,000. It is the second largest city in Yugoslavia, but in terms of industrial potential it holds first place. Other major cities are Split, Rijeka, Osijek, Čakovec, Zadar, Slavonski Brod, Varaždin, Sisak, Šibenik, Karlovac, Dubrovnik, and Pula.

The spacious lowlands of the Pannonian Plain, constituting the traditionally distinct region of Slavonia, occupy the N and NE parts of the republic, between the rivers Drava and Sava. Away to the NW rise the gentle hills of the Hrvatsko zagorje, while to the S and SW stretch the scenic regions of Banija, Kordun and Lika, the Dinaric Alps, and the extensive forests and rugged heights of Gorski Kotar. Nine-tenths of the Adriatic coast of Yugoslavia, with over 1000 islands, lies in Croatia, attracting about 50 per cent of domestic and 80 per cent of foreign tourists. A considerable number of these choose the Croatian littoral because of its well-appointed naturist beaches.

Today Croatia is responsible for 25 per cent of the country's national income, and employs 36 per cent of the labour force. The chief industries are manufacturing, shipbuilding, chemicals, and petroleum refining. Croatia builds three-quarters of Yugoslavia's ships (80 per cent of which are exported), produces and refines 64 per cent of its petroleum and natural gas, and manufactures 87 per cent of its synthetics. Croatian oilfields yield three million tons of petroleum a year, which is enough to satisfy one-quarter of the country's needs. Commercially exploitable natural gas deposits were recently discovered beneath the Adriatic Sea. In 1984 the Croatian economy supplied 23 per cent of Yugoslavia's exports, and almost half of Croatia's national income comes from foreign trade.

Croatians are justly proud of their national parks. The best known is the Plitvice Lakes National Park, followed by the Kornati Isles, and the islands of Mljet, Brioni, Risnjak, and Paklenica. Winter resorts are being developed in the highlands of Gorski Kotar, and northern Croatia with its forests and well-stocked rivers is excellent for shooting and fishing. During the summer there are several drama and music festivals, the best known being the Dubrovnik and Split Summer Festivals and the National Film Festival in Pula.

6 Istria

Istria is the roughly triangular peninsula that projects southward from a line joining Trieste and Rijeka. For much of its history, it has been linked with Venice and has always had the largest Italian minority of the E Adriatic littoral. Nowadays the northern part is administered by the Federal Republic of Slovenia, and the larger southern part by the Federal Republic of Croatia.

A.   Piran to Pula via Buje

ROAD, 94km. Highway N2/E751.—3km *Portorož*.—16km **Buje**.—31km *Baderna* (for Poreč).—14km *Brajkoviči* (for Rovinj).—9km **Bale**.—11km **Vodnjan**.—10km **Pula**.
Frequent buses in about 3 hours.

This route affords access to a series of inland Istrian towns standing on hill sites which have been in continuous occupation since at least Illyrian times. Their history parallels that of the better known coastal towns with the difference that during the Middle Ages they remained longer under the control of the Patriarch of Aquileia. Subsequently they came under the sway of local Istrian bishops and the feudal nobility, and passing to Venice correspondingly later, were subjected to considerably less Venetian influence. At first the inland towns flourished under Venice, despite being remote from the sea and forced to maintain elaborate defences first against Austria and later against the Turks. But in the 16C and early 17C plague decimated the population reducing the region to indigence. Settlers were introduced from Cyprus, Turkey, Greece, S Italy and particularly the rest of the Balkans, where the indigenous Slav population was constantly in flight from the Turks. The towns themselves succeeded in assimilating most of the newcomers and retaining the Venetian language, but the surrounding countryside remained overwhelmingly Slavonic, a situation that bred more recent conflicts in this area between Italy and Yugoslavia. It also led, after the Second World War, when Istria became part of Yugoslavia, to the precipitate departure of almost all the Italian-speaking inhabitants to Italy, resulting once again in depopulation of the towns.

The main road follows the shore of the Piran peninsula as far as *Portorož* (see Rte 2), skirts the salt pans of Sečovlje (right; site of Portorož airport), and follows the river Dragonja as far as (11km) the border between Slovenia and Croatia. You are now entering that part of Istria known as Red Istria from the colour of its soil, which is rich in bauxite deposits. It also produces an excellent variety of the sweet white wine, Malvasia.

The road climbs out of the Dragonja valley passing (2km) the crossroads where a right turn leads to Savudrija, Umag and the coast road (see Rte 6B). 6km Buje a charming small town, in an elevated position that earned it the sobriquet of 'the spy of Istria'. A Roman settlement under the name of *Bullea*, it later belonged to the Patriarchate of Aquileia and then to the counts of Weimar-Orlamunde, before passing to Venice in 1412. In appearance the town is entirely medieval, with fortifications still intact (renewed 15C and 17C) and a maze of narrow streets. In the central square are grouped a fine 15C Venetian Gothic palace with painted façade, a Venetian loggia (16C), a medieval measuring column and the 16C parish church of *Sv. Servolo* (rebuilt in a baroque style in the 18C). The church walls contain fragments and inscriptions from a Roman temple that once occupied the site, and on the W end is a Romanesque relief of an angel. Inside are 14–15C Gothic statues in wood. The detached 16C bell tower (view), patterned on that at Aquileia, bears the arms of local nobles. Just outside the town walls near the main entry is the 15C church of *Sv. Marija* with a contemporary Madonna in wood, Renaissance gates in iron, a 15C Pietà (artist unknown) and eight biblical scenes by the Venetian, Gaspare Vecchio (1711).

Momjan, 6km NE, the next nearest hill-town, has ruins of a 14C castle built into the rock face, a 16C parish church and baroque houses. More interesting is **Grožnjan**, 9km SE of Buje, in a superb position overlooking the Mirna valley, almost 300m up. The small town clustered tightly on its hilltop takes its plan from the Venetian military settlement established here in 1359, when Grožnjan became the seat of one of two military captains of Istria. Parts of the ramparts from this period still stand, together with a 15C town gate and loggia (inset with Roman fragments) and bell tower. On the far side of the town overlooking the valley is the small church of *Sv. Kuzma* (1554) with loggia added in the 18C. The large baroque parish church of *Sv. Marija, Vid, i Modest* and most of the domestic buildings also date from the 18C. Midway along the attractive main street, the Renaissance *Palača Biriani* (1597) has been taken over by a group of Slovene and Croatian artists who work here in the summer and maintain a permanent exhibition gallery (ask neighbours for key if closed).

Continuing S from Buje pass (right) the turning for Umag and Novigrad (see Rte 6B) and descend to (31km) the Mirna, Istria's largest river.

48km long, the river has its source in the hills SE of Buzet and has been known since ancient times. Its first recorded name was *Nengon* and to the Greeks it was known as the *Ister* (also the Greek name for the Danube), from which the name Istria is probably derived. On either side of the river to the N and W of Motovun (see below) stretch the *Motovun Woods*, which were placed under state protection by Venice as early as 1452 and were one of the Republic's principal sources of timber for shipbuilding. Below Motovun the valley in places attains up to 1.3km in width and is subject to extensive flooding, the resulting alluvial plain being rich in truffles.

TO MOTOVUN, OPRTALJ, AND BUZET BY THE MIRNA VALLEY, 44km (with diversions). At the point where our road crosses the river a minor road leads left up the right bank. At (8km) *Livade*, a village on the Mirna, the ways divide.

Motovun (Ital. *Montona*), the finest of the Istrian hilltop towns, stands at 277m, 3km S, and is reached by a zigzag road or by some 1000 steps. Enter by an 18C outer gate and proceed through the newer part of the town to a Gothic *Gateway*; over it is set the town arms and a lion of St. Mark, with open book, and inside another lion with book closed. To the right, just outside, stands an 18C baroque *Loggia* (view). The gate forms part of the **Ramparts** (comp. below) dating from 1350 though later renovated, which encircle the old town; they are embellished on the S side with Gothic arches. Through the inner gateway is the main square with the Renaissance church of **Sv. Stjepan** (1614), whose design is attributed to Palladio. A statue of St. Lawrence by Giovanni Bonazza (1725) adorns the high altar, and the choir stalls are 18C baroque. The treasury (apply to sacristan) includes a silver processional cross and gold chalice (both 15C); a 14C altar cloth, once the property of Bartolomeo Colleoni, was later presented to the church (1509) by Bartolomeo Alviano. Adjoining the church is a crenellated bell tower (1442) with a clock. The *Town Hall*, built originally in the 13C, was in continuous use until the Second World War, though almost completely reconstructed in the last century. Behind the Town Hall (left) access may be had to the ramparts (comp. above) which can be circled in their entirety (*Views W over Motovun Woods, N to the Ćićarija mountains and E to the Učka Massif rising to 1396m). Motovun was the birthplace of Andrea de Antiquis (Andrea Antico), composer and printer, who in the first half of the 16C was a pioneer in the printing of music. It was also the home of Veli Jože ('Big Joe'), a well-known 'giant' of Istrian folklore, whose exploits were chronicled by Vladimir Nazor and others.

From Motovun the gravelled road continues S past the villages of *Rakotole* (see below) and *Karojba* to join (16km) the main Poreč–Pazin highway.

From Livade, an alternative road (left) climbs by more vertiginous bends to (7km) **Oprtalj** (378m), with a 17C Venetian loggia and Town Hall. It was a centre of Italian resistance during Austrian rule. The early 16C Gothic parish church of *Sv. Juraj* (St. George), with a Renaissance W front added in the 17C, has a fine fan-vaulted ceiling with carved bosses and corbels. The statues of SS. Anthony of Padua and Francis of Paola on the high altar are by Giovanni Bonazza, and the painting of the Trinity attended by Saints is by a pupil of Benedetto Carpaccio. In the treasury are 15–16C chalices, a Gothic monstrance and a Renaissance pax. The 15C Gothic church of **Sv. Marija** (lengthened in the 18C) is noted for its *Frescoes, the work of four artists of the Istrian School. The best are on the triumphal arch: Annunciation (top), a group of saints (below), and prophets with two saints (soffit of arch); and (S wall, top left) the Virgin protecting members of the guild whose church this was, signed by Clerigin of Koper ('CLERIGINVS DE IVSTINOPOLI'), and dated 1471. The remaining frescoes, unsigned, are also from the 15C. Those completing the top sector of the S wall, by a second hand, have been almost obliterated. Those on the S wall (below) and on the W end of the N wall, showing scenes from the life of Christ, are by a third artist; and the remainder of the N wall, completed by a fourth artist, depicts five saints and the Virgin and Child.

The tiny Romanesque chapel of *Sv. Jelena* (St. Helen) just off the road 1km S, of Oprtalj, contains frescoes by another Clerigin of Koper (thought to be the grandfather of the artist responsible for Sv. Marija). These date from 1400, and depict (triumphal arch) the Annunciation and (apse) Christ with the four symbols of the Evangelists, Agnus Dei and SS. Helen and Nazarius.—Other frescoes are to be found in the churches of *Sv. Rok* (by Anton of Padova, early 16C) and *Sv. Leonard*, in which there is also an altar painting by Zorzi Ventura of Zadar (17C).

The road continues N from Oprtalj to (19km) Rižana Park and Hrastovlje (see Rte 2) and joins the main Koper–Ljubljana highway at (3km) *Rižana*.

From Livade the main road continues E along the valley of the Mirna to (7km) *Sv. Stjepan*, a tiny spa and curative centre. The sulphur springs, known as *Istarske Toplice*, are considered the second most radioactive in Europe. The road passes under the shadow of towering Mt Zvenje (540m) where Istrian stone has been quarried for centuries; on the right is the main pipeline for Istria's water supply.

9km **Buzet** (151m, 2000 inhab.) is another small Istrian hill town. Owing to its situation on the Mirna and its links with the interior, Buzet has been a communications centre from earliest times, its Roman name, *Piquentum*, becoming *Pinguente* under Venice and Italy. Here for a time the Venetian governor of Istria had his seat. The town is still medieval in character and atmosphere, though only fragments of its fortifications remain, notably the *West Gate* of 1592. The pleasant parish church and bell tower are 18C baroque and *Sv. Juraj* (St. George) has paintings by the school of Carpaccio. The adjacent house (No. 5) is arranged as a small ethnographic exhibit, and there is a town *Museum* (opened on request) with a small lapidary collection. View from the ramparts over the Ćićarija Mts and Mirna valley.

Beyond Buzet a minor road winds in hairpin bends to the lower slopes of the *Ćićarija Mountains* (view down the Mirna valley and over Buzet).

The name Ćićarija derives from the Ćić people who at the invitation of Venice settled here in the 15C and 16C to escape from the Turks. They are Wallachian in origin and speak a Romance dialect cognate with modern Rumanian. Today they are concentrated in villages on the W slopes of the Učka Massif between Pazin and Mošćenice.

7km **Roč** stands on or near the site of the Roman settlement of *Rotium*, of which few traces remain. Of the three churches in the village the parish church of *Sv. Bartolomej* (restored 18C) contains a 16C Venetian painting of the Madonna and Saints together with the Doge of Venice and his consort. The tiny Romanesque chapel of *Sv. Rok* retains 14C frescoes of the Istrian school in its apse. *Sv. Antun* is 14C Gothic. Remains are visible of Venetian fortifications dating from 1420.

An excursion may be made to the tiny fortified town of **Hum**, 7km S of Roč along a narrow lane. In the cemetery, below the ruined fortress, is the 12C Romanesque chapel of *Sv. Jerolim*, whose interior is decorated with *Frescoes. Though damaged, these are among the oldest and best in Istria, dating from the late 12C and showing strong Byzantine influence. Note particularly the Annunciation in the apse and on the S wall the Crucifixion, the Deposition, and the Entombment. The picture of St. Anthony adjoining the Crucifixion is a 16C addition.

Beyond Roč the road winds through increasingly barren karst scenery to (5km) *Ročko polje*, where it converges with the Divača–Pazin–Raša railway line, and (10km) *Vranja*, on the road from Pazin to Opatija and Rijeka (see Rte 6C).

On the far side of the Mirna the road climbs steeply to (17km) *Vižinada*, a sadly neglected little town (view over the Mirna valley to Motovun).

From Vižinada a good, straight, but little used road forks right, following the route of the Roman Via Flavia, to (19km) Poreč (see Rte 6B). At 3km and about 1km off the road (right) on the outskirts of the village of **Božje Polje**, is the 15C Gothic church of *Sv. Marija* (key in Labinci, see below). The church, which once belonged to a now defunct Franciscan monastery, contains a fine rib-vaulted ceiling decorated with contemporary frescoes of the Istrian school. A further 4km down the road in the village of **Labinci** the tiny 13C Romanesque chapel of *Sv. Trojica* (Holy Trinity) likewise contains frescoes (15C) of the Istrian school (key in village, or at Turističko društvo, Poreč).

Continue S from Vižinada—6km crossroads; the road on the right runs to Poreč (15km; see Rte 6B) via (3km) **Višnjan** where the chapel of *Sv. Antun* contains 16C frescoes showing scenes from the life of Christ.

To the left another road runs to Karojba where it divides for Motovun (N) or Pazin (S). About 2km E of the Karojba–Motovun road is the village of **Rakotole**. In the graveyard the Romanesque church of *Sv. Nikola*, erected in the 14C by the Venetian nobleman Barbo of Motovun, contains frescoes (scenes from the life of St. Nicholas) by two unknown Italian artists.

At (10km) *Baderna* cross the main Poreč–Pazin road (Rte 6C).

4km **Lovreč** (also known as *Sv. Lovreč Pazenatički*, or St. Lawrence of Pazin), a historic town, stands on a rocky eminence girdled by its walls (partly 10–11C). As the seat of the Venetian governor of Istria, Lovreč once extended far beyond its present limits and had considerable importance. After the government was transferred elsewhere in

ιe 15C its position declined. Its name derives from the tiny 8C chapel
ın the cemetery, but the main feature of architectural interest is the
Romanesque basilica of **Sv. Martin**, dating from the 9–11C, though
the W front was added in 1838. The two original windows of the N and
S apses are filled with carved stone transennae with an interlacing
pattern. The plain interior is divided by two irregular arcades with
debased Byzantine capitals. The large baroque altar was worked in
oak by a 16C local sculptor. The apses are decorated with 11C
frescoes in a Byzantine style, overlaid in the N apse by 14C work in an
Italian style. Adjoining the church is a 15C Venetian *Loggia* and
opposite it a pillory column of like date, whereas the Romanesque
campanile rests on one of the former town gates. There is a handsome
main square. The chapel of *Sv. Blaž* by the main gate is in a rustic
Gothic style dating from 1460, with traces of frescoes in the interior.
The war memorial, erected in 1961, is by Nenad Krivič.

The road continues due S, leaving on the right a narrow road for
Vrsar and Poreč (Rte 6B) and rises to (4km) a rocky eminence
overlooking the **Limski zaliv** (also called *Limski kanal*), a narrow inlet
extending 10km in from the sea. Steep banks, rising in places to a
height of 130m, give it the appearance of a canyon or small fjord, but it
is the submerged end of the valley of Limska draga which descends
for 55km from Pazin. The river Lim flows into it only in winter. It is a
rich fishing ground and has extensive oyster and mussel beds
administered by the Oceanographical Institute in Rovinj. Its mouth
has been colonised by central European naturists (comp. Rte 6B).

Where the main highway bends sharply left a minor road runs (right) parallel
with the inlet, offering excellent views. This leads to **Kloštar** (c 2km) a village
with ruins of an 11C Benedictine monastery. The monastery was founded by
Romualdo, a hermit, who had lived, according to legend, in one of the many
limestone caves that line the banks of the Limski zaliv. The small church of *Sv.
Mihovil* dates from the 6C but was rebuilt by the Benedictines. The monastery
church proper contains 11C frescoes in the Central European Benedictine style
which, with those at Peroj, are the oldest known frescoes in Istria.

Descending in a zigzag to the floor of the valley, climb again on the far
side, passing beneath the Pazin–Kanfanar railway line, to (5km)
Brajkovići, where a main road forks right to Rovinj (see Rte 6B) and a
minor road left to Kanfanar, Žminj and Pazin (see Rte 6C). From
Brajkoviči to Pula the highway again follows the course of the Roman
Via Flavia.

9km **Bale** (Ital. *Valle*) is a hill town (145m) on the site of a Roman
castrum. The 15C *Kaštel Bembo*, named for the noble family to whom
it passed from the Soardo in 1618, has a graceful Venetian Gothic
façade with a double set of four-light windows adorned with balconies. Entering through the Gothic main gate you quickly come to the
main square where the parish church of *Sv. Julian* (1880) retains a
13C Romanesque campanile. Within, on the S side a late 12C Gothic
Crucifix surmounts the W altar; the adjoining altar has a 15C wooden
screen carved and painted in the Venetian style. The altar in the S
apse containing the relics of St. Julian Cesarello, Bale's patron saint, is
surmounted by an 11C Byzantine Madonna and Child carved in
wood. On the N side a niche at the W end contains an ornamented
pre-Romanesque sarcopahgus (9C). Steps left of the high altar
descend to the crypt, which preserves a stone altar and altar rail
constructed of 6C and 8C fragments from an earlier church and
decorated with Romanesque motifs, and the 14C sarcophagus of St.
Julian. Also in the main square are a Venetian loggia and fontego
(grain warehouse) and the former *Pretorska palača* (Captain's

Residence), now a school. In the little churches of *Sv. Duh* (Holy Spir.
and *Sv. Antun* (on the road to Pula) traces of 15C frescoes have beer
discovered; the Romanesque bell tower of *Sv. Ilija* (on the Rovinj road)
is said to be one of the oldest in Istria (11 or 12C).

Bale is a centre of the Istriots, a people directly descended from the original
Roman population of this area, who speak a Romance dialect of their own. Many
of them live in a large, distinctive type of homestead called a *štancija*, which
houses several families together and has a ground floor for animals. These, in
general, are built to extremely high standards.

11km **Vodnjan**, another Istriot town and road junction. Called
Dignano in Italian, it passed to Venice in 1331, became independent
in 1382 and, apart from being sacked in 1413 by King Sigismund of
Hungary, has had a peaceful and prosperous past. Consequently it is
one of the best preserved of Istrian towns. The attractive main street,
UL. I OG. MAJA, lined with houses dating mainly from the 17–18C and
with a notable Gothic town house at the far end, leads into NARODNI
TRG, the main square. The former *Palača Bradamante* (17C), on the S
side, is now the town hall. To the W of this square lies the old quarter,
a picturesque huddle of narrow streets and houses dating back to the
15C. In the first of two small squares stands the 15C *Kaštel* (formerly
Palača Bettica) in Venetian Gothic; in the second, is the parish church
(18C) with three Romanesque reliefs built into the W wall and a
detached bell tower (view to the coast and Brioni Isles). In the church
the high altar is flanked by two pictures, the Last Supper by G.
Contarini (1598) and a 14C polyptych (school of Paolo Veneziano); in
the N aisle is a Renaissance marble custodial dating from 1451. The
treasury (apply to sacristan) contains a 15C Gothic reliquary
ornamented with miniatures.

From Vodnjan roads lead N to *Svetvinčenat*, *Žminj*, and *Pazin* (see Rte 6C), E to
Barban, *Raša*, and *Marčana* (see Rte 6C), SE to *Galižana* and SW to *Peroj*, and
Fažana (see below).

10km **PULA** is now the chief and largest town (47,000 inhab.) of Istria
and seat of the Kotar (regional administration). A major port and
industrial centre, it is being intensively developed to the S and E as a
tourist centre, with new hotels, camps, and beaches. The principal
attraction for the visitor is its Roman remains.

Post Office: Rade Končara ulica.

Information: *Turist biro*, 4 Trg bratstva i jedinstva, tel. 23276.

Airport: At Valtura, 6km E. *JAT*, 8 M. Balote ulica, tel. 23322.

Buses: Local buses from Trg bratstva i jedinstva to the tourist centre at *Veruda*
and the town beach at *Stoja*. Bus station for all country buses in Trg oslobodjenja.

Ferries connect with Trieste and with all major towns on the Yugoslav Adriatic
coast. Local services call at Istrian coastal towns.—BOATS may be hired to
explore the harbour and offshore islands.

Film Festival annually (Oct) in the Roman amphitheatre.

History. According to legend *Pula*, otherwise *Pola*, was founded by the
Colchians after their unsuccessful pursuit of Jason and the Golden Fleece.
Archaeological evidence shows that there was an Illyrian settlement here from at
least 500 BC. Pliny refers to the place as *Pietas Julia*; it is thought to have been
refounded as a Roman colony by Augustus c 40 BC and named in this way in
honour of Julius Caesar. Its full name was *Colonia Julia Pollentia Herculanea*.
Under the Romans, Pula flourished as a commercial and business town and the
administrative centre of Istria. Its population is estimated to have reached
25–30,000, and the many remaining monuments testify to its wealth and
importance. In the 2C AD Rasparaganus, the banished king of the Roxolans,
found refuge here with his son, Publius Aelius Peregrinus; and in 326 Crispus,

son of Constantine the Great, was brought here and killed on the orders of his father. Pula passed to the Ostrogoths and then to the Exarchate of Ravenna, under which it became a bishopric. In 788 it was joined to the kingdom of the Franks and became the seat of the elective counts of Istria. These gave way to hereditary margraves who remained in Germany, and Pula steadily declined, particularly when, after siding with Pisa against Venice, it was raided and sacked by the Venetians.

In 1230 Pula, together with the rest of Istria, came under the Patriarchate of Aquileia but 28 years later was able to purchase its autonomy. Future prospects were, however, dissipated in internecine struggle, particularly between the monarchical party, led by the Sergi family, and a popular party led by the Ionatasi. The Sergi family, also known as the Castropoli from the castle (Castrum Polae) they occupied, were descended from the Roman family whose name appears on the triumphal arch still standing in Pula. They supported the patriarch in Aquileia, but most of the clan was massacred by the Ionotasi and their allies on Good Friday, 1271. In the struggle between Genoa and Venice, Pula sided with Genoa and was sacked for her pains. In 1331 she submitted to Venice and the Sergi-Castropoli were banished from the town. Now Genoa exacted revenge by raids in 1354, 1374, and 1380. Decline and stagnation followed. The ancient monuments were pillaged, abbeys and churches rifled. In 1630 the Venetians, employing the French engineer Antony de Ville, used the stones of the old Roman theatre to build a fort overlooking the harbour. Plague and malaria were rampant and in 1631 Pula had only 350 inhabitants. Renewal came only under Austria, which in 1866 proclaimed Pula the chief naval port of the empire. Extensive fortifications were built on every hill and island surrounding the harbour, a dockyard and naval arsenal were established, the railway extended from Slovenia and a new centre built, much as it remains today. By 1914 the population had climbed to 60,000. Then, in 1918, came another sharp turn of fortune. Istria passed to Italy. Pula, on the new frontier with Yugoslavia, lost its importance and declined. During the Second World War it was subjected to heavy allied bombing and was occupied by Anglo-American forces until 1947 pending a frontier agreement between Italy and Yugoslavia.

Pula has links with Dante, who is presumed to have stayed here. James Joyce taught at the Berlitz School from October 1904 to March 1905.

The outstanding Roman monument is the magnificent ***Amphi-theatre**, known locally as the *Arena* (adm. May–Sept 8–19, Oct–Apr 10–16). It is the sixth largest of the surviving Roman amphitheatres, ranking in size just below Arles and Catania, and is in some ways the most interesting example of all. The ellipse of the amphitheatre lies upon an axis running from NW to SE with a diameter of 132m, whereas the transverse diameter is 105m. The outer wall reaches 32m at its highest point. There were 15 entrances, of which that from the S nearest the town was the grandest, and the amphitheatre is estimated to have seated c 23,000 spectators.

Probably built by Augustus during the early years of the 1C AD and enlarged by Claudius, the edifice achieved its present form c AD 80 in the reign of Vespasian. In the Middle Ages almost the entire interior was removed, much of it to Venice. A plan to dismantle the exterior wall and re-erect it on the Lido at Venice was frustrated (comp. below). Modern archaeological interest started with the excavations of Marshal Marmont in 1810.

EXTERIOR. The building was situated just outside the limits of the old Roman town beside the Via Flavia which led to Parentium (Poreč), Aegida (Koper), and Tergeste (Trieste). Some of the original flag-stones of the Via Flavia can still be seen at the foot of the amphitheatre wall. The exterior wall is in a remarkably fine state of preservation and can be approached on all sides. It varies in height from four stories on the seaward side to two opposite, where the slope of the terrain was used to support the seating. On the seaward side there is a lower story of massive monumental arches supported by rectangular piers extending for about half the total circumference. Above this is an arcade of equal length. A third arcade of 72 arches encircles the entire

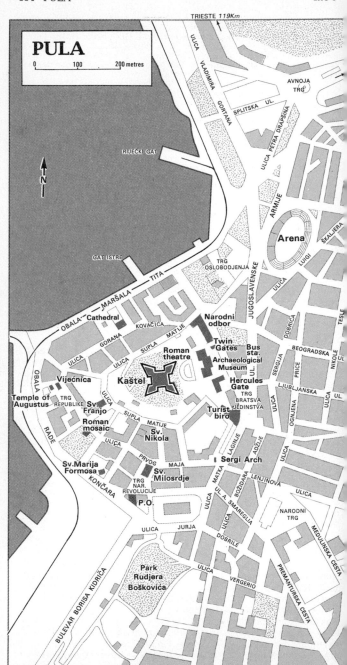

building. The topmost story of 64 rectangular apertures is surmounted by an unusual stone balustrading. The four shallow rectangular towers placed to the four cardinal points were part of a system of waterworks, unique to this amphitheatre, that supplied the building from a neighbouring spring. The water was stored at the top of the towers and carried around the amphitheatre by a channel in the balustrading round the perimeter. The lower part of the towers contained spiral staircases that gave access to the upper tiers of seats. On the external wall of the W tower a plaque, placed in 1584, expresses gratitude to Gabriele Emo, the Venetian senator, who successfully protested against the scheme for transporting the amphitheatre to Venice.

INTERIOR. Admission to the amphitheatre is gained through the S tower. The first impression is of emptiness, for almost the entire contents have been removed over the centuries. The present banked seating was built by the Italians between the two world wars. This sharp contrast with the condition of the exterior was made possible by the complete separation of the two parts in the original construction. The gap between the outermost ring of seats and the perimeter was spanned only by wooden flooring, and the holes for the joists can still be seen in the masonry. The history of the Pula amphitheatre is exactly the reverse of that at Verona, where the outer wall has disappeared, but the interior remains intact.

Pula, the Roman amphitheatre

Around the arena is an excavated passage along which the animals used to run. Their dens beneath the arena now house lighting equipment. At the SE end a line of broken-off rectangular pillars shows the extent of the smaller amphitheatre built by Augustus. A grassy bank at the NW end affords an excellent view of the interior; for those with a head for heights, the top of the W water tower provides an even better vantage point from which the town and harbour are also seen. Here the balustrading and its water channel may be examined. The amphitheatre, once used by the local commandery of Knights of St. John for jousting, now serves for open-air opera productions and for the Annual Festival of Yugoslav Films.

From the amphitheatre UL. MATIJE GUPCA leads to the local bus station in Trg Oslobodjenja, behind which is located the *Karolinin izvor* (Caroline Spring) built in the 18C on the site of a former Roman nymphaeum. Beyond the trg is a small *Park* containing a bronze monument to the fallen of the last war, by V. Radauš. The central figure is typical of the socialist realism era, but the pleasant bas-reliefs on either side portray a traditional theme from Yugoslav folklore.

UL. GORANA KOVAČIĆA marks the N boundary of the old Roman town and winds round to the **Cathedral of Sv. Tomo**, a building that has suffered much during its long history. The original Byzantine basilica was erected in the 6C, possibly on the site of a temple of Jupiter or of thermal baths, and incorporated much Roman material in its structure. In the 15C after heavy damage in raids by both Venice and Genoa, the building had to be almost completely reconstructed, although much earlier material was re-used. In the S wall, is embedded a lintel dated 857 and bearing the monogram of Bp Handegis, with an inscription recording his donation of a doorway to the cathedral. In the 16C a Renaissance W front was added and in the 17C a bell tower, into the foundations of which were incorporated a quantity of seats from the amphitheatre.

The cathedral is entered through a loggia built as a war memorial by the Italians after the First World War against the wall of a Franciscan nunnery. The striking late Gothic lintel over the entrance dates from 1456 and was brought here from the defunct Benedictine church of Sv. Mihovil, whose site is now occupied by the city hospital.

The INTERIOR preserves the basilican plan with the main apse slightly shortened and squared off. The columns dividing the nave from the aisles are a hodge-podge of Roman, Byzantine and other work, whereas the majority of the capitals date from the 15C reconstruction. Many bear heraldic emblems of the craft guilds that donated them. Fragmentary Byzantine mosaics remain just inside the entrance door and in front of the high altar. The altar consists of a 3C Roman sarcophagus and is reputed to contain the relics of the Hungarian King Solomon (died 1074).

Opposite the cathedral the narrow RASPARAGANOV USPON leads up to the **Kaštel**, which crowns the hill in the centre of the old town. This was the site of the original Illyrian settlement and of the Roman capitol, which was destroyed in the 13C for the first castle of the Sergi family. Their fortress was completely reconstructed in 1630–31 by the Venetians according to plans by the French military engineer Antony de Ville and restored first by Napoleon and then (1840) by Austria. Today it houses the *Muzej narodne revolucije Istre* (Istrian Museum of the National Liberation Movement; adm. 9–13 and 15–19).

Steps on the far side of the Kaštel lead down to the Archaeological Museum and Pula's two Roman gateways (see below).

Passing the small square at the cathedral's W end, beyond which can be seen the harbour and naval headquarters, continue along Ul. Gorana Kovačića past attractive houses to the TRG REPUBLIKE, or

Piazza Foro, the site of the Roman Forum. At the N end of the square are two small 1C temples of which the ***Temple of Augustus*** (*Augustov hram*) is an outstanding example, with high, narrow proportions, delicately carved Corinthian capitals (some restored) and a handsome entablature. The *Temple of Diana* (alternatively attributed to Hercules) can only be perceived in outline from the rear, for at the end of the 13C it was bodily incorporated into the Gothic *Vijećnica* (Town Hall). This later became the seat of the Venetian rectors, but was badly damaged by the Genoese in 1379, and later almost completely destroyed. Most of the present building dates from a renewal in 1653; only the E façade remains from the original structure.

From the Trg Republike the main street of the old town, the *corzo*, now named UL. 1 MAJA, leads through the busy shopping centre. In the first street to the left, the steep Uspon Balde Lupetine, are the Franciscan church and monastery. **Sv. Franjo** was built at the end of the 13C in the restrained Gothic style characteristic of the Adriatic seaboard. A curiosity is the double pulpit with one part projecting into the street for preaching to an overflow congregation. The ornate W portal, decorated with unusual shell motifs, is surmounted by a rose window. Within are a beautiful 16C screen of gilt and painted wood behind the high altar, and a 15C Gothic polyptych by Jakob of Pula. To the left of the church is the early 14C cloister (restored), with a small lapidary collection, including a 6C mosaic of saints and the gravestone of the 11C Hungarian King Solomon. Leading off it is a tiny Gothic chapel in which more mosaics have recently been discovered.

In the courtyard of No. 16 Ul. 1 maja (entrance from the rear through small park) is a large and complete Roman *Mosaic Floor* attributed to the 1C BC; part of a Roman villa urbana revealed by bombing, it depicts the punishment of Circe by the sons of Antiope. In the SE corner of the park stands a tiny cruciform chapel, the last remaining fragment of *Sv. Marija Formosa*, a monumental Byzantine basilica (also known as Santa Maria in Canneto).

The basilica, built by St. Maximian, Abp of Ravenna in 546, was one of the more sumptuous buildings of the Adriatic, with marble columns, mosaic floors and a profusion of Byzantine sculpture. In the 14C it was sacked by the Genoese and through succeeding centuries its treasures were removed to Venice. Four exquisite columns of Oriental alabaster from this church can still be seen behind the high altar of St. Mark's in Venice and are famous for their transparency. The remaining chapel, one of two that originally flanked the basilica, served as a mausoleum and resembles that of Galla Placidia at Ravenna; its principal feature is a small Byzantine panel carved in stone, set into the wall over the door. Within are fragments of a 6C mosaic and 15C frescoes.

RIBARSKA UL. leads back to the main street, from which UL. JANA HUSA continues to the Orthodox church of *Sv. Nikola*. Although the exterior dates from the 6C, the interior has been largely reconstructed. Continuing along Ul. 1 maja, pass through the TRG NARODNE REVOLUCIJE, with the church of *Sv. Milosrdje* (Holy Mercy) and the *General Post Office* on the left, and come to the **Sergi Arch** (*Sergijev slavoluk*), which stands just inside the former Porta Aurea of the Roman town. Facing inwards, it consists of a single large arch flanked by paired columns of the Corinthian order. The faces and inner walls of the piers are richly decorated with vine and acanthus leaves and the coffered intrados, ornamented with rosettes, bears a bas-relief showing a snake and eagle locked in combat. In the spandrels are winged victories. The ornamented frieze carries an inscription attesting that the donor was Salvia Postuma, of the Sergi family, and inscribed plinths surmounting the entablature show that the arch was a memorial to three members of the family, whose statues presumably adorned it. The arch is attributed to the 1C BC and was studied by Michelangelo, Fra Giocondo, Battista da Sangallo, and Palladio and also drawn by Piranesi and the Englishmen Thomas Allison and Robert Adam.

UL. MATKA LAGINJE, beyond the arch, traverses the site of the Roman necropolis thought to have inspired Dante's comment on Pula in the 'Inferno' (Canto IX, 113–16), and ends at a Roman theatre, of which only traces remain.

Turn N from the arch and skirt parts of the town walls, whose base and inner side are still to some extent Roman, to TRG BRATSTVA I JEDINSTVA, the main square of modern Pula, a busy centre of banks and tourist offices. In the SW corner its *Hercules' Gate* (Herkulesova vrata), the oldest remaining component of the Roman walls, dating from the 1C AD. At its apex are relief carvings of a club and the head that gives the gate is name. A little beyond stand the *Twin Gates* (or Porta Gemina), dating from the 2C AD, a double arch with a highly decorated cornice but no frieze. Excavations opposite, at the foot of a modern block of flats, have uncovered the foundations of an octagonal Roman mausoleum.

Within the Twin Gates a large Austrian-built structure in eclectic *fin de siècle* style houses the ***Arheoloski Muzej** (Archaeological Museum*, adm. 9–12 and 14–18), with extensive prehistoric, Roman, and medieval collections. GROUND FLOOR. Entrance: Architectural fragments and tomb monuments.—R.1. Temple pediment from Nesactium, altars, tombstones and commemorative monuments.—R.2. Religious monuments: sacrificial altars dedicated to various divinities, including the Vento Boria, the Adriatic north wind.—R.3. Civil Monuments: bases of commemorative monuments, architectural fragments from the Roman theatre and from Nesactium, mosaic from a Roman house, Roman milestone from the Via Flavia.—R.4. Public Monuments: inscriptions with names of civil servants, funerary altars, sarcophagi.—R.5. Early Christian and Medieval Eras: Byzantine and Romanesque capitals; fragments of plutei; a Lion of St. Mark, possibly the oldest in Istria; 5C mosaic pavements.—R.6. Altars, ambo, architectural fragments with braid motifs; mosaics of the early Christian period.

FIRST FLOOR. Prehistoric Collections. R.1. Palaeolithic, Neolithic, and Eneolithic Ages.—R.2. Bronze Age: finds from Istrian necropoleis (1800–1000 BC).—R.3. Stone tables from Nesactium (first millenium BC), Iron Age material.—R.4. Material from Early Christian necropoleis, tools and household articles from the fortified villages of Istria.—R.5. Utensils, etc. from the 7–13C, found in Byzantine and Early Slav cemeteries.

Behind the museum, on the hillside leading up to the Kastel, are the excavated remains of a second *Roman Theatre* dating from the 2C AD. Like the amphitheatre, it was so placed as to make best use of the slope for the cavea.

EXCURSIONS. To **Fažana**, a pleasant fishing village 8km NW by the coast road. The small 12C church of *Sv. Marija od Karmela* (rebuilt 15C, loggia added in 16C) contains well-preserved frescoes in the Gothic manner. The Gothic parish church of *Sv. Kuzma i Damjan* has traces of Renaissance frescoes on its side walls, and the sacristy is decorated with 16C frescoes by an unknown Friulian artist (Crucifixion, Pietà). On the N wall hangs a Last Supper (1578) by Zorzi Ventura of Zadar. On the E side of the village is the tiny Romanesque chapel of *Sv. Elizej*, attributed to the 8C or 9C, with a polygonal apse and carved stone transennae in the windows.

Beyond Fažana a narrow road continues to **Peroj** 3km, a village founded in 1645 by Montenegrin immigrants. Most of the inhabitants retain their Montenegrin dialect and customs. Of the two churches *Sv. Spiridon* is Orthodox and contains icons of the 16–18C, whereas the Catholic church of *Sv. Stjepan* is Romanesque and has fragmentary 13C frescoes.—*Sv. Foška*, another Romanesque church, 3km farther N, has frescoes in the Byzantine manner that are among the oldest in Istria (12C). A large Ascension has been uncovered in the apse; elsewhere a later layer awaits restoration.

About 1 nautical mile offshore from Fažana are the Brijuni or **Brioni Islands**, of which *Veliki Brioni*, the largest, was the summer residence of President Tito. Here, in a newly constituted national park, may be seen some impressive ancient ruins, notably a splendid Roman palace with terraces at *Veriga Bay*, a huge complex known as the Byzantine Castrum at *Dobrika Bay*, and nearby, the ruins of a 6C Byzantine basilica. The park is inhabited by tame deer and hosts a variety of exotic plants.

Off the road to Labin (Rte 4D), beyond (11km) Valtura is **Glavica**, site of Roman *Nesactium*. Once the chief town of the Illyrian tribe of Histra, Nesactium was sacked by the Romans in 177 BC when they defeated Epulo, last of the Illyrian princes. It was later rebuilt by them but did not survive the collapse of the Roman Empire. Extensive archaeological investigation has revealed the prehistoric ramparts, the foundations of some Roman houses and temples, and two 5C Christian basilicas.

B.   Piran to Pula via the Coast

ROAD, 140km. Highway N2/E751 and minor roads. 27km *Savudrija*.—8km **Umag**.—16km **Novigrad**.—16km **Poreč** (*Vrsar*, 9km).—39km **Rovinj**.—34km **Pula**.
Buses frequently in 3–5 hours.

Follow Rte 4A to (13km) the crossroads beyond the Dragonja valley, turn right along a narrow asphalted road and pass through flat featureless country to (14km) *Savudrija* (500 inhab.), a small fishing village and quiet resort set in pine woods and with a rocky shore. The local fishermen's custom of hoisting the boats out of the water on davits when not in use is unique on the E Adriatic coast. The lighthouse (36m), the tallest in Istria, also marks the westernmost tip of the Balkan peninsula (view of Piran, Portorož, and the Bay of Piran). A plaque in the parish church commemorates the defeat here in 1177 of Otto, son of Emperor Frederick I (Barbarossa), by the Venetian fleet under Doge Sebastiano Ziani and Nicola Contarini.

From Savudrija the road turns S to follow the coast, passing (4km) the site of Roman *Siparis*, later Sipar, destroyed in the 9C by the Neretvan corsair Domagoj. Beyond lies the main wine-producing region of Istria, extending S to Vrsar and notable for the white wine, Malvasia, and the red Teran.

4km **Umag** (3000 inhab.), a bustling small resort town is quickly modernising itself, and has facilities for sailing and water-skiing.

Known as *Humagum* in Roman times, Umag passed to the bishopric of Trieste in the early Middle Ages and to Venice in 1268, where it remained until the fall of the Republic. Legend has it that the ship carrying the body of St. Mark to Venice stopped in Umag *en route*. The town was sacked by the Genoese in 1370. Since passing formally to Yugoslavia in 1954 it has been developed as a resort, and light industries established here include a cement factory and a cannery.

The tourist settlement developed on the N side of the town affords a view of the picturesque old quarter typically placed on a low, narrow peninsula. The parish church of *Sv. Pelegrin* has a 14C relief of St. Peregrinus Laziosi built into the S wall and, within, a 15C polyptych on wood, by an anonymous Friulian artist. Houses from the 12C to the 17C survive, particularly in Riječka ul.

Buses to all parts of Istria and the main towns of Yugoslavia. **Ferries** daily to all points N as far as Trieste.

From Umag a good asphalted road runs 13km E to *Buje* (see Rte 4A).

Continue S along the coast road to (11km) the hamlet of *Dajla*, passing (just off the road, right) a neoclassical mansion and baroque church erected in 1839 on the site of a Benedictine monastery. The adjoining farm buildings are an excellent example of the Istrian *štancija*, and the complex is now worked as a co-operative farm. Across rolling vineyards lies Novigrad on its peninsula.

5km **Novigrad** is a sleepy little town (2000 inhab.) of great charm with a history of unbroken continuity from Roman times.

Possibly *Aemona* in Roman times, the town was refounded in the 8C under Byzantium as *Neapolis*. This became *Cittanova* under Venice and Italy and finally *Novigrad* under Yugoslavia. Novigrad had a bishop from the 6C until 1831, and prospered after passing to Venice in 1270, mainly owing to its position at the mouth of the river Mirna which provided an outlet for timber from Motovun. In 1687 the town was sacked by the Turks. After the Second World War, Novigrad marked the southern limit of the disputed Zone B, which passed to Yugoslavia in 1945.

The parish church (formerly cathedral) of **Sv. Pelagij** (St. Pelagius) is a handsome baroque structure of complicated ancestry. The church was totally reconstructed in the 15–16C. The baroque interior dates from 1754, while the exterior and campanile result from 19C alterations. Beneath the high altar, a late-Romanesque crypt remaining from an 11C basilica contains the relics of St. Pelagius, a boy martyred in Istria c 283 under Numerian. In TRG SLOBODE is a small Venetian town hall with clock tower and in UL. JOSIP MILOYAC, leading out of it, the 18C Urizzi mansion containing an excellent lapidary collection and small museum (key from tourist office). Noteworthy are the Romanesque reliefs, showing a rich variety of ornamentation, taken from the original basilica.

Buses to all parts of Istria and the major cities of Yugoslavia. **Ferries** daily to all points N as far as Trieste.

Immediately S of Novigrad cross the wide shallow estuary of the river Mirna by a causeway and climb through pinewoods via (7km) *Tar* to Poreč.

9km **POREČ**, a town of great antiquity, is celebrated for its 6C basilica and fine mosaics. Poreč (3000 inhab.) preserves in exceptional purity the urban plan of a Roman municipium, with the two main arteries, the decumanus maximus and the cardo maximus not only still in use but still bearing their original names. The forum too is still preserved in name and outline at the W end of the town in the large open space known as the Marafor (Mars' Forum).

Post Office: Trg slobode.

Information: 3 Trg slobode, tel. 86126.

Buses run locally in season between hotels Riviera and Plava Laguna. Buses for Istria and the rest of Yugoslavia, from Trg slobode. To *Trieste* and *Graz* in the season.

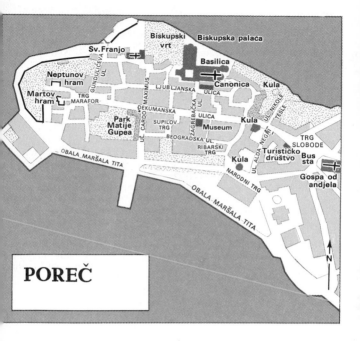

Ferries to all the coastal towns of Istria and also to Zadar and Dubrovnik.

Concerts in season in the Basilica.

History. *Poreč* (Ital. *Parenzo*) is known to have existed in 200 BC as a centre of the Illyrian tribe of Histra. Its name is one of the few thought to be derived from Illyrian. It became Roman in 35 BC under the name of *Parentium*, and was raised to the dignity of a colonia in the 2C AD. With the fall of the Western Roman Empire, Poreč passed to the Goths, then in 539 to Byzantium, during whose rule a bishopric was founded and the present basilica built. Short intervals of Lombard and Frankish rule followed in the 8C, during which time the Slavs began to arrive. After a period of violence and disorder Parenzo became in 1267 the first Istrian town to submit to Venice, under whom it remained for five centuries. As a result of local disputes and plague its fortunes declined sharply, until in the mid 17C the population had been reduced from over 3000 to less than 100. The town was resettled mainly by Croats with some Greeks and Albanians. In 1797 Poreč passed to Napoleon, in 1815 to Austria, and in 1861 became the principal town of Istria and seat of an Istrian assembly. Like the rest of Istria it was occupied by Italy in 1918 and during the Second World War for a short while by the Germans, when a large part of the town was destroyed by allied bombing. Poreč was joined to Yugoslavia in 1945.

One of the outstanding buildings of the Adriatic littoral is the ****Basilica of Euphrasius** (*Eufrazijeva bazilika*; adm. 8–12 and 15–19) a 6C Byzantine cathedral with mosaics in the tradition of Ravenna; described by one expert as 'inferior to the churches of Ravenna in size alone; in beauty of execution it is quite their equal, while in the completeness of its plan with atrium and baptistery it surpasses them'.

The basilica is approached by way of either Zagrebačka or Ljubljanska ul.

History. The complexity of the basilica can best be understood if considered in four stages (see plan). It is thought that the earliest Christian building in Poreč was the so-called 'Oratorium' of St. Maurus (Sv. Mauro), who was probably the first bishop. It was probably part of the Roman house (pl. A), dating from the 3C AD, in which Maurus lived. After the Edict of Milan (313) a small basilica (pl. B; known as the 'Original Basilica') is thought to have been raised on this spot together with a catechumeneum (pl. C) on the N side and a martyrium (pl. D) to the south. The martyrium probably held relics of St. Maurus. In the first half of the 5C this was superseded by a larger church (known as the 'Pre-Euphrasian Basilica') consisting of a rectangular non-apsidal structure flanked on the N by a consignatorium. Finally, the present building was erected in 543–53 on the foundations of the previous one by order of Bp Euphrasius. It is the earliest known Byzantine church where the place of honour in the conch of the centre apse is given to the Virgin and Child, not the Pantokrator.

EXTERIOR. The basilica is entered through an ATRIUM, consisting of an open courtyard surrounded by a covered ambulatory, with three arches on each side. The marble columns probably derived from some local Roman building and support Byzantine basket-shaped capitals of the type found at Ravenna. The atrium was partially restored in 1869 and now has fragments of antique, Romanesque, and Gothic masonry embedded in its walls; on one side of the courtyard is a 9C stone throne.

On the W side opens the octagonal BAPTISTERY (upper part and roof restored in 1881 and again in 1935). The stone inscription on the S wall comes from the sarcophagus of St. Maurus, which was found under the basilica's main altar, and refers to the transfer of the saint's remains to the newly built martyrium. Within is an 18C marble font by the Venetian sculptor Melchior Caffa. Behind the baptistery stairs give access to the *Campanile*, built in 1592 and unusually aligned on the axis of the church.

To the N of the Atrium is the *Bishop's palace*, originally dating from the 6C though the present structure dates from 1694 and is used by the church as offices (no adm.).

The *West Front* of the basilica is best seen from the baptistery door. This façade was once entirely decorated with mosaics of which only the lower part (restored 1897) remains. Here the wall is pierced by three windows flanked on the outside by two pairs of saints. On the piers between are depicted the seven candlesticks of the seven churches of the Book of Revelation. Three marble portals open into the basilica. The lintel of the centre door bears the ornate monogram of Euphrasius.

INTERIOR. The perfect tripartite basilica adheres to the classical Byzantine plan, its restrained beauty wonderfully set off by the rich mosaic in the apse. The NAVE has twin arcades of ten semicircular arches. The columns, like those in the atrium, were probably taken from classical buildings, but the capitals were specially carved and surmounted by the monogram of Euphrasius. The soffits of the N arcade are covered in stucco decorated with coffered geometrical patterns; they probably date from the original construction of the church. Those on the S arcade were destroyed by earthquake in 1440, when the wall above was given inappropriate Gothic windows.

The APSE, polygonal without and semicircular within, is lighted by four Romanesque windows, which has the unusual effect of placing a pier in the central position. Round the apse is the synthronon in white-veined marble with the cathedra in the centre; the walls and semi-dome are covered with *Mosaics and inlay.

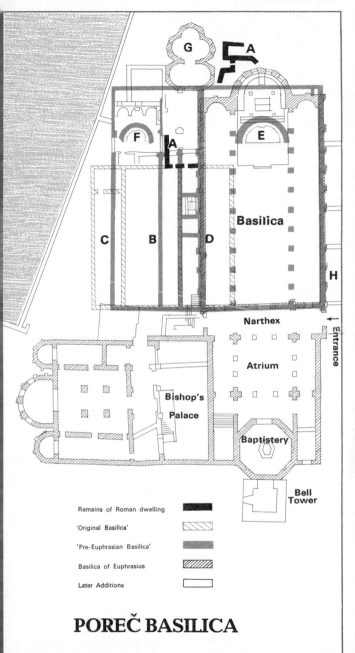

G A

F A

E

Basilica

C B D

H

Narthex

Entrance

Atrium

Bishop's Palace

Baptistery

Bell Tower

Remains of Roman dwelling
'Original Basilica'
'Pre-Euphrasian Basilica'
Basilica of Euphrasius
Later Additions

POREČ BASILICA

Above the sedilia is a sumptuous *dado* made of inlaid porphyry, serpentine, onyx, alabaster, glass, burnt clay and mother-of-pearl, the last used to particularly striking effect to reflect an opalescent light over the curved wall. The panels that make up the dado contain eight varieties of geometrical pattern, arranged symmetrically in pairs. In the centre, above the bishop's throne, a single panel is inlaid with a gold cross on a ground of serpentine and mother-of-pearl, and surmounts a dome between lighted candlesticks. A cornice of acanthus leaves moulded in stucco then separates the dado from the mosaics, which are on a level with the five windows.

The central pier is occupied by an angel holding an orb; the piers between the windows by (left) St. Zachary and (right) St. John the Baptist. In the wall spaces beyond the windows are represented (left) the Salutation of Mary and Elizabeth and (right) the Annunciation. The magnificent centrepiece of the whole composition occupies the semi-dome. On a golden ground the Virgin holds the Infant giving a blessing. To either side are an angel and further figures. On the right St. Maurus, holding an urn, Bp Euphrasius holding a model of his church, together with his son, and the Archdeacon Claudius, holding a book. Those on the left are thought to be early patron saints of Poreč. Below these figures is a large inscription running the full width of the semi-dome, testifying in thirteen hexameters that Bp Euphrasius had pulled down the former church and erected this new basilica for the worship of Christ.

The soffit of the triumphal arch is filled with 12 medallions within wreaths, each portraying a female saint. At the summit of the arch is the Euphrasian monogram in coloured plaster. On the E wall above the triumphal arch, Christ in majesty and the Twelve Apostles. A thin red line marks off the original upper part from the restored portion below.

The altar frontal is of silver gilt and dates from 1452, though the figures of the Virgin and saints on it date from after 1669, when the originals were stolen. The magnificent *Ciborium, dating from 1277, rests on four marble columns, probably from an earlier building, with capitals of a Byzantine type carved in the 13C. The four sides are decorated with Venetian mosaics that are more expressive and natural than the mosaics of the apse, but inferior in artistic design and execution. The front shows the Annunciation, whereas the other three sides bear medallions containing the heads of saints.

The sculptured panels enclosing the sanctuary are of 6C origin but were restored and replaced in their present position in 1837. Immediately in front, protected by trapdoors (usually standing open, if not, apply to sacristan), survive portions of the *Mosaic Floor* (pl. E) of the pre-Euphrasian Basilica, at a depth of about 60cm below the present floor. Their 5C local workmanship shows a strong Roman tradition. Other parts of this floor (not usually seen) have been discovered just inside the main entrance and beneath the sacristy in the former consignatorium.

The mosaics in the N and S apses were badly damaged in the 15C when new windows were pierced. The N apse shows the Face of Christ above clouds as he hands a martyr's crown to each of two saints, while the superior S apse, though in a worse condition, shows a fine unbearded Christ crowning SS. Cosmas and Damian. A 6C altar in the N apse bears an inscription stating that Bp Euphrasius ordered the Basilica to be built in the eleventh year of his episcopate.

On the S side of the church are three chapels, added at a later date. In the largest, dedicated to *Sv. Križ* (The Holy Cross), are walnut *Choir Stalls* (1452) carved in the Gothic style. A curious group of three little chapels is entered from behind the high altar. The first, rectangular, is used as a vestry; the second, oval, with the remains of 15C frescoes, forms the sacristy. It contains a Last Supper by Palma the Younger and a small enamel 18C cross, made on Mt Athos (apply to sacristan to view). The third, the Cella trichora (pl. G), is clover-shaped and has remains of mosaics on its floor. It is thought to have been the martyrium of Euphrasius's basilica or possibly a mausoleum for Euphrasius. Here a 13C sarcophagus, constructed of 6C fragments, contains relics of St. Maurus.

An area just N of the main building has been excavated. Admission is gained from the Atrium by a door just right of the stairs leading into the Bishop's palace. Here are the remains of the three halls of the 'ORIGINAL BASILICA' consisting of (from N to S) the catechumeneum, the basilica proper and the martyrium. In the martyrium we find the oldest *Mosaic of the entire complex, dating from the 3C and a relic of the Roman dwelling that once stood here. In its centre is a fish (ichthys), symbol of Christ, which was inserted into the Roman mosaic probably in the 4C. The remaining mosaics (greatly restored) also date from the 4C.

On the W side of the MARAFOR are the scanty remains of two Roman temples. The larger, popularly known as *Martov hram* (Temple of Mars), is of unknown date and attribution, and although its original dimensions make it the largest Roman temple so far discovered in Istria, all that remains are parts of the stylobate, a few columns and capitals and a reconstructed architrave. The smaller *Neptunov hram* (Temple of Neptune), erected in the 1C AD by Vice-Admiral Titus Abudius Verus of Ravenna, stood opposite; only a few fluted columns from the portico remain but the altar is preserved in the museum (see below).

Beyond the baroque fountain take DEKUMANSKA ULICA and pass (right) a striking 13C Romanesque house with an unusual projecting wooden balcony. In July–Aug it houses 'Anale', an exhibition of contemporary Yugoslav painting and sculpture. Opposite are the remains of a gateway belonging to the former Roman *Comitium*. Further down Dekumanska ul., on the same side, is an attractive block of late 14C Gothic town houses and, at the crossroads where Dekumanska is crossed by Ul. Cardo Maksimus, a cluster of 15C houses in Venetian Gothic, including the *Palača Zuccato*, with the family arms on the wall, and the Palača Radojković.

UL. CARDO MAKSIMUS leads (left) to the abandoned 13C Franciscan church, in plain Gothic with an 18C baroque interior, and to LJUBLJANSKA UL., on the corner of which is the 15C portal of the former bishop's palace. Ljubljanska ul. in turn leads past the 18C *Palača Vergotini*, with pleasant courtyard, to the entrance to the Basilica (see above). The **Canonica**, just to the S of the Basilica, is a rare and outstanding example of secular Romanesque architecture, dating from 1251. Although reduced in size the remaining part has been well preserved and restored and has a simple but harmonious frontage with two-light windows, each carved out of a single block of stone.

Continue along Dekumanska to the next crossroads and the baroque *Palača Sinčić* (1719) now occupied by the **Porestine muzej** (adm. 9–12 and 17–20). The ground floor houses Roman architectural fragments, including an altar (1C AD) from the Temple of Neptune. In a side room prehistoric finds include a ritual cup and knife from the Early Bronze Age and Etruscan pottery. Upstairs are further Roman and Greek objects including mosaics found at nearby Črvar and a small head of Zeus. The pictures are mainly of a local noble family named Carli.

Further E is Poreč's small shopping centre. On the right No. 5, dating from 1497, is a fine example of Venetian Gothic with three-light windows. The pentagonal *Kula* (Fortress Tower, 1448), at the far end of the street marks the end of the old town. Most of the medieval walls have been destroyed, but a good idea of them can be had in Ul. Nikole Tesle on the N side of town.

Beyond the tower is the modern part of Poreč where the cinema, the bus station and the information bureaux are situated. Also here are the 18C baroque church *Gospa od Andjela* (Our Lady of the Angels) and a memorial to People's Hero Joakim Rakovac. In the TRG SLOBODE is a pleasant round tower, erected in 1475, that houses a café dansant. In BEOGRADSKA UL., notable among a number of 13–15C houses, a 13C Romanesque house known as *Dva sveca*, has an unusually large archway on the ground floor (now used as a shop).

From Poreč the coast road continues S for 9km to *Vrsar* (Roman Ursaria), a fishing village recently much affected by tourism. The *Kaštel Vergotini*, the 18C summer palace of the bishops of Poreč (now abandoned), overlooks the village from its highest hill. The 12–13C parish church of Sv. Marija is Romanesque. Traces of former town walls remain, particularly the W gate, and a 4C early-Christian basilica with mosaic floor is undergoing investigation. Beyond Vrsar a road continues to the mouth of the Limski Kanal, where there is a naturist camp; the offshore island of *Kuvrsada* (also naturist) can be reached by boat direct from Vrsar.—A minor road leads directly from Vrsar to the main Piran–Pula highway, but most motorists will prefer to return to Poreč and use the main road.

From Poreč another road runs E to (13km) *Baderna*. Hence follow Rte 6A to (14km) *Brajkovići*, then turn right to the coast at Rovinj.

12km **ROVINJ**, a popular and growing resort (9000 inhab.), occupies a typical rocky promontory rising from the sea. The town has a large Italian minority and is the centre of Italian studies in Istria. The outstanding natural beauty of its surroundings, particularly to the S, has attracted a colony of artists; to the N in 1968 the International Naturist Federation opened a settlement (Valalta).

Post Office: Ulrea rismondo.
Information: Società turistica di Rovigno, tel. 81207.

History. First mentioned in the 8C, *Rovinj* (Ital. *Rovigno*) follows the pattern of other Istrian coastal towns in its early history. It came under the sway of Venice in 1283 and in the days of sail was a trading port for timber and bauxite. With the coming of steam it was eclipsed by Trieste and Rijeka.

TRG MARŠALA TITA, the main square, opens from the harbour. On the corner stands the 17C baroque *Vijećnica* (old town hall), with a clock tower, and opposite it the fine baroque *Vrata Sv. Križa* (Holy Cross Gate), by Balbi (1680), one of three remaining gates that lead into the old Venetian quarter of the town. The *Gradski muzej* (adm. 10–14), housed in a baroque mansion adjoining the gate, contains pictures by Bonifazio, portraits of the Hütteroth family, a library, furniture, and, on the top floor, paintings by modern Yugoslav artists.

Just within the gate (left) are the *Narodni odbor* (new town hall) and administrative offices. Regain the shore by the *Vrata pod zidom* (Old Wall Gate) and continue by OBALA PINO BUDICIN to the *Vrata Sv. Benedikta*, the oldest of the three (1554) which adjoins a small chapel also dedicated to St. Benedict. A little farther on, in OBALA JUGO-SLAVENSKE MORNARICE, the pretty little *Loža* (1592) overlooks the sea. The rocky foreshore beyond is used for bathing. Steps lead up to the parish church.

The church of *Sv. Eufemija*, built in baroque style in 1736, dominates the town. A 14C marble relief of St. Euphemia flanks the side door and within stands the 6C sarcophagus of the saint (adapted

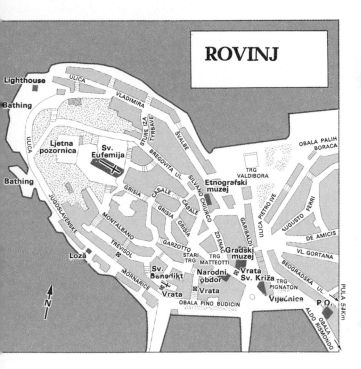

in the 15C). The lofty bell tower (31m) was built to plans by A. Manopole in 1677, in imitation of St. Mark's in Venice and affords excellent views over the harbour and neighbouring islands.

Behind the main square, in TRG VALDIBORA, are the market and a striking monument to the fallen of the Second World War, by I. Sabolić (1956). The OBALA PALIH BORACA leads to the *Marine Biological Institute* (responsible for the oyster beds in the Limski kanal) with an aquarium, then to the hospital. On the E side of the town a modern quarter has developed round the curious heptagonal chapel of *Sv. Trojstvo* (Holy Trinity), a 13C Romanesque baptistery that has survived its former church. The NW window has early Gothic decoration.

The islands just off the coast are beautiful and repay exploration (boats may be hired). The closest is *Otok Katarina*, a favourite spot for bathing or evening entertainment. Also popular is *Crveni Otok*, sometimes known as Sant'Andrea from its church. Here the Hütteroth Mansion, once a 13C Benedictine monastery, has been converted into a hotel. There are a number of pebbly beaches, one frequented by naturists, and round about there are smaller islets: *Banjol*-(Island of Love), *Sv. Ivan*, with lighthouse and church, and *Sturag*.

On the mainland opposite, S of Rovinj and extending between the twin headlands of Montauro and Punta Corrente, is an extensive park shaded with Mediterranean pine. Along the shore here are Rovinj's main beaches and hotels, and the rocky coast to the S is excellent for underwater fishing. Beyond the park is an international student centre.

From Rovinj return to the Piran–Pula highway at (15km) *Bale*, then join Rte 6A to (20km) **Pula**.

C.   Poreč to Pazin and Rijeka

ROAD, 91km. Highways N2–1 and N12/E63.—13km *Baderna*. 14km *Beram*.—5km **Pazin**.—22km *Boljun*.—4km *Vranja*.—15km *Veprinac*.—8km *Matulji*.—10km **Rijeka**.
   Buses to Pazin, but not beyond. Pazin is on the Divača–Pula railway.

This route runs almost due E from Poreč. It cuts across the heart of the Istrian peninsula, touching upon some of the more remote towns of the interior before regaining the coast near Opatija. Beyond Vranja the road becomes narrow and mountainous, and careful driving is necessary.

A good asphalt road runs E to (13km) *Baderna* on the main Piran–Pula highway (comp. Rte 6B), and to (8km) *Tinjan*, where a minor road branches right to the village of *Sveti Petar u Šumi*, with a 13C Benedictine monastery (Romanesque and Renaissance cloister) and fine baroque church, and Kanfanar (described below). At the next junction (6km) another minor road forks left for Karojba and Motovun.

1km **Beram** stands on a hill (308m) above the main road (left) and should be visited for its frescoes. A great Illyrian necropolis was discovered here by the Austrian archaeologist Pulcher at the end of the last century. In the Middle Ages Beram was fortified. The parish church of *Sv. Martin* has a Gothic sanctuary (1431) with contemporary frescoes and a Glagolitic inscription on the font. A number of Glagolitic manuscripts discovered in the church are now in the University Library at Ljubljana. In the cemetery, 1km outside the village, is the guild church of *Sv. Marija na Škriljinama** with the best cycle of frescoes in Istria, by Vincent of Kastav (thought to be the father of Ivan of Kastav, responsible for the frescoes at Hrastovlje). The original 15C church was altered in the 18C when the triumphal arch was removed, the rib-vaulted ceiling replaced by a wooden one, and windows pierced in the walls. The outstanding fresco sequences are the Dance of Death over the W door and the Adoration of the Magi on the upper part of the N wall. Also on the upper part of the N wall is a Last Supper, whereas the panels on the lower wall depict (left to right) the Temptation of Christ, a trio of saints (Apollonius, Leonard, and Barbara), St. Martin, St. George, the Entry into Jerusalem, Christ Praying on the Mount of Olives, and (beyond the window) the Kiss of Judas. On the S wall are fourteen panels arranged in two tiers. Those in the upper tier, depict (left to right) the Birth of Mary, Mary's Offering in the Temple, Mary's Betrothal, the Annunciation, the Journey to Bethlehem, the Birth of Christ, and the Infant Christ in the Temple. Shown in the lower tier are (right to left) the Massacre of the Innocents, the Flight into Egypt, St. Sebastian, St. Michael, Christ Disputing in the Temple, the Baptism of Christ, and SS. John and Florian. The name of the painter and the date of completion are indicated in a Latin inscription just above the door in the S wall.

Returning to the main Poreč–Pazin road you pass the obelisk and memorial to the native hero Vladimir Gortan, shot by the Italians in 1929. A plaque marks his birthplace.

The road climbs steeply in a series of hairpin bends to a point above the deep chasm into which the river Fojba plunges to vanish underground for the rest of its way to the sea.

5km **Pazin** (3000 inhab.) stands dramatically on the cliffs (262m) that overhang the Fojba gorge. Strategically placed on an important road junction in the centre of the Istrian peninsula, Pazin (Ital. *Pisino*; Ger. *Mitterburg*) marked for centuries the boundary between Venetian and Frankish (later Austrian) territory and was the seat of the counts of Pazin.

History. *Pazin* is first mentioned in 938 in a charter of the emperor Otto II granting the town to the bishops of Poreč. In the 12C it passed to Maynard of Schwarzenburg, who became its first count. In 1248 the title passed by inheritance to the counts of Gorica (Gorizia) and, in 1374, to the Habsburg dynasty, although the town was briefly occupied by Venice in 1344 and again in 1508. In 1766 the title passed to Antonio Laderchi, marquis of Montecuccolo, near Modena, with whom it remained until the Second World War. In 1825–61 Pazin was the administrative centre for all Istria.

The garrison commander of Pazin in the 15C was Leonhart Herberstein, father of Sigismund von Herberstein, the diplomat and writer. The castle and some of the turbulent history of Pazin have been described by Jules Verne in 'Mathias Sandorff' and by the Croatian novelist, Vladimir Nazor, in 'Krvavi dni' (Time of Blood).

Dominating the town is the massive **Kaštel**, founded in the 9C and so many times reconstructed in the 13–16C that architecturally it is interesting only for individual details. In the interior is an *Ethnographic and Historical Museum* (adm. 10–18) with a collection of bells of the 12–18C. The front courtyard and battlements afford views into the Fojba gorge and to the Učka Massif in the east.

In the Prelaz Jurja Dobrile is the parish church of *Sv. Nikola*, founded in 1266, but largely reconstructed in baroque style in 1714, when the separate bell tower was erected. The vaulted ceiling of the sanctuary (1441) is decorated with frescoes, notable for their fine colouring and realism; the work of an anonymous Tyrolean artist, they depict scenes from Genesis and the life of Christ.

FROM PAZIN TO PULA, 47km. A good country road runs S along the old border between Venice and Austria to (6km) *Lušetići*, a hamlet whence a poor road forks right to Sv. Petar u Šumi (4km; described above). Continuing S you come to (8km) **Žminj** (379m), once a thriving small border town, though now reduced to less than 500 inhab., which commands a multiple road junction. The 16C parish church of *Sv. Mihovil* (restored 18C) contains Venetian paintings of the 16–18C, a baroque pulpit in marble and, among its ancient vestments (apply to sacristan), a 16C red damask cope. Next to the church the small chapel of the *Sv. Trojstvo* (Holy Trinity) has frescoes of 1471. Gothic in manner and painted by an anonymous Tyrolean artist, the majority are badly damaged. On the N wall, Last Supper; W wall above the door, the Flight into Egypt; and, upper part of the E wall, the Ascension. Older frescoes, also damaged, adorn the guild church of *Sv. Antun Opat* (St. Antony Abbot), a tiny Gothic structure built by the mason Armirigus in 1381. Painted under Venetian influence, the best preserved of them are in the apse.

From Žminj a byroad runs SE to *Barban* (14km) on the main Pula–Rijeka road (Rte 6D).

7km **Svetvinčenat** is another old frontier town. The *Main Square rivals that of Koper as the finest in Istria. At its far end the 16C Renaissance church of the *Navještenje* (Annunciation) contains in its 19C interior a Madonna and Saints attributed to Palma the Younger and an Annunciation by an unknown 16C Venetian artist. The pulpit dates from the same period. To the left of the church is the *Kaštel Grimani*, a handsome rectangular fortress founded in 1485 and rebuilt in a Renaissance manner in 1589. The interior was badly damaged during the Second World War. Right of the church are the Renaissance *Vijećnica* (town hall) and *Loggia*, probably 15C, flanked by a number of contemporary town houses.

In the town cemetery is the unusual 12C Romanesque church of *Sv. Vincent*, with three apses but no aisles. The walls are decorated with frescoes painted in the 13C by Ognobenus of Treviso (OGNOBENUS TRIVISANUS) under Byzantine influence. The best preserved, depicting (left to right) the Baptism of Christ, Christ Enthroned, and the Mother of God Enthroned, are in the conches of the three apses.

The road continues straight to join the main Piran–Pula highway at (16km) *Vodnjan* (see Rte 6A).

PAZIN TO ROVINJ, 40km. Follow the road to (14km) *Žminj* (comp. above) and turn SW to (6km) **Kanfanar**, a small railway junction where the branch line to Rovinj leaves the main Divača–Pula railway. The town grew up mainly in the 17–18C as a result of the evacuation of Dvograd (see below). The parish church of *Sv. Silvestar* (1696) contains objects brought from the basilica at Dvograd, notably a 13C Gothic pulpit decorated with reliefs of St. Sophia holding twin towns in her hands and, on the inner wall, of the Madonna. The lectern is supported by a single slender column. Notable also are a 14C painted door, a pair of wooden statues dating from the 15–16C and, among illuminated manuscripts (apply to sacristan), a 15C Liber anniversariorum. Beside the road to Barbat and Lovreč, 2km N of Kanfanar, is the small 11C chapel of *Sv. Agata*, with Romanesque frescoes decorating the apse and triumphal arch.

In the valley of Limska draga, 3km W of Kanfanar, is the ruined and deserted town of **Dvograd** (or Dvigrad), which is reached by a rough narrow track. Its foundation dates from Illyrian times when fortifications were set up on twin mounds controlling the passage through the valley. In the Middle Ages the twin towns were known as *Moncastello* and *Parentino* and were later joined under the name Duecastelli (or Docastelli), whence the modern Croatian form. The town belonged to the Patriarchate of Aquileia until the 15C, when it passed to Venice. It was sacked by the Genoese in 1381 and by the Uskoks at the beginning of the 17C. In 1630 it was assailed by a virulent epidemic of malaria and its population hastily evacuated to Kanfanar.

The ruins stand in a romantic situation in the deserted valley and give a remarkable impression of the town as it was when abandoned. Two fortified gates and a ruined tower guard the entrance, but the main object of interest is the excavated foundations of the 11–12C basilica of *Sv. Sofija*. The innumerable holes in the ruins are said to have been dug by treasure seekers and testify to a curious local legend: the village of *Morgani* (or Mrgani), 2km W of Dvograd, is supposed to have been named after Captain Henry Morgan, the pirate Governor of Jamaica, and it was widely believed for a time that his treasure was buried in Dvograd.

Just outside the town beside the road from Kanfanar is the ruined 10C Benedictine abbey of *Sv. Petronilla*. On the other side, on the road to Morgani, the Romanesque guild chapel of *Sv. Marija od Lakuća* has well preserved 15C frescoes and the smaller chapel of *Sv. Antun* has more frescoes by the same hand.—7km *Brajkovići* and thence to (13km) Rovinj, see Rte 6B.

PAZIN TO PLOMIN 28km. A secondary road runs SE passing (3km) a turning (left) for the village of **Lindar** (view of the Učka massif). The N wall of the Gothic parish church of *Sv. Katarina* is decorated with well-preserved rustic frescoes (1409) depicting the rare motif of a Living Cross.—Continuing E you climb to a mountain ridge (views) on which stands (6km) **Gračišće** (454m) a small fortified town that flourished in the 15–18C. The walls are partially preserved and a Venetian loggia (1549) stands just inside the gate. In the main square are the chapel of *Sv. Marija* (1425), the 15C Gothic 'Bishop's Chapel' and the slightly later *Palača Salomon*. Beyond the square the baroque parish church (1769) has carved stalls, whereas *Sv. Eufemija* contains a 13C wooden Crucifixion. The steep, picturesque street running S of this church preserves almost intact its 15C aspect. The town commands views of the Raša Valley, Čepičko polje (Čepić Plain) and Učka Massif.

2km **Pićan** is another small hilltop town with well-preserved fortifications. Known as *Petin* in Roman times, the town was a bishopric from the 5C to 1788. Up to the 16C it was a stronghold of the old Slavonic rite and Glagolitic texts. The former *Cathedral* was totally reconstructed in a baroque style during the 18C (view from the campanile). The painting over the main altar is by V. Metzinger (1738); the treasury preserves a 15C silver cross and a 16C monstrance. In the cemetery the small Romanesque church of *Sv. Mihovil* has good 15C frescoes on the N wall: Mount of Olives, Kiss of Judas, and Christ before Pilate.

From Pićan the road descends in steep turns to the floor of the Raša valley. Crossing the Raša and the Kozjak–Raša railway line, climb again to (12km) **Kršan**, where a narrow country road leads left to Čepic and its fertile plain, or right to Labin (see Rte 6D). Join the main Pula–Rijeka highway at (3km) Vozilići, whence to (2km) *Plomin*, see Rte 6D.

Continuing E from Pazin the road crosses the Divača–Pula railway line twice and runs beside it to (8km) *Cerovlje* where a secondary road forks left to Draguć (9km) and Buzet (11km, Rte 1).

Draguć was once fortified and still has a ruined castle, but its main interest lies in its two frescoed churches. The older of the two, the Romanesque cemetery chapel of *Sv. Elizej*, contains poorly preserved rustic frescoes from the 13C. The early 15C church of *Sv. Rok*, erected as a votive offering to combat the plague, is covered with paintings by Anton of Padova (i.e. Kašćerga, a village c 10km SW of Draguć), who was also responsible for frescoes at Hum and Oprtalj. The side walls and roof were painted in 1520 and that behind the high altar (SS. Fabian, Roch, and Sebastian) in 1537. Note particularly the large Adoration of the Magi on the lower N wall and the three square panels above, representing (left to right) Baptism of Christ, Temptation in the Wilderness, and St. Margaret (?). On the S wall (top left) Votive Offering Against the Plague and (bottom left and centre) the Birth of Christ and Flight into Egypt; and the large Imago Pietatis over the W door.

You now bear right, cross the River Fojba and follow one of its tributaries E.—At 3km a gravel track leads (right) to the hamlet of *Gologorica*, where the church of Sv. Marija contains the remains of 14C frescoes in rustic Gothic style.

6km **Paz** lies at the foot of the ruined castle of the Walterstein. In the parish church is a late Gothic custodial (1496) with an inscription by Walter Walterstein. The cemetery church of Sv. Vid contains Venetian-style frescoes by Master Albert (1461).—The road now winds down towards the valley of the river Boljunšćica, a tributary of the Raša, where it meets the minor road that runs S through the Čepić Plain and the heart of the Ćić country to Kršan and Labin (see Rte 6D).

On this road, beyond Šušnjevica (6km), the church of Sv. Duh (Holy Spirit) at *Nova Vas* has 16C frescoes by Blaž of Dubrovnik, whereas those in the church of Sv. Kvirin at *Jasenovik*, the next hamlet S, were painted by Master Albert (15C; restored 1965).

Climbing once more the road passes beneath the Divača–Pula railway line and runs below (3km) *Boljun*, another small walled town in decay. The ruined fortress dates from the 15–17C and the parish church (note the high altar) and town hall are also of the 17C.

4km *Vranja* has late Gothic frescoes (1470) in its parish church. The left branch here runs through Ćićarija to Buzet, but you fork right to climb by spectacular hairpin bends to the pass of *Poklon* (968m) in the centre of the Učka Massif. The scenery changes from barren karst to Alpine meadows and woods, which in turn give way to thick forest. A good country road runs through the forest (right) in c 10 minutes to the comfortable *Hotel Učka*. 1.5km farther on is the more modest Hotel Poklon. From either of these it is possible to reach the summit of Učka (1394m) on foot in c 1½ hours. Alternatively the gravel road may be followed by car for a further 7km to within a few hundred metres of the summit. Both hostels are centres for hunting in the season (especially wild boar) and skiing in winter.

Beyond the pass the road broadens and improves as it drops rapidly through oak, beech, and pine woods, with views over the Kvarner to Rijeka and the offshore islands.

15km **Veprinac** clings to the side of the mountain. A baroque loggia by the main gate gives excellent views over Opatija and the Kvarner. The parish church (Sv. Marko) has carved choir stalls and pews. Frequent buses during the season link Veprinac with Opatija and Rijeka.

Continue along the E slope of the Učka Massif and parallel with the coast, with Opatija directly below. At (8km) *Matulji*, whose railway station serves Opatija, join the main Trieste–Rijeka highway (see Rte 1) to (10km) **Rijeka**.

D.   Pula to Rijeka

ROAD, 102km. Highways N2/E75 and N12/E63.—28km *Barban*.
—15km *Labin*.—14km *Plomin*.—20km *Mošćenička Draga*.—7km **Lovran**.—6km **Opatija**.—12km **Rijeka**.
Buses several times daily in 2½ hours.

This route follows the mountainous E coast of Istria, touching upon Yugoslavia's oldest and perhaps most elegant seaside resort, Opatija.

Leaving Pula by TRG AVNOJA and UL. 43 ISTARSKE DIVIZIJE, drive NE parallel with the coast. At 6km a narrow road leads off right to Valtura and Nesactium (comp. Rte 6A).

A flat, straight road continues to (28km) **Barban**, overlooking the Raša valley. Originally attached to the margraviate of Pazin, Barban passed to the Habsburgs in 1374 and during the 16C to Venice as the patrimony of the Loredan family. Parts of the medieval fortifications still stand, but the extensive *Kaštel* has been incorporated in later buildings, including the *Palača Loredan* (1606). The campanile of the parish church rests on one of the castle towers. The *Church* itself contains Venetian pictures of the 16–18C and a late-Gothic stone custodial. Of the two surviving gates the *Vela Vrata* dates from 1718 and the *Mala Vrata* from 1720. Near the latter is a Venetian *Vijećnica* of 1555, with loggia and clock tower. Gothic frescoes have been preserved in the two guild churches of *Sv. Antun Opat* and *Sv. Jakov*, both 15C.

The road descends by hairpin bends into the Raša valley with views S to the fjord-like Bay of Raša and N to the Učka Massif. The Raša was for centuries an important frontier line, marking first the boundary between the Roman provinces of Istria and Liburnia and later the limits of the kingdom of Croatia under King Peter Krešimir IV. It was regarded by many, including Dante, as the E boundary of Italy. Crossing the river and railway line, pass through the coal-mining villages of *Raša* and *Krapan*, whence galleries extend 200m under the sea.

15km **Labin**, a town of 6000 inhab., is sharply divided into its ancient and modern components. At the bottom of the hill lies the modern mining community of *Podlabin*. The old town crowded on its narrow hilltop is one of the prettiest in Istria, but the hill on which it stands has been so extensively undermined by galleries and tunnels that it is subsiding almost daily. Many of its buildings have been declared dangerous, the population is being evacuated to the newer part and there is a possibility that it may one day collapse in ruins.

History. Known to have been inhabited in prehistoric times, probably by the Celts, the town was called *Albona* by the Romans, and Pliny attests its status as a municipium. In the 7C it was sacked by the Slavs, who began to settle the area at this time, but it passed to Charlemagne and the Franks. For a short time during the 10C Labin represented the westernmost town of the kingdom of Croatia under King Peter Krešimir IV, but it later passed to the Patriarchate of Aquileia and in the 15C to Venice. In 1921, under Italy, a miners' strike turned into an armed uprising that led to the proclamation of a short-lived 'Republic of Labin' before order was restored. Labin was the birthplace of Mathias Flacius Illyricus (Matija Vlačić-Franković; 1520–75), theologian of the Reformation.

The focal point of the town is the spacious main square where the local bus deposits visitors. The once celebrated 17C loggia was dismantled in 1965 owing to subsidence, and plans for its reconstruction elsewhere have not yet been completed. Beyond the round fortress tower on the N side of the square the *Town Gate* (1587) leads into a maze of twisting streets. The *Palača Scampicchio* (1570; right), with courtyard and colonnaded balcony, adjoins the parish church of *Sv. Marija*, originally 14C Gothic, but reconstructed in a Renaissance style (1582) on Scampicchio's initiative. His portrait is built into the W front over a bricked-up Gothic window. The church also is suffering from subsidence. The former *Pretorska palača* (Captain's Residence), opposite, is occupied by nuns of the Paulician order, while the somewhat overblown baroque *Palača Battiala-Lazzarini* (1717), just beyond, houses the small Town Museum (adm. 10–4). Here is a claustrophobic reconstruction of one of the mining galleries, which visitors can negotiate complete with helmet and lamp. A little further on the street emerges on the battlements of the medieval fortifications, whence there is a superb panorama of the Kvarner Bay, the islands of Cres and Lošinj and, on a clear day, of Krk, the Velebit Mountains and the North Croatian coast. Returning via UL. MARTI-NUZZI notice the 17C baroque mansions of the Vlačić-Franković, Manzin, and Negri families and the dilapidated church of *Sv. Marija od Zdravlja* (keys from nunnery), with some baroque wooden statuary.

Buses run hourly to the small harbour and resort of **Rabac**, 5km SE of Labin. A car ferry sails in the season from Brestova to Porozine on the island of Cres (Rte 12).

The main road continues NE and at (12km) *Vozilići* joins a road from Pazin (see Rte 6C), turning SE to skirt the narrow Plomin Bay.—2km **Plomin**, now a deserted backwater, retains its medieval system of fortifications (13–17C) in fair preservation.

First Illyrian and then a Roman castrum, known as *Flanona*, Plomin was sacked by the Avars in the 6C and resuscitated only after 1012, when it came under the Patriarch of Aquileia. After joining Venice (1410) it was sacked on repeated occasions in the 16C by the Uskoks of Senj.

At the S edge of the town (view over the Kvarner Bay) is the tiny 11C Romanesque church of *Sv. Jurje* (St. George), built to a cruciform plan with a small bell tower. In the S wall are fragments of a primitive relief together with the oldest Glagolitic inscription in Istria (11C or 12C). In the centre of the town is a later and larger church of *Sv. Jurje* (1474) with Renaissance altar and stalls.

The road runs beside the strangely green waters of Plomin Bay before twisting N again high above the shore. On the right between the mainland and the island of Cres is the *Vela Vrata*, one of the two main navigation channels leading into the bay and harbour of Rijeka. After passing through (13km) *Brseč*, a compact little township and birthplace of Eugen Kumičić (1850–1904), the Croatian novelist, descend to the shore and enter the region of the Kvarner or Quarnero. Although geographically a part of Istria, the coast between here and Opatija, sometimes known as the OPATIJA RIVIERA, is linked administratively and economically with Rijeka.

7km *Mošćenička Draga*, is a popular small resort with a pebble beach. An obelisk on the shore commemorates the landing here in 1945 of Yugoslav forces to begin the liberation of Istria. High up on the hill above the town is the old settlement of **Mošćenice** (180m), which is reached by 760 steps from the S end of the beach or by road (3km). The quaint old town is entered by a gate surmounted by the arms of the Habsburg family and the date of its repair, 1634. The plain 17C loggia in front is known as the 'stražarnica' (look-out) from its traditional use for keeping watch on the sea. The baroque parish church of *Sv. Andrija*, situated in the main square, contains 17C choir stalls and, over the high altar, sculptures by I. Contieri, an 18C Paduan. Just inside the main gate, in a private house, are preserved an ancient olive press, a horse-operated mill, and other primitive equipment, still used in November and December.

Following the coast road N, with attractive pebble beaches to the right and the Učka Massif towering on the left, pass through the resort villages of *Kraj*, birthplace in 1870 of Viktor Car Emin, the Croatian novelist, and *Medveja*.

7km **Lovran**, an attractive resort (3000 inhab.), still has an Austrian *fin de siècle* flavour. The surroundings are noted for their luxuriant vegetation and wide variety of flora, the cause in 1845 of a botanical expedition to the town by King Frederick Augustus II of Saxony. Lovran came to prominence as a seaside resort at the turn of the century after the railway had been constructed from Vienna to Trieste and Rijeka.

Post Office: Šet M. Tita.

Information: *Turističko drustvo*, šet. M. Tita, tel. 731041.

Buses (local) from the front to *Mošćenička Draga* and to Opatija and *Rijeka*. Long-distance services to *Labin*, *Pula*, and the rest of Istria.

History. Named *Lauriana* after the laurel that grows in great profusion in these parts, the town existed in Roman times, though its name first receives mention only in the 7C. In 799, Eric of Strasbourg, nephew of Charlemagne, was killed here in a battle with the Avars and Slavs. Later Lovran formed part of the kingdom of Croatia, then passed to the Patriarchate of Aquileia and in 1374 to the Habsburgs, when it was ruled first by the noble family of Walsee and then by the counts of Pazin. During the 16C Lovran was sacked repeatedly by the Venetians and the Uskoks and in the 17C the population was decimated by plague.

The MODERN QUARTER is centred on the front and the excellent beaches (shingle and pebble), where most of the hotels are situated. It is joined to Opatija by an attractive promenade, at the S end of which is the tiny Romanesque chapel of *Sv. Trojstvo* (Holy Trinity), later reconstructed with ornamented doorway and traces of 15C frescoes within. The MEDIEVAL QUARTER, formerly fortified, lies above the main street on the lower slopes of Učka. The *South Gate* is all that remains of the walls. In the main square the parish church of *Sv. Jurje* (St. George), basically 14–15C Gothic, was later twice enlarged. The choir walls and the triumphal arch are decorated with 15C frescoes (discovered 1952) showing Alpine influence (Crucifixion and Last Judgment). Also in the square are a Romanesque bell tower and fortress tower, probably 12C; among baroque town houses, note especially St. George's House, named for the equestrian statue that adorns the tympanum, opposite the church, and (W side) the house with a Turk's head in relief and the town arms.

Above the town marked paths offer pleasant walks on the lower slopes of **Mt Učka** amid groves of cherry, chestnut, laurel, beech, and pine. Places that can be visited include the hamlets of *Oraj* reached in about 1½ hours; *Liganj* (¾ hour); *Lovranska Draga*, 1½ hours; *Dobreč*, ¾ hour; and *Poljane*, 1½ hours. Marked paths also lead higher to some of the peaks of the Učka Massif. *Mali Knezgrad* (615m) can be reached in c 2 hours via Liganj, and *Veliki Knezgrad* (615m) via Liganj and Ivulići. The name Knezgrad ('princetown') is said to commemorate the death here (but comp. Rte 7) of Charlemagne's nephew, Eric of Strasbourg, in 799. The summit (1409m) can be reached on foot in about 4½ hours via Liganj and Ivulići or 3½ hours via Dobreč.

Continuing N along the coast, the main road passes through the villages of Ika and Ičići, now virtually suburbs of Lovran and Opatija.

 6km **OPATIJA**, a prosperous, well laid-out holiday town (10,000 inhab.) with a strong Central European flavour, is Yugoslavia's leading tourist resort. Its geographical situation gives it a particularly benign climate, since it is cooled in summer by the proximity of the Učka Massif, while in winter the mountain acts as a barrier to the cold winds from the north. The sea here is also exceptionally rich in minerals and the air in iodine, which makes Opatija an important convalescent centre, particularly for rheumatism and heart diseases. A clinic has been established for sea-water cures. Visually Opatija remains Austrian in character. Its architecture is in a rich variety of eclectic, imitative and florid styles which give the town an air of 19C opulence.

Post Office: 2 Kumičićeva ul.

Information: *Turističko društvo*, 183 M. Tita, tel. 711310; *Turistički Savez Općine*, 8 Park I majo, tel. 711700.

Buses run through the town to *Rijeka* and *Lovran* every 15 minutes. Bus station for all local and long-distance buses at Slatina at the S end of the main street (Ul. Maršala Tita); connections with all parts of Yugoslavia and with *Trieste, Venice,* and *Vienna.*

Amusements: OPERA FESTIVAL annually in July and Aug.—FESTIVAL OF POPULAR MUSIC annually in Oct.—CASINO at the Hotel Rosalia.

History. *Opatija* (Ital. *Abbazia*) takes its name from the Benedictine Abbey of St James founded here in the 15C. Its existence as a resort dates from 1844 when Iginio Scarpa, a Rijeka businessman, built the Villa Angiolina. Opatija's popularity was given a tremendous fillip by the construction of the railway from Vienna to Trieste (1857) and its extension to Rijeka (1873). It became a favourite resort of Viennese high society and ex-Empress Maria Anna of Savoy, consort of Emperor Ferdinand, holidayed here repeatedly during the 1860s. Later Emperor Francis Joseph kept it in the fashion by purchasing a villa for Katarina Schratt, his mistress, in nearby Volosko.

Of the ancient abbey, only the small chapel of *Sv. Jakov* (St. James) survives near the promenade. After reconstruction in 1774 and enlargement in 1937, little of the original structure of 1506 remains. Adjoining is Scarpa's *Villa Angiolina* (open to the public); its beautiful park (now called **Park 1 maja**) is maintained as a botanical garden. The fine selection of exotic flora includes giant evergreen sequoias, giant magnolia, Japanese orange and banana, grape myrtle, wild cinnamon, Chinese forsythia, gingo, tropical lilies, and eucalyptus. There are also Lebanon, Deodara and Mount Atlas cedars, tamarisk, agave, balsam, japonica, bougainvillea, and palm trees. The excellent PROMENADE extends for 12km from Lovran in the S to Volosko in the N, and marked paths lead up to Vrutka Park (view), Veprinac (Rte 6D), and the Učka summit (see above).

Beyond Opatija the main coast road continues N through *Volosko*, formerly a fishing village but now a picturesque suburb of Opatija, and *Preluk*. 12km the suburbs of **Rijeka** (see Rte 7) are reached.

7 Rijeka and its Environs

Rijeka, thanks to its protected harbour, strategic position, and excellent communications with the interior, is the largest port of Yuoslavia, second city (200,000 inhab.) of Croatia, and a major industrial, commercial, and cultural centre. Ringed on the landward side by high mountains, it stands at the mouth of the small River Rečina at the head of Rijeka Bay, which in turn forms part of the Kvarner Gulf. Relatively few of its ancient monuments survived an earthquake of 1750, and the town suffered heavy air raids in the Second World War. As the headquarters of Yugoslavia's passenger fleet, it has become for many visitors the gateway to the Eastern Adriatic.

Post Office: 14 Rade Končara ul.

Information: *Turistički Informativni Centar*, 9 Trg republika, tel. 23786.

Airport: at Omišalj, on the island of Krk.

Car Ferries: For Porozina on the island of Cres and for points on the Zadar–Dubrovnik–Corfù–Igoumenitsa line.

Buses from Beogradski trg for *Kastav, Matulji, Opatija, Lovran, Mošćeniška, Draga; Martinscica, Bakar, Kraljevica*; and for the villages of the Gorski Kotar. From Trg Ząbica for other points in Istria, the Adriatic coast, and major cities of Yugoslavia. Also for Trieste, Venice, Graz, and Vienna.

History. The town of *Rijeka* is first mentioned in the 13C as Terra fluminis sancti Viti (later *St. Veit am Pflaum, Fiume*, like Rijeka all meaning 'river') although it grew up on the site of the much older Roman settlement of *Tarsatica* (comp. the suburb of Trsat) which seems to have been destroyed by Charlemagne in 800. From the possession of the lords of Duino, it passed by marriage (1399) to the lords of Walsee and in 1471 to the Habsburgs, who retained it for three centuries. During this time, together with Trieste, Rijeka flourished as an Austrian port and became a commercial threat to Venice, provoking Venetian attacks (1508, 1599, 1612) as well as attention from the Uskok pirates of Senj. In 1527 Rijeka was granted its own statute and in 1719 (with Trieste) was declared a free port by Charles VI. In 1776 Empress Maria Theresa united Rijeka with Croatia under the Austrian monarchy, but in 1779 the city was declared autonomous, with responsibility for its external affairs transferred to the crown of Hungary, and its history becomes turbulent and complex. The Hungarians, seeing an opportunity to establish an outlet to the sea, built new roads to the interior and favoured the Italian minority at the expense of the Croats. This was interrupted by Napoleon's occupation of the area in 1809–14 (the English bombarded Rijeka in 1813), after which Rijeka with the legacy of a road to Karlovac reverted to Vienna. During the Hungarian Revolution of 1848, the Croats under Ban Jelačić sided with the Habsburgs and afterwards regained the port, with Jelačić as governor. The 'Settlement' between Croatia and Hungary in 1868, however, awarded Rijeka once more to the Hungarian government in Budapest, and Hungarian domination persisted until the First World War. During the war many Fiumani joined the Italian forces. In 1919 Rijeka became a focus of world attention when Italian irredentists, led by the poet D'Annunzio, occupied the town and attempted to set up a regency. Under the Treaty of Rapallo (1920) Fiume became a free state and in 1924, as a result of the Rome Agreement, part of Italy; Sušak was incorporated into the new state of Yugoslavia. The border ran down the Mrtvi kanal with the Yugoslav Baross harbour separated from the port of Fiume only by a wall. The two parts of the town were reunited after the Second World War.

Rijeka was the birthplace of Vinko Jelić, the 17C musician, and of Ivan Zajc (1832–1914), who was instrumental in establishing a Croatian national musical tradition, particularly in opera.

The busiest part of Rijeka for most of the day is the **Harbour**. The OBALA JUGOSLAVENSKE MORNARICE leads NW to TRG ŽABICA with the long-distance bus station and, on the E side, the ostentatious unfinished *Kapucinska crkva* (church of the Capuchins, 1906) in wedding-cake Gothic.

Farther on, the broad busy UL. BORISA KIDRIČA passes the railway station (left), the principal hospital (right), and the attractive town park, *Djardin*, at Mlaka, before giving way to the Bul. Marksa i Engelsa, which leads to Kantrida and the road for Preluk, Volosko, and Opatija.

Just before Kantrida, to seaward of the railway, are the diesel-engine works that began as the *Stabilmento Tecnico Fiumano* in 1856. Here their founder (and later owner), Robert Whitehead (1823–1905), a native of Lancashire, invented the modern torpedo in 1866 for the Austrian navy. The paper-mill farther on was another English foundation (1893), and beyond once stood a hostel for 3000 people, constructed by the Hungarians to accommodate emigrants in transit from central Europe to America.

On the other side of the harbour UL. IVANA ZAJCA, following the railway line, leads past the baroque church of *Sv. Nikola* (Orthodox) and the main *Tržnica* (market place) to the so-called *Mrtvi kanal* or dead channel, a sealed off arm of the Rečina that marked the frontier between Italy and Yugoslavia between the two world wars. At the junction of Sarajevska and Titogradska ul. is the neoclassical *Narodno Kazalište 'Ivana Zajca'* (People's Theatre), designed by H. Helmer and F. Fellner (1886).

Just behind the harbour lies the uninspired TRG TOGLIATTI whence the KORZO NARODNE REVOLUCIJE (or simply *Korzo*), Rijeka's most attractive street and the main shopping centre, brings you to the General Post Office opposite the entrance to the old quarter.

Enter what is left of **Stari grad**, the badly bombed old city, by an ornamental gateway known variously as the *Gradski toranj* (City Tower) or Južna or Morska vrata (South or sea gate). The gateway itself was probably built in the 13C, when the sea came up to this point; the baroque tower was added in 1654 (inscription); and the cupola dates from 1801 when the whole structure was renewed. The arms over the arch are of imperial Austria, and a niche above enshrines busts of Leopold I (left), who granted Rijeka new arms in 1659, and Charles VI (right; face damaged). Inside extends TRG IVANA KOBLERA, where a stone column represents the base of a former flagstaff, erected, according to the inscription, by Captain Tivan Tozich in 1565. A relief shows St. Vitus, Rijeka's patron, holding a model of the city. Behind stands the 16C *Palača komunaričkoga*, the town hall from 1532 to 1835, which became a music school (plaque) under the direction of Ivan Zajc.

From the square, UŽARSKA UL. leads SE through the heart of the old quarter to the **Cathedral** (*Sv. Marija*), an old foundation completely rebuilt in a baroque manner in 1695–1726. The detached bell tower

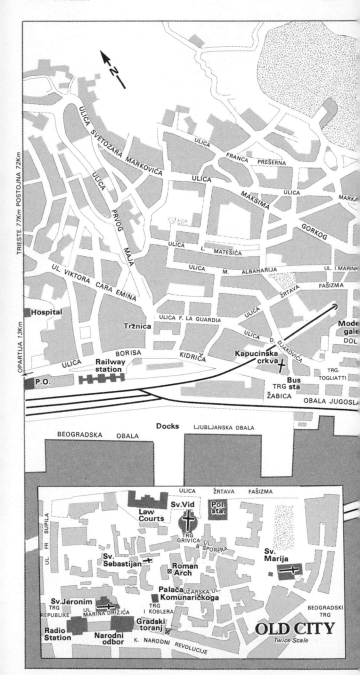

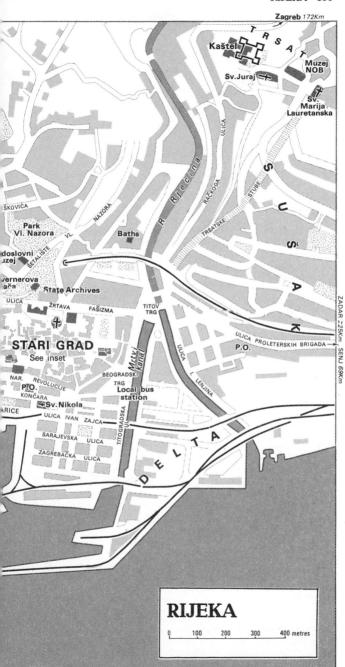

T R S A T

Kaštel

Muzej
NOB

Sv.Juraj

Sv.
Marija
Lauretanska

R. Riečina

RAČKOGA

S

NAZORA

ŠKOVIĆA

U

STUBE

Park
Vl. Nazora

VL.

Baths

TRSATSKE

Š

doslovni
uzej

ŠETALIŠTE

S

vernerova
ača

State Archives

A

ULICA

ŽRTVAVA FAŠIZMA

TITOV
TRG

K

ULICA PROLETERSKIH BRIGADA

P.O.

STARI GRAD
See inset

Mrtvi
kanal

ULICA
I. LENJINA

ZADAR ≈25Km

SENJ 69Km

NAR. REVOLUCIJE

P.O.

BEOGRADSKI
TRG

KONČARA

Local bus
station

Sv.Nikola

ARICE

ULICA IVAN ZAJCA

TITOGRADSKA

SARAJEVSKA ULICA

D E L T A

ZAGREBAČKA ULICA

RIJEKA

0   100   200   300   400 metres

(1377), in a style of transition between the Romanesque and the Gothic leans considerably to the E. In GRIVICA TRG at the far end of Ul. Jurja Sporera the baroque Jesuit church of *Sv. Vid* (1638–1742), has an octagonal groundplan and large cupola modelled on Santa Maria della Salute in Venice. A cannonball embedded in the wall to the left of the main entrance is said to be a memento of the English bombardment in 1813. Inside, in the chapel of the Čudotvorno raspelo (Miraculous Cross), is a 13C Gothic crucifixion in wood. The relics displayed are of St. Victor. Farther W, in the decayed UL. MARKA MARULIĆA, is the Renaissance church of *Sv. Sebastijan* (1562). From here you pass through a battered *Roman Arch* of the 1C AD, to regain Trg Ivan Koblera by the narrow UL. STARA VRATA.

From Trg Ivana Koblera pass to the small TRG RIJEČKE REZOLUCIJE and the 18C baroque church of **Sv. Jeronim** (Jerome), practically all that remains of an extensive Augustinian monastery founded in 1315 and abolished in 1788 by Emperor Joseph II. Its main buildings, altered in 1815 to serve as municipal offices, now house the town archives. Within the church a chapel to the left of the sanctuary admits to the vaulted sacristy, from which entrance is gained to the baroque monastic *Cloister*. Here have been collected many inscribed tomb slabs of Rijeka's noble families removed from the church floor. Off the cloister is the attractive Gothic *Rauber Chapel*, built in 1482 by Nikola Rauber, a Rijeka Captain. Its proportions have been spoiled by additional chapels and an oversized baroque altar, but it preserves its painted vault.

At the corner of the long, narrow Trg Republike and the Dolac stands the excellent *Reference and Lending Library* (c 200,000 vols), based on a former Jesuit College collection begun in 1627. Above is a small **Museum of Modern Yugoslav Art** (Moderna Galerija; adm. 9–12, 13–17) with an imaginative policy that enables much foreign work to be exhibited.

UL. FRANA SUPILA, following the line of the former W wall of the old town, mounts by steps to the neoclassical **Guvernerova palača**, built in 1896 to a design by Alajos Hauszmann, architect of the Palace of Justice in Budapest. The seat of the Hungarian governor until 1914, it was occupied by D'Annunzio during his brief rule and from its balcony in 1924 the Italian annexation of Fiume was proclaimed in the presence of Victor Emmanuel III. The Italian governors occupied it until 1943 when it became temporarily the headquarters of the regional People's Council; it is now a national monument, and also houses the **Pomorski i Povijesni Muzej Hrvatskog Primorja** (Maritime and Historical Museum; adm. 9–12, 17–19).

The public rooms have been restored as far as possible and arranged as they were when the governors were in residence. The sumptuous furniture, made specially for the mansion, has suffered from its multiplicity of masters; pieces bearing the arms of Austria were systematically defaced by order of D'Annunzio. The museum is divided into several sections regarding archaeology, history, folklore, and maritime life. Violins in the Crvena sala (Crimson Room) are the work of Franjo Kresnik, a local maker, who after studying the methods of Stradivarius claimed that the master's secret lay in the lacquer he used. The *Maritime Collection* displays ship models, documents, and portraits.

In a separate building next door is housed the *Muzej Narodne Revolucije*, with documents and other material concerning the war of liberation.

ŠETALIŠTE VLADIMIRA NAZORA leads uphill to a small park in which stands the building containing the *State Archives* of Rijeka and the archives of Istria and the Kvarner. Adjoining it is the *Prirodoslovni muzej* (Natural History Museum). A little behind the park, on the hill called *Kalvarija* (Calvary), can be seen remains of the so-called Liburnian Wall, erected by the Romans (2C AD ?) against the Illyrian Iapidae. The hill gives a fine view of the town and harbour.

Descend the broad UL. ŽRTAVA FAŠIZMA, which follows the line of the demolished town wall SE past the *Law Courts*. The extensive suburb of **Sušak** lies to the E of the Rečina and is joined to the city by the spacious TITOV TRG, straddling the river. On the S side of the square stands the *Liberation Monument* (1955) in bronze and stone, by Vinko Matković, a native of Rijeka.

UL. PROLETERSKIH BRIGADA leads SE from here past the Hotel Kontinental to the suburbs of Kostrena and Pećine and the highway to Dalmatia, while RAČKOGA UL. runs N through the Rečina gorge (view) to the main road for Karlovac and Zagreb.

The castle and quarter of **Trsat** are reached from the NE side of Titov trg, where a baroque archway (1745) bearing a relief of the Madonna marks the beginning of the TRSATSKE STUBE, a flight of 538 steps. These were designed to provide a suitable approach for pilgrims to the church of St. Mary Laureta.

The lower flights were built in 1531 under a bequest from Petar Kružić, Captain of the fortress of Klis in Dalmatia and a Croatian warrior noted for his exploits against the Turks. The while the steps were completed (1725) by Gabriel Eichelburg, who was also responsible for the archway at their foot. A Gothic votive chapel (1531) stands at their head.

According to legend the Santa Casa, or house of the Virgin, was transported here from Nazareth in 1291, and remained three years before being carried across the Adriatic to Loreto. The arrival is said to have been witnessed by an old lady named Laureta, whence the name of the church.

The church of **Sv. Marija Lauretanska**, built by Count Nikola Frankopan of Krk in 1453, was enlarged in 1644 and almost completely reconstructed in 1824. The Gothic triumphal arch remains from the earlier building. A good wrought-iron screen (1705) separates the sanctuary from the nave. On the baroque high altar (1692) is a painting of the Mother of God, presented by Urban V in 1367. In the N aisle are the tombs of the founder and his wife Elisabeth (died 1513). Ex-votos adorn the walls.

Adjoining the S side of the church is a FRANCISCAN MONASTERY, founded from a bequest by Count Martin Frankopan, also in 1453, and enlarged in the 17C. The *Refectory*, off the pleasant cloister, is elaborately decorated. The far wall, by the Swiss painter Fra Serafin Schön, depicts a mystical supper; the side walls (Miracle of the Loaves and Fishes, Manna in the desert) and ceiling (Assumption) are by the Venetian artist Cristoforo Tascha (1705). The *Treasury* (on view only by special request), on the second floor, contains a incunabula, vestments (chasuble donated by Maria Theresa), a silver reliquary donated by Barbara Frankopan, and two 15C Gothic chalices.

UL. PETRA ZRINSKOG from the church leads to the **Kaštel** of Trsat (133m) on the site of an encampment of the Iapidae and a Roman observation post. By 1288 it was in the possession of the Frankopan family, who retained it until 1487. It then passed to the Habsburgs and in 1779 to the town of Bakar. Marshal Laval Nugent of Austria purchased the castle in 1826 and restored it in the romantically eclectic style it has today.

The quadrangular keep has circular towers at three corners and the entrance-tower at the fourth. The well-preserved N tower affords fine views over the town and bay of Rijeka and into the Rečina canyon. Arcades (added by Nugent) surmounted by a loggia cross to the E

tower, now a café-restaurant. The small Doric temple, incorporating
Roman columns from Pula, was erected by Nugent as a family
mausoleum. The striking bronze chimaera, in front, bearing a banner
inscribed 'DECREVI' and the arms of the Nugents and the related
Sforza, is one of a pair by the Viennese sculptor, Anton Fernkorn
(1813–78).

Adjoining the castle is the 13C church of *Sv. Juraj*. About 1km to the E, between
Ul. Slavka Krantzeka and Ul. Željka Marča, the extensive *Park narodnog heroja*,
with a monument to the Unknown Warrior by Z. Kolacio and Z. Sila, commands
excellent views over the town.

A pleasant EXCURSION may easily be accomplished in a day to Platak (regular
bus service and excursion buses) in the Gorski Kotar. Take the road for Karlovac,
passing through the Rečina canyon and rising rapidly by a series of hairpin
bends to the karst plateau of Grobničko polje.—At (7km) *Čavle* a minor road
forks left for **Grobnik** (451m), at the far NW end of the Vinodol Valley (see Rte 8),
a fortified settlement in medieval times and one of the seats of the Frankopan
counts. Their castle (good well head) and much of the old town walls (15–17C)
survive. The parish church of Sv. Filip, half Gothic, half baroque, has inscriptions
in Glagolitic. The belfry was erected in 1572. The bare plateau, near by, was
used by the Germans as a military airfield; a memorial stone commemorates the
battle by which the Partisans destroyed it in Sept 1944.
    Climbing further from Čavle, at 17km, diverge left from the main road on to a
steep and narrow byroad and climb to *Platak*, a small winter and summer resort
(1129m) frequented for walking, skiing, and hunting. On foot the neighbouring
peaks of Mt Snježnik (1506m; refuge hut) and Mt Veliki Risnjak (1528m; refuge
hut) may be reached respectively in c 1 hour and 2½ hours.

8   Rijeka to Zadar

ROAD, 223km. Highway N2/E65, the *Jadranska Magistrala*
(Adriatic Highway).—17km *Bakar*. 5km *Kraljevica*.—14km **Crikvenica**.
—10km *Novi Vinodolski*.—23km *Senj*.—40km *Jablanac*.—24km
Karlobag.—45km *Starigrad-Paklenica*.—21km *Posedarje*.—24km
Zadar.

CAR FERRY daily in c 7½ hours with more frequent service in
summer.

Rijeka, see Rte 7. Leave the town by UL. PROLETERSKIH BRIGADA and
ŠETALIŠTE XIII DIVIZIJE, passing through the residential suburb of
Pećine and reaching the shore at the mouth of the small bay of
Martinšćica. Skirting the bay with its shipyard (Viktor Lenac),
continue SE on the Jadranska Magistrala with the high range of the
Velebit Mts on the left and views out to sea of Cres and Krk.
    The road swings left in a broad curve, crossing the branch railway
linking Bakar with the Rijeka–Zagreb line at Škrljevo, and affords
superb views into the elliptical, almost landlocked *Bakarski zaljev*.
The Bay of Bakar (c 5km long) owes its steep sides and fjord-like
appearance to its formation by subsidence, and is the largest such bay
in the Kvarner. Circle the bay under the steep slopes of the Velebit
(leaving on the left a road for Škrljevo and Trsat), passing terraced
vineyards that produce an excellent sparkling wine called Bakarska
vodica, and at 16km double back and descend to the sea.
    17km **Bakar**, an old maritime town (2000 inhab.), has declined like
so many places along this coast into a sleepy backwater, although a
modern oil refinery stands just outside.

Bakar may be the Volcera of Ptolemy. Part of the Frankopan county, it was unsuccessfully besieged by the Turks in 1527 and by the Venetians in 1616. After a period of union with Fiume, it was united to Croatia. Bakar was blockaded by the British in 1812–13. From its shipyards was launched the first steamship of the Austrian navy. In his story, 'La Beffa di Buccari', D'Annunzio describes an exploit in which three Italian torpedo boats crept into the harbour in 1918 and fired torpedos at Austrian ships at anchor.

The old quarter, reached by steps, preserves its medieval character with narrow twisted streets and closely packed houses. *Sv. Andrija*, dominating this quarter, has an altar painting of the Holy Trinity by Girolamo da Santa Croce (also a 14C Romanesque cross, a 16C reliquary of St. Ursula, and baroque chalices in the treasury). Higher up the hill is the crumbling *Castle* (1405?) of the Frankopans (Rte 9), who held Bakar from 1225 to the 15C, and later of the Counts Zrinski (see below), who held it in 1557–1671. The ruined interior (key from house opposite) affords excellent views over the town and Bay of Bakar. Between the church and the castle lie the *Hospicij* (Hospice) of 1526, renovated 1716; the *Plovanija* (Vicarage) of 1514; the so-called *Turska kuća* (Turkish house), an uninspired copy of Muslim architecture built by a local sea captain; the *Biskupija*, a former palace of the bishops of Modruš (coat of arms dated 1494); the 18C Petazzi Mansion; and the so-called *Rimska kuća* (Roman house), the 18C baroque residence of the Bakar Captains. *Sv. Kriz* (17C) half-way down the hill, has a late Gothic Crucifixion on the main altar. The baroque church of *Sv. Margareta* (1668), was endowed by the Zrinski family and contains pictures by V. Metzinger (1757). In the house of the former town magistrate is the cell in which Tito was confined before being sent to prison at Ogulin.

Return to the Adriatic Highway passing (right) Bakar's disused railway station.

A minor road forks left here to *Hreljin* (6km), a former fortified settlement of the Frankopans and later the Zrinskis. Remains of the medieval castle, town walls and houses can still be seen, though the population migrated outside the walls in the 18C.

The treasure of the ancient parish church of Sv. Juraj (modernised in the 16–17C) has now been transferred to the large new parish church by the main road (15C Gothic monstrance and some baroque reliquaries).

Hreljin lies in the **Vinodol** ('wine valley'), a long, fertile valley running roughly parallel with the coast and located amid the lower slopes of the Velebit Mts. In the Middle Ages the name also came to signify a political region stretching from Grobnik in the NW to Novi Vinodolski in the SE and including the coastal region as well. In 1225 this region came into the hands of the Counts Frankopan of Krk who made it their main centre after being driven from Krk in 1480. The main towns at this time were Grobnik, Trsat, Bakar, Hreljin, Drivenik, Grižane, Bribir, Ledenice, and Novi Vinodolski, all of which signed the famous Vinodol Statute in 1288. In the 16C when Dalmatia and the Kvarner islands were subject to Venice, the coast between Zadar and Karlobag under the Turks and Senj, Rijeka, and Istria under the Habsburgs, this small region represented the only access to the sea left to Croatia and it has always been noted for its Croatian national sentiment. Nowadays the Vinodol, as a geographical term, embraces only the southern part of the valley from Hreljin to Novi Vinodolski and does not include the coast.

From Hreljin the so-called Caroline Road, built by Emperor Charles in 1728, leads NW through Škrljevo, Kukuljanovo, and Čavle to Rijeka, and SE to Grižane, Bribir, and Novi Vinodolski, and a tortuous mountain road (gravel) winds through the Velebits to Gornje Jelenje on the main Rijeka–Zagreb road.

5km *Bakarac* was once the port for Hreljin but is now a sleepy village. The two tall *tunere* projecting over the sea are the only working tunny ladders left on the mainland.

These tunny ladders were once characteristic of every bay of the Kvarner. The local fishermen kept a 24-hour watch in two-hour shifts from ladders 6–10m high for shoals of tunny; once a shoal was within the bay, the entrance would be closed with nets and the tunny hauled in; the dramatic final stages attracted many sightseers, but Bakarac and the island of Krk are now only places where the custom survives.

1km **Kraljevica** (1900 inhab.) lies on a small inlet near the mouth of the Bay of Bakar. Today a growing resort, it was once an important Frankopan centre. Its Italian name is *Porto Re*. Charles VI initiated the harbour as an Austrian military base. In the 19C it enjoyed some prosperity when its main shipyard was run by Pritchard Brothers of England. It was again under English management between the two world wars. President Tito worked here as a young man (1925–26) shortly before his arrest for illegal agitation (plaques in yard and on the house where he lived). The shipyard, named after him (Titovo brodogradilište) now does mainly repair work.

The twin castles of the Zrinski family (see above) are the town's most prominent monuments. The *Stari grad*, near the harbour, has three stories built round two courtyards with simple baroque arcading. In the near one a well-head bears the Zrinski arms, the inscription C.P.A.Z. (Comes Petrus a Zrinio), and the date 1651. A baroque belfry (1790) is built on to the façade. The adjoining church of *Sv. Nikola* (patron saint of the Zrinski family) is part Gothic and part baroque, with a rib-vaulted ceiling. The more interesting *Novi grad*, begun in 1650 by Petar Zrinski, stands on a small promontory near the water's edge. Modelled on the late-Renaissance palaces of Italy, it is rectangular in plan with cylindrical towers at the corners and an imposing double-arcaded courtyard inside. A well-head in the courtyard bears the arms of the Frankopan and Zrinski families. The revolt of these two families against the Habsburgs was supposedly plotted in this castle beneath the rose window of the great hall (hence the expression 'sub rosa'). After the smashing of the revolt and the execution of Krsto Frankopan and his brother-in-law, Petar Zrinski, at Wiener Neustadt (1671), both castles were damaged. In the mid-19C the castle was bought by the Jesuits who added a floor and modernised it, and it now serves as a hostel for workers from the shipyard. The war memorial in the main square is by Zvonko Car (1952).

A road (N29) runs from *Kraljevica* to *Krk*, on the island of the same name (see Rte 9).

The Adriatic Highway continues SE high above the shore between the straight of Mala vrata, here only 500m wide, and the Velebit Mts. Here the island of Krk is closest to the mainland, and clearly displays its bare and rugged NE shores. The small island at the N end of the strait is *Sv. Marko*, with the ruins of a Venetian fortress erected to guard against the Uskoks of Senj (see below). Its striking triangular shape is a well-known landmark to Adriatic sailors.

At about 2 and 6km out of Kraljevica minor roads fork left to *Križišče* whence a mountain road leads up via *Fužine* to *Lokve* and *Delnice* on the main Rijeka–Zagreb road (trains from Rijeka). With an Alpine climate and terrain, these three small resorts (each with mountain chalets) attract visitors for skiing, hunting, fishing, walking, and mountain climbing. At Delnice in particular there are many ski-runs as well as a ski-lift and two ski-jumps, with picturesque lakes at Lokve (Lokvarsko jezero) and Fužine (Jezero Bajer).

14km **CRIKVENICA** is a pleasant, thriving seaside town (3700 inhab.) nestling on a well-protected slope between the Adriatic Highway and the sea. It is a modern and, by Yugoslav standards, relatively sophisticated holiday resort, with good hotels (including one specialising in sea-water cures), a modicum of entertainment and an excellent and well-equipped sandy beach. There are also good natural beaches extending to the Kačjak Peninsula to the N and to Selce (see below) to the S.

Post Office: opposite the bus station.

Information: *Turističko društvo*, opposite the harbour, tel. 831234.

Buses to *Rijeka*, *Pula*, and *Istria*; to *Ljubljana*; *Zagreb*; and *Belgrade*; to *Senj*, *Zadar*, *Split*, and *Dubrovnik*.

Car Ferries to *Šilo* on the island of Krk.

Near Crikvenica is the birthplace of Julije Klović (Julius Clovius, 1498–1578), Croatia's most famous miniature painter, who was educated at the monastery here. Nikola Car, a hero of the national liberation struggle, was born in the town.

Although Crikvenica seems to have been inhabited more or less continuously since Roman times, its sole relic of the past is the so-called *Kaštel* or Frankopan castle (1412), in reality a fortified Pauline monastery of a single story erected by Nikola Frankopan (died 1439) on the bank of the small river Dubračina. A second story was added in the 19C and the Kaštel now stands at the entrance to the park.

Regular excursions are run from Crikvenica to the islands of Krk (Rte 9) and Rab (Rte 10); and to Opatija (Rte 6D), the Postojna Caves (Rte 3), Plitvice Lakes (see below), and Vinodol Valley on the mainland.

A minor road runs due N from Crikvenica along the valley of the River Dubračina to join the highland road from Križišće to Bribir in the Vinodol (Hydro-electric station 'Vinodol' at the junction). At the hamlet of (2km) *Badanj*, left of the road, are the ruins of one of the medieval castles of the Frankopans. In (7km) *Drivenik*, lying about 1km off the main road at the end of a rough track, is a much better preserved example dating from the 13C (added to in the 16C), with four horseshoe-shaped corner turrets and a rectangular entrance tower. Adjoining it is the medieval church of Sv. Dujam (badly restored in the 19C) and at a little distance the Gothic church of Sv. Stjepan.—At Badanj a poor and tortuous gravel road forks right to join the Kirižišće–Bribir road 5km from Bribir.

3km **Selce** is a small resort on the lines of Crikvenica, of which it forms virtually a suburb. It can also be reached by a local road (3km) along the shore. Just outside Selce another local road runs N to Bribir in the Vinodol.

6km **Novi Vinodolski**, also known as *Novi*, is the chief town (2100 inhab.) of the Vinodol region and an ancient centre of Croatian national consciousness. It is noted for its rich folklore, national costumes and folk dances, most of which can be seen during the colourful carnival known as the Mesopust (three days ending with Ash Wednesday). The town has developed into a successful small holiday resort.

History. Here was signed (1288) the famous Vinodolski zakon (Vinodol Statute), the oldest complete Croatian historical document, in which the overlordship of the Frankopans was formally recognised and the rights of the Vinodol citizens set out. In 1614, during the Uskok Wars, the town was ferociously sacked by Admiral Marcantonio Venier for aiding the Uskoks of Senj.—Ivan Mažuranić (1814–90), former Ban of Croatia and author of a classic narrative poem ('Smrt Smail-age Cengiića') was a native; his brother Antun (1805–88) was a pioneer in the scientific study of the Croatian language.

The older part of the town on the high hill overlooking the Adriatic Highway has suffered from indiscriminate demolition and rebuilding in the 19C. The 13C Frankopan *Castle* in the main square, where the Vinodol Statute is thought to have been signed, has been much reduced in size and renovated; Kvadrac, one of its towers, affords views over the town and Velebit channel. The 18C parish church of *Sv. Filip and Jakov* has a Gothic sanctuary (1520) dating from an earlier building (Tomb of Christophorus, Bishop of Modruš, 1499, before the main altar; 15C Gothic relief of the Madonna in wood on side altar). Opposite it, in the former residence of the bishops of Senj and Modruš, is the *Narodni muzej* (Town Museum; adm. Mon and Thurs 9–11). The museum combines local history, ethnography, and art and is as noteworthy for the loving care with which it has been assembled as for its contents (voluminous catalogues available in half a dozen languages, including English). Exhibits include a photocopy of the Vinodol Statute (see above), mementoes of the Mažuranić family, an early baroque altar frontal and the folk costumes of Novi Vinodolski.—The neighbouring Mažuranić birthplace is marked with a plaque.

Below the Adriatic Highway and to the S lies the modern part of Novi Vinodolski with its enormous promenade (bust of Ivan Mažuranić), beach and hotels. At the edge of the park are the ruins of Lopar, a Roman fortress. On a hill above the harbour are the extensive ruins of a 15C Pauline monastery and church.

Excursions can be made from Novi Vinodolski to the islands of Krk and Rab and to Senj (see below) and the Plitvice Lakes (see below).

A winding country road runs N from Novi Vinodolski to *Bribir* (5km) in the Vinodol valley (see above), with the remains of medieval town walls and a square tower from the former Frankopan Castle (1302). The tower (key from the town hall) affords views over the Vinodol valley and down to Novi Vinodolski and the sea. The baroque parish church (1740) has a picture of the Washing of Christ's Feet by Palma the Younger and the treasury contains a gold Romanesque cross (c 1200), the work of the goldsmith Milonigus. Beside the church is a monument to Josip Pančić, first president of the Serbian Academy of Sciences, a native of Bribir. Also born in Bribir was the Croatian literary scholar and critic Mihovil Kombol.

S of Novi Vinodolski the Adriatic Highway hugs the coast at the foot of the Velebit Mts, which here descend abruptly into the sea. Offshore is the barren coastline of Krk (Rte 9), and the intervening channel widens to form the beginning of the VELEBITSKI KANAL, or *Podgorski Kanal*, that extends for 150km to Maslenica Bridge near Zadar.

Just S of Novi Vinodolski, an asphalt and gravel road (left) ascends in zigzags into the Velebits and across the Velika Kapela Mts to Ogulin in the interior. Called the *Rudolf Road*, it was built in the 18C to link inland Croatia with the coast. At 9km, perched at a dizzy height on the mountainside, is the ruined medieval castle of *Ledenice* (visible also from the coast), an important stronghold until sacked by Venice in 1614 during the Uskok Wars.

23km SENJ, the largest and oldest town (4000 inhab.) beneath the Velebit Mts, with a colourful and turbulent past, owed its prominence in earlier times to good communications with the interior and strategic command of the Velebitski kanal and the sea. It was for long the home of the Uskok corsairs (see below). Unlike most towns on the coast, it was never occupied by Venice and in consequence has a strongly continental flavour. It was badly damaged by allied air raids during the Second World War. Senj is the nearest town on the coast to the National Park of Plitvice and its famous Lakes.

Post Office: on the waterfront.

Information: *Turističko društvo Velebit*, tel. 881030.

Car Ferries: to *Baška* on the island of Krk (Rte 9) and *Lopar* on the island of Rab (Rte 9).

History. *Senj* is thought to have been founded in 432 BC by the Celtic tribe of Senones who came from the region round Modruš, 40km inland. As *Senia* it was a Roman trading port of some importance and is mentioned by Pliny. In the 9C Senj passed from the Franks to Croatia; in 1154 it was made a bishopric; in 1271 the Frankopans became hereditary captains; and in 1388 the town received its own statute. Later (1469) it was attached directly to the throne of Matthias Corvinus, king of Hungary and Croatia, but in 1526, as a result of the battle of Mohač, it passed to the Habsburgs. An era of notoriety ensued. The Turks had overrun Greece, Bulgaria, Serbia, Bosnia, and parts of Croatia. Large numbers of Slavonic refugees from these lands gathered in Senj and soon became known under the collective name of Uskoks (Ital. *Usocchi*), the Serbo-Croatian word for runaway or refugee. At first, under the aegis of Austria, they constituted virtually an élite and autonomous frontier force against the Turks, but they soon turned to the sea, and throughout the 16C and early 17C operated as pirates, the scourge of Venice and the Venetian fleet. Their legendary exploits and superhuman courage earned them a European reputation. Austria, as a natural rival to Venice, turned a blind eye, particularly in view of the Uskoks' role against the Turks, but in 1615 Uskok depredations finally led to the so-called Uskok War between Venice and Austria. By the Peace of Madrid (1617), the Uskoks were disbanded by Austria and resettled inland. To the Venetians they were lawless brigands; to Austria turbulent but useful irregulars; but in Croatia and Serbia they were and are regarded as Slav patriots, hostile to Turkey and Venice alike and tolerant of Austria only as their titular overlord. After their dispersal Senj, with an Austrian garrison, went into a long decline, which was aggravated by the growth of Trieste and Rijeka.

Senj, always a centre of Croatian culture, had the earliest known Croatian printing press (in Glagolitic) in 1493–1508. The town was the birthplace of many prominent writers, including Pavao Ritter-Vitezović (1652–1723), S.S. Kranjčević (1865–1908), Vjenceslav Novak (1859–1905), Milan Ogrizović (1877–1923), and Milutin Cihlar Nehajev (1880–1931). The folk ballads relating the heroic deeds of the Uskoks are among the most beautiful in Yugoslav literature.

Senj is also noted for the *Senjska bura*, a N wind that blows down from the Velebit Mts and out to sea with such ferocity that it inspires universal dread. The Uskoks, the only sailors ever to have mastered it, used it as a cover for their raids. It gives Senj the lowest average temperature on the Adriatic seaboard.

The focal point of Senj has moved from the old city to the *Harbour* and sea front, which lie directly on the Adriatic Highway. Opening from the harbour a busy little square surrounds the War Memorial ('On Guard'), by I. Vukušić; on the far side the dilapidated 16C *Palača Posedarić* preserves the family arms in its badly altered façade. Two houses adjoin it at the rear, the first Renaissance in style and the other (1541) with a Gothic doorway. POTOK, the old main street of the town, passes the house (plaque) in which was born Vjenceslav Novak.

The pleasant TRG MARKA BALENA, the main square or *Velika placa*, is mainly baroque in character with an early-19C drinking fountain known as *Cilnica*. On the E side rises the massive **Kaštel**, a Frankopan castle erected in 1340. After 1469 the building became the residence of the Senj captains and housed the city's garrison. In 1896 it was given a new façade and became a school. The entrance corridor is adorned by an elaborate 15C coat of arms of Matthias Corvinus, king of Hungary and Croatia. The **Velika vrata**, or *Great Gate* (1779), adjoining the castle, was erected to mark the completion of the Josephine Road from Senj to Karlovac under Emperor Joseph II of Austria (as the inscription above records). The distances marked on the left gatepost are in German miles.

Outside the gate a path continues (right) past the town wall and over the Kolan kanal to Nehaj Fortress (see below). To the left a road follows the line of the walls past the ruined Gulden tower (left) and the Neda textile works (right) to the E end of Stara cesta (comp. below).

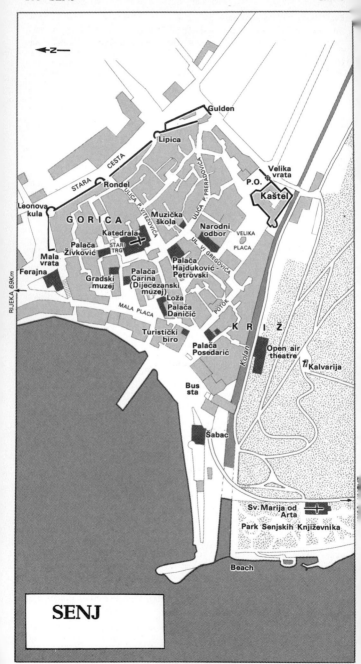

SENJ

UL. VL. GREGOVIĆA, running at right angles to Potok behind the three baroque houses that close the W side of the square, has several ancient houses. Carved on the lintel of No. 2 is a pair of rustic heads, male and female, a typical feature of Senj; No. 3 has a Gothic doorway with a coat of arms; and the corner of the end house bears a carved cross as a spiritual protection against damage by wheeled traffic. In the corner of the main square adjoining Ul. Vl. Gregovića is the **Narodni odbor** (Town Hall) and former *Franciscan Monastery* (1558), built round a Renaissance cloister by Captain Ivan Lenković. The second story was added in 1698 and the monastery restored in 1816 (after fire) and adapted to its present use in 1896.

The modest baroque bell tower on the corner of Ul. P. Preradovića, is all that remains of the monastery church (bombed 1943), which was the traditional burial church of the Uskoks. The house to the E, on the corner of UL. VL. PAVELIĆA, has a well-preserved lion of St. Mark in the entrance way and is thought to have been the home in the 13–14C of the Venetian ambassador. On the other side, a few steps down, is the 15C *Palača Hajduković-Petrovski*, with the excellent Lavlje dvorište or Lion Courtyard, so named from the corbels that support the balcony. A carved well-head in the courtyard bears the arms of (?) the Duke of Zweibrücken. The *Music School* (Niža muzička škola) immediately opposite the bell tower, occupies the former 14C church of Sv. Ivan Krstitelj (John the Baptist), of which Gothic details can still be seen on the façade; inside are 15C frescoes. Behind the school is Uskočka ulica, a picturesque narrow cul-de-sac, with a double-arcaded courtyard, the best remaining example of a local style of architecture.

From UL. P. VITEZOVIĆA you may shortly reach KAPTOLSKI or STARI TRG. Dominating this small square is the **Cathedral of Sv. Marija**, a Romanesque single-nave church of the 12C with aisles added in the 18C, when the building was remodelled in baroque. Bombing during the Second World War revealed part of the original façade with blind arcading in brick, which has been restored. The interior, also restored after bombing, is baroque, except for a Gothic triumphal arch and sacristy of 1497. Above the sacristy, half obscured in a niche, is the fine Gothic sarcophagus of Bishops Ivan and Leonardo de Cardinalibus de Pensauro (1392–1401). In the S aisle is a 15C stone custodial and by the door a good baroque font.

The quarter to the NW of the cathedral, behind the modern bell tower (1900), is GORICA, the oldest section of the city with a maze of narrow streets and houses dating back to the 15C. Here, in a narrow street beside the cathedral, the birthplace of the poet, S.S. Kranjčević is marked by a plaque. House No. 24 has a Glagolitic inscription on the lintel (1477) and No. 25, adjoining, with an arcaded courtyard, is thought to have housed the first Glagolitic printing press (1493, see above). Beyond Gorica are the surviving town walls (see below). Opposite the W front of the cathedral is the *Palača Živković* (1487), with a handsome Renaissance doorway and a small statue in a niche. The Živković arms are just inside the door. The street beside the palača descends to a small square just within the *Mala Vrata* (Little Gate), though the actual gateway has been destroyed. In the square is the house (plaque) in which Milutin Cihlar Nehajev was born. Beyond the gateway is a large 18C baroque edifice known as the *Verein* (or Ferajna) in which, in 1835, was opened one of the earliest Croatian reading rooms.

Steps descend to the left towards the harbour. Stara cesta, the broad street to the right, skirts the remaining section of the CITY WALLS (12–15C) with three circular towers. The *Leonova* or *Papina Kula* is named after Pope Leo X (1513–21) who financed its erection. *Rondel* has been badly modernised. Beyond *Lipica* or Salapan you may regain the Velika vrata (comp. above).

The 16C *Palača Vukasović*, to the SW of the cathedral, houses the **Gradski Muzej** (Town Museum; adm. 10–12 and 17–19), containing a lapidary and archaeological section, Partisan relics, and a collection devoted to the history of literature in Glagolitic and Senj's literary past. A little farther down Ul. M. Ogrizovića, on the opposite side, the 18C *Palača Carina* with a typical Uskok head sculpted over the doorway, is now the palace of the bishops of Senj-Modruš. The ground floor houses the **Dijecezanski Muzej** or Diocesan Museum, in which are displayed the Gothic Kaptolski križ in silver and wood, a similar but larger Gothic cross in beaten silver, a set of silver votive tables, church plate and vestments, a small lapidary collection, and the Diocesan Library with a number of early codices and incunabula. In the spacious TRG ŽRTAVA FAŠIZMA or MALA PLACA, which owes its irregular shape to wartime bombing, the 15C *Palača Dančić* has a good Venetian Gothic three-light window on the third floor. The adjoining *Town Loggia* (16C) has been transformed as a dwelling but is to be restored. In the narrow UL. I. VLATKOVIĆA, behind these two houses, is the 14C Gothic chapel of *Sv. Marija Mandaljena*; the tiny cul-de-sac opposite is hemmed in with old houses, one with a relief of the Madonna.

Return to the waterfront and follow the shore S. The former SW limit of the city walls is marked by the *Šabac*, a round fortress tower, near the water's edge, now the harbourmaster's office. Beyond the canal, between the Magistrala and the sea, extends the pleasant green *Park Senjskih književnika* (Senj Writers' Park) with busts of native literary figures. The church of *Sv. Marija od Arta* (key from diocesan museum) inside the park (1489, restyled in baroque), known as the Sailors' Church, contains a large number of 18–19C ship models. Beyond the church a path leads to the town beach, equipped with cabins, showers, and a cemented foreshore. Traces are visible of the artillery battery that once covered the shipping channel and commanded the islands of Krk and Prvić.

Opposite the park a footpath winds uphill, past a handball court and a rustic Calvary of 1740, to the imposing **Castle Nehaj** (Fear Not). This was built by Ivan Lenković, most famous of Senj city captains, between 1538 and 1558, when the Turks were at the height of their power in the Balkans and had repeatedly attacked Senj. Lenković had all buildings outside the city walls destroyed and incorporated much of the masonry into his castle. Fragments and incriptions from the 13C monastery of St. Peter and the Benedictine Abbey of St. George, can still be traced. The square keep built to face the cardinal points of the compass, with corbelled turrets at each corner, has an additional machicolated turret above the entrance.

The interior has recently been restored. A well-head in the courtyard bears the arms of Lenković (1558) and of the town of Graz, under whose jurisdiction Senj was placed by the Austrian court. The ground floor housed the men's quarters; today it and the courtyard are used for concerts. The first floor, formerly officer's quarters and the site of the powder magazine, has been adapted as an Uskok Museum, with ethnographic material and a collection of antique weapons. The second floor, which constituted the firing platform, has been restored to its former condition, with its heavy cannon (some of which have done duty as bollards on the quayside). The roof affords superb views of the entire Kvarner, extending as far as Istria on a clear day, and inland of the peaks of the Velebit Mts and the pass of Senjska draga.

FROM SENJ TO PLITVICE AND THE PLITVICE LAKES, road, 89km, Highways N5 and N6, buses daily in c 3 hours; numerous excursions in summer. The Josephine Road leads inland from the Velika vrata towards the Velebit Mts. After 2km it climbs by a series of hairpin bends through typical karst scenery to the passes of Senjska draga and Vratnik (887m), with superb views back to the coast and islands. The prominent memorial at Vratnik is the tomb of Kajetan Knežić (died 1848), builder of the road. At (21km) *Žuta Lokva* a road diverges left for Karlovac and Zagreb; continue through the green and fertile valley of Lika via (19km) *Otočac*, and (16km) *Vrhovine*, on the Zagreb–Split railway line.

31km **Plitvice National Park**, an area of outstanding natural beauty, comprises woodlands, meadows, lakes, waterfalls, rivers, and caves (guided tours twice a day in season). Although visitors are given every facility for access, the park is strictly administered as a nature reserve, all flora and fauna being protected. Particular attention is paid also to the protection of the abundant travertine (a crystalline calcium carbonate formed by the deposits of the lake and river waters) in the park, which is essential to the balance of natural forces. A new (1976) road has been opened E of the lakes, leaving the beautiful road that runs along their shores for the exclusive use of the electric vehicles operated by the Park Authority. Delightful walks may be taken through the woods, particularly at the W end of the park where in virgin forest trees reach heights of 50m and more. Excursions can also be made to some of the hilltops, caves and smaller river valleys in the park.

The *Plitvice Lakes (Plitvička jezera)*, a continuous chain of sixteen lakes and innumerable waterfalls, form a system c 6km long of unrivalled natural beauty. They are best visited in the spring, when the water-level is high; in the autumn, when the colouring of the foliage is particularly brilliant; and in the middle months of winter when many of the falls freeze over to form gigantic icicles and ice barriers.

Running from S to N, the lakes take their source from two small streams, the Crna (Black) and Bijela (White) Rijeka (river), which join in the hamlet of Plitvički Ljeskovac to form the River Matica. This feeds **Prošćansko Jezero** (*Lake Prošće*), the highest lake (636m), 68 hectares in area. A road running along its entire E bank and a footpath on the W bank afford excellent views of many inlets and coves, of which *Limunska draga* (Limun Cove), at the extreme S end, is the most striking. Prošćansko jezero then falls by a series of small lakes and waterfalls, notably the *Labudovac Fall*, to *Galovac jezero*, and this cascades in turn into *Gradinsko jezero* and **Jezero Kozjak**, largest of all the lakes (83 hectares) with a depth of 46m. The *Galovac* and *Kozjak Falls* are particularly beautiful; a closer view is obtained from the footpaths that cross at these points. The road from Lake Prošće closely follows the lakeside as far as Lake Kozjak, then bends away to the village of Plitvička jezera, below which are the main bathing beach and facilities for hiring boats. Beyond the village a lower road keeps close to Lake Kozjak as far as the *Milanovac Falls* where it crosses to the other shore and continues for Zagreb, whereas the upper road remains at a distance from the shore until it reaches Lake Gavanovac. The footpath on the W side, however, follows the water's edge right round the lake. At the N end of Lake Kozjak lie the lower group of lakes *Milanovac*, *Gavanovac*, and *Kaludjerovac*, which feed one another in a series of superb cascades tumbling in quick succession down a rapidly deepening gorge lined with limestone caves. Most spectacular are the waterfall of the Plitvice River (70m) which here flows into the

lakes and the magnificent plunge of the *Sastavci* (76m) into the canyon of the River Korana, with which the series ends. Numerous footpaths and observation points give ample opportunity to observe the falls from various angles and the wild Korana Canyon can also be explored on foot.

Cascades in the Plitvice National Park

Other excursions can be made from Senj to the islands of Krk (Rte 9), Rab (Rte 10), and Pag (Rte 11); to Zavratnica fjord (see below); and to the Velebits for mountain walking (information about marked tracks and mountain huts from the *Planinarsko društvo Zavižan*).

The rugged grandeur of the coast has a forbidding air in all but the finest weather as the Velebits fall straight into the sea. The road, with a vastly improved surface, winds and twists at their foot all the way to the end of the Velebitski kanal, and there are excellent views out to sea of the impressively barren NE shores of the Kvarner islands.

10km **Jurjevo**, a small village at the water's edge, is the starting-point for excursions to Oltari and *Mt Vučjak* (1644m) in Zavižan National Park (mountain hut) in the Velebits Mts. A twisting mountain road gives access to the park (on foot c 3 hours).

From Zavižan another footpath leads through beautiful wooded uplands (c 1½ hours) to the mountain hut Rosijeva koliba, just below the summit of *Mt Gromovača* (1675m), the highest peak in this section of the Velebits. Footpaths descend from here to the village of Gornja klada (c 2 hours) on the Adriatic Highway and to Jablanački Alan and the road to Stirovača National Park (see below). At Oltari a left fork in the road leads to Otočac (pass of 1040m) and inland Croatia.

The road swings inland slightly and climbs away from the shore to a height reaching 300m, with views to the islands of *Prvić, Grgur,* and *Goli,* and the northern shores of Rab. Threading hamlets, many of them with twin-named settlements down on the sea-shore, you pass under a cable railway at (24km) *Stinica.* The railway ascends to 1300m in the Velebits and is used to bring down timber from the vast forests of Jablanački Alan. The intended addition of passenger cars to the railway would provide convenient access to the Velebit mountain region.

6km **Jablanac** (300 inhab.), with a history dating from the 12C, is reached by a winding asphalt byroad. Set in a quiet, deeply indented little bay, it has a car ferry to the island of Rab (see Rte 10), here at its closest to the mainland. On the headland just S of the harbour are the scanty ruins of a castle (1251) built by Ban Stjepan Šubić, and 2km S of the village is the fjord-like inlet of *Zavratnica* (20 min on foot, or by boat), with steep rocky sides and exceptionally clear water.

Jablanac is the starting point for excursions to Jablanački Alan (1612m) and Štirovača National Park (mountain hut) in the Velebits and for longer trips to Rosijeva koliba and Zavižan (see above). Beyond Štirovača the road divides for Otočac (left) and Karlobag (right).

Continue S. To seaward, Rab disappears and is replaced by the bleak outlines of Pag (Rte 11), which after about 10km comes close inshore.—At (19km) *Cesarica* the road descends to the sea again to run along the shore of the Velebitski kanal.

15km **Karlobag** (400 inhab.) is the largest of the villages along the Velebitski kanal, a regular halt for long-distance buses and the terminal of a car ferry to Pag. The settlement grew up around the *Fortica,* a massive 14C castle rebuilt in 1579 after being sacked by the Turks; its extensive remains are visible on a hill overlooking the town. The baroque Capuchin monastery dates from the 18C when Austria attempted to build up Karlobag as a port for the inland district of Lika. From Karlobag a fair asphalt road climbs steeply (gradient 1 in 5 in places) to *Gospić* (40km), the main town of the Lika region.

Just S of Karlobag you pass the ruins (right) of Vidovac, an old lookout tower and a ruined Gothic church. Successive small fishing villages lead on to (45km) *Starigrad-Paklenica,* an unprepossessing village with no visible centre and a mushroom growth of summer bungalows, simple restaurants, and pensions. Starigrad's main interest is its position at the entrance to *Velika Paklenica Canyon* and *Paklenica National Park.*

A narrow gravel road leads 4km into the mouth of the canyon, whence you must continue on foot. A reasonably easy ascent follows the course of the river Velika Paklenica and leads in c 2 hours to a mountain hut with beds and facilities for simple meals (the local honey is recommended). A number of caves may also be visited on the way up, of which *Manita Peć* (165m long, torch needed) is the best known. From the mountain hut excursions may be made through the Velebit uplands to the neighbouring peaks of *Štirovača* (1292m), with refuge hut (open in the summer only), (1639m), *Babin Vrh* (1740m), *Sveto Brdo* (1753m) and *Vaganski Vrh* (1757m), the highest peak of the Velebit range.

Beside the lower course of the Velika Paklenica and to the left of the Adriatic Highway is the small pre-Romanesque church of *Sv. Petar* with an irregular number of lesenes on its outer walls and a single semicircular apse. The unusual Romanesque campanile has an open ground story and four Romanesque windows at the top, and the graveyard contains a curious roofed structure that once served as a baptistery and Bogomil gravestones with primitive carvings. Where the watercourse meets the sea stands the ruined tower of *Večka kula* built by the Venetians as a defence against the Turks.—Beyond Starigrad-Paklenica is the adjoining village of Seline and the entrance to *Mala Paklenica*, a smaller canyon also accessible by footpath.

At 11km **Rovanjska**, where the unusually shaped pre-Romanesque chapel of Sv. Juraj (10–11C) at the water's edge has a charnel house and cupola, round the head of the Velebitski kanal and bear right in the direction of Zadar. Highway N2–2 (left) goes to Obrovac (see Rte 14B). The new suspension bridge over *Maslenićko ždrilo*, the narrow cleft joining the landlocked Novigradsko more (Sea of Novigrad) to the Velebitski kanal, affords excellent views in both directions.

10km **Posedarje** (1100 inhab.), on the shores of the Novigradsko more, is a pleasant seaside village with a shingle beach. In the village is the medieval Romanesque chapel of *Uzašašće Marijino* (The Assumption) and on an islet close inshore the Gothic church of *Sv. Duh*.

From Posedarje a minor road runs NE towards the island of Pag (see Rte 11). At (4km) crossroads, a gravel road (right) leads to *Vinjerac* on the shores of the Velebitski kanal, with the small ruined fortress and medieval church of Sv. Marko, remnants of a former Pauline monastery. The road continues through barren karst, passing (9km) just inland of *Ražanac*, a rundown village with the remains (walls and tower) of a 16C Venetian fortress built to resist the Uskok pirates and the Turks. Here a road runs SW to *Krneza* (6km), a hamlet whence a track leads to *Ljubač* on the seashore, where the modern church preserves a 14C Gothic monstrance from *Rt Ljubljana*. This picturesque cape, 3km walk beyond the village, was the site of a medieval Croatian town destroyed by the Turks in the 17C. The considerable ruins include remains of the 13C Romanesque basilica of Sv. Marija.—Continuing by the main road you reach (8km) the suspension bridge linking the mainland with the island of Pag (see Rte 11).

Cross the fertile plain of Ravni Kotari, where the road is frequently encumbered by peasant carts, to (24km) **Zadar** (see Rte 13).

9   The Island of Krk

Approaches. BY LAND: Highway N29 from *Kraljevica*, on the mainland over the new bridge to *Omisalj*, on the N shore of the island.

BY SEA: Car ferries from *Črišnjeva* on the Dalmatian coast, to *Voz*, on the N shore; from *Crikvenica* to *Šilo*, a little to the E and from *Lopar* (on N coast of Rab) to *Baška in the S*.

BY AIR: From major Yugoslav cities to Rijeka airport, at the N end of the island.

KRK is the largest and most populous island (15,000 inhab.) in the Adriatic, 38km long, up to 18km wide and with an area of 409km^2. It is the only island having a river (the Ričina, flowing into Baška) in addition to seasonal streams, and it has two small lakes, Omišaljsko jezero, near Njivice, and Ponikve jezero between Malinska and Krk. Agriculture and fishing are the principal occupations, and tourism, though growing, has not yet spoiled the character of the island. Six of the seven major centres (Dobrinj is the exception) are on the coast. The island is famed for its traditional adherence to Croatian culture, retention of the Glagolitic liturgy until well into the 19C, a vigorous folklore, and colourful folk costumes. The city of Krk, however, retained until recently a Romano-Venetian dialect, called Vegliot, carried over from an earlier era. Krk has an excellent network of good signposted roads.

History. The first known inhabitants of Krk, the Liburnians, gave way about the end of the 2C BC to the Romans. Strabo refers to the island as *Cyractica* and Pliny as *Curicta*, and Ptolemy also mentions the city of Curicum (presumably today's Krk), from which the modern Croatian name is derived. Caesar is thought to have had a base on Krk and he was defeated by Pompey in a naval battle (49 BC) just off the island. With the arrival of the Slavs in the 7C the Roman population withdrew into the city of Curicum, which in the 8–10C became the *Vecla* of Byzantium (whence the Venetian and Italian name for the island, *Veglia*). So strong was this Roman element that its language survived in a dialect form until the 19C. For a century or more Krk oscillated between Venice and Croatia until 1133, when Count Duymus, having defeated a large force of pirates with Venetian assistance, achieved insular autonomy under token Venetian protection. Duymus reputedly founded the Frankopan (Frangipane) dynasty. Under the Counts of Krk the island preserved a fluctuating state of independence and prosperity until 1480, when, whether owing to Frankopan misrule or Venetian perfidy, Count Ivan was driven out and replaced by direct Venetian rule. The severe economic decline that followed was aggravated by plague in 1499 and by the depredations of the Uskoks during the 16C and 17C and not halted until the fall of Venice in 1797. Austrian rule was kinder to Krk than the Napoleonic interregnum (1805–13), and ended only with the First World War. In 1918 D'Annunzio tried unsuccessfully to occupy the island before it passed to Yugoslavia. During the Second World War it was again occupied by Italy and then Germany (from 1943) until freed by Partisan forces in March 1945.

As a centre of the Glagolitic movement, Krk for centuries played an important role in the preservation of Croatian national identity and was a major influence on the early development of Glagolitic printing.

The city of **Krk** has for centuries been the cultural, administrative, and political centre (1300 inhab.) of the island but is now much reduced in population and importance. Its great antiquity, however, and good state of preservation makes it the most interesting town on the island.

Post Office: Titov trg.

Information: *Kvarner-Express* on the waterfront, tel. 851035.

Krk Festival of Folklore, annually in August.

The spacious TITOV TRG opens between the harbour and a well-preserved section of the *Town Walls* (15–16C). In front of the walls is a small market place. The *Glavna Straža* (1493), a rectangular watch tower at the far end, was erected by the Venetians as the town's main gate and now houses the Gradska kavana. A sundial and the coats of arms of four doges adorn the wall, and a lion of St. Mark embellishes the central boss of the vaulted interior. Following the walls towards the sea, you quickly reach a 15C hexagonal bastion into which is built a Roman gravestone bearing the old arms of Nikola Frankopan carved on its upper part and the date 1407.

Turn left along the waterfront, still following the line of the walls into which have been built the Narodna banka, a fish restaurant and the information office. Ahead is the main steamer quay. Turn left through the *Mala vrata* (Little Gate) into the fascinating labyrinth of the old town. UL. JUGOSLAVENSKE ARMIJE, to the right, is a typical medieval street that approaches the unusual architectural complex of Krk cathedral.

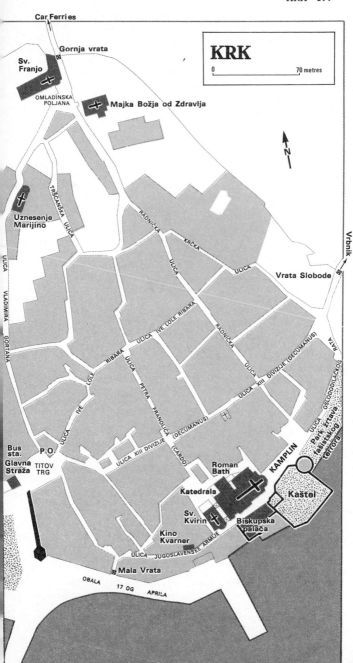

KRK

0   70 metres

Car Ferries

Gornja vrata

Sv. Franjo

OMLADINSKA POLJANA

Majka Božja od Zdravlja

N

Uznesenje Marijino

TRŠĆANSKA ULICA

ULICA VLADIMIRA GORTANA

RADNIČKA

KRČKA

ULICA

ULICA

Vrata Slobode

Vrbnik

RADNIČKA

ULICA IVE LOLE RIBARA

ULICA IVE LOLE RIBARA

ULICA PETRA FRANOLIĆA (DECUMANUS)

ULICA XIII DIVIZIJE (DECUMANUS)

RATA

ULICA OSLOBODILAČKOG

Park žrtava fašističkog terora

Bus sta.

Glavna Straža

P.O.

TITOV TRG

ULICA XIII DIVIZIJE (CARDO)

KAMPLIN

Roman Bath

Katedrála

Kaštel

Sv. Kvirin

Biskupska palača

Kino Kvarner

ULICA JUGOSLAVENSKE ARMIJE

Mala Vrata

OBALA 17 OG APRILA

Beyond the triple apses of Sv. Kvirin (see below), a narrow vaulted passage leads to the W door (right) of the **Cathedral of Uznesenje Marijino** (The Assumption), erected by Bp John in 1186–88. The early-12C NAVE, nine bays in length, is divided from the aisles by Romanesque arches of uneven height supported on reused columns, some Roman, some from the 5C basilica that preceded the present building. The majority of the *Capitals, however, were specially carved for the cathedral and are fine examples of the Byzantine type, being mainly variations on the Corinthian order. A significant exception is the second from the W end in the N arcade, an outstanding Romanesque example carved with birds and beasts. The W end earlier terminated in a narthex which was demolished in the 13C when the present W wall and two responds were added.

The CHOIR, an addition of the 16C remodelled in 1743 after a fire, is closed by an excellent Renaissance balustrade of red breccia flanked by contemporary octagonal ambones of the same material. The next bay to the E on the N side is occupied by a 17C baroque pulpit of wood carved in relief. In the floor an elaborate 14C memorial to Bishop John, the founder, shows the prelate in low relief; there is also a memorial to Ludovicus Cicuta, commander of a galley that Krk sent to Lepanto. The four paintings in the choir are by Cristoforo Tasca (1706). Off the N AISLE the 14C Gothic *Chapel of Sv. Vid* (St. Vitus) has elaborate rib-vaulting with the Frankopan arms, both old and new, emblazoned on the bosses. The NW chapel is built over a Roman bath whose mosaic floor can be seen beneath a trap door.—In the first chapel of the S AISLE opposite is a celebrated Gothic *Reredos in silver by P. Colero (1477) depicting the Madonna in Glory, a gift of the Frankopans. The picture of the Entombment (sometimes attributed erroneously to Titian), at the end of this aisle, is by Giovanni Antonio Pordenone.

Immediately opposite the W entrance of the cathedral across the vaulted passageway is the LOWER CHURCH (formerly *Sv. Margareta*) of the unusual 10–11C Romanesque basilica of *Sv. Kvirin** (St. Quirinus), built on two levels and oriented from N to S. The simple interior with massive square-ribbed vaulting supported by rectangular piers was restored in 1963 after long use as a wine vault. An expressive wooden crucifixion stands in the central apse. The *Bell Tower*, Romanesque below with a hideous baroque superstructure and onion dome added in 1776, provides access to the beautiful UPPER CHURCH, a model of harmony and simplicity. The arcades are supported by plain columns with cushion capitals. On the altar stands a wooden figure of St. Quirinus (a 4C bishop of Siscia, now Sisak) flanked by two panels of a Gothic polyptych depicting St. Quirinus and St. John. Traces of frescoes have been uncovered in the apse to the right.

In 1960 an Early Christian baptistery was discovered beneath the courtyard on the N side of the cathedral with a polygonal immersion font and mosaics. Inquire at the Bishop's Palace for details.

UL. PETRA FRANOLIĆA, beyond the covered passage, follows the course of the Roman cardo maximus through the centre of the town (comp. below).

The long, low building between the cathedral and the sea is the **Bishop's Palace**, in which there is an ecclesiastical museum containing several fine exhibits, notably a large *Polyptych on wood (1333–45?) by Paolo Veneziano, brought here from Jurandvor. Adjoining the Bishop's Palace and forming one side of the small square known as KAMPLIN (Poljana XXVI udarne divizije) is the large **Kaštel** of the counts Frankopan of Krk.

The origins of the family are obscure. Duymus (Dujam, Doimo), the first to receive historical mention, defeated a force of pirates off Krk in 1133 and achieved local autonomy for Krk under the nominal suzerainty of Venice. The title of *count* was first assigned to his two sons, Bartholomaeus (Bartolommeo) and Guidonis (Vid, Guido). In 1193 the counts of Krk were granted the fief of Modruš (Modrussa) by King Bela III of Hungary-Croatia, and their growing influence on the mainland was immensely increased when the grateful Bela IV, who had taken refuge on Krk in 1242 in his flight from the Tartars, granted them the fief of Senj. These honours earned them the disfavour of Venice and a period of exile from Krk, but after 1260 the Frankopans played the role of peacemakers between Venice and Hungary-Croatia from a unique position as simultaneous feudatories of both powers. In 1358 by the Treaty of Zadar, Krk was ceded by Venice to Hungary-Croatia. Count Ioannis (Ivan, Giovanni) maintained his former rights and in addition was appointed Ban (viceroy) of Dalmatia, Croatia and Slavonia. Although all their possessions were now in Hungaro-Croatian hands the Frankopans retained their seat in the Gran Consiglio of Venice. Count Nicolaus (Nikola, Nicolò), the son of Ioannis, was temporarily ejected from Krk when he and the population took opposite sides in Hungary's dynastic struggles of 1387–1400. Informed by Pope Martin V in 1425 (so the story went) that his family was descended from the famous line of Roman Frangipani, Nicolaus exchanged the old arms of the counts of Krk, gold stars on a white ground, for the twin lions of the Frangipani, a device which henceforth was used exclusively by the whole family. (The Salvonic name may be derived from Franko and 'ban' or viceroy.) After Nicolaus' death, the elder son, Ioannis (Ivan, Giovanni), who inherited Krk, began to quarrel with his brothers on the mainland and placed the island under the protection of Venice, abrogating his title to it completely in 1480. The mainland Frankopans continued active in Senj, Modruš and the Vinodol valley throughout the 16C and early 17C. With the rise of Austria the Frankopans became identified with Croatian nationalism and the last of the line, Fran Krsto Frankopan (born 1643), was executed at Vienna in 1671 for raising a rebellion against the central government.

The castle is roofless and empty. The oldest part, the plain square tower opposite the cathedral, dated 1191, was once the tribunal and prison of the commune of Krk. A wall of later and cruder construction connects this with a well-preserved circular tower of the 16C in the SE corner. The seaward flank consists of a curtain wall topped by forked battlements, constructed in 1407 by Count Nikola. The interior forms a garden to the Bishop's Palace, but the round tower and battlements afford excellent views of Krk and across the bay to Punat and the island of Košljun.

UL. ŽRTAVA OSLOBODILAČKOG RATA continues beside a small park extending above the shore. The road bends sharply left to join the decumanus. On the right is the *Vrata slobode*, or Porta Pisana, one of the three main entrances to the old walled town, though the gateway has disappeared. Beyond, it is a short walk to the town beach on the small bay of Dražica (shingle with sandy bottom).

The picturesque UL. XIII DIVIZIJE follows the line of the Roman decumanus through the middle of the town, crossing Ul. Petra Franolića (the former cardo), in the main shopping area. Any of the ancient streets to the right lead to Omladinska Poljana, an irregular open space at the N end of the town. The 12C Romanesque basilica of *Majka Božja od zdravlja* (Our Lady of Health), with a Liburnian cippus standing in front, is entered through the Bell Tower, essentially Romanesque but as with Sv. Kvirin, deformed by the addition of an unsuitable spire. The interior was restyled in baroque in 1730, when the columns were stuccoed and varnished and the apse painted, but it is hoped to restore the church to its Romanesque appearance. As in the cathedral the columns are reused and of irregular height, but the capitals are good; a fine example, depicting an eagle devouring a lizard on each of its four sides, may be noted on the N side. The Gothic church of *Sv. Franjo*, opposite, was erected in the 14C and extended in 1626, when the present roof and an organ loft were added. The tall trifoliated windows are filled with 19C Viennese stained glass. At the E end a vaulted chapel with corbels carved in the shape of human heads shows traces of Gothic frescoes. The high altar bears a painting of the Madonna and Saints by Bernardino Licinio (1531). The 19C pulpit is of inlaid wood. Gravestones in the floor include the carved slab of Iohannes Bernardini captain of another Krk galley at the Battle of Lepanto. The Renaissance cloister on the N of the church has a pleasant well-head. The tower dates from the rebuilding of the monastery in 1626 with additions of 1743.

Just N of OMLADINSKA POLJANA is the third of the original landward gates in the town walls, *Gornja vrata*, or Porta di Su, again without its gateway.

Return to Titov trg by UL. VLADIMIRA GORTANA, passing (left) the Benedictine nunnery of *Uznesenje Marijino* (The Assumption). Among the picturesque Romanesque and Gothic houses in this street are the Kotter house, with lion-head corbels, and an excellent example of 'na koljeno' door and counter (comp. Rte 22).

EXCURSIONS FROM KRK

A. KRK TO PUNAT, 7km. Leave Krk from the E, passing the town beaches of Porta Pisana and Dražica and skirting the Bay of Krk. Just to the right of the road (3km) is the tiny pre-Romanesque church of *Sv. Dunat*, cruciform in plan with a primitive dome of Byzantine type. It was badly damaged in the war.

At (1km) **Kornić** branch right from the main road (comp. below), continuing round the bay.

3km **Punat**, a neat attractive village (1700 inhab.) and the most populous settlement on the island, stands on the small shallow Puntarska draga, an almost landlocked inner bay linked with the larger Bay of Krk by Usta, a narrow strait (150m) wide. A bridge that once spanned this strait gave its name to the town (Villa di Ponte). Francesco Orlich, president of Costa Rica (1962–66), was born in Punat. The baroque parish church (1773) of *Sv. Trojstvo* (Holy Trinity) has a baroque high altar from Sv. Nikola in Senj (1787) with a Baptism of Christ by Maggiotto (1713–94). In the S aisle is a 15C polychrome statue of St. Anne. The 18C houses on the hillside facing the bay are typical of the domestic architecture of the Kvarner islands, with characteristic vaulted staircases (balature) leading up to small terraces on the first floor. An 18C olive press (Toš) stands in the centre of the town.

An elaborate carnival and regatta called *Puntarska noć* is held on the second Saturday in August each year.

The small wooded islet of **Košljun** in the bay is reached by boat in 5 minutes. Here an abandoned 12C Benedictine abbey was granted to the Franciscans by Ivan Frankopan, last count of Krk, in 1447. The present buildings of the **Franciscan Monastery**, erected at the beginning of the 16C, incorporate parts of the earlier structure. The monastic church of the *Navještenje* (Annunciation) consists of an aisleless nave with an open tiebeam roof and a vaulted Gothic choir. The triumphal arch is covered by a huge canvas of the Last Judgment by E. Ughetto (1653), more notable for size than for quality. Over the high altar is a polyptych of five panels by Girolamo da Santa Croce (1535); behind the altar the friars' choir is adorned with a Christ in the Manger (school of Raphael). Just inside the main entrance on the left s the gravestone of the church's benefactress, Katarina Frankopan, daughter of Ivan and the wife successively of Doges Francesco Dandolo and Andrea Foscolo, who was formerly buried in the chapel of Sv. Bernardin. The Stations of the Cross were painted by Ivan Dulčić (1961).

The 12C Gothic chapel of *Sv. Bernadin*, reached from the Renaissance cloister (well-head, Roman child's sarcophagus and gravestones) houses the monastic *Museum*. Notable among the paintings (16–17C Venetian) are works by Franjo Juričić (1671–1718), a local artist. There is a good collection of Krk folk costumes. In the *Library* (opened on request) are an early copy of Ptolemy's atlas (1511), the papal bull granting Košljun to the Franciscans, a fragment of one of the earliest printed books in Croatian (1483), Katerina Frankopan's will (1520), and c 100 incunabula; a large collection of manuscripts in Glagolitic and Latin dates back to the 11C. Beside the door stands a primitive local boat called a *ladva*, hollowed out of a tree, and said to have been in use up to the end of the 19C.

B. KRK TO BAŠKA, 18km. To Kornić, see above. At (5km) *Kuka* branch right; the road climbs steeply by zigzags to 300m. The barren plateau of Teskavac and *Mt Obzova* (568m), the highest point on the island, rise on the right. The road gradually descends the fertile valley of *Suha ričina*, where the river Ričina almost dries up in summer, to the coast.

12km **Jurandvor** is an attractive village with typical vaulted terraces and wide courtyards. Just SE of the village stands *Sv. Lucija*, the 11C pre-Romanesque church of a former Benedictine abbey. Built into its Romanesque bell tower, which has lost its top story, are four sculptures depicting the symbols of the evangelists. The bell dates from the early 14C. The church is entered through the vaulted base of the tower; its plain nave contains architectural fragments. Off the S side is the Gothic chapel of *Bogorodica od ruzarije* (Our Lady of the Rosaries), built in 1498 by the Juranić family. On the wall is a cast of the Bašćanska ploča (Baška Tablet; original in the Yugoslav Academy at Zagreb). The slab, decorated with early Romanesque relief carvings of vine leaves, bears an inscription in Glagolitic recording the gift of land for the abbey by King Zvonimir of Croatia (1076–89). Excavations around the church in 1955–62 revealed remains of a Roman villa and traces of a 6–7C church.

1km **Baška** (900 inhab.), the most southerly village on the island, is strung out along a sheltered bay at the mouth of the river Ričina. Beside its long sand and pebble beach, one of the finest in the Kvarner, extend small hotels and villas. The main street runs along the shore to the picturesque old quarter with curious houses (note the unusual chimneys), some of the 16C. Those on the seaward side were originally raised on piles above the water. The baroque parish church of the *Sv. Trojstvo* (Holy Trinity; 1722), contains a Last Supper by Palma the Younger and the Virgin with Saints and Angels by M. Marziale (c 1495). On the baroque high altar from Senj, the Coronation of the Virgin is by Franjo Juričić (18C). In the main square is the small Renaissance church of *Sv. Antun* (1482) with a painting by Celestin Medović (1859–1920); and behind the Hotel Velebit the small Romanesque chapel of *Sv. Marko*. In the fields behind the beach the small 16C church of *Sv. Mihovil* (key from parish priest) contains a tryptych by Paolo Campsa (1514).

Baška has sea connections with the island of Rab, to which excursions are easi.
made in a day. More locally, the cave of Škuljica, accessible only by boat, open.
in the cliff just opposite Prvić. The narrow *Senjska vrata* between the islands of
Krk and *Prvić*, notoriously the most dangerous strait in the Adriatic, has been the
scene of countless shipwrecks. The lighthouse on the barren Prvić affords
excellent views.

C. KRK TO VRBNIK, 12km. Beyond (5km) *Kuka*, the forks left through
the fertile plain of Vrbničko polje, known for grapes and tomatoes.—
7km Vrbnik (1300 inhab.), situated on a steep cliff overlooking the
Velebitski kanal, is the only major settlement on the Ę side of the
island. In the 14–15C it was a stronghold of the Counts Frankopan
(castle ruins in Vrbničko polje, fragmentary town walls), but it
declined in importance with the rise of Krk. The parish church of
Uznesenje Marijino (The Assumption), erected in the 15–16C on an
E–W axis but rebuilt in baroque to face N and S, preserves Gothic
elements in the choir. The Last Supper in the predella of the altarpiece
was painted by Marin Cvitković (1599), a native of Kotor. In the
Ružarija, a vaulted side chapel, is the fine 15C Renaissance altar of Sv.
Marija Ružarica (Mary of the Rosaries) depicting the Virgin and Child
with 15 rosettes illustrating the life of Christ.

Beside the detached Renaissance tower (1527), now disfigured by an ugly spire,
the tiny chapel of Sv. Marija (key from the parish priest) has a 15C polyptych
depicting St. Anne, a pietà carved in relief, and a Madonna, all in wood and
Gothic in feeling.
    In the nearby Zadružni dom the *Dinko Vitezić Library* (c 15,000 vols) preserves
a number of Glagolitic manuscripts, incunabula, and rare books. The most
outstanding book on display is one of two copies extant (the other is in
Cambridge) of the beautifully illustrated *Atlas of Johann David Kochler,
printed in Nuremburg in 1612. There are also photocopies of the Glagolitic
Vrbnički statut (Vrbnik Statute) of 1388 and Petrisov zbornik (Petris Miscellany)
of 1468. In the temporary charge of the parish priest are the First Vrbnik Missal
(1456) in Glagolitic with illuminations; the Second Vrbnik Missal (1463) also in
Glagolitic with outstanding miniatures and curious initials in Latin; a rare copy
of Transitus Sancti Hieronymi, printed (probably in Senj) in 1508; and four 15C
breviaries thought to have been composed also in Vrbnik. It is hoped eventually
to house these works with an ethnographical collection in a single museum.
    Vrbnik produces a white wine called Zlahtina. The plant where it is pressed
and bottled may be visited on request.

The N and NE SHORES of the island are served by roads which divide
at 2km N of Krk.

D. KRK TO ŠILO (Crikvenica), 20km. The right branch passes just E of
(14km) **Dobrinj**, one of the four early fortified villages on the island
and the only settlement of importance not on the coast. The unusual
defensive system consists of a ring of linked houses built with thick
outer walls specially strengthened. The parish church of *Sv. Stjepan*,
rebuilt in the 18C, preserves fragments from the 12C and a rectangular Gothic choir with a rib-vault (1602). The treasury contains a 14C
altar frontal embroidered with gold and silver thread, depicting the
Coronation of the Virgin; 15C silvered crosses; a 16C ciborium; and a
gold reliquary of St. Ursula. Beyond Dobrinj lies the bay of Soline
where the Frankopans had extensive salt works and which is now
occupied by oyster beds. *Sv. Vid*, by the Dobrinj fork, is the
pre-Romanesque church whose foundation in 1100 is described in the
'Dobrinjska listina', one of the earliest documents in Croatian.—
Beyond Sv. Vid the road continues to (6km) *Šilo*, a small resort linked
by car ferry to Crikvenica (Rte 8) on the mainland by which it is
administered.

E. KRK TO OMIŠALJ (Kraljevica), 26km. The left branch of the road from Krk runs NW to (13km) **Malinska** (300 inhab.), a small resort with a pleasant promenade, three pebble beaches, and an open-air theatre. During the first week in August it is the principal venue of the Krčki Festival, a concert of local folk songs and dances with visiting groups from other parts of the country. In *Porat*, a hamlet across the bay (15 minutes by boat), is a 15C Franciscan monastery. A favourite excursion from Malinska is by boat to Glavotok (see below)—4km *Njivice* stands peacefully on a bay in pretty wooded surroundings.

9km **Omišalj** (800 inhab.) comprises a picturesque but dilapidated old quarter on a lofty hill overlooking the sea, and the new tourist quarter known as *Zagradi*, on the shore. The town was once a centre of the Frankopan family.

In the spacious main square stands the parish church of *Sv. Marija*. The plain Romanesque W front with a good relief carving in the tympanum is embellished with a fine rose window inserted in 1405 by the mason Sinoga. The cupola and rectangular choir were added in the 16C and numerous side chapels at the same time or a little earlier. The interior is surprisingly harmonious and the cupola imposing from within, but the effect is spoiled by indiscriminate painting of the walls in 1925. In the S apse is a 15C polyptych of St. John by Jacobello del Fiore. A stone carved with pre-Romanesque basketwork is built into the interior of the pulpit. The detached Renaissance bell tower erected in 1533–36 is disfigured by an inappropriate spire. The small Gothic church of *Sv. Ivan* (1442) beside it serves as the sacristy. On the E side of the square is the Gothic church of Sv. Jelena (1470).

A narrow street runs down to the left of the parish church to the small square of Dubac perched just inside the remnants of the town walls. On one side is the Romanesque church of *Sv. Antun* with a loggia. The square commands superb views over the deeply indented Omišaljski zaljev (Bay of Omišalj) and out over the Kvarner to Rijeka, Opatija, and the Učka mountains of Istria. Clearly visible also is the neighbouring bay of *Sepen* (or Sapan) to the SW (reached by boat or on foot) with the massive overgrown ruins of a 5C early Christian basilica and remains of an extensive Roman settlement (*Fulfinium?*).

The Stomorina, Omišalj's annual harvest festival (15 August) is the biggest and most colourful of the Krk festivals. Folk costumes are worn and the many indigenous Krk songs and dances performed, including one famous song, Turne moj lipi (My beautiful tower), said to have been sung by Ivan, last Count Frankopan of Krk, when he was exiled by Venice.

Beyond Omišalj the road continues through a flat plain covered with scrub, passing Rijeka's airport, several petrol stations, a fruit and vegetable stand and climbs to the rocky NE tip of the island. From the summit of the ridge glimpses may be had of the typical Kvarner tunny ladders (see Rte 8) in Peškera bay before the road serpentines down to the quiet sheltered cove of *Voz*.

F. KRK TO GLAVOTOK, 14km. A narrow road runs NW to (14km) *Glavotok* on the westernmost tip of the island. About 300m from a pleasant shaded beach, with a café set among the trees, is the Franciscan Monastery endowed by Ivan Frankopan in 1473. The church in Franciscan Gothic erected in 1507 was extended to the E in the 17C and the façade remodelled in 1879. The bare interior consists of a single nave with an open tie-beam roof and barrel-vaulted choir. On the high altar, Sts. Francis and Bonaventura by Girolamo da Santa Croce.

In the neighbouring bay of *Čavlena*, accessible only by boat, the pre-Romanesque church of Sv. Krševan has a cupola and triple apses

10   The Island of Rab

Approaches. BY SEA: Car ferries from *Jablanc* to *Mišnjak* and from *Baška* (on Krk) and *Senj* to *Lopar*. Passenger boats from *Rijeka* and *Zadar*.

RAB (8900 inhab.) 22km long and 3–10km wide, and of very irregular shape, consists of three parallel ranges of limestone hills, which result in great variations in vegetation and climate. On the NE side, *Kamenjak* (Tinjarosa), the longest and highest range, runs the length of the island, rising in the centre to 409m. This bleak rocky barrier protects the island from the cold N and E winds giving it a mild climate. In the centre the parallel *Mundanija* is much shorter and lower, and to the S and W is the smaller ridge of Kalifront. Between these ridges are two long fertile valleys (Supetarska draga and Kamporska draga), watered by over 300 natural springs—a rare phenomenon on an Adriatic island—the presence of which has turned the people towards the land rather than the sea. In addition to olives and grapes they grow grain and vegetables, and silk culture is by local tradition supposed to have been introduced to Europe by a native of Rab. The NE side of the island is almost bare of vegetation but the peninsula of Kalifront in the W is noted for its luxuriant woods. Juniper, fig, cypress, jasmine and agave are also found in abundance.

History. The first known inhabitants of Rab were the Liburnians who, with a few Greek settlers, were conquered by the Romans in early imperial times. With variant names on the root *Arba*, the town is mentioned by both Ptolemy and Pliny the Elder and early became a bishopric. Under Byzantium about the 8C Rab came into conflict with Croatia and was eventually absorbed into the Croatian kingdom of King Tomislav (910–28). In the year 1000 Doge Pietro Orseolo subjugated the islands of Dalmatia and the Kvarner to safeguard the communications of the Venetian merchant fleet. During the three centuries' struggle that followed between Croatia and Venice, Rab passed repeatedly from one side to the other. Like the other cities on the seaboard, it developed a complex system of self-government by a bishop and a city captain, called a prior and later knez (prince). Throughout this period the city's autonomy was recognised by its overlords and Rab prospered. But in 1409, when King Ladislaus of Naples sold Zadar and Dalmatia to Venice, Rab quickly followed. Power remained nominally in the hands of the nobles, but Venice exercised effective control. In the 15C the island population was decimated by plague and has never since recovered its numbers. Rab passed to Austria (1797) and in 1805 to Napoleon's France. From 1815 to 1918 it was again administered by Austria and then joined to Yugoslavia. During the Second World War Italy and Germany occupied the island, which was liberated in April 1945 by the Ninth Division of Tito's partisan army. Rab had begun to develop tourist facilities before 1900 and is now one of the best organised and prosperous of the Adriatic islands, with a growing population.

Rab was the birthplace of the Jesuit theologian and natural scientist, Mark Antun Dominis (Marcantonio De Dominis, 1560–1624), bishop of Senj, archbishop of Split and later, during his apostacy, dean of Windsor. His pioneer work on the spectrum was acknowledged by Newton, and he was the first to prove the influence of the moon on tides. Also born in Rab were Ivan Krstitelj Rabljanin (Giovanni Battista di Arbe) the 16C bell-founder, and the painters Stjepan Crnota (Stefano Cernotto, 16C), a pupil of Titian, and Matej Pončun (Matteo Ponzoni, 17C), a follower of Palma the Younger.

Rab, the sole town (800 inhab.) on the island, perched on a sloping peninsula at the mouth of the deeply indented Bay of Sv. Fumija with four graceful belfries pointing slender fingers to the sky, is the most beautiful town of the Kvarner, especially striking from the SW seaward approach. In spite of its great popularity with holidaymakers it retains an unspoiled medieval atmosphere of great authenticity and charm. At the S end of the peninsula lies the oldest quarter, called *Kaldanac*, with crooked, narrow streets winding uphill to the cathe-

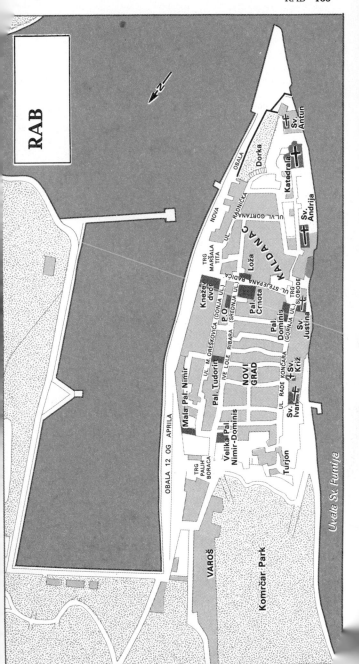

RAB

Sv. Antun

Dorka

Katedrala

Sv. Andrija

OBALA

NOVA

RADNIČKA

UL.VL.GORTANAA

KALDANAC

TRG MARŠALA TITA

UL. STJEPANA BADICA

Loža

Pal. Crnota

Knežev Dvor (DONJA UL.)

P.O.

SREDNJA UL.

Pal. Dominis

UL. RADE KONČARA

Sv. Slobode TRG

Sv. Justina

Mala Pal. Nimir

UL. M. OREŠKOVIĆA

IVE LOLE RIBARA

Pal. Tudorin

GORNJA UL.

NOVI GRAD

Sv. Ivan

Sv. Križ

Velika Pal. Nimir-Dominis

Turjon

OBALA 12 OG APRILA

TRG PALIH BORACA

VAROŠ

Komrčar Park

Uvala Sv. Fumija

dral. To the N lies *Novi grad* (the 'New Town'), dating mainly from the 14–17C and still the social centre; and beyond this again the *Varoš*, the newest section where most of the hotels are located.

Post Office: Trg M. Tita.

Information: Tourist biro, 1 Trg M. Tita, tel. 871123.

Opening from the NOVA OBALA (or NOVA RIVA), the popular TRG MARŠALA TITA, gay with café tables, is a favourite vantage-point opposite the entrance to the inner harbour. On the N side is the **Knežev dvor** (Prince's Palace), former residence of the Rab town governors, now the offices of the tourist bureau. The handsome rectangular Romanesque tower (13C) that forms its main part, preserves its original entrance and a window on the second floor. A two-light window on the first floor and two windows above present contrasting additions in Renaissance and Venetian Gothic styles, and the W side has Renaissance details.

The quay, known from here on as OBALA 12 OGA APRILA, continues to TRG PALIH BORACA and the hotel quarter of Rab. At right angles to it UL. STJEPANA RADIĆA mounting from Trg Maršala Tita to Trg slobode (comp. below), divides the Kaldanac from the Novi grad.

Behind Knežev dvor is UL. MARKA OREŠKOVIĆA or DONJA UL. (Lower Street), the lowest and quietest of three that run the length of the Novi grad. Turn N and come immediately to the Galzigna-Marčić mansion, the Renaissance doorway of which bears the family motto. Along the street numerous architectural details (doorways, windows, coats of arms) may be noted. At the far end on the right the ornate late-Venetian Gothic doorway of the *Mala Palača Nimir*, with the Nimir arms in the tympanum and a good Renaissance balustrade above, admits to an arcaded courtyard containing architectural fragments. The remainder of the mansion has been demolished and the basement houses a restaurant. The adjoining garden, partially enclosed by remnants of the town walls, now forms part of a restaurant.

The wide TRG PALIH BORACA, open to the harbour on the E, marks the boundary between the Novi grad and the Varoš. On the N side are hotels; on the rising W side paths and steps lead into the pleasant town park of Komrčar (comp. below) from the small informal market (fruit and vegetables; occasionally lace and other handicrafts). A bronze war memorial, by Vinko Matković, marks the site of the land gate to the town. Most of the fortifications have been destroyed, but steps behind the market lead up to *Turjon*, a 14C bastion, now occupied as a dwelling.

Leaving the square again on the S side follow UL. IVE LOLE RIBARA or SREDNJA UL. (Middle Street), the busy main shopping street of the town. Immediately on our right is the imposing Renaissance *Velika Palača Nimir-Dominis* (mainly 15C) with well-proportioned windows (one Gothic) and doorway, bearing on the lintel and upper façade respectively coats of arms of the Dominis and Nimir families. On the N wall, facing the square, is a Roman head of Jupiter. This palace, the largest in Rab, was the birthplace of Marcantonio De Dominis (comp. above). It now has the town pharmacy on the ground floor. UL. IVE LOLE RIBARA, with numerous souvenir shops, is crowded morning and evening; attractive narrow residential streets rise (right) in steps to UL. RADE KONČARA, from which water descends in cascades after rain. Halfway along, two vaulted houses span the street on broad arches, the first bearing the Benedetti arms. Beyond them (left) the *Palača Tudorin* has a handsome Renaissance window on the N side with ion-head corbels supporting the sill. The intersection with UL. STJEPANA RADIĆA just above Trg Maršala Tita, marks the centre of Rab. On the corner stands the Renaissance *Palača Crnota* (Cernotta) with a richly ornamented main door in Ul. Stjepana Radića. The finely executed arms in the tympanum are an outstanding example of the transition Gothic-Renaissance style of the E Adriatic. On the other side of Ul. Stjepana Radića the *Palača Kašić* (Cassio), for a time the residence of Rab's bishops, has a simpler doorway in similar style. Adjacent, on the corner of the main street is the *Loža* (1509), a plain Renaissance structure with a wooden roof supported on six columns. The 14C *Clock Tower* facing the Loggia was renovated in 1831.

Here the main street changes its name to RADNIČKI PRELAZ as it enters Kaldanac. Passing (right) the tiny Gothic church of Sv. Nikola, now abandoned, the street narrows and darkens beneath vaulted houses on single arches before joining UL. VLADIMIRA GORTANA. Many of the ruined houses in this quarter were built before the terrible plague of the mid-15C and have only recently been reoccupied. At its lower end Ul. Vladimira Gortana joins RADNIČKA UL., which runs from Trg Maršala Tita past the Renaissance courthouse to *Dorka* a small park enclosed in a section of town wall. Turn uphill, passing the extensive ruins of the *Episcopal Palace* (since 1828 when the bishopric was merged with Krk, the residence of the parish priest). Steps mount to the ridge on which stand the churches of Rab.

The former **Cathedral of Sveta Marija Velika*, consecrated in 1177, is an excellent example of a small Romanesque basilica. The W front (well seen from the campanile), built of local stone and breccia in alternate courses of pink and white, is decorated at the base with two stories of blind arcading. The marble Renaissance doorway, pierced in 1490, has a simple Pietà by Petar Trogiranin (1514) in the tympanum. In the dignified Interior the nave arcades are borne on columns with undistinguished Byzantine capitals. The spacious choir raised on six steps has sumptuous Gothic **Stalls* (1445) carved in walnut; on the front ends the angel of the Annunciation (left), with the arms of the Nimir family, and the figure of the Virgin Mary (right), with the Crnota arms. Further steps lead to the sanctuary. The high altar has a 17C baroque frontal of inlaid marble depicting St. Christopher (patron saint of Rab). The remarkable *Ciborium*, hexagonal in plan, rests on six marble columns with Byzantine capitals. The three sides of the canopy towards the front are uninteresting Renaissance work, but the three at the rear are outstanding examples of early Croatian decorative carving probably 9C or 10C from an earlier church. The low pyramid roof has an elaborately carved finial.

In the N AISLE, the apsidal chapel of *Sv. Križ* has a baroque crucifix on the altar and late Gothic altar rails attributed to Andrija Aleši of Albania. At the square E end of the S AISLE the altar of Gospa žalostna (Our Lady of Sorrows), is surmounted by a Madonna showing Byzantine influence (Italo-Cretan; 15C?). A gravestone built into the wall (right) bears a carved head of Bp Ivan Skafa of Rab by Aleši (1456). The altar rails bearing the Skafa arms are also attributed to him. In the chapel of the *Sv. Sakrament*, a Byzantine marble icon (13C) shows Christ enthroned. The simple Gothic chapel of *Sv. Petar*, contains a hexagonal font (1497) by Petar Trogiranin and more altar rails attributed to Aleši. Two pilasters inside the W door, showing angels with candelabra are also Aleši's work. These separated fragments were probably once part of a destroyed Skafa chapel. The stucco work on the ceilings was recently removed in order to reveal the open Gothic roof.

The magnificent *Bell Tower, standing apart from the cathedral, is a masterpiece of 12–13C Romanesque architecture that may challenge comparison with any of its kind elsewhere. T.G. Jackson, the English architect, took this tower as his model when completing the cathedral belfry at Zadar. The tower rises c 28m from a base 6m square. An effect of increasing lightness is obtained by the disposition of the windows. The ground story is pierced by a single light in each face, above which in succession are two single lights, two double lights, a triple light, and at the top a four-light aperture. The additional tracery is given correspondingly richer decorative ornament. The top two stories are finished with a delicate cornice of acanthus leaves and the tower is surmounted by a Romanesque balustrade and a pyramidal spire (rebuilt in 1495). The summit (closed to visitors 1988) affords magnificent views.

In the *Cathedral Museum* (in the Bishop's Palace, 6 Ulice gortana) is preserved a *Reliquary of silver parcel-gilt with a gabled lid containing the head of St. Christopher, by which in the 11C Rab was miraculously saved from a besieging army of Sicilian Normans. The casket, attributed to the 12C, is of very fine workmanship; the skull inside wears a crown said to have been the gift of Queen Elisabeth the Younger of Hungary. Here also are four copper plates bearing champlevé enamels of Saints, executed probably in Limoges in the 12–13C, perhaps part of another reliquary; and a polyptych by the school of Paolo Veneziano, formerly in the cathedral.

Immediately behind the cathedral, above the tip of the promontory, is the nunnery of *Sv. Antun*, founded in 1493. Except for the original choir the present church is of the 16C with rustic baroque altars and a picture showing Rab in earlier times. There is a bas-relief of St. Anthony over the entrance to the nunnery.

UL. RADE KONČARA or GORNJA UL. (Upper Street) leads back along the ridge. Almost immediately you come on the left to the Benedictine nunnery and church of SV. ANDRIJA, entered through a small courtyard paved with carved gravestones. The nunnery was founded in the 11C and an aisled basilica was probably erected a century later, though it received its present Renaissance form mainly in the 15C. The polyptych in the N aisle is a poor copy of a Vivarini, the original of which has been removed to Boston. Adjoining is a Venetian ambry in Florid Gothic. The belfry is the oldest of Rab's celebrated towers, a smallish Romanesque structure erected in 1181. In the small TRG SLOBODE a tree planted in 1921 commemorates the Treaty of Rapallo. The 16C baroque church of *Sv. Justina* is adjoined by Rab's third bell tower. The Death of St. Joseph, inside, long attributed to Titian, is a good example of 17C Venetian painting. The *Palača Dominis*, opposite, with beautiful Gothic windows, bears the arms of the Dominis and Nimir families.

The W side of the square commands excellent views over the Frkanj peninsula and the bay of Sv. Fumija; steps descend to a path along the shore that leads to the town beach.

The street narrows between picturesque old houses. The small 16C baroque church of *Sv. Križ* on the left is in a poor state of repair but has a stuccoed ceiling by the Sommazzi (1798). Adjoining in a pleasant garden are the foundations of the Romanesque church of *Sv. Ivan*. Its simple Romanesque bell tower still stands. At the town hall, the street divides. To the right a slope and steps descend to Trg palih boraca (see above); other steps mount to the ruins of the former castle (and the restored church of St. Christopher within the walls), where one of the towers offers an excellent view of the bay. On the far side a gate leads into the beautiful **Komrčar park** laid out with pleasant walks. A path runs along the ridge to *Sv. Franjo* (1491), once the church of a vanished Franciscan monastery and now the chapel of the town cemetery, with a decorated façade and emblazoned memorials.

Rab, the old town

EXCURSION FROM RAB

A pleasant walk may be taken through Komrčar Park and past the town beach to the head of the Bay of Sv. Fumija (also reached by boat). Here, on the shore, stands the Franciscan monastery of **Sv. Fumija** (Euphemia), built in 1446 by Juraj Dimitrov of Zadar, that gave the bay its name. In the pretty cloister, surmounted on two sides by an upper story, are displayed a fine 15C Gothic sarcophagus, said to be of Manda Budrišić, a Bosnian noblewoman who founded the convent of Sv. Antun in Rab; the memorial slab of Petar Car (de Zara), founder of Sv. Fumija; and, among Roman and medieval fragments, a 7C crux gemmata. The simple Franciscan Gothic church of *Sv. Bernardin Sijenski* (St. Bernardin of Siena; 1456) was restyled in the baroque taste in the 16C, and the ceiling paintings were executed in 1669. There is a beautiful 13C Byzantine icon on the main altar flanked by two paintings of saints (15C). One of the altar rails incorporates a stone slab decorated with pre-Romanesque knotwork carving. In the chapel of Sv. Križ (Gothic windows from the original nave), S of the choir, is a late Gothic Crucifixion (wood; 15C); the tasteless chapel opposite is relieved by a polyptych of the Madonna and Saints by Ant. and Bart. Vivarini (1458). The *Museum*, in the convent, contains 14–15C illuminated codices and two dozen incunabula. Also exhibited are a small Roman statue of Diana and a Gothic figure of St. Francis in wood.

Beyond the monastery a pleasant footpath through the shallow valley of Kamporska draga leads in c 20 minutes to the *Slovensko groblje* (Slavonic Cemetery), a memorial to 5000 victims of an Italian concentration camp established here in 1942. The project was designed by Edo Ravnikar (1955) and the central mosaic is by Marijan

Pregelj. To the W extend the cool, shady *Dundo Woods*, of Italian oak, cypress and pine with a scattering of cork oaks. Footpaths serve the small bays along the W shore of Kalifront peninsula. Due W, a further 20-minute walk brings you to the shallow, deeply indented Bay of Kampor with its broad almost deserted sandy beach.

TO SUPETARSKA DRAGA AND LOPAR. A good secondary road (local bus) winds round Rab harbour to *Mundanija* at the foot of Mt Kamenjak, whence it continues through the valley of Banjol.—8km. The former Benedictine monastery and church of **Sv. Petar** (200m right), founded in 1059, was confirmed in its possessions in 1071 by King Petar Krešimir of Croatia, but abandoned by the 16C. The conventual buildings form a residence for the parish priest. The church is a Romanesque basilica with three apses, although the purity of its design has been spoiled by heightening the aisles in 1761 and enlarging the windows. The handsome stone canopy over the W door rests on brackets carved with animal heads, but the tympanum is now empty. In the pleasant interior the five pairs of columns dividing the nave from the aisles exhibit five kinds of capitals representing variations on acanthus leaf ad other vegetation motifs. The Romanesque bell tower was truncated in 1906 because it was unsafe. The two bells date from 1299 and 1593.

1km farther is the upper part of *Supertarska draga*, with a view across the sandy bay of the lower village (cafè) by the water. The road then hugs the N shore of the bay before swinging right to wind over the barren Kamenjak plateau to (5km) **Lopar** (1000 inhab.), the second largest settlement on the island. It is connected with Jablanac, Misnjak, Senj and with Baška on Krk by ferries, May–Sept. Legend states that the stone carver, Marin Biza (St. Marinus), who with his workmen founded the Republic of San Marino, was born in Lopar. In the bay of *Crnika*, on the other side of the narrow isthmus joining Lopar Peninsula to the main island, is the so-called Rajska plaža (Paradise beach), a magnificent crescent of golden sand extending for nearly 2km. Elsewhere around the Lopar Peninsula there are similar but smaller beaches accessible only by boat.

Other excursions from Rab may be made by boat to numerous attractive bays on Kalifront; *Gavranišće*, with its naturist beach; *Matovica*; *Suha punta*; *Krištofor*; *Planka*; and *Sv. Mara*. The quiet village of *Barbat* lies in the opposite direction. Organised excursions are run to Lošinj by boat; to the Plitvice Lakes by bus and hydrofoil; to Jablanac, Zavratnica Bay, and *Lun*, a hamlet on the N shore of Pag which is traditionally administered by Rab. A walk to the summit of Mt Kamenjak takes c 2 hours from the town of Rab.

11 The Island of Pag

Approaches. BY LAND: A bridge 300m long connects the island to the mainland at *Posedarje*, on the Adriatic Highway (N2/E65).

BY SEA: Car ferries from *Karlobag* to *Pag* and from *Metajna* and *Jablanac*.

PAG (8500 inhab.), the third largest island of the Kvarner, consists of one long ridge extending for 59km which exceeds 10km in width only across parallel peninsular ridges. Its deeply indented coastline extends for 260km. Like most of the Kvarner Islands, Pag rises abrupt and barren on the mainland side, reaching 349m in Mt Sv. Vid in the centre, and is flatter and more fertile in the west. There are extensive olive groves on Lun Peninsula in the N and large quantities of white wine, called žutica, are produced in the district around the town of Pag. The two most famous products are a hard, piquant ewe's milk cheese, known simply as Paški sir, and hand-made lace (čipka), of great delicacy and beauty. Salt beds, in use since Roman times, were once in almost every bay; now they are concentrated in Solana Bay immediately to the S of Pag town. A good road runs the full length of the island, asphalted almost all the way. The tranquillity of the island, hitherto relatively untouched by tourism, is not likely long to survive the road link.

History. The chief Roman settlement of the island was *Cissa*, a fortified castrum on the site of present-day Caska. A Roman port was also founded at *Novalia* and among other settlements was *Pagus*, which subsequently gave the island its name. With the coming of the Croats (7C) Novalja became the new centre of the island, but in 1071 King Petar Krešimir divided the island administratively between Rab in the N and Nin in the S, and in the 12C the centre was moved to 'old' Pag, then located 2km S of present-day Pag. Dispute over control of the island between Rab and Nin, and later Rab and Zadar, was temporarily resolved by the intervention of Venice in 1192 and more satisfactorily in 1244, when Bela IV of Hungary and Croatia proclaimed Pag an autonomous city with privileges similar to the other ancient cities of the seaboard. This autonomy was short-lived, however, for Pag, Rab, and Zadar almost immediately passed under the sway of Venice and Pag was divided once more, a situation in which it remained, under Venice and Hungary-Croatia alternatively, for another 150 years. In 1393 Pag was sacked by an expedition from Zadar and although the city was awarded compensation by Sigismund in 1396, it was not until 1409, when Dalmatia passed to Venice, that Pag at last gained effective local autonomy free of Rab and Zadar. In 1443 'new' Pag was laid out and old Pag abandoned. In 1538 Lun, Novalja, and Caska were regained from Rab and thenceforward the island became a political and administrative entity under Venice. In 1602 the Uskoks here surprised the galley of Crist. Venieto, carrying off the admiral and his men to execution in Senj. After 1797, with a short Napoleonic interval, Pag passed to Austria for 120 years. The First World War was followed by three years of occupation by Italy, then under the Treaty of Rapallo, union with Yugoslavia. During the Second World War Pag was occupied first by Italy (1941–43) and then Germany.

From the early Middle Ages Pag has always had a pronounced Croatian character and like Krk has preserved a vigorous folklore. Bartul Kašić (1575–1650), author of the first Croatian grammar (Rome, 1604), was born on Pag.

The main settlement is **Pag**, a small town with 2400 inhab. lying at the SE end of the bay of the same name and at the neck of the inlet in which the famous saltpans are situated. Laid out in 1443 with a regular street plan, Pag is a rare and relatively pure example of early Renaissance town planning. Its inhabitants have a reputation for seriousness and hard work.

In 1443 the citizens of old Pag (Terravecchia) asked permission from Venice to reconstruct their capital on a better site. On 2 March Doge Francesco Foscari gave consent and on 18 May Count Pietro Failiero laid foundation stones of the walls and church. Juraj Dalmatinac may have been the overall planner but if his hand is possibly to be seen in some of the public buildings, most of the detail was left to his pupils with mediocre results.

Two straight main streets at right angles meet at NARODNI TRG, the spacious central square, dividing the town into four. The large parish church of **Uznesenje Marijino** (The Assumption), 1443–88, modelled to a large extent on its predecessor in Old Pag, presents a curious mixture of Gothic, Renaissance and even Romanesque elements. The plan is basilican but without apses, and the W front Romanesque in feeling. The W portal, Renaissance in style and embellished by egg and dart mouldings, is enclosed by an ogee arch. The high relief in the tympanum depicts the Virgin shielding the townspeople under her cloak and is an accurate portrayal of 15C local costume, particularly the women's headdresses. Above the W door a finely carved wheel-window is flanked by Gothic figures of Mary and the Archangel Gabriel (representing the Annunciation); beneath them are SS. Michael (left) and George (right). The last three are unfinished.

The tower was begun in 1562 but discontinued before the final story had been raised. The church is entered from Vela ul. by one of two Renaissance doors pierced in a wall decorated with blind arcading. The Renaissance arcades spring from capitals carved with ingenious variations of traditional acanthus leaf, scroll, and animal motifs. There are twin hexagonal pulpits. In the baroque stuccoed ceiling three medallions portray St. George and the Dragon, the Assumption, and the Martyrdom of St. Sebastian. Each of the aisles terminates in a simple Gothic chapel (Gothic Crucifixion in the S chapel).

The 15C **Kneževa palača** (Prince's Palace) has a fine side entrance (from VELA UL.) in Venetian Gothic. The carving on the lintel is worthy of attention and the tympanum carries the coat of arms of Toma Zorzi, prince in 1467. The well-head in the courtyard is also finely carved. Adjoining the Kneževa palača are fragments of a similar gateway of the unfinished *Biskupska palača* (Bishop's Palace). The palace was intended for Antun Palčić, Bishop of Osor, a native of Pag, who is known to have commissioned Juraj Dalmatinac for the work. The Prince's palace has also been attributed to him on stylistic grounds.

At the far end of Vela ul. can be seen remnants of the town walls and the small Renaissance church of *Sv. Juraj*. In ŠTROSMAJEROVA UL. the cruciform 15C church of *Sv. Margarita*, with a triple bellcot, adjoins the nunnery. In the treasury are a 14C silver cross, a silver-gilt reliquary and a silver hand reliquary of St. Margaret fashioned in florid Gothic. Round the corner, in SAMOSTANSKA UL., a pleasant doorway bears another ornate Zorzi coat of arms (1468).

About 3km S of Pag on the W side of the salt lagoon are the ruins of **Old Pag**, known as the *Stari Grad*. The Romanesque-Gothic church of *Uznesenje Marijino* (completed 1392), whose W front was the model for the later church in new Pag, is fairly well preserved. In the tympanum of the Gothic doorway is an equivalent figure of Mary protecting the citizens of Pag. Higher up there is a similar wheel-window and statues; here, however, two angels flank the window, with Sts. Peter, George, and Martin below. The altar is 17C baroque. Nearby are the cloister of the former *Franciscan Monastery* (founded 1589), and a ruined bastion.

The road N from Pag leads over the bridge, passing numerous salt warehouses (some from Venetian times) and the town beach, and follows the shore of **Pag Bay**. To the left the abrupt ridge rises to 349m in Sv. Vid and a narrow strip of fertile fields divides the road from the landlocked bay. After 15km the road swings away from the bay on to the flattening ridge, affording views towards Cres and Lošinj.

8km **Novalja** is a sprawling village with a sandy beach. Its early history as the port (navalia) for the Roman town of Cissa is obvious from scattered fragments of Roman masonry in the cemetery; remains of a large basilica have been discovered (not yet excavated). Parts of a Roman wall have been built into the Palčić Mansion in the main square and an imperial aqueduct, known locally as the *Talijanova buža*, runs for part of the way between Novalja and Stara Novalja to the north. On *Rt Gaj*, NW of the village, a mosaic floor and walls belong to a 5C basilica.

In nearby *Caska* (3km) are the remains of an aqueduct, a Roman acropolis, and the ruined medieval church of Sv. Juraj, but much of the former Roman town of *Cissa* now lies underwater. The round tower at the water's edge is a modern structure used for tunny spotting.

N of Novalja, *Stara Novalja* stands on the small bay of the same name. *Lun*, remote at the far end of a narrow tongue of rock (20km), is more usually visited as an excursion from Rab.

A major road runs S past the Pag salt flats, continuing to (23km) *Rt Fortica* and the bridge that links Pag to the mainland.—At (7km) *Gorica*, a rough gravel road diverges (right) to *Povljana* (7km more), with a shingle beach. Just S of the village beside the sea stands the small pre-Romanesque church of *Sv. Nikola* (9–11C).

The island of *Vir* (600 inhab.) just SW of Povljana can be reached by road from Zadar or from ports between Povljana and Rijeka. The Romanesque church of Sv. Ivan (12–13C) stands in the graveyard and a ruined 17C Venetian fortress on the shore nearby.
  The island of *Maun* to the NW is inhabited only seasonally by Pag shepherds pasturing their sheep.

12 The Island of Cres

Approaches. BY SEA: Car ferries from *Rijeka* and *Brestova* to *Porozine*, on the N shore of the island, and from *Pula* and *Zadar* to *Mali Lošinj*. Air services to *Mali Lošinj* airport from *Zagreb*.

CRES, although sparsely populated (4000 inhab.), is the second largest island (404km^2) in the Adriatic, exceeded in size only by neighbouring Krk. It is 67km long, and together with Lošinj, to which (across an artificial strait) it is joined by a bridge, forms the beginning of the outer chain of islands that end in the Kornat archipelago. The E side consists mainly of bare rock exposed to the fury of the N wind (bura) and descending steeply to the sea, and the highest point of the generally mountainous island is Gorice (648m) in the N between the town of Cres and Porozine. All the settlements are on the W side where the land slopes gently to the sea and the climate is milder, though even here soil is sparse and the ground infertile. The main crops are olives, vegetables, and grapes, though most of the vineyards were wiped out by phylloxera at the turn of the century. Fishing plays an important part in the island economy, the catch being canned at Cres and Martinšćica. Although there are no springs or rivers on the island, Vransko jezero (Lake Vrana) is the largest freshwater lake in the Adriatic and supplies both Cres and the island of Lošinj.

History. Extensive remains show that Cres has been occupied since Neolithic times. With Lošinj, it bore the Greek name of *Apsyrtides*, said to preserve the memory of Absyrtus, brother of Medea, who was murdered during the flight of the Argonauts and his dismembered body flung into the sea. In Classical times two settlements are mentioned, *Crpesa* (now Cres) and *Apsoros* (Osor), the larger of the two. Although sacked by Attila in the 5C and by the Saracens under Sahib Kalfun in 841, Apsoros, later *Ossero*, continued to grow in size and importance, having meanwhile under Byzantium become a bishopric before 530. In 924 the island became part of the Croatian kingdom under Tomislav but between 998 and 1018 the two principal cities, constantly troubled by piratical raids, sought the protection of Venice, under whose rule they remained until 1358. For much of this time Ossero was ruled by hereditary counts, notably the Morosini (1180–1304), instead of the more usual elective ones. For half a century Cres again belonged to Hungary-Croatia, but with the sale of Dalmatia (1409) returned to Venice until the republic's fall in 1797.
  Osor meanwhile began to decline. Its prosperity had largely depended on command of the artificial strait between Cres and Lošinj, the main route for shipping from the north Adriatic until the 15C. With its unhealthy climate, which led to the spread of malaria and the plague, Osor could not survive the growing preference for open-sea sailing and was eclipsed. In 1459 the centre of Venetian rule was moved to Cres which grew rapidly, while Osor, repeatedly pillaged by the Uskoks in the 16C and 17C and also by Genoa, sank to a village. In 1797 the island passed to Austria, then briefly to France (1805–14) and back to Austria (the bishopric was suppressed in 1818) until the end of the First World War.

Under the Treaty of Rapallo (1921) Cres was awarded to Italy until the Second World War. It was the scene of fierce fighting because of its strategic importance and was attacked by British naval units in September 1944. In 1945 it was joined to Yugoslavia for the first time.

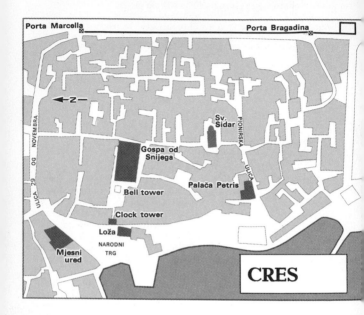

Cres, the main settlement on the island, is a delightful small fishing town (1850 inhab.) not much visited by foreigners. Situated on a magnificent natural harbour on the W side of the island, it packs a deceptively large number of streets into a small area; and although built by Venice, its main interest lies less in monumental or patrician architecture than in domestic dwellings with details typical of the Kvarner. Almost all the inhabitants are bilingual in Croatian and Italian, in which the town is called *Cherso*.

Post Office: on the waterfront.

Information: *Turističko društvo*, 11 Dure Salaja, tel. 820833.

NARODNI TRG opens on the picturesque double harbour with its numerous fishing boats. Here a large *Loža* (Loggia; 15–16C), is used as a market, and a 16C *Clock Tower* surmounts the main gate into the old town. UL. 29 OG. NOVEMBRA, the main street, curves N and E past the *Mjesni ured* or Town Hall, which incorporates a Venetian Gothic window from its predecessor on the site. The ground floor is arranged as a historical collection, with inscriptions, medieval wooden figures of SS. Jerome and Isidore, and coins. The street ends at the *Porta Marcella*, a fine Renaissance gateway, decorated with the coats of arms of Doge Pasquale Cicogna (1585–95) and the Marcello family and a defaced lion of St. Mark. A broad avenue follows a long section of the town *Walls*, erected by the Venetians between 1509 and 1610, to the *Porta Bragadina*, a similar gate also with a lion of St. Mark.

You may complete the circuit of the old town, rejoining the quay near the habour mouth. A hotel occupies the former Venetian *Fontico* (15C) or grain warehouse. The handsome 15C *Palača Petris* on the corner of PIONIRSKA UL., houses the *Creski Muzej*, with archaeological and ethnographic collections. Farther along Pionirska ul., which leads into the oldest quarter of the town, are two other Venetian Gothic mansions. A narrow street leads left to the church of *Sv. Sidar* (St. Isidore), with a Gothic W front and a Romanesque apse decorated with blind arcading. Inside are a polyptych and a wooden effigy of St. Isidore (both 15C).

About 50m to the N stands **Sv. Majka Božja Sniježna** (Mary of the Snows) another 15C church with a detached bell tower that is prominent from the harbour. The handsome Renaissance West Doorway has a good Madonna in the tympanum with an Annunication above. In the plain interior are a 15C Gothic Pietà in wood and a picture of Cres in the 17C. In the parish offices behind the church (opened on request) are a polyptych by Alvise Vivarini (1486?) showing St. Sebastian with Saints, a wooden Renaissance Crucifixion, Venetian pictures of the 16–18C, reliquaries and a baroque chalice (1617).

Just S of the town is a 14–15C **Franciscan Monastery** with two cloisters; the smaller one, with gothic arcades, is particularly attractive. The *Church*, in essence Franciscan Gothic, has a Renaissance W doorway. Behind the high altar are good Gothic stalls (15C). Entered through a Renaissance arcade from the S side of the choir is a large rib-vaulted chapel. A Gothic wooden Crucifixion adorns its altar, and a slab bearing an effigy of Antun Marcello, a 16C bishop of Novigrad, is built into the wall behind. The *Library* (open to men only), in addition to 15 incunabula and manuscripts from the 14–18C, possesses a Madonna in low relief by Andrea da Murano (1470?). The Benedictine nunnery farther along the shore is not open to visitors.

Excursions by boat from Cres may be made to the neighbouring coast of Istria (see Rte 6) and to Martinšćica and Osor down the W coast (see below). Across Valun Bay (c 1 hour by boat) is *Valun* (Inns) a tiny hamlet favoured with good shingle beaches. The Valunska ploča (Valun Tablet), built into the sacristy wall of the parish church, bears an 11C inscription in Glagolitic and Carolingian Latin. The white wine from Lubenice, close by, is the best known of Cres wines.

A recently paved road connects Cres with (24km) *Porozina* in the N, and car ferries to Brestova and Rijeka.

TO OSOR, 33km. The road runs S with good retrospective views.—8km. Turning right for Valun (see above).—7km *Vrana* affords views (right) to *Vransko jezero* (Lake Vrana), 5.5km^2 in area and 84m deep. The lake offers excellent freshwater fishing (pike, eels, and carp).

2km *Martinšćica*, a scattered little village with excellent shingle beaches, lies 6km to the W. The Franciscan Monastery, frequently rebuilt, was founded in the 15C. On the high altar is a painting of St. Jerome by Baldassare d'Anna (1636) and in the refectory six paintings representing the twelve apostles (17C Venetian school). The adjoining 17C Sforza Palace (rebuilt as dwellings) retains only a well-head with the Sforza arms.

16km **Osor**, once a Roman city of 20,000 inhabitants, now a sleepy village with less than 100, commands the narrow strait, Cavanella, that divides Cres from Lošinj. In the main square is the early Renaissance *Cathedral* (1465–98), begun by Bp Antun Palčić, with a handsome Lombardesque W front. The W door closely resembles that at Cres. The interior suffered from bombardment by British naval units. On the high altar is a Madonna enthroned with Sts Gaudentius and Nicholas (School of Palma the Younger); Gaudentius (died 1044) was bishop of Ossero. The bell tower, built in 1675 by the mason Gallo of Krk, offers éxcellent views of the islands of Krk and Lošinj. The *Museum* occupying the former Venetian town hall contains fragments of masonry, Roman busts, burial urns and pottery; also Illyrian jewellery, pottery, and weapons, all excavated locally. In the former *Bishop's Palace* opposite (coat of arms on wall) are the parish offices where the cathedral treasure (seen on request) includes vestments, plate and 15C Gothic sculpture. In the courtyard is a well-head with pre-Romanesque ornamentation.

The 15C Gothic church of *Sv. Gaudencije* has traces of frescoes in the choir and a curious 15C statue of its patron bishop behind the high altar. Outside the city gate, with a lion of St. Mark built into the wall, the small Gothic church of *Sv. Marija* (1414) has a Romanesque apse, beside which foundations were exposed in 1950–54, of a 6C double basilica with baptistery, thought to be Osor's first cathedral (fragmentary mosaics). Nearby a larger Roman mosaic floor has been covered again. Beyond the church the cove of *Vijar* marks the outer limits of Apsoros. Traces of the Roman walls can be seen, but little else remains above ground of the city. Sir Richard Burton dug here in 1877 while British Consul in Trieste. Just beyond Vijar is Osor's harbour with a pleasant promenade, and, in the pine wood beyond, an autocamp. On the other side of the village stands the ruined Benedictine monastery of Sv. Petar (11C).

From Osor a narrow gravel road runs SE to Punta Križa at the S end of the island.

13 The Island of Lošinj

Approaches. BY LAND: Lošinj is connected to Cres by a bridge over the narrow Osorski Zaljev.

BY SEA: Car ferries from *Rijeka* and *Brestova* to *Porozine*; from *Pula*, *Zadar*, 6Venice, and *Rimini* to *Mali Lošinj*; hydrofoil in summer from *Rijeka* to *Mali Lošinj*.

Air service to *Mali Lošinj* from Zagreb.

Lošinj (8500 inhab.), the smallest of the principal islands of the Kvarner, is 30km long. Two steep and rocky ends are joined by the long narrow isthmus of Privlaka, which also encloses the deeply indented bay of Mali Lošinj. In the N the precipitous ridge of Osoršćica, rising to a height of 589m at Televrina peak, is separated from Cres only by a narrow artificial canal. In the W the Kurila peninsula is continued, geologically, in the islands of Vele- and Male-Srakane and Unije. In the S, Grgošćak peak (243m) marks the highest point, and Lošinj's rocky spine finds its continuation in a cluster of small islands at its southern tip, of which Ilovik is the most prominent. Susak, to the W, is geographically associated with Lošinj, but in geological terms is something of a curiosity (see below). Although poor for crops, Lošinj is noted for the luxuriance of its vegetation and the pine woods on its western shore. Fishing and ship-building continue to occupy the islanders, and a merchant shipping line is based at Lošinj.

History. Lošinj was known in classical times as one of the components of the Apsyrtides and until relatively recently had no history separate from that of Cres and Osor. The first record of its name (*Lussin*) is in 1384. With the decline of Osor in the 15C Lošinj became more independent, but did not develop its own trade links until the 17C. In the 18C Lošinj turned decisively to the sea for its living and by the end of the century, when Austria displaced Venice as master, had over

100 ships, a shipyard and a nautical school. Napoleon's continental blockade and British reprisals harmed the industry but its fortunes were restored under Austria during the Russo-Turkish war of 1828 and the Crimean War, when numerous ships were chartered by Russia and later by Britain and France. Lošinj's apogee came in the 1870s when its fleet of 150 ships ranged the Mediterranean, and six shipyards employed over 600 men. The change from wood and sail to steel and steam was successfully made and Lošinj was home port for many large ships until the First World War. With the rise of Trieste and Rijeka its shipping industry declined. Chosen by leading Austrian physicians in 1886 for its dust-free air and even humidity, by the end of the century Lošinj was second only to Opatija as a health and holiday resort. Between the wars, under Italy, its development was retarded, but since 1945, as part of Yugoslavia, Lošinj has regained its place as one of the leading holiday islands of the northern Adriatic.

Mali Lošinj, long known as *Lussinpiccolo* but despite its name the principal town (6000 inhab.), rises in a natural amphitheatre at the head of its beautiful bay. Owing to its early rise as a tourist resort, it resembles Opatija rather than the other island towns in the E Adriatic, having a strong Austrian flavour mingled with its Mediterranean elements.

Post Office: Obala Maršala Tita.

Information: *Tourist biro*, 7 Obala Maršala Tita, tel. 861547.

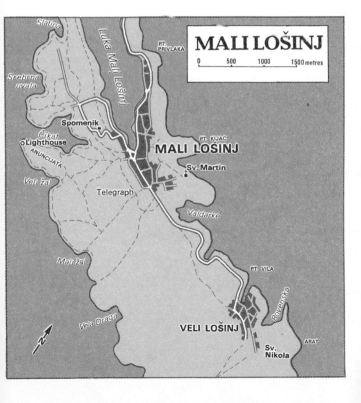

The deep basin of the excellent harbour is lined by two pleasant broad promenades, OBALA MARŠALA TITA and OBALA JUGOSLAVENSKE NARODNE ARMIJE, converging in TRG MOŠE PIJADE, the main square. The memorial to the national liberation struggle on the front is by Dušan Džamonja (1956). Beyond the parish church, on the top of the hill, stand extensive ruins of a 15C Venetian fortress known locally as the *Kaštel* or Fortizza (views over Lošinj, Cres, and the Kvarner Bay).

A winding road and numerous paths lead through pleasant pine woods to the attractive bay of *Čikat*, the main recreation area and the peninsula of Annuncijata, with many good walks through the woods or along the indented shore.

A road winds over the hill to the sister community, reached alternatively on foot in 45 minutes by a pleasant shaded path along the shore.

Veli Lošinj, once the larger of the two settlements, as its name indicates (comp. *Lussingrande* in Ital.), is now a quiet village (1000 inhab.) situated picturesquely on an almost landlocked little harbour. Just behind the harbour, the so-called *Uskok Tower* (1455) was built with forked battlements and machicolations by the Venetians against piratical Uskok depredations. On the other side of the harbour the large parish church of *Sv. Antun* (1774) contains a Madonna with Saints by Bartolomeo Vivarini (1475), in poor condition and badly placed. On the adjoining altar is a baroque Madonna and Child in marble (17C). The floor is paved with memorial slabs of local sea captains from the 17C to the present day. In the sacristy are a St. Francis by Bernardo Strozzi and a St. Gregory by Francesco del Cossa.

Beside the church a seaside walk leads round to the tiny fishing hamlet of *Rovenska*, the oldest settlement at this end of the island with a picturesque harbour. On the hill above it, reached in about 30 minutes is the part-Gothic church of *Sv. Nikola*, a 15C foundation with 18C votive pictures showing local people in the folk costume of the period. In *Sv. Marija*, on the hill opposite, are two paintings by Francesco Fontebasso (18C). Above the church the former villa (1885) of an Austrian archduke has become a hospital for allergies, for the treatment of which Lošinj's climate is particularly suitable. At Rovenska and in the town there are similar hospitals for children. The former garden of the villa, planted with many Mediterranean species, is now a public park.

From Mali Lošinj, Obala Maršala Tita continues N as a country road along the narrow isthmus separating Mali Lošinj Bay from Lošinjski Kanal to serve the N part of the island.

14km *Sv. Jakov* has two parish churches, of which the later (16C) contains a Gothic Crucifixion and a 16C triptych.

2km **Nerezine** stands on the site of the oldest settlement on the island. The Franciscan monastery (1509–15) has a pleasant cloister and Renaissance bell tower (1590) and its church (choir added in the 19C) contains a large St. Francis with Saints by Girolamo da Santa Croce (16C), and a 15C Venetian Madonna. Just outside the village is the 16C fortified tower of the Draža (de Drusa) family, who endowed the monastery. From Nerezine, *Televrina* (588m), the highest point on the island, can be reached on foot in about 1½ hours.—4km *Osor* (comp. Rte 12) lies across the swing bridge that connects Lošinj with the island of Cres.

The most interesting of the smaller islands encircling Lošinj is **Susak** (200 inhab.). Alone of the Adriatic islands, it is composed entirely of clay and sand, not rock. It lies 10km W and is reached by boat from Mali Lošinj. Susak is intensively cultivated with terraced vineyards producing good red wine (pleskunac). Sardine is fished in quantity. The isolation of the inhabitants has produced a distinct local dialect and traditional customs, seen to best effect at weddings, vintage, and carnival time. The folk costumes of the women are characterised by brightly coloured tights, and short flared skirts. An 11C cross from a vanished Benedictine monastery adorns the parish church; inside there is a 12C Romanesque Crucifixion.

To the S of Lošinj is *Ilovik* where the fishing village (350 inhab.) is reached from Veli Lošinj. On the adjoining islet of *Sv. Petar*, which protects the harbour, are the remains of Roman summer villas, and the ruins of an 11C Benedictine monastery enclose a cemetery. A ruined Venetian tower (1597) recalls the depredations of the Uskoks. *Unije* (300 inhab.), largest of the lesser islands, off Kurila peninsula to the W of Lošinj, has boat connections with Osor and Mali Lošinj. The village on the W side of the island has an inn and seasonal restaurants.

14 Zadar and its Environs

A. Zadar

ZADAR, the largest and most important town (80,000 inhab.) of northern Dalmatia, stands on a narrow peninsula at the western edge of the Ravni Kotari, a broad flat plain unique on the E Adriatic seaboard. For centuries the principal town of Dalmatia, Zadar was displaced at the turn of the present century by Split and lost further ground by becoming a remote outpost of Italy between the two world wars. Though the town suffered heavily from allied bombing, many of its more precious monuments were unharmed, and rebuilding has been accomplished with taste.

Post Office: Poljana V. Gortana.

Information: *Turističko Informativni Centar*, Omladinska, tel. 22146.

Airport: 6km E. *JAT*, 7 Ulica Natka Nodila, tel. 22385.

Sea Connections: Car ferries for *Preko* on the island of Ugljan; and for Trieste, Rimini, and Ancona in Italy, and N to Rijeka and S to Dubrovnik and Greece.

Buses to all parts of the coast and to the main towns inland.

History. *Zadar* entered recorded history in the 4C BC as *Idassa*, when Greeks from Pharos (present-day Hvar), according to a contemporary inscription, repelled invaders there. From the 9C BC, however, Zadar had been a stronghold of the Illyrian tribe of the Liburnians who, sometime around the 1C BC, threw in their lot with the Romans. In 69 BC Roman *Jadera* became a municipium and eleven years later received a Roman colony. With the fall of the Western Roman Empire the city passed to Byzantium and in 752 became the chief town of the theme of Dalmatia and seat of the Byzantine duke. Byzantine sovereignty, although only nominal in later centuries, continued until 1105. Constantine Porphyrogenitus listed the city under the name of *Diadora*. Zadar began paying tribute to the Franks in 803, but returned to Byzantium as a result of the treaty of Aachen in 810. Later in the 9C and throughout the 10C the city was forced to pay tribute to the Croats. As the most important and populous city of Dalmatia, Zadar became the chief object of the struggle between Venice and first Croatia and then the dual kingdom of Hungary-Croatia. Zadar (Italian *Zara*) first swore allegiance to Venice in 998, after the triumphant Dalmatian campaign of Doge Pietro Orseolo, but quickly reverted to Croatia again. In 1084 the Venetians tried to reassert their claim, but in 1105, Zadar acknowledged king Koloman of Hungary-Croatia. After his death in 1116 Venice prevailed until 1178, when it was again rejected by the Zadrians with the aid of Hungary-Croatia. The most significant battle occurred in 1202 when Venice tricked the members of the Fourth Crusade into storming Zadar as a precondition for assisting the Crusaders with transport to Constantinople. Despite several uprisings, Zadar remained in Venetian hands until 1358, when the Hungarians compelled Venice to renounce all claims to the city and to Dalmatia. Ironically, in 1409 both city and province were sold to Venice by King Ladislaus of Naples and ceased independent existence. As the administrative centre of Venetian Dalmatia, Zadar had an uneventful history, apart from occasional Turkish forays to her walls. Zadar passed to Austria in 1797 and in 1808 to Napoleonic France. In 1813 the port was blockaded by the British navy while the Austrians attacked and recaptured the city from the land, and it remained in Austrian hands until 1918. By the Treaty of Rapallo in 1921 Zadar was attached to Italy as a solitary enclave on the Dalmatian mainland. Later, as a centre of Italian operations during the Second World War, Zadar was heavily bombed by the British and American air forces. Liberated by Partisan units in October 1944, it has since been a part of Yugoslavia.

Among famous natives of Zadar are Juraj Matejev Dalmatinac (died 1473), also known as Georgius Dalmaticus and (erroneously) Giorgio Orsini, the Dalmatian sculptor and architect, and Andrea Meldola lo Schiavone (Andrija Medulić; 1500?–63), the painter. Two other prominent sculptor-architects, Lucijan (1420?–1502) and Franjo (1420?–79) Laurana (Luciano and Francesco de Laurana), although born outside the city, both received their early education at Zadar. Zadar was also the birthplace and home of a group of 16C writers, Petar Zoranić (born 1508), Brno Krnarutić (1515?–72), Juraj Baraković and Sime Budinić, who were among the founding fathers of Croatian literature.

The broad long RADNIČKA OBALA, where boats moor and buses terminate, is a convenient starting place for touring the town. At its NW end the Hotel Beograd adjoins a massive *Bastion* (late 16C), erected on the site of a medieval fortress when the fortifications were rebuilt by Venice. The interior (steps by hotel) is laid out as a small park (café in summer). Beyond the bastion the pre-Venetian town walls extend the length of Radnička obala, to the seaward end of which the former Venetian *Custom House* (rebuilt 1791) was moved in 1920.

The *Lančana vrata* (Chain Gate), from which in medieval times a massive chain barring the harbour was stretched across to the Porporella opposite, admits to the town. Immediately inside the gate on the left is the *Veliki Arsenal* (1752), with a double staircase rising to a classically simple façade. Opposite, a hexagonal corner tower and part of the outer wall of a 14C fortress (now a park; 18C Turkish cannon in the embrasures) were uncovered by bombing, which also created the large open square beyond. The three wells (well-heads 1761), which have given it the name of TRG TRI BUNARA, are fed by the former fortress moat, and the medieval house just behind the third well (popularly but erroneously called the *Mali Arsenal*) incorporates the former main entrance to the fortress. The façade bears four defaced coast of arms and a 15C lion of St. Mark. On the far side of the square, a small Rotunda (1582) alone remains of the church of *Gospa od Kastela*, or Gospa od zdravlja (Our Lady of Health). The wrought-iron gates bear the arms of Abp V. Zmajević (1718–45), who is buried here, and in the tasteful baroque interior is a Gothic ambry (1413).

Leaving the square by UL. BORISA KIDRIČA pass (right) the marine headquarters of Jugotanker, with parts of the city wall behind. Beyond, ISTARSKA OBALA provides the embarkation point for the car ferry to Ancona. At the far end of the street (left) the former church and monastery of *Sv. Nikola* (1760), with a good courtyard and Romanesque bell tower, is to be restored after long use as barracks. The Army Club opposite occupies the former seat of the Austrian governor of Dalmatia, with just behind, the bastion of Sv. Nikola (view out to sea).

Entered from the tiny and almost concealed Trg Vranjanina is the **Franciscan Church and Monastery**, supposedly founded by St. Francis himself while on his way to Syria in 1213. Although the first Gothic church to be built in Dalmatia (1283), it preserves of the original style only a restored two-light window in the rebuilt W front

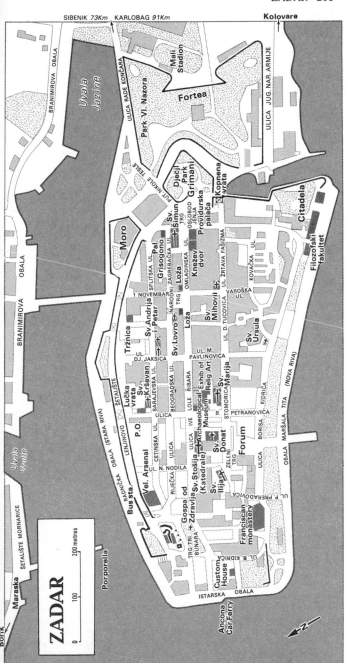

ZADAR

(1780), the choir, and the partly Gothic Detrico chapel. Within, a lavishly decorated Romanesque column supports the stoup to the left. In the N aisle the *Detrico Chapel* (1480) bears the elaborately carved Detrico arms, attributed to Nikola Firentinac, over the entrance, and on the N wall a large allegorical painting by Lazzaro Bastiani (late 15C). In the S aisle, above the centre altar: Palma the Younger, St. Francis. In the choir behind the altar are outstanding Gothic *Stalls (1394) by Giovanni da Borgo Sansepolcro. On the returned stalls are depicted St. Chrysogonus (Patron of the city) on a horse, with Fra Benedict, who ordered the stalls (below), and on the other side St. Francis receiving the stigmata, with a bust of Louis of Anjou.

From the choir opens the *Sacristy* where the Treaty of Zadar (comp. above) was concluded in 1358 (memorial plaque 1958). On the wall (right) the fine polyptych (15C), attributed to Dujam Vušković of Split, came from the Franciscan monastery at Ugljan. The two enormous chests are of oak (1724). Over the door to the choir hangs a small bronze crucifix by Ivan Meštrović.
  In the adjoining monastic *Treasury*, the large wooden Crucifixion (13C?) is unusually carved in low relief and painted. Also displayed are the Dead Christ with Angels, a painting from the Bassano workshop; a Madonna (15C), tempera on wood; SS. Jerome, John the Baptist, and Simeon, three figures from a polyptych by Pietro de Riboldis (1433); two additional screens from the choir stalls; and, in cases, three illuminated codices (13C, 14C, and 15C). Notable among the church plate are a 14C silver processional cross decorated with miniatures and three 15C silver-gilt chalices.—A door in the W wall of the treasury admits to the small Renaissance chapel of *Sv. Ante* (Anthony), the former chapter house, and thence into the graceful cloister (1556), built by local masons Ivan Trifunić and Ivan Stijović. A late 15C well-head stands in the centre and gravestones of the 15–17C have been built into the walls.

Continue round the monastery to the excavated NW end of the Roman forum (see below) and turn left along UL. J. SUNDEČIĆA. Immediately on the left is the Serbian Orthodox church of *Sv. Ilija* (Elijah), erected 1773, with a small collection of late icons (16–18C) and, adjoining it, the *Palača Janković*, with a baroque façade. In the small TRG 27 MARTA stand the *Teologija*, an Austrian built seminary of 1867, and, enclosing the S side of the square, the **Slavensko** (or Ilirsko) **sjeme-nište** (Slavonic Seminary), founded by Abp V. Zmajević; a plain baroque building dating from 1748, with a pleasant cloister (well-head with Zmajević arms; view of S side of cathedral).

The ***Cathedral of Sv. Stošija** (Anastasia), the largest and finest Romanesque church in Dalmatia, is less ancient than its appearance would suggest, owing to stylistic conservatism. It was restored and given a new roof in 1924–28.

Constantine Porphyrogentius refers to a cathedral on this site in the 10C and Pope Alexander III visited it in 1177. In 1202 the city was sacked by the Crusaders when many churches are said to have been destroyed, though it is not certain that the cathedral was among them. In 1285, however, the cathedral was rededicated by Abp Lorenzo Periandro. The main apse probably remains from the older church while the remainder, reconstructed in the 12C, may have undergone extensive repairs in the 13C after the visit of the Crusaders. At this time the building was also lengthened, and the W front, completed in 1324, ranks among the latest Romanesque work in Europe.

EXTERIOR. The WEST FRONT, the finest single feature of the cathedral, has affinities with the better-known Tuscan churches of Pisa and Lucca, with the difference that the lower part is completely unador-ned, except for the three portals. The upper part is decorated with four stories of blind arcades, the middle two flanking a great wheel window (restored), a device that gives it extraordinary harmony, though the gable story is, unusually, broken by a second and later rose window. The device is continued along the N wall by an arcaded gallery beneath the eaves. The large centre *Portal* consists of five recessed orders; in the tympanum, the Virgin and Child are flanked by SS. Anastasia and Chrysogonus. The statues of the four apostles that flank the portal are earlier than the rest of the work. The fine N portal has a sculptured agnus dei in the richly ornamented tympanum and figures of the Virgin Mary (restored) and the angel Gabriel on either side. The two similar figures flanking the S portal are replacements made in the late 19C by T.G. Jackson, the English architect.

The spacious INTERIOR (50m × 18m) is basilican in plan. The nave, three times wider than the aisles, is divided from them by arcades having round arches, supported alternatively by piers and marble columns. The two columns nearest the W door have spiral fluting and capitals of pre-Romanesque design. The next two are rectangular and have Corinthian capitals. The four columns at the E end are Roman with good Corinthian capitals. Above the arcades is an ornamental string-course. The triforium has six small arches in each bay with arcaded balustrades.

The second chapel of the S AISLE has a coloured marble altar by the Venetian artist Vivarini (1719); a wooden crucifixion once part of a great rood, now lost, by Matteo Moronzoni (1426); and the entrance to the Early Christian Baptistery, destroyed during the war, of which traces of the hexagonal floor-plan remain. At the end of the aisle, the Sacristy of 1398, formerly the chapel of St. Barbara, contains Venetian paintings of the 16–17C and the cathedral *Treasure*, with reliquaries, vestments, and liturgical objects of the 9–15C.

The raised CHOIR, lined on both sides by elaborate late Gothic *Stalls (1418–50), is the work of the Venetian artist Matteo Moronzoni (restored 1883). The more sumptuous seats were for the bishop and the town governor. The Gothic *Ciborium* (1332) over the high altar is loftier than that of **St. Mark's** in Venice, and rests on four marble *Columns individually decorated with fluting and diaper work; one of the capitals has little figures worked into the foliage. The rib-vaulted canopy is finished with a horizontal cornice of acanthus leaves and bears an inscription with the date and name of Abp Ivan Butovan, during whose tenure the W front was also completed. Behind the high altar the spacious apse (10C?) retains its Byzantine *Synthronon* with the Cathedra (bishop's throne) raised on five steps, and slabs from an old altar rail have been built into the high altar.

The CRYPT, beneath the choir, is probably contemporary with it. Fragments of 9C ornament have been built into one column. On the spot beneath the high altar a stone sarcophagus contains relics of SS. Agape, Chionia and Irene, martyred in Salonika under Diocletian. The simple altar is formed of a damaged slab with a 13C relief of St. Anastasia at the stake.

In the N AISLE there is a 17C altar frontal of St. Dominic and a painting by Palma the Younger. The apse has poorly restored 13C frescoes depicting Christ and St. Thomas Becket. The altar here contains a 9C sarcophagus, presented by Bp Donat, with the relics of St. Anastasia, and its frontal has a 15C Gothic relief of the saint in marble.—In the S AISLE is the Rococo altar of the Holy Sacrament (1719) by A. Viviani and on the next altar to the W a Madonna by Blaž Zadranin (Blaise of Zadar, 1447), thought to be the same as Blaž Jurjev Trogiranin (of Trogir); this came from the rotunda in Trg tri bunara, which retains a copy. Two doors, one Gothic, one in Renaissance style with the arms of Abp Valaresso, formerly led into the baptistery. It will be reconstructed when funds are available. In the S apses are more 13C frescoes and a door leading to the Gothic SACRISTY (1398), formerly the chapel of *Sv. Barbara*. Here are a polyptych showing six saints by Vittore Carpaccio (1480) and a late 13C icon of the Madonna. Between the sacristy and the main apse, a barrel vault remains from an earlier church.

The **Bell Tower** rises above Ul. Ive Lole Ribara at the E end of the cathedral. Begun in 1480 by Abp Valaresso and interrupted after only one story had been built, it was completed in 1892 according to plans by T.G. Jackson, who took the tower at Rab as his model.

Behind Sv. Stošija turn right along UL. BOŽIDARA PETRANOVIĆA, which crosses a large irregular open space created by bombing in the Second World War. This is the site of the **Roman Forum**. Excavations have established that the forum measured 95m long by 45m wide, and that the capitol at the NW end was almost as long again.

Ul. Božidara Petranovića and STOMORICA represent the decumanus and cardo maximus of the Roman town. Looking NW from their intersection you can see the low walls of a row of taverns and parts of the cloaca or drainage system. Steps descend to the level of the porticus, with its Roman paving, and a further step marks the level of the original pavement of the forum. Low walls to the left define the E end of a large *Basilica*, with a semicircular apse; the W end has been destroyed to make way for a well. The floor of the forum is strewn with fragments of Roman masonry from the lapidary collection formerly housed in Sv. Donat. The remains of a Roman triumphal arch are from Podgradje (Roman Asseria) near Benkovac (see Rte 14B), and there are large numbers of the characteristic Liburnian gravestones (cippi) with their foliated tapering tops. More spolia can be seen built into the base of Sv. Donat, which stands on the floor of the forum. Beside the bishop's palace in what is now Zeleni trg a lofty Roman column (10m high by 1m in diameter) stands in its original position. Originally a votive column, it served as a pillory in the Middle Ages when the small pre-Romanesque plaque (9C) near its base and the gryphon on top were added. Beyond the column where the forum is crossed by Ul. J. Sundečić steps lead up to the former capitol, now partly occupied by the complex of buildings joined to the church of Sv. Ilija. Immediately behind these buildings are the excavated foundations of a massive *Temple* dedicated to Augustus, Juno, and Minerva. Extensive remains of the surrounding peribolus may be seen SW of here behind the new block of flats. Further foundations of the peribolus can also be seen NE of the Palača Janković.

The **Archaeological Museum** (adm. 10–12 and 16–19; Sun 9–12; closed Mon), located in a modern building (1972) adjoining the Forum on the E, contains prehistorical, classical, and medieval antiquities found in northern and central Dalmatia. The Prehistorical Collection occupies the Second Floor and includes material from the Palaeolithic, Neolithic, Bronze, and Iron Ages; as well as material from Nin (see Rte 14B), including numerous Illyrian and imported Greek vases. The First Floor hosts the Roman Collection, with glass, pottery, mosaics, inscriptions, architectural and sculptural fragments, and Early Christian oil lamps ranging from the 1C BC to the 6C AD. The Ground Floor is devoted to the High Middle Ages, especially Croatian culture from the 7C to the 12C. Displayed here are pottery, metal objects, and coins from the necropolis of Nin; Early Croatian sculptures and reliefs from Zadar (including the pluteus from the church of St. Dominic, a pluteus and portal from the church of Sv.

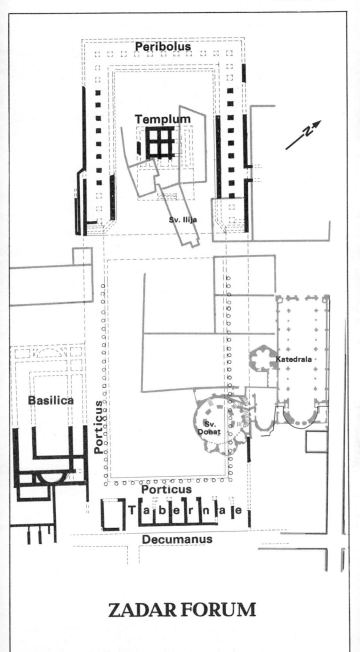

ZADAR FORUM

Lovro, a ciborium from the cathedral, carved wooden beams from Sv. Donat, and objects from outlying churches (such as a ciborium from Sopot).

Romanesque altar closure slab from Sv. Nedjeljica, now in the Archaeological Museum, Zadar

The monumental round church of ***Sv. Donat** (St. Donatus; adm. 10–12 and 16–18) on the NE side of the forum is one of the more curious and original buildings in Dalmatia. The church, circular in plan and 27m tall, consists of a plain drum with narrow lesenes spaced at regular intervals and with three apses on the E side, decorated with shallow blind arcades that rise from ground level to just under the eaves. In the centre rises a smaller concentric drum topped with a gently sloping conical roof. The foundations consist of fragments of Roman masonry laid directly on the floor of the forum.

The exact date of the church's construction and the origins of its style are uncertain, but it was probably built in the 9C (Constanine Porphyrogenitus provides the first mention of it in 949), although not necessarily by Bp Donat, whose name became popularly linked with the church only in the 15C; the original dedication was to the Holy Trinity. Its style links it with Charlemagne's chapel at Aachen, St. Vitale at Ravenna, and the church of SS. Sergius and Bachus at Istanbul; but differences, notably in the apses, seem to point to the local Croatian architecture of the period. A number of minor changes have been made to the church in recent centuries (in 1798–1870 it served the Austrians as a military magazine and under the Italians it became a museum), but its form remains substantially unaltered.

An irregularly shaped narthex on the W side admits to the main doorway, composed of antique fragments. The lofty INTERIOR gives an impression of massive strength. Within the circular outer wall a concentric arcade rises in two stories to form an ambulatory with a gallery above, leaving the central space open to the full height of the inner drum. The round arches are supported on huge rectangular stone piers set directly upon the forum pavement; similar piers support the roof, whereas the arches opening towards the apses are borne by two Roman columns with composite capitals from the colonnade of the forum. Two similar columns in the gallery above have been truncated to make them fit; here one capital is Corinthian. Among the many Roman fragments built into the structure the most interesting are two Roman altars dedicated to Juno and Jupiter on the pier next to the main entrance. Two flights of stairs give access to the upper gallery. Those on the right are thought to be original, although reconstructed in 1733; those on the left were added at the same time. The access doors both bear the Zmajević arms. The upper gallery is entered from a vestibule of 1752, with an entrance also composed of Roman fragments, and is identical in plan with the ground floor below.

The *Bishop's Palace* (1830), attached to the W side of Sv. Donat, incorporates the episcopal offices and Institute for the Conservation of Ancient Monuments.

On the E side of the forum the badly damaged church and former Benedictine nunnery of **Sv. Marija** was founded in 1066 by Čika, a Zadar noblewoman said to have been the stepsister of King Petar Krešimir IV of Croatia, who granted the new foundation many privileges. In 1091 the present church, an aisled basilica, was consecrated and King Koloman commemorated his entry into Zadar in 1105 by endowing the construction of a bell tower and chapter house. In 1529–36 the church was enlarged and given a graceful Lombardesque façade with a Renaissance doorway and a wheel-window. The E end was rebuilt and a cupola added in 1762.

The bare INTERIOR has been re-roofed since the war. The Romanesque arcades acquired a rococo facing of stucco in 1744. The spacious triforium, also richly stuccoed, served the nuns as their matroneum; the arches are closed by wrought-iron lattices. On the N wall is a baroque memorial with a bust of Simon Comfanfogna (1707). The Benedictine device and a Latin inscription commemorating the foundation of the nunnery surmount a closed aperture through which deceased nuns were passed from the nunnery into the church. On an altar in the S aisle is a Gothic Pietà (15C).

A Romanesque doorway left of the church gives access to the convent, now occupied by the **Zlato i srebro Zadra** (*Exhibition of Religious Art in Zadar*; adm. 9–12 and 16–18, Sun 9.30–12; closed Mon), a well-displayed collection of religious articles produced by local artisans of the 11–16C. Exhibits include silver and gold reliquaries and liturgical objects, wood and stone sculptures, and several fine paintings, most notably a polyptych by Vittore Carpaccio (1480).

The handsome Romanesque *Bell Tower (1105), the oldest of such dimensions in Dalmatia (restored 1438–53), has well-proportioned groups of windows culminating in fine four-light windows at the top. An inscription records its endowment by King Koloman.

Behind the bell tower is the *Chapter House* (1105–11), with a barrel-vaulted roof reinforced by cross ribs, an early example of a method of construction that became a Dalmatian idée fixe, surviving as a glorious anachronism in Šibenik cathedral. In the SE corner stands the Romanesque *Tomb of Vekenega* (died 1111), daughter of Čika and abbess when the campanile and chapel were built (as the inscriptions attest). A narrow flight of stairs mounts to *Vekenega's Chapel* on the first floor of the campanile. Detached columns in the corners support two massive diagonal ribs carrying the roof, one of the earliest examples of rib vaulting in Europe. On the faces of the cushion capitals are carved the letters of Koloman's name: R.CO/LLO/MAN/NVS. Contemporary frescoes on the walls, difficult to see, show Christ Triumphant and the Deposition. A door in the S wall, whose lintel is a fragment of a Roman frieze, leads to stairs to the top of the bell tower with views over Zadar and out to sea.

Walk NE along Ul. Božidara Petranovića to the small TRG VLADI-MIRA GORTANA. On the right side is the *Narodni muzej* (adm. 8–12; Wed 16–19; Sun 8–11; closed Sat) with memorials of the Second World War. The street terminates in the *Lučka vrata*, or Harbour Gate, which incorporates fragments of a Roman triumphal arch, a plaque commemorating the battle of Lepanto (1571), and an equestrian relief of St. Chrysogonus. The 16C lion of St. Mark on the side facing the quay was defaced after the Second World War during squabbles between Croat and Italian nationalists. Turning back, take Sarajevska ul. E.

The Romanesque church of **Sv. Krševan** (Chrysogonus), dedicated to Zadar's patron saint, is second only to the cathedral in interest and beauty. Built in the 10C on the site of an earlier church and reconstructed in its present form in 1175, it was attached to a Benedictine monastery until its dissolution in 1807. The monastic buildings disappeared in the bombing. The W front is plain with the mere stump of a tower, begun in 1546 and never completed, but the S wall is beautifully decorated with shallow blind arcades resting on spirally fluted columns. Particularly striking is the central *Apse where arcades resting on slender columns with cushion capitals form a high open gallery, with blind arcading beneath. Just N of the apses a two-light Romanesque window from the former monastery has been built into the wall.

The S door admits to the plain but well-proportioned INTERIOR, basilican in plan, with arcades supported alternately on piers and columns. In the N apse and on the wall adjoining, Romanesque frescoes (restored) depict the Birth of Christ, the Last Judgment, the Annunciation, and Saints. The incongruous baroque high altar (1632) bears marble statues of Zadar's patron saints (1717); built into the reverse side is an early 15C Gothic relief of St. Anne. In the S aisle an altar dedicated to St. Zoilus has a painting attributed to Giovanni Battista Piazzetta. Over the S door is a memorial with marble bust to Marino Zorzi (died 1675), a Venetian governor.

Continue by Sarajevska ul. past the *Palača Gverini* and, on the next corner, the *Palača Fanfogna*, with interesting details. On the opposite corner are *Sv. Andrija* (Andrew) and an adjoining Renaissance façade, all that remains of the church of *Sv. Marcela* (1540).

In Sv. Andrija the apse and S wall are decorated with poorly-preserved 11C frescoes in Byzantine style. A door in the apse leads into the curious pre-Romanesque church of *Sv. Petar Stari* (9C?) with nave and single aisle divided by a simple arcade. Many Roman fragments went into its construction and traces of 11–12C frescoes remain.

The colourful **Tržnica**, one of the biggest markets in Dalmatia, occupies a small square and several adjoining ruins adapted since the war for the purpose. In the E corner are the vine-clad remains of one wall of the church of *Sv. Marija Velika*, which held the sarcophagus of St. Simeon until it was demolished to make way for the new fortifications in 1543; its roofless chapel of *Sv. Rok* now serves as a meat market. Beside them stands the uncompleted W front of what was intended to become the church of St. Simeon, bearing the date

(1600) and the emblems of benefactors. On the NE side of the square the 16C *Gate of Sv. Rok* through the Venetian walls, later blocked up, was reopened in 1847 to Radnička obala and the quays. Immediately on the left here is the *Bastion of Sv. Rok* and farther to the right, where the quayside ends, the *Bastion Moro*, now built over. Between the two, opposite the footbridge to Voštarnica (see Rte 14B) a 19C opening, by a newsagent's kiosk, leads back through the walls. Immediately inside the gateway steps mount (left) to a pleasant walk along the top of the town walls.

Taking UL. 1 NOVEMBAR recross Ljubljanska ul. passing, at the corner, the remains of the *Palača Cedulini*, with an interesting Venetian Gothic doorway. On the opposite side the Romanesque *Palača Ghirardini*, has a typical Dalmatian 15C balconied window from the workshop of Nikola Firentinac.

Turn left to NARODNI TRG, the Platea Magna of the Middle Ages and main square and gathering place of Zadar, crossed on the far side by UL. IVE LOLE RIBARA, the Corso and main shopping street of Zadar, which runs from the cathedral to Sv. Šimun (see below). The N and W sides of the square are dominated by the pompous, neo-classical *Vijećnica* (Town Hall), with reliefs showing scenes from Zadar, erected by the Italians in 1936. It also houses the *Naučna biblioteka*, an important library founded by Pier Aless. Paravia in 1855.

A wing of the town hall encloses the small 11C church of *Sv. Lovro* (Lawrence), now partly ruined (key from the Institute for the Conservation of Monuments). It takes the form of a miniature basilica with aisles divided from the nave by four columns; two with Roman capitals also have reversed Roman capitals as bases, while the other two have pre-Romanesque capitals of which one represents a man with outspread arms. The nave is barrel-vaulted with transverse ribs, but the aisles are covered with semi-domes resting on squinches.

The former **Loža gradske straže** (Guardhouse), an elegant loggia, erected in 1562, has been attributed to Gian Girolamo Sammicheli, nephew of Michele. The *Clock Tower* was added by the Austrians in 1798. The Guardhouse now contains the *Etnografski muzej* (adm. 8–12; Sun 9–12; closed Sat) founded in 1945 and notable for an excellent collection of folk costumes. On the SE corner of the square stands the **Gradska Loža** (Town Loggia), designed by Gian Girolamo Sammicheli and built in 1565. The inscription over the door refers to a restoration in 1792. The building, originally open on all four sides, has been adapted for mounting art exhibitions, but still contains the stone magistrates' bench ornamented with reliefs and coats of arms.

The picturesque, narrow KLAIĆEVA UL. leads into one of the few old quarters of the town which escaped bombing. A number of houses with attractive façades include the Palača Papafava (No. 1), with courtyard, and the Palača Civalelli. At the end on the left is the Franciscan Gothic church of **Sv. Mihovil**, with an excellent original W portal (1389), probably the work of Paolo (Vanuzzi) da Sulmona. In the tympanum is a relief of St. Michael, with Sts Anastasia and Chrysogonus on either side. Above this is a Madonna and Child, and on the gable is a Roman relief of three heads on which haloes have been carved at a later date. The choir, the work of Andrija Desina, a local architect, bears traces of Gothic frescoes in various states of preservation, and a large painted Crucifixion (13C) in low relief on wood, the companion piece of which is in the Franciscan monastery. By the entrance is a stone font (15C) supported by four angels.

In VAROŠKA UL. straight ahead and UL. SIMA MATAVULJA beyond are the oldest houses in Zadar, some of the 12–13C with Romanesque doors and windows. There are also good later houses in Ul. Dimitrija Tucovića (16C), notably the baroque Palača Fozze (18C).

Turn left along UL. ŽRTAVA FAŠIZMA, the E continuation of Stomorica, and pass (left) the Venetian *Palača Nassis*, the main portal of which has the Nassis coat of arms in the tympanum. Ahead the Land Gate leads out to the old harbour (see below). Make a detour left along UL. ANDRIJE MEDULIĆA to the *Moderna Galerija* (open daily 8–12) housing a small collection of late icons and works by modern Yugoslav painters; here an international photographic exhibition entitled 'Man and the Sea' is held biennially. Above the gallery is the *Prirodoslovni muzej* (Natural History Museum), with a collection of Mediterranean fish and birds. The street ends in the irregularly shaped Trg Oslobodjenja where a tall *Roman Column* incorporates drums from two temple columns brought here from the forum in 1729. A railed pit enclosed the excavated foundations of the Roman triumphal arch which marked the E limit of the ancient town.

The square opens into the Poljana Petra Zoranića, which is lined on one side by the *Providurska palača* (1607), the former residence of the Venetian Governor-General of Dalmatia. The upper story was added by the Austrians in the 19C. A well-head in the courtyard bears the Austrian imperial arms.

Adjoining is the former *Knežev dvor* (13C) or residence of the town governor, also reconstructed by the Austrians (1804), with a Venetian well-head in the arcaded courtyard. A little farther on, in Omladinska ul., the 18C Venetian *Kamerlengo* has a baroque façade. No. 7 in this street has a Romanesque façade and a Renaissance courtyard.

The baroque church of **Sv. Šimun** (Simeon) is a 17C reconstruction of the older church of St. Stephen, whose name was changed when the sarcophagus of St. Simeon was transferred here from the church of Sv. Marija Velika (1632). The Bell Tower, on the N side, is crowned by four busts of prophets removed from the unfinished church of St. Simeon in the market square. The INTERIOR is mainly Renaissance in feeling with a nave and two aisles divided by arcades with fluted columns and rich Corinthian capitals. An unusual feature is that it has two triumphal arches, one (added in 1705) marking the choir, the other the sanctuary. On the high altar stands the sumptuous *Sarcophagus of St. Simeon*, a superb example of the silversmith's art.

According to legend a ship was driven ashore at Zadar either in 1213 or 1273, from which landed a nobleman bearing apparently the body of his brother, which he deposited at the cemetery. Shortly afterwards he died and from his papers it appeared that the body was that of Simeon the Just, who had held Christ in his arms in the Temple. The body was taken to the church of Sv. Marija Velika and accredited with miracles. At the request of Queen Elisabeth the Younger, daughter of Ban Stjepan Kotromanić (II) of Bosnia, who visited Zadar with her husband King Ludovik (Louis d'Anjou) of Hungary and Croatia in 1371, five nobles of Zadar commissioned the goldsmith Francesco di Antonio da Sesto of Milan to build a silver sarcophagus for the relic. With the assistance of Andrija Markov of Zagreb, Peter son of Blaž of Rača, Stipan Pribčev, and Mihovil Damjanov, the work was begun in 1377 and completed in 1380.

An oblong coffer with a pitched roof and gable-ends rests on two bronze angels (1678), cast from cannon captured from the Turks, which replaced four original angels in silver. The sarcophagus is covered with silver panels embossed with religious and historical scenes. On the front, Presentation of Christ in the Temple (after Giotto), flanked by the finding of the body of St. Simeon (left) and the triumphal entry of Louis the Great into Zadar (right). On the lid, a full-length effigy of St. Simeon. The ends are notable, both for their workmanship and for the detailed picture of contemporary life. On the left, the storm-tossed boat that brought St. Simeon's body to Zadar; on the right (supposedly) the wife of Ban Pavle Šubić taking the oath after being accused of adultery. The arms of King Lewis appear in the gable at both ends. Panels on the reverse depict (left) the handing of a casket to St. Simeon by Queen Elisabeth; (right) the death of Ban Stjepan Kotromanić, Elisabeth's father; and (centre) an inscription giving the date and name of the maker. On the lid, amid scenes depicting the miracles wrought by the saint, the artist has included a self-portrait. The sarcophagus is opened annually on 8 October. Inside, further panels depict miracles done by the saint while, enclosed in glass, the mummified body wears a silver crown and an embroidered apron, the gift of Djurdje Branković, despot of Serbia.

An earlier sarcophagus of St. Simeon in stone (13C), also with a lifesize effigy, stands against the S wall of the choir. On the N side are a 17C Venetian chair and a memorial bust (1746) of Rossini, the engineer who restored Zadar's fortifications. The sacristy, entered from behind the altar, contains a number of 17C paintings. In the TREASURY (apply to sacristan) an outstanding Gothic chalice, the gift of Elisabeth the Younger of Hungary, is decorated with the Angevin arms. There is also a 17C silver dish.

Of some interest in the NAVE are a gilt stucco relief of the Madonna and Child (18C) at the E end of the N aisle; an ornate silver frame, in the S aisle opposite, by Matej and Luka Boričević (1564); and a 13C Romanesque relief of the Birth of Christ built into the wall next to the S door.

In Zagrebačka ul. on the N side of the church, houses with interesting details include the 15C *Palača Petrizio* and the *Palača Grisogono*, a rare example of a secular Romanesque building, with an upper story added in the 15C.

Return to Trg oslobodjenja, the SE corner of which is dominated by the *Bablja kula*, a tall pentagonal tower from the fortifications of the 13C. Behind the tower are a remnant of the 13C wall and an earlier wall; some remains of the Roman city wall in the courtyard of a Children's Clinic (Dječji dispanzer) recall a still earlier stage of fortification. The large raised space on the far side of the square with a line of five well-heads (Trg pet bunara) is in fact the roof of an enormous cistern constructed in 1574 over the former moat. It provides access to the contemporary *Grimani Bastion*, the massive pentagonal key-point of the city's eastern defences. Filled up in 1829, the bastion now forms a children's playground, around which are scattered fragments of masonry from various vanished buildings.

The main road leaves the town on the N side of the bastion, but on foot it is more convenient to descend by steps on the S side to the **Kopnena vrata**, or *Land Gate*, constructed in 1543 to a design by Mich. Sammicheli. The imposing façade in rusticated Doric is embellished with inscriptions and the coats of arms of its Venetian builders. The keystone of the centre arch bears the arms of Zadar (St. Chrysogonus on horseback), and a large lion of St. Mark fills the niche above.

At the seaward end of the former moat, and enclosed by the city bastions, is the pretty little harbour of **Foša**, crowded with small fishing and pleasure craft. A former guardhouse (1786) on a small mole has been transformed into a fish restaurant.

Beyond the broad road that separates it from the Grimani Bastion rises the **Velika utvrda**, or *Fortea*, erected in the late 16C as an advance post for defence. This great bastion is laid out as the pleasant *Park Vladimira Nazora* in which a former barracks (1789) is now the grammar school. The main entrance to the Fortea, on the E side, displays the arms of Sforza Pallavicino, its builder, comprising a seven-headed hydra crowned with laurel leaves.

The tree-lined avenue to the S leads shortly to *Kolovare*, Zadar's nearest beach, much patronised by the locals. Farther on, beyond a large polygonal well, the *Carev Bunar*, built in 1546 to supply water to ships, the rocky shore offers opportunities for bathing, but access is steep and safe only for experienced swimmers only. The large suburb of *Arbanasi* was settled by Albanians from the Lake Skadar region in the early 18C and a form of Albanian is still spoken.

To the left of the Land Gate a stone parapet skirts the Fóša at the foot of the walls. At the harbour mouth stands a large corner bastion known as *Citadela*, flaunting the usual lion of St. Mark high up on the wall and the date, 1574. The broad acacia-lined OBALA MARŠALA TITA, also known as the *Nova obala* or *Nova riva*, runs the length of the town on the seaward side. Constructed in 1874 when the S walls were demolished, the promenade is a favourite resort of Zadrians especially for the evening corzo, when the sunsets are often spectacular. The large neoclassical building on the right, erected by the Austrians in 1905 as a girls' college, houses the *Filozofski fakultet* (Faculty of Arts), a constituent college of the University of Split. Farther along we reach the hotel and kavana Zagreb, opposite the entrance to which (on the landward side) are excavated foundations of the small pre-Romanesque church of *Stomorica* (or Sv. Ursula), with an unusual plan consisting of a rectangular entrance hall and five apses.

The main residential suburb of *Voštarnica* beyond the main harbour can be reached either by footbridge or by passenger ferry from the bus station to the breakwater opposite. Along the shore are a small shipyard, yacht marina, and the *Maraska Distillery* where the famous maraschino is made (visit by application to the Turistbiro). Beyond the distillery is a small bathing-place and c 7km further the main beach of *Borik*. On the other side of Voštarnica, in Ul. Ivana Gundulića, the church of Sv. Ivan incorporates fragments from earlier churches, including a Romanesque relief of the agnus dei, a 15C relief of St. Francis receiving the Stigmata, and a medieval altar rail, whereas the parish office contains a marble relief of St. Jerome attributed to Andrija Aleši.

B.   Excursions from Zadar

ZADAR TO NIN, 18km. Buses several times daily throughout the year. Just beyond (15km) *Zaton*, on a tumulus (left) stands the tiny 11C church of Sv. Nikola, a typical example of early Croatian architecture, with a nave and triple apses forming a cruciform plan; the crossing was surmounted with a fortified watch tower at the time of the Turkish invasion.—2km Crossroads. To the left *Privlaka* (6km) occupies the site of the Roman Brevilaqua, and preserves a pre-Romanesque church. Its sandy beaches mark it for tourist development. Crossing a small stone bridge, with salt flats on the right, the road enters the historic but devastated settlement of (1km) **Nin**, which stands on an artifically created island.

Nin, once the Roman municipium of *Aenona*, later Nona, became the chief town of Croatia in the 9–11C and preferred seat of Croatia's early peripatetic kings. Its prosperity continued under joint Croatian-Hungarian rule, but in 1328, as a result of deteriorating relations Nona sought the protection of Venice. In 1571 it was partly evacuated and slighted to avert Turkish invasions and in 1646 it was wholly abandoned and deliberately set on fire, from when it has steadily declined to its present sad condition. Nin was the seat of Bp Gregory (Grgur Ninski), the leading champion of the Slavonic liturgy at the Council of Salona in 1059.

Ruins of the former town walls stand desolate on all sides amid a litter of Roman masonry. The rebuilt church of **Sv. Anzelm** is interesting only for the reliquaries from the former cathedral. In a case on the high altar, two silver caskets are believed to date from the 8–9C, and two more in front (14–15C) contain relics of SS. Anselm and Marcella. A hand and two feet in silver gilt, the gift of Prince Pavao Šubić, were made in 1309. Behind the altar is a carved and gilded wooden sarcophagus on which a casket contains relics of St. Ambrose.

A chapel remains on the S side of the church from the earlier Gothic cathedral, hideously decorated but preserving on its altar a 15C statuette called Our Lady of Zečevo, the object of a local cult. Pilgrimages are made each May on the day of St. Saviour (Spasov dan). A memorial stone to Bp Divnić bears his effigy and the date 1530. Two Gothic heads representing Sts Anselm and Ambrose have been set over the N door.—Beside the church is a good Romanesque Campanile in undressed stone, with two-light windows set in the higher stories.

The *Museum* (adm. 9–12 and 13–17) holds a small collection of prehistoric and Roman ornaments and copies of some of the objects found at Nin but since removed. Close by is **Sv. Križ**, the church of the Holy Cross, erected in the 9C as the first cathedral of Nin. Cruciform in plan, with small apses between the chancel and the transepts and a central drum, Sv. Križ is a perfect specimen of the miniature rustic churches erected by the Croats during the period of their allegiance to Byzantium. Above the W door a bevelled lintel richly ornamented with interlacing knots and scrolls in the Byzantine fashion, records tho building of the church by the Croatian Župan Godežav. The 13C church of *Sv. Ambroz*, formerly Benedictine and now a mere shell, has a good W front incorporating an unusual window in the shape of a cross. Behind the church are part of the town walls and a gateway called *Rimska vrata*. The *Roman Remains*, on the N side of the town, were partially excavated at the beginning of the present century. The existence of an amphitheatre, forum and temple, was established, but the best finds were removed and because the excavations were never finished, the visible remains are fragmentary.

ZADAR TO OBROVAC VIA THE ZRMANJA CANYON. By road and boat (frequent excursions organised from Zadar in summer); or by road (45km) and on foot. A whole day should be devoted to the round trip. Take the Adriatic Highway (Rte 8) to (25km) *Posedarje*, where boats can be hired. The boat crosses the almost landlocked Novigradsko more (Sea of Novigrad) and then pushes up the river Zrmanja through the impressive ZRMANJA CANYON, the bare rocky sides of which rise in places to nearly 200m. The ruined towers seen at intervals were erected by the Turks against the Venetians. The alternative is to continue along the main highway to the bridge over the Maslenićko ždrilo. Here a right fork joins the main road from Starigrad just short of (11km) *Jasenice*. This runs below the Velebits (views, left) and parallel with the Zrmanja canyon (right) which may be reached on foot across scrubland. At the T-junction turn right again and descend into the Zrmanja valley.

20km **Obrovac** is the usual terminal point for excursions. On a hill overlooking the town and the canyon is the 13C castle of the Gusić-Kurjaković family, now empty. The town is half Catholic and half Orthodox, and the town cemetery on a bank of the Zrmanja c 1km downstream is accessible only by water, funeral processions of both faiths taking place by boat. During the Turkish occupation of the interior, Obrovac marked the western limit of Turkish power in Dalmatia (1527–1685).

ZADAR TO KARIN AND NOVIGRAD, 46km, buses twice daily. Leaving Zadar by BENKOVAČKA CESTA follow the course of a Roman aqueduct, considerable remains of which front the town cemetery, with a memorial to the Borelli family by Ivan Rendić (1888).—Beyond (13km) *Donji Zemunik*, branch left from the Benkovac road.—9km *Smilčić* is the site of one of the largest Neolithic settlements in the Balkans (1km W; excavated in 1957–62). In the village itself rich finds have been made from the Illyrian, Roman, and early medieval periods. Most are now in Zadar museum. A number of villas of the 17C and 18C formerly belonged to noble families from Zadar.

From Smilčić a road (left) leads directly in 10km to Novigrad (see below); or (turning left again after 2km) to *Islam Grčki* (7km), with the fortified 17C home of Serdar Stojan Janković, a prominent opponent of the Turks and hero of many epic folk songs.

Continue to Dubraja and (12km) **Karin** (Roman *Corinium*) at the SE end of the *Karinsko more*. This small 'sea' opens out of the Sea of Novigrad and like the latter is shallow, rich in fish, and almost landlocked. At the mouth of the small river Karišnica is the *Franciscan Monastery*, founded in 1429, but badly damaged by the Turks and rebuilt in 1736. The church retains a Gothic choir and the attractive Renaissance cloister has a decorated well-head. Among architectural fragments from the medieval Croatian town of Karin, preserved in the monastery, is a pre-Romanesque Croatian cross with knot-work carving. Karin Fair (2 July) attracts residents from all over Ravni Kotari, many of whom wear national costume.

From Karin the road continues NE around the Karinsko more to Obrovac (see above). Return to Dubraja and (1km beyond) turn right for Novigrad. At (4km) *Pridraga* the 11C pre-Romanesque church of Sv. Martin has triple apses decorated with lesenes and shallow blind arcading. About 100m away stand the foundations of an earlier Croatian church with six apses arranged in a circle.

5km **Novigrad** a picturesque small town, stands on an attractive winding inlet above the S shore of the Novigradsko more. It is well known for its oysters, mussels, and tuna fish. In the huge *Castle*, built in the 13C by the Gusić-Kurjaković family, Queen Elisabeth the Younger of Hungary, together with her daughter, Maria, were imprisoned in 1386–87 as a result of dynastic quarrels over the throne, and here Elisabeth was murdered. Parts of the town walls can still be seen, and the pre-Romanesque church of *Sv. Kata* in the graveyard has stone fragments ornamented with interlacing knotwork, birds, and animals built into the W front.

Excursions may be made by boat up the Zrmanja canyon to Obrovac or to Posedarje (see above).

ZADAR TO BENKOVAC, 34km. To *Donji Zemunik*, see above. Branch right for Benkovac.—At 30km a track (right) passes under the railway line to *Raštević* (1km), a further km beyond which the ruined medieval castle of Kličevica stands on a spur of rock overlooking a narrow canyon.—4km *Benkovac*, a bustling small town (1500 inhab.), with pleasant broad streets, was for the period between the two world wars, when Zadar was Italian, the cultural and administrative centre of the Croatian Ravni Kotari. There is a market every Monday and on the 10th of each month a colourful fair. High above the town stands the well preserved 14C castle of the Benković family.

A little beyond Benkovac, just left of the road to Knin, is the hill of Podgradje, site of the Roman city of *Asseria*. The extensive site has been well quarried and little remains except the lower courses of the Roman walls on the N. The gravestones round the primitive small church of Sv. Duh (Holy Spirit) consist of Roman fragments, some of them bearing ornament and inscriptions. The hilltop commands views of the surrounding plain and of the chain of beacon towers, used to give warning of the Turks, that extends over the hills on all sides.—To the N of Benkovac, on the road to Smilčić, is the village of (3km) *Kula Atlagić*. Here the Catholic church (Sv. Petar) has Romanesque features and a pre-Romanesque S wall with primitive blind arcading, while the Orthodox church of Sv. Nikola (1440), Gothic in style, contains a large 18C iconostasis displaying icons in both Byzantine and Western styles.

C. The Zadar Archipelago

The Zadar Archipelago consists of over 200 islands of greatly varying size and character, extending from Silba in the NW to Kurba Vela in the SE. Many are very fertile, being specially rich in figs, olives, and grapes, and the fishing grounds around them are generally reckoned the richest in the Adriatic. They also represent an area of great natural beauty which, because of its relative inaccessibility, remains largely unspoiled. Accommodaton is generally simple and informal and transport slow. Although frequent ferries ply from Zadar to all the main islands and towns, many of the more interesting places have to be visited by small boats hired locally, of which, fortunately, there is no shortage. The islands are here described from NW to SE.

Silba (400 inhab.). The most northerly island of the group, lying no more than 4 nautical miles from Ilovik and 8 nautical miles from Lošinj (see Rte 13), covers an area of 15km². Olives, almonds, grapes and figs are grown, and goat's milk cheese produced. Silba has shingle and sandy bays and is a favourite haunt of artists and writers from Zagreb. The only settlement, dominating both shores from a ridge, is *Silba*, a picturesque fishing village that prospered as a maritime centre in the 17–18C but subsequently fell into decline. Baroque paintings by Carlo Ridolfi adorn the parish church, the parish offices and the church of Gospa od Karmena; his canvas in Sv. Marko (1637), dated 1640, includes a self-portrait. Gravestones of former sea catains are carved with reliefs of ships. Walls and one tower survive of the 16C fortress built to guard against pirates. A curious stone look-out tower, called the Toreta, was erected in the last century.

Immediately E of Silba is the larger but less visited island of **Olib** (580 inhab.), with an area of 26km². The main occupations of the islanders are fishing and, on the open E side of the island, the growing of grapes and olives. On the wooded W side lies the only village, *Olib*, with a low fortified tower. In the treasury of the parish church are a Gothic cross, monstrance and pyx. The cemetery church has two baroque altars and a 16C polyptych.

To the W and S of Silba is a group of four islands, all inhabited but with little to offer the casual visitor: *Premuda*, *Škarda*, *Ist*, and *Molat*. Molat is the largest, with three small villages and a memorial in Uvala Jazi to mark the site of a notorious Italian prison camp of 1941–43. The parish church has a Gothic chalice and Renaissance and baroque crucifixes in its treasury and a baroque painting of SS. Simeon and Michael on the altar. The waters around these islands are particularly suitable for underwater fishing.

The largest island of the Zadar Archipelago is the well-named **Dugi Otok** (5500 inhab.), meaning 'Long Island', situated in the chain of islands farthest from the mainland. Nowhere exceeding 5km in width, and extending for 44km, it has an area of 124km². The seaward shore consists of a high, barren ridge rising sheer from the sea to over 330m, whereas the gentler shore facing the mainland is partly wooded. On this side all the villages are situated. The islanders, traditionally occupied with agriculture and fishing, are increasingly involved with tourism.

In the N is *Božava*, a picturesque fishing village with a good pebble and sand beach. The small church in the cemetery (1469) contains a 15C Crucifixion in wood and two ornamented stone slabs from an earlier, pre-Romanesque building (9–11C). Pleasant excursions can be made to the deeply indented bay of *Soliščica*, with a good beach at *Soline*; the long sandy beach at *Saharun*; and the smaller islands of *Zverinac* (18C Fanfogna villa in village), *Sestrunj* and *Rivanj*, all visited by regular boats. Of the small villages S of Božava (regular boat services from Zadar), the farthest, *Savar*, has a church incorporating a 9C pre-Romanesque chapel.

Offshore lies the small island of *Rava* (300 inhab.) with many coves for bathing and fishing, and beyond Rava the larger island of *Iž* (comp. below).

The southern line of villages on Dugi begins with *Luka*, with a pleasant rock and sand beach. In the church is a 15C painting of the Dead Christ. Two of the local limestone caves, Strašna peć and Kozja peć, are rich in stalactites and stalagmites. *Zaglav*, to the S beyond Žman, is picturesquely situated on a high cliff. The Franciscan Gothic church of Sv. Mihovil (1458), preserves two processional crosses and a rustic Crucifixion, but the attached Glagolitic monastery was rebuilt in the 19C.

Sali, a thriving fishing centre (1200 inhab.) with a fine natural harbour, is the largest settlement on Dugi Otok, with a cannery and fishmeal factory. The parish church of *Uzašašće Marijino* (The Assumption) has a narrow 15C nave with recently uncovered wall paintings of galleys and a more spacious E end added in 1584. The reredos incorporates an earlier painted panel of the Madonna. Among old houses round the harbour, are the Renaissance Gverini house on the N side and the 17C baroque Petriccioli house, now the Pension Kornat. A small festival with donkey races is held on the second Sunday in July.

Sali is the centre for excursions to the southern part of Dugi Otok and the Kornat Islands. The deeply indented bay of Telašćica (10km long) at the SE end of Dugi is entered by boat from Sali via the strait, Mala proversa, on the N side of which stand the foundations of a Roman summer villa. A frequent halt is the tiny bay of Mir near the salt lake of Mir. The impressive cliffs on the W can be seen from the far side of the lake, but are better viewed from the sea.

Immediately S of Dugi Otok begins the large complex of 125 islands known collectively as the **Kornati** (Kornat Islands or Kornat Archipelago), named from the largest one among them, Kornat. Consisting almost entirely of barren rock, they are uninhabited except for a few seasonal settlements when the owners of the land, mainly from Sali and Murter, bring sheep to graze and cultivate the miniscule plantations of figs, olives and vines that the islands are able to support. *Kornat Island* 24m long, is the largest uninhabited island in the Adriatic, although a ruined medieval fortress on Tarac hill (opposite Levrnaka island) and the foundations of an early Christian basilica below bear witness to past habitation. Other large islands in the group are Žut, Sit, Levrnaka, Jadra, Lavsa and Vela Kurba. The Kornati are particualrly famous as rich fishing ground and for their scenic beauty, the most interesting being the outer line of islands running from Levrnaka to Kurba Vela. Frequent excursions are organised in summer from Sali, Zadar, Biograd, and Šibenik.

Iž, a fertile and populous island (1800 inhab.), lies midway between Dugi Otok and Ugljan. It has celebrated olive groves and is the only island in the northern Adriatic to produce its own pottery. It won local fame during the Second World War as the first island to take arms against the Italian occupation. There are two main settlements. *Veli Iž* is an attractive fishing village. Among its older houses are the former residence of the Canigietti family and the Fanfogna house, adapted as a school. In the less compact *Mali Iž*, the small circular church of Sv. Marija Iška (9–11C) above the harbour, was enlarged in the 17C. The neighbouring Kaštel Begna is a fortified summer mansion.

Rather different in character from the rest of the archipelago are the two large inshore islands of Ugljan and Pašman.

Ugljan is the most densely populated island (10,252 inhab.) in the Adriatic. With a length of 22km and 54km^2 in area, it is steep and rocky on the N and seaward side, but exceptionally rich and fertile in the populous E. It lies under 5nm from Zadar.

At the N end is the scattered village of *Ugljan*, predominantly agricultural in character, with a Franciscan Monastery (1430) attractively situated on the edge of the harbour. The rustic cloister has excellent Romanesque capitals brought from Zadar (four angels, three fishes with a single head, eight heads interwined with foliage, etc.), and preserves the gravestone of Šimun Begna, Bp of Modruč and Senj (1537). The simple Gothic church of Sv. Jeronim attached to the convent was dedicated in 1447. In the sacristy is a Gothic trefoil stoup and there is a Gothic Crucifixion in the small chapel above. The parish church on a hill overlooking the village has good plate, including a Gothic cross, pyx and chalice, all in gold, and a later gold chalice dated 1515.

A pleasant excursion may be made by boat (1¼ hours) or on foot (¾ hour) to the sandy bay of *Muline*, where the foundations of an early-Christian basilica and mausoleum have been excavated and extensive remains of a Roman villa show tiled and mosaic floors.

At a midway point on the island and immediately opposite Zadar is *Preko*, the largest of the island villages (2400 inhab.). The small 12C church of Sv. Ivan has part of a Roman frieze built into the W wall. About 60m offshore from Preko is the beautiful small island of *Galovac* with a Franciscan Glagolitic Monastery (1443) noted for its luxuriant garden. Over the high altar of the church (1596) is a Madonna and Child with Saints by Zorzi Ventura of Zadar (17C). Preko is the starting point for the climb to the *Fortress of Sv. Mihovil* (1–1½ hours), whose ruins dominate the island. Erected in 1203 by the Venetians after the sack of Zadar by the Fourth Crusade, the fortress was restored by Hungarians in the mid-14C. Incorporated into the fortress is the 10C church of a former Benedictine monastery. Unsurpassed views from the fortress (262m) extend over the surrounding islands and to the mainland opposite.

Kali the second largest village (2300 inhab.) on Ugljan and the most picturesque, is crowded with the fishing vessels of the prosperous local zadruga or co-operative. Visitors can usually arrange to go out with the fleet (two nights and a day).

Kukljica, the southernmost village has a good beach which is attracting visitors.

Divided from Ugljan only by a strait (10m wide) dug in 1883, **Pašman** is similar in size and geological formation. Its 3800 inhab. are occupied in farming and the island is as yet largely untouched by tourism.

The northern villages of Ždrelac, Dobropoljana, and Nevidjane, afford good beaches for excursions. In *Pašman* half way down the E coast the baroque parish church has a medieval choir and two Gothic processional crosses in the treasury. In the village of *Kraj* the Franciscan Monastery of Sv. Jeronim has a relief of St. Jerome (1554; school of Andrija Aleši) above the W door, an attractive baroque cloister (1683), and 15–17C paintings in the refectory.

The largest village is **Tkon** (800 inhab.) at the S end opposite Biograd. The parish church has a Madonna attributed to the 15C Zadar artist, Petar Jordanić. The walled monastery of *Čokovac* on a high hill overlooking Tkon can be reached in 40 minutes on foot, or with less effort in 15 minutes from Ugrinići, a coastal hamlet nearer Kraj (comp. above).

Founded by Benedictines from Biograd after their town was razed by Venice in 1125, the monastery was repeatedly attacked until after the peace of Zadar in 1358, when most of the present buildings were erected. It became a leading centre of the Salvonic rite and Glagolitic writing. The monastery was closed by the Napoleonic invaders and reopened only in 1956 as the sole Benedictine monastery in Yugoslavia. During the war it served as a secret HQ of British intelligence agents in this part of the Adriatic.

The monastic church, a plain Gothic edifice dedicated to Sv. Kuzma i Damjan, was begun in 1367. The W doorway has a statue of the Madonna and Child in the tympanum with the date of the church's completion (1418) and the arms of Bp Maripetro of Split. A contemporary statue of one of the dedicatees stands on the W gable. In the interior hangs a large Gothic Crucifixion. The sacristy is a Romanesque fragment of the original foundation.

15   Zadar to Split

ROAD, Highway N2/E65. 30km **Biograd.**—46km **Šibenik.**—61km **Trogir.**—27km **Split**.

Frequent buses.

The Adriatic Highway continues through relatively flat countryside that is rapidly being developed for the tourist trade (villas, hotels, and campsites are already too numerous). There are still good sea views all the way to Trogir, after which the road turns inland, passing through the industrial suburbs of Split. Šibenik, now a major industrial centre, has an interesting medieval quarter on the water. Trogir is one of the better-preserved Venetian settlements in Dalmatia and one of the more pleasant towns on the Yugoslav coast.

Leaving Zadar by PUT N. TESLE, turn right at the crossroads to follow the coast road S with views out to sea of Ugljan and Pašman.—11km **Sukošan** is a dilapidated village with a good sandy beach. The 17C parish church of *Sv. Kasjan* has a decorated pre-Romanesque altarpiece built into the wall over the side entrance, and similar pre-Romanesque decoration can be seen on the doorposts of the cemetery church nearby. Ruins of the summer palace of Abp Valaresso of Zadar

(15C) remain near the harbour. A byroad leads inland from Sukošan to join (8km) the road from Zadar to Bankovac.

Continue S with the island of Pašman on the right and pass through (8km) *Krmčina* with remains of the Roman aqueduct from Vrana to Zadar. On the low peninsula of Tukljaća just before the road forks right to Turanj is a well-preserved small pre-Romanesque church (11C). A Glagolitic inscription on the lintel mentions the Mogorovići, one of the 12 tribes of Croatia that concluded the treaty of union with Hungary in 1102.—23km *Turanj* takes its name from the large fortress erected in the 17C as a defence against the Turks. A corner tower and part of the battlemented walls still remain, and other parts have been incorporated into the houses along the front.

6km **Filipjakov**, a pleasant village, was once the harbour for the Benedictine abbey of Rogovo, c 1km inland. Its small church (Sv. Rok; 12–14C), easily reached by a good country road, contains a fine painted Gothic Crucifixion (key from parish priest at Filipjakov).

5km **Biograd** or *Biograd na moru*, just off the highway to the right (1km) is reviving, after centuries of neglect and stagnation, as a pleasant seaside resort (2400 inhab.) with a modern centre and a pine-shaded beach. So thorough were the two destructions of Biograd that all that remains of the historic small town is a few fragments in the modest town museum.

Biograd, meaning 'white city' (Alba Civitas in the early Middle Ages) became one of the seats of the peripatetic kings of Croatia and in 1050 was made a bishopric by Petar Krešimir, who later installed his court here permanently. Koloman was crowned here in 1102 (Rex Hungariao, Croatiae et Dalmatiae) as a result of the union with Hungary, but in 1125 the town was razed by Doge Michieli. After the sack of Zadar by the Fourth Crusade (1202) a number of refugees here founded 'New Zadar' (Zara Nueva), which, when they returned home, became Zara Vecchia, still its name in Italian. Later fortified against the Turks, the town was abandoned and burnt in 1646 during the Candian War.

A good asphalt and gravel road, lined with cypresses, leads inland through the former Borelli estates, now a state co-operative, in the fertile Vransko polje, reclaimed from marshland in 1897. At 6km turn right, catching sight of Vransko jezero (Vrana Lake).—At **Vrana** (4km further) is the enormous ruin of the *Castle* of first the Knights Templar (1138–1311) and, after their suppression, of the Knights of St. John (1311–92). The castle fell into disuse after the coming of the Turks (1538) and was dismantled during the Venetian occupation of 1647. Even more interesting is the *Turkish Han* or Caravanserai (1644) of the native vizier and Kapudanbaša (Admiral) Jusuf Mašković, one of very few Turkish buildings still standing on the Adriatic coast and one of the best examples of a caravanserai in Yugoslavia, although dilapidated and used as a farmyard. A triple archway with Oriental arches gives access to a broad courtyard, with a Turkish well. A second courtyard is lined on three sides by travellers' rooms on two floors each with a chimney. A walk round the outside of the han gives an idea of its massive construction and a view of two Moorish windows in the W wall.—The return to the coast may be made at Pakoštane (see below).

The Adriatic Highway now runs a little inland.

5km **Pakoštane** is a village with a good sand and shingle beach, shaded by pine trees, where the Club Mediterranée maintains a permanent camp. Within 15 minutes walk is the semi-salt *Vransko jezero*, the largest lake in Dalmatia (31km^2) rich in mullet, mackerel and eels. It offers excellent duck shooting in the season. A minor road runs past the lake to Vrana (see above).

Beyond the narrow neck of land dividing Vransko jezero from the sea lies (17km) **Pirovac** on the deeply indented bay of the same name, with a pleasant pebble and sand beach and remains of 16C defensive walls. In the chapel of the Draganić-Vrančić family in the cemetery is a rich Gothic sarcophagus (1447) by Andrija Budčić and Lorenzo Pincino.

About 4km beyond Pirovac an asphalt road branches right to **Murter** (19km^2), a populous small island linked to the mainland by a bridge over the Murterski kanal. Crossing the bridge at (6km) *Tijesno*, a pleasant village straddling the channel at its narrowest point, the road continues to (7km) *Betina* and 2km *Murter*, the main settlement (2150 inhab.) on the island. The baroque parish church (Sv. Mihovil) has a high altar by Pio and Vicko dell' Acqua (1770). Murter is a favourite starting point for excursions to the Kornat Islands (see Rte 14C).

12km **Vodice** is an inexpensive small resort (2900 inhab.) very popular with Yugoslavs. The road swings inland to cross (7km) the handsome bridge across the Krka estuary.

5km **ŠIBENIK**, one of the leading cities of the Adriatic coast, with a fine cathedral, lies on a long, narrow and almost landlocked lagoon near the mouth of the river Krka. Electro-chemical and other industries N and S of the old centre have encouraged a rapid rise of population in recent years and the town (40,000 inhab.) is an important port exporting bauxite and a lively centre, though not well situated for sea-bathing. May and October tend to have the greatest rainfall.

Post Office: 39 Vladimira Nazora ul.

Information: *Turističko društvo*, 2 Trg Republike, tel. 22075.

Amusements. Children's festival every other year (odd years).

History. Šibenik, a Slav settlement, grew up round the fortified hill of Sv. Ana, and is first mentioned in 1066 when a special assembly was called here by Petar Krešimir IV. Despite two short periods of Venetian occupation during the 12C, its Slavonic character remained and was augmented after the destruction of Biograd (1125), when most of the inhabitants fled to Šibenik. In 1167 Stephen IV of Hungary-Croatia gave the city a charter, and in 1298 it was made a bishopric by Pope Boniface VIII. Like other Dalmatian cities, Šibenik became involved in the struggles between Hungary-Croatia and Venice, and was ruled for a time by the Croatian feudal lords of Kačić and Šubić and later by King Stjepan Tvrtko of Bosnia. In 1412 Venice gained the upper hand, fostering two centuries of prosperity and learning in Šibenik. At the same time it suffered heavily from the Turks; seven major attacks culminated in 1647 when the town was heavily besieged by Tekely Pasha of Bosnia and successfully defended by Baron C.M. Degenfeld. From 1797 to 1815 Šibenik formed part of Napoleon's Illyria before passing to Austria until the First World War. In 1918 it was briefly occupied by Italy but it joined Yugoslavia in 1921 as a result of the Treaty of Rapallo. In Aug 1936 Edward VIII here embarked in the yacht 'Nahlin' for Istanbul, at a time when Anglo-Italian relations precluded departure from Venice. The town was occupied by Italy and Germany in 1941–44.

Among the best known natives of Šibenik are Juraj Šižgorić (1420–1509) the scholar and humanist; Antun Vrančić (Antonius Verancius, 1504–73), Abp of Gran and Primate and Viceroy of Hungary-Croatia; his nephew, Faust Vrančić (1551–1617), philosopher and inventor; the engravers, Martin Koluminć-Rota (Martinus Rota Sibenicensis, 1532?–82/3) and Natale Bonifacio (1548–92); Ivan Tomko Mrnavić (1580–1637?), scholar and historian; the painter Nikola Vladanov (1390?–1466?); the short-story writer, Simo Matavulj (1852–1908); and the Italian writer, Nicolò Tommaseo (1802–74).

On the waterfront a pleasant promenade, busy morning and afternoon with local boats bringing children to and from school, and in the evening with the Corzo, faces the Kanal Sv. Ante across the landlocked bay. The church of *Sv. Nikola* (1451), by Ivan Pribislavić, has a coffered wooden ceiling (1762) and ex-votos in the form of model ships.

Beyond the modern Town Hall, pleasant gardens front a section of the old fortifications that extend from a large pentagonal *Tower* to the cathedral steps. A pair of 18C French cannon and a bell, cast in

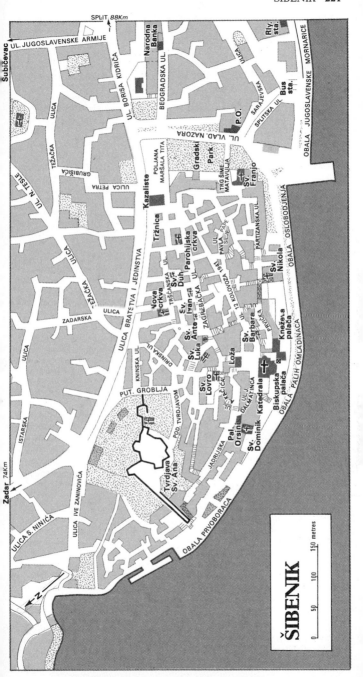

SPLIT *88Km*

Šubićevac

UL. JUGOSLAVENSKE ARMIJE

UL. BORISA KIDRIČA

BEOGRADSKA UL.

Narodna Banka

Rly. sta.

OBALA JUGOSLAVENSKE MORNARICE

SARAJEVSKA

SPLITSKA UL.

Bus sta.

P.O.

UL. VLAD. NAZORA

POLJANA MARŠALA TITA

Gradski Park

TRG ŠIME MATAVULJA

Sv. Franjo

TEŽAČKA

UL. N. TESLE

GRUBIŠIČA

ULICA PETRA

Kazalište

Tržnica

Parohijska crkva

PAVLA PAPE SILJE

PARTIZANSKA UL.

OBALA OSLOBOĐENJA

ULICA

ŽEŽIĆA

ZADARSKA

ULICA BRATSTVA I JEDINSTVA

ULICA

Nova crkva

TRŠČANSKA

Sv. Duh

Sv. Ante Ivana

ZAGREBAČKA

Sv. Nikola

Sv. Barbara

12 KOLOVOZA 1911

PANČIKA

Kneže-a palača

ULICA

ZADARSKA

ULICA

KNINSKA UL.

DRINSKA UL.

Sv. Luka

Loža

PUT. GROBLJA

POD TVRDJAVOM

Sv. Lovro

KRKIĆA

UL. DALMATINCA

Katedrala

Biskupska palača

OBALA PALIH OMLADINACA

ISTARSKA

ULICA IVE ZANINOVIĆA

JADRUSKA

Pal. Orsini

Sv. Dominik

Tvrdjava Sv. Ana

Zadar *74Km*

ULICA S. NINIČA

OBALA PRVOBORACA

OBALA PRVOBORACA

N

ŠIBENIK

0   50   100   150 metres

Ancona in 1266 and recently dredged from the sea, stand in front of the Gothic *Mliječna vrata*, and busts of local partisan heroes line the walks. The next rectangular tower that projects to seaward once held the Venetian law courts and dungeons. The Renaissance *Morska vrata* opens between the Governor's and the Bishop's Palaces, affording the most picturesque approach to the cathedral. A better first impression of the exterior is, however, gained by continuing along the waterfront as far as *Sv. Dominik*, a church rebuilt in 1906, but preserving old fragments behind and, inside, paintings by Palma the Younger and Matteo Ponzoni, from which you turn back to mount a broad flight of steps.

The ***Cathedral of Sv. Jakov***, a striking amalgam of Gothic and Renaissance styles with many individual features, stands in an enclosed square (Trg republike) just above the quay. The building was begun in 1431 on the site of an older church after a design sometimes attributed to Antonio di Pier Paolo Dalle Masegne, by the Italian architects Francesco di Giacomo, Lorenzo Pincino, and Antonio Busato with the assistance of local masons. The side walls and W front were erected to the height of the W and N portals (the decoration of which was completed by Bonino da Milano), when in 1441 local dissatisfaction was expressed with both the old-fashioned (Gothic) style and the cost. Juraj Matejević Dalmatinac (Giorgio Orsini) was appointed master of the works, and under his direction the side walls were completed and the choir added. The apses, baptistery (1462), and sacristy (1454) followed, after which Orsini retired to Italy leaving the work to assistants. After his death in 1475 had brought work to a halt, the building was resumed in 1477 under Nikola Firentinac, who completed the aisles and the W front and placed the dome above the crossing. The nave roof was completed to his design by Bartolomeo di Giacomo da Mestre and his son Pietro, who virtually finished the building. The wheel-window in the W front was carved by Ivan Mastičević (Giovanni da Zara; 1536) and the church was consecrated in 1555. In 1850–60 the cupola and the nave vault were restored.

The WEST FRONT shows clearly the three stages of construction. Its unusual but successful resolution of Gothic and Renaissance elements became the model for the composite style that survived so long on the Adriatic coast. The richly ornamented *W Portal* is by Bonino da Milano. On either side a fluted column carries a two-storied tabernacle. The jambs are carved with figures of the apostles culminating in a keystone depicting Christ blessing. The graceful upper part with semicircular gable and quadrants over the aisles in Lombardesque fashion is purely Renaissance in feeling, though the large wheel-window in the centre is Gothic in detail.

The NORTH or LION PORTAL (Lavlja vrata), in the centre of the Gothic N wall, is partially composed of Romanesque elements from the earlier church. Octagonal columns on a pair of lions support on their spreading capitals Romanesque statues of Adam and Eve. Gothic tabernacles above hold figures of SS. Peter and Paul, by Juraj Dalmatinac. Above the pointed windows a rich cornice of interlaced trefoils resting on corbelled heads is topped with a continuous horizontal cable moulding, another surprising blend of Romanesque, Gothic, and Renaissance motifs.

The Gothic elements appear less dominant from the far side of the square, from which you can see also the singular barrel vaulted roofs of the nave, aisles, and transept, and the octagonal cupola. The system of tongued and grooved stone employed on such a scale is unique to Šibenik and an impressive feat of construction.

A narrow opening gives access to the EAST END where the three *Apses*, rising from different levels, are given cohesion by a magnificent *Frieze of 74 portrait heads of contemporary figures. On the NE angle a lively scroll and inscription record the laying of the foundations of the choir and apses in 1443 by Juraj Dalmatinac.

In the beautiful **Interior**, seen to advantage in the early morning, the nave and aisles are divided by graceful Gothic arcades resting on six pairs of columns with modified Corinthian capitals. An unusual frieze is carved with acanthus leaves blowing in the wind, above which a low triforium in classical style rises to a plain clerestory. An undecorated barrel-vault binds together the disparate elements to produce a harmonious effect of proportion and spaciousness. The aisles are vaulted.

In the S AISLE are the Tomb of Juraj Šižgorić, executed by Andrija Aleši (1454) to a design by Juraj Dalmatinac; and a Crucifixion by Juraj Petrović (1455). In the N AISLE are the tomb of Ivan Stafilić (16C), a painting of Sts Fabian and Sebastian by Filippo Zanimberti (early 17C), and two angels in marble relief by Nikola Firentinac (Nicola Fiorentino). The wooden pulpit is by Girolamo Mondella (1624).

The raised CHOIR, approached by concentric steps between a balustrade, has seats of carved marble. The delicate balustrading of the galleries is carried round two of the piers to form a pair of ingenious ambones. The altar rails are by Nikola Firentinac. The decorated apses are pierced by windows in a transitional style between Gothic and Renaissance.

From the S apse stairs descend to the remarkable *BAPTISTERY, by Juraj Dalmatinac, a little gem of Italian late-Gothic design. It is square in plan but the walls are curved to form shallow apses. At the four corners low columns support the domed roof. Niches above the columns were intended for statuettes of prophets, but only two are filled (Simeon and David). Above, profusely decorated ribs taper to a central boss carved with the image of God the Father. The conches of the apses are carved and Gothic tracery fills the spandrels above. Angels with flowing draperies occupy the segments of the dome. The marble font, carried by a trio of putti, is the work of Aleši. The outer door leads into a graceful loggia at the foot of the steps to the Morska vrata.

The *Sacristy*, approached by a long flight of stairs, is ornamented in the manner of the apses and furnished with carved chests by Mondella.

On the NE side of the square stands the dignified **Loža** (Town Loggia; 1532–42), a long arcaded building of two stories in the style of Sammicheli, restored after bomb damage. The small church of *Sv. Barbara* (1447–51), opposite the E end of the cathedral, was built by Ivan Pribislavić and has a relief of St. Nicholas by Bonino da Milano on the N wall. Adjoining the SE corner of the cathedral is the **Biskupska palača** (1439–41) with a late Gothic arcaded court and, in an inner court, an excellent traceried three-light window. The figure above represents St. Michael, patron saint of the city. Two polyptychs by Nikola Vladanov (1340?–1466), a Šibenik painter, are kept in the palace chapel. The former *Kneževa palača* (15C), next to the Bishop's Palace, bears a fine statue of Niccolò Marcello (1609–11) and the elaborate coat of arms of the Šubić family. It now houses the **Muzej Grada Šibenika** (adm. 10–12 and 18–20; Sun 9–12; closed Mon), with archaeological collections, an altarpiece attributed to Paolo Veneziano, and exhibits devoted to the history of Šibenik.

The *Statue of Juraj Dalmatinac*, at the W end of the cathedral square is the last work of Ivan Meštrović (1961). The narrow UL. JURAJ DALMATINCA mounts in steps past two Venetian Gothic houses, and bears left above the *Velika čatrnja* (Great Well) built perhaps by Giacomo Correr (1446) and decorated with coats of arms and a Lion of St. Mark. This, the oldest part of the city, is embellished with a great number of interesting doorways, coats of arms, and inscriptions. The *Palača Orsini*, residence of Juraj Dalmatinac, was burnt down in the 16C, but the excellent doorway still stands, carved, presumably by Dalmatinac himself, with a bear, symbolising the sculptor's assumed Italian name (Orsini), and with the tools of his trade. Turn back and diverge almost immediately left along UL. ANDRIJE KAČIĆA. An archway by a quaint artificial grotto of 1926 leads to the monastery church of *Sv. Lovro* (1677–97), with baroque altars by Pio and Vicko dall'Acqua and (in the sacristy) an inscribed silver chalice presented by Marshal Marmont (1808). A staircase by the W end of the church gives access to the monastery, where a collection of paintings (15–18C) is exhibited. Among them are a 15C Madonna and Child (school of Bellini), the Assumption attributed to Dom. Robusti, and a portrait of Napoleon (the only one in Yugoslavia) by Andrea Appiani. The Codex of Bp Kosirić (16C) is illustrated with many fine drawings, although many more have been stolen.

Continue past the nunnery of *Sv. Luca* and the fine Gothic *Palača Foscolo* to the small 15C church of *Sv. Ante* (recently restored). Behind is the attractive little TRG PUĆKIH KAPETANA with a well. Steps on the left lead up through a maze of narrow streets to the 12–13C Fortress of *Sv. Ana* (rebuilt 16–17C), now used as a signalling station. In picturesque Tršćanska ul. is the so-called *Nova Crkva* or church of *Sv. Marija Milosrdje* (Our Lady of Compassion) built (1516) in transitional Gothic-Renaissance style, with a richly decorated interior. The coffered ceiling (1623–32) is by Girol. Mondella, Ivan Bojković, and Andrija Sisanović, the wall paintings by Mihovil Parkić (1619) and Antun Moneghin (1628). A Venetian Gothic guildhall adjoins the church and in the wall of the courtyard between them is a good Pietà by Nikola Firentinac (1502). Another relief, showing the burial of Christ, by Ivan Pribislavić, adorns the bell tower (by Ivan Skoko, 1742–59).

ZAGREBAČKA UL., the medieval main street to the S, retains many churches and patrician houses. Midway is the Renaissance church of *Sv. Ivan Krstitelj (John the Baptist, 15–17C), with a graceful ornamented staircase and balcony on the S side by Nikola Firentinac and Ivan Pribislavić (1460). A lintel by Pribislavić beneath the balcony, depicting St. John, shows the city and cathedral of Šibenik in the background. The baroque bell tower, erected to celebrate the withdrawal of the Turks from Dalmatia, incorporates a Turkish clock of 1648. Beyond the Renaissance *Palača Mišić* lies the small KREŠIMIROV TRG, with a local market and the *Palača Draganić*, behind which a narrow alley leads left to the church of *Sv. Duh* (Holy Spirit), a small gem of Dalmatian Renaissance architecture built by Vicko Piakarić in 1592–93. The Serbian Orthodox church of **Uspenje Bogorodice** (The Assumption), also known as *Parohijska crkva* (1390), originally belonged to the Benedictines but was presented to the Orthodox church by Marshal Marmont during the rule of Napoleon (1805) and is now the seat of the Orthodox bishop of Dalmatia. The W front has a remarkable baroque bell-cot (late 16C) incorporated into the wall; within are a number of Italo-Cretan icons.

The limits of the old town are marked by the spacious POLJANA MARŠALA TITA, dominated by the *Narodno Kazalište* (theatre) and a modern civic centre incorporating a Venetian bastion with a large relief of St. Michael.

The open TRŽNICA (market) lies along Ul. K. Tomislava, which is the main exit to Knin and N Dalmatia. Hence streets lead uphill to the residential quarter and the massive *Šubičevac Castle*, also known as the *Forte Barone* (in honour of Baron C.M. Degenfeld who in 1647 defended the city against attack by the Turks), with excellent views over the town and harbour. Behind the castle a monument (K. Angeli Radovani) and memorial park mark the spot where Rade Končar and 25 partisans were executed by the Italians in 1942, and a path ascends to *Sv. Ivan*, the highest of Šibenik's three forts.

To the SW of Poljana Maršala Tita the *Town Park* and quayside enclose a picturesque section of the old town in which many ancient houses display interesting doors, windows and balconies. The 14C Gothic *Franciscan Church*, adjoining the park, has been remodelled inside, with a richly painted coffered ceiling by Marco Capogrosso (1674), and baroque wooden altars made in Venice by Iseppo Ridolfi (1635) to designs by Girolamo Mondella. The bell tower was erected by Ivan Skoko in the 18C and the monastery library possesses a good collection of codices and incunabula. The silver on display includes several reliquaries.

Immediately opposite the old town the narrow *Kanal Sv. Ante* gives access to the Bay of Šibenik from the sea. On the NE side of the strait is the bathing beach *Jadrija* (ferries every half hour in the season), whereas to the SW is the Fort of *Sv. Nikola* (1540–47) built by Gian Girolamo Sammicheli. This operates together with Sv. Ana (comp above) as a siqnal station controlling navigation in the strait.

Frequent ferries run from Šibenik to the islands of Zlarin and Prvić. **Zlarin**, the largest and best known of the small group of islands off the coast at Šibenik, is situated immediately opposite the entrance to Šibenik harbour. *Zlarin*, the only village (920 inhab.), is noted for the beauty of the local costume, now seen only on feast days, and its coral fishery, the only one in Dalmatia. The local co-operative also sells coral jewellery. The baroque Parish Church was built by Ivan Skoko (1735–49), though the bell tower is older. In the church of Gospa od Rašelja (15C, restored 1714) is an altarpiece by the Dall' Acqua brothers (1767). Of the baroque summer villas the Palača Žuliani (early 17C) is the most interesting.

Prvić lies just to the N of Zlarin and slightly closer inshore. *Prvić luka*, the larger and more attractive of its two villages, has a 15C parish church where Faust Vrančić (comp. above) is buried. His summer home (15-minute walk), containing his portrait (1605) and a Madonna (school of Titian), lies half way between Prvić and *Šepurine*, the other village.

EXCURSION FROM ŠIBENIK. To **Skradin, the River Krka, Drniš, and Knin** (77km). The journey may be made entirely by road or by a combination of road and boat. Inquire at the Turistlko društvo for details.

Leave Šibenik by UL. BRATSTVA I JEDINSTVA and STARA CESTA and cross the Adriatic Highway. The road now climbs through karst country with views left over the Prukljansko jezero and Krka estuary.—At (11km) *Tromilja* the road divides; for Drniš, see below. Keeping left you come almost immediately (1km) to a second fork where the road divides for Skradin and Skradinski buk.

A road on the left descends by hairpin bends to a bridge over the River Krka and (7km) **Skradin** (*Skradinski buk*), a sleepy small town. Known to the Romans as *Scardona* and a city of some consequence under the Croatian Šubići, the Venetians, and the Turks (1522–1684), Skradin declined after the 17C and in the 19C was notoriously malarial. Juraj Ćulinović (Giorgio Schiavone, c 1436–1504) was born here. The Serbian Orthodox church of *Sv. Spiridon* has a good 16C Venetian iconostasis with three life-size figures; and, among the icons of the Italo-Cretan school around the walls, a Last Judgment by Gregory Margazinis (1647). Leading NW from Skradin is the road for Zadar by which you will return from Knin (see below).

The Krka Falls may be reached in half an hour by boat from Skradin, or by car by returning to the second fork and continuing to (8km) *Skradinski buk*. The volume of water is greatest in spring and early summer. The falls comprise 17 steps dropping nearly 50m in four stages over a distance of about 500m. Outcrops of rock and clumps of vegetation spread across the river allowing close access to individual rapids. At the top end, near the main observation platform is a cluster of old water mills. One is still used to pound the woollen blankets of the local peasants; the water-powered oak hammers can be seen in action.

A further excursion may be made up river by boat (hired at the falls). From the broad lagoon above the falls, where the Krka is joined by its tributary the Čikola, the river narrows between water meadows enclosed by steep limestone cliffs. After half an hour it widens again to reveal the beautiful island of **Visovac**, thickly planted with cypress and poplar. The *Franciscan Monastery and Seminary* (sometimes shown on request) includes in a small collection of pictures (mostly 17–18C) a Madonna (1576) and an Annunciation (17C) in mother-of-pearl inlay. The library has one of three known copies (others in the British Museum and the Bodleian) of an illustrated translation of Aesop's fables, published by Boninus de Boninis (Dobrić Dobrićević) of Dubrovnik in 1487 and a collection of Turkish documents (signed decree of Sultan Mehmed IV). Visovac and its surroundings provided the setting for Simo Matavulj's celebrated novel, *Bakonja fra Brne* (1892). Upstream there is good fishing for brown trout and eels.

Continuing upriver you pass the mouth of the Voša tributary on the left and high on the cliffs to the SW the ruined circular *Uzdah-kula* (tower of sighs), a Turkish stronghold during the 16–17C. You then enter the deep narrow *Visovrački kanjon* with the ruins of *Kamičak Castle* on the right, said to be the birthplace of Petar Svačić (1090–97), the last Croatian king, and come in c 15 minutes to Roški slap (Roški Falls; rfmts on W bank). The falls resemble those at Skradinski but have a smaller fall of 26m spread over 132m. A bridge carries the road from Drniš to Djevrske.

Above Roški slap the river is again navigable as far as the monastery of Arhand-jelovac, but in general it is difficult to find a boat and the upper reaches are best visited by road (see below).

By car the next objective is Drniš. Return to Tromilja and take the road that follows the river Čikola, with views into the canyon and across to the ruined castle of Ključ.

30km **Drniš**, a small country town beside the river Čikola on the edge of the fertile plain of Petrovo polje, has a colourful market on the fifth day of the month. The place was the main bridgehead of the Turkish advance into N Dalmatia early in the 16C, and grew to a population of over 20,000 during the two centuries of Turkish rule, when it was known as 'little Sarajevo'. Few monuments remain. A ruined castle on the hill overlooks the town (view) and a roofless minaret. The only mosque remaining in Dalmatia has been converted into a church (*Sv. Ante*) but preserves Turkish honeycomb decoration. A *Town Museum* (adm. 8–12, 4–6) has been opened in the house of Božidar Adžija, a communist intellectual shot during the Second World War. Here is a collection of sculptures presented to the town in 1960 by Ivan Meštrović. Other works by Meštrović can be seen at the Dom kulture, the local hospital, and in the town park.

Meštrović was born at *Otavice*, a pretty village in an idyllic pastoral setting beside the river Čikola, 10km E of Drniš off the Knin main road. On a hill, to the S, stands the **Meštrović Mausoleum** (ask for the house of Ante Meštrović to obtain key and a guide). Designed by the sculptor for himself and his family, the mausoleum was built in 1926–30 of stone with cast bronze doors, on which the heads of the members of the family are depicted. Within, niches are decorated with religious scenes carved in low relief, and a single low altar is surmounted by an unusual Crucifixion, in which a youthful Christ is enfolded in the arms of a guardian angel who forms the cross.

Continuing N from Drniš, the road passes between Mt Promina (left; 1147m) and Mt Svilaja (right; 1206m) keeping parallel with the Drniš–Knin railway line.—11km *Biskupija*, a hamlet just off the road (right), preserves considerable remains of five medieval churches and a monastery (9–11C). The site is associated with the reign of King Zvonimir of Croatia who died here in 1089. Its excavation (1886) marked the beginning of autonomous Croatian archaeology and the rich finds of medieval jewellery, pottery, sculpture, and architectural fragments, formerly displayed at Knin, are now to be seen in Split. In 1938 a memorial church was erected with sculptures by Ivan Meštrović and mural paintings by J. Kljaković.

14km **Knin** a railway junction and market town, is picturesquely sited on the upper reaches of the Krka river. It was the seat of the last Croatian king, Petar Svačić (1090–97), and here on 4 December 1944 the Partisans won a decisive victory over the Germans. The town is dominated from the hill of Sv. Spas by a huge *Fortress*, one of the largest in Yugoslavia, comprising three sections, Romanesque, Gothic, and 18C Venetian. The Gothic portion was reconstructed and heightened by the Turks in the mid 16C and the Venetians restored the whole in the early 18C. The baroque entrance gate with the lion of St. Mark dates from 1711.

A pleasant excursion from Knin is to the *Topoljski Slap* (Topolje Falls) on the river Krčić, 2km SW of the town.

From Knin cross the river Krka and follow the Obrovac road for 7km before turning W along the Krka. In the hamlet of (21km) *Ivoševac* stand two enormous arches known popularly as Šuplja crkva, the remains of the Roman praetorium of the castrum *Burnum*. A narrow road leads S to the falls of Brljan and Manojlovac, the second particularly fine, with a width of 200m and a drop of 60m. About 1.5km downstream are the Rošnjak (or Sondovjel) and Miljacka falls, the latter with a drop of 24m.

7km **Kistanje** is the starting point for a short excursion to the Orthodox monastery of Sv. Arhandjel, known as Arhandjelovac. A gravel road runs left in 4km to the brow of the Krka valley, with views of the river and monastery and SE to Mt Promina. To the NE are visible the round tower and ruins of the medieval Čučevo Castle, built by the Šubić family, and opposite it, on the far side of the river, the 15C castle of the Nelepić family. A path leads down to **Arhandjelovac**, which stands in delightful surroundings beside the river. The monastery was founded in 1345 from a bequest by Princess Jelena Šubić, sister of Stefan Dušan of Serbia, and altered in 1402 and 1683. The church is in Byzantine style, cruciform in plan with a large green cupola over the crossing. The iconostasis is Greek 17C work with 18C Russian gates. The best icons however, St. Jerome (1562) and Three Hermits in the Wilderness (16C), are in the library. Here also is the illuminated 14C Mokropoljsko evandjelije (Mokropolje Gospel), discovered locally in 1954, A Russian gospel of 1689 with MS illustrations, and a Bulgarian paterikon of 1346. A collection of embroidery includes a fine epitra-chelion (stole) embroidered in gold with figures of 32 saints.

From Kistanje the road continues W through more fertile country to (10km) *Djevrske*, where a side road leads left to Roški slap (comp. above). A little beyond Djevrske another road leads left to the village of **Bribir** (5km). The hill of Glavice is the site of Roman *Varvaria* and medieval *Bribir*, seat of the Šubić family, the most powerful Croatian nobles of Dalmatia in the 13–14C. Bribir was partially explored in 1912–13, but renewed excavations are still continuing. The Roman walls stand in places to a height of 5m and the Forum and several villas have been excavated. Among Croatian buildings, the most interesting are the 13C church of Sv. Marija, beneath which one of the Šubić graves has been found, and a large Franciscan monastery. The round tower at the summit is a relic of Turkish occupation and the adjoining fortifications were erected by the Venetians in the 17C.

Returning S to the main road continue to (12km) Skradin (see above) and thence to (15km) Šibenik.

The Adriatic Highway curves round the Krka estuary to return to the shore at Ražine.

8km *Brodarica*. Across a strait (400m wide) from the hamlet lies the village and island of **Krapanj** (boat every hour) with an attractive waterfront. There is a sponge fishery and factory in the village, founded in 1700 by a Greek Franciscan monk on the model of Greek fisheries. The Franciscan monastery, founded in the 15C, has a contemporary Madonna in the church and a Renaissance cloister. In the refectory an extensive collection of sponges, shells, and coral, with Greek and Roman pottery brought up from the seabed, is arranged below a Last Supper by Francesco da Santacroce.

Hugging the coast the road continues in a series of serpentine bends with views out to sea of the Šibenik archipelago.

17km **Primošten** is an attractive old place picturesquely situated on an island once joined to the mainland by a bridge, now by a causeway. The church was excellently restored in 1967 and given a beautiful modern sanctuary. There are numerous pebble and shingle beaches around the village and the Esperantists have a permanent international camp in one of the bays. 7km **Rogoznica** is similar to Primošten, but quieter and set on a deep inlet just off the main highway (2km).

26km **TROGIR** (6000 inhab.) occupies a compact island, joined to the mainland by a bridge over an artificial channel and to the larger island of Čiovo by a bascule bridge across a narrow strait, a situation similar to that of Taranto in Italy. One of the more attractive and interesting towns on the Adriatic, Trogir has a marvellously preserved medieval quarter. Many Romanesque and early Gothic houses are still lived in and, though individual buildings have been deprived of symmetry and beauty by inept repair, the general aspect of an early medieval town survives.

Post Office: Ulica Rade Koncara.

Information: *Turističko društvo*, Palača Cipiko, tel. 73554. *Turistički Savez Opcine*, Titova Obala, tel. 73412.

History. *Tragurion* was founded in the 3C by Syracusan Greeks and as Tragurium was developed by the Romans into a major port. The rise of Salona overshadowed the city for a while, but with the latter's destruction by the Slavs and Avars (614) it rose to prominence again, particularly under the aegis of Byzantium. In the 9C a prosperous Trogir began to pay tribute to the Croatians,

Trogir, the waterfront

but in 998 it was captured by Doge Pietro Orseolo II of Venice, and from then on shared the vicissitudes of the cities of Dalmatia. In the 12C Trogir recognised Hungary–Croatia, Venice, and Byzantium in turn, seeking always to preserve a degree of autonomy, which did not save it from being sacked in 1123 by the Saracens or in 1171 by Venice. In 1242 King Bela IV of Hungary took refuge in the city from the Tartars, whose leader, Caydan, brought his troops to the very gates. Periods of submission followed: to Bosnia, the counts Šubić of Bribir, Venice, Hungary, and even a brief period of independence. In 1398 the Genoese fleet took refuge here after their defeat at Chioggia, but in 1420 Trogir was besieged and taken by Admiral Loredano of Venice, and thereafter, as *Traù*, the town led a peaceful existence under the Republic. In 1797, with the fall of Venice, Trogir passed to Austria, then to France (1806–14) and then back to Austria until the end of the First World War, when Yugoslavia came into being.

Famous natives include Blaž Trogiranin (15C), the painter; Ivan Duknović (Giovanni Dalmata da Traù, 1440?–1509?), the sculptor; Koriolan Cipiko (Coriolanus Cipicus, 1425–93), the humanist; Petar Berislavić (1450–1520), soldier-bishop and Ban of Croatia; Trankvil Andreis (Tranquillus Andronicus, 1490–1571), diplomat and friend of Erasmus; and Ivan Lučić (Ioannis Lucius, Giovanni Lucio, 1604–79), author of the first analytical history of Dalmatia, 'De Regno Dalmatiae et Croatia' (1666).

Trogir is separated from the mainland by a dike cut in the Middle Ages to strengthen the city's defences against the Turks. From the main highway and bus station, cross a stone bridge and pass between the pleasant gardens that occupy the site of the ring of walls demolished during French rule. Opposite the bridge, pass through the late-Renaissance *Kopnena vrata* (Porta terrae firmae), adorned above the keystone with the coat of arms of Antonio Bernardi (1656–60), the

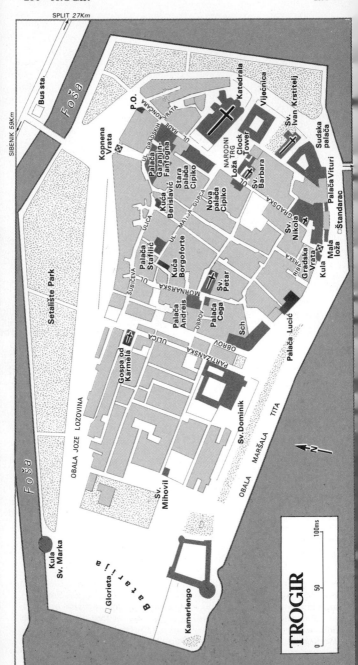

SPLIT 27Km

SIBENIK 59Km

Foša

Bus sta.

Foša

Šetalište Park

OBALA JOZE LOZOVINA

Foša

Kula Sv. Marka

Glorietta

Batarija

Kamerlengo

Sv. Mihovil

Gospa od Karmela

ULICA PARTIZANSKA

OBALA MARŠALA TITA

Sv. Dominik

OBROV

Palača Lučić

Palača Cega

Palača Andreis

UL. SUBIČEVA

Palača Stafilić

Kuća Borgoforte

UL. MORNARSKA

Sv. Petar

Sch

Kuća Berislavić

UL. MATIJA GUPCA

Stara palača Cipiko

Nova palača Cipiko

UL. GRADSKIH VRATA

UL. RADE KONČARA

P.O.

Kopnena Vrata

Palača Garanjin-Fanfogna

NARODNI TRG

Loža Clock Tower

Sv. Barbara

GRADSKA

RIBARSKA

Sv. Nikola

Gradska Vrata

Kula

Mala loža

Štandarac

Palača Vituri

Palača Ćipiko

Sudska palača

Sv. Ivan Krstitelj

Viječnica

Katedrala

TROGIR

0   50   100ms

Venetian governor who built it. The figure on top of the gate is St. John Orsini, the city's patron; the empty niche formerly held a Venetian lion. At the first junction turn left along UL. GRADSKIH VRATA to UL. RADE KONĆARA. In the pleasant small square on the left, the Post Office faces a 13C Romanesque house. The baroque *Palaca Garagnin-Fanfogna* houses the **Muzej Grada Trogira**, illustrating the history of Trogir; and the **Galeria Cate Dujšrin-Ribar**, with works by the painter, a native of Trogir.

Ul. Rade Konćara broadens in front of the cathedral before entering *NARODNI TRG, the spacious main square round which many of Trogir's most important buildings are harmoniously grouped. On the N side stands the *Cathedral of Sv. Lovrijenac* (St. Lawrence), a Romanesque basilica, begun c 1180 on the foundations of an earlier church ruined by the Saracens, and completed towards 1250. The S wall, decorated with blind arcading, terminates in an unusual dwarf loggia added when the pitch of the aisle roofs was altered. The interior division into five bays is marked externally by pilaster strips. The plain central Romanesque S Portal, or *Kneževa vrata*, approached by steps, bears an inscription dated 1213. The E end, with three apses ornamented with slender columns (spirally fluted on the main apse) and blind arcading, and pierced with well-proportioned round-head windows, is a model of its kind.

Enclosing the full width of the W end is a *Narthex*, or Galilee, consisting of three large rib-vaulted bays rising to the height of the aisles. The walls are embellished with slender, rounded shafts and more blind arcading finished with a frieze of acanthus leaves, and a graceful balustrade encloses the flat roof. Above the SW bay soars the **Bell Tower**; an intended companion on the N side was never built. The first story above the balustrade was built before 1422. The second, added by Matej Gojković, is a splendid example of traceried Venetian Gothic, and the third, completed by Trifun Bokanić in 1598, combines Gothic detail with Renaissance feeling well enough for the four evangelists by Alessandro Vittoria at the corners of the tall crowning pyramid to harmonise successfully.

A high Romanesque arch gives access to the vaulted interior which conceals the magnificent **WEST PORTAL**, a work of simple conception and rich detail, marvellously executed. Basically the work of an otherwise unknown local master, Radovan (Raduanus), whose name and the date (1240) are inscribed on the lintel, the portal is Romanesque in conception and design, but with Gothic elements where the work was continued by pupils. The portal rises from a low marble step decorated with blind arcading. Flanking the doorway, classic consoles support a lion and lioness, above which stand life-size figures of Adam and Eve. A gabled moulding, added in the 14C, to enclose a niche containing a statue of St. Lawrence and frame the whole, springs rather clumsily from the outer capitals.

Two richly carved orders within are supported at the bottom by figures in Eastern dress apparently imitated from some lost Roman triumphal arch. The outer jamb has three apostles to either side framed in vine-leaf medallions, whereas its inner sides are decorated with a profusion of beasts. On the inner jamb the months are depicted in scenes from rural life, and the inner faces are decorated with exquisite scroll-work. Two delicately sculptured limestone shafts at the inner edge are carved with lively hunting scenes. The winged cherubs in the impost blocks were added by Nikola Firentinac. The lunette and the inner arch tell the story of the Nativity: in the centre the Virgin with the infant Saviour in the manger with below, the

Trogir, the main portal of the Cathedral

washing of the child by Joseph; to the right the three kings approach
on horseback, to the left shepherds tend their flocks. On the arch the
Annunciation at the bottom (left and right) and the Adoration of the
Magi at the top, with flying angels between. The outer arch shows ten
scenes from the life of Christ, beginning with the Baptism (bottom
right) and rising in alternate left and right panels to the Crucifixion.
Two small Romanesque transennae on the W wall depict a sinner
being devoured by snakes, and a griffin devoured by lions.

The **Interior**, sombre and mystical, is basilican in plan, the narrow-
ness of the aisles accentuated by their great height and the weight of
the piers supporting the Romanesque arcades. The nave was vaulted
in 1427–40. Paintings on the piers of the nave include a representation

of the 14C Bp Augustin Kažotić (Cazotti) by Palma the Younger (1599) and Mary Magdalen and a Pietà by Padovanino. The octagonal *Pulpit* (13C) is supported on marble columns with Romanesque capitals. The carved walnut *Choir Stalls* worked in Venetian Gothic style by Ivan Budinić, a local artist, show invention of design and exuberance in execution. Set into the end pillar on the N side, beside the high altar, is a Venetian Gothic tabernacle (15C) with doors carved with a Crucifixion scene. The altar is covered by a striking 13C *Ciborium*, supported on four marble columns with fine capitals and culminating in an octagonal cupola rising in two stories with open colonnades to a pyramidal roof. The figures of the Annunciation above the columns are signed Mauro (14C). The main apse retains a synthronon, ornamented with blind arcading, but the bishop's cathedra in the centre is missing.

A majestic triumphal arch opens from the N Aisle into the *CHAPEL OF IVAN ORSINI*, one of the outstanding creations of the Renaissance in Dalmatia, built by Nikola Firentinac (1468–97; otherwise Nicola di Giovanni da Firenze, a pupil of Donatello). The Annunciation figures added above the cornices came from some earlier monument. The chapel is rectangular with a coffered barrel vault, richly decorated by Nikola himself and Andrija Aleši. A central tondo is filled with a half-length figure of Christ, whereas each panel bears a cherub's head and wings. Above the altar rests the Gothic marble sarcophagus (1348) of John Orsini, first Bp of Trogir (died 1111), a patron saint of the city. The lower part of the walls is divided into 17 high relief panels representing half-open double doors from which emerge cherubs bearing torches. Above, elaborate niches, separated by engaged columns surmounted by putti, contain statues of saints and, on the rear wall, Christ flanked by Mary and John the Baptist. SS. Thomas and John the Evangelist (left) are the work of Ivan Duknović (a local sculptor who later made his name in Rome as Giovanni Dalmata). The lunette above the windows is filled with a Crowning of the Virgin.

Farther E is the Sacristy, constructed in 1446–50, with an elaborately carved and inlaid Wardrobe by Grgur Vidov (1458). Here are displayed items from the *Treasury*. Among the paintings are a St. Martin by Salvator Rosa.

The Gothic chapel of *Sv. Jeronim* (Jerome), built in 1438, opens from the W end of the N aisle.

From the Galilee opens the BAPTISTERY, the principal known work of Andrija Aleši (1467). Over the door a relief shows the Baptism of Christ. The small chamber has a coffered vault, similar to that of Sv. Ivan Orsini, but slightly pointed, with fluted niches and a frieze of putti bearing garlands, in the manner of Juraj Dalmatinac. In the lunette, St. Jerome (relief). The sacristan will also admit to a spiral stair leading to the flat roof and thence to the top of the Bell Tower (view).

Opposite the cathedral porch is the 15C **Nova Palača Cipiko**, in the Venetian Gothic style (attributed to Nikola Firentinac and Andrija Aleši), with two notable three-light windows and a handsome doorway in Ul. Matije Gupca. In the vestibule are the Cipiko arms and a large wooden figurehead in the shape of a cock, captured from the Turks by the Trogir galley at the battle of Lepanto. It houses the *Turističko društvo*, through which entrance may be gained to the courtyard, with Renaissance arcading, an open gallery and a well-head decorated with the Cipiko arms. In this palace a previously unknown chapter of the Satyricon by Petronius, called Trimalchio's Feast, was discovered in 1650. Formerly an arch spanned Ul. Matije Gupca joining this palace to the **Stara Palača Cipiko** (Old Palace). Its façade has two three-light windows in Venetian Gothic, of which that on the left is a modern copy. A doorway in Gradska ul, gives access to the courtyard with a doorway at the top of a flight of stairs by Nikola Firentinac and a laurel-wreathed head by Ivan Duknović, said to be of King Matthias Corvinus of Hungary. Hanibal Lučić, the 15C poet from Hvar, often stayed here.

On the S side of the square is the fine city **Loža** (Loggia) erected in the 15C and restored in 1890. Some of the columns supporting the roof are antique, while of the capitals one is Roman, three Byzantine and two of Renaissance work. On the rear wall a relief by Ivan Meštrović (1936) depicts Ban Berislavić on horseback, and on the E wall a large relief by Nikola Firentinac (1471) showing Justice with St. John Orsini, holding a model of the city, and St. Lawrence. The composition was ruined in 1932 when the central lion of St. Mark was dynamited (it bore the equivocal text 'Iniusi punientur et semen impiorum peribit'). The incident provoked a minor international crisis between Italy and Yugoslavia. The judge's bench and table date from 1606. The near wall of the loggia is formed by the small church of *Sv. Barbara* (or Sv. Martin), which is entered from Gradska ul. (key from Turističko društvo). Built in the 9–10C it is a good example of an early Croatian church of Byzantine influence, narrow and lofty, with a semi-dome over the chancel and utilising Roman spolia (probably from Salona) for its columns and capitals. The altar rail has pre-Romanesque plaited decoration and an inscription records a gift to found the church by a certain Croatian lady, Dobrica.

The **Clock Tower**, which forms the E wall of the loggia, was once the Romanesque chapel of Sv. Sebastijan, remodelled in the Renaissance manner by Nikola Firentinac (1447) with figures of Christ and St. Sebastian over the doorway. In the interior, now used as a souvenir shop, survive the Romanesque apse and a lintel with pre-Romanesque ornamentation. The windows of the shop look on to the foundations of the pre-Romanesque church of *Sv. Marija*, dating from the 8C, with a curious plan having six apses. The large **Vijećnica** (Town Hall), formerly the Venetian governor's residence, closing the E end of the square, was erected in the 15C but remodelled in 1890. It bears the city arms in the centre, with those of St. John Orsini and an unknown noble over the two side doors. In the courtyard (good well-head) is a handsome 15C staircase by Matej Gojković, who may be portrayed in the stone head beneath the stairs. Numerous coats of arms adorn the walls, and the only lion of St. Mark remaining in Trogir.

Part of the S side of the Vijećnica is now used as the Kavana Radovan, beyond whose garden is the 13C Romanesque church of *Sv. Ivan Krstitelj* (John the Baptist). Contemporary with the cathedral, which it resembles in many constructional details, the church was once attached to a Benedictine abbey. The exterior, decorated with blind arcading under the eaves, has a Romanesque agnus dei above the W door and an unusually placed triple bell-cot added in the 14C. The interior houses a small *Museum of Religious Art* containing the tomb of Korijolan Cipiko, with a relief of the Deposition by Nikola Firentinac (1470); a large painted Crucifixion (15C); a polyptych in a Gothic frame and a Madonna of the Rosary by Blaz Trogiranin (15C); two painted doors from an organ case by Gentile Bellini, depicting SS.

Jerome and John the Baptist; a cast of Meštrović's John the Baptist (original in the baptistery at Split); illuminated manuscripts and codices; and silver and gold liturgical items, some of which were donated by Queen Elisabeth of Hungary, who was born in Trogir. Traces of frescoes have been found on the walls.

A promenade follows the line of the shore. Walk past the neo-Gothic *Sudska palača* (Courthouse), erected by the Austrians, on the right to a complex of buildings marking the line of the town walls. Beyond an attractive row of gabled fishermen's cottages, the former *Palača Vituri* (15–16C) incorporates in its tall balconied tower a medieval watch tower. It is now part of the Benedictine nunnery, the belfry of which (comp. below) rises behind. The beautiful **Mala Loža** (small loggia), erected by governor Alessandro Lipoman (1524–7) for the shelter of strangers awaiting admission to the city, serves as a fish market. Between the loggia and a tower remaining from the medieval fortifications opens the *Gradska vrata* (Porta civitatis, or Porta marina) with an inscription recording its erection in 1593 by governor Delfin Delfino and the original wooden gates still in place.

Just inside the gate is the entrance to *Sv. Nikola*, erected in the 15–16C on the site of the Romanesque church of Sv. Dujam, traces of which can be seen behind the altar. The bell tower (1593) by the Bokanić family has unusual stone lattices in the upper story to screen bell-ringing nuns from prying eyes. Immediately behind the church a door admits to a court in various Gothic styles. Two inscriptions are built into the walls, one in Greek of the 3C BC, the other concerning Ban Berislavić. The nunnery *Treasury* is notable for a rare marble *Relief of Kairos, the Greek god of luck (1C BC?; shown on request). This figure became the symbol of the 1936 Olympic Games. Among icons and paintings are exhibited a painted wooden polyptych (c 1400) and a Gothic Crucifixion.

Continuing along the shore, pass the stone *Štandarac* (1605) or flagpole, and the *Palača Lučić*, home of Ivan Lučić the historian; the façade has been modernised, but there is a good Renaissance courtyard and doorway. Trogir's principal school occupies a neo-Gothic edifice on the corner of Partizanska ul, a broad straight street following the course of an old moat, which divided the original town from Pašike, a later medieval extension. On the opposite corner rises the conspicuous Campanile of the **Dominican Church**, built in the 14C by Bitcula, sister of Bl. Augustine Gazotich (Augustin Kažotić, Bp of Zagreb; died 1323), a native of Trogir. The Virgin and Child in the lunette was carved by Niccoló Dente (1372). Within, the nave has a flat ceiling and the short chancel a pointed barrel vault. On the S wall the Subota tomb is by Nikola Firentinac (1469). There is a Circumcision (1607) by Palma the Younger, and a 15C polyptych of six panels. The Renaissance *Cloister* (apply to sacristan), bombed in the last war and now restored, houses a lapidary collection.

The imposing **Kaštel-Kamerlengo** in the SW corner of the town, a large Venetian fortress, complete with battlements and machicolated towers, was erected in 1424–37 to guard the harbour. The nine-sided principal tower (20m), called *Donjon*, is a reconstruction of a Genoese fort (1380) on the same spot. The interior is open and in summer becomes a cinema. At the side is a bronze war memorial by I. Mirković (1951). Across the *Batarija*, now used for football and gymnastics, stands the graceful classical *Glorietta* of Marshal Marmont, Napoleon's governor of Illyria. The bell tower (right) of the former church of *Sv. Mihovil*, destroyed during the Second World War, was built by Jerko Bokanić (1595). The landward end of Batarija is marked by the 15C round tower of Sv. Marko with conspicuous batter and machicolations. Here turn right along FORTIN. On the corner of Partizanska ul. (comp. above) is a fragment of a former bastion and a few steps down on the right is the small baroque church of *Gospa od Karmena* (Our Lady of Mt Carmel; 1618), with a 14C Gothic relief over the door and a Gothic Crucifixion inside. The whole quarter E of here, in an area roughly bounded by Fortin, Obrov, and the main square, repays exploration.

The small 16C church of *Sv. Petar*, in UL. OBROV, has a statue of St. Peter in the tympanum. In the Renaissance interior (coffered and painted ceiling) are paintings (16–18C), two Gothic crucifixes, a rustic wooden figure of Christ (15C) and a 17C baroque organ case. On the opposite side of the street are two Venetian Gothic mansions, the *Palača Cega* (left) and the *Palača Andreis*. MORNARSKA UL. and ŠUBIĆEVA UL. are lined with houses exhibiting Romanesque, Gothic and Renaissance features. You may regain the Land Gate by the latter street passing Berislavić's house on the corner of the street bearing his name; or return to the main square by UL. MATIJE GUPCA, in which stand the Venetian Gothic *Palača Stafilić* and the *Borgoforte Mansion*.

A bascule bridge crosses the strait to the island of Čiovo, linking Trogir with its suburb, also called *Čiovo*. The churches of Sv. Jakov and Gospa kraj mora (Our Lady by the Sea) contain late-Gothic polyptychs (15C), and Sv. Ante na Dridu (1432) a painting of SS. Anthony and Paul in the Desert by Palma the Younger. A minor road serves the village of Arbanasi. At 4km stands the 15C Dominican Monastery of *Sv. Križ* (Holy Cross), built by Ivan Drakanović and Nikola Mladinov, where the beautiful late Gothic cloister has an upper story on the S side, and (E side) the chapel of Sv. Jerolim (Jerome) in Venetian Gothic with a remarkable painted ceiling. The plain Gothic church has a fine Crucifixion (15C) over the main altar; the rustic 15C choir stalls have carved bench-ends (Cipiko arms). The two paintings on the N altars are by Matej Pončun (Ponzoni) of **Rab** (born Rab 1584, died Venice after 1663).

Continue S on the Adriatic Highway. 6km the road forks, the highway continuing (left) directly to Solin while the old road (poor surface) runs nearer the sea along the so-called **Kaštelanska Rivijera** with its eight Kaštela (fortresses).

The **Kaštela**, fortified mansions rather than castles, were built by the nobility of Trogir and, to a lesser extent, of Split between 1476 and 1556 as a defence against Turkish invasions. As a refuge for the local peasantry, they attracted the formation of villages. Only seven of the original 14 remain. The belt of land enclosing the villages is exceptionally fertile and the traditional vineyards are giving way to orchards and market gardens. The kaštela are becoming increasingly popular tourist resorts, particularly with Yugoslavs. A frequent bus service runs betwen Split and Trogir.

Pass the village of *Divulje* on the right, whence a gravel track leads up the mountainside to Bijaći (or Bihać), a residence of Croatian princes in the 9C (pre-Romanesque church of Sv. Marta, extensively restored) destroyed by the Turks. Skirt the *Airport* of Split. Beyond *Resnik* continue to (4km) **Kaštel Stafilić** (*Nehaj*) where the westernmost fortress of *Nehaj* projects into the sea. Begun by the Lodi brothers of Trogir (1548) and continued by the Papalić family of Split, it was never completed. *Kaštel Stafilić* itself was built by Stjepan Stafileo in 1508, as the coat of arms and inscription indicate. The baroque parish church with its prominent bell tower (18C) was built by I. Macanović. A continuous promenade extends for 4km along the shore to Kaštel Lukšić.

The two villages of (1km) **Kaštel Novi** and Kaštel Stari are now continuous with Kaštel Stafilić. Both kaštels were erected by the Cipiko family of Trogir: Kaštel Stari, the oldest of all the fortresses by Koriolan Cipiko (1476–81) after his return from the Turkish wars in Asia Minor, and Kaštel Novi by his nephew, Pavao Cipiko, in 1512. *Kaštel Novi*, a plain tower in poor condition (Cipiko coat of arms), was the birthplace of the sculptor Marin Studin (1895–1960), whose war memorial, Herald of Victory, stands between Kaštel Novi and Stari. In Kaštel Novi village is an 18C town loggia and the Renaissance church of Sv. Rok (1586). **Kaštel Stari** is a larger and more attractve village served by a railway station (3km N). The *Kaštel* has a pleasant Renaissance courtyard and handsome façade facing the sea, and in the village is the Renaissance church of Sv. Josip.

A pleasant excursion may be made to *Biranj* (647m), one of the peaks of the Kozjak Massif, c 1½ hours distant, on the road passing the railway station.

3km **Kaštel Lukšić** stands on the border between the former lands of Trogir and Split. The *Kaštel*, built by the brothers Jeronim and Nikola Vitturi of Trogir (1487), with a Renaissance courtyard, is the largest still standing (now a school). The old parish church, a modest Renaissance structure by Ivan Rudičić (1515), has rustic baroque altars. The new parish church houses the Altar of Abp Arnerius (Bl. Arnir) by Juraj Dalmatinac (1444–45), from the Benedictine nunnery in Split. Beneath the recumbent figure of the archbishop, a relief depicts the stoning of Arnerius by the people of Poljica. West of the village, beside the promenade that links it with Kaštel Stari, are the ruins of *Kaštel Rušinac* (built 1482 by Mihovil Rosani of Trogir) and a small church with the grave (1681) of the lovers Miljenko and Dobrila, popular subjects of folk myth.

About an hour's walk from Kaštel Lukšić, on the lower slopes of the Kozjak Massif, lies the village of *Ostrog* with the pre-Romanesque church of Sv. Juraj (9C) and the 12C Romanesque church of Sv. Lovro.

1km **Kaštel Kambelovac** is an attractive fishing village with a handsome round tower (the Kaštel) erected by the Cambi family of Split in 1566 and rebuilt a century later (coat of arms and inscriptions); a Renaissance villa of the Cambi (1589) adjoins it. At the W end of the beach a villa (1911), in its own park, once a favourite resort of King Petar II and his mother Queen Marija, was later used by President Tito before becoming the Ana Roja Ballet School.

1km **Kaštel Gomilica**, the most striking of the fortresses, occupies a tiny island joined to the mainland by a drawbridge. The entrance is guarded by an impressive square machicolated tower erected by the Benedictine nuns of Split in the early part of the 16C. Within, a conglomeration of small houses and narrow streets constitutes the village. The parish church of *Sv. Jerolim*, has a baroque Crucifix by F. Bakotić (18C). The tiny Romanesque church of *Sv. Kuzma i Damjan* may be 12C.

3km **Kaštel Sućurac** the most easterly of the Kaštela, despite its attractions as a holiday spot is in danger of being engulfed by Split's industrial expansion. The fortress built by Archbishop Gualdo of Split in 1392 was the earliest of the kaštela, but this was destroyed and rebuilt in 1489–1503, and only fragments remain. The present episcopal palace is a late reconstruction incorporating Venetian Gothic and baroque portions. In the parish offices is an inscribed 7C lintel from the hamlet of *Putalj*, 3km to the N.

Putalj also figures in two charters issued by Princes Trpimir and Mutimir of
Croatia in 852 and 892, the originals of which are preserved in the village
archives. A small museum is devoted to the liberation struggle and Second
World War, with a bronze relief on the wall by Joka Knežević. A strenuous
excursion can be made to the summit of *Mt Kozjak* (779m) preferably with an
overnight stay in a mountain hut near the top (inquire at information office).

Across the water the long, wooded peninsula of Marjan gives way to
the industrial suburbs and shipyards of Split. Rejoining the main road
at (5km) *Solin* (see Rte 15), continue through rapidly expanding
residential areas to (6km) **Split**.

16 Split and its Environs

SPLIT, the largest and fastest growing city (210,000 inhab.) of
Dalmatia and Yugoslavia's second port, stands on a broad peninsula
at the at the E end of the Kaštelanski zaljev. Bursting from the
confines of the great Roman palace of Diocletian, the city spreads
fanwise round a broad semicircular harbour and extends eastwards
behind three attractive bays. Seen from the S approach, it is attractively bounded by the wooded Marjan peninsula and backed by a fine
range of mountains. Stark skyscrapers on the periphery are a
reminder of the industrial quarters and commercial port that lie,
largely hidden behind a ridge, on the N shore. The centre presents a
fascinating palimpsest of sixteen centuries' organic growth. In the old
town, though motor traffic is absent, Split rivals Naples for noise, with
the shortest gap between the last evening revellers and the grind of
iron-bound wheels on marble pavements as the first vendors come to
market.

Post Office: 9 Ivana Lučića-Lavčeviča ul.

Information: *Turistički biro*, 12 Titova obala, tel. 42142.

Airport: At Kaštel Stafilić, 22km N; *JAT*, 8 Titova obala.

Buses to all coastal towns and to main cities inland.

Sea Connections: Car ferries for *Trieste, Venice, Rimini, Ancona, Pesaro, Bari,
Pescara, Rijeka, Zadar, Dubrovnik, Corfù, Igoumenitza*; for *Rogač* on the island
of Šolta; *Supetar* on the island of Brač; *Vira* and *Starigrad* on the island of Hvar;
and *Vela Luka* on the island of Korčula. Passenger service to *Milna, Bol, Jelsa,
Vrboska, Drvenik Veli, Drvenik Mali,* and *Trogir*.

Summer Festivals: *Melodies of the Adriatic*, featuring famous Yugoslav singers
singing about the sea (first week in July); *Dalmatian celebrations*, with folk and
classical music.

History. The city is said to derive its name from the Greco-Illyrian settlement of
Aspalathos, but the recorded history of Split begins with the building of
Diocletian's palace in AD 305. After the Slav destruction of Salona (c 614) the
inhabitants sought refuge within the palace walls and never went back;
continuity was established by transferring the bishopric and the relics of St.
Domnius. By the 9C Aspalathos was one of the leading cities of the Byzantine
theme of Dalmatia, and as Byzantine power waned, it evolved into a free city
with its own statutes and charter. In 998 Venice appeared on the scene briefly
and in 1069 Croatia, but from 1105 the city acknowledged the nominal
suzerainty of Hungary-Croatia. The next three centuries were a time of
economic and cultural flowering during which most of the present old town took
shape, while in external affairs the city played off the Croats and Hungarians
against Venice and periodically went to war with its nearest rival, Trogir. In 1241
the Tartars appeared before the walls in pursuit of King Bela IV of Hungary, but
followed him to Trogir without attacking. By the 14C the rivalry of Hungary and
Venice for possession of Dalmatia had grown intense and *Spálato* as it now came
to be called, placed itself under the protection of Venice (1420). For a while the

city continued to prosper and the arts in particular flourished under the influence of the Renaissance, but the increasing threat from the Turks, who had taken the fortress of Klis in 1537, and the slow decline of Venice led to stagnation and impoverishment. In 1797 Split passed with the rest of Dalmatia to Austria, under whose power it remained, except for the French interregnum (1805–13), until the end of the First World War.

Split was the birthplace of Thomas Archidiaconus (1200–68), author of 'Historia Salonitana'; of Marko Marulić (1450–1524), historian and author of the poem 'Judita'; of Jeronim Kavanjin (1641–1714), the poet; and of Ivan Lukačić (1574–1648), the composer. Marcantonio Dè Dominis was Abp of Split in 1602–15. In 1757 the city was visited by Robert Adam, whose observations and drawings of the palace became the basis of the celebrated Adam style of architecture. Ugo Foscolo studied at the seminary here. Franz von Suppé (1819–95), whose overtures have outlived their operas, was a native. Ivan Meštrović began his career in Split and his fellow sculptor and friend, Toma Rosandić (1878–1958), was born and died here.

I. The Old Town

The **Old Town** comprises the original settlement (Stari grad) inside Diocletian's Palace and a quarter of almost equal extent (Novi grad) immediately to the W, which together form a fascinating complex of narrow streets, the product of an urban tradition of sixteen centuries. The ****Palace of Diocletian** (*Dioklecijanova palača*) determined the shape and development of the centre and remains the most important single element of the city. It is the largest and most perfect example of Roman palatial architecture extant and its frequent departures from classical rules give it a special place in the evolution of European building from trabeated to arched construction.

Built for Diocletian (Emp., 284–305), who had been born near Salona, the palace was begun in 295 and completed during his reign (305). He retired to it on his abdication and he died here in 313. The palace passed to the State and a textile factory for the army was established inside its walls. Galla Placidia, daughter of Theodosius the Great, found sanctuary here, and Julius Nepos was probably assassinated in the palace in 480. In the 7C the palace was wrecked by the Avars when they sacked Salona, but it afforded refuge to the Salonitans, becoming the nucleus of a new walled town, with houses constantly rebuilt from the ruins left by barbarian raids. In the 13–14C its walls were further fortified. Many of the accretions were destroyed by allied bombing during the Second World War, and the opportunity has since been taken to effect further restorations (begun in the last century). More recently the palace vaults have been excavated and restored.

The palace, constructed of white limestone from Brač, covers a sloping site of c 3 hectares, being very similar in extent to the Escorial. It is almost rectangular in plan, the E and W sides measuring 215m; the S wall 180m; and the N wall 177m. The S wall rises to 28m, whereas the N wall, based on higher ground, is only 15m high. Originally the walls were reinforced with 16 towers, rectangular except for the three pairs guarding the land gates, which were octagonal. Three of the corner towers alone stand today; that at the SW was washed away in 1550 by the sea, which originally lapped the entire S side. The general layout of the interior was a combination of fortified *castrum* and villa rustica, with a *decumanus* running E and W and a *cardo* meeting it at right angles from the N gate. The quarters of the slaves, servants, and garrison occupied the N half, while the Imperial apartments and offices of state filled the seaward half S of the decumanus.

Although visitors arriving by sea generally gain their first impression of the palace from the S façade on the waterfront, a better appreciation of its disposition and extent is gained by starting the tour proper from the N side. The NORTH WALL, exposed for the greater part of its length, is bordered by gardens. The imposing **North Gate**, known since the 16C as the *Porta Aurea* or Golden Gate (Zlatna vrata), was the main entrance; to it led the main highway from Salona. Only traces remain of its flanking octagonal towers. The doorway lacks its ornamental casing. The corbelled blind arcading above, with unequal

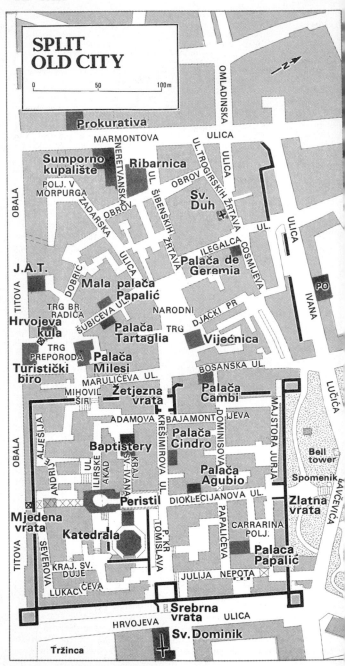

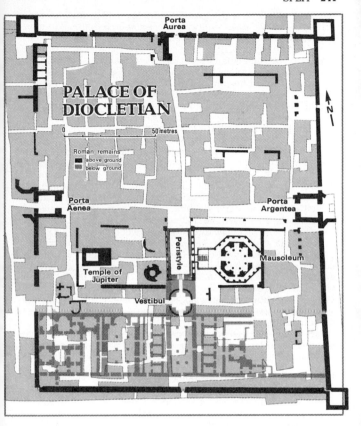

PALACE OF DIOCLETIAN

Porta
Aurea

0   50 metres

Roman remains
above ground
below ground

N

Porta
Aenea

Porta
Argentea

Peristyle

Mausoleum

Temple of
Jupiter

Vestibul

arches, is surprisingly bold for its period, but has lost its ornamental columns. The niches probably held statues. Within, grooves for a portcullis are still visible. The inner entrance was equipped with hinged gates, leaving a rectangular *propugnaculum* into which strangers were admitted for identification before being allowed to proceed. The gallery at the top, designed to acommodate the guard, now forms the tiny church of Sv. Martin (see below).

Facing the gateway is a colossal bronze statue (1929), by Ivan Meštrović, of Grgur Ninski (Gregory of Nin), the 10C Croatian bishop who defied the pope in defence of the Croat liturgy. The statue stood in the peristyle until the occupying Italians removed it; it was placed in its present position in 1954. To the W rises the elegant baroque bell tower of a Benedictine nunnery burnt down in 1877. The foundations of the 11C basilica of *Sv. Eufemija*, its church, have been cleared; of this the small Gothic chapel of Sv. Arnir (Arnerius), by Juraj Dalmatinac (1445), remains intact. Across the road is the small pleasantly shaded *Gradski Park*.

Pass round the NE Tower and descend HRVOJEVA UL, as far as the East Gate (*Porta Argentea*, or Srebrna vrata), a simpler version of the

N gate. It was restored to its present condition in 1946 after bombs had destroyed the Venetian fortifications and church that had hidden it from view since the 17C. Its protecting octagonal towers are impressive in their ruin. Opposite the gate the 13C church of *Sv. Dominik* (rebuilt in 1682 and enlarged in 1932–34) contains a Gothic Crucifixion, a baroque altarpiece by Palma the Younger, and a Christ in the Temple, by one of his pupils. You pass (left) the colourful **Pazar**, an extensive open market, gay with fruit stalls and frequented by itinerant souvenir vendors from the south. The SE Tower of the palace, now a café-restaurant, commands a panorama of the harbour.

Turn right along the busy TITOVA OBALA, a spacious palm-lined promenade along the waterfront. The seaward side affords an excellent view of the **South Façade** of the palace, once washed by the sea. The plain lower courses are now concealed by a row of houses and shops (18C and later). Higher up an open gallery, often misnamed *Crypto-porticus*, ran the full length of the façade. The detached columns, of which 38 of the original 52 survive, rest on carved corbels and carry an entablature effectively interrupted by three tripartite loggias. The arched openings between the columns are mostly filled by the walls and windows of houses.

The *South Gate* (*Porta Aenea*, or Mjedena vrata), functional in design, served purely for convenient access from the sea. Inside is a vaulted hall connecting the waterfront directly with the peristyle (see below). To the left is the entrance to the so-called ****Podrumi** (Underground Halls) of the palace (adm. 8–20; guide available). These halls, impressive in scale, represent one of the larger vaulted structures in existence. Their main function was to raise the floor of the southern quarter of the palace to the level of the remainder. The pillars of cut and dressed stone and the brick vaults are of excellent workmanship. During the Middle Ages the basements were filled with rubble and refuse and though their existence was rediscovered around 1900, their restoration first by the Konzervatorski zavod and latterly by the Urbanistički biro has been carried out since 1946. The halls reproduce in their layout the disposition of the imperial apartments above (no longer extant). A longer, narrow, cross-vaulted *Gallery*, corresponding to the 'Cryptoporticus' above (wooden beams on display from the original Roman scaffolding), gives access (right) to a series of small rooms and, farther on, to a huge *Hall* of basilican plan with an apse. A smaller apsidal hall, beyond, forms part of a complex of chambers, circular, cruciform, rectangular, and quadrifoliate, all with massive stone walls supporting barrel or groin vaults or domes.—The E side of the underground halls is still being excavated.

A flight of steps (lower half original) mounts from the central hall to the ****Peristil**, the main forecourt of the palace, which opens from the interrupted cardo just S of its intersection with the decumanus. This attractive piazza, three steps lower than the surrounding streets, with a frequented open-air café, is still a social centre of the city, affording today's citizens access on the E side to their cathedral, as it did their Roman forebears when the same building was the emperor's mausoleum. The peristyle (35m by 13m) comprises parallel open arcades made up of granite columns with fine Corinthian capitals, from which spring semicircular arches. The S end is closed by a magnificent *Prothyron*, tetrastyle in antis, tied to the colonnades by a continuous entablature. The entablature surmounts the arches of the lateral arcades, becomes conventional over the side doors of the prothyron and, below the apex of the pediment, springs in an arch over the two centre columns, an effect seemingly derived from the Temple of

Hadrian at Ephesus. It makes a fine backdrop for operatic performances in summer.

The W side of the colonnade has been incorporated into the façades of
a row of patrician houses, resulting in a fascinating and unexpectedly
felicitous blend of Roman and Renaissance architecture. In a bay of
the open E colonade rests an Egyptian sphinx of black granite (c
15BC), one of two that originally flanked the entrance to the
mausoleum.

Steps lead up between a pair of votive chapels, *Gospa od Pojasa*
(1544) and *Gospa od Začeća* (1650), to the former **Vesibulum** of the
palace, a rotunda once domed and lined with marble and mosaics,
now a favourite venue of young footballers and (because of its
acoustics) amateur singing groups. In the space behind the rotunda,
now devoid of Roman remains, stands an 11C Romanesque house,
beautifully restored and occupied by the *Urbanistički biro*. Farther to
the right an open arch of the palace façade looks on to the harbour.
The opening to the E from the rotunda leads to the tiny space in which
three Roman mosaic floors have recently been discovered; a similar
opening to the W leads to the maze of narrow streets immediately
above the palace vaults.

On the E side of the peristyle 22 steps mount through the Bell
Tower, which supersedes the mausoleum forecourt once guarded by
sphinxes (comp. above). The Romanesque Bell Tower (53m), a
landmark so characteristic that it has been incorporated into the city's
badge, remains one of the more striking on the coast, though its patina
was lost and many of the original details replaced in the reconstruction of 1882–1908. It is guarded by two (restored) Byzantine *Lions*,
though the sculptured groups they bear are copies (originals in the
museum, see below). Beneath the arched lower story are three
Romanesque reliefs attributed to a pupil of Radovan. They depict the
Annunciation, the Nativity, and (below) SS. Peter, Domnius, and
Anastasius, the last signed Otto, who is also thought to have carved
the reliefs on the arch of the vault. The summit commands a fine view
of town and harbour.

The reconstruction, effected under Alois Hauser by Dalmatian and Italian
masons, faithfully copied the old lines, except that the crowning octagon was
altered, not very happily. The original lower story was of the 13C; the second
was consolidated and the next two added in 1501–25 (possibly by Bartholomeo
di Giacomo da Mestre). The tower was struck by lightning in 1719. Replaced and
similary damaged in 1789, it was restored the following year to the form on
which the re-building was modelled.

The *MAUSOLEUM OF DIOCLETIAN, converted in 652 by John of
Ravenna, first Bp of Split, into the **Cathedral of the Blessed Virgin
Mary**, is known popularly as *Sv. Dujam* after its subordinate dedication to St. Domnius, the Salonitan martyr. The building, octagonal
in plan and well preserved, is raised on a podium within a dignified
Corinthian colonnade. Two or three panelled ceiling slabs remain in
situ and holes in the wall above show that the walk had a pentise roof.
The inter-columniations are filled with Christian sarcophagi, notably
the ornate tomb of Prior Peter (9C). On the S side is the entrance
(apply to sacristan) to the crypt chapel of *Sv. Lucija*.

The rich Roman *Portal* is decorated with animals and vine leaves.
The magnificent double *Doors of walnut backed with oak display
some of the finest Romanesque woodcarving in Europe, executed in
1214 by Andrija Buvina, a local master. On either door 14 recessed
panels, individually framed in intricate scroll or knot wood, are

*Detail showing the Flagellation of Christ: Juraj Dalmatinac's
monument to Sv. Staš in Split Cathedral, 1448*

separated by a continuous vine motif, in which dogs, birds, and
people pluck bunches of grapes. Many of the human figures are
naked, an unusual feature for the time of their composition. The
panels illustrate the life of Christ. On the *Left Door*, Christ's birth
and early life; Annunciation (top left); Nativity; Journey of the
Magi; Adoration of the Magi; Massacre of the Innocents; Flight into
Egypt; Presentation in the Temple; Baptism; Wedding at Cana;
Temptation in the Wilderness; Miracles of the Gadarene swine;
Christ and the Woman of Samaria; Healing the Blind; Raising of
Lazarus. On the *Right Door* the scenes read upwards and show

Christ's Passion: Mission of the Disciples; Christ weeping over Jerusalem; Entry into Jerusalem; Last Supper; Washing the Disciples' Feet; Agony in the Garden; The Betrayal; Christ before Pilate; Scourging; Crucifixion; Deposition; Entombment; Descent into Hell; Ascension.

The circular *INTERIOR, structually unaltered and somewhat cramped and gloomy for its present use, is divided into eight bays by a double tier of ornamental columns standing forward of the wall. The lower tier has Corinthian capitals (restored) with a splendidly ornamental cornice, whereas the composite order above, standing forward of pilasters, carries another elaborately carved entablature, which returns over each column. A fine *Frieze*, below the entablature, depicts scenes from the chase with medallion portraits of Diocletian and his consort Prisca. The intact domical vault is remarkable for the fan-like pattern of its bricks. Between the columns are eight niches, alternatively rounded and square. The entrance is flanked by two stoups. The exquisite Romanesque *Pulpit*, to the left, stands on six marble columns: note the capitals deeply carved with winged beasts twined in foliage. The hexagonal upper part is decorated with blind arcading resting on paired columns with rich capitals; each arch contains a sculpture. The lower cornice supports a crouching lion grasping a winged serpent, from which rises a spirally fluted column bearing a lectern in the form of an eagle grasping a pair of birds. The W niche has been opened into the exterior colonnade to accommodate a baroque altar dedicated to St. Domnius.

The niches on either side of the high altar are filled with Gothic canopied shrines. On the N, *Sv. Staš*, by Juraj Dalmatinac (1448), contains the sarcophagus of St. Anastasius, carved with a violently realistic Flagellation of Christ. On the S, *Sv. Dujam*, by Bonino da Milano (1427), has frescoes beneath the canopy by a local painter, Dujam Vušković(1429); these were discovered in 1958 when a baroque surface was removed. The altar, an Early Christian sarcophagus with a relief of Christ as the Good Shepherd, bears a reclining marble figure of St. Domnius. A reredos of five panels portrays the Virgin and Child with saints.

A Y-shaped Gothic Crucifixion (14C) hangs above the high altar. Behind extends the rectangular CHOIR added in the 17C by Abp Marcantonio De Dominis. The magnificent *Stalls* are composite. Their Romanesque *Screens (the oldest in Dalmatia; c 1200), attributed to Buvina, show a variety of interlacing patterns and lattice-work surpassing that of the doors; certain motifs have an Oriental look. The bench-ends carved with rampant lions are 15C Venetian work (the seats and cornices were added later). The paintings above include scenes from the life of St. Domnius, by Pietro Ferrari (1685), and works by Matteo Ponzoni.

From the S side of the choir opens the TREASURY. A notable collection of codices, includes the Evangeliarum Spalatense, a rare 8C copy of the Gospels; the Supetarski Kartular (11C); a missal and an evangelistary, both illuminated in the 12C and bound in engraved silver covers; the 12C illuminated Homilies of Origenes; and Archdeacon Toma's celebrated Historia Salonitana (13C). Also interesting: a silver monstrance (1532) in the shape of a ciborium; a Gothic morse, or brooch; a gilt cross (12C); two 15C ampullae; and several fine 15C chalices. Among the vestments are two embroidered chasubles of red velvet and a collection of lace.

By the small S door of the cathedral is the 16C tomb of Janko Alberti, above which hangs a 15C Crucifixion.

From the opposite side of the peristyle the narrow KRAJ SV. IVAN leads to the *Temple of Jupiter (Jupiterov hram) later adapted as the cathedral *Baptistery*. A small prostyle building on a raised podium, it has lost its portico but the cella (5m by 8m) is in an excellent state of preservation. The steps are guarded by a headless sphinx of black granite, one of the pair from the mausoleum (comp. above). Outside the temple stands a Renaissance sarcophagus (1533). The 5C column attached to the house opposite is not from this temple. The engaged corner pilasters at the rear have delicate capitals. The finely carved portal is surmounted by an elaborate cornice borne on voluted consoles. Within, plain walls rise to another elaborate cornice and are roofed with a fine coffered barrel-vault, each panel decorated with flowers or fantastic heads in high relief. Both this roof and the doorway exercised a profound influence on the architecture of Dalmatia. The *Font* is constructed of 11C marble plutei decorated with pre-Romanesque carvings, the front slab bearing a low relief scene depicting an early Croatian ruler (as Christ?) on a throne. Behind are the sculptured sarcophagi of Abps John of Ravenna (650–80) and Lovro (1059–99). The gilded bronze of John the Baptist is by Meštrović.

Inside the complex of 13–15C houses that form the *Radničko sveučilište*, or Workers' University (on your left as you return to the peristyle), can be seen the circular foundations of another of several temples that stood in this area.

The northern half of the area enclosed by Diocletian's palace is more purely medieval than the south, with hardly any Roman buildings remaining, and consists of a mass of tiny twisting streets of great fascination and charm. At the NE corner of the peristyle, an office of Dalmacijaturist occupies the converted Renaissance chapel of *Sv. Rok* (1516). To the E the wide POLJANA KRALJA TOMISLAVA still preserves the paving and dimensions of the Roman decumanus with the column bases of a Roman stoa along the S side. This is now a favourite pitch of flower, postcard and souvenir sellers whose bright parasols make a splendid show here and around the East Gate. On the N side of the street (entered from Poljana Grgura Ninskoga) stands the baroque church of *Sv. Filip Neri* (1735). UL. JULIJA NEPOTA just beyond it preserves a number of early Gothic houses and is lined to the E by Roman arches of the palace wall.

Running from the peristyle to the North Gate is the narrow DIOKLECIJANOVA UL. (the former cardo), one of the more picturesque streets in Split. Beyond the *Palača de Agubio* (16–16C; left), with Venetian Gothic doorway and Renaissance courtyard, pass beneath a Gothic vault and turn right. PAPALIĆEVA UL. was recently renamed after the lovely Venetian Gothic *Palača Papalić* (15C) by Juraj Dalmatinac, with its flamboyant gateway, four-lighted traceried window and intimate courtyard with loggia and well-head. The palača now houses the **Muzej grada Splita** (adm. 9–13, Thurs 9–16, closed Sun). On the ground floor the Armoury displays 15–18C weapons. Beside the entrance is a statue of Leonardo Foscolo, the Venetian general who defeated the Turks at Klis in 1648. The collection includes both Turkish and European small arms and two rare examples of guns with wicks, the forerunners of flintlocks. On the walls are coats of arms of the city's nobility. The rooms upstairs illustrate the history of Split in the 12–16C with models, drawings and plans, etc. Exhibits include statutes of the city, original sculptures from the cathedral bell tower with other Romanesque fragments, a Gothic Crucifixion and a Gothic Madonna.

Continuing along Dioklecijanova ul. walk past the entrance to Cararina poljana, where performances are held during the Split summer festival, and come almost at once to the North Gate. Here a vaulted passageway leads left to UL MAJSTORA JURJA in which steps (right) give access to *Sv. Martin*, a tiny pre-Romanesque church (9C), 11m by 2m, inserted into the gallery above the North Gate. The pre-Romanesque reredos (11C?) is carved in stone. The entrance steps give an excellent view across UL. Majstora Jurja of a recently discovered palača attributed to Juraj Dalmatinac. The unusual N façade is pierced by three Venetian Gothic windows on the first floor with a loggia below, and the interior has been restored and modernised to house a branch of the Workers' University.

From the peristyle KREŠIMIROVA UL. the constricted, congested alley that forms the main shopping street, runs W past the handsome baroque *Palača Cindro* (17C) to the **West Gate** (*Porta Ferrea* or Želijezna vrata), a bottleneck to pedestrian traffic. The gallery of the propugnaculum is occupied by a medieval church, *Gospa od zvonika* (Our Lady of the Belfry), whose pre-Romanesque belfry (c 1100) is the oldest in Dalmatia. The entrance is by steps in Bajamontijeva ul. (right). The charming baroque interior has murals by V. Meneghello and a marble relief of the Madonna protecting the townsfolk (1480).

You pass out of the Roman palace by a narrow cut (Ispod ure) into the spacious irregular NARODNI TRG, the social centre of Medieval Split and still the city's busiest and most attractive square. It is thronged during the evening corzo, and the Kavana Central in the SE corner is particularly favoured by the local citizens. Looking back towards the East Gate you see the medieval *Clock Tower* with its 16C clock and in front of it a walled-up *Loggia* (15C) enclosing a pharmacy. The most striking building in the square is the old **Vijećnica** (Town Hall) with its triple-arched Gothic loggia on the ground floor. This retained its 15C form when the building was radically rebuilt under the Austrians (late 19C). The first government of the People's Republic of Croatia was constituted here in May 1945. The building now houses the **Etnografski muzej** (adm. 8–14 and 17–19; Sun 10–12) with the finest collection of folk costumes and artefacts on the coast.

The costumes are exhibited on the *First Floor* in two sections according to regions. The Dinaric costumes of the interior are in general the more sumptuous and imaginative, especially those of the Ravni Kotari, Knin, Vrlika (especially blouses and aprons), Konavli and the Dalmatinska zagora. There are also Alka costumes from Sinj. The costumes of the Littoral tend to be more subdued and subject to foreign influences, but note especially the women's costumes of Split; the costumes (male and female) of Šibenik; and the lace of Pag, Priošten, and Novigrad. On the second floor are utensils, furniture, tools, weapons, interesting basket-work and an outstanding display of jewellery.

The Renaissance *Palača Karepić* (16C) is joined to the Vijećnica by a small Gothic bridge over the street.

From Narodni trg picturesque medieval streets radiate in all directions. BOSANSKA UL. follows the line of the vanished W wall of the palace with the 15C Gothic *Palača Cami* at its lower end and a number of old town houses near the top. Even more interesting is its continuation S, MARULIĆEVICA UL., lined with medieval houses and with a statue of St. Anthony Abbot (1394) on the corner. From the W end of the square ILEGALACA UL. passes (left) the ornate Renaissance doorway (1583) of the former monastery of *Sv. Marija de Taurello* (relief of the Madonna in the tympanum). The court within is bounded on one side by the small 14C Gothic church of *Sv. Duh*, the key to which is to be found in an adjoining courtyard reached through a door in the far corner (ring for sacristan). The roof and walls of the apse are

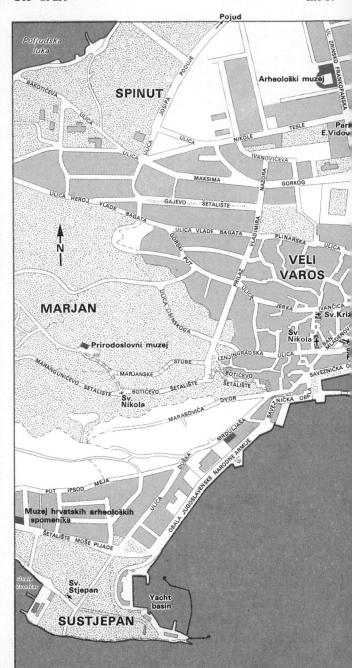

SENJ *34Km* SIBENIK *88Km*

SPLIT

| 0 | 100 | 200 | 300 | 400 metres |
| 0 | 100 | 200 | 300 | 400 yards |

MAKARSKA *63Km* DUBROVNIK *217cm*

MAKARSKA *63Km* DUBROVNIK *217Km*

Galerija umjetnina

ŠETALIŠTE

STARČEVIČEVA ULICA

GRANIČARA

ULICA

ULICA

TSKA

RADNIČKO

DOBRI

STARCEVICEVA ULICA

UL CIRIL METODOVA

SLAVIČEVA UL

LIVANJSKA UL

ULICA ŽRTAVA FAŠIZMA

GORIČKA

MAŽURANIČEVO

ŠETALIŠTE

BALKANSKA

ISTARSKA

ULICA

ULICA

VINOGRADSKA

rodno azalište AZALIŠNI TRG

POLJ 27 MARTA 1941

UL. SINJSKIH ŽRTAVA

ZAGREBAČKA ULICA

MANUŠ

TOLSTOJEVA

WASHINGTONOVA

ULICA

MODLAKINA

ULICA

ULICA

KLAIC POLJ

P.O.

ULICA IVANA LUČIĆA LAVČINA

Gradski park

G R I P E

SKA UL

STARI GRAD

NARODNI TRG

mporno palište

Sv. Dominik

Sv.

ULICA IVE LOLE RIBARA

PRILAZ VIII KORPUSA

ŠUPILOVA ULICA

PARTIZANSKA

VRZOV DOLAC

TITOVA

Turist biro

TRPOVIEJA

OBALA

Tržnica

LUČAC

OBALA LAZARETA

Bus sta. Jadrolinija

P.O.

ULICA PRVOBORACA

ULICA

P.O.

ULICA

Sv. Klara

GAT PROLETERSKIH BRIGADA

OBALA BRATSTVA I JEDINSTVA

Railway station

BLANKINIJEVA

RADE KONČARA

ŠET. I. MAJA

BAČVICE

TRG OKTOBARSKE REVOLUCIJE

ULICA MATIJE GUPCA

JADRANSKA

PRERADOVIĆEVO

PRILAZ XXV DALM DIVIZIJE

GAT SV DUJE

ŠETALIŠTE I MAJA

Lighthouse

Uvala Bačvice

Beach

OSLOBODJENJA

decorated with frescoes, and over the high altar is a painting of the Descent of the Holy Ghost by Pietro Novelli. Here is buried Andrija Aleši, the sculptor. Over the main entrance to the church (in Ul. Trogirskih žrtava) is a Romanesque relief of Christ Enthroned. At the junction with Cosmijeva ul., the Renaissance *Palača de Geremia* preserves in the courtyard a Roman sarcophagus depicting the battle of the Lapiths and Centaurs.

To the W and SW of Narodni trg a maze of narrow shopping streets leads out to Marmontova ul., forming the W boundary of the old town, and to the Poljana V. Morpurga. ŠUBIĆEVA UL., with (right) the Venetian Gothic *Mala Palača Papalić* (15C), by Juraj Dalmatinac, and (left) the baroque *Palača Tartaglia* (17C), leads down to the busy TRG PREPORODA, adorned with a statue of Marko Marulić by Ivan Meštrović. The square is dominated by the striking Renaissance-baroque *Palača Milesi*, where there is an excellent bookshop. The POMORSKI MUZEJ (Maritime Museum, adm. 9–12; closed Sun), with collections and models illustrating the maritime history of Dalmatia occupies a medieval tower. Opposite stands the *Hrvojeva kula*, part of the 15C Venetian fortifications, through which a gateway leads out to Titova obala and the waterfront.

II. Western Split

At the W end of Titova obala opens TRG REPUBLIKE, a somewhat incongruous arcaded square built by the Austrians, with the Kavana and Hotel Bellevue at its southern end. Split's principal taxi rank stands in front of the restored church of *Sv. Frane*, a miniature pantheon of Split notables, with the gravestones of Marko Marulić, Archdeacon Toma, Jeronim Kavanjin and Ivan Lukačić. The church contains a Crucifixion by Blaž Trogiranin and a 15C Gothic statue in wood of St. Lucy. A charming Gothic cloister adjoins the S side.

Behind the church the shady suburb of **Veli Varoš** occupies the lower slopes of Mt Marjan. In KOZJAČKA UL. is the little pre-Romanesque church of *Sv. Nikola* (12C), domed and cruciform in shape; and a little to the N the baroque church of *Sv. Križ* (Holy Cross) has a Gothic painted Crucifixion and Madonna. LENJINGRADSKA UL. leads to the foot of Mt Marjan and the *Marjanske stube*, a sequence of steps leading up through pleasant woods to the small **Zoološki vrt** and PRIRODOSLOVNI MUZEJ (Natural History Museum, opens 8–sunset). The zoo has a comprehensive collection of native animals and birds, and some Asian and African fauna; the museum has good collections of fossils, marine life, and particularly beetles (over 10,000 specimens). Its terrace commands fine views of the city and harbour. A winding road (closed to motor traffic) leads higher to an even better viewpoint at the summit of *Mt Marjan* (170m). From the museum more steps descend to the small 13C church of *Sv. Nikola*, and beyond to Saveznička obala (comp. below).

From Trg Republike the broad SAVEZNIČKA OBALA follows the shore, changing its name to OBALA JNA on the W side of the harbour. The promenade continues to the delightful little peninsula of **Sustjepan**, with a fine yacht basin, park, and outdoor swimming pool. Here, bear right on Šetalište Moše Pijade, where a handsome modern building houses the **Muzej hrvatskih arheoloških spomenika** (adm. 9–16, closed Mon), an attractive collection of Croatian archaeological finds. The exhibits are mainly pre-Romanesque from the period of early Croatian independence (9–12C) and include two excellent rectangular ciboria: one from Bijaći near Trogir and the other of white marble, with a beautifully carved canopy, from Biskupija near Knin. From Biskupija comes also a rare hexagonal ciborium and, from the church of Sv. Križ at Nin, a hexagonal limestone font. Notable are a transenna carved with a Madonna and a 9C stone crucifix. The jewellery (especially earings and necklaces) and medieval weapons are worthy of notice, as is an 8C censer found at Stara Vrlika.

The Šetalište Moše Pijade continues W to the tip of the Marjan peninsula. About 2km from the old town is the **Galerija Meštrović**, the former villa of the sculptor Ivan Meštrović (1883–1962), which he designed for himself in 1937, and which since 1952 has contained a permanent exhibition of his works (adm. 9–sunset). The villa, a long low building of dazzlingly white Brač limestone, was designed as a combined mansion and gallery in an uneasy and ostentatious mixture of neo-classicism and modernism. The formal gardens were also intended as a setting for sculptures. The interior is arranged in chronological order to illustrate Meštrović's career and development.

In a pleasant pine grove a little farther on stands the **Kaštelet** (adm. 10–12, 15–19; closed Mon), the 17C summer villa of Jeronim Kavanjin, adapted and restored by Meštrović. The showpiece is the *Chapel*, designed and built by Meštrović and decorated by his series of walnut panels carved in relief to illustrate the life of Christ. The panels, though carved over a long period (1914–54) and not in sequence, show extraordinary unity of style. They were designed to throw deep shadows by the natural lighting of the chapel (no artificial light being provided on the sculptor's insistence) and are best seen on a sunny morning.

Beyond the Kašelet the road continues along the foot of Marjan to the bay of *Kašjuni* (pebble beach), with views out to sea of the islands of Brač, Šolta, and Čiovo. The pine-clad slopes are criss-crossed here with pleasant shady paths leading to the top of Marjan. At the W end of the bay a by-road doubles back and climbs to the little 15C church of *Sv. Jere* (St. Jerome), with a relief of the saint by Andrija Aleši. Cells cut into the rock beside the church were once inhabited by hermits. A little farther on, this road widens to form a platform below the 15C church of *Bethlehem* (altar by Aleši) and then divides for (left) the summit and (right) Sv. Nikola. Continuing round the foot of the hill you come to the very tip of the peninsula, Rt Marjana, and the **Institut za oceanografiju i ribarstvo** (Oceanographical Institute) with a small *Aquarium*. The road continues round the N side of Marjan through pinewoods to the beautiful little bay of *Bene* (bathing; bus from the centre), with a rocky foreshore and sandy bottom, and thence to the residential suburb of *Spinut* with a pebbly beach and the yacht marina of the Split sailing club.

III. Northern and Eastern Split

The most direct road to the northern part of the city is MARMONTOVA UL., passing the neo-Renaissance Prokurativa on the left and the Secessionist building of the Split spa (Kamil Tončić) on the right. Adjoining the latter is the colourful *Ribarnica* (Fish market). At the top lies KAZALIŠNI TRG. On the S side stand two sections of bastion from the 17C Venetian walls. To the W stands the neo-classical *Hrvatsko narodno kazalište* (Croatian National Theatre, 1893) and to the N the church of *Gospa od zdravlja* (Our Lady of Health; 1937), with overpraised frescoes (1959) by Ivan Dulčic. The broad ARINJSKO-FRANKOPANSKA UL., one of the two main arteries leading N from the centre to residential suburbs, leads to the stadium of the Hajduk Football Club. In U.l. Maksima Gorkog, No. 19 is the former studio of Emanuel Vidović (1897–1953), the landscape painter, now a small gallery exhibiting his works. A bust by Frano Kršinić (born 1897) stands on a pedestal in the small *Vidovića park*.

The far side of the park is bounded by Lovretska ul. in which No. 15 is the **Galerija Umjetnina** or Art Gallery (adm. 9–12, 16–18; Sat 9–12), founded in 1931. On the top floor a collection of 15–19C icons typifies the stereotyped techniques of the later Cretan and Venetian schools and illustrates the activities of the Boka Kotorska school, where the art was continued by certain families from generation to generation. Here also are two painted panels, Orpheus and Narcissus, from a chest by Andrea Meldola 'Schiavone' (Medulić); a relief of St. Jerome by Aleši; two paintings, St. Francis of Paola and the Holy Family with St. Anthony of Padua, by Frederiko Benković (Bencovich Schiavon); and a polyptych (school of Veneziano).

On the lower floors are paintings by local painters of the 19C and 20C (Medović, Bukovac, Kraljević, Račić, Vidović, Job), and sculpture by Meštrović, Rendić, Rosandić, Kršinić and others. The museum also possesses drawings by Koko-schka and George Grosz.

Continue up Zrinjsko-Frankopanska ul. to (left) the **Arheološki muzej** (Archaeological Museum, adm. 9–13, Sun 10–12; closed Mon). Founded in 1820, and moved here in 1914, the museum owes its expansion to Don Frane Bulić, the native archaeologist, and its interest to the fine Roman collection from Salona (described below).

The greater part of the exhibits are housed under open verandas round the garden in roughly chronological order. From the entrance turn left. A few Greek stelai from Vis lead on to ROMAN ANTIQUIT-IES, notably the enormous tomb of Pomponia Vera (in park to the right) from Salona and a relief from Tilirium (Trilj, near Split) believed to illustrate the victory of the Romans over the Illyrians. The headless statue of Tiberius is a copy. Of many Roman sarcophagi, two of the finest in the far left corner show *Meleager Hunting the Calydonian Boar (somewhat weathered) and the Legend of Phaedra and Hippoly-tus. A portrait of a seaman (Gaius Utius) adorns the sarcophagus at the entrance to the following gallery. Here (far left) are a relief of Hercules and the Nemean lion, and reliefs connected with the cult of Mithras. Part of the main gate of Salona stands at the end of this section, with a relief of a goddess detached from it. Cross the garden in front of the museum preceded by a headless Egyptian sphinx (14C BC?) to the EARLY CHRISTIAN ANTIQUITIES. In the gallery (right) are damaged mosaics from Salona and a marble mensa and altar rails from the Salona basilica. The original capitals from Diocletian's mausoleum are also on display. At the far end, in the corner, are two outstanding early Christian sarcophagi, depicting the *Crossing of the Red Sea and Christ as the Good Shepherd, and four capitals from the baptisery at Salona. On the return to the main entrance pass two mosaic floors from Salona, one a Triton medallion and the other portraying Orpheus.

In the main building are pottery, jewellery and artefacts from neolithic to Roman times. Various statues of minor interest stand in the vestibule and a Greek frieze shows a group of seven dancing girls.

A short distance beyond the museum, TOPUSKA CESTA forks left from the main road and leads to the small bay of *Poljud* (bathing). On the N side stands the Franciscan monastery of *Gospa od Poljuda* (Our Lady of Poljud), rebuilt in 1450 and fortified against the Turks a century later, when the existing towers were built. In the spacious cloister are two well-heads (one of the 15C bearing the rebus of the Delfini family) and fine memorials removed from the church, notably those of Bp Thoma Nigris (1527) and Katarina Zuvetić (15C), both with full-length effigies. The church has as reredos a monumental *Polyptych by Girolamo da Santacroce (1540), showing the Madonna and Child with saints, and another painting by the same artist of the Madonna; a Madonna with SS. Peter and Clare is attributed to Girolamo's brother, Francesco. A picture in a side chapel, a poor copy of a lost original, depicts eminent writers who have praised the Virgin, including Mahomet holding a scroll with a quotation from the Koran; tradition holds that this painting helped to protect the monastery from attack by the surrounding Turks. The *Treasury* includes a portrait of Bp Nigris by Lorenzo Lotto (1527) and two crosses, one Gothic (15C) and one baroque by Fulgencije Bakotić, a local sculptor; also two codices illuminated by Fra Bone Razmilović (1675) and incunabula annotated by Marko Marulić.

SUTROJIČIN PUT, opposite the Museum, leads to the pre-Romanesque church of *Sv. Trojstvo* (The Holy Trinity), a rare surviving example of a round early Croatian church with six apses, though the dome has fallen. Roman fragments are apparent in the walls and four apses are decorated with shallow lesenes.

Immediately N and E of the old town extend the inner suburbs, many of whose streets and houses date back to the 17–18C. Between *Dobri* and *Manuš* a large wedge-shaped bastion remains from the Venetian fortifications. *Gribe*, a massive star-shaped fortress of the same date, stands on a hill on the edge of *Lučac*. The area N of these suburbs is being developed as the new civic centre of Split in the modern manner. UL PRVOBORACA, the main road for Omiš and the coast, passes to the S of Lučac; beyond it stands the Franciscan nunnery and church of *Sv. Klara*, with Byzantine icons and a painted Gothic Crucifixion (13C) in its treasury. Still farther S is the suburb of Bačvice.

Bačvice is usually reached by the OBALA BRATSTVA I JEDINSTVA along the waterfront. Passing the railway and bus station on the left, leave the quay and follow PRILAZ XXVI DALMATINSKE DIVIZIJE. In the *Park Pomoraca* above the breakwater is the Hotel Dalmacija with a popular dance terrace and, on top of the cliff, the striking slender *Lighthouse* by B. Carić, erected in memory of sailors killed in action, with a monumental relief by Andrija Krstulović. A sharp bend in the road leads to *Uvala Bačvice*, a fine sandy beach, above which extends a quarter of villas and hotels. In the Šetalište I Maja is the new home of the *Muzej narodne revolucije* with Partisan relics of the Second World War. Farther along the shore are the beaches of *Firule*, *Zenta*, and *Trstenik*.

Excursions from Split

Solin (Salona) 5km. Leave Split by the broad UL ŽRTAVA FAŠIZMA. After 1km the road divides, the older road (left) leading through industrial quarters to the new docks and the Kaštelanska rivijera. The main road (right) runs beside a surviving part of Diocletian's Aqueduct. The roads rejoin to cross the Jadro just outside the village of *Solin*. The site of **Salona** lies on sloping ground between the modern highway to Trogir and the local road that diverges left to Kaštel Sućurac. The view, over an endless complex of smoking factories, is nothing to write home about.

Salona is first mentioned in 119 BC as a centre of the Illyrian tribe of the Delmats, where the Roman consul Caecilius Metellus wintered. The place became a Roman colony after fighting for Julius Caesar against Pompey. Under Augustus it developed as the capital of the Roman province of Illyria, later Dalmatia, and reached the height of its prosperity as a seaport with c 60,000 inhab. under Diocletian, who is generally supposed to have been born hereabouts. One of the finer provincial cities of the Roman Empire, Salona was noted for its cosmopolitan citizenship. During the Diocletian persecutions Domnius, A Syrian, and Anastasius from Aquileia were martyred, together with the priest Asterius and four soldiers of the emperor's guard. Their graves became cult centres over which were later raised large basilicas. A century later the city suffered the first attacks of the Huns and the Goths and was torn internally by civil strife; after the fall of the Western Roman Empire it was occupied by the Ostrogoths under Theodoric. Byzantium later asserted her claim but c 614 the city was attacked and totally destroyed by the Avars and Slavs, the population fleeing to Trogir and Split. The remains provide an important record of the development of Christianity under the Romans. They have been excavated over a long period notably in the late 19C by Don Frane Bulić (1846–1934).

The visible remains are dispersed over a wide unshaded area and are best visited on a cool day. *Tusculum*, an eccentric summer villa built by Prof. Bulić, standing a short way from the car park, forms the administrative office of the site (guide service), with a souvenir shop and a garden café. Roman and Romanesque fragments are incorporated in the villa and columns and capitals in the garden came from the cathedral bell tower in Split.

Just N of the Tusculum extends the Christian *Necropolis of Manastirine* overlying part of which are the well-preserved foundations of a 5C basilican church. The Basilica incorporates the burial place of St. Domnius, Salona's patron saint and martyr. His tomb, a vaulted crypt entered from a square marble-paved chamber, can be seen in the sanctuary in front of the main apse. To the W is the well-preserved sarcophagus of Bp Primus, nephew of Domnius. Since the sanctuary was separated from the rest of the church c 600 by a stout wall erected to protect it from barbarian incursions, it is necessary to walk round to view the narthex, nave and aisles, with their stylobates and broken off columns still in place. On the ground at the W end is the original lintel bearing the inscription: DEVS NOSTER PROPITIVS ESTO REI PVBLICAE ROMANAE. The ground here is littered with about 100 sarcophagi plundered by the Avars; many of the best have been removed to the Archaeological Museum in Split.—To the N of the basilica are the remains of an early Roman *Wine Press*.

A complex similar to Manastirine but less well preserved is the necropolis of *Marusinac*, about a 10-minute walk on the other side of the car park. Here the grave of St. Anastasius was enshrined in a mausoleum (foundations visible) beside which in the 5C were built two linked basilicas, one hypaethral, the floor of which, a mosaic with geometrical designs, is well preserved.

From the Tusculum a cypress avenue leads S across a road that follows the line of the northern *City Wall*, traces of which may still be seen at the side. Immediately inside the wall are the remains of the largest complex of Christian buildings so far discovered, which include two basilicas (basilicae geminae) joined by a common narthex. In the centre the spacious 4C *Basilica Urbana*, reconstructed in the 6C, has well-preserved stylobates and column bases and a prominent apse. From the narthex, steps lead up to auxiliary buildings, through which early initiates passed in sequence: a *Catachumeneum*, an octagonal *Baptistery*, with cruciform immersion font lined with marble and descending in steps, and a rectangular *Chrismatorium* for confirmation. Mosaics from these rooms and from the church are now in Split. To the S is the *Basilica of Bp Honorious* a rectangular structure erected in the 4C and later made cruciform under the influence of Byzantine models. It is thought that some of the well-known church assemblies of Salona were held in this building. Of the remaining buildings in this area, which include a bishops palace and a well defined chapel, the most interesting consists of a gymnasium and *Thermae*, which have been excavated to show the hypocausts under the steam rooms. The floor of the frigidarium is still intact and in the NE chamber are traces of frescoes.

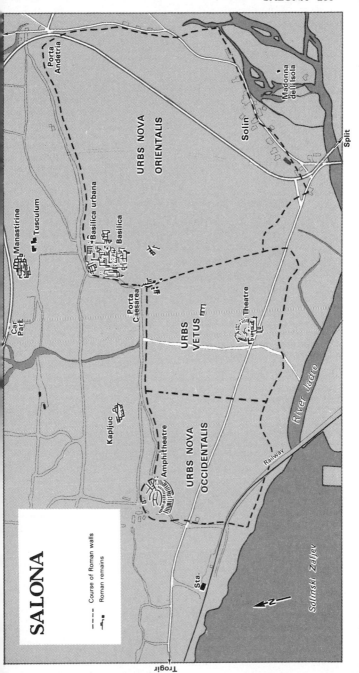

SALONA

---- Course of Roman walls
🛕 Roman remains

Continuing S and then right along the gravel road, pass (down steps to the left) the former *Porta Caesarea*, marking the division between old and new Salona. The western and older half is the Greco-Illyrian quarter (Urbs occidentalis); that to the E (Urbs orientalis) the more purely Roman section. Ten minutes' walk brings you to Kaplijuč, another Christian necroplis just N of the Kaštela road, beside the stream of the same name. The remains of a 4C basilica stand beside the necropolis, dedicated to the Five Martyrs of Salona. At the W end of the city are the scanty remains of the 2C *Amphitheatre* with seating for 15–18,000 spectators. Only the foundations, the outline of the great entrance, and the central arena remain.

Immediately beyond the amphitheatre lies the road for Kaštel Surćurac, beside which c 500m W, is the *Hortus Metrodori*, Salona's largest necropolis, though little remains visible. In the opposite direction, towards Solin, are the ruins of a Roman *Theatre* on the very edge of the road, with the scanty remains of a temple opposite. The area between the theatre and the basilica urbana to the N is the site of the forum. To the E one of the city gates, *Porta Andetria*, opens on to the main road for Klis and Sinj; beyond the road, on the site of yet another necropolis, *Suplja crkva*, a pre-Romanesque basilica which may have been the coronation church of King Zvonimir of Croatia, has recently been excavated.

TO KLIS AND SINJ, 34km. Highway 11/16. Take the Trogir road (comp. above) and at Solin bear right. The road rises in stages through the foothills, with magnificent views of *Kozjak* ridge to the left and of the jagged peaks of *Mosor* to the right, culminating in Debelo brdo (1043m) and, farther away, Ljubelj (1330m). Threading a tunnel, turn sharp left before the summit of the pass to (9km) **Klis**. Beyond the village and dominating the pass, the castle occupies a romantic position (400m) on the cliff.

Klis was occupied in Roman times and was later the estate of Prince Trpimir (845?–64) of Croatia. In the Middle Ages it was held by the Šubić family and in 1242 King Bela IV sought refuge here from the Tartars. With the arrival of the Turks in Dalmatia its strategic position gave it added importance. The basic fortifications were erected by Marko Pavlović and Ivan Karlović in the 15C, but they were completed by the Turks after their capture of the castle in 1537. Petar Kružić, a celebrated Uskok captain from Senj, lost his life in the battle. Klis remained the key-point of Turkish domination of inland Dalmatia until Leonardo Foscolo retook the castle for Venice in 1648, after which its importance declined.

The Castle, reached by footpath, consists of a triple enceinte at different levels. The remaining buildings occupy the innermost ring, entered through a massive baroque gateway. They include a small historical museum (mainly pictures and documents) and, a rarity in Dalmatia, a small Turkish mosque, later converted to Christian worship as Sv. Vid. From the top of the ramparts there are splendid views over the valley to Mosor and S to Split and the islands.

The road continues across a rock karst plain to (21km) *Brnaze*, a village on the edge of the fertile Sinjsko polje, where you turn left. Sinj aerodrome (right) formerly served charter flights for Split.

4km **Sinj**, a pleasant town of 4200 inhab. planted with trees, achieved its present appearance mainly in the 18C after the departure of the Turks. It is celebrated for the *Siniska Alka*, an annual competition or tourney to celebrate a famous victory over the Turks on 15 August 1715. Fifteen mounted 'knights' or Alkari, dressed in 18C costume, tilt a ring in the shape of a stirrup (the 'alka') to symbolise the capture of the Turkish general on horseback, a colourful and stirring ceremony that attracts huge crowds. The costumes used at the tourney can be seen in the *Alkarski muzej*, with the horses' harness and the riders' weapons. Also displayed are Turkish weapons and the saddle of Serašćer Mehmet Pasha, the defeated Turkish general. The conjoint *Town Museum* has a section devoted to the National Liberation Struggle. A small collection of *Persian furniture, put together by a former Yugoslav ambassador to Persia, includes a beautiful inlaid games table, a rich trellis screen, and a large bureau with a trellised front and inlaid with mother-of-pearl.

A *Franciscan Monastery*, not far away, houses a good collection of finds from the neighbouring Roman site of Aequum (now Čitluk). Outside are Roman gravestones, including a good mausoleum gate covered with reliefs (also a 14C font and a Bosnian cross dated 1703). A separate museum is devoted to sculpture, reliefs, and coins, with a notable marble head of Hercules, heads of Diana and Minerva, and a statue of Hecate. A good local Ethnographic Collection includes folk costume, musical instruments, jewellery and bygones.

17   Split to Dubrovnik

ROAD, 223km. Highway N2/E65. 26km *Omiš.*—37km **Makarska**. —41km *Kardeljevo.*—60km *Orebić.*—49km **Dubrovnik**.

Frequent **buses**.

Car ferries from Makarska to Sumartin on the island of Brač; from Drvenik to Sućuraj on the island of Hvar; and from Kardeljevo to Trpanj on the peninsula of Pelješac.

A fine stretch of the Jadranska Magistrala runs close to the coast all the way.

Leave **Split** by PRVOBORACA ULICA and pass through vineyards to (3km) *Storbreč*, where the road regains the coast. This was the site of Greek Epetion. Villages here are gradually being developed as quiet holiday resorts, with clean shingle beaches and accommodation in pensions or private rooms.

At (17km) **Sumpetar** are two Gothic chapels. *Sv. Stjepan* in the cemetery has a pre-Romanesque altar rail and a Renaissance bust of St. Stephen.—Continue S with views offshore to the island of Brač and round the headland at Dugi rat, with its massive fertiliser factory. The Bay of Omiš and mouth of the River Cetina come into view ahead.

6km **Omiš** (2200 inhab.), a somewhat shapeless small town, huddles at the foot of the towering Omiška dinara ridge on the left bank of the Cetina. The Adriatic Highway divides the town into two, the newer part, with a long sandy beach, lying on the broad delta S of the road, and the old town clinging to the rock to the N of it. During the 12–14C Omiš was the lair of a band of gusari, or corsairs, first under the princes Kačić and subsequently the princes Šubić of Bribir. It passed to King Tvrtko of Bosnia and Matko Talovac of Dubrovnik, before surrendering to Venice in 1444; and it suffered considerably from Turkish incursions until 1684.

A medieval gate gives access from the highway to the main street and crowded houses of the old quarter. The baroque parish church of *Sv. Mihovil* (St. Michael, 16–17C) in the main street has a fine W door (1621) and detached bell tower. Within are a baroque Crucifixion and two paintings by Matteo Ingoli of Ravenna (1585?–1631). Farther along a Renaissance house contains the modest *Gradski muzej*, where the lapidary collection includes a Roman relief of Dionysus and the 13C memorial slab of Prince Miroslav Kačić. The collection of historial documents includes the Omiška dukala (1579), an illuminated parchment decree. Folk costumes and relics of the Second World War are also displayed. A little beyond the 18C chapel of *Sv. Rok* steps ascent to the clock tower and church of *Sv. Duh* (1585), with a painting by Palma the Younger of the Descent of the Holy Ghost. More steps mount from the clock tower to the ruined *Peovica-Mirabella Fortress*, affording excellent views of the town and coast and into the Cetina Canyon. The *Starigrad Fortress*, perched on a rock pinnacle higher up to the E, can be reached in c 30 minutes by a stiff climb. The main street continues to the pleasant main square on the bank of the River Cetina, with a Venetian štandarac (stone flagpole). A footbridge crosses the Cetina to the suburb of *Priko*, where the pre-Romanesque church of *Sv. Petar* stands. The 10C exterior is decorated with lesenes and blind arcading. It has a curious gabled tower enclosing a small cupola. The S wall is pierced by three stone transennae.

A pleasant excursion up the River Cetina to *Radmanove mlinice* may be made by road or, better, by boat through the impressive Cetina Gorge. Beyond the dam of the Zakučac hydro-electric works stands the mill house and former summer villa of the Radman family, now a pension and restaurant (fishing and bathing in the park).

From Priko a road leads to *Gata*, former capital of the tiny independent republic of Polijica, which extended to Žrnovnica in the NW and from the sea to the Cetina. Its independence, dating from the 11–12C, was ended by Napoleon in 1807.

Beyond Omiš the Adriatic Highway runs along the foot of the Omiška dinara (872m) with the island of Brač visible offshore. At (19km) the bay of Vrulja begins the *MAKARSKA RIVIERA. Beaches of fine shingle and pebbles, bleached white by the sun, extend for nearly 40km. Pinewoods along the shore reach into the foothills of the *Biokovo Mts*, the highest range of the Velebits, which rise in Sv. Jure to 1762m. The villages are especially popular with Yugoslav and central European visitors.

Approaching Makarska, pass (left) the caves of Vepricá and the shrine of *Gospara od Vepricá*, a modest emulation of Lourdes initiated by a local bishop in 1908. The road into town (Radnička cesta) leaves the highway by a small pyramid that originally honoured Marshal Marmont. In 1818 its inscription was replaced by another commemorating the visit of Francis Joseph I of Austria.

18km **MAKARSKA**, the only coastal town of size (8000 inhab.) between Split and Dubrovnik, is a delightful resort on a sheltered bay extending from the peninsula of Sv. Petar in the NW to the headland of Osejava in the SE at the foot of the awesome Biokovo Mts. A pleasant park occupies Sv. Petar, on the N side of which extends the beach of Donja luka; the town and harbour are father South. Unlike most Dalmatian towns Makarska has a predominantly modern appearance, many of the oldest buildings (in a baroque style dating from the 17C) having suffered from air attack.

Post Office: on the waterfront.

Information: *Turist biro*, tel. 61688.

Car ferries to *Sumartin* on the island of Brač.

History. The Roman settlement of *Murcurum* was probably destroyed by Totila the Ostrogoth in 548. Makarska became a centre of the Slavonic Neretvans or Narentines, a widely feared nation of corsairs based on the river Neretva. They defeated the Venetian fleet off Makarska in 887. In the 11–14C the city formed part of Croatia (later Hungary-Croatia), passed for a century to the Kotromanić princes of Bosnia, and after a brief interval under Venice was occupied by the Turks (1499–1646), who made it their principal port on the Adriatic. Venice regained the city and in 1797 it passed to Austria. Makarska was demolished by the Turks, suffered from bombing during the Second World War; in 1962 it was damaged by an earthquake. Andrija Kačic-Miošić (1704–60), poet and scholar, was educated and lived in Makarska.

From MALA OBALA, SE of the quay, steps lead up to KAČIČEV TRG, the main square. In the centre stands a statue by Ivan Rendić (1890) of Andrija Kačić-Miošić, author in 1756 of a successful collection of patriotic verse, which had a marked influence on the development of Croatian literature. A large fountain (1770), bearing the city arms, stands in front of the baroque parish church (cathedral until 1828) of *Sv. Marko* (1700–76). The church contains a Venetian high altar of marble (18C) and a silver reredos (1818) portraying the Madonna of the Rosary; and paintings in the sacristy, including portraits of former bishops and 16C icons. In a small square to the N of the church is the market.

To the N of the quay, Titova (Velika) obala preserves a single baroque mansion, and the church of *Sv. Filip Neri* (1769), built by Bp Blašković. A number of Roman gravestones are kept in the courtyard.

From the SE end of Mala obala, PUT ŽRTAVA FAŠIZMA runs past the *Sports Centre*, built in 1959 as a winter training centre for national and foreign teams, to the **Franciscan Monastery**, founded in 1400 and reconstructed in 1614. The baroque bell tower was added in 1715. Inside are a well-head decorated with the coat of arms of Bp Blašković and the charming rustic cloister, with an open loggia running round the top. The simple church was once used as a mosque by the Turks. The *Malakaloški muzej*, off the cloister, displays an outstanding collection of seashells from all parts of the world.

Excursions may be made on foot from Makarska to the Biokovo Mts. A country road leads to the nearby village of *Makar*, whence footpaths climb to *Velo Brdo* (636m), *Vožac* (1421m), with a mountain hut, and *Sv. Jure* (1762m) the highest point on the Dalmatian coast.

The Adriatic Highway continues a little inland, whereas a minor road along the shore serves the narrow but attractive pebble beaches that comprise the southern half of the Makarska Riviera.

5km **Tučepi** stands back from the shore on the main road, but its name is commonly applied to the resort of *Kraj* that stands beside the sea. The tiny 13C church of *Sv. Juraj* exemplifies the early Croatian Romanesque style and incorporates Roman capitals. The Hotel Kaštelet occupies the 18C *Palača Grubišić*.

7km **Podgora** is a pleasant fishing village with an attractive harbour. During the war it was the first headquarters of the Partisan navy, founded here in September 1942, and was the object of 40 bombing raids. It also suffered damage from the earthquake of 1962. Above the harbour a striking monument, 30m high, takes the form of a symbolic seagull with wings outspread. It was designed by Rajko Radović in 1962 to mark the 20th anniversary of the new Yugoslav navy. An unusual church by Ante Rožič (1964) takes the shape of a tent.

11km **Igrane**, with a long sand and pebble beach, is overlooked by the roofless 17C fortress tower of Zale; lower down, beside the harbour, stands the 18C baroque Palača Simić-Ivanišević. Above the main road, amid olive groves, is the early pre-Romanesque basilica of *Sv. Mihovil* (St. Michael; 11–12C). 3km **Živogošće**, the last village of the Makarska Riviera, is said to be the only place on the Adriatic where nightingales sing. To the SE of the village are the 17C *Franciscan Monastery* and the baroque church of *Uznesenje sv. Križa* (Assumption of the Holy Cross, 1766), with a painted ceiling.

Continue along a magnificent section of the coast, where the Velebit Mts descend directly into the sea. Offshore the island of Hvar comes its closest to the mainland off (4km) *Drvenik*, whence a car ferry plies to Sućuraj. The long peninsula of Pelješac, previously glimpsed far off over Hvar, now fills the seaward view. 8km **Zaostrog** has a Franciscan Monastery of the 16–17C. The church contains baroque altars and choir stalls, an organ by Petar Nakić (1694–1770), and busts of Andrija Kačić Miošić and Ivan Despot by I. Rendić. There is a Roman mosaic floor in the garden.—12km *Brist*, birthplace of Kačić-Miošić (monument in the parish church by Meštrović), and (2km) *Gradac* (Laguna) with an excellent shingle beach ('Gornja Vala') and a ruined fortress tower (1661), are the last villages before the road veers inland to cross the estuary of the river Neretva.

8km **Kardeljevo** (3000 inhab.), just S of the main road, was formerly called *Ploče*. It is being developed as a modern port to serve the hinterland of Bosnia and Hercegovina. A car ferry to Trpanj, on the Pelješac peninsula affords the shortest route from Split to Korčula. The road now runs parallel to the Kardeljevo—Sarajevo railway and one of the arms of the river Neretva. The marshy delta land has been reclaimed for agriculture and, such is its fertility, produces two crops a year. The local reeds are extensively employed for basket-making. A unique design of boat, called a trupica, with a flat bottom and raised ends, is found locally on the Neretva river.—A (3km) *Rogotin* the road divides, one arm running along the right bank of the Neretva to Metković (22km) whereas the newer Adriatic Highway crosses the river to follow the left bank (comp. below).

Metković is a river port and the growing industrial centre (4500 inhab.) of the region. The town is a late successor to the Roman *Narona*, which was second to Salona in Roman Dalmatia and destroyed at the same time by the Avars (614). The village of *Vid*, 4km NW of Metković, occupies the site of the city and preserves numerous remains, including a large mosaic floor. There is also a small archaeological museum. The extensive marshes NE of Metković known as the *Hutovo blato*, are rich in bird life, particularly ducks (shooting in the season). The Ornithological Museum in Metković possesses over 300 species collected in this area.

The main road at Rogotin crosses the River Neretva, which it follows almost to (10km) *Opuzen*, once a possession of Ragusa and from 1685 the site of the Venetian Fort Opus (now ruined), that marked the S limit of Venetian possessions in Dalmatia. The house of Stjepan-Steva Filipović, executed by the Germans at Valjevo in 1942, is marked by a plaque. *Podgradina*, with the castle of Břstanik (1373, rebuilt 1878), is visible on the left as the road climbs high above the Posrednica with a superb view of the marsh delta, before returning to the coast at the landlocked bay of Klek-Neum. The bay is named for two villages, Klek at the NW end of the bay and Neum in the SE. The territory between them was ceded to the Turks by Ragusa under the Treaty of Passarowitz (now Požarevac) in 1718, providing the Turks with an outlet to the sea while placing a protective corridor between Venetian possessions in Dalmatia and the territory of Ragusa. After 1878 this strip of coast passed to Bosnia-Hercegovina and since the Second World War it has been administered again from Sarajevo as Bosnia's only outlet to the sea. In *Klek*, just off the main highway, is the ruined Monković tower and chapel from the 17C; the fortress Smrden-grad stands just outside the village, near a Bogomil cemetery (14–15C). Skirting *Neum*, an over-developed resort town, continue S along the barren shores of the Kanal Malog Stona, with views of the Pelješac peninsula across the narrowing channel. A bridge spans a wide inlet, affording views of a pretty inhabited islet; just beyond we get a fine glimpse of Mali Ston (see below).

At 42km, by a petrol station, a good minor road turns off right to the peninsula of Pelješac.

PELJEŠAC is all but an island; only since 1956 have all its settlements been linked by road. Traditionally it has looked to the sea for communications and a livelihood. With a width varying between 3 and 6km and 65km long, it is one of the most delightful and least explored territories left on the Adriatic coast, and has an abundance of reptilian life.

In ancient times the peninsula (Rhatanae Chersonesus) was settled by both the Greeks and the Romans and later was held by Byzantium. With the coming of the Slavs it was incorporated into the state of the Neretvans, then into the principality of Zahumlje and in 1333 passed to Ragusa, which held it until its fall in 1808. The peninsula reached the peak of its prosperity in the 18C and early 19C when its fleet based at Orebić, traded all over the world. When steam replaced sail, Pelješac declined into obscurity.

BY ROAD TO OREBIĆ, 71km.—6km **Mali Ston** together with Ston (see below) forms part of the most remarkable complex of fortifications on the Adriatic, designed to block off the neck of the peninsula from the mainland. When complete it extended for a distance of just under 6km, and with a total of 41 towers and 7 larger bastions. The fortifications were begun by Ragusa in 1334, when they acquired Pelješac, and completed in 1506. Among the architects were Župan Bunić (1445), Michelozzo Michelozzi (1461–64), Juraj Dalmatinac (1465), Olivier Francuz (1472–78), and Paskoje Miličević (1488–1506).

Mali Ston was laid out as a square with a grid of streets running N–S and E–W and enclosed within walls (1336–58), most of which still stand. Entrance to the harbour (1490), which was modelled on the old harbour of Dubrovnik, is gained through the *Morska vrata* (1358), with a relief of St. Blaise. Over the arch, while a large fortified salt warehouse, *Slanica* (1462–81), stands on the shore beside it. In the centre of the village is the 14C parish church (later rebuilt) with a bell cast in 1491. Mali Ston controls extensive oyster and mussel beds, situated in various parts of the Kanal Malog Stona and in the bay of Bistrina on the opposite shore.

On rising ground just S of Mali Ston stands the massive fortress of *Koruna* with five towers facing the sea. Hence the main defence wall of the peninsula runs to the high hill of *Pozvizd* (250m; footpath), crowned by another fortress midway between Mali Ston and Ston. It affords an unparalleled view of the SE part of the Peninsula and of the remaining fortifications. The road runs at the foot of the hill parallel with the wall to a third massive fortress, the Veliki kaštio in Ston.

2km **Ston**, an attractive but melancholy little town (1200 inhab.), had suffered considerably from the improving efforts of earlier generations and lost all its walls and many of the public buildings erected under Ragusa, even before it was all but annihilated by 28 Allied bombing raids during the last war.

The *Veliki Kaštio* occupies one corner of the main square, in the centre of which the neo-Gothic church of *Sv. Vlaho* (St. Blaise) replaces the former Gothic cathedral (destroyed by an earthquake in 1850). Relics from the previous building include an icon of the Virgin by Andrea Riccio (1470–1532); wooden statues of SS. Blaise, Peter, and Paul; and a Gothic font. On the far side of the square are the Venetian Gothic *Palača Sorkočević-Djorkić*, now a hotel; the Gothic *Chancery* of the Republic of Ragusa; and, a short way down the main street, the former *Biskupska palača* (1573), in which Gothic and Renaissance elements are mixed. The loggia houses examples of pre-Romanesque stone carving and a number of statues of St. Blaise. Farther down the main street, beyond a large open space, the *Franciscan Nunnery* (1347) has a beautiful cloister in the South Italian Gothic and a late Romanesque church (*Sv. Nikola*). Both were damaged by bombing and are being restored. In the sacristy are a painted Crucifixion attributed to Blaž Trogiranin (15C), a Gothic silver censer, a silver-embossed missal and a Gothic figure in wood of St. Nicholas. At the far end of the main street, beyond the limit of the former city walls, the 15C parish church of the *Navještenje* (Annunciation) has a loggia containing two bells cast by Ivan of Rab (1528).

On Starigrad and on Sv. Mihajlo, two hills overlooking the town, can be seen extensive remains of the two Roman castra of *Turris Stagni*, as it was then called, while Sv. Mihajlo was also the site of early medieval Ston. Near the top of the hill is the pre-Romanesque church of *Sv. Mihajlo* with Romanesque *Frescoes among the oldest in Yugoslavia; two other medieval churches survive intact.

To the SE of Ston are the extensive salt flats which for centuries have formed the basis of the town's economy. Beyond them a narrow gravel road runs to *Broce* on the Stonski kanal, with an abandoned Dominican monastery and church (1629), three other churches and the ruined villa (1539) of the bell and gun founder, Ivan of Rab.

The Pelješac road runs SW out of Ston and, leaving the bathing beach and autocamp of Prapratna on the left, turns NW along the peninsula's central spine of hills. Between the villages of Gornja and Donja Dubrava narrow gravel tracks lead off (left) to *Žuljana* on the open sea, with two baroque churches and a sandy beach, and (right) to *Brijesta*, on a deep protected inlet of the kanal, with a square fortress tower (1617) and the baroque church of Sv. Liberan.—At (29km) *Drače* you touch the N shore briefly and then cross the S shore, passing through *Janjina* (600 inhab.), the largest of the inland villages, and *Popova Luka* to *Trstenik*. A short distance away is the village of *Dingač*, which gives name to one of the better-known red wines of Yugoslavia.—At (15km) *Potomje* a road forks to Kuna and the fishing village of *Crkvice*. In *Kuna*, in the Župa hills, is a Franciscan monastery (1705) with a baroque church containing several works by Celestin Medović (1850–1920), whose birthplace this was. More paintings are displayed in his house, and there is a monument to the artist by Ivan Meštrović (1955). From Kuna a rough road continues to Trpanj, also reached by a by-road from Župane Selo, though it is better to continue to the junction with the main Trpanj–Orebić road, whence Trpanj is 3km down a steep descent.

The small port of **Trpanj** (800 inhab.) on the NW shore of Pelješac, opposite the estuary of the river Neretva, is reached by regular car ferry from Kardeljevo on the mainland (see above). The high altar of the church of *Gospa od Karmena* is decorated with the arms of the Gundulić family of Dubrovnik. The parish church has a richly ornamented window from an earlier 16C building. Beside the ruined medieval fortress overlooking the harbour are the remains of a Roman bath. A by-road leads to the hamlet of *Donja Vručica* with the summer villa of the Dubrovnik noble and poet, Dinko Ranjina (1536–1607).

Beyond Županje Selo the main road descends a long precipitous shelf of rock to the S shore.

19km **Orebić**, a delightful and peaceful village (600 inhab.) in surroundings of great natural beauty, faces the island of Korčula, which is reached by regular ferries. An air of prosperity and even sophistication is imparted by the sea-captains' houses that line its main street, although real wealth has long since departed. As a resort (with shingle beaches) it is noted for its benign climate, being well-protected by the mountains rising behind it, and its profusion of subtropical vegetation.

As the seat of a Dubrovnik knez (prince), the medieval village (comp. below) was known as *Trstenica*, but when the shore settlement became the centre of the Pelješac merchant fleet in the 16C it took the name of Orebić after a seafaring family from Bakar in the Kvarner.

In the centre of the village is the *Pormorski muzej*, which illustrates the history of Orebić's merchant fleet, by models, paintings and documents. Two of the more interesting *Captains' Houses* (for admission inquire locally) have been arranged as informal museums. The house ot Mr Matko Župa, an 18C villa with painted walls and ceilings, contains an eclectic collection of furniture by Chippendale and Biedermeier, pottery by Wedgwood and the Russian court potter Kuznetsov, and excellent copper and pewter. The house of the Fisković family reproduces the conditions of life in the 18–19C and also includes interesting icons and 19C costume. The baroque church of the *Navještenje* (Annunciation) has an early Christian relief on the porch.

About 2km W of the village is a 15C *Franciscan Monastery* in a mixture of Gothic and Renaissance styles, with a fortified cloister and loggia. The relief of the Madonna over the W door of the church is by a pupil of Mino da Fiesole; a similar relief within is by Nikola Firentinac. The monastery also has ex-votos donated by local sailors. Higher up the hillside is the site of *Trstenica*, with the ruined Kneževa palača and a baroque loggia. The Gothic church of Gospa od Karmena was later converted to a baroque edifice and contains baroque gravestones and more ex-votos. Beyond the monastery a fair road leads to the neighbouring villages of *Kučišče* (Gothic chapel with bell from 1522) and *Viganj* (Dominican Monastery with cloister, 1671), which shared the management of the merchant fleets with Orebić. Captains' houses may be seen in both places; of particular interest is the Lazarević house (c 1700) in Kučišče.

Orebić lies at the foot of Zmijino brdo and the highest peak on the Pelješac peninsula, *Sv. Ilija* (960m), which can be climbed in about 1½ hours.

Continuing S the Adriatic Highway passes through the village of *Djunta-Doli* (16C tower, Bogomil tombstones) and skirts the shore.

11km **Slano** is a curious village, one of whose main occupations is the gathering of medicinal herbs. At the annual fair (2 Aug) folk costumes are worn and an ancient dance called the Lindjo is performed. The Franciscan church of *Sv. Jeronim* (1420) contains ornamented tombstones of the Ohmučević family of Bosnia, whose pleasant summer villa stands in the village. In the hills behind Slano, at *Zavala* (14km), is the large limestone cave of Vjetrenica, with stalagmites and stalactites and several underground lakes.—To the S of Slano the grey karst gives way to more vegetation, with views across the Koločepski kanal to the Elaphite Islands (Šipan, Lopud, and Koločep).

13km **Trsteno** is celebrated for its excellent *Botanical Park*, the oldest in Yugoslavia, laid out in the Renaissance manner in 1502 by the Gučetić family of Ragusa. It is adminstered by the Biological Institute of the Yugoslav Academy of Sciences. Occupying the slope between the Adriatic Highway and the sea, the park is reached by an avenue of cedars and cypresses. The exotic species include oleander, jasmine, eucalyptus, cinnamon, camphor, magnolia, bougainvillea, etc., together with varieties of cactus and palm. A rare oak (quercus lanuginosa), 600 years old, stands behind the villa; in front of it a long pergola is covered with climbing plants. The villa, once the residence of the writer Nikola Vitov Gučetić (1549–1610), contains a small historical collection relating to the family, a small lapidary collection and an arboretum. The baroque fountain in the park depicting Neptune with sea nymphs was erected in 1736. In the village stand a pair of colossal plane trees (platanus orientalis) said to be 400 years old and the only specimens in continental Europe. The larger of the two has a girth of 11m.—A painting of St. Michael in the Gothic parish church is sometimes wrongly attributed to Titian.

3km **Orašac** until 1399 marked the boundary between Ragusa and Bosnia and was a favourite resort of the Ragusan nobility. Here are a small Dominican monastery (1690) and the former villa (1700) of the Austrian Resident in Ragusa, Filippo Saponaro. The massive ruined palace of Arapovo is said to have belonged to the Gonfalier, Pietro Soderini, of Florence. The twin villages of *Veliki Zaton* and *Mali Zaton*, on opposite sides of a pretty inlet, also have private chapels of the Ragusan nobility, and Mali Zaton a summer villa of the Sorkočević family.

The highway turns inland to follow the course of the Rijeka Dubrovačka or River Ombla and returns on the other side to Gruž and (28km) **Dubrovnik** (Rte 22).

18 The Island of Brač

Approaches. Car ferries from *Split* to *Supetar* and from *Makarska* to *Sumartin*. Passenger service from *Split* to *Bol*.

The island of **BRAČ** (14,000 inhab.) is the most northerly of the Southern Dalmatian group and the third largest in the Adriatic, 40km long and 10km wide. It is divided from the mainland by the Brački kanal, 5km at its narrowest point, and from the island of Hvar to the S by the equally narrow Hvarski kanal. Over most of its surface Brač exhibits the typical rocky landscape of the karst region, particularly in the S, where a range of mountains rises to 780m in Vidova gora, the highest island peak in the Adriatic. Although there are no springs, the island is relatively fertile in the centre and E, and produces morello cherries, almonds, figs, and olives in abundance. Its goats'-milk cheese was praised by Pliny and its wines are renowned, particularly the white Vugava and the red Murvica. Brač limestone, quarried along the N shore, is remarkable for the purity and durability of its whiteness and was utilised for Diocletian's palace, the cathedral tower at Split, and the cathedral at Trogir. It was chosen, after much research, for the Canadian Vimy Ridge Memorial in Flanders. Ponies and mules still provide the chief mode of transport in the interior. They are pastured for much of the year in a semi-wild condition and rounded up periodically in colourful fashion.

In spite of its size and relatively large population the island has never had a town, although Supetar was recently designated the administrative centre and is a town in name. The inhabitants are more rural and conservative than on neighbouring islands and have preserved ancient customs, dialects and a way of life that differ from the other parts of Dalmatia. The strong indigenous tradition of stone carving can be seen in dozens of cemeteries and small churches scattered about the island.

History. Brač has been continually inhabited since Neolithic times. To the Greeks it was known as *Elaphos* for the stags found on it, and the Latin name of *Brattia* may derive from *brentos*, the Illyrian word for stag. The chief settlement in ancient times was on the site of Škrip, but in the early Middle Ages, owing to the danger from pirates, the entire population withdrew inland and the centre shifted to Nerežišća. Brač passed to Byzantium and in the 11C was occupied by the Neretvans. It passed to the Kačići of Omiš, to Split (1240), Hungary, Bosnia and finally to Venice in 1420, under whose greater security the population began to move back to the coast. For much of this time Brač was administratively united with the neighbouring island of Hvar. All but two of the main settlements on the island date from after the 15C. During the 16C Brač received numbers of refugees fleeing from the Turks on the mainland, particularly from the small republic of Poljica. With the fall of Venice, Brač passed to Austria, was for a while a base for the Russian fleet and after a brief period of French rule returned to Austria. It was united to Yugoslavia in 1918.

The principal settlement, **Supetar**, has daily bus services to all parts of the island, and local boats to the villages on the N coast. Supetar is a modern little town (1500 inhab.) that originated as the port for Nerežišća and later, thanks to its proximity to Split, replaced it as the island's administrative centre. It is now a growing resort, with fine sandy beaches. The parish church retains baroque west doors (1733), the central one surmounted by a statue of God the Father blessing. Inside is a baroque Venetian painting of the Virgin and St. Anne, a portrait (in the sacristy) of the parish priest by a local painter, F. Tironi (1783), and a Renaissance monstrance (in the treasury). The painted processional standards lining the walls, with representations of saints at the top, are guild emblems. An ornate baroque well-head (1734) stands in an adjoining courtyard.

A pleasant promenade runs W of town to the beach and wooded headland of Sv. Nikola with the town's *Cemetery*. Among the fine headstones are a number of apprentice works by Ivan Rendić, notably the Franasović Memorial with a good Pietà. The cemetery is dominated by the exotic Petrinović Mausoleum by Rendić's contemporary, Toma Rosandić, an uneasy blend of Byzantine and Oriental elements. Two Early Christian sarcophagi against the N wall are decorated with low relief crosses.

From Supetar a minor road lined with cypresses runs W, parallel with the N shore, to (7km) the quiet village of **Sutivan** (Vesna). On the waterfront are a windmill, the baroque *Palača Kavanjin* (1705), now used as a hotel, the fortified Renaissance *Palača Natali* (1505), and the *Kaštel Marjanović* (1777), all of modest pretensions and with later additions and alterations. In the baroque parish church of *Sv. Ivan* a mannerist work depicting Our Lady of The Rosaries (17C Italian) is interesting. The handsome baroque bell tower with an onion dome is by B.P. Bertapelle (18C).

In the opposite direction from Supetar a similar road runs E to (6km) **Spliska**, a delightful small village set in pine woods at the head of its own bay. In the centre the massive *Kaštel Cerineo* (1577), with machicolated corner towers, contains a Madonna by Bernardino dei Conti (c 1500), a pupil of Leonardo da Vinci, and a 16C portrait of Mauro Cerineo Morruso. A Madonna and Saints signed by Leandro Bassano adorns the high altar of the parish church. From the harbour the stone for Diocletian's palace was shipped and the quayside is now usually piled with Brač limestone awaiting despatch. The quarries lie about 15 minutes walk inland; in *Rasohe* quarry is an unusual 4C Roman relief of Hercules cut in the rock.

A tortuous narrow gravel track leads uphill inland from Spliska to the hamlet of **Škrip** (3km), the oldest settlement on the island. On the E side of the village is the 18C parish church of *Sv. Jelena* with a good baroque W front, though the effect of a fine wheel-window has been somewhat spoiled by the addition of other windows. A statue of the Madonna and Child occupies a niche over the W door and on top of the gable is the Risen Christ. The aisleless interior has a stuccoed apsidal chapel enclosing the high altar, and four baroque side altars bear paintings by Palma the Younger. The bell tower exhibits styles from Gothic to baroque. Adjoining is the much altered *Kaštel Cerineo* (1618), with fortified towers at opposing corners (view). Three Roman sarcophagi stand beside the castle. To the E of the church is the single tower of the *Kaštel Radojković*, with a vaulted lower storey which is largely Roman. Beside it can be seen the massive masonry of a *Cyclopean Wall* thought to have been constructed by the Illyrians (3C BC). In the nearby cemetery is the curious Romanesque church of *Sv. Duh* (11–12C), to which a double bell-cot was added in the 14C and aisles in the 16C. Ornately carved gravestones of the Cerineo family can be seen inside the church, and in the cemetery the simpler stones of various artisans and craftsmen, bearing carved emblems of their trade.

Beyond Spliska the coastal road continues to (6km) **Postira**, a large village spread out on a hillside with an attractive fishing harbour and waterfront, and sandy beaches. The parish church of *Sv. Ivan Krstitelj* (John the Baptist) has a curious fortified apse with embrasures and machicolations dating from the 16C, when the Turkish threat was most imminent. The house in which Vladimir Nazor was born (plaque) has Renaissance elements. A favourite excursion is to the lovely sandy bay of *Lovrečina* about 2km to the E, where the ruins of an early Christian basilica, with an unusual ground plan, preserve two sarcophagi. The hamlet of **Dol**, lying 3km inland, is pleasantly reached on foot by a steep gravel track, through olive groves. The pre-Romanesque church of *Sv. Mihovil* with shallow blind arcades in the interior and a W door constructed from a sarcophagus is one of the oldest of this type on the island (11C?). The Gothic church of *Sv. Petar* retains its 14C bell. The parish church has a late but surprisingly pure baroque W front (1866) and the fortified Renaissance Palača Gospodnetić a fine baroque coat of arms over the main gate.

THE MAIN ROAD from Supetar runs inland to serve the remaining villages on the island. Leaving Supetar as above, turn off the Spliska road after 1km and wind up through olive groves with retrospective views to the Brački kanal and mainland. A feature of the landscape here as elswhere in Brač are the turret-like heaps of stones known as *gomile*, removed from the land by the peasants, a mute testimony to the struggles to maintain a viable agriculture—6km. The roofless pre-Romanesque church of *Sv. Luka* stands just off the road. On the inside W wall, N of the door, is a rare 11–12C graffito of a sailing ship cut into the plaster, the oldest such drawing in Dalmatia; two smaller ones can be seen on the N wall—1km further on a T-junction offers a shortcut (left) to Nerežišća (see below), but you want to bear right to (3km) *Donji Humac*, set on a low hill. The parish church of **Sv. Fabijan i Sebastijan** has a Romanesque nave with Gothic elements dating from a reconstruction in the 14C and aisles added in the 18C, when Ignacije Macanović of Trogir worked on the bell tower (1766). A marble reredos shows the Madonna with SS. Fabian and Sebastian and above the apse is a 13C Romanesque fresco of Christ Enthroned, with the Madonna and St. John the Baptist. In the treasury is a silver-gilt Renaissance processional cross with saints on the four arms.

The little pre-Romanesque church of *Sv. Ilija* standing about 1km W of Donji Humac, incorporates re-used Roman material (part of a Roman memorial in the S wall). The remains of a sizable Roman mausoleum can be seen outside the N wall.

From Donji Humac a road leads W through the hamlet of *Dračevica* to (8km) **Ložišća** where the late baroque parish church (1820) has an elaborate bell tower designed by I. Rendić; to the NE of the village is the Romanesque chapel of Stomorica (11–12C).—1km **Bobovišća** consists of a picturesque small habour and the village c 1km inland. The parish church contains two Venetian paintings in the sacristy, a Pietà (school of Palma the Younger) and Our Lady of Mt Carmel (18C), and the treasury contains a Renaissance processional cross and fine 18C lace of local workmanship. On a hill overlooking the village is the 14C church of *Sv. Martin* with a Renaissance reredos carved in relief by a follower of Nikola Firentinac. Beside the harbour of Bobovišća the large fortified Palača Marinčević-Gligo has baroque details to relieve the plain exterior.

8km **Milna**, a growing community (1300 inhab.), situated on a fine natural harbour, was founded in the 17C. In 1807 during the Napoleonic wars, it served for a time as a Russian naval base. The large *Parish Church* (1783) is an excellent example of Dalmatian baroque with an impressive W front (statue of the Assumption in the central niche) and an exuberantly stuccoed interior. Cherubs emerge from half-open doors on the keystone and sideposts of the triumphal arch, a motif borrowed from the chapel of St. John in Trogir cathedral. A gold Venetian Annunciation (18C) adorns the high altar. The detached 17C bell tower with open upper stories derives from an earlier church. In the centre of the village is the fortified mansion known as *Angleščina*, erected in the 17C by the Cerineo family. The name derives from a tradition linking mansion and family with a 14C English crusader.

Turning SE from Donji Humac you shortly reach (2km) **Nerežišća**, a sprawling village, until 1828 the administrative centre of Brač, known for its wine and goats' milk cheese. On rising ground stands the baroque parish church of *Gospa od Karmena* (1752) by Ignacije Macanović, the cluttered W front an adaptation of a earlier façade (1593). The contemporary bell tower anachronistically recalls the Romanesque towers typical of Dalmatia. On the sumptuously baroque altar is a 17C Venetian painting of the Madonna with SS. John and Catherine. The N aisle has a Madonna of the Rosaries by Carlo Ridolfi and a 17C Annunciation. In the square in front of the church stands a stone flagpole (štandarac), decorated with the Lion of St. Mark, and there is a large but damaged relief of the Venetian lion on a nearby wall (1545), flanked by the arms of two local governors, Alvise Tiepolo and Giovanni Morosini.

Over another low hill behind the parish church extends the oldest quarter, with many picturesque houses with courtyards, outside staircases and attractive balconies; the largest, the baroque *Palača Harašić*, has a fine balcony enclosing the S and E sides. Nearby are the tiny Gothic chapel of *Sv. Rok*, and, in the graveyard, the 14C Gothic church of *Sv. Nikola*, with an attractive rose window. In the newer quarter at the bottom of the hill, are two Gothic churches, Sv. Margarita and Sv. Petar, the latter containing a sculptured reredos depicting the

Madonna and Child by Nikola Lazanić (1578), a local artist. Two similar reliefs may be seen just outside the village in the pre-Romanesque church of Sv. Juraj (on hill to the N) and (S) in Sv. Jakov.

Beyond Nerežišća the road climbs higher to the barren karst plateau in the centre of the island. At 3km, a narrow gravel road forks right to the summit of *Vidova gora* (778m) with superb views over the island and S to Hvar and Korčula. Excursions may be made to the mountain from Nerežišća, on foot · or horseback.—10km **Pražnice** is gradually being depopulated as its inhabitants move to the coast. In the modern parish church two reredos illustrate the excellence of the local stone-carving tradition. A early Renaissance relief (1467) adorns the 14C Gothic church of Sv. Ciprijan in the cemetery, and a somewhat cruder one of Pope Clement (1535) the small church of Sv. Klement.

Pučišća, the largest settlement (1700 inhab.) on the island, is today the main source of Brač building stone, with three large quarries nearby and a fine natural harbour, on an inlet 3km from the open sea. The modern *Parish Church* has over the high altar a wooden relief of St. Jerome by Franja Čiočev, part of an older altar (1578). On the fine wooden baroque altar of St. Anthony is a painting of St. Roch by Palma the Younger; and, in the treasury, a silver-gilt processional cross and an embroidered chasuble (1629). The small Renaissance church of *Gospa od Batka* (Our Lady of Batko, 1533) contains the graves of members of the Bokanić and Radojković families, active throughout Dalmatia in the 16–17C as sculptors and builders. On the high altar is a Renaissance reredos in stone relief attributed to Nikola Radojković, and in the chapel of Sv. Juraj at *Velika Braćuta* just outside the village a relief of St. George of similar period. The war memorial by Valerija Michieli, a local sculptor, is the best of its kind on the island.

The right branch beyond Pražnice passes the abandoned hamlet of **Straževnik**, where the early 12C Romanesque church of *Sv. Juraj* has a bell-cot thought to be the oldest in Dalmatia. The unusual Romanesque and Gothic W door, with six stylised acanthus leaves carved on the lintel and a cross in the tympanum, was added in the 14C. The reredos has two stories, the upper part (Christ with angels) Renaissance work by a pupil of Nikola Firentinac (15C) and the lower (St. George and the Dragon) dating from about a century later—4km **Gornji Humac** is another inland village with a dwindling population. In the cemetery church of Sv. Marija a good reredos of three relief panels from the school of Firentinac shows the Madonna and Saints; a baroque wrought-iron gate divides the chancel from the nave. Over the entrance to the parish church is a late Gothic relief of St. Michael, part of an earlier triptych of which a second portion, depicting the Madonna, is kept in the small church of Sv. Rok.

In Gornji Humac the road divides again, the left branch (comp. below) continuing E. Turn right and traverse the ridge of mountains dividing the interior from the S shore, descending by sharp hairpin bends. About 3km beyond Gornji Humac you pass (left), some distance off the road, the small Gothic church of *Sv. Mihovil*, which contains a Renaissance reredos of St. Michael and the dragon. With the high peak of *Draževo brdo* (627m) on your right, swing gradually W parallel with the shore.

13km **Bol**, the only major settlement (1000 inhab.) on the S shore, is an attractive small resort famous for its golden beach, *Zlatni rat*. The charming small square above the harbour is flanked by the small medieval church of *Sv. Ante* (late Gothic monstrance in the treasury). Adjoining is the 15C Gothic *Palača Lode*, also kown as the Kašil. A short distance behind the square is the parish church of *Gospa od Karmena* (1785), with a baroque gable. At the E end of the village stands the *Dominican Monastery* (1475). The Gothic church (enlarged in the 17C) has a painting of the Madonna and Child with Saints on the high altar (workshop of Tintoretto) and a choir ceiling decorated with baroque paintings by Tripo Kokolja (1713). A pre-Romanesque tympanum from Sv. Ivan (see below) is inserted above the entrance to the cloister. The monastery holds an icon of the Adoration of the Magi and a copy of Titian's St. John the Baptist, and possesses an extensive numismatic collection. In the treasury is a baroque chalice from Florence (1666). Near the monastery is the pre-Romanesque church of Sv. Ivan with a W front and apse altered in the 13C.

At the W end of the village an avenue of pine trees leads to the pleasant shaded beach of Potočine (pebble and shingle) and in about 10 minutes to *Zlatni rat, a tongue of fine pebble and shingle beach projecting 600m into the sea. The latter, although it is more or less constant in length, changes its shape and direction in relation to the wind and currents of the Hvarski kanal, assuring bathing in calm water irrespective of local conditions.

To the W of Bol are a number of pleasant smaller places best visited by boat. The hamlet of *Murvica* (6km) has an excellent shingle beach and good inn and is the starting point for walks into the hills to the picturesquely sited nunnery of *Stipančić* (c ½ hour), now abandoned and *Dragonjina* (or *Zmajeva*) *špilja*, a nearby cave with medieval monsters and animals carved in the rock (15C ?). A little farther W and reached by a separate footpath is the ruined hermitage of *Dračeva luka*, founded in 1519 by Marin de Capitaneis of Split, with its church situated in a cave. The more interesting hermitage of *Blaca*, farther W still, can be reached only by taking a boat to the tiny bay of Blaca (c 1½ hours from Bol) and walking up the valley. The hermitage, founded in 1588, occupies a beautiful situation at the head of the valley beneath vertical cliffs. The last inmate, a keen astronomer, left a fascinating collection of old clocks. Among many pictures are lithographs by Poussin. During the war Blaca was used for a while as a British radio station and military hospital; and, on 15 February 1961, it provided astronomers with an admirable view of the total solar eclipse.

The left branch from Gornji Humac leads through the narrow cultivated valley of *Cuča Dol* to the E tip of the island.

13km **Selca** occupies a striking situation at the head of the long narrow bay of Radonja and is an important centre of stone quarrying. In the main square is the colossal parish church built by local masons to designs by Adolf Schlauf of Vienna. Projected in 1925 and begun in 1942, the neo-Romanesque building provides a graphic illustration of island pride and local stone-masons' craft. On a hill outside the village stands the pre-Romanesque church of *Sv. Nikola*, an excellent example of early Croatian architecture with a cupola and a suspended arch projecting over the W door. At the seaward end of the bay is the little port of **Sumartin**, whose Franciscan monastery contains some 17–18C Venetian paintings.

A minor road through groves of olive and fig trees crosses the E tip of the island to (7km) **Povlja**, on one arm of a many-branched bay of the same name. In the centre of the village, beside the harbour and adjoining the parish church, are the remains of a large early-Christian *Basilica* (4–5C), discovered in 1960. The main body of the basilica has been preserved only in outline, though parts are incorporated into later buildings. The main apse, with an excellent three-light window, forms the base of a fortress tower, itself an adaptation of an earlier building made in the 16C as a defence against the Turks. The *Baptistery* survives complete and is still used. The immersion font is roofed with a cupola above an octagonal drum. The building was converted into a church around 1100 to serve the Benedictine abbey of Sv. Ivan (St. John) of Povlja, when the cruciform basin was used as the saint's tomb. Abbey and church were abandoned in the 14C but the church was later adopted to parochial use. During later enlargements the baptistery was reinstated to its proper use. Traces of frescoes have been brought to light on the pendentives of the dome and elsewhere. The remainder of the church is modern, but the abbey *Chapter House* has been incorporated into the present sacristy and the stone bench for the monks is still in position. The church treasury contains a simple Gothic monstrance and in the parish offices can be seen the Povaljska listina (1250), an abbey muniment that is the oldest Cyrillic document in Serbo-Croatian.

Off the W coast of Brač lies the small island of *Šolta*, dotted with tiny villages (car ferries from Split). The older settlements are all inland, and the largest, *Grohote* (1000 inhab.), in the middle of the island, is the main administrative centre. There are some Roman ruins in the village, including sections of mosaic floors, and beside the parish church the remains of a 6–7C early-Christian basilica. The 14C church of Sv. Mihovil just outside the village is decorated with Gothic frescoes. The coastal villages date mainly from the 16–17C, after the threat from pirates had receded. On the NE coast are *Stomorska* (15C Madonna and Child on the high altar of the parish church), *Nečujam* (small museum dedicated to Marko Marulić, the poet from Split) and *Rogač* the port for Grohote. At the W end of the island is the holiday and fishing village of *Maslinica*, with a 17C fortress tower and the plain baroque Palača Marchi (1708).

19   The Island of Hvar

Approaches. Car ferries from *Split* to *Starigrad* and *Vira*, and from *Drvenik* to *Sućuraj*. Passenger service from Rijeka and Split in the N and from Dubrovnik in the S to Hvar.

Hvar is the longest island (68km) in the Adriatic and the fourth largest in size, with an area of 300km^2. A range of mountains rising from the sparsely populated S shore to a peak at Mt Sv. Nikola (627m), is paralleled in the N by the flat and fertile plain of Velo polje. The majority of the population (12,000 inhab.) lives at the broader W end of the island, and although the main towns are situated on the coast the chief occupation is agriculture. Wine, olives, figs, and honey are produced, and lavender and rosemary are cultivated on a large scale. An exceptionally favourable climate gives Hvar the highest number of hours of sunshine in the Adriatic and mild winters, so that the island, sometimes compared with Madeira, is both a summer and a winter resort.

History. Abundant archaeological finds on Hvar have given name (Hvarska kultura) to the early-Neolithic culture centred in Dalmatia. Circa 385 BC Syracusan Greeks founded a colony (Pharos) on the site of Stari Grad, and another colony, Dimos, grew up at Hvar. Curiously the Slavonic name for the island has always been Hvar, derived from the Greek, whereas the Venetian and Italian name, Lesina, is from a Slavonic root meaning 'woody'. After a short period under the Illyrians, during which Hvar was ruled first by King Agron and then by Demetrios (husband of Queen Teuta), the island passed to Rome in 219 BC. The mixed Roman and Illyrian population did not survive after the arrival of the Slavs in the 7C and the island was subsequently disputed between the Neretvans and Byzantium. In the 11C Hvar acknowledged the sovereignty of the Kings of Croatia and thereafter of Venice (1145–64), Byzantium (1164–80), and Hungary—Croatia (1180–1278). In 1278 it accepted the protection of Venice. The city of Hvar replaced Stari Grad as the capital, being granted its own statute in 1331. In 1358, by the Treaty of Zadar, the island passed to Hungary again. After another period of uncertainty at the beginning of the 15C Hvar passed decisively to Venice (1420) and prospered as an agricultural producer and an important naval station midway between Venice and Corfù. In spite of several popular revolts during the 16C and widespread destruction at the hands of the Algerian Bey, Ulez-Ali, in 1571, this prosperity survived well into the 17C. Decline set in by the 18C, and the final blow came in 1776, when Kotor superseded Hvar as a naval station. In 1797 Hvar passed to Austria, France

(1805–12) and even Britain (1812–13) before reverting to Austria, again until 1918. After an illegal Italian occupation, which lasted until 1921, Hvar became part of Yugoslavia.

A notable feature of Hvar society during the 16C and 17C was its devotion to literature and the theatre, and the number of writers it produced. Chief among them were Hanibal Lucić (1485–1553), author of *Robinja* (The Slave-girl), the first secular drama in Croatian, and Petar Hektorović (1487–1572), whose eclogue on fishing *Ribanje* had considerable literary influence. Others included the 16C historian, Vinko Pribojević, the poets, Jerolim Bertučević and Mikša Pelegrinović (died 1563), Marin Gazarović (Gazzari), and Martin Benetović (died 1607). Hvar was also the birthplace of Gian Francesco Biondi (Ivan Franjo Biundović, 1574–1645), the Venetian diplomat and author who spent many years at the court of James I. Apart from numerous novels Biondi wrote a history of the Wars of the Roses (1637) that was immediately translated into English. The Hvar theatre was built in 1612.

The city of **Hvar**, the principal settlement and administrative centre (3200 inhab.), is a delightful small port at the foot of twin hills near the W end of the island. Extensive rebuilding after the Turkish sack of 1571 gave the town a strong Venetian flavour, and it maintains the spacious atmosphere of a prosperous past. It is one of the most popular Yugoslav holiday resorts.

Post Office: Nova Obala.

Information: *Turistički biro*, Nova Obala, tel. 74132.

The **Harbour** comprises a modern quay along the E shore and the tiny *Mandrać*, an enclosed basin for smaller boats constructed before 1459. The name suggests an affinity with 'Mandraki', the Greek diminutive (literally 'sheepfold') commonly used for such small harbours in the Dodecanese. At right angles to the quay and completely bisecting the town, the long and spacious **Pjaca** extends from the Mandrać to the cathedral. In Roman times this space formed an inlet of the sea which in the Middle Ages became the *Campo* dividing the fortified city (*Grad*), on the steep hill to the N, from the newer suburb (*Burg*) in the S. It was fully paved only in 1780 and is now the largest square in Dalmatia, over 4000m² in extent. A large circular well (1520) in the centre is still used.

The Hotel Palace, in the NW corner of the square, occupies the site of the Governor's Palace, demolished by the Austrians. The magnificent 16C *Loža survives, however, with graceful arcades, decorative Corinthian columns, and a lion of St. Mark in the upper balustrade. The obelisks on the roof were added in the 17C. The loggia was enclosed in 1868 and now serves as a café to the hotel. Another survivor is the clock tower, *Leroj*, formed in the 15C from the SE tower of the city walls, and reconstructed after hurricane damage in 1725. The bell on the roof dates from 1562, but the clock was replaced during 19C restoration. The white marble base of the *Štandarac* (municipal flagpole; 1735) stands before the Loža.

On the N side of the square stands the Gothic *Palača Gazzari*, restored in the 19C. Just before it opens (left) *Gradska vrata*, the main gate into the Grad, surmounted with machicolations, a feature generally of the 13–14C CITY WALLS that enclose the **Old City** on all sides. To the left the spectatular Venetian Gothic façade of the unfinished *Palača Hektorović* (15C) rests on the city wall. Its interior is gained through a vaulted arch inside the gate, and gives access to the tiny derelict church of *Sv. Kuzma i Damjan* with a coffered Renaissance ceiling. From the Gradska vrata steep steps rise through the heart of the medieval town to the castle on top of the hill, with fascinating narrow streets leading off to either side.

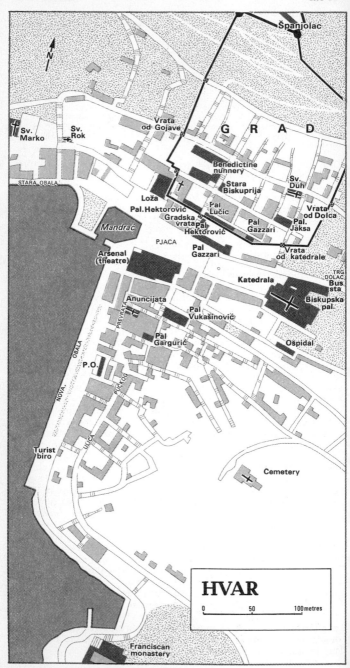

Španjolac

G R A D

Sv. Marko

Sv. Rok

STARA OBALA

Vrata od Gojave

Benedictine nunnery

Stara Biskuprija

Sv. Duh

Loža

Pal. Hektorović

Gradska vrata

Pal Lučić

Pal Hektorović

Vrata od Dolca

Pal Gazzari

Pal. Jaksa

Mandrać

PJACA

Pal Gazzari

Vrata od katedrale

Arsenal (theatre)

Katedrala

TRG DOLAC Bus sta

Anuncijata

Pal Vukašinović

Biskupska pal.

OBALA

Pal Gargurić

PREVRATA

NOVA

P.O.

PUCKOG

Ošpidal

ULICA

Turist biro

Cemetery

HVAR

0   50   100 metres

Franciscan monastery

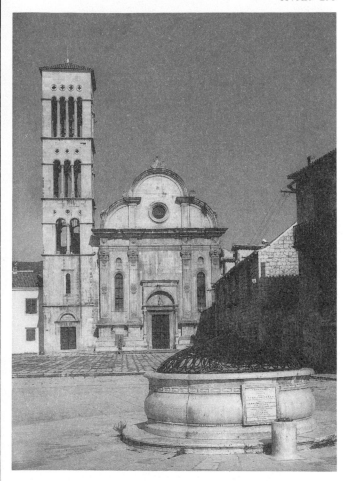

Hvar, the Pjaca

Immediately on the right in the street that follows the line of the city wall parallel with the main square a number of patrician houses were built into the wall when fortification was no longer necessary under the Venetians. These houses then marked the southern limit of the city and overlooked the main square. The nearest is the large Venetian Gothic *Palača Lučić-Paladini* (15C), with the Lučić arms over the door and a Gothic façade to the S (go through main door to garden to view). Note especially the *Balcony. Adjoining are the modest house of the poet, Petar Hektorović, and the *Palača Gazzari*, part of which straddles the street on a vaulted arch. In front of its ruined N portion (14C) is a large octagonal well-head (1475) bearing a Lion of St. Mark with a closed book. The street bends to reach the massive Renaissance *Palača Jakša just above the Vrata kod katedrale* (1454), another town gate.

Pass (right) the *Old Bishop's Palace* (15C) and in the cross street (left) the 17C baroque church of the Benedictine nuns where the altarpiece (Madonna and Saints) is by Liberale Cozza (1750). The convent occupies the former mansion of the poet, Hanibal Jučić, on the next corner. Come to the main E–W artery of the old town, at the W end of which the 14C *Vrata od Gojave* has curiously fashioned sides constructed to allow the passage of pack animals. In the same street, to the right, are a small Gothic and Renaissance house that bears the arms of the Piretić family and the 15C church of *Sv. Duh* (Holy Spirit), in late Gothic style with a Romanesque relief of a saint in the tympanum and a wheel window above. In the interior (key from house next door) are a Madonna with St. Nicholas, by Padovanino, and a small Descent of the Holy Ghost by the Spanish-born painter, Juan Boschetus(1523). At the far end of the street is the 14C *Vrata od Dolca*, the East Gate. The road beyond affords a fine *View of the crenellated walls ascending the hillside.

To the N of the main street the remaining houses soon give way to rocky terraces planted with cypress, agave, and pine trees, through which paths wind to the handsome Kaštil, known also as Španjola, on the summit of the hill (109m). The original castle was erected in the 13C, but the present building, with a massive redoubt projecting to the SE and round towers at the corners, dates from a rebuilding in 1551. In 1571, during the raid by Uluz-Ali, much of the population took refuge in the castle and survived unharmed. The castle retained its strategic importance until the first half of the 19C when the Austrians built the barrack-block that stands gaunt and ruined within.

The **Cathedral of Sv. Stjepan** was begun in its present form in 1560 but, delayed by the Turkish incursions, was completed only in the first half of the 17C. An earlier cathedral on the site, mentioned in 1326, started as a Benedictine abbey in the 12C, probably when the bishopric was founded. Portions of the old church and its furnishings survive in the choir. The W Front, already baroque in feeling, imitates the composite Dalmatian style of Šibenik Cathedral. The *Bell Tower*, built by Nikola Karlić, Pomenić and Milić-Pavlović of Korčula in 1532, is in a severely retarded form of Romanesque.

The aisles are furnished with 11 baroque marble altars (17C). To the left of the entrance (W wall) is a large Gothic reredos, with a small panel above of the Scourging of Christ (perhaps a copy by Nikola Jurjev, a local pupil, of Juraj Dalmatinac's relief at Split). N Aisle. A pietà by Juan Boschetus is incorporated into a larger canvas by A. Gradinelli, 1728. The baroque chapel of Bishop Andreis (1678) contains the sarcophagus of St. Prosperus. The entrance to the CHOIR is flanked by unusual Ambones incorporating miniature altars below. The elaborate Gothic stalls (15C, restored 1579) are of walnut. On the high altar: Palma the Younger, Madonna with St. Stephen. In the S Aisle are a 13C icon of the Pisan school and several carved gravestones set into the floor.

The much-rebuilt **Bishop's Palace**, adjoining the cathedral on the N side, now houses the *Biskupski Muzej* (adm. 9–12 and 17–19). Of prime interest is the sumptuously ornamented *Pastoral staff of Bishop Pritić (Patrizius, 1509–22) in gilt brass, the work of Pavao Dubravčić, a local silversmith; the church plate includes a Gothic monstrance and chalice, both the gifts of Bp Tomasini (15C), a 16C pax, and numerous baroque vessels and chalices. Vestments include a rare 15C *Cope embroidered with the heads of saints, and a crimson and gold chasuble dating from the end of the 18C. The lace garments (16–18C) are numerous and there is a 16C figure of St. Michael in stone.

A little behind the cathedral is the small square of Dolac (well-heads) from which the island buses depart. The old Put Grablje leads to the 16C Renaissance summer *Villa of Hanibal Jučić*. The interior now houses part of the Institute of

Conservation; the surrounding park (well-head with the Lučić and Gazarović arms) has been laid out as a botanical garden. On Mt Sv. Nikola, above the road for Stari Grad and reached by a gravel track, stands *Fort Napoleon*, erected by the French in 1811.

Facing the harbour at the SW corner of the main square stands the fine **Arsenal**, completed around 1559 with a large vaulted arch forming a covered dock for the city galley. The building was destroyed by the Turks in 1571 and completely renewed in 1611 under Governor Pietro Semitecolo. An inscription over the E door recording this date also calls it 'the first year of peace', a reference to a serious rebellion which Semitecolo had resolved in the previous year. In 1612 an upper storey was added to the Arsenal in the form of the *Kazalište, the oldest theatre in Yugoslavia and one of the earliest still extant in Europe, and in the same year a *Belvedere* was added on the N side with a spacious terrace overlooking the square. This wing was subsequently adapted as a granary and named Fontik. The Arsenal proper has been turned into a cinema. The theatre, now also an art gallery, may be visted (adm. 10–12 and 17–18; Sun 10–12) and has a charmingly painted baroque interior (restored 1800) and covered galleries. The painted wooden figurehead of a dragon in the vestibule is from the galley sent by Hvar to the Battle of Lepanto (1571).

Behind the Arsenal, steps lead up to the huge baroque *Palača Vukašinović* (17C), now a children's home. *Nova Obala*, the pleasant palm-lined promenade and quay, runs S from the Arsenal past the Post Office and travel agencies. UL. PUĆKOG PREVRATA, the main street of the old *Burg*, running parallel, presents a fascinating medley of architectural styles. From it a maze of narrow alleys, staircases, cul-de-sacs and small squares lead off to the east. Beyond two fine Gothic and Renaissance houses (left) lies the small Renaissance church of the *Anuncijata*. The relief of the Annunciation in the tympanum is attributed to Nikola Firentinac; inside are a 16C icon (on the high altar) and four 18C processional candlesticks with rococo wood carvings. Pass a cluster of Gothic and Renaissance houses, then below the 15C Venetian Gothic *Palača Gargurić* (left), and, at the Hotel Slavija, descend steps to the promenade.

Beside a small bay (bathing) at the S end of the promenade is the **Franciscan Monastery**, founded in 1461. The elegant Bell Tower, is identical with that of Sv. Marko (see below) and resembles that of the cathedral save that it terminates in an octagonal lantern topped with a small cupola, less harmonious and effective. It was completed c 1507 by Blaž Andrijić and Franjo and Nikola Španić of Korčula. The simple Gothic church, dedicated to *Gospa od Milosti* (Our Lady of Mercy), was completely renovated after being burnt by the Turks in 1571. The relief of the Madonna in the tympanum of the graceful W door is attributed to Nikola Firentinac. The church is entered from the attractive Renaissance cloister built by the mason Rade of Šibenik (1489) and consists of a single nave divided from the raised choir by a screen. In the choir are Renaissance Stalls by Franjo Čiočić and Antun Spia (1583) and the floor is paved with memorial stones, of which the most interesting are those of the Lucić (dated 1575), Kačić, and Hranotić families. A large and over-restored polyptych by Francesco da Santacroce (1583) on the baroque high altar encloses a small painting of Our Lady of Mercy said to antedate the foundation of the monastery. Paintings by Santacroce also decorate twin altars at the W end of the choir. Six scenes from the Passion on the upper part of the screen are the work of the 16C dramatist and poet, Martin Benetović, who was also organist. On the N side of the church stands the beautiful Gothic chapel of *Sv. Križ* with altar rails by P. Andrijić and a Crucifixion by Leandro Bassano. On the 2nd altar on the S side is a painting by Palma the Younger of St. Francis receiving the Stigmata (1617). The *Refectory*, housing the treasury and museum (adm. 9–12 and 16–18), is dominated by an enormous *Last Supper, an outstanding painting traditionally attributed to Matteo Rosselli but now thought to be by Matteo Ingoli. Other paintings from the 16–18C are on display with a selection of illuminated church books, a Ptolemy atlas (1524) and coins, liturgical objects (two Gothic chalices), vestments, and lace.

STARA OBALA, or *Fabrika*, a jetty constructed in the 16C, now forms the beginning of a beautiful promenade encircling the wooded headland of **Veneranda**, which protects the town on the west. The ruined Dominican church of *Sv. Marko*, nearby, fell into decay after 1806, leaving only the bell tower, a replica of the Franciscan tower on the other side of the bay. The shell of the church, containing the gravestones of many Hvar notables, has been adapted to house a small archaeological collection. Continue along the shore past the old Venetian military hospital (*Ospedal*) and come (right) to the ruined monastery and church of *Sv. Veneranda*, partially destroyed by a Russian naval bombardment in 1808 and afterwards fortified by the French. It has been transformed into an open-air theatre. Still farther round the headland the promenade leads to the principal formal bathing place (concreted foreshore, sand, and pebble beach).

The **Pakleni otoci** (lit. Hell's Islands) extend for about 7 nautical miles SW of the harbour and protect it from the open sea. Of the 11 islands in the group none is permanently inhabited, but there are seasonal settlements on *Sv. Klement*, the largest, with a good sandy beach (Palmižana), and the islands are growing increasingly popular with tourists. *Jerolim* is reserved for naturists.

A winding road runs inland from Dolac square to the outlying towns and villages. Climbing through the hills behind the town it traverses pinewoods, olive groves, and delightful fields of lavender and rosemary to the N coast. As far as Stari Grad the road was engineered during the Napoleonic occupation.

20km **Stari Grad**, the second largest settlement (1600 inhab.) was founded by the Greeks (as Pharos) c 385 BC and remained the island's chief town until in the 12–13C it was displaced by Hvar. Strikingly situated at the E end of a 8km-long fjord in natural surroundings of great beauty, it has recently developed as a popular tourist resort.

In a small square behind the waterfront stands *Tvrdalj* (c 1520), the fortified mansion of Petar Hektorović, the Renaissance poet. Tvrdalj is a delightful and idiosyncratic creation, with a charming fishpool as its centrepiece, enclosed by a vaulted and arcaded terrace. The sides of the pool are embellished with reliefs and Latin inscriptions, and in addition to a tower with a dovecote there is also an unusual 'sparrowcote', expressive of the designer's whimsical intention. The small ethnographical collection (adm. 9–11) has been arranged in one wing. The square is adorned with a bust of Hektorović by I. Mirkovic (1956). In the street adjoining the Tvrdalj on the W side, a house in the Austrian 'Jugendstil' (1896) contains a small *Maritime Museum and Art Gallery* displaying works by Meštrović, Rendić, and Juraj Plančić (1899–1930), who was born in Stari Grad. The Hektorović family chapel of *Sv. Rok* (1569) stands in the street to the E which leads uphill to the fortified *Dominican Monastery*, founded in 1482 and rebuilt in the 16C after Turkish depredations. The church contains an Entombment by Tintoretto and St. Hyacinth by Baldassare d'Anna, also (at the W end) a Crucifixion by Giacomo Piazzetta (1703) of Venice. In the monastery is a catalogued lapidary collection and upstairs in the library two paintings by Giovanni Crespi and a number of votive paintings donated by sailors. The 15C Gothic church of *Sv. Nikola*, farther up the hill, has a wooden baroque high altar by Antonio Pori (17C) bearing life-size figures of Sts Nicholas, Andres the Martyr, and Anthony.

The baroque parish church of *Sv. Stjepan* (1605) contains a good triptych by Francesco da Santacroce, a 16C font and a rococo organ loft. The 18C bell tower incorporates Greek masonry and a stone relief of a Roman vessel. Parts of a *Cyclopean Wall* of Greco-Illyrian date can be seen in nearby Kiklopska ul. (inquire at Turistički biro). In the small square, just S of the parish church, is the Romanesque and Gothic church of *Sv. Ivan*, thought to occupy the site of the island's first cathedral. Foundations of an early-Christian baptistery (5–6C), recently discovered beside this church, have been covered up again until the site can be opened to view.

From Stari Grad a good asphalt road continues E through *Veliko polje* the most fertile plain of the island, given over mainly to vineyards. A small grass airstrip runs parallel to the road. A by-road to the S serves the two large villages of *Vrbanj* (altarpiece by Baldassare d'Anna in the parish church) and *Svirće*, with attractive rustic houses dating back to the Middle Ages.

10km **Jelsa**, the main settlement (1600 inhab.), on the N coast, is spread out on both sides of a fine natural harbour, with a pleasant park, good beaches and unusually green surroundings. On the W shore stands the newer quarter, the result of a minor 10C shipping boom. The old quarter embraces the head of the bay to the S. At its head just behind the promenade, in a beautiful little square, stands the fine baroque church of *Sv. Ivan* (16C) with a wheel window in the W front. In the area behind the church are a number of old houses, notably those of the Skrivaneli and Kačić families. A short walk brings you to the parish church of *Sv. Fabijan i Sebastijan*. The original church dating from before 1331 was heavily fortified in 1535 and became the choir of a larger building with a nave and aisles; the W front and bell tower were added during the last century. The lofty Gothic Choir has a painted ceiling and a magnificent baroque altar in painted wood by Antonio Pori (17C). The treasury contains a Gothic Crucifixion in wood, a late Renaissance Crucifixion in silver-gilt and vestments (16–18C). On the E side of the harbour a pleasant promenade leads to the wooded peninsula and sandy bathing beach of *Mina*, beyond the cemetery and 17C church of the former Augustinian monastery.

The sloping hills behind Jelsa offer numerous walks. With a local guide visits may be made to the well-preserved foundations of a former Greek look-out *Tower* (5–4BC); a ruined Roman fort called Grad or Galešnik, farther E (both about an hour's walk); and near the summit of the mountain ridge to the S *Grapčeva špilja*, a large cave from which the rich finds date back to 3000 BC. Another excursion (bus or car) may be made to the picturesque old village of *Pitve* and thence via a rough tunnel (roughly 1500m in length) that pierces the mountains and emerges on the steep, sparsely populated S shore of the island. From here the road serpentines down the mountainside (views offshore to Šćedro and Korčula) to the hamlet of *Zavala*, with pleasant beaches.

Vrboska, in a deeply indented bay 4km to the NW of Jelsa, can be reached from Jelsa by bus or boat. The long inlet curves into the heart of the picturesque village, which, with its island and three bridges linking the opposite banks, resembles a corner of old Venice, an impression strengthened in the oldest quarter by the survival of 15C houses in Venetian Gothic. The remarkable fortified church of *Sv. Marija*, a massive crenellated building, has huge semicircular bastions at the E end and a spur bastion attached to the NW corner. The fortifications, erected c 1580 around a church dating from the previous century, were designed as a refuge for the populace in the event of attack by pirates or Turks. In the interior are numerous 17C paintings; the floor is paved with grave slabs. From the sacristy the ascent may be made to the roof for a closer look at the fortifications and for the view. A short distance to the W stands the baroque parish church of *Sv. Lovrinac* with a polyptych of St. Lawrence by Paolo Veronese (c 1575) on the high altar, a Madonna of the Rosary by Leandro Bassano, and three paintings by Celestin Medović (19C). The W front of the Gothic chapel of *Sv. Petar* (1469) on the waterfront bears a small statue of St. Peter by a pupil of Nikola Firentinac.

From Jelsa a good road traverses the length of the island (views to the Biokovo Mts on the mainland) to (50km) **Sućuraj**, the small fishing village whence a car ferry plies to Drvenik on the mainland.

20 The Island of Korčula

Approaches. Car ferries from *Orebić* on the Peljesac Peninsula to *Dominče* for *Korčula*, and from *Split* to *Vela Luka*. Passenger service from *Rijeka* in the N and *Dubrovnik* in the S.

KORČULA, the most southerly of the major islands of the Adriatic, is in many ways the most attractive. Geologically it is a continuation of the Pelješac Peninsula, from which it is separated by a channel 1km in width. It is the sixth largest island in the Adriatic, 47km long from E to W, with the N and S shores almost parallel 5km apart. It is also the most densely populated, with 28,000 inhabitants. Except at either end the settlements are inland, and though they are never more than 3km from the sea, they are rarely within sight of it. The island is clothed with extensive pinewoods, and in the past had a strong tradition of shipbuilding, but this has been superseded by agriculture and, in post-war years, by tourism. Stone-quarrying and carving is another traditional pursuit and quarries are still in use at the E end of the island. Korčula is the only island in the Adriatic on which the wild jackal has survived.

History. *Korkyra Melaina* was founded as a Greek colony by the 4C BC. The epithet 'black' in reference to dense pinewoods, passed with the island (Corcyra Nigra) to the Romans in 33 BC after two centuries of bitter struggle with the Illyians. About the 6C Korčula became subject to Byzantium and in the 9C was colonised by the Slavonic Neretvans. In AD 1000 Korčula, after strong resistance, submitted to Doge Pietro Orseolo II and was occupied by Venice for a time. Shortly afterwards it acceded to Croatia and after 1102 to Hungary-Croatia, but was reoccupied for Venice in 1125 by Popone Zorzi, who became governor of the island. In 1180 the island reverted to Hungary-Croatia and in 1214 established its own independent statute, said to be the oldest in Dalmatia. The Zorzi family, with Venetian aid, returned in 1254 and attempted, without success, to establish themselves as hereditary rulers, though the governorship did pass from father to son until the Venetian departure in 1358. During this period of Venetian rule there took place off Korčula the great naval battle (1298), in which Venice suffered the greatest defeat in her history at the hands of the Genoese Admiral Andrea Doria, when Marco Polo was captured by the Genoese. By the Treaty of Zadar in 1358 Korčula was ceded to Hungary and during the next half century owed allegiance to many masters, including Stjepan I Tvtko of Bosnia and the Republic of Ragusa; in 1420, in common with Dalmatia, it returned to Venice. A period of great prosperity followed during which were erected most of the public buildings in the city of Korčula, but the protectionist policies of Venice later damaged the island's principal industry, shipbuilding, and this with the depredations of the plague led eventually to decline. After the fall of Venice in 1797 Korčula went through turbulent times, being occupied successively by Austria (1797–1805), France (1806), Russia (1806), France (1807–13), and Great Britain (1813–15) before reverting to Austria (1815–1918). During the First World War the island was occupied by Italy, which prolonged its occupation until 1921, when Korčula was joined to Yugoslavia, and again during the Second World War by Italy and Germany.

Natives include the Andrijić family of architects, sculptors and masons (notably Marko and Petar), who were active in the 15–16C; Petar Kanavelić (1637–1719), the poet; and the modern sculptors Frano Kršinić (1897–1982) and Petar Palavičini (1886–1958). Korčula also claims on slender evidence to be the birthplace of Marco Polo.

The administrative centre (2800 inhab.) and the principal town, although not the largest, is **Korčula**, a delightful medieval city occupying a tiny peninsula at the E end of the island. The old town, less than 500m in length and only half that distance in width, is extraordinarily small for the wealth and importance it enjoyed in former times (6000 inhab. in its prime) and is even more cramped on its small peninsula than the average town of the period. It stands on a low conical hill, which gives it an almost symmetrical appearance on the seaward side. Within the almost elliptical shore the streets are laid out to a plan, a main street running for three-quarters of its length down the middle like a central spine, with regularly spaced side streets placed like ribs at a slight angle. All but two rise in steps and are angled to catch the morning and evening sun, while avoiding the hot rays of midday and the prevailing winds. Korčula has preserved almost intact its medieval aspect, with over a quarter of its houses Gothic and a significant proportion Renaissance; and although the plague caused large areas of the town to be deliberately burnt in the 16C, many interesting details remain to be seen.

Post Office: outside main gate.

Information: *Turistički biro*, Plokata.

Entertainments: On 27 July a knightly ritual dance, the *Moreška, is performed in the city of Korčula symbolising the struggle between the Moors and Turks, a survival of a traditional Mediterranean ritual that came into being probably in the 16C. The participants are recruited as boys and the performance is athletic and spirited. Visitors in summer are often granted a sight of practice dances.

The **Walls**, which formerly girdled the city, were erected by local masons in the 14–16C and partly dismantled in the last century. A good idea of them and of the shape and extent of the town can be gained by first walking round the outside. Start from the S end of the *Yacht Harbour* where the massive cylindrical *Kula Balbi* (late 15C), now used as a reservoir, has patriotic insriptions recalling recent tyrannies in place of its original lion of St. Mark. This is overlooked by the taller, more slender *Torjun*, or Kula Lombardo (1449), with a double ring of stone brackets round the top, on which depended the defence of the governor's palace. Continuing N, pass the Lučka Kapetanija with a rebuilt arcade, and the town well, still the only water supply for many houses, and come to a broad neo-baroque *Staircase* (1907) which mounts through the vestigial walls to the W side of the town. The staircase is flanked by twin obelisks raised in honour of governors Alviseo Jelani (1589) and Pelegrin Pasqualigo (1680). A truncated square tower on the S side contains the former *Morska Vrata* (Sea gate; 15C), adorned with coats of arms. On the inner side is an inscription placed by Governor Leoni in the 16C

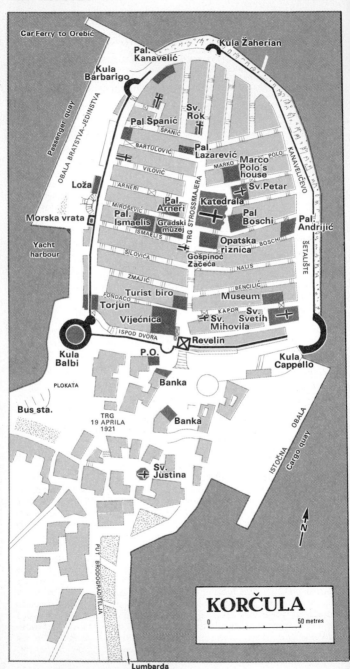

KORČULA

0   50 metres

erroneously attributing the foundation of Korčula to the Trojan hero, Antenor (1200 BC). Beyond the staircase stands an open **Loža** (1546) with a wooden roof supported on columns. A palm-lined promenade leads along the waterfront to *Kula Barbarigo* (1485–88), a handsome, machicolated tower, with the Barbarigo arms displayed on the wall.

Passing inside the walls, notice (right) the *Palača Kanavelić*, in 15C Venetian Gothic, with its courtyard enclosed by a crenellated wall, and the *Kula Zakernjan* (or Tiepolo; 1481–83), with excellent views across the strait to the Pelješac Peninsula. On the E side of the town the walls have been lowered to form a mere balustrade along which the Kanavalićevo šetalište runs as a tree-lined esplanade above the rocks. The little angled lane on the right has splendid Venetian fragments. The esplanade passes the Renaissance *Palača Andrijić*, the home of the well-known family of masons and sculptors (note also the fine sculptured arms on the adjacent house to the S), to the little guild church of **Svi sveti** (All Saints; 1306).

On the high altar is an expressive *Pietà in carved and painted wood by Rafael Donner (18C), which is enclosed by a 15C Baldachin with a pyramidal roof in imitation of the larger one in the cathedral. On the left is a Byzantine Crucifixion; on the right a polyptych by Blaž Trogiranin (early 15C). The ceiling is covered with paintings (c 1713) attributed to Tripo Kokolja of Perast in the Boka Kotorska, but more interesting are the Christ and twelve apostles on the gallery, by a local artist.

A stone bridge crosses the street from within the N side of the church to the adjoining Gothic *Guildhall*, a plain, rectangular building with a paved floor, timbered roof resting on Gothic stone brackets, and a late-Gothic ambry set into the N wall. The hall has been restored and contains a collection of the guild's treasures (adm. 9–12 and 16–19) notably nine late-Byzantine Icons believed to have been brought from Crete at the end of the Candian War (1699). Note especially *SS. George (17C ?), Christ Pantocrator (15C ?) and Christ and the Virgin Mary with SS. Anne, John the Baptist and Joachim (16C ?). Adjacent stands the upright of a large painted cross attributed to the School of Dubrovnik (late 14C). At the far end of the hall is a large canvas of the Last Supper by a local artist (17C). At the opposite end stands a flag-standard surmounted by a silver Gothic *Crucifix by Ivan Progonović (1430–5), the Dubrovnik silversmith. Documents, processional candlesticks, furniture and a painted wooden Crucifix in Byzantine style (17C) are displayed left of the entrance door. Two reliefs showing guild members adoring the cross, one Gothic (14C), the other baroque, can be seen on the wall outside.

At the round *Kula Cappello* (1493–99) with its old cannon, turn right to the main entrance to the town.

The entrance is approached by a stone bridge erected in 1863 to replace a wooden one that spanned the former moat separating the town from the mainland. The bridge and its scarp provide the main venue of the Moreška dances. The **Kopnena vrata** (main or land gate) is surmounted by the massive rectangular tower of *Revelin* (14C), the oldest part of the fortifications still standing. It has the lion of St. Mark and various coats of arms displayed on the outer face. Inside opens the miniature TRG MARŠALA TITA, a tiny square proportionate to the cramped scale of Korčulan streets. Looking back you see the baroque *Triumphal Arch* erected on the inner side of the main gate (1650) to honour the victories of Leonardo Foscolo, the Venetian Governor-General during the Candian War. To the left is the *Vijećnica*, or Town Hall (1520), with a graceful Renaissance loggia on the ground floor (a second story was added in 1866), complete with stone benches and the judge's table. The fluted column standing in front was erected in 1569 to Governor Ivan Michieli, who paved the square in that year. On the opposite side of the square stands the small guild church of *Sv. Mihovil* (St. Michael; 1603), with a charming triple bell-cot. Inside are a Renaissance pulpit and an altarpiece attributed to the 18C Venetian painter Domenico Fedeli ('Maggiotto').

The narrow main street, GLAVNA UL., rises up steps to the narrow, elongated cathedral square (TRG SV. MARKA or STROSS-MAJERA), with its *Štandarac* or stone flagpole (1515) standing at the near end. Immediately on the left is the Renaissance *Palača Gabrielis* (early 16C) with a handsome balcony, now the home of the **Gradski muzej** (Town Museum, adm. 10–12 and 16–18). The rather thin collection includes a plaster cast (original in Zagreb) of a Greek inscription (4C BC) found at Lumbarda; ethnographic, lapidary, and nautical displays; and a room devoted to the wartime resistance movement that includes photographs of the British military mission to Korčula. In the lower hall is a fine bronze Door Knocker by Tiziano Aspetti (16C) depicting Neptune between two lions.

The **Cathedral of Sv. Marko** (15–16C), an attractive hybrid of various Gothic styles fills most of the E side of the square. The building was begun early in the 15C on the site of an earlier Romanesque edifice, of which only the three apses remain. Hranić Dragošević, a local mason, completed much of the church and the first two stories of the bell tower by 1426. Work was continued by Ratko Ivančić of Korčula and the Dubrovnik mason, Ratko Brajković, who finished the third story of the bell tower in 1440 and thereafter shared in work on the interior. In 1441 Giacomo Correr of Trani in Apulia assumed direction of the building and is thought to be responsible for the final plan. He may also have sculpted the W door. The Korčulan mason, Marko Andrijić, finished the main building, adding the sumptuous decoration of the W gable end and the double lantern on the top of the bell tower. In 1525 the chapel of St. Roch, in the form of an extra aisle, was added to the N side by Marko Milić Pavlović another local mason.

The W front consists of a conventional gable end to the nave and S aisle but with the N aisle displaced by the bell tower and an extra, flat-roofed extension attached to the N side. The cramped effect is accentuated by the acute angle at which the front stands in relation to the S wall, but the result is not unharmonious. The façade is enlivened by three magnificent features. The Italian Gothic W Door, with cabled jamb shafts and moulded brackets bearing lions couchant, with the naked figures of Adam and Eve on the underside, has a figure of St. Mark (possibly by Bonino da Milano) in the tympanum. An excellent, traceried wheel-window has four heads set in the rim. The *Cornice to the gable, by Marko Andrijić, is decorated with a profusion of fantastic beasts and Gothic blind arcading filled in with scallop shells. This unusual mixture of late-Gothic and Renaissance elements culminates in a rich finial at the apex, beneath which is a female bust, the identity of which has excited much fruitless speculation. The Bell Tower is topped by an arcaded parapet of trefoiled arches from which rises a sumptuously decorated octagonal lantern with a smaller lantern on top.

The rather gloomy **Interior** consists of a nave and aisles only five bays in length, of which one and a half bays in the N aisle are occupied by the baptistery in the base of the bell tower. This and the fact that its E and W walls are not at right angles to the sides gives an overcrowded air to the whole. The unusual timbered roof, which had been plastered over at the beginning of the 19C, was renovated in 1961. An excellent Gothic and Renaissance *Baldachin by Marko Andrijić (1486), shelters the high altar, behind which (difficult to see) is an early painting by Tintoretto of St. Mark with SS. Bartholomew and Jerome.

The S Aisle contains an altarpiece of the Holy Trinity by Leandro Bassano; a sarcophagus of Bishop Malombra with a full length figure of the bishop and the arms of Malombra and Bishop Niconisius; a Byzantine icon of the Madonna and Child (13C ?); and a rack of halberds, dedicated in 1483, said to have been carried by the women of Korčula when Uluz-Ali, the Bey of Algiers, was deflected from attacking by a ruse.

In the N Aisle, notice the Renaissance Giunio chapel in the N apse; a remarkably handsome Gothic door to the sacristy (attr. to Antoine de Vienne; 14C), with a relief of St. Michael in the tympanum and lintel brackets portraying boys playing musical instruments. In the chapel of St. Roch on the N side are three paintings of saints by Carlo Ridolfi (1642) and, on another altar, carved wooden figures of saints and a Madonna by a local sculptor, Franjo Čiočić-Čučić of Blato (1576).

Just to the S, opposite the town museum, stands the large *Biskupska palača* (Bishop's Palace), originally built in the 14C but with a baroque façade added some time in the 17C. The palace now houses the well-arranged and labelled **Opatijska riznica** (Cathedral treasury, adm. 8–12 and 17–19). Display cases in the entrance corridor contain liturgical items and jewellery from the 15–18C, a fragment of a Byzantine cross from the 4C and a collection of medals. R.1 is devoted mainly to works by Dalmatian painters. On the right-hand wall is a *Polyptych and five panels by *Blaž Trogiranin* (1431). On the opposite wall, paintings of the Madonna and Child and St. Damian, both of the school of Dubrovnik (late 15C). Also exhibited in this room are two panels from an altar painting by *Pellegrino da San Daniele* and illuminated manuscripts (one 12C). A side door leads to the private chapel of the Bishops of Korčula, with reliquaries, and a terrace with a small lapidary collection. R.2 contains mainly works by Italian painters of the Rennaissance, including a painting of a Young Man by *Vittore Carpaccio*, a Madonna and Child by *Giovanni Bellini*, the Virgin and Saints attributed to the school of Titian, and an Annunciation attributed to the school of Veronese. R.3, devoted to the baroque, contains a Mystical Marriage of St. Catherine by the 17C Neapolitan, Bernardo Cavallino; two 15C English alabaster reliefs, a remarkable ivory statuette of Mary Stuart (said to be 18C) and a marble relief of the Virgin Mary (school of della Robbia); and a portrait of Bp Spanić by *Tripo Kokolja* (c 1700). In R.4 are displayed embroidered *Vestments, of which the 15C dalmatics are outstanding.

In the street to the S (second door left) a large kitchen has been re-equipped with period furniture and displays a quantity of amphorae raised from the sea.

The plain church of *Sv. Petar* behind the N apse of the cathedral is the oldest in Korčula. Originally Romanesque, it was reconstructed in 1338 and later given a Renaissance door. It contains wooden figures of the 12 apostles (17C Venetian) and a rustic Crucifixion (17C) by a local sculptor. In the adjoining street is the house displayed to visitors as *Marco Polo's House*, in reality a mainly 17C dwelling of no particular interest.

The most notable of the private houses is the *Palača Arneri* opposite the cathedral, a Gothic palace with excellent façades on three sides and a fine Renaissance courtyard in the side street. A statue of

Leonardo Foscolo stands in a niche in one corner, brought here from the triumphal arch inside the main gate. Opposite the entrance to the Palača Arneri is the ruined Renaissance *Palača Miloš;* in the next street to the N, the Gothic and Renaissance *Palača Lazarević,* now used as flats; and behind the Town Museum the Renaissance *Palača Ismaelis* or Šilovića dvor (formerly an orphanage), with the ornate family arms over the entrance and an excellent courtyard with a double-tiered gallery round all four sides.

The suburb to the S of the town walls, which began in the 16C and grew in the 17C when many inhabitants fled the plague, is now the shopping and administrative centre of Korčula. On the S side is the small baroque rotunda of *Sv. Justina,* which contains parts of a 16C polyptych attributed to Pellegrino da San Daniele; from here a pleasant seaside walk leads round to the open-air swimming pool, beach, and hotel quarter. Another shore walk leads W from Plokata past the hospital to the Dominican monastery and church of *Sv. Nikola* (1509). A parallel street climbs steeply by steps, continued through pleasant pine-woods to *Fort Wellington* (or *Sv. Vlah*), an imposing tower (refreshments) built by the British in 1813 (views of the town, and across Pelješac strait to Orebić).

The road to the town beach (comp. above) continues to *Lumbarda,* a quiet village 6km to the E, a favourite place for excursions with good sandy beaches and a modest restaurant. The road leads past (2km) *Sv. Antun na Glavici* (1420), a small medieval church, which is reached by stone steps between an avenue of cypresses 250 years old and of great beauty (views). Lumbarda was the birthplace of two of Croatia's best-known modern sculptors, Frane Kršinić and Ivan Lozica, and is the home of a third sculptor, Ivan Jurjević Knez (born 1921), whose studio and workshop may usually be visited on request. A few of Kršinić's works may also be seen at the house in which he was born (plaque). Lumbarda may also be reached by boat (c 1 hour), through part of the archipelago of small islands known as the **Skoji**. Of these the most interesting is *Badija,* with its former Franciscan Monastery founded in 1392 by refugee monks from Bosnia. The beautiful *Cloister (1477), is one of the finest in Dalmatia, in which late Gothic and Renaissance elements are mixed in perfect harmony. The church has a W front in imitation of the cathedral at Korčula, but the ornament is of inferior workmanship. Gravestones in front of the church, engraved with the emblems of various trades, include that of Hranić Dragošević, one of the architects of the cathedral. The monastery is now a holiday residence for physical training instructors, but may be freely visited. *Vrnik,* another island closer to Lumbarda, has quarries, of which one is still worked.

A good road leads from Korčula through the centre of the island, linking the main settlements. Climbing steadily out of Korčula, the road passes through the inland villages of (5km) *Žrnovo,* with views N to the Pelješac Peninsula, and (9km) *Pupnat,* the oldest settlement on the island, before emerging briefly on to the S coast at *Pupnatska Luka.*

9km **Čara,** another old settlement, was a favourite summer resort of Korčula nobles, whose villas can still be seen, notably the Kaštil Španić (16C). In the parish church is an altarpiece attributed to one of the Bassano family and in *Gospa u polju* (Our Lady in the Fields), a medieval chapel about 1km from the village, are five English alabaster reliefs (14C or 15C).

3km **Smokvica** has a fine loggia in front of the church and is the centre of the district in which the excellent white wine *Pošip* is produced.

13km **Blato,** the largest place on Korčula, is a country town (5100 inhab.) with a surprisingly continental atmosphere for an island settlement so close to the sea. The town is bisected by a magnificent avenue of lime trees that passes the town park, with a monument to national hero Ivan Cetinić by V. Mačukatin (1959). In the centre of the old quarter in a large square stands the parish church of *Svi Sveti* (All Saints). To the original Gothic church (14C) the nave and aisles were added in the 15C, whereas the W and S fronts and bell tower were rebuilt more than a century later. The high altar has baroque furnishings and two paintings by Girolamo da Santacroce (All Saints, and Madonna and Child). The chapel of St. Vincent has a baroque altar by Petar Bertapelle of Vrboska. The handsome *Loggia* at one end of the square, replacing an earlier one, was largely the work of Spaso Foretić (1700–30). On 23 April the 'Kumpanija', a knightly ritual dance with swords, is performed in the main square to accompaniment of bagpipes and drums. Not far from the square the modest baroque Arneri house (1699) contains a small historical museum.

5km **Vela Luka**, a busy little port and light-industrial centre (4300 inhab.), lies on a deeply indented bay between heavily wooded peninsulas at the W extremity of the island. A small museum illustrates with ship models the maritime history of Korčula. On the islet of *Glavica* in the bay stands the 14C Gothic church of Sv. Ivan. The main attraction of Vela Lucá, however, lies in the beauty of its surroundings.

21 The Outer Islands (Vis, Lastovo, Mljet)

A. Vis

Approaches. Car ferry from Split to Vis (serving Yugoslav citizens only).

The island of **Vis** is the farthest from the Dalmatian coast (36 nautical miles) and although only 90km^2 in area has over 8000 inhabitants. The shores of the island are steep and difficult of access, except for the bays of Vis in the NE and Komiža in the SW, and the interior is crossed by two mountainous ridges running parellel with the axis between these bays. Mt Hum, SE of Komiža, is the highest point (587m). The benign climate is conducive to sub-tropical flora, including palms, eucalyptus, agave and cactus, and citrus fruits; the fertility of its valleys has encouraged the growing of early fruits and vegetables. Vis wines have been lauded since ancient times, and Plavac, Opolo, and Vugava are known throughout the country.

History. Vis became the site of the first Greek colony in the Adriatic when, in the early 4C BC, Dionysios the Elder of Syracuse here founded the colony of *Issa*. Later an independent *polis*, Issa minted its own money and founded further colonies at Lumbarda (Korčula), Trogir, and Stobreč (near Split). In 47 BC the island fell to Rome and after the division of the empire passed to Byzantium. It was colonised by the Slavs during the 8C. Venice attacked it for the first time in 997, acquired it by purchase, together with the rest of Dalmatia, in 1420, and ruled it peacefully from Hvar until the republic's demise in 1797. Austria was succeeded in 1805 by Napoleonic France and the island's strategic position midway between Italy and the Dalmatian coast became of importance; this, allied with its impregnable cliffs and isolation, made it a natural site for a naval base, a fact first realised by the British. In 1811 a British force dislodged the French in a naval battle and fortified Vis harbour; Austria, to whom it was handed over in 1815, made it the 'Malta of the Adriatic'. A battle off Vis in 1866 between Austria and Italy was one of the biggest of the 19C, resulting in complete victory for the Austrian fleet (manned largely by Slavs) under Admiral Teghethoff. Vis came to prominence again during the Second World War, when from June 1944 it became the general staff HQ of Tito's National Liberation Front and the centre of the Allied military effort in support of Yugoslavia.

The main town, also called *Vis*, at the head of a deeply indented bay on the NE coast, is still a garrison town (2900 inhab.) and closed to foreign visitors. If you arrive by sea in your own boat, however, you can glimpse, among other things, the ring of fortresses built by the British in 1811–14 (George, Wellington, Bentinck, and Robertson). The small island of *Host* at the entrance to the harbour is named for Captain William Hoste, who commanded the small British force that defeated the French here in 1811.

Komiža, on the W side of the island, is a prosperous small fishing town (2500 inhab.) backed by an amphitheatre of high mountains and spread out round a broad sandy bay. Although it was first settled by the Benedictines from Biševo (see below) in the 13C, its appearance was determined mainly in the 16–17C by the many balconied houses lining its streets.

On the quayside in the centre of the town is the machicolated *Kaštel* built by Venice in 1585, with a clock tower rising above one corner. Here a small art gallery has been arranged to display paintings of Djuro Tiljac (1895–1965), a former pupil of Kandinsky. Just S of the Kaštel and beside the cannery is the small baroque church of *Sv. Rok*, adapted from a lookout tower. A broad palm-lined promenade curves N round the shore to the market place, overlooked by the Renaissance *Palača Zanetova* (16C) with a Madonna and Child in a niche in the façade. UL. Marinkovića leads past the lobster and crab farm on the seashore (*Jastužero*), which may be visited on request, to the main bathing beach (pebble). The tripartite Renaissance church of *Gospa Gusarica* (late 16C), with a triple bell-cot just beyond the beach, is entered through a yard with an octagonal well-head (1705) decorated with reliefs showing religious subjects. The interior furnishings are baroque except for a polyptych of 11 panels on wood (probably 16C).

On a hill behind the town stands the *Benedictine Monastery* surrounded by a defensive wall with a fortress tower (1645). A second tower forms the base of the bell tower (views). The church of *Sv. Nikola*, also known simply as *Mustar*, has a Gothic nave by Andrija Vitaljić and a Romanesque aisle remaining from earlier buildings, but is otherwise of the 17C. Inside are baroque altars of painted wood and gravestones decorated with escutcheons and relief carvings. A small museum behind the church contains 16–17C vestments, baroque paintings and statuary, and an ethnographical collection.

AN EXCURSION may be made (daily at 8 in summer taking 45 minutes; a boat hired locally takes approx. 2 hours) from Komiža to the small island of *Biševo* lying about 5 nautical miles offshore, whose chief attraction is the beautiful *MODRA ŠPILJA (Blue Grotto). This is a large cave 31m long, 17m wide and 18m high, but with an entrance only 1.5 by 2.5m, and can only be entered by small boat on a calm day (or by swimming). It is best visited between 10 and 12 noon, when the sun is near its zenith. The reflection of the sun's rays from the seabed imparts to the water in the cave a silvery blue phosphorescent light of great brilliance, and objects within are bathed in an ethereal aquamarine that flickers in the play of the ripples. In beauty it compares with the more famous grotto on Capri.

Excursions can also be made from Komiža to the tiny outlying island of *Svetac*, 16 nautical miles to the W of Vis, with one small village (50 inhab.). Nearby is the uninhabited islet of *Brusnik* and, a further 15m to the W, the uninhabited islet of *Jabuka*. Both have an indigenous species of lizard (Lacerta taurica melisellenisi), are volcanic and contain enough iron ore to deflect compasses, and have rich grounds for tunny and especially lobster fishing.

B. Lastovo

Approaches. Car ferry from *Split* to *Ubli* (serving Yugoslav citizens only).

Lastovo, a small island 6 nautical miles S of Korčula, from which it is separated by the Lastovski kanal, lies at the centre of an archipelago of 45 uninhabited islets extending to E and W. Roughly rectangular in shape, it is 10km long and 5–6km in width. The shores of the island are rocky and difficult of access, and the interior is heavily wooded and dotted with fertile valleys growing vines, the characteristic wines being plavac and maraština. Olive, almond, and walnut trees grow in profusion and the climate is favourable to citrus fruits, palms, and subtropical species. Owing to steady depopulation over the last two centuries inhabitants number only c 2000, most of whom live in the village of Lastovo.

History. Known to the Greeks as *Ladesta*, the island was later colonised by the Romans, who founded their town on the site of present-day Ubli. In the early Middle Ages this became Byzantine *Lastobon*, to which the Slavs migrated in the 8C, but in 998 the town was destroyed by Doge Pietro Orseolo II and the inhabitants fled to the far side of the island. Except for a short inverval under Hungary-Croatia, Lastovo now formed part of the small state of Zahumlje (in the area of present-day Hercegovina) until in 1252 it acceded to the Republic of Ragusa. Under the terms of its statute (1310) as an autononous commune it had strict laws of inheritance by which it was forbidden for any outsider (even from Dubrovnik) to settle on the island, while women had equal rights of inheritance with men. As a result Lastovo has the most purely Slavonic population of any of the islands. In 1808 the French took over the island, then the British (1813–15) and subsequently Austria (1815–1918). By the Treaty of Rapallo (1921) Lastovo was one of the few islands in the Adriatic to be granted to Italy and did not become part of Yugoslavia until after the Second World War.

Thanks to its isolation and self-sufficiency Lastovo preserves a number of folk customs, of which the most colourful is the annual Lenten Carnival or *Poklad*, a ritual pageant performed in the streets in February. On this occasion national costume is worn.

The best-known native of Lastovo was Dobrić Dobričević (Boninus de Boninis; 1454–1528), pioneer printer and Venetian diplomat, whose most important works were published at Brescia in 1483–91.

Ubli (250 inhab.), the main port, is a nondescript village overrun by soldiers from the local barracks. An early-Christian basilica (5–6C) has recently been excavated and restored and a number of sarcophagi are displayed on one side of the site.

A bus leaves daily in the morning for Lastovo and returns at lunch time, taking a winding gravel road that affords ever-changing views of the N coast and the offshore islands, culminating in a striking view of Lastovo itself, spread out on a steep hill and tumbling down to the valley below.

10km **Lastovo**, the principal settlement (1700 inhab.), lies in a natural amphitheatre on the lower slopes of Glavica hill, and although adjacent to the sea is all but cut off from it by steep cliffs to the N. The village looks inward and S to face the broad fertile valley from which it draws its livelihood. The narrow precipitous streets and hundreds of steps winding up and down the hillside give it a peculiar charm, made somewhat melancholy by the evident decay resulting from depopulation.

The majority of the 29 churches still standing on Lastovo are in this village, though only a few are of interest. The road enters the village at the Turistički biro, opposite which is the small 16C church of *Sv. Rok* built as a talisman against the plague, with a good Renaissance reredos and a painted wooden statue of St. Roch by Fran Čiučić of Korčula (1576). A few steps up the hillside is the larger church of *Sv.*

Vlaho (St. Blaise), endowed by Ragusa as the republic's official church on the island. A side chapel and new W front were added to the original 14C Gothic chapel in 1719. The stone seats and terrace in front of the church were for the Ragusan governor and his aides at official ceremonies, while similar seats for the governor and three judges can also be seen in the main apse. The baroque altarpiece of St. Blaise with SS. Cosmas and Damian is by Anton Sciuri (1605).

Continuing along the main street, pass a large mansion incorporating fragments of the former governor's palace and the 14C church of *Sv. Ivan*.

The handsome parish church of **Sv. Kuzma i Damjan**, on the right, is surrounded by a spacious terrace. The main Gothic building dates probably from the late 15C, the Renaissance side chapels and W door from a century later; the triple bell-cot, decorated with lions' heads, dragons, and the head of a man, was erected by Jerolim Pavlović in 1734. This unusually late appearance of Gothic decoration is thought to have been inspired by the W front of Korčula cathedral, and there seems little probability in the persistent legend tht the head represents King Uroš I of Serbia. The neo-Gothic bell tower was built by the Italians in 1942.

The most striking features of the interior are the twin altars in the side aisles enclosed by stone Baldachins with pyramidal canopies (early 16C) in imitation of that in Korčula cathedral. On the N altar is an icon of the Madonna and Child probably painted in Dubrovnik (15C?), and on the S altar is a 16C Pietà (perhaps by Juan Boschetus). The painting of SS. Cosmas and Damian on the high altar is by Giovane Lanfranco. At the W end of the church are a Renaissance font and a bronze urn for holy water, the gift of Dobrić Dobričević.

The treasury (apply to sacristan) includes 15–16C objects of Ragusan workmanship. among the best are a silver-gilt chalice with a portrait of St. Blaise; a silver-gilt processional cross by Marul Ivaneo (1574); two censers of beaten silver; two small reliquaries of silver and glass; two silver reliquaries of the legs of SS. Boniface and Constant and one of the arm of St. Valentine; a Renaissance pyx. Among baroque works are monstrances and a pax with a relief showing the Deposition.

On the far side of the terrace is a small rustic loggia (18C), around which can be seen some of the chimneys characteristic of Lastovo. Steps beside it lead down to the little 15C Gothic church of *Sv. Majija ua Grži*, with a triple bell-cot and a triptych on wood in the Byzantine manner on the high altar (school of Dubrovnik, 16C). On the E side of the village the guild church of *Sv. Antun* consists of a 14C Gothic chapel forming the choir and an attractive baroque W end added in the 17C. From the open space behind the church there is an impressive *View down to the Pržina valley, with its vineyards and olive groves and up to upper Lastovo and the French fort on the hilltop, now a meteorological station. Steps and narrow streets descend to lower Lastovo at the foot of the hill. Beyond the modern winery (visits arranged on request) is the cemetery with late-15C church of *Sv. Marija u poliu* (St. Mary in the Field). The altarpiece is a painting of the Madonna and Saints by Francesco Bissolo; the figure kneeling in the left foreground is probably the donor, Dobrić Dobričević.

C. Mljet

Approaches. Car ferries from *Trstenik* on Pelješac to *Polače*.
Passenger service from *Dubrovnik* to Okuklje, Sobra, Kozarica and *Polače*.

Mljet, the most southerly of the larger Dalmatian islands, lies parallel with the S half of the Pelješac Peninsula, from which it is divided by the Mljetski kanal, 5 nautical miles in width. Nowhere exceeding 3km across, but 32km long, it is relatively sparsely populated (2000 inhab.)

and is noted for the unspoiled character of its landscape, three-quarters covered with virgin Mediterranean forest. This is particularly luxuriant in the SW end (mainly Aleppo pine), around the twin lakes of Veliko and Malo jezero, which forms a national park. The larger villages are all inland and the principal occupation is agriculture, but in modern times there has been a gradual migration towards the coast with a resultant increase in fishing. Mljet is the only European habitat of the mongoose, which was imported here from India to rid the island of poisonous snakes.

History. In Roman times the island, known as *Melita*, is thought to have been used as a place of exile and there is a theory that this, rather than Malta, is the Melita on which St. Paul was shipwrecked on his way to Rome. In the 6C Mljet came under Byzantium, was later occupied by the Neretvans and became a part of the Slavonic states of Zahumlje and then Bosnia. In 1333 Ban Stjepan of Bosnia sold the island to the Republic of Ragusa, whose fate thereafter it shared.

Mljet, the Malo Jezero and former Benedictine monastery

Most visitors land at the hamlet of *Polače*, which has become the main disembarkation point for the two lakes and the national park. The name is taken from a Roman palace inside whose ruins the present settlement stands; parts of the walls and two defensive towers can still be seen (3–4C AD). According to early Ragusan sources this was the palace of Agesilaius of Anazarbo, who was exiled here by Lucius Septimius Severus and later freed by Caracalla at the urging of Oppian.

From Polače an asphalt road runs across the narrow neck of the island to (2km) *Govedjari* and *****Veliko jezero**, a beautiful salt-water lake surrounded by dense pinewoods. On the far side of the lake, on a small island, the *Hotel Melita* occupies the former *Benedictine*

Monastery, founded by monks from Apulia in 1151 under a bequest by Župan Desa of Zahumlje. The two-storied building has a Renaissance cloister and a machicolated tower at one corner. The monastery church (*Sv. Marija*) is a good example of Apulian Romanesque, though it was enlarged with the addition of a Renaissance loggia and bell tower in the early 16C (Gundulić arms on the loggia). The W front and eaves are decorated with blind arcading. The narthex has Gothic relief carvings of St. John the Baptist and angels. Inside is a painting of the Vision of St. Benedict attributed to Petar Mattei-Matejević (1701). Among the many Dubrovnik notables who were members of the order were the writers Mavro Vetranović (1482–1576) and Ignjat Djurdjević (1675–1737), who left a description of Mljet in his long poem 'Marunko'.

An asphalt and gravel road leads E from Polače to the remaining villages on the island, most of which are at the E end.—18km **Babina polje** (800 inhab.), at the foot of the island's highest mountain, *Veli Grad* (514m), is the largest settlement and the former capital, with a number of interesting old churches. These include the pre-Romanesque church of *Sv. Andrija* with a richly ornamented transenna, the pre-Romanesque and Gothic church of *Sv. Mihovil*, the 13C Gothic churches of *Sv. Pankraija* and *Djurdje* (St. George) and the 15C parish church with Renaissance and baroque additions (Romanesque processional cross in the treasury). Several baroque houses in the village include the former *Knežev dvor* (Governor's Palace).

The Gothic church of Sv. Trojic (Holy Trinity) in (26km) *Prožura* was built by the Benedictines from Lokrum (15C) and has a bronze Romanesque crucifix in the treasury. There is also a 17C defensive tower in the village.—In (15km) *Korita*, at the end of the road, are the 15C Gothic church of Sv.Vid (Gothic chalice), a 17C defensive tower and a number of baroque houses from the 18C.

22   Dubrovnik and its Environs

DUBROVNIK occupies a small, rocky peninsula at the foot of Mt Srdj with modern suburbs fanning out to E and W and over the lower slopes of the mountain. Although comparatively small (31,000 inhab.), it is the most famous city of Yugoslavia, a distinction it derives from its long history as the independent republic of *Ragusa*. The exceptional beauty of its streets and buildings moved even George Bernard Shaw to hyperbole, and it stands high among the more attractive cities of the world, being rivalled in the Adriatic only by Venice. Two centuries of economic decline saved the town from the architectural philistinism of the 18–19C, and though prosperity has returned with tourism, good taste has so far kept excesses to a minimum. The old centre constitutes one of the more perfectly preserved medieval entities in Europe, made incomparably more enjoyable by the exclusion of motor traffic.

Post Office: 14 Put Maršala Tita.

Information: *Turistički Informatvni Centar (TIC)*, 1 Placa, tel. 26355.

Airport: At Čilipi, 23km SE; *JAT*, 7 Put M. Tita, tel. 23575.

Sea Connections: Car ferries to *Ancona, Bari, Corfù, Igoumenitsa*, and points N to *Rijeka*. Passenger service to the islands of *Koločep, Lopud, Šipan* and *Mljet*. During the summer launches make excursions to *Cavtat, Trsteno, Mljet, Korčula*, and the *Elaphite Islands* (inquire at TIC).

Amusements: MUSIC: The Dubrovnik Symphony Orchestra plays two or three times a month; in winter in the Sala doma sindikata (Sv. Klara); in summer in the court of the Rector's Palace. The DUBROVNIK SUMMER FESTIVAL, with national and international orchestras, ballet, opera, and theatre companies, annually July –Aug. For information and tickets apply to 1 Ulica od Sigurate, or local travel agencies.

History. When the Greco-Roman city of Epidaurus (today Cavtat) was sacked by the Avars and Slavs (early 7C) its population took refuge on the small rocky island of Lausa (later Rausa and then *Ragusa*), which was separated from the mainland by a narrow channel. At about the same time Slavs settled on the wooded slopes of the mainland side of the channel, whence the name *Dubrovnik* (from *dubrava*, a glade). In time the intervening channel was filled in and the two halves united and encircled by defensive walls. The city remained nominally under the suzerainty of Byzantium, having beaten off attacks by the Saracens (886–87), the Bulgaro-Macedonians under Czar Samuilo (988), and (in alliance with William II of Sicily) the Serbs (1184). A see was founded in 990. As a result of the sack of Constantinople by the fourth Crusade, Ragusa was forced in 1205 to acknowledge the supremacy of her Adriatic rival, Venice. In 1292, the city, still constructed largely of wood, was ravaged by fire; the present urban plan stems from the major rebuilding that followed. Venetian rule ended in 1358, when the whole of Dalmatia, together with Ragusa, was ceded to Hungary-Croatia. Rugusa, by superior diplomacy, won better terms from her new overlords. After 1420, when Dalmatia was sold back to Venice, it became independent in all but name, retaining a nominal link with Hungary as a safeguard against Turkish or Venetian aggression until 1526, after which an agreed annual tribute was paid to the Turks. Benefiting from valuable trade concessions as intermediary between the Ottoman Empire and the Mediterranean, Ragusa's prosperity was such that the word 'argosy' (derived from Ragusa) entered the English language as a synonym for a treasure ship. By the 17C however, wars, and the shift of trade to the New World, were affecting Ragusan and Mediterranean prosperity generally. On 6 April 1667 a catastrophic earthquake killed over 5000 citizens (including the Rector) and levelled most of the public buildings. The ruins had to be defended against looters from the South. Though with great effort a measure of recovery was achieved, the Republic was only a shadow, when, in 1797, like Malta, it attracted the cupidity of Napoleon's eastbound fleet. Menaced in 1806 by a Russian advance from Corfù to bases in the Boka Kotorska, Dubrovnik surrendered to a French force from Makarska. A month's siege by the Russo-Montenegrin fleets (during which 3000 cannon balls fell on the city) was lifted by a French force from Split. Marmont arrived as governor and in 1809 the Republic's independence was formally ended by Napoleonic decree. In 1815, by the terms of the Treaty of Vienna, Dubrovnik passed to Austria until 1918.

The territory of the Republic of Ragusa extended from Klek-Neum in the N to Sutorina (Boka Kotorska) in the S and for a mere few kilometres inland. It included the islands of Šipan, Lopud, and Koločep (after 1080), Mljet (1141) and Lastovo (1216), the town of Ston (1298) and the Pelješac Peninsula (1399). Ragusa also ruled Korčula, Brač, and Hvar for a brief period (1414–17), but was forced to cede them to Venice.

The *Republican Constitution* of Ragusa, like that of Venice, was strictly aristocratic. The population was divided into three classes: nobility, citizens, and artisans or plebians. The last had no voice in government and citizens were permitted to hold only minor offices, all effective power being concentrated in the hands of a small hereditary nobility. No intermarriage was permitted. The supreme governing body was a Grand Council (Veliko vijeće or Consilium majus), on which every noble took his seat at the age of 18. Executive power was vested in the Minor Council (Malo vijeće or Consilium minus), consisting first of eleven members and (after 1667) of seven, chief among whom was the *Knez* or Rector. Both bodies had come into existence by 1235 and in 1253 a consultative body, the Senate (Vijeće umoljenih or Consilium Rogatorum), was added, consisting of 45 invited members (over 40 years of age) and including the members of the Malo vijeće. Under Venice the Knez was Venetian, but after 1358 always a Ragusan, and to prevent any abuse of power he held office for only a month, becoming eligible for re-election only after two years.

The government of the Republic was liberal in character and early showed its concern for justice and humanitarian principles. In 1272 the laws, based on Roman practice and local customs, were codified into a single statute (including town-planning and quarantine regulations), in 1301 a medical service was introduced, in 1317 a pharmacy, in 1347 a refuge for old people, and in 1432 a foundling hospital, while in 1418 slave trading was abolished. Having lost 11,000 lives during the Black Death of 1348, the city survived the epidemic of 1430 thanks to organised quarantine and cremation of infected corpses. After Constantinople fell to the Turks, Ragusa became a refuge for numerous wealthy and noble families from Macedonia, Serbia, Bosnia, and Croatia.

The cultural life of the Republic, though wide and varied, did not equal its political and mercantile achievements. No native artist ever achieved international recognition but evidence of good taste in the employment of architects and sculptors from other parts of the Adriatic coast or from Italy is everywhere apparent. The literary tradition is respectable if seldom brilliant. Ilija Crijević (Elius Lampridius Cervinus; 1463–1520) was crowned poet laureate in Rome in 1482 for his study of Virgil and a cycle of love poems in Latin, and other Latinists, such as Jakov Bunić (Bona Bonus), achieved recognition. Of greater importance was the considerable body of work in the Dubrovnik dialect of Serbo-Croatian, created between the Renaissance and the 18C. Although mainly imitative of Italian models, this literature did produce two writers of more than local interest, Marin Držić (1508–67), author of a large oeuvre of Renaissance pastoral dramas and comedies (notably *Skup*— The Miser, and *Dundo Maroje*—Uncle Maroje), and Ivan Gundulić (1589–1638), author of *Osman*, a long epic poem on relations between Turks and Christian Slavs. Other leading figures were Šiško Menčetić (1457–1527), Džore Držić (1461–1501), Mavro Vetranović (1482–1576), Dinko Ranjina (1536–1607) and Dinko Zlatarić (1558–1609) from the earlier period, and from the 17C Junija Palmotić (1606–57), Dživo Bunić Vučić (1594–1658), Stijepo Djordjić (1579–1632), and Vladislav Menčetić (1600–66 ?). The last Dubrovnik writer of any note was Ignjat Djurdjević (1675–1737).

The natural sciences produced two outstanding men in Marin Getaldić (Marino Ghetaldi; 1568–1626), who determined the specific weights of metals, and Rudjer Bošković (1717–87). Mathematician, physicist and astronomer of genius, author of Theoria Philosophiae Naturalis (1758), Bošković founded the Observatory of Milan and was a member of the French Academy. In London as a Fellow of the Royal Society, he made the acquaintance of Dr Johnson, Boswell, and Sir Joshua Reynolds. Juraj Dragišić (Georgius Argenteneusis Salviatus; 14500–1520 ?), was tutor to the sons of Lorenzo de' Medici and defending counsel for Giovanni Pico della Mirandola against the Inquisition. Benedikt Kotruljić or Kotruljević (1400–68), a minister at the court of Aragon, was author of one of the first scientific treatises on trade and commercial practices. A more recent native of Dubrovnik was the Croatian playwright, Ivo Vojnović (1857–1929), who wrote several works about the decline of the ancient Republic.

I   The Old City

The riches of Dubrovnik are concentrated into a small compass, but even so visitors whose time is limited are advised to begin with the area between the Jesuit Church and the Ploče Gate at the E end of the town, with perhaps a walk round the walls to gain some idea of the whole layout.

Most visitors will approach for the first time from the W, arriving at the irregular open space of PILE (described below), where city buses arrive and depart and where a taxi rank contributes to the bustle. An excellent preliminary view of the massive walls encircling the city may be gained from a few paces up Put iza grada on the landward side. Steps lead down beside the bridge to a pleasant small park in the former moat, which descends to the water's edge (view of forts Bokar and Lovrijenac).

A stone bridge with twin Gothic arches, designed by Paskoje Miličević (1471), the Republic's official architect, leads via a wooden drawbridge to the Pile Gate, one of the two main land entrances to the city. A statue of the city patron, St. Blaise, is set over the arch and on the inner side can be seen the heavy iron balls and windlass that used to operate the drawbridge. The entrance to Fort Bokar (see below) is just inside the gate. Within the outer gate a flight of steps and a ramp provide alternative descents to the Gothic inner gate (1460), which was modelled on the Fishmarket Gate in the old harbour. The Balustrade of the steps and a second statue of St. Blaise set in a niche are both the work of Ivan Meštrović. A small gate gives access to the moat. Immediately inside the inner gate is the W end of Placa, the main artery of the old city (see below).

The ****City Walls** of Dubrovnik are among the finest and most complete in Europe and majestically symbolise the strength and stability of the ancient republic. They comprise an inner and an outer section. The inner ring, with a circumference of just under 2km and rising to a maximum height of 25m, with a thickness attaining 6m in places, is furnished with three round and 12 rectangular towers, five bastions, two corner towers and one major fortress. On the landward side, this is protected by a lower outer wall having ten semicircular bastions and the casemated fortress of Bokar, with a moat running round the outside.

The walls were begun when the city was founded and the earliest remaining fragments date from the 10C, although the first complete enceinte was thrown up only in the 12–13C. In the 14C the works were extended on the Ploče side and 15 square towers added. The fall of Constantinople in 1453 led to a reappraisal of the system, during which the curtain walls were trebled in thickness and many of the towers rebuilt. A century later, in answer to threats from Venice, some bastions were added on the seaward side, together with the fortress of Revelin, and the last reconstruction took place (1647–63) as a response to the Candian War between Venice and Turkey. Among the numerous architects and builders involved, the most prominent were Jean de Vienne (1381–87), Michelozzo Michelozzi (1461–64), Juraj Dalmatinac (1465–70) and Ivan Giorgi (1668–71).

Access to the walls is gained by a flight of steps to the left of the Pile Gate. Another entrance is to be found at the Ploče Gate on the E side of the city. Adm. daily 8–18.

Walking NE along the top of the steeply rising wall flanking the Franciscan Monastery, you soon reach the magnificent round tower of *Minčeta*, built in 1455–61 to designs by Michelozzi and Dalmatinac. It rises from the highest and most massive of the corner towers. The battlements afford one of the finest *Views of the old city. From the N wall you have a constantly changing panorama of the landward side of the city, with its regular streets running almost N and S. Beyond the N entrance gate to the city is the semicircular tower of *Sv. Jadov*, once the NE corner tower of the walls. Its present shape dates from the 16C. The projecting complex of bastions that enclose the Dominican Monastery (comp. below) was added in the 14C and brings you to the Old Ploče Gate. A further short section of wall takes us to the 13C tower of *Sv. Luka*, the oldest tower still standing; farther on, the tower of *Sv. Dominik* (1387), opposite the S door of the Dominican church, overlooks the harbour.

Descend to the street behind the Clock Tower, pass between the Rector's Palace and the Cathedral (described below), and regain the walls by steps just inside the *Vrata od Ponte*, on the far side of the harbour. A straight section of wall skirting the S side of the harbour precedes to the massive *Tvrdjava of Sv. Ivan*, the largest single component of the walls, erected in four stages between 1346 and 1557. From here a massive chain used to be stretched across the harbour to the tower of Sv. Luka. Traverse the S walls with excellent views out to sea. The bastions of *Sv. Spasitelj* (1647–57) and *Sv. Stjepan* (1658–63), facing SE and enclosing the oldest quarter of the city, where the last to be rebuilt. From the high bastion of *Sv. Margarita*, beyond a re-entrant angle, you can see the exterior of the sector just traversed, which rises from jagged rocks. This section, that following, and the bastion of *Zvijezda* (Star), suffered heavily from the earthquake of 1667 and parts had to be repaired afterwards, though the largest fortification on this side, the *Mrtvo zvono* (1509–74), designed by Paskoje Miličević, was not affected. Descend to the tower of *Sv. Marija*, with views ahead of Fort Lovrijenac and the coast, and come to *Kalarinja* (completed 1430) the SW corner tower, with

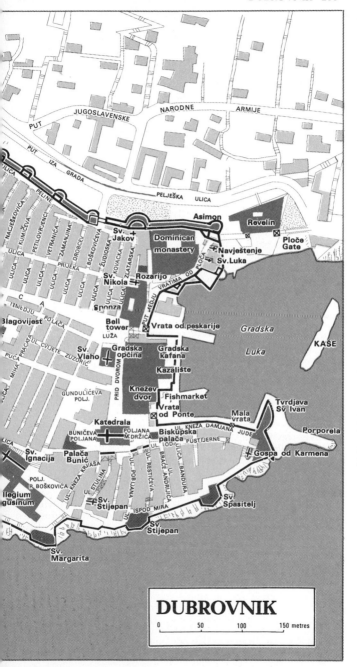

PUT JUGOSLAVENSKE NARODNE ARMIJE

PUT IZA GRADA

PUT

ULICA

PELINE

PELJEŠKA ULICA

NALJEŠKOVIĆA

KUMIČIĆA

PETILOVRIJENCI

VETRANIĆA

TAMANJINA

DROBCE

BOŠKOVIĆEVA

ŽUDIOSKA

KOVAČKA

ZLATARSKA

PRIJEKA

Asimon

Revelin

Ploče
Gate

Sv.
Jakov

Dominican
monastery

Navještenje

Sv. Luka

Sv.
Nikola

Rozarijo

PUT MEDJU VRATIMA OD PLOČA

IZMEDJU

POLAČA

C A

Blagovijest

Sponza

Bell
tower

Vrata od peskarije

Gradska
Luka

KAŠE

LUŽA

PLACA UL CVJETE ZUZORIĆ

PUCA

Sv.
Vlaho

Gradska
općina

Gradska
Kafana

GUNDULIĆEVA
POLJ.

PRID DVOROM

Kazalište

Knežev
dvor

Fishmarket

Tvrdjava
Sv Ivan

Katedrala

Vrata
od Ponte

Mala
vrata

Porporela

BUNIČEVA
POLJANA

POLJANA
M.DRŽIĆA

Biskupska
palača

UL KNEZA DAMJANA JUDE

Sv.
Ignacija

Palača
Bunić

UL OD
PUSTIJERNE

Gospa od Karmena

POLJ.
R. BOŠKOVIĆA

UL- KNEZA KRVAŠA

UL STULINA

UL-POB JANA

UL. RESTIĆEVA

BRAĆE ANDRIJIĆA

ULICA BANDURA

llegium
gusinum

Sv.
Stijepan

ISPOD MIRA

Sv.
Spasitelj

Sv.
Stijepan

Sv.
Margarita

DUBROVNIK

0   50   100   150 metres

Bokar fortress below. Turn NE to the large rectangular *Puncijela* tower (1305–50), with an unusual pillared stair (good view of Pile), beyond which the cloister of the former nunnery of St. Clare is seen, and regain the Pile Gate.

An entrance within the Pile Gate gives access to **Fort Bokar**, a handsome round fortress (1461–1570) designed by Michelozzi, that stands just below Kalarinja on an outcrop of rock. It is said to be the oldest casemated fortress in Europe and contains a small lapidary collection and numerous cannon.

Within the Pile Gate an open space called POLJANA PASKOJE MILIČEVIĆA extends on the right. In the centre stands the *Velike česma*, a 16-sided reservoir and drinking fountain by Onofrio di Giordano della Cava, which formed part of the town waterworks, designed and partly constructed by this Neapolitan architect in 1438–44. The dome was added later. In the corner of the square and next to the Pile Gate is the delightful small church of *Sv. Spas* (St. Saviour), designed in thanksgiving for deliverance from the earth-quake of 1520 and built in 1520–28 by Petar Andrijić of Korčula, with a typically Dalmatian Renaissance W front (wheel-window) and a Gothic interior. On the N wall is a painting of the Ascension by Pietro Antonio da Urbino (1528).

Adjoining is the **Franciscan Monastery**. The church, erected in 1343, has a late-Gothic *South Portal* by the brothers Petrović (1499), facing the Placa. In the tympanum is a Pietà flanked by SS. Jerome and John the Baptist, and surmounted by God the Father. The detail of the elaborately crocketed finial and windblown acanthus decor-ation is admirably emphasised by the plain wall. The Gothic *Bell Tower* (1424) was given an unfortunate cupola after the earthquake had toppled its spire. The lofty INTERIOR (reputed once to have had ceiling paintings by Titian) was reconstructed after the earthquake of 1667. To the left of the high altar is the *Sacristy* with a carved lavabo and vestment cupboards of walnut with inlaid portraits of Christ and saints. It is extended E by the beautiful little Gothic chapel of the Bunić (Bona) family (1472). A huge Gothic ambry for reliquaries surmounts the altar; its triple doors, painted as a triptych, form the altarpiece.

The *CLOISTER (adm. 8–12 and 16–20) is entered from the passage between the W front and Sv. Spas. A remarkably original creation by Mihoje Brajkov of Bar (1317–48), it escaped damage in the earth-quake and remains the chief glory of the monastery. Each bay of the covered walk is enclosed by an arcade of six closely set round arches borne on coupled octagonal columns. The joint capitals of the paired columns display a variety of fantastic beasts, monsters, and mytholo-gical creatures in the best traditions of Romanesque art. The tympana above have circular openings, the central one of each side surrounded by a rich border of acanthus leaves, the remainder containing a quatrefoil. The elegant ornamented balustrade above is the work of Ratko Brajković (1433). A richly decorated Gothic sarcophagus of the Gučetić family is set into the wall of the SE corner. Two-light windows flank the door into the Gothic *Chapter House*, which is now used as the monastery TREASURY (adm. 9–12, 16–18). The well-labelled exhibits include a 15C silver-gilt cross and silver thurible, an 18C crucifix from Jerusalem in mother-of-pearl on olive wood, and an interesting display from the monastery's extensive library (30,000 volumes, 20 incunabula, 1500 MSS), notably the manuscript of Gundu-lić's epic poem 'Osman', a first edition of 'Judita' by Marko Marulić (Venice, 1521), a 15C copy of the Statute of Zadar, an illuminated martyrology (1541) by Bernardin Gučetić (Gozzě) and illuminated psalters. Among the pictures is one of Rudjer Bošković (see above) painted in London in 1760; and a painting showing the town before the earthquake. The Gothic chapel of the Djordjić family contains a charming fragment of a reredos and the adjoining niche a 16C wooden statue of St. Nicholas. The *Pharmacy*, or apothecary's shop, established in 1317, the oldest to survive in Europe, has been restored, with early ceramic jars (Faience and Delft), apparatus, furniture, and 16C pharmacy registers.

The beautiful wide street of **PLACA**, or *Stradun* (300m; pedestrians only) runs from the Pile to Ploče gates, following the line of the channel that once bisected the town. The street came into being in the 12C, was paved in 1468 and reconstructed after the earthquake of 1667. The limestone pavement, polished by use, shines like glass after rain. The Placa is the main street and traditional venue of the evening corzo. The houses on either side, though preserving an ancient ground plan, also date from the 17C, their elevation and style being uniform. Their shops mostly have the characteristic 'na koljeno' combined door and counter.

The 'na kojeno' consists of a door and window in a single frame spanned by a semicircular arch. The door was kept closed and goods handed over the sill, which served as a counter. The recipient took them on to his knee (hence the name 'on to the knee'). The distinctive shape of the 'na koljeno' with its stone frame is to be found in many parts of the Kvarner and Dalmatia, but particularly in Dubrovnik, where it has been adopted almost as a local trademark.

The irregularly shaped LUŽA, the hub of public life in the days of the old Republic, makes a fitting architetural climax to the walk down the Placa and is a favourite meeting place for natives, visitors, and pigeons alike. The N side of the square is occupied by the striking *Plača Sponza*, a harmonious blend of Gothic and Renaissance architecture probably inspired by the Rector's Palace nearby. A graceful loggia stands forward of the façade.

As the ancient custom house, mint, and main warehouse (variously known at different times as the Fontik, Divona or Dogana) this was one of the more important buildings in the city and remained in continuous public use until the end of the 19C. For many years the first floor was used for social gatherings and the meetings of learned and literary societies. The palace dates from 1516–22, when plans by Paskoje Miličević were executed by the Andrijić family from Korčula, notably the sculptor Petar Andrijić. Authorities differ as to whether it was designed and built in a mixture of styles or whether the Gothic middle story remains from an earlier building.

The INTERIOR is built round a spacious court arranged as a double cloister, with round arches below and slightly pointed ones on the first floor. A pithy Latin inscription set in the far wall refers to the public scales that formerly stood here (Cheating and tampering with the weights is forbidden, and when I weigh goods God weighs me). The adjoining coat of arms enclosed in a wreath held by two angels is by Beltrandus Gallicus (1520). The ground floor houses a museum devoted to the National Liberation Movement (soon to move, 1987) and contains the original 16C mechanism and jacks of the town clock, whereas on the upper floors are stored the extensive Republican archives. The courtyard is used for exhibitions and festival concerts.

In the centre of the square stands *Orlando's Column*, with a statue of the Paladin Roland by Antun Dubrovčanin (1418), symbolising a free city; from it state decrees were proclaimed. The upper part bore the Republic's standard, and the forearm of Orlando was the standard measure of the Ragusan cubit (shown more accurately by a line in the base). The baroque church of **Sv. Vlaho** (*St. Blaise*), the patron saint of Dubrovnik, was built by Marino Gropelli in 1706–14 to replace a building of 1368 lost by fire. It faces N instead of W. The spacious interior, modelled on San Maurizio in Venice, is rectangular with a central dome, and preserves some of the treasures from the earlier church. In the reredos is a celebrated silver *Statuette of St. Blaise, holding a model of 15C Dubrovnik. The painted organ loft behind the high altar is by Petar Mattei Matejević (early 18C); the glass windows by Ivo Dulčić (1971). High on the walls are placed stone statues of SS. Peter and Jerome, by Nikola Lazanić of Brač (late 16C), and above the side door a wooden figure of St. Anthony, of unknown date.

Along the E side of Luža a continuous line of buildings extends from the Sponza across the width of the harbour, fronting upon the long open space called PRID DVOROM. A Gothic archway adjoining the Sponza marks the beginning of Put medju vratima od Ploča leading to the Outer Ploča Gate and supports the **Loža zvonara**, an open loggia in which were hung bells for sounding alarms or summoning assemblies. Erected in 1463, the loggia was restored to its former appearance in 1952 after conversion by the Austrians into an admiral's residence. The graceful *Bell Tower*, 35m tall, dating from 1444, was dismantled and rebuilt in 1928. The modern clock, with bronze jacks in the form of soldiers that strike the hour, is a faithful copy (with the addition of a figured time indicator) of one dating from 1478 (remains in Sponza palace). The great bell in the tower (the only original detail) was cast by Ivan Rabljanin in 1506. The adjoining *Glavna Straža* (Main Guard), incorporating a Gothic upper story of 1490 from the Ragusan admiral's house, was constructed in 1706–08, when the baroque portal was inserted after a design by Marino Gropilli. The charming *Mala česma* (little fountain) of Onofrio, an octagonal basin with defaced sculptural panels, from which rises a 'baroque-Gothic' column recalling the fountains of Viterbo, was completed by Pietro di Martino da Milano (mid 15C). The undistinguished *Gradska općina* (Town Hall; 1864) incorporates the pleasant *Gradska kavana*, with a loggia overlooking the harbour on the far side (see below) and a cinema above, and the *Narodno Kazalište* (theatre).

The *Kneževdvor*, or *Rector's Palace*, embodies (like the Sponza) a blend of Gothic and Renaissance styles so harmoniously fused as to epitomise Ragusan architecture at its best. Here the Rector of the Republic had his official seat and hence supreme political power was wielded. A castle on the site, which became the early Rector's residence, was destroyed in 1435 when fire exploded a magazine. A new palace was commissioned from Onofrio di Giordana della Cava and built in South Italian Gothic. This in turn was partly destroyed by another expolsion in 1463 and plans for its renovation were commissioned from Michelozzo and Juraj Dalmatinac. Their Renaissance solutions were rejected, although it is probable that Michelozzo's designs formed the basis of the subsequent rebuilding of the ground floor by Salvi di Michiele in 1468. Slight damage caused by the earthquake of 1667 was made good by Jerolim Skarpa of Korčula.

The upper floor of the façade is pierced by eight graceful Gothic windows with traceried heads, probably as Onofrio built it in 1435 but reassembled during the rebuilding of 1468. The plain Gothic portions at either end are the remnants of two towers between which has been inserted the handsome loggia of Michelozzo, built by Michiele. The columns and four of the *Capitals (first, second, sixth, and seventh from the right) are Gothic in manner, though the first depicts Asklepios in the setting of a medieval pharmacy. The loggia is vaulted with graceful Gothic ribs which spring fanwise from carved Renaissance corbels. Arcaded marble seats line the rear wall and that to the left. The Gate of Mercy, where alms were distributed, opens in the S wall. Entrance is gained by the main *Portal*, a Gothic arch with fanciful capitals and imposts; the figure of St. Blaise in the niche above is by Pietro di Martino and there is a fine bronze knocker in the shape of a lion's head.

The inner *COURT has a Renaissance arcade on three sides; on the fourth, an imposing staircase leads to an arcaded balcony. Below the stair arch are a Venetian Gothic fountain and a doorway (angel in niche above) leading to the offices of the Conservation Department in the former repository of the State Archives. The Bust of Miho Pracat (Michaeli Prazzato) by Pietro Giacometti da Recanati (1638) was the only monument to a citizen ever erected (or even allowed) by the medieval state; Pracat, a 16C merchant adventurer from Lopud, bequeathed his riches to the Republic. A small staircase leads to the mezzanine and former hall of the Lesser Council, which now houses temporary exhibitions and the city's *Naučna biblioteka*, a research library of 90,000 volumes (78 incunabula) and many manuscripts. Two of Onofrio's original capitals flank the entrance, one depicting Justice with a pair of lions, the other the Rector administering justice to the citizens.

On the FIRST FLOOR the *Hall of the Great Council* and the adjoining *State Rooms* house the **Gradski muzej** (adm. 9–13 winter, 9–16 summer). The entrance to the Hall at the head of the main staircase bears an admonitory inscription to forget private affairs and attend to public business. Some 18C sedan chairs are temporarily exhibited here. They bear the coats of arms of the Gjorgjić (Giorgi), Zamanja (Zamagna) and Gučetić (Gozze) families. The State Rooms are furnished with baroque and rococo furniture, portraits of Republican notables, and faience. The Louis XVI Hall (R.III) contains 18C paintings of pastoral scenes by Ioan Cingeri, and a copy of Rubens' *Thomyris and Cyrus*. The Rector's Study (R.IV) preserves the former state seals and keys of the city gates. The paintings include the *Baptism of Christ* by Mihajlo Hamzić (1509), a Ragusan pupil of Mantegna; and *Venus and Adonis* by Paris Bordone, a Venetian painter.

The EAST WING contains the rooms of the palace guards, on the mezzanine, and a small *Pinacotheca* with works by local painters of the 15–16C (notably Blaž Jurjev Trogiranin, the first important personality in local painting and a major figure in the late Gothic art of Dalmatia; and Dobro Dobričević Marinov, who introduced the Renaissance), and by artists from Italy and Northern Europe (Annibale Carracci, *Cain and Abel*; School of Tintoretto, *Holy Family*). There is also an extensive collection of Ragusan coins, seals, coats of arms, and measurements.

The baroque **Katedrala**, designed by Andrea Bufalini of Urbino and built in 1672–1713, stands in the centre of POLJANA MARINA DRŽIĆA. Its predecessor, a 13C Romanesque basilica said to have received a benefaction from Richard Coeur-de-Lion (supposedly shipwrecked on the island of Lokrum in 1192 when returning from the Third Crusade), was destroyed in the earthquake of 1667. The cathedral is cruciform in plan, with the high altar unusually towards the W and a high dome over the crossing. The exterior is decorated with a balustrade enclosing the roofs of the aisles and surmounted by statues of saints carved by Marin Radica of Korčula early in the present century. The interior is light and spacious. A large polyptych of the Assumption, by Titian (after 1552), occupies the wall above and behind the high altar. In the sanctuary are four paintings by Pado-vanino and over the entrance to the treasury a work by Andrea del Sarto. Among many altarpieces by lesser Italian masters in the nave is a Flemish triptych, which served as a portable altar when Ragusan ambassadors went to pay the annual tribute in Constantinople (they alone holding the privilege of hearing mass in Turkey).

The *TREASURY (open Tues and Thurs, 11–12), to the left of the high altar, contains some 138 reliquaries, most of which are carried in procession round the city on the feast of St. Blaise (3 Feb). Entry has always been a jealously guarded privilege, in the days of the Republic needing permission of the bishop, the Grand Council, and the treasurer, each of whom kept a key to one of the three locks. The collection occupies a beautiful baroque chapel designed by Gropelli and painted by Mattei-Matejević. The head of Christ is by Pordenone. On the altar stand the three major reliquaries of St. Blaise: the *Reliquary of the Skull, in the form of a Byzantine crown of enamel and silver filigree work set with 24 12C enamels; a 12C silver-gilt arm reliquary, set with nine Byzantine enamels (originally 18); and a 17C silver filigree leg reliquary with the arms of the Republic in enamel. Behind is a large late-Gothic silver *Cross enclosing part of the true cross, decorated with reliefs in silver-gilt by J. Matov (16C), and a silver statuette of St. Blaise. Cases display a superb *Ewer and Basin of silver by W. Jamnitzer of Nuremberg (c 1550), a baroque casket enclosing a supposed fragment of Christ's swaddling clothes, another with the hand of St. Bridget, a Gothic reliquary containing the lower jaw of St. Stephen of Hungary, and silver-gilt rib cage of St. Blaise. A bronze English lectern with a Latin inscription reading 'Remember, Henry, that thou too must die' is said to be of the time of Henry VIII.

The former *Biskupska palača* faces the cathedral; built in Tuscan Renaissance style, it was previously the home of the Sorkoč family. It is planned to house a Museum of Religious Art in the SW corner of BUNIĆEVA POLJANA, behind the cathedral; the *Palača Bunić* has a good portal with the Bunić (Bona) arms in the tympanum and a Renaissance court within. GUNDULIĆEVA POLJANA, the larger adjoining square, accommodates the principal fruit and vegetable market (Tržnica), to which peasants from surrounding districts sometimes come in local costume. The monument to Ivan Gundulić in the centre, by I. Rendić (1893), depicts scenes in bronze relief from his epic poem 'Osman'.

UL. UZ JESUITE leads to the foot of the imposing staircase (modelled in 1738 on the 'Spanish Steps' in Rome) that mounts to Sv. Ignacija, the baroque church of the Jesuits, designed by And. Pozzo (1725) in imitation of the Gesù in Rome. The belfry boasts a bell cast in 1355. The focal point of the spacious interior is the apse painted by the Sicilian G. Garcià (1738). The *Collegium Ragusinum*, dominating the S side of Poljana Rudjera Boškovića (and indeed much of Dubrovnik), was designed by two local Jesuits in 1735 and is perhaps the least tasteful building in the city. In the steps leading to the main entrance is a relief (1481), thought to be from the church of Sv. Bartula (Bartholomew) which once stood at the far end of the square. According to legend St. Francis slept in the vestibule of this church during a week's halt en route for Constantinople. Its portal, richly decorated with pre-Roman carving, survives in Ul. Kneza Krvaša.

Pustijerna, one of the older and more picturesque quarters of the city, lying to the E between the harbour and the city walls, largely escaped the devastation of the earthquake. It repays detailed exploration, but since this involves a serpentine progress up and down its stepped streets, it is best reserved for a cool day. From the Collegium Ragusinum UL. KRVAŠA (comp. above) descends past one of the older houses in the city, with Romanesque door and window frames, to

Vrata od Pustijerne, the Romanesque gate that marks the extent of the 10–11C walls (also reached from behind the cathedral by steps). In UL. STULINA, which mounts again almost parallel, are two town houses of the Restić (Resti) and Saraka families and, at the top, the ruined church of *Sv. Stjepan*. The original building, dating from the 8C or earlier, is mentioned by Constantine Porphyrogenitus in his account of the founding of Ragusa; only the lower courses of this remain. Over the S door is a pre-Romanesque carving of a cabled double arch enclosing twin crosses. The narrow winding UL. ISPOD MIRA runs inside the walls at the head of delightful small streets lined with old houses. On the corner of Ul. Pobijana is the Renaissance *Palača Bunić*. In Ul. Restićeva are the Gothic *Palača Zamanjina* and the Renaissance *Palača Skočibuha*, built by the brothers Josip and Ivan Andrijić (1549–53) to designs by Antun iz Padove (Antonio da Padova). Perhaps the finest street of Pustijerna is UL. BRAĆE ANDRIJIĆA where Gothic and Renaissance mansions make up the complex *Palača Restić*. The pleasant baroque church of *Gospa od Karmena* (Our Lady of Mt Carmel; 1628–36) lies at the end of UL. ISPOD MIRA in the shadow of the fortress of Sv. Ivan, with the city arms over its W door. The interior (key from Bishop's Palace) contains 17C paintings by minor Italian artists.

Dominating the entrance to the old harbour is the **Fortress of Sv. Ivan**. On the ground floor an *Aquarium* (adm. 8–20) is stocked with fish from various parts of the Mediterranean. On the upper floors is the *Pomorski muzej* (summer 8–13 and 17.30–18; winter 8–14), a maritime museum in which the four sections are devoted to the Republican period; the age of steam; the Second World War; and to techniques of sailing and navigation.

From UL. KNEZA DAMJANA JUDE, the plain *Mala vrata* gives access to the old harbour (comp. below), but it is more interesting to return to the Cathedral by UL. OD PUSTIJERNE, an almost subterranean street spanned by numerous vaults and lined with ancient houses. In UL. BANDUREVA, a narrow cul-de-sac, are the handsome Renaissance town houses of the Kaboga and Sorkočević (Sorgo) families (left) and the Bunić family (right).

Between the Cathedral and Rector's Palace, the *Vrata od Ponte* (1476) gives access to the peaceful **Old Harbour**, now used only by little fishing boats and pleasure craft. The breakwater (*Kaše*) was built by Paskoje Miličević in the 15C, but by the 16C the harbour had already been superseded by Gruž. To the right a narrow way along the walls leads round Fort Sv. Ivan to the *Porporela*, a favourite swimming place of the local youth. The Veliki arsenal, built to house four state galleys, was demolished in 1863 to make way for the Gradska općina (described above), but parts of it, incorporated into the Gradska kavana, are still visible. Beyond the cafe, opposite the mole whence excursion boats ply to Lokrum, the Harbourmaster's Office occupies the site of the former Mali arsenal.

The Gothic *Vrata od ribarnice* (or perkarije), erected in 1381–87 as the second of the original gates (with a statue of St. Blaise on the harbour side), readmits to the town by the narrow PUT MEDJU VRATIMA OD PLOČA, the street linking the inner and outer Ploče gates (as its name states). Just to the left steps lead up to the walls; turn right, between the high city wall and the side of the Sponza palace.

A stone staircase with a Renaissance balustrade mounts left to the **Dominican Church and Monastery**. The Church was erected between 1315 but had to be rebuilt after the earthquake of 1667 and again after the French occupation, when it was used as a stable and storehouse; its last renovation was in 1883. The plain interior consists of a huge single nave with a triple Gothic arch near the E end opéning into the sanctuary and two side chapels, the only part of the original building that survives. The fine *Rood comprises a 15C Crucifixion by Paolo Veneziano, flanked by paintings of the Virgin Mary and St. John by Lorenzo di Marino Dobričević (15C).

Two altarpieces by Francesco di Maria (17C) adorn the S wall. The Romanesque S door (13C) has a Gothic frame added in 1419. A 15C statue of St. Vincent Ferrer surmounts the next altar. Behind the high altar is a Gothic portal (damaged) with the Mečetić (Menze) arms in the tympanum and arms of the Zamanjina, Držić, and Restić families round it. The Gundulić Chapel, left of the high altar, was designed by Luka Paskojev (1536).

Along the N wall are an altarpiece showing a Miracle of St. Dominic by Vlaho Bukovac (a local 19C work in the Sicilian manner); and a late-Gothic stone pulpit (15C). The W wall incorporates a curious Renaissance triple arch with scalloped semi-domes, by Ludovik Maravić, into the base of which are built carved Gothic tomb-slabs.

The graceful late-Gothic CLOISTER, erected by local masons to a modified design of Maso di Bartolomeo of Florence, has interesting bosses in the vault and tomb slabs in the walls, but is somewhat marred by the over-clever interlaced orament in alternate tympana and in the balustrade above. The S side was surmounted by a balcony in 1520 inscribed with the date and the words of the Te Deum. The garth is planted with orange trees; the Venetian well-head in the centre of 1559 was given a Renaissance superstructure in 1623. In the corner, over the sacristy, rises the Bell Tower, begun in 1390 and completed in 1531 in a curiously retarded Romanesque style, continued somewhat unfortunately by the later baroque lantern.

The CHAPTER HOUSE was divided in 1668 into an outer (Djurdjevic) chapel and an inner treasury. Both rooms, together with the church SACRISTY (built by Paskoje Miličević in 1485), are used today to house an interesting collection of PAINTINGS, MANUSCRIPTS, AND LITURGICAL OBJECTS. Especially noteworthy are an early 16C polytych of the Dubrovnik School (attributed to Lorenzo Dobričević); an altarpiece showing Mary Magdalen wth St. Blaise, the Archangel Raphael, and a donor, by Titian (c 1554); and the manuscripts and incunabula, just a small part of those preserved in the fine monastic *Library* (16,000 volumes, including 217 manuscripts and 239 incunabula).

Adjoining the Dominican church is the former Renaissance church of *Sv. Sebastijan* (1466–69), transformed into a prison by the French (note the barred windows on the street façade). Facing is the deconsecrated church of *Rozarijo* now an art gallery, built in 1594 and restored after a fire in 1642. The French turned it into a salt store but it was restored in 1962 as the headquarters of the Društvo prijatelja Dubrovačke starine (Society of Friends of Old Dubrovnik). The beautiful interior is divided by two tall Renaissance arcades, ornamented with heads of nuns and angels. An ornate portal, probably the entrance to a vanished chapel, stands within the vestibule.

PUT MEDJU VRATIMA OD PLOČA slopes uphill past the S door of the Dominican church (left), its Romanesque style disguised by the florid arch in which it was later framed. Further on (right) stands the tiny church of *Sv. Luka*, of pre-Romanesque foundation. The Gothic figures of saints in the tympanum are attributed to the brothers Petrović (late 15C); the lintel gives the date (1786) of the last renovation. Adjoining is the larger chapel of *Navještenje* (Annunciation), built by Petar Andrijić in 1536 in a mixture of late-Gothic and Renaissance styles (good portal and blind arcading on the gable;

restored 1910). The altarpiece is an Annunciation by Mattei-Matejević. A few steps brings you to the twin-angled arches of the *Inner Ploče Gate* the first (Romanesque) through the wall of *Asimon Tower*, the second widened by the Austrians. The framed statue of St. Blaise over the outer arch is the oldest of many in the city. A stone bridge (1449) across the moat leads through another arch and along the foot of the massive **Revelin**, one of two vast fortresses built outside the walls to protect the city from surprise attack. A small belvedere (Trg oružja) at its foot affords a marvellous view of the old harbour and town and accomodates a war memorial by Franjo Kršinić (1954).

Revelin, entered from Put iza grada, was begun in 1463 (it is said as a preparation for the landing of Pius II's projected crusade from Ancona), and completed c 1500, but in 1538 new plans drawn by Antonio Ferramolino, an engineer sent from Genoa at Ragusa's request, were implemented and the fortress finished in eleven years. Under Austria the building was adapted as barracks, but it has been renovated for use as a concert hall. Its enormous terrace also makes a fine natural stage for performances in summer.

Pass out of the Old City by the fortified and embrasured *Outer Gate of* **Ploče**, built by Miho Hranjac in 1628, and over a wooden drawbridge and twin-spanned stone bridge (15C) by Paskoje Miličević similar to those at Pile Gate.

Just beyond the square in front of this gate, along a cul-de-sac to the right, extends the former **Lazaret** (17C), restored in 1968–69. The far end had been adapted as a covered market. Put Frana Supila leads past the prominent grammar school and a modern art gallery to the Excelsior Hotel and the Argentina Hotel. Here the main road rises (left) to join the Adriatic Highway (one way only in the downward direction), while a branch continues (right) past the *Villa Shahrazade*, built by an eccentric millionaire for his mistress (magnificent walled garden; entered from the Argentina) and the *Villa Dubrovnik*, used as a residence for official visitors, to the former monastery of *Sv. Jakov*. Here the Institute of Arts and Sciences has established research laboratories into corrosion of sea water and desalination methods. The cloister (12C) has charm but the church is dilapidated. The road ends at the Hotel Belvedere.

By the side of the Rozarijo (comp. above) a narrow passage leads to the street and northern quarter of the city known as **Prijeko**, the original Slavonic settlement on the mainland of the dividing channel. The little pre-Romanesque church of *Sv. Nikola* on the left, has a Renaissance W front of 1607 and preserves a Gothic figure of St. Nicholas in wood, a 15C painting, and a stone slab with pre-Romanesque carving that serves as the altar frontal. ZLATARSKA UL. in front of the church mounts to *Sv. Jakov na Pelinama*, the only Romanesque church to have survived, which sheltered the Dominicans in 1225–28 on their first arrival. Within (key from Gradski muzej) is a 15C painting of the Madonna.

UL. PELINE runs W inside the walls along the top of the quarter's narrow stepped streets. ŽUDIOSKA UL. is named for the Jewish ghetto that once stood here and has, in its lower section, an unobtrusive 15C synagogue, said to be the oldest in the Balkans, which functioned throughout the Second World War. At the top of BOŠKOVIĆEVA UL. a modern opening in the walls leads into Put iza grade. By Boškovićeva, named for the birthplace (plaque) of the scientist Rudjer Bošković, you may descend again to PRIJEKO which, running parallel to Placa, is lined with balconied houses. Most date from after the earthquake, in which this district was hard hit, but two Gothic mansions midway along survived. A short distance up UL. OD SIGURATE is the *Sigurata* (Transfiguration), a little pre-Romanesque church with later aisles

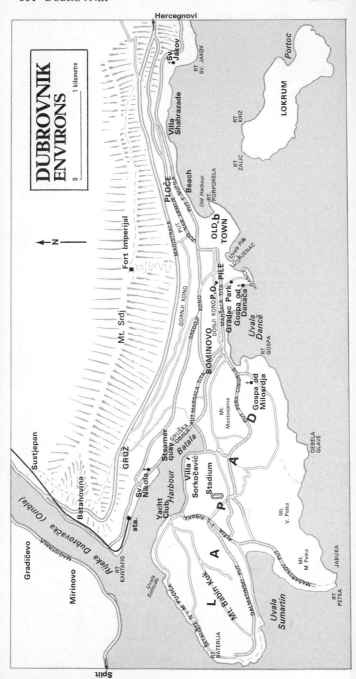

DUBROVNIK ENVIRONS

and a baroque W front. Descend beside the Franciscan monastery to Poljana Paskoje Miličevića.

Enclosing its S side is the former nunnery of SV. KLARA, founded in 1290. Restored after damage in 1667, it was dissolved by the French in 1806 and used as barracks. Under Austria the church too was occupied by the military. Since the last war the whole complex has been rearranged to accomodate the *Radnički dom* (trade union house, with a congress hall) and the Jadran cinema. The Renaissance cloister with double arcades has been excellently restored to house the *Jadran Restaurant*, in the centre of which stands a profusely decorated well-head from the former prefect's residence on Lastovo.

The busy UL. OD PUČA, parallel with Placa to the S, is the principal shopping street. About halfway along (left) the ugly Serbian Orthodox church of *Blagovijest* (Annunciation); 1877) displays Byzantine and Italo-Cretan icons; four doors farther along is the parish office with a *Museum of Icons*. The collection, well displayed and labelled, consists mainly of provincial work (15–18C) of various schools; also portraits of Dubrovnik worthies, including eight works by Vlaho Bukovac, a 19C painter from Cavtat. Turning back, repass the Serbian church and, beyond the small baroque church of *Sv. Josip*, built to replace an earlier one destroyed in the earthquake of 1667, turn left. At the top of ŠIROKA UL. stands the attractive baroque church of *Domino* (1707) with an angled façade. It preserves as its sacristy an aisle of an earlier building destroyed in 1667. The church, reopened for worship in 1968, contains a St. Jerome by Andrea Vaccaro and Annunciation by B. Linterino. There is also a wooden statue of St. Apollonius attrib. To Petar Bogdanović.

In UL. ZA ROKOM nearby, the small 16C church of *Sv. Rok*, turned into a warehouse by the French, was restored around 1900, and has an altarpiece of the Annunciation by Mattei-Matejević.

The steep UL. OD DOMINA mounts by steps to a highly picturesque quarter with many houses of the 13C and 14C. In U. OD RUPA stands **Rupa**, an enormous granary built in 1542–90 (restored 1940), with 15 huge storage chambers hewn from the rock which give a steady temperature of 17.5°C. The cavernous interior with a vaulted ground floor and arcaded upper stories houses the *Lapidary Collection* (adm. 9–13; closed Sat) of the Gradski muzeji, comprising fragments from the many churches that suffered in the earthquake and from the former town loggia. Examples of pre-Romanesque stone carving show a more pronounced Mediterranean influence than is found farther north, and there are Roman pieces from Cavtat. Here also is a small ethnographical collection, with embroideries, pottery, dolls in national costume, and other local handicrafts.

UL. OD KAŠTELA passes through the oldest part of Dubrovnik, settled by the first refugees from Epidaurus. Between the street and the walls is the former Benedictine nunnery of *Sv. Marija*, used as barracks after its dissolution by the French and now turned into flats. Over the entrance is a late-Gothic relief of the Annunciation with the arms of the City and of the Pucić (Pozza), Gučetić (Gozze), and Buchia families. Higher still stands a baroque statue of St. Catherine. The outline of the former churches of Sv. Marija and Sv. Srdj can be seen inside. Another dissolved nunnery, *Sv. Katarina* of the Dominican order, stands in Štrosmajerova ul.; it is now the MUZIČKA ŠKOLA and is frequently used for musical performances in the summer festival. Two fine reliefs by the brothers Petrović (c 1500) occupy the tympana of the two entrance gates. In the garden the picturesque ruins of the

Benedictine monastery of Sv. Šime (Simon) command from their upper terrace an excellent view of the city. A recently excavated crypt in the grounds is thought to have belonged to the church of *Sv. Petar Veliki*, one of the oldest in the city (7–8C). ŠTROSMAJEROVA UL. leads back past the *Palača Gučetić* to the Jesuit church and the Cathedral.

II   The Western Suburbs

You may now take a more detailed look at the square outside the Pile Gate (described above). On the N side stands the baroque *Palača Pucić* (Pozza) now the headquarters of the Atlas travel agency. Off the S side opens *Brasalje* (i.e. Bersaglio) the former shooting range, a large, open space shaded by plane trees, with the Kavana Dubravka on one side. A fountain by I. Rendić (1900) stands in the centre, decorated with figures from the Gundulić play, 'Dubravka'. Steps lead down from the far side of Brsalje to the picturesque little suburb and harbour of PILE, whence several flights of steps mount to the formidable fortress of *Lovrijenac on its gigantic spur of rock. It is probable that this rock was fortified in the 11C, but the fortress, first mentioned in 1301, was radically reconstructed twice in the 15C. It acquired its present form in 1571–76, partly from plans by Giovanni Battista Zanchi of Pesaro. Since 1866 it has been successively an Austrian barracks, a hotel, and an Italian prison. It was restored in 1933 for the International Pen Club Congress of that year and again in 1950, and now serves for performances during the festival. Entrance is gained (9–12, 16–19) through a narrow door with a locally famous inscription on the lintel: NON BENE PRO TOTO LIBERTAS VENDITUR AURO. The triangular interior contains three stories, of which the ground floor consists of a handsome courtyard ringed with Renaissance arcades. The upper terrace just under the battlements affords excellent views of the old city and the coastline to the NW.

In the small bay to the W of Lovrijenac is the modest beach of *Pile* (cabins, shower), beyond which a flight of steps leads up to the charming park of *Gradac* with its Aleppo and marine pines. The terrace at the entrance also acts as an open-air stage during the summer festival. Perched on rocks at the water's edge and reached by a footpath from the park is the little votive church and Franciscan nunnery of *Gospa od Danača* (Our Lady of Danče). The Gothic and Renaissance church (1457), with a triple bell-cot, has a good W door with ornately decorated capitals to the jambs, beside which is an inset stoup with a relief showing God the Father. In the tympanum of the S door is a relief of the Madonna. In the interior (entered through the nunnery) are two good paintings: a polyptych on the high altar by Lovro Dobričević (1465), depicting the Madonna flanked by SS. Blaise and Anthony (left) and SS. Nicholas and Julian (right), with God the Father above; and on the N side a triptych by Nikola Božidarević (1521), showing the Madonna flanked by Pope Gregory (left) and St. Martin (right). A self-portrait of the artist is incorporated in the panel of St. Martin as a reflection in the saint's sword-blade. A high relief of the Madonna and Child removed from the tympanum of the W door serves as an altar. In former times the church was particularly associated with the shoemakers' guild, whose gravestones can be seen in the adjoining cemetery. The open and unspoiled peninsula of *Danče* offers excellent rock bathing and opportunities for skin diving. An asphalt road returns to Put Maršala Tita opposite the *Post Office* and *Hotel Imperial*.

Gruž and Lapad may be reached viâ PUT MARŠALA TITA on foot or by bus. Passing (left) the Renaissance *Palača Crijević* (or Pucić), now the headquarters of the festival orchestra and choir, and the old General Hospital (Opća bolnica), go over the hill to the district of BONINOVO, with a pleasant clifftop walk amid sub-tropical vegetation, commanding views out to sea. On the right are the open-air cinema and Kavana Slavica, beside which a path leads to Donji kono and the large *Palača Skočibuh-Bonda* (1576–88), now a library. The Russians exploded a barrel of gunpowder in the palace in 1806 and it was restored somewhat ineptly in 1938. The chapel in the grounds (1627) was intended to be a copy of the Santa Casa of Loreto. The road divides.

To the left, Put Pera Čingrije passes the bathing beach of Boninovo to branch left though the centre of the Lapad peninsula or right to cross the lower slopes of *Velika Petka* (196m). Just beyond this second fork is the little church of *Gospa od Milosrdja* (Our Lady of Mercy), with votive pictures donated by local seamen, and on the lower slopes of Velika Petka the ancient church of *Sv. Mihajlo* (12C) with its interesting old graveyard. Not far from here is the new hospital of Dubrovnik.

Put Maršala Tita descends past the Hotel Stadion, built round an open-air Olympic swimming pool and now the main bus station, to BATALA, where the road divides.

To the left (Lapadska obala) is the *Palača Majstorović* and the Renaissance *Palača Getaldić* (Ghetaldi), with boathouse and raised chapel, a few yards farther on. Midway along the shore, opposite the steamer quay of Gruž, is the handsome **Palača Sorkočević** (Sorgo; 1521), which now houses the *Historical Institute of the Yugoslav Academy of Arts and Sciences*. The palace, typically Ragusan in style (Renaissance below and Gothic above), has a beautiful *Forecourt with spirally fluted columns overlooking a large fish pool. The great salon, with a fine carved lavabo, opens at either end into two small rooms decorated in period style. An open loggia, adorned with baroque murals, connects with a later wing where the fine library is situated; it overlooks a pretty garden court, enclosed by the family chapel where the altar is adorned by a statue of St. Blaise by Juraj Dalmatinac. The spacious terraced garden is planted with orange trees. A little beyond is the smaller *Palača Pucić* (Pozza) in a similar style, but without the courtyard and garden. At the far end of the shore road is the Orsan yacht club, beyond which a narrow road leads to the small bay of Solitudo; Aleja I.L. Ribara crosses the peninsula of **Lapad** to the bay of Sumratin with its beach and numerous hotels.

The road to the right at Batala continues as Gruška obala to **Gruž**, the busy main harbour and steamer quay for Dubrovnik. On the right, rather hidden by their high walls, are several former summer residences now turned into flats and somewhat dilapidated. The Gothic and Renaissance *Palača Gradić* (Gradis) is conspicuous because its boathouse, with a chapel above, still spans the older part of the road. An entrance beyond the arch gives access to the main reception hall with a stuccoed ceiling, decorated with the emblems of prominent Dubrovnik families, and a small selection of the original furniture. About 30m farther is the *Palača Bunić* (Bonus), with small boathouse, and farther still, behind the pharmacy, the imposing PALAČA GUNDULIĆ (1521), with a most attractive loggia over the boathouse and a partly Gothic chapel (1507). By the small *Tržnica* (market) the road divides round a small park. To the right the Renaissance *Villa Natali*, a summer residence of the Sorkočević family, has a pleasant arcaded façade. Opposite the Hotel Petka are the coastal steamer quays with the international quays beyond, in front of the guild church of *Sv. Nikola* (1527).

Excursions from Dubrovnik

To the **Rijeka Dubrovačka** (R. Ombla), 5km (infrequent local bus; best by hired boat). The Rijeka Dubrovačka is an indented seawater creek or estuary (formed from a sunken valley) immediately to the N of Gruž, into which the *Ombla*, an underground karst river, flows at its E end. The estuary (4km long) was once a favourite resort of Ragusan nobles who built many summer villas here. Now it is very built up, with blocks of flats on one side and industry on the other and a vast marina at the end of the estuary. Little of the vanished splendour remains, although charming details survive. In sequence along the S bank, in *Batahovina* are the Palača Kaboga and Palača Stay; in *Sustjepan* the Romanesque church of Sv. Stjepan (11–12C) with a triple bell-cot and a triptych by Frano Milović (1534); in Čajkovići the Palača Bozdari; in *Komolac* the Palača Gundulić, Sorkočević, Getaldić, and Bizzarro. Komolac also hosts a large new marina. Between Komolac and Rožat on the opposite bank is the 'source' of the river Ombla (really a continuation of the river Trebišnjica in Hercegovina), which issues from the cliff in most impressive fashion. The general view, however, is obstructed by a hydro-electric power station constructed since the Second World War. Along the N bank in *Rožat* are a Franciscan Monastery (1393, restored 1704), with a 16C Renaissance cloister, and the Palača Restić; in *Obuljeno* the Palača Sorgo-Gučetić; in *Mokošica* the Palača Zamanja and Palača Gučetić-Djordjić; in *Gradićevo* the Palača Gradić; and in *Marinovo* the Palača Bucinjolo. Freshwater fishing is possible at the mouth of the Ombla.

To **Mt Srdj** (12km, by asphalt and gravel road or 2½ hours on foot; the cable car is closed). By car take the Put Iza Grada, then the Put jugoslavenske narodne armije above the suburb of Ploče. Where the road (2km) divides, fork left to join (1km) the main Adriatic Highway, to the village of (2km) *Dubac*. Turn left along the road for Trebinje, turn left again at (3km) *Brgat*, and take a winding road to the summit of (2km) *Žarkovica* (313m), with superb views of Dubrovnik, the coast and the offshore islands. Hence a narrow gravel track leads to the top of (2km) **Mt Srdj** (412m), crowned by the *Fort Imperial*, built by the French in 1808.—Alternatively you may walk up to the Gornji kono from the gate behind the church of Sv. Jakov and thence by a steep winding path to Mt Srdj (2½ hours) and Žarkovica (3 hours).

To **Trebinje**, 32km; frequent buses from the Hotel Stadion. Trebinje is the nearest town of Hercegovina to Dubrovnik and is much visited for its Oriental quarter and relics of Ottoman rule. To (8km) *Brgat* see above. At (14km) *Duži* turn right and continue to (10km) **Trebinje**, a small town on the river Trebišnjica in a fertile plain. The old fortified town was built at the instigation of Sanjakbey Osman-pasha Resulbegović in 1706, soon after Trebinje had become the capital of the Sanjak of Hercegovina, and stands with most of its walls and gates intact. The architecture is a mixture of Oriental and Mediteranean elements, as Dubrovnik masons were employed. Within the walls are the two mosques *Careva džamija* and *Osmanpašina džamija*, a clock tower (Sahat-kula) and the Sanjakbey's residence, but their condition and that of the Turkish quarter generally is poor and only one mosque and the bey's house (museum) are open to the public. About 3km E of Trebinje is the Arslanagić Bridge, a fine Turkish structure.

To **Cavtat** (by bus from the Pile Gate), 19km by road or by boat from the Old Harbour in 50 minutes. From the E gate climb past Put JNA to the Adriatic Highway, passing inland of the three small resort villages of *Kupari, Srebreno,* and *Mlini.* In Kupari is the miniature castle, Toreta (1623), of the Djordjević family and in Mlini the Renaissance Palača Stay. Beyond *Plat,* with its hydro-electric power station worked by water from the river Trebišnjica, fork right from the main road.

19km **CAVTAT** is an attractive holiday resort, noted for its luxuriant trees and exotic shrubs. Cavtat was the Greek and later Roman colony of Epidaurus until its sack in the 7C by the Slavs and Avars. Its dispossessed inhabitants founded the city of Ragusa, and the old city (Civitas vetus) was subsequently incorporated into the Republic. The central **Kapetanov dvor** (1555–58), or Captain's residence, is now a museum containing the collections bequeathed by Baltazar Bogišić (1834–1908), lawyer and bibliophile. More than 10,000 engravings include works by Lucas Cranach the Younger, Martin Rota-Kolunić, Andrea Medulić (Schiavone), Stefano della Bella, Chodowiecki, and Natale Bonifazio; the excellent library contains early printed works by Boninus de Boninis (Dobrić Dobričević, 1454–1528) of Lastovo, and Andrija Paltašić (Andrea de Paltasichis, 1450–1500) of Kotor. The house and studio of Vlaho Bukovac (1855–1922), a native of Cavtat, has been turned into a small museum and gallery of his works, and there are further paintings by him in the baroque church of *Sv. Nikola* (1732). The *Franciscan Monastery,* with a Renaissance cloister, and the church of *Sv. Vlaho* both date from 1483; in the latter is a large polyptych of St. Michael (1509–10) by Vicko Lovrin of Kotor, in a richly carved gilt frame, the sole surviving work of this gifted Renaissance painter. On a hill overlooking the harbour and monastery is the town cemetery beautifully planted with cypresses and dominated by the grandiose *Račić Mausoleum* by I. Meštrović (1920–22).

The district of Konavli, immediately SE of Cavtat, is noted for the fertility of its fields and the rich costumes of its inhabitants, often seen in the market at Dubrovnik.

To the **Island of Lokrum,** 15 minutes by boat from the old harbour. **Lokrum,** a small island covered for most of its area by dense pinewoods, is a favourite spot for picnics and swimming excursions. Its shores are rocky and in many places steep, however, and suited only to good swimmers.

A legend persists that Richard Coeur de Lion was wrecked on the island in 1191 while returning from the crusades. In gratitude for his rescue, it is said, he offered to endow a church on the island but was persuaded to divert his funds to the cathedral of Dubrovnik. In later centuries the island was repeatedly claimed by Venice, who even landed troops in 1631, but their withdrawal was effected by cannonade from Dubrovnik. In the 19C Lokrum belonged for a while to the Habsburg Archduke Maximillian and later to the heir-apparent, Rudolph, who often stayed on the island.

Boats usually ply to the small bay of *Portoč* from where a footpath ascends to the ruined *Benedictine Monastery,* founded in 1023. The ruined church incorporates the N wall and apse of the earlier Romanesque basilica, a Gothic W front and part of a semicircular Renaissance chapel, together with pre-Romanesque and Romanesque fragments from two earlier churches. Adjoining the 16C cloister is the residence built by Maximillian, now the *Prirodoslovni muzei* (Natural History Museum) with a botanical garden containing sub-tropical and Mediterranean species. On the highest point of the island is the ruined *Fort Royal*, built by the French in 1806 and later extended by the Austrians. There is is small lake, *Mrtvo jezero*, at the S end of the island.

To the Elaphite Islands (Koločep, Lopud and Šipan). By boat (daily) from Dubrovnik to Koločep (25 minutes), Lopud (50 minutes), and either Sudjuradj (1¼ hours) or Šipanska Luka (2 hours).

The **Elaphite Islands**, a group of seven islands between the S end of Pelješac Peninsula and Dubrovnik, are separated from the mainland by the narrow Koločepski kanal. Settled by both Greeks and Romans, the islands were subsequently incorporated into the medieval Slavonic state of Travunia and passed in the 11C to Ragusa. From 1457 the islands were ruled by a separate knez or rector and remained an important part of the Republic until its fall in 1806. Koločep was an important centre of coral fishing until the 18C with trading posts as far afield as France and the Levant. Lopud was noted for its mercantile enterprise and at the height of its prosperity in the 16C its ships accounted for a quarter of Ragusa's fleet; her galleys participated in Spanish raids on Tunis, Algiers, Portugal, and particularly the armada against England. During the Napoleonic wars, England occupied the islands from 1813–15.

Only three of the islands are inhabited, of which **Koločep** (from the Greek Calaphodia) is the smallest (250 inhab.) and closest to Dubrovnik. The boat arrives at *Donje Čelo* (Koločep), the larger of the two villages on the island, with a pleasant park and a good shingle and sandy beach. The Gothic parish church (13–15C) has Roman and pre-Romanesque sculpted fragments in its walls and is overlooked by a 16C fortress built to repel the Turks. Beside the footpath leading to Gornje Čelo is the village cemetery with the pre-Romanesque church of Sv. Nikola, and farther on the little church of Sv. Antum Opata (St. Anthony Abbot) containing a Gothic Polyptch (1434–35) of the Crucifixion, the only surviving work of the Ragusan painter, Ivan Ugrinović (died c 1461). In the bay of Raca at *Gornje Čelo* is the 12C pre-Romanesque church of Sv. Antum Padovanski (St. Anthony of Padua) with a cupola over the nave and a bell-cot at the W end. The bell (1586) is decorated with reliefs.

The central island of **Lopud**, the most important of the three, has been developed as a comfortable small holiday resort (400 inhab.) with modern amenities. From 1457 to the fall of the Republic it was the seat of the Ragusan knez for the islands. The name derives from the Greek Delaphodia.

Most of the interesting buildings on the island date from the 16–17C, when it is said to have had 30 churches, two monasteries, and innumerable residences and summer villas erected by both local and Dubrovnik nobles.

Two 16C castles (now in ruins) give the place a picturesque air, one on the narrow peninsula to the W of the town (known as the 'Spanish' castle). A short distance away from the latter is the abandoned *Franciscan Monastery* (1483) with a pleasant but overgrown Renaissance cloister and 16C fortifications. The Gothic monastic church of Sv. Marija od Špilice (Mary of the Cave) is now parochial. Among its paintings are an excellent polyptych on the high altar by Pietro di Giovanni (1523) of Venice, a triptych from the workshop of N. Božidarević, parts of a polyptych by Girolamo de Santa Croce, a Crucifixion by one of the Bassano family of Venice, a 17C garlanded Madonna, and a Mannerist work depicting St. Anthony of Padua. The 15C Gothic stalls are the work of local craftsmen, as are the Gothic altar rails. The church plate, kept in the parish office, includes a large Gothic chalice (15C) with an elaborately decorated base and flying angels attached to the sides, a 15C silver processional cross and silver-gilt monstrance of later date.

On the hill in the highest part of the town is the 15C late-Gothic *Kneźev dvor* (Rector's Palace), now abandoned; a number of noble residences in varous states of repair include the *Palača Djordijić*, with a pretty garden, the *Palača Brantić* (16C), and the ruined summer residence of Lopud's most famous citizen, the merchant Miho Pracat. On the W side of town is the abandoned *Dominican Monastery* and church of Sv. Nikola (1482) with belfry, and by the harbour the small 17C baroque church of *Sv. Trojstvo* (Holy Trinity), endowed by the ship owner, Vice Bune, who is buried here.

The 15C Gothic church of GOSPA OD SUNJA (with 17C additions), once the principal church of the island, is situated on the S side of the island about 30 minutes' walk from Lopud. There is a late-Renaissance high altar of painted wood (16C), which a curious erroneous legend links with Henry VIII of England, and contemporary side altars. The high altar is also set off by Gothic altar rails and there is a Renaissance front. The paintings, mostly in poor condition, include a large Madonna attributed to Palma Vecchio, a Madonna attended by Saints attributed to Nataline da Murano, a painting of the Holy Family signed A.B.D., an Annunciation by an unknown Umbrian artist and several pieces of a large polyptych by the Ragusan Matej Junčić (1452), the only work extant by this artist. Of the many pre-Romanesque churches scattered about the island, the small church of *Sv. Ivan* with primitive cupola and lesenes (beside the path to Sunj) is the best preserved and contains a number of examples of pre-Romanesque stone carving.

Šipan (700 inhab.), the largest of the Elaphite Islands, has two main settlements with smaller villages in between. The larger of the two is *Šipanska Luka*, with the handsome Gothic Kneźev dvor (Rector's Palace, 1450) built by local masons, the 15C Gothic Palača Sorkoče-vić and the massive Palača Pracat. The parish church of Sv. Stjepan contains interesting paintings. Beside the gravel track that leads to Sudjuradj is the 16C summer residence of the archbishops of Ragusa, of which one half, with wall paintings, has recently been restored. This part was originally erected (1557) by Abp Becadelli, a friend of Michelangelo. The ruined castle in the nearby hamlet of *Renatova* is said to have been built by René of Anjou, king of Naples. A little farther along the track is the unusual fortified church of Sv. Duh (1577) with towers and battlements.

5km *Sudjuradj* is an attractive small fishing village. It derives its name from the Romanesque church of Sv. Djurdje (George), which has a loggia attached to the W front. Behind the harbour are the Palača Skočibuh (1539), with a machicolated tower (1577) and paintings by G. Vasari, and the Palača Sagrojević, another fortified mansion. The parish church of Sv. Marija is situated in *Pakljena* about 1km E of Sudjuradj. Built in 1323, it was enlarged in the 16C: on the high altar is a triptych of the Assumption in imitation of Titian by the Ragusan Hristofor Nikolin (1552–54), and on other altars a Madonna and Child by an unknown French artist (15C), a painting attributed to the school of J. Cornelis van Oostsanen (16C) and a polyptych by a Dubrovnik painter. Skočibuh, Stjepović, and Sagrojević tomb slabs adorn the church. Adjoining is the ruined Benedictine monastery of *Sv. Mihajlo*, with a 16C tower and fragmentary carvings of the pre-Romanesque to Gothic periods.

23 Ljubljana to Zagreb

ROAD, 135km. Highway N1/E70. 30km *Ivančna Gorica.*—30km *Karteljevo.*—6km *Otočec ob Krki.*—69km **Zagreb**.

RAILWAY, via Zidani Most in c 2½ hours.

This route passes through eastern Slovenia and northern Croatia, lovely regions of wooded hills and fertile valleys peppered with small farms and villages.

From central **Ljubljana** follow KARLOVSKA CESTA to Highway N1/E70. This is the main N–S artery of Yugoslavia, and traffic is often heavy.

30km *Ivačna Gorica*: exit for **Stična**, a village with a ruined Cistercian abbey, founded in 1136, combining Romanesque, Gothic, Renaissance, and baroque elements. The walls surrounding the monastic buildings were built for defence as well as for seclusion, as this area was for many centuries the frontier of Christian Europe.

From Stična an alternative route follows the lovely Krka Valley to (49km) **Novo Mesto**, passing (5km) *Muljava*, where there is a fortified church containing 15C frescoes; (18km) *Žužemberk*, with imposing remains of a 16C castle (walls and cylindrical towers); and (14km, right) *Dolenjske Toplice*, a small spa.

30km *Karteljevo*: exit for (6km) **Novo Mesto** (202m, 14,000 inhab.), capital of the Dolenjska district and one of the lovelier small Slovene towns. The old quarter is situated on a bend in the River Krka. It has a fine town hall and parish church. The *Cathedral*, with a 15C Gothic presbytery, contains a painting of St. Nicholas ascribed (somewhat dubiously) to Tintoretto. The *Dolenjski Muzej* (7 Muzejska; adm. 9–12, 17–19, Sun 9–12, closed Mon) contains interesting archaeological, ethnographical, and historical collections, and a gallery with regional works of the 16–20C.

From Novo Mesto a road (Highway N4) climbs in a series of curves over the Gorjanci Massif, via (29km) *Metlika* and (15km) *Ozalj*, charming little towns with medieval castles, to (17km) **Karlovac** (see below).

6km **Otočec ob Krki** is famous for its 16C Renaissance castle, situated on a romantic islet in the middle of the Krka. The castle was originally built as a defence against the Turkish incursions; it was one of many fortifications that stood along the edge of what was known as the Bela Krajina, the White Borderland. The nearby Carthusian monastery of *Pleterje* was established in 1407 and preserves a Gothic church and remains of ramparts.

Kostanjevica (10km E), a village of 600 inhab., has a baroque parish church preserving a Romanesque doorway of the 13C, and a small gallery (Gorjupova Galerija) with works by Slovene artists. 2km further on is another fortified monastery, the Cistercian *Kostanjevica*, established in 1234. The church, built in a transitional style between Romanesque and Gothic, has a baroque façade; the large cloister is also baroque. Today the monastery hosts two important cultural events, the Dolenjsko Festival and 'Living Form', an international exhibition of wood sculpture.

54km **Samobor** (6000 inhab.), a picturesque town amid wooded hills, is overlooked by two medieval ruins: *Ikric Castle* (12C) and the *Fortress of Susegrad* (13C). The most interesting building in the town itself is the Gothic church of *St. Michael*, later baroqued. In the *Municipal Museum* (adm. 9–13, closed Thurs) are collections of historic documents and clocks. 2km N, near the village of Bregana, is *Mokrice Castle* (16C; visible from the highway), today a hotel.

15km **ZAGREB** (135m, 730,000 inhab.), the capital of Croatia, is approached by a cloverleaf. It grew up on the wooded slopes of the Medvednica (literally, 'Place of Bears') around two rival towns, Kaptol and Gradec. The old city rises on the left bank of the River Sava; the modern quarters extend to the east, west, and south.

Post Office: 13 Jurišićeva.

Information: *Turistički savez Zagreba*, 5 Kaptol, tel. 426311; *Turistički informativni centar Turističkog saveza Zagreba*, 14 N. Zrinjskog, tel. 411883: *Turistički savez Hrvatske*, 8 Amruševa ulica, tel. 432312.

Airport: at Pleso, 17km W; *JAT*, 17 Zrinjevac, tel. 443322.

British Consulate: 12 Ilica, tel. 424888.

United States Consulate: 2 Braće Kavurića, tel. 444800.

History. Kaptol, which derives its name from the Croatian term for 'cathedral chapter', was established as the seat of an archbishop in the 11C—about the time that Gradec was established as a fortress of the Croatian nobility. The rival towns, one loyal to the Crown, the other to the Church, quarrelled continuously (witness such place names as *Krvavi potak*, and *Krvavi most*, respectively 'Torrent of Blood' and 'Bloody Bridge') until the 16C, when the common threat of Turkish conquest compelled the inhabitants to bury their hostilities. The name, Zagreb ('Behind the Cliff'), is documented for the first time in the early 16C; but it was not until 1557 that the city became the capital of Croatia, and even then 19 years were to pass before the parliament and the executive power were moved here from their traditional seat at Varaždin. During the Second World War Zagreb was the capital of the fascist state ruled by the despot Pavelić, whose trained thugs, the Ustase, murdered more than 300,000 of their Serb countrymen, mainly because they were members of the Orthodox Church, as well as almost all of Croatia's Jewish population. Today Zagreb is the leading industrial town of Yugoslavia and an important centre of learning. Its university, established in 1669, is the oldest in Yugoslavia.

The modern TRG REPUBLIKE, which is the main square of the town and just a short (and pleasant) walk from the station, is a convenient starting point for visits to the *Gornji Grad* (or 'Upper Town') or historic city center, as well as to the *Donji Grad* ('Lower Town'), where the major museums are located.

Gradec, which encompasses the W quarters of the Gornji Grad, is most easily reached by the funicular (built in 1890 and electrified in 1934) just off the square, in the Ilica. The upper station, in STROSS-MAYEROVO ŠETALIŠTE, stands practically in the shadow of the **Lotršćak Tower**, one of the last vestiges of the 13C fortifications of Gradec. From the top of the tower a bell used to announce the closing of the town gates at night; today a cannon is fired every day at noon. Beyond the Lotršćak Tower lies a maze of quiet streets lined with elegant houses and palaces built by the Croatian nobility in the 18C. Quite nearby, in KATARINSKI TRG stands the former Jesuit convent of *Sv. Katerine*. The church, dating from the 17C, has a baroque interior. At No. 2 in the square is a small gallery (*Galerijia suvremene umjetnosti*; adm. 10–13 and 17–19) containing works by modern artists, including Picasso, Vasarely, and Léger. Beyond lies JEZUITSKI TRG with a fountain and, on the right, the buildings that formed the *Jesuit Seminary* (17C), now an art gallery.

A central position in the fortified triangle of Gradec is occupied by Radićev trg. The square develops around the little church of **Sv. Marka**, originally of the 13C, but rebuilt in subsequent centuries following damage by fire and earthquake. Most of the present structure, including the Gothic south portal, dates from the 14C or 15C. The baroque bell tower was added in the 17C, and the brightly coloured tile roof inlaid with coats-of-arms (of Croatia, Dalmatia, Slavonia, and Zagreb itself), in the mid-19C. The interior contains

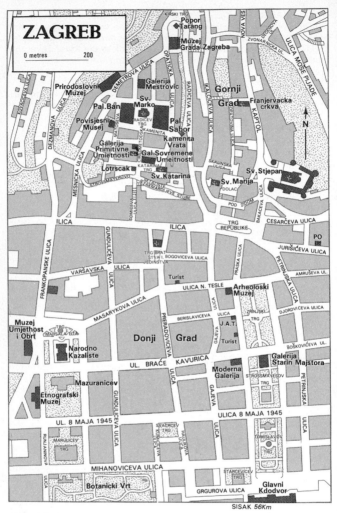

paintings and sculptures by the 19C masters Meštrović and Kljaković.
The stained-glass windows were gifts from local patricians.

Tradition holds that Matija Gubec, leader of a peasant revolt of 1573, was
executed in the square in front of this church. According to the legend the
ill-fated rebel was led into the square by his captors and here formally invested
with a red-hot iron crown; his body was subsequently dismembered and his
followers were summarily massacred.

Behind the church is the *Hall of the Croatian Parliament*, erected in
1908; on the other side of the square is the *Governor's Palace* (1800),
today the seat of the Prime Minister.

From the E end of the square KAMENITA ULICA leads down to the **Kamenita Vrata**, or Stone Gate, with a small shrine. This magnificent gateway was also part of the old fortifications of Gradec.

Midway along, the elegant OPATIČKA ULICA diverges N past a number of monumental palaces. At No. 2 is the 17–18C *Gradjanska Kuća*, the courtyard of which contains a bastion and part of the old town walls. At No. 10 the Institute for Historical Studies occupies the early 19C *Paravić Palace*, with a fine wrought-iron gate. The contemporary *Dvorana Palace* (No. 18), built in 1830 by B. Felbinger for Count Drašković, today houses the Yugoslav Academy of Arts and Sciences. At No. 20 is the former *Convent of the Poor Clares*, built in 1650, from which the street receives its name (Opatička ulica in fact means 'street of the nuns'). Today it is the seat of the **Muzej grada Zagreba** (Municipal Museum of Zagreb, adm. 9–13; Tues and Thurs 9–13 and 16–19; Sun 10–13; closed Mon), illustrating the historical, economic, and social development of the town and its surroundings from antiquity to the present day. At the end of the street rises the 13C **Popov toranj** ('Priest's Tower'), an advanced fortification of Kaptol, later converted into an astronomical observatory.

From here the stately DEMETROVA ULICA, perhaps the most aristocratic street of old Zagreb, leads shortly to the 18C Amadé Palace. The first floor houses the **Prirodoslovni muzej** (Natural History Museum), divided into two sections, the Museums of Mineralogy, Petrography, Geology, and Paleontology (adm. 9–13; Tues and Fri 9–13 and 16–19; closed Mon); and the second floor the National Zoological Museum of Croatia (adm. 9–13, Tues and Fri also 15–18 in winter and 16–19 in summer).

The *Studio of Ivan Meštrović*, at 8 Mletačka ulica, contains a collection of works by this eminent 20C Yugoslav sculptor.

The elegant MATOŠEVA ULICA is lined with 18C baroque palaces, notably the Walter Palace of 1778 (No. 11), and the Oršić-Rauch Palace (c 1750), seat of the *Povijesni muzej Hrvatske* (Historical Museum of Croatia; adm. 9–16, Wed 8–16, Sat 8–13, Sun 10–13), with weapons, flags, old prints, portraits, documents, etc.

Kaptol, which stands a little to the E and below Gradec, is best reached by returning to Trg Republike and then walking up through the *Dolac*, or marketplace. Traces of the 15C fortifications may be glimpsed in the four cylindrical towers around the cathedral, a fifth tower adjoining a nearby school, and a portion of the ramparts to the N. The **Cathedral** (Sv. Stjepan), which dates from the 11C, was destroyed and rebuilt in the 13C, and damaged by earthquake in 1880 and extensively restored at the end of the century. In the Treasury are numerous items of interest, including an ivory diptych of the 10–11C that was smuggled out of the country in 1927, sold to the Cleveland Museum (USA), and recovered the following year. The fortified 18C **Bishop's Palace**, adjoining the cathedral, is perhaps the most impressive of the quarter's numerous ecclesiastical buildings and patrician palaces. It was built in the 18C over the 16C fortificaitons erected against the Turks. The courtyard encloses the Gothic Chapel of St. Stephen (13C), with fragments of coeval frescoes.

The most interesting monuments of the lower town are the neo-baroque **National Theatre**, with its spacious square and fountain (by Meštrović); the *University*; the *Zrinjevac* and *Maksimir Parks* (the latter with a zoo); the *Kazališna kavana*, or Theatre Café, a traditional meeting place of artists and writers; and, of course, the excellent museums for which Zagreb is famous. The latter are grouped in and around two lovely garden areas. From Trg Republike it is a short walk to the wooded TRG ZRINJSKOGA and (right) the **Arheološki muzej** (Archaeological Museum; adm. 8.30–13.30; Mon, Wed and Fri 8.30–13.30 and 16.30–19.30; Sun 10–13; closed Sat), with an excellent prehistoric collection and sections devoted to Egyptian, Greek, and Roman antiquities.

The collections are laid out on the Ground, Second, and Third Floors, the First Floor being used for temporary exhibitions. GROUND FLOOR: Coin collection (100,000 pieces); Greek and Roman sculpture from Southern Italy, Nin, Salona, and Lissa. SECOND FLOOR: Roman antiquities (glass, pottery, jewellery, arms, and inscriptions) and some very fine Greek red- and black-figure vases. Medieval material, including Slav pottery (5–8C), arms and ornaments of the Croatian period (9–11C), an inscription of Croat prince Branimir (888), gold jewellery. THIRD FLOOR: Prehistorical material dating from the Stone Age, Middle Bronze Age, Iron Age, and Celtic period. Egyptian collection (the most important in Yugoslavia), with mummies, papyri, and tomb treasures.

Not far away, on the same side of the park, is the **Moderna galerija** (Modern Gallery; adm. 10–13 and 17–20; closed Mon), with works by 19–20C Croatian artists and a few examples of French Impressionism.

Across the street, in STROSSMAYEROV TRG, stands the *Jugoslavenska akademija znanosti i umjetnosti* (Yugoslav Academy of Science and Art). This was founded by the eminent 19C bishop Strossmayer (statue in the square by Meštrović), a champion of freedom from Austro-Hungarian rule and a theoretician of Serbo-Croatian (or Catholic-Orthodox) unity. The academy, which occupies a neo-Renaissance building, houses the ***Strossmayerova galerija starih majstora** (Strossymayer Gallery of Old Masters; adm. Tues 17–19, Wed–Sun 10–13), with more than 200 works, mainly by Italian artists from the Trecento to the late Settecento.

The permanent collection is displayed on the second floor. Among the more important works are R.1: Donatello, Madonna and Child; Cosimo Rosselli, Madonna; Neri di Bicci, Madonna; Jacopo del Sellaio, Adoration. R.2: Matteo da Milano, Breviary of Alfonso d'Este; Luca della Robbia, Madonna; Ridolfo Ghirlandaio, Madonna and Child with St. John. R.3: Vincenzo Catena, Madonna and Saints; Giorgione, Mars and Venus; Gentile Bellini, St. Stephen and St. Benedict; Vittore Carpaccio, St. Sebastian; Filippo Mazzola, Ecce Homo. R.4: Paolo Veronese, Allegory, Christ and the Woman of Zebedeus; Palma the Younger, Deposition. R.5: El Greco, St. Mary Magdalen. R.6: Fedrighetto (Federico Benković), Sacrifice of Abraham; Giovanni Battista Piazzetta, St. Anthony. R.7: Pieter Brueghel the Elder, Country Wedding; Master of the Virgo inter Virgines, Holy Trinity; Albrecht Dürer, St. Ann; 16C German School, St. James and St. Catherine. R.8: Antoine-Jean Gros, Mme de Recamier; Jean Auguste-Dominique Ingres, Portrait of a Young Woman; Jacques Louis David, Portrait of Public Magistrate; R.9: Jan Lievens, Rembrandt's Father; Eugène Delacroix, Moroccan Market. R.10: Bartholomeus Van der Helst, Portrait of a Gentleman; Antonie Van Dyck, St. Andrew; David Teniers the Younger, The Inn.

The building also houses the Academy Archives, containing the world's largest collection of Glagolitic and Cyrillic manuscripts. In the atrium is the Baska Stone, the oldest known Glagolitic inscription (11C).

TOMISLAV TRG, adjoining Strossmayerov trg on the S, receives its name from the 10C Croatian king Tomislav, whose monument stands in the middle. Temporary exhibitions are held in the *Umjetnički paviljon*.

From here a 15-minute walk past the *Botanical Gardens* and the *Marulićev trg* brings you to the **Etnografski muzej** (Ethnographical Museum; adm. Tues, Wed, and Thurs 9–15; Fri, Sat, and Sun 9–13; closed Mon), which has excellent folklore and costume sections (the costumes of nearly every region of Yugoslavia are represented), a fine collection of musical instruments, and several fascinating reconstructions of Croatian peasant houses. Further E on the park are the *****Muzej za umjetnost i obrt** (Museum of Arts and Crafts; adm. 10–13; Tues–Sun 10–19, Mon 13–19), with an excellent collection of religious art, furniture, musical instruments, silver, porcelain, and glass; and the *Opera House*. From here the return may be made to the Trg Republike via the Frankopanska Ulica and the Ilica.

EXCURSIONS. The Croatian Zagorje region, of which Zagreb is a part, is a place of extraordinary natural beauty and historical importance. Whereas Dalmatia was annexed by Venice during the late Middle Ages and other areas of Croatia were occupied by the Turks after the battle of Kosovo, the Zagorje was the last bastion of the Croatian kings, and this aspect of its history should be borne in mind when visiting the region.

A pleasant excursion may be made by car (the road is clearly signposted) or by city bus to **Gračani** and **Šestine**, two villages of narrow streets and old houses picturesquely set in the *Zagrebačka Gora*, the wooded hill country that extends to the N of Zagreb. On Sunday the older villagers dress in traditional costumes; those of the women are particularly colourful.

Also interesting is **Kumrovec**, a small hamlet some 60km NW of Zagreb, the birthplace of Marshal Tito, whose home has been turned into a museum.

Krapina, 60km N on the Zagreb–Celje rail line, gives its name to *Homo Krapiniensis*, a relative of Neanderthal Man, whose fossil remains were discovered in the nearby cave of Hušnjakov Breg. The medieval castle is now a museum. The Franciscan convent and church of St. Catherine date from the 17C. In September the village hosts a lively and entertaining Festival of Dialect Song (Kajkavske Popevke).

Belec (Highway 12 N to 59km *Novi Marof*, then left), in the lovely Ivanščice region, has a ruined *Castle* of the 14C or earlier and a parish church (Sv. Jurje u Jańsvini) bearing traces of Romanesque origins. Especially interesting, if not exactly beautiful, is the church of *Marija Snježna* (Our Lady of the Snows): built in the late 17C, it has a plain exterior and a rich baroque interior (1739–41) whose gold and silver ornaments, flamboyant carvings, and illusionistic frescoes are without rival in Croatia.

There are several hot springs in the Zagreb area. The more famous are **Varaždinska Toplice**, known to the Romans as *Aquae Iasae* (58°C); **Krapinske Toplice**, the Roman *Aquae Vivae* (40°C); **Stubičke Toplice** (65°C, radioactive); and **Tuheljske Toplice** (33°C, slightly radioactive).

Rijeka, 172km away on the Adriatic coast, is conveniently reached by Highway 12. This road, which will soon be supplemented by a motorway (the first section, from Zagreb to Karlovac, is already open) crosses the most scenic part of Croatia, which reaches the height of its beauty in the great forest of Gorski Kotar (cf. below).

26km *Jastrebarsko* (250m, 3000 inhab.) was made a free city by King Bela IV in 1257, and it remained a fortress of the Croatian kings until the 16C. Its name, in fact, derives from *Jastreb*, 'falcon', the symbol of the royal house of Croatia (crest on the Castle).

24km **Karlovac** (112m, 48,000 inhab.) was established by Archduke Charles of Styria in 1579 to defend Slovenia and other Croatian lands from the Turks. It stands in a strategic position at the confluence of the Kupa and the Korana, not far from where the latter is joined by the Mrežnica. Little remains of the Castle, although its general lines (it was built in the form of a six-pointed star) can still be glimpsed in the street plan of the present town. With the withdrawl of the Turks in the 18C Karlovac became an important commercial centre, a point of transit between the ports of Bakar and Rijeka and their mountainous hinterland. Today it is an important industrial town. In the baroque *Frankopan Palace* (17–18C) there is a small museum that gives a good idea of the development of the town and its environs. The Roman Catholic church of the *Holy Trinity* (17C) and the Orthodox church of *St. Nicholas* (18C) provide further examples of the local baroque taste.

Beyond Karlovac the road enters the wooded mountains of the **Gorski Kotar**, the western watershed of the Danube. Much of the region is included in the *Risnjak National Park*. A few km further is *Severin na Kupi*, with a former Zrinjski and Frankopan castle, made over into a manor house in the 19C. *Skrad* (700m) is a health spa. *Delnice* is a popular resort.

128km **Rijeka**, see Rte 7.

24 Zagreb to Belgrade

A. By Motorway

ROAD, 380km. Highway N1/E70.—76km *Kutina*.—42km *Okučani junction*.—14km *Nova Gradiška*.—54km *Slavonski Brod*.—54km *Županja*.—69km *Sremska Mitrovica*.—71km **Belgrade**.

RAILWAY, in c 5½ hours.

This route traverses the Sava Valley, a vast monotonous lowland. This broad basin is part of Slavonia, an important farming district and the northernmost region of Yugoslavia to be conquered by the Turks, traces of whose presence may still be glimpsed. The highway, known as the *Bratstvo i jedinstvo* (Fraternity and Unity) Motorway, runs through four of the six Yugoslav republics, and is the country's principal N–S artery. Traffic is intense and largely made up of long-distance lorries, so the greatest caution is necessary, especially when overtaking.

Zagreb, see Rte 23. From the city centre follow DRŽIĆEVA ULICA SE to BEOGRADSKA ULICA and Highway N1/E70. The road runs through lonely forests, passing an occasional farm.

58km exit for (22km) **Sisak** (99m, 38,000 inhab), near the confluence of the Sava and the Kupa. The town, which stands on the site of the Roman *Septimia Siscia*, became the seat of a bishop in the 2C and a fief of the powerful Croat prince, Ljudevit Posavski, in the Middle Ages. It was fortified against the Turkish invasions in the mid 16C; today it is an important industrial centre. The *Castle* is now an historical museum; in the environs may be seen some fine wooden houses with imaginatively carved details.

18km **Kutina** (9000 inhab.), on the SE slopes of the Moslavačka Gora, has a fancy baroque church dedicated to *Marija Snježna* (Our Lady of the Snows, 1767–69).

42km **Okučani junction**, Highway N1/E70 is crossed by Highway N16/E661. The latter leads N to the spas of *Lipik* and *Daruvar*, passing through the attractive little town of **Pakrac**, nestled on the River Pakra at the foot of the wooden Psunj. Little remains of its medieval *Castle*, destroyed in 1922; but the Serbian Orthodox *Cathedral* of the Holy Trinity, the *Bishop's Palace*, and the Roman Catholic church of the *Assumption*, all built in the 18C, are worthy of attention; and the town centre has many elegant 18C and 19C houses. To the S Highway N16/E661 leads via *Bosanska Gradiška* to **Sarajevo**, Rte 27.

14km **Nova Gradiška** (4km N; 132m 10,000 inhab.), situated on the southern slopes of the Psunj massif, is a starting point for excursions to the Požega basin, the *Vallis Aurea* of the Romans.

At the centre of this fertile plain, surrounded by the hills of Psunj, Papuk, Krndija, and Požeška Gora, lies the pretty market town of **Slavonska Požega**, documented since 13C. It was held by the Turks from 1536 until 1691, during which period the Gothic church of *Sv. Duh* (Holy Spirit) was made into a mosque. Almost all of the other major buildings—including the Jesuit and Franciscan convents, the Županija Palace, and the parish church—were built after 1691, when the baroque was enjoying wide favour. The small Museum is instructive. The environs offer fine walks, bathing at Velika, hunting and fishing. Požega is famous for its wine (Kutijevo) and its cognac (David and Trenk).

54km **Slavonski Brod** (95m, 50,000 inhab.), on the site of the Roman *Marsonia*, was also a Turkish town from 1536 to 1691. It has remains of an 18C fortress, a Franciscan convent and church of 1725, and a baroque parish church (1754). There is a museum in the *Magistrate's Palace*; and swimming, hunting, and fishing in the environs.

32km junction with Highway N17/E73 from Osijek (Rte 24B).

20km N on this road is **Djakovo**, the former see of Bishop Strossmayer. Built on the site of a Roman town, it was a fief of the Bosnian bishops until 1526, when it fell to the Turks. It was retaken in 1687 (only 13 houses were inhabited) and later recovered its status as a bishopric. The immense *Cathedral*, built in 1882 to plans by the eminent neo-Gothic architect Baron Schmidt, has a picture in the apse of Bishop Strossmayer in the company of Sts. Peter and Paul.

The road crosses the rich but dull plain of Slavonia.

22km *Županja* (8000 inhab.) has an interesting wooden fortress

69km **Sremska Mitrovica** (82m, 78,000 inhab.), a big industrial town, stands on the site of the Roman *Sirmium*, capital of the province of Lower Pannonia and birthplace of the emperors Aurelianus, Probus, Gratianus, and Constantius II. Marcus Aurelius lived here, as did Diocletian; and Theodosius was crowned here. The town was destroyed by the Avars in 582. Excavations have brought to light a great deal of Roman material, much of which is in the archaeological museum in Zagreb. Fragmentary *Baths* and an early *Byzantine basilica* can be seen in the town center; other archaeological finds are preserved in the Museum. The *Muzej Crkvene Umetnosti* (Museum of Religious Art), on the Sava, occupies an old Orthodox church with a handsome carved, gilt iconostasis.

71km **BELGRADE**, see Rte 25.

B. Via Novi Sad

ROAD, 462km. Highways N1–3, N3, N7, and N22–1.—80km *Bjelovar*.—64km *Virovitica*.—77km *Našice*.—51km *Osijek*.—36km *Vukovar*.—43km *Bačka Palanka*.—37km *Novi Sad*.—74km **Belgrade**.

RAILWAY, bypassing Bjelovar and Novi Sad, in c 7½ hours. Bjelovar may be reached by changing at *Križevci*; Novi Sad by changing at *Indjija*.

This route traverses a region that is only beginning to be discovered by tourists: the autonomous **Vojvodina** ('Dukedom'). It is a mixed land ethnically, composed of Serbs, Croats, Slovaks, Ruthenes, Rumanians, and large numbers of Hungarians; before 1918 a considerable part of the region belonged to Hungary. The countryside is flat, fertile, and dominated by a sense of vastness, which finds an echo in the spacious, sometimes sprawling character of the towns and villages.

Here, as in the preceding route, traces of the Turkish occupation can be seen.

Zagreb, see Rte 23. Leave the city by VLAŠKA ULICA and MAKSI-MIRSKA CESTA, which lead into Highway N1–3.

59km *Žabno*, a road diverges left to **Križevci** (148m, 7500 inhab.), in the Kalnik foothills, a free city governed by representative assemblies from the 13C onward and one of the few Slavonian strongholds that managed to hold out against the Turks. Its more noteworthy monuments include remains of the old walls; the Gothic church of *Sv. Kriz* (Holy Cross) with 18C baroque additions, a baroque parish church, a Pauline convent, and the Greek-Catholic *Cathedral* and *Bishop's Palace* (formerly a Franciscan church and convent). There is also a small museum. Walks, mountain climbing, and hunting in the environs.

21km **Bjelovar** (135m, 21,000 inhab.), mentioned in the 15C documents as a market town, developed rapidly in the 17C when it became an important military base and administrative centre.

27km **Djurdjevac**, turn right on Highway N3, which runs along the foot of the Bilo Gora.

37km **Virovitica** (122m, 14,000 inhab.) became a free city in 1242, but its development was interrupted, from 1522 to 1684, by Turkish occupation. In the early 19C the Pejačević family built a classical palace in place of the medieval fortress, and today this is still the town's main attraction. There are also an 18C Franciscan covent and parish church.

27km **Našice** (157m, 20,000 inhab.) was established in the 13C as a fief of the Knights Templar. From 1532 to 1686 it was under Turkish domination. The chief monuments are the Gothic Franciscan church (with baroque additions) and covent; and two neo-classical palaces with English gardens, dating from the early 19C.

51km **Osijek** (94m, 95,000 inhab.), the Roman *Mursa*, lies on the right bank of the Drava. It was conquered by the Turks in 1525 and held until 1687. The birthplace of Croat bishop and patriot J. J. Strossmayer (1815–1905), today it is the principal centre of Slavonia. The more important monuments date from the period subsequent to the Turkish occupation. The **Citadel**, called the *Tvrdjava*, stands in a park at the point where the upper and lower towns merge. Within are a guardhouse and an 18C clock tower; a richly sculptured column commemorating the plague of 1729; and, in the former courthouse, the *Muzej Slavonije* (Museum of Slavonia, adm. 10–12), with collections of archaeological material, furniture, ceramics, clocks, and glass. All around the fortress are lavish baroque churches and palaces, the most interesting of which are the military headquarters and barracks, the Jesuit and Franciscan covents, and the churches of *Sv. Kriz* and *Sv. Michovil* (the latter with two bell towers). The *Galerija Likovnih Umetnosti u Osijeku*, at 9 Bulevar Jugoslavenske Narodne Armije (adm. 9–12 and 17–20; Sun 10–13; closed Mon), has a small collection of paintings from the 18C to the 20C, and copies of Renaissance masterpieces. In the upper town the Capuchin covent (18C), the parish church, the neo-classical *Županija Palace*, and the Pejačević family tomb are worthy of notice. There are also several nice parks, a bathing beach on the Drava, and fishing and hunting in the environs.

EXCURSIONS. To (25km) **Valpovo**, with water sports, hunting and fishing, and a medieval castle.

To (22km more) **Donji Miholjac**, on the Hungarian frontier, where there is another castle in a large garden.

To (37km) *Djakovo*, a medieval town which in June hosts a famous Folklore Festival.

32m **Borovo**, the road joins the Danube and is crossed by Highway N16/E661, which leads S to (15km) **Vinkovci** (90m, 35,000 inhab.), on the site of the Roman colony of Aurelia Cibalae. Some remains of baths and fortifications can be seen in the town, and objects found in the Roman necropolis are displayed in the Museum. There is also a fine baroque square with two 18C churches.

4km **Vukovar** (108m, 28,000 inhab.), was the centre of the Vukovska Županija, the fief of the Vuka. Like so many other Slavonian towns, it suffered from the Turkish occupation of 1526–1687. Its more noteworthy buildings include an 18C Franciscan covent and parish church, an Orthodox church with baroque interior, the baroque palace of the Etz family, and the monumental *Županija Palace* of 1777. There is also a small Museum.

37km **Ilok** (133m, 5000 inhab.) has remains of medieval fortifications, a 15C Gothic church with the monumental tombs of Nikola and Lovre Iločki, and a baroque Franciscan covent incorporated in the complex of the town walls. Across the Danube lies Bačka Palanka (21,000 inhab.), originally a quarter of Ilok, autonomous since the early 17C.

Clearly visible to the S is the *Fruška Gora*, a long, low range of hills, covered with thick forest, which runs E–W for about 70km. The forest harbours many deer, wild boar and wild cat, and the lower, fertile slopes produce excellent wines. The hills also constitute a natural fortress commanding the Sava and Danube plains—a fact which the Serbian Orthodox Church was early to recognise. There are 20 or more monasteries in the area, the main concentration being on the S slopes (see below).

43km **NOVI SAD** (80m, 240,000 inhab.), a spacious modern city on a bend of the Danube, has played an important role in Serbian history since the 18C. Today it is the capital of the autonomous province of Vojvodina, the second largest city of Serbia, and a prosperous industrial, commercial, and university town.

Post Office: Poštanska ulica.

Information: *Turist Biro*, 27 Dunavska ulica, tel. 51888.

History. Formerly known as *Petrovaradinski sanac* (Petrovaradin's Trench), the city was renamed *Novi Sad*, 'New Plan', by a royal decree of 1748 which also granted it the status of free city. It quickly became a centre of culture (it was nicknamed the 'Serbian Athens' in the 19C). Its theatre is the oldest in Serbia, and its castle (the Petrovaradin, described below) was the site of a famous battle of 1716 in which Prince Eugène of Savoy defeated a Turkish army.

There is not much in the way of monuments at Novi Sad, except for the *Orthodox Cathedral* and *Bishop's Palace*, the latter containing some interesting paintings by 18 and 19C artists. The museums, in contrast, are excellent.

The *****Zbirka strane umetnosti** (Museum of Foreign Art; adm. 8–12 and 16–19) is located in a baroque house at 29 Dunavska ulica. GROUND FLOOR: paintings by Giovanni Battista Langetti (Death of Cato), Antonio Tempesta (Stigmatisation of St. Francis), Jacob Jordaens, Federico Barocci (Holy Family with St. John), Johan Georg de Hamilton, Pier Francesco Mola (Landscape), Rembrandt (*Portrait of the Artist's Father), Josse Suttermans, Alessandro Magnasco (Soldiers Resting, Soldiers among Ruins, Dead Christ), Paolo Veronese

(Christ at Cafarnao; Adoration of the Magi), Pieter Paul Rubens
(*Seneca), Frans Franken, Jan Brueghel (Lunch in the Woods), Paris
Bordone (Madonna and Child), Cornelis de Vos, Monsù Bernardo,
H.P. Oosterhuis, C. Molenaer (Winter Landscape), Pordenone (Vir-
gin of Mercy), Cesare Gennari (Holy Family with St. John), and H.
Swanevelt. FIRST FLOOR: antique furniture: rococo, Louis XV, Louis
XVI, Empire Style, and Chippendale.

The *Galerija matice srpske (literally the Gallery of the Serbian
Queen Bee; adm. 9–13, Tues and Thurs 8–19, closed Mon), the oldest
Serbian cultural institution, founded at Pest in 1828 and moved to
Novi Sad in 1864, is located in a modern building at 1 Trg
Proleterskih Brigada; it is devoted to religious art and to Serbian and
Vojvodina painting of the 18–20C. FIRST FLOOR: 18C paintings and
prints. *Icons from the Orthodox monasteries of the Fruška Gora
region (17–18C); baroque icons and fragments of iconostases: works
by Cristofor Zefarović, Teodor Kračun and Jakob Orfelin (18C); 18C
religious prints. SECOND FLOOR: 19C paintings and prints, including
portraits by Konstantin Danil, Katarina Ivanović, Novak Radonić, and
Pavle Simić; works from the Biedermeier (Nikola Aleksić, Pauce
Djurković) and Impressionist (Djorde Krstić) periods; and contemporary paintings by Stevan Aleksić, Paja Jovanović, and Uroš Predić.

The Spomen Zbirka Pavla Beljaškog (adm. 9–17; closed Mon and
Tues), located next to the Galerija matice srpska at 10 Trg
Proleterskih Brigada, is devoted to painting, archaeology (pre-
Roman, Roman, and Early Christian finds), and handicrafts.

On the knoll some 40m high on the right bank of the Danube
stands the huge *Castle of Petrovaradin (today part of a separate
township of the same name) with a network of fortifications which
rival the Kalemegdan in Belgrade and the Tvrdjava at Niš for size.
The site was fortified by the Romans and then by the Byzantines; in
1237 the Hungarians gave the area to the Cistercians, who erected a
fortified monastery. This was taken by Suleiman the Great in 1526
and recaptured by Eugene of Savoy in 1692. From that year the
Austrians began the construction of the present fortress, most of
which dates from the 18C. The Austrians considered it the largest
and most formidable of the empire, calling it the Gibraltar of the
Danube. 16km of tunnels were dug on four levels beneath the
fortress; the various buildings housed offices, workshops, and a
hospital. The dungeons have held some distinguished prisoners,
among them the Serbian leader Karadjordje and Marshal Tito. In a
former office building are the Muzej grada Novog Sada and the
Vojvodjanski muzej (Museum of the City of Novi Sad and Museum of
the Vojvodina; adm. 8–6.30; closed Mon) with sections dealing with
archaeology, political history (mainly the Partisan Revolution) and
natural history (ornothology). The barracks have been converted into
a hotel with a restaurant overlooking the Danube, an ideal spot to
dine on a summer's evening.

EXCURSIONS. To (11km SE) Sremski Karlovci (80m, 7000 inhab.), on the banks of
the Danube, seat of Serbian metropolitans in the 18th and 19C and one of the
prettiest small towns in Serbia. Its main square, named after the 19C romantic
poet, Branko Radičević, is adorned by a marble fountain of 1770. Around it are
several handsome buildings: the neo-classical Town Hall (1806–11), the baroque Cathedral (1752–62, with a 19C façade), and several 18C houses. The
cathedral is decorated with frescoes and has a carved iconostasis with icons by
18C Serbian artists. The neo-Byzantine Patriarchate (16 Ulica Maršala Tita)
houses a Museum of archaeology, history, and ethnography; and a gallery with
works by local painters of the 18–20C. There is another small museum devoted
to Radičević just off the square.

Petrovaradin, the immense Austrian fortress on the Danube

Leave Petrovaradin along the right bank of the Danube. Beyond *Sremska Kamenicá* the road winds up the green slopes of the Fruška Gora, passing beneath the summit of *Iriški Venac*, a hill surmounted by a monument to the Partisans (1951).

18km **Novo Hopovo Monastery**, reached by a turning on the left, was founded in the mid 16C, rebuilt in the 18C, and radically restored after the last war. The 16C church, a work of the Morava school, has a beautifully carved exterior and a graceful 12-sided dome encircled by colonettes. In the narthex six levels of frescoes by Montenegrin artists (1654) illustrate the celestial hierarchies and the life of Christ; the latter is also the subject of the refined cycle in the naos, painted in 1608 by artists from Mount Athos.—Return to Iriški Venac and turn right.

9km **Remeta Monastery**, in a secluded valley, was established in the 13C as a Catholic convent. The church has paintings of 1568 and a tall baroque bell tower; the conventual buildings have been converted into a reform school.

From here it is a short drive on the Irig road (signposted) to (3km) **Krušedol Convent**, the largest and most important of the Fruška Gora, founded in the late 15C by Djuradj Branković, who ruled Serbia for about ten years and later became an archbishop. The church is a work of the Morava school. The interior is adorned with 16C frescoes (heavily restored in the 18C) and contains the tombs of several princes and Serbian patriarchs, notably King Milan Obrenović (died 1901). The spacious monastic quarters house a small museum of religious art and mementos of the Obrenović family.

To see more of the Fruška Gora, continue along the same road.

8km **Irig** is a small, pretty village enjoying a splendid view over the S slopes of the Fruška Gora and the surrounding plains.

11km **Ruma** (111m, 21,000 inhab.), a large agricultural town on the main road from Novi Sad, was the site of one of the earlier prehistoric settlements in Serbia.

Proceed W to (23km) **Ležimir**, another small village high up in the hills, with several monasteries, unfortunately much damaged during the Second World War. The most interesting of these are *Šišatovac* (16C), *Kuveždin* (18C), *Petkovica* (16C, with frescoes of 1588), and *Divša* (15C, with a baroque church of 1753).

Beyond Ležimir the road bears N, descending in curves to the Danube, where it joins the road from Ilok. Petrovaradin lies 41km to the right.

74km **BELGRADE**, see Rte 25.

III SERBIA

Serbia, which includes the autonomous provinces of Vojvodina and Kosovo, covers an area of 88,361km² (35 per cent of Yugoslavia's territory) in the eastern part of the country. Apart from the Pannonian Plain in the north, it is mostly hilly or mountainous, with many river valleys. The highest mountains are Kopaonik, Tara, Zlatibor, Zlatar, Šara, and Prokletije. Natural lakes are few in number and small, but in the last 30 years the Danube, Drina, Lim, Vlasina, and other rivers have been dammed to create artificial reservoirs for power generation, and these are now recreation and sports centres. The rivers ultimately flow into three seas: the Adriatic, Black and Aegean. The Danube (with its tributaries, the Sava, Tisa, Morava, Timok, and others) drains the largest area—about 94 per cent of the republic.

Serbia has a population of 9,314,000: 5,694,000 living in Serbia proper, 2,035,000 in the Autonomous Province of Vojvodina, and 1,584,000 in the Autonomous Province of Kosovo. 67 per cent are Serbs, 14 per cent ethnic Albanians, 4 per cent ethnic Hungarians, 2 per cent Croats, 2 per cent Muslims, 2 per cent Montenegrins, 5 per cent self-declared 'Yugoslavs', and 4 per cent persons of other nationalities, including Slovaks, Rumanians, Ruthenians, Bulgarians, Turks, and others.

Belgrade, the capital of Serbia and of Yugoslavia, has a population of 1,570,000. Situated at the confluence of the Sava and Danube rivers, in the course of its long history it has been captured 60 times and destroyed 38 times. Other large towns are Novi Sad (capital of Vojvodina), Priština (capital of Kosovo), Niš, Subotica, Kragujevac, Zrenjanin, Leškovac, Peć, Prizren, Smederevo, Sombor, Kruševac, Titovo Užice, Valjevo, and Šabac. The rural population has declined from 72 per cent in 1954 to 25 per cent (in Kosovo from 80 per cent to 25 per cent and in Vojvodina from 68 per cent to 29 per cent). Nevertheless Serbia is Yugoslavia's biggest food producer. Owner-farmers work 82 per cent of the land. Co-operative farms, particularly the agro-industrial complexes, while working 18 per cent of the land, turn out 44 per cent of the produce appearing on the market.

Where economic development has proceeded at a less satisfactory pace, such as in the Autonomous Province of Kosovo, special funds have been created and work organisations from more developed regions have been called in to accelerate development through co-operative efforts and joint ventures. Priority has been given to the production of raw materials, food and energy, and to the development of transportation.

The diversity of Serbia's natural beauty, its many places of historical and cultural interest, its mineral springs, and its hunting and fishing grounds draw thousands of visitors every year. The main attractions are the archaeological sites at Vinča, Gamzigrad, Lepenski Vir and Stirmium, and the magnificently frescoed medieval monasteries at Studenica, Žiča, Mileševa, Sopoćani, Dečani, Peć, Manasija, and Ravanica. Modern winter sports centres have been built on Mts Kopaonik and Šara; country holidays are also becoming popular.

25 Belgrade and its Environs

BELGRADE (Serbo-Croatian, **Beograd**; 76m, 1,570,000 inhab.), the capital of Serbia and of Yugoslavia, is situated at the confluence of the

Sava and the Danube, commanding the plains and the entrances to the principal passes through the hills. It is a large, modern city of tall buildings and tree-shaded boulevards, offering little in the way of monuments but containing several fine museums.

Post Office: 2 Takovska ulica; *International telephone centre*: 17 Zmaj Jovina ulica.

Information: *Turist Biro*, under the Terazije, tel. 635343; *Central Tourist Office*, 8/IV Moše Pijade ulica, tel. 339780.

British Embassy: 46 General Ždanova, tel. 645055.

United States Embassy: 50 Kneza Miloša, tel. 645622.

Airport: at Surčin, 12km W, tel. 601555; *JAT*, 17 Bulevar Revolucije, tel. 331042 (International flights), 332179 (domestic flights).

History. The site on which the city stands was inhabited as early as the Stone Age. It was colonised by the Greeks, the Illyrians, the Celts, and the Romans, the latter granting it, in the early 2C, the rights and privileges of a colony. The Roman town was destroyed by the Huns (5C) and rebuilt by Justinian, only to be devastated again by the Avars (7C). In the 10C it reappeared under the dominion of Byzantium but bearing the Slavonic name *Beli Grad* (White Fortress). In 1124 it was taken by the Hungarians, in 1284 by the Serbs, in 1319 by the Hungarians again, in 1403 by the Serbs, and in 1427 again by the Hungarians.

The decline of Serbia was accompanied by the rise of the Ottoman Empire, which launched a first, unsuccessful assault on the city in 1439–40 and another in 1456 (the defending army in this instance was commaned by the Hungarian general Janos Hunyadi and the Franciscan saint John Capistran). A new attempt in 1521, led by Suleiman the Great in person, met with success. In 1688 Belgrade was taken by the Austrians, but it was lost two years later; in 1717 it was retaken by Eugène of Savoy; in 1739 the Turks returned. Serbian patriots managed to take the city on two occasions: in 1806 under Miloš Karadjordje and in 1815 under Miloš Obrenović. In 1830 Serbia was made an autonomous province of the Ottoman Empire, but a Turkish garrison remained in Belgrade (Serbia's capital since 1841)—an unacceptable situation which led to a grave incident involving the death of a young Serbian boy, in 1882. Finally, on 18 April 1867, after some fighting and much diplomacy, the Turkish pasha Ali Riza surrendered the city to the Serbian prince Mihailo Obrenović.

During the First World War Belgrade changed hands twice, with heavy bombing and street fighting each time. In the Second World War it was bombed both by the Germans and the Allies and occupied by the Germans from 1941 to 1944.

As late as 1918 Belgrade was a quiet and fairly small place; today there are not many old buildings, and most of the new ones are unimpressive.

The busy TRG REPUBLIKE, adorned with an equestrian monument of *Prince Miloš Obrenović* by the Florentine sculptor Enrico Pazzi (1882), is the centre of the city and a good place from which to begin a visit. On the E side stands the *National Theatre* (1868, restored after the First World War and again in 1988), on the site of the Istanbul Gate which once gave access to the old town. To the W lies the Ulica Kneza Mihaila, today a pedestrian way closed to motor traffic and lined with shops and cafés. It ends at the Kalemegdan park, described below.

The N side of the square is occupied by the ****Narodni muzej** (entrance 1 Ulica Vase Čarapića; adm. 10–17, Thurs 10–19, Sat 10–17, Sun 10–14; closed Mon). The *National Museum*, established in 1844, is devoted to art and archaeology. The collections were seriously damaged in the First World War, but have since been restored and considerably enlarged.

The GROUND FLOOR is occupied by the archaeological collections. **Prehistoric Section.** Cases 1–4: Neolithic pottery, weapons, tools, utensils, and votive statuary, mostly representative of the Starčevo Culture (before 2800 BC) and the Vinča culture (1800–2000 BC). Cases 5–7: Bronze Age material from the Bubanj-Hum Culture (from the Niš area), decorated vases from Vučedol, votive cart from Dupljaja (1500–1000 BC); Iron Age material from the Halstatt and La Tène Cultures (silver and gold jewellery, necklaces and bracelets).

Classical Section. *Gold masks, jewels, and bronze vases (6–5C BC) from the Greek necropoleis at Radovište and Trebenište, near Ohrid (Macedonia); amber objects and gold jewellery from Novi Pazar; Mycenaean and Corinthian vases; Greek weapons and utensils; terracottas from Tanagra and Sicily; marble copies of Phidias's Athena Parthénos and bas-relief with Dionysiac procession, from Bitola. Hellenistic utensils and jewellery (4–2C BC) from Stobi (Macedonia) and Budva (Montenegro). Roman finds, including a fine 2C AD processional helmet, votive effigies of Danubian horseman and of the god Mythras, silver vases from Rudnik (3–4C), fibulae and other objects from Stobi, portrait busts including a famous bronze *bust of Constantine found at Niš, and the highly celebrated *Belgrade Cameo (4C). Early Christian finds: sarcophagus with the story of Jonah (from Belgrade), 6C mosaics, 5C capitals and decorative fragments from Stobi.—Coins used in Serbia from the tetradrachma of Damastion (4C BC) to 1868. Greek and Roman tomb inscriptions.

The FIRST FLOOR is devoted to art in Serbia from the Middle Ages to the late 19C. At the foot of the stairs, two sculptures by Meštrović. On the landing, all round the stairwell, pottery, weapons, utensils, and religious objects connected with the Slavic Migrations (9–11C).

Medieval Rooms. Vestibule: copy of the Gospel of Prince Miroslav (1180–90). R.1: Frescoes from the church of Djurdje Stupovi (1168). R.2. Frescoes from the churches of Gradac (late 13C), Prizren (13C), Sisojevac (14C), and Peć (14C). R.3. Late 14C frescoes clearly influenced by Byzantine art of the period of the Palaeologues, architectural fragments. R.4. *Romanesque archaeological fragments from Milentija. R.5. Serbian silver objects and the famous *Illuminated Codex of Emperor Dušan (14C). R.6. Liturgical objects and icons. R.7. Serbian icons of the 17–18C. R.8. Italo-Cretan icons of the 16–17C and Serbian and Macedonian icons of the 18C. R.9. icons of the Kotor School (17–18C).

18–19C Serbian Painting. Baroque artists trained in the Viennese School, icons and fragments of an iconostasis of 1772, works by Dimitrije Popović. Neo-classicism: Biedermeier style: works by Konstantin Danil and Pavel Djurković, P. Simić and Stevan Aleksić. Romanticism: Djura Jaksić, Stevan Todorović, Novak Radonić (Portrait of Mrs Bokmaz); Realism: Djordje Milovanović (Still Life), Dimitrije Popović, Ljubo Aleksandrović (Grape Picker), Djordje Krstić (The Anatomist, the Drowned Woman), Paja Jovanović (Portrait of a Lady), Uroš Predić (The Gay Company). Impressionism: Leon Koen (Woman with White Hat), Marko Murat.

The SECOND FLOOR is devoted to **20C Art in Serbia** and to **Foreign Painters**. On the landing, marble sculptures by Ivan Meštrović (The Mother). Serbian painters from 1904 to the Second World War. School of Paris and Impressionist circle: Nadežda Petrović, Milan Milovanović, K. Milićević; artists of the twenties and thirties: Sava Šumanović, Petar Dobrović, Milan Konjović, Ignjat Job, Marin Tartaglia, Zora Petrović, Milo Milunović, Milena Pavlović-Barilli, M. Čelebonović, Petar Lubarda, Ivan Tabaković, Ivan Radović, Pedja Milosavljević.— Foreign Painters. R.1. Italo-Cretan icons, works by Giovanni di Paolo, Paolo Veneziano (Maestà, Birth of Christ), Spinello Aretino (Maestà). R.2. Lorenzo di Credi (Adoration of Christ), Francesco Trevisani, Francesco Bassano, Tintoretto (*Madonna with Donor), Palma the

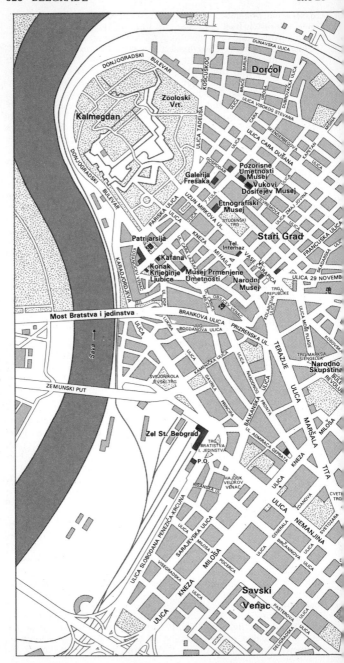

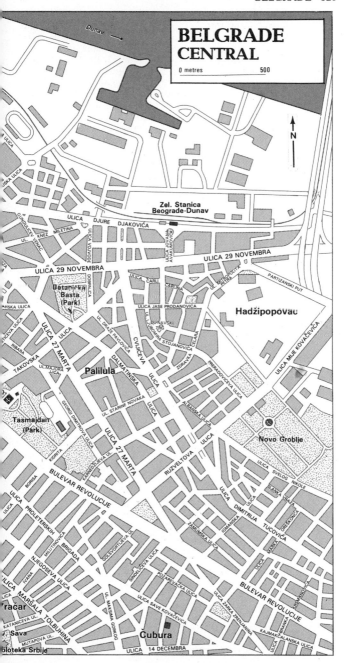

BELGRADE CENTRAL

0 metres 500

Dunav →

Zel. Stanica
Beograde-Dunav

N

ULICA DJURE DJAKOVIĆA

ULICA 29 NOVEMBRA

KNEZ MILETINA

GUNDULICEV VENAC

UL. KNEZ VRANAC

ULICA VOJVODE DOBRNJCA

ULICA JOVANA AVAKUMOVIĆA

ULICA 29 NOVEMBRA

ULICA. CARLI CAPLINA

UL. MITROPOLITA PETRA

PARTIZANSKI PUT

Botanička
Basta
(Park)

ULICA JASE PRODANOVICA

Hadžipopovac

AHSKA ULICA

TICEVA ULICA

RIBARA

ULICA 27 MARTA

TAKOVSKA

UL. MAJORA ILIĆA

UL. DRAŽE PAVLOVIĆA

DUNAVSKI 168

UL. IBRAHIM STOJANOVICA

CELIRA

CVIJICEVA

DALMATINSKA
ULICA

Palilula

ZDRAVKA

PRIBADOVICEVA ULICA

ULICA MIJE KOVAČEVIĆA

UL. STARINE NOVAKA

ULICA

ALBANSKA ULICA

ULICA

Tasmajdan
(Park)

KIDMITA

KARNEGIJEVA UL.

GEORGI DIMITROVA ULICA

ULICA 27 MARTA

Novo Groblje

BULEVAR REVOLUCIJE

RUZVELTOVA ULICA

ULICA SVELOG NIKOLE

SLANKA VRAČA

ULICA

BORISA

ULICA PROLETERSKIH

MILUTINOVICA

BRIGADA

ODLSVORTLJEVA UL.

SIMOPLCEVA ULICA

ZAMUNSKA ULICA

ULICA DIMITRIJA TUCOVICA

IGUMANSKA

MARICA

ORLJESKOVICA

NJEGOSEVA ULICA

IVANA

ULICA MAKSIMA GORKOG

POZAREVACKA ULICA

ULICA SAVE KOVACEVICA

ULICA ŽARKA ZRENJANINA

BULEVAR REVOLUCIJE

ISKALOVICA

BRANKA

KATANICEVA UL.

rača

r Sava

ULICA MARŠALA TOLBUHINA

MUTAPOVA UL.

Ćubura

KAJMAKCALANSKA ULICA

oloteka Srbije

ULICA 14 DECEMBRA

Elder, Alessandro Magnasco (Landscape with St. John), Daniele Crespi, Antonio Zanchi, Vittore Carpaccio (SS. Roch and Sebastian). R.3. Josse van Cleve, Cornelis de Vos, Jan Brueghel dei Velluti, Pieter Paul Rubens (*Diana), Arthur Moor, Josse Suttermans, Adam Frans ver der Meulen, David Teniers the Younger, J. De Lairesse. R.4. Abraham van Beyeren, Anthonis van Ravenstein the Younger, Adriaen de Gryef (Still Life), Jan Victoors, Adriaen van der Werff, Pietersz Berchem, Franz van Mieris the Elder, Anthonie Palamedesz, Jan van Goyen, Caspar Netscher. R.5. Canaletto (*Madonna della Salute), Michele Marieschi, Giovanni Paolo Pannini, Honoré Daumier, Vincent Van Gogh, Camille Corot (Italian Landscape), Eugène Boudin. R.6. Auguste Renoir (Moulin de la Galette; Bagneuse; Portrait of A. Maillot), Edgar Degas (*Dancer, *After the Bath). R.7. Camille Pissarro, Henri de Toulouse-Lautrec (Portrait of a Young Lady), Van Gogh, Claude Monet (Rouen Cathedral), Alfred Sisley, Paul Gauguin (Tahitian Woman), Gustav Moreau. R.8. Henri Matisse (Woman at the Window), Pierre Bonnard, Maurice Utrillo (Rue Saint-Vicent); Piet Mondrian, Pablo Picasso (*Head of a Woman), Maurice Vlaminck, Raoul Dufy, Marc Chagall, André Derain, Georges Rouault, Lovis Corinth, Kees Van Dongen, Edouard Vuillard.

ULICA VASA ČARAPIČA leads NW to STUDENSKI TRG, which takes its name from the University Building on the W side, today housing the offices of the administration. In the garden at the centre of the square were discovered remains of Roman Baths, now covered over. The monument to writer D. Obradović by Rudolf Valdeć (1914); that to botanist J. Pančić is by Djoka Jovanović (1897). On the N side (at No. 13) is the **Etnografski Muzej** (*Museum of Ethnography*; adm. 10–17; closed Mon), containing examples of Bogomil and Serbian tombstones, wooden sculptures, musical instruments, national costumes, popular paintings, and a vast and curious collection of painted eggs.

The **Galerija Fresaka** (20 Cara Uroša ulica, adm. 10–17, Thurs 10–19, Sat 9–17, Sun 10–14, closed Mon), has an instructive collection of copies of the frescoes from the Orthodox monasteries of Gračanica, Studenica, Sopoćani, Dečani and Kalenić. Here also are reproductions of sculptural decorations from Studenica, Trogir, and Split.

Nearby in GOSPODAR JEVREMOVA ULICA, a street of Balkan-type houses, is Belgrade's only extant mosque, a 17C building named the *Bajrakli Džamija* ('Flag Mosque') because the signal for the hours of prayer was given by waving a flag. At No. 19 in same street, the *Muzej Pozorišne Umetnosti* (adm. 9–14; closed Sun) traces the history of Serbian theatre by means of sketches, models, photographs, etc. Next door, at No. 21, is the **Vukov i Disitejev Muzej** (adm. 8–14, closed Sun), situated in one of the older houses in Belgrade, where Dositej Obradović and Vuk Karadžić (creator of the modern Serbian language and orthography) opened the first lycée in 1808. Today the museum is devoted to life in the city under the Turks, as well as to the two great educators: in fact the house was once occupied by a pasha and his harem, and retains the haremlik and sellamlik divisions.

Gospodar Jevremova ulica ends in the SKADARLIJA, one of the more attractive streets of Belgrade, closed to traffic. During the 19C it was the centre of the gipsy quarter and the haunt of artists and writers whose bohemian life style is ideally reflected in the various cafés, restaurants, and galleries. Musical and theatrical events take place in the street during the summer.

7 JULA ULICA, which cuts across the N quarters of the town, has a small *Jewish History Museum* (adm. 10–12, closed Mon) and two

Secession Stil buildings (Nos 39 and 41). Near the end of the street is the Orthodox *Cathedral*, dating from 1837–45. Within are a large painted iconostasis, the tombs of the founders of the Obrenović dynasty, princes Miloš (1780–1860) and Mihailo (1839–1868). The modern Patrijaršija, facing the cathedral, houses the *Muzej Srpske Pravoslavne Crkve* (Museum of the Serbian Orthodox Church; adm. 8–13, Sat 8–12; closed Mon) with icons, religious manuscripts, and vestments.

Across the 7 Jula ulica are the *Kafana kod Znaka* (Question Mark Café), a focus of bohemian life popular with artists, writers, and actors; and the *Konak Knejginje Ljubice*, built in 1829–31 by Prince Miloš Obrenović for his wife Ljubica. Restored and furnished in the original style, the Konak houses temporary exhibitions in its basement.

The nearby **Muzej Primenjene umetnosti** (Museum of Applied Art, adm. 12–19, Sat 10–19, Sun 10–14, closed Mon) contains objects illustrating the evolution of the decorative arts in Europe from the Gothic age to the present day, with particular emphasis on Serbia.

At the top of the old town extends *Kalemegdan Park*, an immense public garden much frequented by Belgraders. Once this was the parade grounds of the Turkish garrison; the N part, today transformed into a Zoo, was the Turkish cemetery. The ****Kalemegdan Fortress**, on a bluff above the junction of the Sava and the Danube, commands magnificent *Views across the great river and its fertile plain, which stretches for hundreds of kilometres up into central Europe. One of the largest fortifications in existence, it took its present form in the 18C, when Belgrade was in the hands of the Austrians. Within are a *Roman Well* (actually dating from around 1731), a huge *Monument to France*, by Ivan Meštrović, commemorating the aid offered by that country to the Serbs and other South Slavs during the First World War; the *Messenger of Victory*, another monument by Meštrović; an art pavilion, where temporary exhibitions are held, and an open-air café. The *Citadel* houses the *Military Museum of the Yugoslav People's Army*, one of the finest of its kind anywhere. Below the fortifications are two small churches: the Ružica, once a Turkish Arsenal transformed into a church in 1838; and Sv. Petka, formerly a place of pilgrimage with a miraculous reputation. Nearby is the baroque gateway named after Prince Eugène of Savoy and erected in 1717 to commemorate his important victory over the Turks.

Return to the Trg Republike and turn S to the TERAZIJE, a large square where several main avenues meet. On the W side is the *Moskva Hotel*, a Secession Stil building by J. Ilkić (1906). The *Terazije Fountain*, focal point of the square, was erected in 1860 in honor of the return to Serbia of Prince Miloš Obrenović. Further S lies TRG MARKSA I ENGELSA, whence begins BULEVAR REVOLUCIJE, a broad modern avenue lined with monumental buildings, notably (right) the former *Royal Palace* (1882), today the seat of the Praesidium of Parliament; and (across the street) the early 20C *Narodna skupština*, or National Assembly Building.

Some 2000m S of the Terazije lies the **Muzej 25 Maj** (Museum of May 25, entrance at 6 Botićeva; adm. 9–15, summer 9–16, closed Mon), displaying gifts presented to Marshal Tito on his birthday and other occasions; behind it extends the large garden of the former presidential residence. The latter now houses the ***Tomb of Marshal Tito** (1892–1980), an extraordinary example of tasteful simplicity.

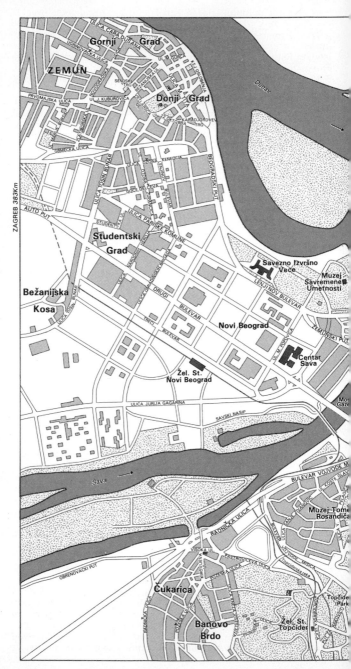

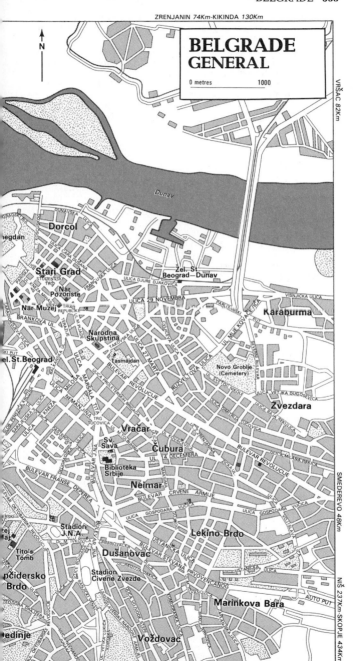

ZRENJANIN 74Km-KIKINDA 130Km

BELGRADE GENERAL

0 metres   1000

N

VRŠAC 82Km

Dunav

Dorcol

egdan

Stari Grad

STUDENTSKI TRG

Nar Pozoriste

Nar Muzej

BRANKOVA UL.

Žel. St Beograd—Dunav

ULICA DJURE DJAKOVICA

ULICA 29 NOVEMBRA

VISNJICKA ULICA

Karaburma

Narodna Skupstina

el.St.Beograd

Tasmajdan

ULICA 27 MARTA

BULEVAR REVOLUCIJE

Novo Groblje (Cemetery)

ULICA VETJKA DUGOSEVICA

Zvezdara

TRG TUCOVICA

Vračar

Sv. Sava

Čubura

UL. 4 DECEMBRA

BULEVAR REVOLUCIJE

Biblioteka Srbije

BULEVAR FRANSE DEPEREA

Neimar

BULEVAR CRVENE ARMIJE

ULICA GOSPODARA VUCICA

ULICA GOSPODARA VUCICA

Stadion J.N.A.

Lekino Brdo

Tito's Tomb

Dušanovac

BULEVAR OKTOBARSKE REVOLUCIJE

pčidersko Brdo

Stadion Civene Zvezde

USTANICKA ULICA

PRVOVEN-ČANOG

Marinkova Bara

AUTO PUT

SMEDEREVO 48Km

NIŠ 237Km-SKOPJE 434Km

edinje

Voždovac

KRAGUJEVAC 118Km

Topčider Park, a few blocks further S, is a good picnic spot. Here the former residence of Prince Miloš has been converted into a *Museum of the First Serbian Rebellion* (1804). In the E part of the park is a pretty church once used as a royal chapel.

Košutnjak Park, nearby, is now largely a summer camp. The fountain near the entrance, called the Hajdučka Česma, was once an assembly point for rebellion. The monument farther on marks the spot where Prince Mihailo Obrenović was assassinated in June 1868.—Continuing SE you reach the village and monastery of **Rakovica** (18C; extensively restored), containing the memorial chapel of the revolt of 1806.

Novi Beograd, on the left bank of the Sava, is, as the name suggests, the area of most recent construction. Here are located the new university campus; government ministries and other offices; and the **Muzej savremene umetnosti** (Museum of Contemporary Art; adm. summer 10–19, winter 9–16, Sat and Sun 10–19; closed Tues), which affords a good general view of painting, sculpture, and graphic arts in Yugoslavia from 1900 to the present.

EXCURSIONS. To **Avala** (16km S by the Kragujevac road), a wooded hill offering fine views over the Danube, Sava, and Šumadija. Formerly the site of a Turkish fortress, the hilltop is now crowned by Meštrović's *Monument to the Unknown Soldier* (1938), considered one of this contemporary sculptor's better works.

To (175km) **Subotica**, one of larger towns in Yugoslavia, where the Hungarian influence is very apparent. The town (reached by taking Highway 22/E75 N from Novi Sad) is one of the principal cultural centres of the Vojvodina. It has an ornate and bizarre *Town Hall* and a good *Ethnographical Museum*.

To (82km) **Vršac**, situated on hills amid vineyards near the Rumanian border (from Belgrade, take Highway N1–9/70NE). The city stands on the site of several prehistoric settlements and a Roman colony. Its most important monument is the 15C *Tower of Vršac*. The city developed particularly after the departure of the Turks in 1717, as various 18C palaces suggest. There are two interesting churches: the *Uspenska* and the *Saborna*, both with fine iconostases. High to the E of the town is a volcanic hill crowned by the ruins of a late medieval fortress commanding vast *Views over the Danube plain.

*Tour of the Danube by Hydrofoil**, through majestic scenery to the Iron Gates, a deep gorge now blocked by a huge dam that has modified, but not spoiled, the surrounding landscape. Tour information from the Turist Biro at the Terazije. Most locations can also be reached by road (Highways N1/E75, N24, and N25–1).

The first river port at which the hydrofoil calls is **Smederevo**, a large (40,000 inhab.) industrial centre and agricultural market built, it is believed, on the site of the Roman *Mons Aureus*. It became the capital of the despotate of Serbia in the 15C when the Serbs were ousted from Belgrade by the Hungarians; at this time the despot Djurdje Branković built the colossal *Castle*, one of the largest and best-preserved fortresses in Europe. In 1459 Branković's castle was taken by Sultan Mehmet I, and it remained in the hands of the Turks until 1867. Although damaged several times, particularly during the Second World War, it still testifies to the power of its builder. Within, in the N corner, is the former royal palace, now a ruin, defended by a chain of towers and surmounted by a keep; today it is used as an open-air theatre.—In the town is a former monastic church, erected in the 15C by the Morava school builders in brick and stone, with three polygonal apses and a central dome. Within, 17C frescoes illustrate the Life of Christ and the Psalms.

Beyond Smederevo the Danube becomes very wide and flows past several large islands, touching on the first foothills of the Carpathians. The ruined castle of **Ram**, on the right bank, dates from the 16C, although the site on which it stands was fortified much earlier. From here on, the river marks the frontier between Yugoslavia and Rumania. The hills become higher and wilder.

Golubac Castle, on the Danube near Belgrade

Golubac Castle, on a rocky point high above the water, overlooks the Isle of Moldava. It is one of the largest and most beautiful of the Danube castles, with nine ruined towers and crumbling machicolated ramparts. Built in the early 14C on the site of the Roman *Castrum columbarum*, it was taken by the Turks in 1391 and retaken by the Serbs in 1867. Since that time it has fallen into ruin. On the Rumanian side of the river lie the remnants of another stronghold, *Laslovar Castle* (15C).

Beyond Golubac begins the spectacular tract of the Danube known as the **Iron Gates**, the narrowest part of the Djerdap Gorge, 3km long and 500m wide, beyond which the river reemerges into the plains. Near the small port of Donji Milanovac, in a recess in the riverbank at **Lepenski Vir**, excavations have revealed traces of inhabitation dating from as early as 7000 BC. A village of 85 huts, situated 35m below the present level of the river, has been excavated and raised to safe ground, respecting the original arrangement; the reassembled remains (dating from 5480–4610 BC) are now visible in a covered pavilion; No. 54, the largest and best preserved of the huts, retains the original hearth. In the *Museum* (adm. 8–12 and 13–17) are tools, utensils, etc. recovered during the excavations. Especially noteworthy are the so-called *Lepenski Vir Sculptures*, dating from 5350–4700 BC. These are large stones carved with anthropomorphic and geometric forms and kept for ritual purposes near the hearth.

Lepenski Vir was apparently inhabited by a fishing and hunting community; there is no evidence of agriculture or stock-breeding.

Beyond *Donji Milanovac* the river narrows and enters the defile of Kazan, the depths of which are inhabited by sturgeon weighing up to 250–300kg. Set into the rock high up the mountainside is the *Tabula Traiana, a large inscription surrounded by reliefs of figures and eagles, erected in AD 103 to mark the completion of a Roman road that was begun by Tiberius in AD 28 and to commemorate Trajan's campaign against the Dacians. The monument has been raised from its original site; the road, which ran along the edge of the gorge partly carved in the rock and partly supported by beams, is now below the waterline.

The **Djerdap Dam, built jointly in 1964–72 by Yugoslavia and Rumania with contributions from the other countries touched by the Danube and by the Soviet Union, is one of the more impressive pieces of civil engineering in Europe. The dam, which cost a total of 500 million dollars, is 448m wide at the base, 1278m at the top, and rises 30m above the level of the Danube; on the left and right banks are two locks 310m long and 34m high; and hydroelectric plants with a yearly capacity of 10.5 billion KW. The dam has raised the level of the Danube by 35m, creating an enormous lake 135km long and permitting ships of up to 5000 tons to navigate the river from the Black Sea to Belgrade. In the vicinity of the dam, at *Karataš*, recent excavations have revealed traces of a large and important Roman frontier post, a castrum erected in the reign of Trajan and restored and enlarged under Justinian (530).

26 Belgrade to Skopje

A. Via Niš

ROAD, 437km. Highway N1/E75.—89km *Velika Plana.*—13km *Markovac.*—34km *Svetozarevo.*—11km *Ćuprija.*—10km *Paraćin.* —80km **Niš.**—39km *Leskovac.*—69km *Vranje.*—54km *Kumanovo.* —38km **Skopje.**

RAILWAY, c 7 hours.

N1/E75 (Rtes 23, 24A) continues from Belgrade to the Greek border. From the capital city to (237km) Niš it is a modern motorway; thereafter divided and undivided tracts alternate and, as usual, careful driving is necessary.

On the whole the countryside is uninteresting until you enter the wild, narrow gorge of the Južna Morava, near (237km) Niš. Most remarkable, in contrast, are the Serbian Orthodox monuments of the Morava valley, which constitute the region's chief attraction. These require a word of explanation.

Following the death of the last Serbian emperor, Uroš V (1335–71), the most important of the new Serbian states grew up in the northern region of the former empire, along the River Morava. Here Prince Lazar (who died on the battlefield of Kosovo in 1389) and his son Stefan (1389–1425) founded several convents, which, by virtue of their architectural features and the style of their fresco decorations, constitute a distinct school of Serbian art. The main features of the Morava School are the triple-apsed naoi of its churches; the combined use of brick and stone in its masonry work; and the refined, graceful style of its paintings. The most important examples are found in Manasija, Kalenić, Sisojevac, Naupara, Ljubostinja, and Ravanica. Although none of these lies along the main road, all may be reached fairly conveniently, offering a welcome break in an otherwise monotonous journey. The monuments of Niš, birthplace of Constantine, are also interesting.

Belgrade, Rte 25. Leave the city from the S, by BULEVAR JUGO-SLOVENSKE NARODNE ARMIJE, then enter N1/E70 for Niš. The road crosses the low hills of Šumadija.

89km **Velika Plana**, exit for *Koporin* (8km S by country road), a 15C monastery with a Morava School church containing coeval frescoes (Passion and New Testament scenes).

13km **Markovac**, exit left for (33km) Despotovac and the monastery of Manasija.

The fortified monastery of **Manasija*, originally known as Resava from the stream that runs past it, was built in 1406–18 by order of the despot Stefan Lazarević as his own burial place and as the seat of the monks whom he engaged to reform the Serbian language. It immediately became an important cultural and literary centre; later it was devastated by the Turks. Its high defensive walls, reinforced by 11 imposing towers (two of which guard the entrance), are still intact, giving the complex the appearance of a Byzantine fortress. Within are parts of the conventual buildings and the lovely church of the **Holy Trinity*, a masterpiece of the Morava School. Unlike most churches of this school, which combine stone and brick masonry, it is made almost entirely of ashlar. The interior, which follows a Greek Cross plan, has a narthex (built in the 18C to replace the original, destroyed by an explosion), a naos with three apses, a central dome over the crossing, and four corner domes. The frescoes, which are contemporary with the church, although partly ruined, are colourful and highly express-ive. They are considered among the chief monuments of Serbian Orthodox painting, and were executed by Greek artists or by local painters trained at Salonika. The subjects of the paintings are as follows: on the W wall, to the left the entrance, portrait of the founder with a model of church; above, Dormition of the Virgin; side walls, Life of the Virgin and Passion; piers, medallions of Saints; side apses, Saints and Parables; central apse, procession of Saints.

A minor road running through attractive countryside connects Manasija with the monastery of Ravanica, described below.

34km **Svetozarevo** (116m, 24,000 inhab.), formerly an important station on the caravan route to Constantinople, has a small gallery of naive art.

11km Ćuprija (123m, 12,000 inhab.), at the confluence of the Ravanica and the Morava, lies on the site of the Roman *Horreum Margi*, the only traces of which are to be seen in the *Museum* (4 Lole Ribara; artefacts and a few small statues, bronze copies of Hellenistic originals). A turning (left) leads N, past a pretty village, to (12km) the monastery of Ravanica.

The fortified monastery of **Ravanica* was founded around 1376 by Prince Lazar, whose body was brought here after the battle of Kosovo (1389). Today Ravanica stands behind a long, white wall of distinctly Oriental appearance; in the past it was protected by ramparts and towers, like Manasija, and parts of these fortifications have recently been excavated and restored. The church belongs to the Morava School and is built to a Greek Cross plan with five cupolas and apses on the N and S arms as well as at the E end. The walls, made of alternating bands of brick and stone, are adorned by elaborate bas-reliefs, especially around the windows and doorways and on the cupolas. The narthex dates from the 18C, when the church was restored after being several times devastated by the Turks. The interior contains much-ruined frescoes: on the W wall, above the entrance, Ascension of the Virgin, and on the left, Prince Lazar and his family; around the walls and in the vault, life and miracles of Christ, Church feasts, and Passion episodes; in the central apse Saints, Communion of the Apostles, and in the vault, Virgin and Child with angels.

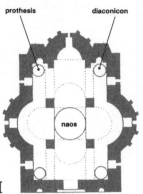

RAVANICA CHURCH

10km **Paraćin** (136m, 17,000 inhab.), on the site of the Roman *Sarmatos*, is known today for its textile and glass industries.

14km **Pojate**, turning for (31km) Kruševac.

Kruševac (146m, 35,000 inhab.), the capital of Prince Lazar in the 14C, was not subdued by the Turks until long after the battle of Kosovo (it probably fell in 1455, and it remained in Turkish hands until 1833). In the centre of the town is the ruined medieval castle, within which stands the *Lazarica palatine church*, established by Prince Lazar in 1380 and restored (with excessive zeal) by Prince Miloš Obrenović in the 19C. It belongs to the Morava School type (Greek Cross plan with central cupola, brick and stone masonry, elebroate decorative carvings around doors and windows, etc.); but the frescoes have been lost: like the ramparts, they were destroyed by the Turks.

80km **Niš** (193m, 133,000 inhab.) is the Roman *Naissus*, birthplace of the emperor Constantine (274–337). For many centuries it was an important station on the road from Belgrade to Constantinople and Athens—which of course made it strategically important, too. The emperor Claudius defeated the Goths here in 269, but Atilla destroyed the city in 441. It was rebuilt in the 6C by Justinian, only to be devastated again in 615. The Turks captured it in 1454 and held it until 1877; since then it has been a target in several other campaigns, particularly during the last war. Today it hosts many important industries and a university.

Post Office: 1 Voždova.
Information: *Turistički savez opštine*, 7 Nade Tomića, tel. 22108.

Though it is not a pleasant place in itself, Niš has several interesting monuments. At the N end of the bridge on the Nišava lies the **Tvrdjava**, an immense fortification built by the Turks between 1690 and 1720. Elaborate carvings and Arabic inscriptions adorn the main gate; within, in a public garden, stand the former arsenal, now a gallery of modern art; a domed haman; and a mosque. Excavations have brought to light remains of the Roman fortification and of the Byzantine citadel. The park also contains a monument commemorating the liberation from the Turks (1877) and Roman sculptures and inscriptions unearthed in and around the town.

The **Arheološki Muzej** (Archaeological Museum; 59 V Kongresa KPJ ulica, adm. 9–16; Sun 9–13; closed Mon) contains prehistoric material from the Stone, Bronze, and Iron Age; Roman glass, pottery, coins, and statuary; and Byzantine coins and sculpture, all from local excavations.

Surely the most curious monument of Niš is the **Ćele Kula**, or Tower of Skulls (on the Sofia road, adm. summer 7–19, winter 9–16), a Turkish construction of 1809 originally covered with 952 skulls, arranged in 56 rows, of Serbian rebels killed in battle. Lamartine, who saw it on the way back from his Oriental tour in the 1830s, described it as 'a white tower rising in the middle of the plain and gleaming like marble'. Only gradually, he realised its full significance: 'I drew close and let a Turkish child following me hold my horse while I dismounted and sat in the shade of the tower to rest. Raising my eyes to the monument in whose shade I was sitting I saw that it was made not of marble but of even rows of human skulls. The skulls, bleached by sun and rain...completely covered the victory monument. Some of the skulls still had some hair on them which fluttered in the wind like leaves on trees'. After the expulsion of the Turks (1877) the tower was enclosed in a chapel, and today only a few of the skulls remain.

Continuing beyond the Ćele Kula you reach (left) the excavations of **Medijana**, a 4C Roman town containing, among other things, a villa of Constantine. The small Museum (adm. summer 7–19, winter 9–16) contains a fine mosaic and other objects. More antiquities can be seen in the suburb of *Jagodin male*, where an early Christian cemetery with vault tombs bearing traces of frescoes has recently been brought to light.

EXCURSIONS. To **Kladovo**, 215km N by Highway N24, through one of the lesser-known regions of Serbia.

56km **Knjaževac** (216m, 6000 inhab.), on the Beli Timok, has remains of a 14C castle.

41km **Zaječar**, a road leads left to the village of Gamzigrad, near which lie the imposing ruins of a Roman *Castrum* built in the 3–4C and restored under Justinian. The ramparts, forming a trapezoid measuring 300m by 230m, are reinforced by 20 cylindrical towers (some of which survive almost intact) and pierced by four gates. Within are remains of several buildings, including a palace with fine mosaic floors, and a thermal complex.

61km **Negotin** possesses a small museum (*Muzej Radi Svakog Dana*, Voivode Mičića ulica, adm. 7–18, Sun 9–13; closed Mon) with Roman antiquities. Beyond, the highway follows the Danube (across the river is Rumania) to (58km) *Kladovo*, Rte 25.

To **Priština**, 137km SW by Highway 25, traversing the upper Morava valley.

29km **Prokuplje** (266m, 16,000 inhab.), on the River Toplica, at the centre of a wild region famous for its game, is overlooked by a Byzantine fortress on a hill. The church of *Sv. Prokopije*, built in the 9–10C and enlarged by King Milutin in the 14C, has 13C frescoes. Next door is the 15C oratory of *Jug Bogdan*, with coeval frescoes.

37km **Kuršumlija** (365m, 3000 inhab.), has two churches, *Sv. Nikola* and *Sv. Bogorodica*, built by order of King Stefan Nemanja, in the 12C. 71km **Priština**, see Rte 26B.

39km **Leskovac** (230m, 45,000 inhab.), a very old Serbian settlement, today is an important industrial centre. The *Narodni Muzej* (6 Ulica Učitelja Josifa; adm. 7–14 and 16–18) has ethnographical and archaeological sections, the latter with finds from the excavations at Caričin Grad.

The imposing ruins of **Caričin Grad*, a fortified, 6C Byzantine town destroyed by the Slav invasions of the 7C, lie some 32km away. From Leskovac, take the road SW to the village of (24km) *Lebane*, then turn right to *Prekopčelica*; the ruins lie 8km beyond. Excavations were begun in 1913 and are still going on; they have revealed what was apparently an important town, believed by some to be *Iustiniana Prima*, Justinian's capital in this region.

The site lies on a hillside, about a 15-minute walk from the road. Outside the *Walls* (well preserved, with ramparts, towers, and five of the city gates) are remains of *Baths* and a 6C *Basilica* with a nave, two aisles, narthex, atrium, and apse. Here considerable portions of the mosaic pavement have survived, especially in the narthex, nave, and sanctuary. The tessellations depict a variety of subjects, notably, at the E end of the nave, a peasant representing the Good Shepherd with his flock (a rare subject for the period) and a hunter spearing a lion; and, in the N half of the nave, some splendid mounted Amazons and centaurs, and another scene of the chase with a hunter in pursuit of a wounded bear. All the work is finely executed.

Access to the town proper is gained by the imposing S gate, whence a broad main street leads up past the foundations of what is known as the *Cruciform Church* (right), a late 6C edifice believed to be a private chapel and memorial to a military governor. On the other side of the street, beyond the ruins of some private dwellings, is a modest three-aisled *Basilica* thought to have been used for worship by tradesmen and artisans who lived in the neighbourhood.

Some 50–60m further on, one comes to a large circular space and crossroads—evidently the *Forum*—around which are remains of several public buildings, including another large *Basilica*. From here broad streets down which local cattle graze lead to the N, E, and W, past the substantial ruins of many houses.

The *Acropolis*, at the highest point of the town, is enclosed within a second set of ramparts. Here are to be found the most important ecclesiastical buildings: on the left, the large *Cathedral*, a three-aisled basilica with a narthex, atrium, and baptistery; on the right, the *Bishop's Palace*; and, away to the E, the *Crypt Basilica*—with a single apse, no nathex, and three doorways leading directly from the atrium into the nave and aisles—beneath which was an unusually large crypt where important clerics, and perhaps some secular dignitaries, were buried.

The road traverses the *Gradelička klisura*, a wild canyon, nearly 50km long, formed by the Južna Morava. In the hills to the E is the spa of *Vranjska Banja*.

69km **Vranje** (280m, 26,000 inhab.), an important place on the roads to Bulgaria and Macedonia in Turkish times, today is an agricultural and industrial centre. Vestiges of the Turkish era include a haman, a Turkish bridge, the Djorenska fountain, and two residences of the paša, one of which (built in 1765 by Paša Rajif Beg

Džinić and unaltered since) houses the *Narodni Muzej* (National Museum; 1 Pionirski ulica; adm. 9–15, Sat 9–13; closed Mon), with important prehistoric material (including some Stone Age idols dated 5000 BC), Roman and Byzantine finds, and an ethnographical section. On a hill NW of the town are the extensive remains of a castle, *Markovo kale*, built by the Serbs and fortified by the Turks.

As you cross into Macedonia you enter a new tract of motorway, at the beginning of which a road branches left to Kriva Palanka and the Bulgarian border.

14km NE on this road lies the church ***Staro Nagoričane**, once part of a monastery founded by King Milutin in 1313. The church (dedicated to St. George), was built over an 11C Byzantine edifice, signs of which can still be seen. Mostly made of brick and stone, it follows a Greek Cross plan and has five graceful cupolas. The façade and flanks of the church are decorated with a pleasing mixture of brickwork patterns and inlaid ceramic; the designs are often in the form of a cross. Within are magnificent frescoes, among the finest in Macedonia, executed by two of King Milutin's court painters, Mihajlo and Eutihije (signed on the robes of the warrior saints on the N wall and on a pillar on the S side). In the narthex are a cycle of paintings that illustrate the Orthodox Calendar, and portraits of King Milutin and his child wife, Simonida. The Queen wears the huge earrings with which she is often represented, the King holds a model of the church. In the naos are two fine sequences, depicting the Legend of St. George and scenes of the Passion, where the episodes are treated as theatrical representations, in the cupola, Prophets, Evangelists, and Christ Pantokrator; in the apse cycles of the life of the Virgin and life of St. Nicholas; on the iconostasis a magnificent Vergine Pelagonitissa (Prilep style) and St. George. In nearly all the paintings in the church considerable attention is devoted to detail, and there is every effort to make a full narrative.

54km **Kumanovo** (334m, 46,000 inhab.), where the Serbs won their definitive victory over the Turks in the First Balkan War, is a large, modern town with a considerable Muslim population and an interesting gipsy quarter. Nearby, on the outskirts of the village of *Konjuh*, is a curious round church thought to date from the 6C, 'discovered' by local peasants in 1919.

11km W of Kumanovo, in a magnificent position on the forested E slopes of the Skopjška Crna Gora, stands **Matejić Monastery**, dating from the mid 14C and once heavily fortified. The church of the Holy Virgin, a building of brick and stone with five cupolas, was built by order of Helena and her son Uroš V 1356, though there are records of a monastery here 50 years earlier. The fissure in the NW wall was made by the Skopje earthquake. Inside the church are traces of frescoes in a miniaturistic style.

Beyond Kumanovo the road and railway proceed in a straight line across the *Ovče Polje* ('Plain of Sheep'), considered the breadbasket of Macedonia. In the spring, this region is bright with opium poppies, a crop unknown in other regions of Yugoslavia. Other crops typical of Macedonia are tobacco, peanuts, and sesame.

38km **Skopje**, see Rte 26B.

B.   Via Kragujevac and Priština

ROAD, 438km. Highways N23, N22, N25, N2/E65.—79km *Topola*. —39km *Kragujevac*.—54km *Kraljevo*.—49km *Ušće*.—32km *Raška*. —62km *Titova Mitrovica*.—36km **Priština**.—87km **Skopje**.

RAILWAY, c 8½ hours; change for the bus for Priština at Kosovo
Polje.

This route, which links the national capital with that of Yugoslav
Macedonia, is of the highest artistic interest. Like Rte 26A, it
traverses the area of the great Serbian Orthodox monasteries,
perhaps the finest of medieval ecclesiastical architecture in the
Balkans. That they are so little known makes these monuments even
more remarkable.

Belgrade, Rte 25. From the city centre follow BULEVAR JUGO-
SLOVENSKE NARODNE ARMIJE S to N23. The road passes beneath the
mausoleum of Avala, winds up to the Ralja pass, then descends to a
fertile lowland.—*Arandjelovac* (286m, 5000 inhab.), reached by a
turning on the right, is a much-frequented spa.

79km **Topola** (235m, 4800 inhab.) is a pleasant town on the River
Kamenica, amidst the forested highlands of the Šumadija. It is the
home of the Karadjordjević dynasty, the former royal house of
Yugoslavia. The public gardens (with a monument to Djordje Petrović, founder of the dynasty, by P. Palavicini) occupy the site of
Karadjordjević Castle, the only extant part of which is the *Konak*
(residence), now a historical museum. The adjoining Orthodox church
dates from the same period, as does the guardhouse, which has been
transformed into a restaurant. The *Mausoleum* of the royal family
(adm. Apr–Oct, 8–19; Nov–Mar, 9–16) stands on the hill of Oplenac,
overlooking the town. The church, dedicated to St. George, was built
in a neo-Byzantine style by Peter I in 1912, damaged in the First World
War, and rebuilt during the 1920s.

A road on the right leads to *Stragari* (8km) at the centre of an area with several
Serbian Orthodox monasteries, the most famous of which is **Blagoveštenje** (the
Annunciation), dating from the 14–15C, with coeval frescoes (saints, life of
Christ) touched up in the 17C.

39km **Kragujevac** (183m, 71,000 inhab.), the chief city of the Šumadija
region, played an important role in the insurrections of the Serbs
against the Turks, and from 1818 to 1839 was the capital of the
Principality of Serbia. Today it is of little interest to the casual visitor.
The former *Palace of Prince Miloš* (2 Svetozara Markovića ulica),
houses a Museum with archaeological, historical, and ethnographical
collections; and the *Šumarica Memorial Park* has monuments
commemorating the 7000 victims of a German reprisal of 1941.

54km **Kraljevo** (208m, 40,000 inhab.) is a 19C town, a former seat of
the Obrenović dynasty. At the centre of the town is the residence of
Prince Vasin, built in the same style as the palaces of Belgrade and
Čačak. The *Muzej-Galerija Fresaka* (3 Karadjordjeva ulica; adm.
8–12, Tues and Thurs 8–12 and 15–17; closed Mon) has copies of
frescoes from the Serbian Orthodox monasteries in the environs, as
well as archaeological, historical, and ethnographical collections.

To (59km) **Kruševac**. Highway N5 follows the valley of the Zapadna Morava
through a district containing several fine monasteries of the Morava School (cf.
Rte 26A).

29km **Trstenik**, on the right bank of the Zapadna Morava. 3km N, in a
delightful setting amidst forested hills, is the *Convent of Ljubostinja*, founded
in the late 14C by Princess Milica, consort of Prince Lazar, whose tomb is in the
church. The church itself is an outstanding example of the Morava School, with
narthex, naos, and apsidal transept. The walls of the exterior are adorned with
many fine carvings, especially around the doors and windows. Within, only
fragments of the original fresco decoration survive, of which the best are in the
narthex; notice especially, on the W wall, the portraits of Lazar and Milica, on the
N side of the door; and of their sons Stefan and Vuk, on the other side. Princess
Milica established this convent following the death of her husband on the

battlefield of Kosovo, and retired here together with many other noblewomen widowed by the Kosovo disaster; the conventual buildings include the magnificent timbered *Konak* where she resided until her death.

25km N, on the slopes of the Gledićke planine, lies the **Convent of Kalenić**, founded between 1407 and 1413 by a Serbian nobleman called Bogdan. The church, dedicated to the Presentation of the Virgin, is a masterpiece of the Morava School. The harmonious exterior is enlivened by colourful stone and brickwork, and adorned with minutely carved decorations round doorways, windows, and arches. These include geometric patterns, vegetable and zoomorphic motifs, biblical and mythological scenes, and a splended relief of the Virgin and Child on the S side of the narthex. Many of the designs are derived from miniature work and wood carving. Within, a domed narthex precedes the triapsidal naos with its central cupola. All around are magnificent *frescoes, coeval with the church. In the narthex, life of the Virgin, Nativity, Saints, and portrait of the founder; in the naos (entered by a fine sculpted doorway), Miracles of Christ and Church Feasts; in the cupola, archangels, prophets, and Pantokrator; in the chorus, Passion and Miracles of Christ; in the S apse, Marriage at Cana, in the diaconicon (right), praying Madonna; in the prothesis (left), Deposition. Here Serbian painting reaches its highest level of delicacy and refinement. Notice that the proportions of the compositions are calculated to combine with the dimensions of the building in the most balanced way possible: for instance, the scenes in the naos and apse are subtly graded (they become larger and larger as they approach the top of the cupola). This is especially noticeable in the Marriage at Cana, a masterfully constructed narrative scene that is interesting also because it shows the bride and bridegroom performing an old Serbian ritual ceremony: the groom is about to prick the finger of his bride, a preliminary to the ancient custom of mixing blood and wine and pledging each other. The warrior saints in the naos, another 'anomaly' found in Serbian pictorial cycles of the post-Kosovo period, represent the secular power of the

Kalenić, the monastery church

church and coincide with a time of peril.—The iconostasis dates from the mid 19C.

14km **Stopanja**: a turning on the right leads in 7km to **Veluće Monastery**, founded in the late 14C. The church, another work of the Morava School builders, has a typical brick and stone exterior with splendid sculptural decorations around the doors and windows. The frescoes, dating from the 14C and 16C, are primitive in comparison to those at Kalenić. Those of the narthex represent the Last Judgment and family of the founder; those of the naos (much faded) the Life of Christ and Procession of Saints. A richly carved doorway joins the narthex to the naos.

59km **Kruševac** (146m, 35,000 inhab., see p 338). 12km S is the church of *Naupara*, founded by Prince Lazar in the 14C on the model of the Lazarica; it retains its original decorations.

6km SW lies the **Monastery of Žiča**, founded in the early 13C by King Stefan Prvovenčani (the First Crowned), and made the seat of the Patriarchate by his brother, St. Sava, organiser of the Serbian Orthodox Church. Here the Serbian sovereigns were crowned. The church, much altered in the course of the centuries (the red intonaco of the exterior, restored in 1954, is original), belongs to the Raška school. The exonarthex is no longer extant; the narthex, naos, apse, and transept are intact. The frescoes, mainly dating from the 14C, are also interesting. They include an illustration of the Christmas Hymn of St. John Damascene, with the portraits of the royal family and allegories of the earth and the desert, beneath the belfry; and a Translation of the Virgin and Procession of Saints on the W wall of the narthex. In the naos, transept, and apse can be seen traces of the original, 13C fresco decoration (Saints, Crucifixion). Adjoining the naos are the chapels of Sv. Sava of Jerusalem (N) and Sv. Stefan (S), the latter with frescoes of the life of St. Stephen.

The road winds along the narrow Ibar Valley, between wooded hills. Overlooking the valley on the left are the ruins of *Maglić Castle*, the medieval stronghold of the archbishops of the Serbian Orthodox Church and one of the grander hilltop fortresses in Yugoslavia. The 14C ramparts, fortified by seven towers, enclose an imposing octagonal keep.

49km **Ušće** lies at confluence of the Ibar and its tributary, the Studenica.

A road on the right leads in 11km to the ****Monastery of Studenica**, the largest and richest of all Serbian monasteries, built amidst high mountains and dense forests, today still a prosperous place with many monks and a good deal of land. Within its walls are three churches and spacious conventual buildings. The most important church is *Sv. Bogorodica*, the church of Our Lady, founded by the Serbian king Stefan Nemanja and finished in 1191. It is the masterpiece and prototype of the Raška School, with an exonarthex, exceptionally tall narthex and naos, elongated chorus flanked on the left by a prothesis (where the Orthodox service begins) and on the right by the diaconicon (or sacristy), and an octagonal cupola on a square drum over the crossing. The beautifully polished marble exterior is is unique in medieval Serbian ecclesiastical architecture; it is adorned, as is customary, with intricate carvings.

Entrance to the interior is gained through the exonarthex, added by King Radoslav around 1230 and today used as the *treasury* (walnut coffin of King Stefan Prvovenčani with inlaid designs in ivory and mother-of-pearl; 16C evangelistary; 15C copper bas-reliefs; 16C iconostasis; books, icons, chasuble and liturgical vestments of the 17–18C). On the right of the exonarthex is a chapel with frescoes of 1235 showing the Translation of the Body of Stefan Nemanja. A magnificent marble doorway with finely carved surround and a relief in the lunette of the Virgin and angels leads into the narthex, adorned with frescoes (Last Judgment, Last Supper, Washing of the Feet) of

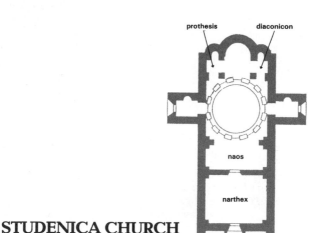

prothesis   diaconicon

naos

narthex

STUDENICA CHURCH

1569. Hence another elaborately carved doorway leads to the naos. The frescoes here were executed in 1208–09, possibly by a single artist. They are divided into an upper part, with gilded background; a middle part, with yellow background; and a lower part, with blue background. All that is left of the original paintings is a Crucifixion and part of an Annunciation. The others scenes (Life of Christ, Procession with King Stefan offering a model of the church to the Virgin, and Dormition of the Virgin) were repainted in 1569.

Apparent here are all the fundamental elements of monumental painting in Serbia: its epic quality, its emphasis on physical strength, and its clear definiton of character through the rendering of features. Most of the frescoes were repainted in the late 16C when the monastery was restored. The most important image is the monumental Christ in the Crucifixion on the W wall.

Stefan Nemanja abdicated at Studenica before retiring to Mt Athos. When he died his body was returned here and entombed near the S wall; above it is a portrait of him holding a model of the church. His feast day is May 24, and there is a pilgrimage here to celebrate the event.

The small white church next to that of the Virgin is the *Kraljeva Crkva* (King's Church) dedicated to SS. Ann and Joachim, built by King Milutin in 1314 to a strictly Byzantine plan: Greek Cross with central cupola. Its frescoes, coeval with the building, are considered among the finer works of Serbian art by virtue of their design, composition, chromatic range, and documentary importance. They too are laid out on three levels, comprising, from the bottom up, portraits of Saints (on the right King Milutin, offering a model of the churh, between his wife Simonida and St. Anne), the life of the Virgin (the principal cycle, solemn yet gay), and the life of Christ. The best-known episode is the Dormition, above the entrance, on the left, inside the naos.

Studenica, view of the monastery

Between the two churches is the more modest church of *St. Nicholas* of the 13C, which recalls the architecture of Dalmation churches. Within, only a few traces of the late 13C frescoes (Entry into Jerusalem, Angel at the Sepulcre, St. John) survive.

Beyond Ušće the Ibar becomes a rapid torrent. *Jošanička Banja* preserves the Turkish haman; the water temperature of the mineral springs is 70°C. At *Brvenik* a minor road on the right leads in 12km to Gradac.

The **Monastery of Gradac** was founded in the late 13C by Helen of Anjou, wife of Uroš I and mother of kings Dragutin and Milutin. The church of the Annunciation (relief above main door) combines Gothic and Byzantine elements, suggesting that craftsmen familiar with Western religious architecture may have had a hand in its construction—as at Studenica. Within are badly damaged frescoes, notably a Crucifixion on the W wall, the Dormition of the Virgin on the N wall, and several scenes from the life of the Virgin in the narthex. Remains of the conventual buildings and of the defensive walls have been brought to light by recent excavations.

On the other side of the Ibar is the 14C church of Nova Pavlica, with well preserved frescoes.

32km **Raška** turning (right) for (21km) **Novi Pazar** (499m, 40,000 inhab.), a picturesque Muslim town on the left bank of the Raška.

Post Office: 157 Ulica 28 Novembar.

Information: *Turistički informativni biro*, Ulica 28 Novembar, tel. 21678.

History. Novi Pazar owes its origin to the Serbian fortress of Raš, built in the mid 9C on the frontier of the Byzantine Empire. Here, in the late 12C, Stefan Nemanja established the capital of his kingdom (transferred by Milutin, in the early 14C, to Skopje). The name *Pazar* ('market') appears for the first time in the 15C, when the town became a base for the Turkish conquest of the North; it reached the height of its development in the 16–17C and declined in the 18C. Burned three times by the Serbs in the 19C, it was abandoned by the Turks only in 1912.

MESTNI TRG, the main square of the town, is very Turkish in appearance. Here can be seen the well-preserved 18C *caravanserai*, consisting of four buildings grouped around a vast courtyard. The **Mosque of Altum Alem**, which lies at the S end of the town, is the most important Turkish religious edifice of the region. Built in the 15C, it follows a square plan with dome, minaret, and vestibule; notice especially the mihrab, within, and the characteristic Balkan edifices of the courtyard. The *Zavičajni Muzej* (Ulica Stevana Nemanje) has sections devoted to history, archaeology, and ethnography, the latter with a series of popular costumes. The *Turkish fortress*, overlooking the town, was erected in the 15C, and sections of the ramparts and of an octagonal tower are still standing. For centuries the fortress was the seat of the Turkish sandžak.

3km N of Novi Pazar on the Raška road lies the church of **Petrova** (St. Peter), the only extant Serbian church which predates the Nemanjić dynasty. Founded in the 8C, it follows a Byzantine-Dalmatian model, circular in plan with central cupola and three radial apses. For nine centuries it was the seat of the Orthodox see of Raška. The interior, dark and mysterious, consists of a single, circular nave, with the tombs of several Serbian princes round the walls. During a recent restoration, fragments of 13C frescoes, in sombre red and black tones, were brought out on the walls; and the tomb of a 5C BC Illyrian prince was discovered beneath the floor. The tomb contained a considerable treasure (including gold jewellery, amber masks, statuettes, ceramic objects, etc.), much of which can now be seen in the National Museum in Belgrade. A fine old cemetery, with massive tombstones, surrounds the church.

Another interesting excursion point is the ancient city of **Ras**, the ruins of which lie 7km W of Novi Pazar. This may be combined with the monastery of Sopoćani, which lies a few kilometres up the valley (signposted). Ras is first mentioned in documents of the 9C. It became the capital of the kingdom of Raška, and then, with the Nemanja, the capital of Serbia. Although it was virtually destroyed by the Byzantines in the 12C, it remained the capital of the Nemanjić kings until 1314. After that it lost its importance and fell into decline. Sections of the ramparts remain.

The ****Monastery of Sopoćani**, 9km SW, was built around 1260 by King Uroš I as his burial palce. It was severely damaged in 1689 and completely abandoned in the 18C, after which it was allowed to fall into ruin. In recent years it has been carefully restored, but the magnificent frescoes, unfortunately, still show traces of prolonged exposure to the elements.

The church of the *Holy Trinity*, in a Romanesque style adapted to a Raška School plan, is a large building with a narthex, naos, semicircular apse, and cupola. In the 14C the emperor Dušan added an exonarthex which subsequently collapsed, except for the belfry. On the exterior, under the eaves, run blind arches; beneath these are small mullioned windows in simple stone surrounds. Within, the narthex and naos are adorned with monumental **frescoes, solemn and majestic paintings which, in their quality and style, are considered to foreshadow the Italian Renaissance. They are certainly the highest achievement of Serbian painting. The frescoes in the narthex date from 1270. Their subjects (the legend of St. Joseph, genealogy of Christ, and Last Judgment) are new to Serbian iconography. The scene of the death of Queen Ann, mother of Uroš I, and that of the Dormition of the Virgin (with the praying figure of Uroš's queen, Helen of Anjou) are particularly moving. In the little chapel on the S side of the narthex are late 13C scenes representing the life of King Stefan Nemanja as a monk of Mt Athos and the translation of his body to the monastery of Studenica. The frescoes of the naos, executed around 1265 in a mosaic-like technique with bright colours and a strong nervous line, are the finest compositions of all. On the entrance wall is the monumental Dormition of the Virgin; on the N wall the Birth of Christ, Descent into Limbo, and Transfiguration; on the S wall the Crucifixion, Presentation at the Temple, and Christ among the Learned Men. In the apse are the Fathers of the Church, Communion of the Apostles, and Resurrection scenes.

On the left side of the church are the scant remains of former monastic buildings.

66km **Titova Mitrovica** (42,000 inhab.) lies near the Trepča lead and zinc mines, to which it owes its prosperity. It has a small Municipal Museum with archaeological material found in the environs. Above the town (½ hour walk) stand the ruined castle of *Zvečan*, originally a Roman fortification, rebuilt in 12C and fortified by the Turks after the battle of Kosovo (1389).

This historic conflict, which sealed the Turkist conquest of Serbia, receives its name from the *Kosovo Polje* (literally 'field of blackbirds'), the alluvial plain, formed by the River Sitnica and its tributaries, which extends roughly from Titova Mitrovica to Priština. Here, in June 1389, Prince Lazar and his Christian allies were vanquished by the Muslim legions of Sultan Murad I, both leaders perishing in the fighting. The circumstances surrounding the battle are unclear, and it is thought that the actual fighting lasted several days, the Turkish victory coming only after a series of draws. According to one interpretation the Serbian armies were defeated by their own internal rivalries, which resulted in the defection of Serbian nobleman Vuk Branković with 12,000 cavalry. Another theory suggested that the Serbs attacked before they were ready (it is known, for instance, that many allies and vassals of Prince Lazar did not come in time), moving against an enemy whose numbers were far superior. Whatever the case may be, legend and speculation, as well as a lack of reliable evidence, have obscured the true facts, and the main interest of the battle today lies in the epic cycles of lays and ballads which grew out of it, as well as the messianic tenor it gave to later Serbian nationalism.

36km a turning left leads to (3km) **Priština** (631m, 136,000 inhab.) the modern capital of the autonomous Kosovo region, spread out across the slopes above the Kosovo plain. Formerly a capital of King Milutin (1282–1321) and other sovereigns of the Nemanjić dynasty, today it is the cultural centre of the over-whelmingly Albanian population of the region and a university town. No signs of royal occupation remain; however, the old (and somewhat rundown) Turkish quarter contains some konaks, a 15C imperial mosque, a haman of the same period, and a 19C clock tower. There is also a small museum.

Gračanica, the monastery church

8km S of Priština is the ***Monastery of Gračanica**, a foundation of King Milutin, once the seat of the bishops of Lipljan (comp. below). Built between 1313 and 1321, it was burnt down by the Turks in the late 14C and later reconstructed. In 1539 it received the first printing press in Serbia. The church, the only part of the monastery to survive intact, is perhaps the finest example of the Central School of Serbian ecclesiastical architecture. It is an elaborate structure of brick and stone, with five cupolas rising above arched gables. The interior is entirely covered with frescoes, the oldest of which are contemporary with the church and are executed, like those at Staro Nagoričane and in the King's Church at Studenica, in the courtly style of King Milutin. The best frescoes, in the narthex, date from 1321 (those in the exonarthex, itself a later addition to the church, date from the 16C). On the arch of the entranceway, royal portraits (notably of King Milutin, holding a model of the monastery; his queen Simonida; and Helen of Anjou, wife of Uroš I), a Nemanjić family tree (the first to be painted), and a liturgical calendar; on the entrance wall, Last Judgment. A somewhat later date is ascribed to the frescoes of the naos—on the S wall, the Dormition of the Virgin; on the side walls, on three levels, Saints, stories of the life of Christ, and Church feasts; in the cupola, Pantokrator; in the apse, saints adoring the Mystic Lamb, Communion of the Apostles, Christ and the Virgin, and the Ascension. The little chapel on N side contains some scenes from life of St. Nicholas and an extraordinary painting of St. John the Baptist, considered one of finer portraits in Serbian art. Above the narthex runs a small gallery, really a kind of royal box that the sovereign occupied while remaining invisible to the congregation. A secret door and stairway to this may be seen in one of the piers.

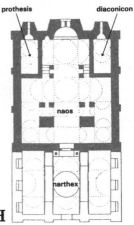

GRAČANICA CHURCH

Between the monastery and the village of Lipljan, nearby, are ruins of the Roman city of *Ulpiana*, established in the 2C BC, destroyed by a fire, and rebuilt in the 4C by Justinian, who called it *Iustiniana Secunda*. Finds from the site are displayed in the museum at Priština.

The road skirts *Uroševac*, a thriving town with several mosques, and enters Macedonia.

From 11km S of Uroševac a mountain road winds through lovely scenery to **Prizren** (62km) and **Peć** (76km), Rte 32.

87km **SKOPJE** (330m, 500,000 inhab.) is the capital of Macedonia. It is a bustling, modern city situated on the banks of the River Vardar. The old town, distinctly Oriental in appearance, extends to the N; the new city and the industrial quarter to the S. Many of the buildings in Skopje were constructed after the disastrous earthquake of 26 July 1963, which destroyed much of the city and claimed over 1000 victims.

Post Office: Ulica M. H. Jasmin.

Information: *Turistički informativen centar*, 1 Kej D Vlahova, tel. 238455; *Turistički sojuz na Makedonija*, 39 Ulica Maršala Tita, tel. 231348.

Airport: 22km SE; *JAT*, Gradski zid, blok V, Tel. 239175.

History. The Roman city of *Scupi* was for centuries the garrison of the Seventh Legion, and from the 4C onward it was the seat of the bishops of Dardanija. Devastated by the Goths and by a long series of earthquakes, it was rebuilt by the Emperor Justinian, who was born in Scupi in 483. Justinian's city was contested at length by the Byzantines and the Slavs. In the 9C it fell to the Bulgars, whose king, Samuel, made it the capital of his short-lived empire, brought to an early end by the Byzantines. In 1282 it was taken by the Serbian king, Milutin, and the emperor Dušan made it the capital of the Serbian empire. After a brief period of independence under the Serbian prince, Vukašin, it fell in 1392 to the Turks, who renamed it Uskup and held it until 1912.

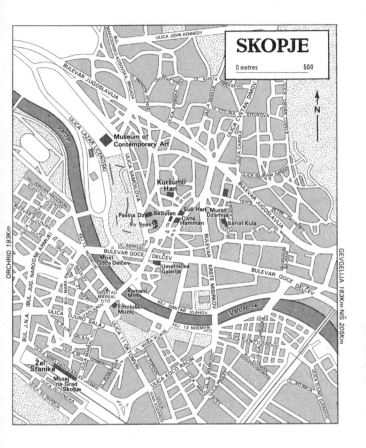

PLOŠTAD M. TITO, a broad, centrally located square on the right bank of the Vardar, is a good place to begin a visit to the city. At No. 10 is the **Etnološki muzej** (Ethnological Museum, adm. 8–14; Tues and Fri, 8–18), devoted to Macedonian folklore (costumes, tools, jewellery, etc.). From here the modern city stretches away to the S. A short walk along ULICA MARŠAL TITO brings you to the *railway station* and, inside, the *Muzej na grad Skopje* (Municipal Museum of Skopje; adm. 9.30–17; Sun 9.30–13; closed Mon), documenting local history from the Second World War to the present day. The old station building, destroyed by the earthquake of 1963 (the clock marks the time of the first tremor, 5.17) has been left as a memento of the catastrophe.

From Ploštad M. Tito, cross the Vardar by the **Kameni Most**, a narrow stone bridge built by the Romans, restored by Czar Dušan in 1348, and remodelled by Sultan Murad II in the 15C. From here the main street of the old town, SAMOILOVA ULICA, leads up to the castle, passing a number of old Turkish houses and new buildings constructed after the earthquake. All round extends the Čaršija or bazaar, bustling with activity like the one in Sarajevo, but much larger, comparable with the great bazaars of Turkey and North Africa. Nearly every street is devoted to a specific craft, and many of the tradesmen and craftsmen squat in front of their shops, which are barely larger than cupboards. A few blocks along, on the right, stands the **Daut Paša Haman**, built in the 15C by Daut Paša, the Grand Vizier, and once one of the finer bath complexes of the Ottoman Empire. It now houses the *Umetnička Galerija*, containing medieval frescoes and icons, and, mainly, works by local artists of the 18–19C. Further on, beyond the bridge over Bulevar Goce Delčev, is the Church of *Sv. Spas* (the Holy Saviour, adm. 8–12, 15–17; closed Sat and Sun pm), an edifice of 1689 remodelled in the 19C. It is surrounded by imposing walls with a wooden belfry. The foundations of the church are below ground level, because of the Turkish law that no Christian church could be taller than their houses; within are a fine wooden iconostasis wth Old and New Testament scenes, executed between 1812 and 1824 by artists of the Debar school; fresco fragments contemporary with the original building; and 18–19C icons. Situated on the portico that runs round the church are the tombs of the bishops of Skopje; and at the center of the courtyard, the tomb of Goce Delčev, leader of an anti-Turkish insurrection of 1903.

Immediately beyond, on the right, is the **Mustafa Pašina Džamija**, a 15C mosque with a large, arched portico, broad dome, and slender minaret. An Arabic inscription above the entrance bears the date of construction, 1492. The Interior is adorned with floral decorations, and the minbar and mihrab are made of marble. Adjoining the mosque is the hexagonal mausoleum of Mustafa Paša (1519); and behind this, the finely decorated sarcophagus of his daugher, Umi. Across the street, on the left, entrance is gained to the **Kale**, or citadel, established by the Byzantines in the 6C and rebuilt by the Turks, to whom it owes its present appearance. Within its walls is a public garden from which you may enjoy a good view over the town.

Adjoining the Kale to the N is the *Museum of Contemporary Art* (adm. 10–17; Sun 9–13; closed Mon), with 20C works mainly by local artists.

The **Kuršumli Han**, located a few metres E of the citadel, is one of the finer canavanserai ever constructed. Legend dates it to the time of the emperor Justinian, but it was probably built by merchants from Dubrovnik during the Turkish era (16C). Today it hosts the *Archeološki Muzej* (adm. 9–17), with statues, reliefs, and inscriptions from Scupi and other Macedonian sites.

The **Pakrivena Čaršija** is the most characteristic street of the Turkish quarter, lined with artisans' workshops. On the left are the *Suli Han* and, immediately afterward, the *Ćifte Haman*, both built during the 15C. Across the street, in the *Bezisten* or covered market (19C), more local handicrafts can be seen. Further on is the *Kapan Han*, a small but handsome caravanserai with a central paddock and double portico.

In the neighbourhood of the ULICA PETRE GEORGIEV, a wide street laid out after the earthquake of 1963, can be seen the *Isa Begova Džamija*, a 15C mosque (left); the Sultan Murat Džamija, erected by

Murad II in 1436 (in the lane opposite, on the right); and the *Sahat-Kula*.

EXCURSIONS. There are a number of interesting monasteries in the hills around Skopje; some are rather remote, but all are worth visiting.

The ***Monastery of Sv. Pantelejmon** (5km SW, near the village of Nerezi; adm. 10–15) was founded in 1164 by Alessio Comneno, a prince of the Byzantine imperial dynasty. Little remains of the conventual buildings, but the church, built to a Greek Cross plan with a large, central cupola and four smaller cupolas in the corners, contains superb frescoes, among the finest in Macedonia, executed in the 12C by an artist from Constantinople. They express a delicacy and a human quality that is rare in Byzantine painting. The subjects are: on the W wall, Dormition of the Virgin and, below, Birth of Christ; on the N wall of the naos, Passion scenes; on the S wall, Resurrection of Lazarus, Presentation of Christ at the Temple, and Transfiguration; in the apse, Saints, Communion of the Apostles, and Madonna and Child; in the cupola, Pantokrator. In the narthex are an image of St. Michael obtained by reworking a Roman bas-relief, and more fresco fragments. An inscription on the entrance door to the naos commemorates the foundation of the church.

The ***Monastery of Sv. Nikita** (14km NW) lies near *Čučer*, a pleasant village of white-washed houses on the slopes of the Crna Gora (Black Mountain). It was built in the early 14C by the Serbian king Milutin, on the site of an earlier convent, and has been destroyed and restored several times. The church, at the centre of a walled paddock, is a small, austere building in alternating bands of brick and stone, of the Serbian Byzantine type with apsidated naos and a single, central cupola. The frescoes of the interior are the work of the painters Mihajlo and Eutihije, who also executed the paintings in Sv. Kliment in Ohrid and Staro Nagoričane near Kumanovo, and who may have worked in Salonika, Constantinople, and on Mt Athos, as well. In the naos, on three levels, saints, Serbian Kings, and the life and Miracles of Christ; in the apse, Celestial Hierarchies, Communion of the Apostles, Theotokos (Mother of God). On the entrance, Dormition of the Virgin, on the left wall, St. Nicholas, and on the right, Marriage at Cana.

Matka Monastery (16km SW, just off the Tetovo road) is situated amidst thick forests in the austere valley of the Treska, near the village of Saraj. The church, dedicated to the Virgin, is a small, 14C edifice adorned with frescoes of 1497.

A little farther up the valley (c 1km), the River Treska has been dammed at the entrance to a deep gorge, forming an artificial lake on the banks of which lies the **Monastery of Sv. Andrija** (or Andrejaš), of which all that remains is an elegant little church with three apses and a cupola on pendentives. The monastery was founded by Andrej, second son of King Vukašin, in 1389 (the year of the Battle of Kosovo), and is named after his patron saint. The frescoes, by the painters Jovan and Grigorije, represent Saints and Passion scenes.

*Markov Monastery (22km SE) is splendidly situated amidst thick forests in the valley of the Markova Reka. The church, dedicated to Sv. Dimitrije, was begun in 1345 by King Vukašin, and was finished by his son, King Marko Kraljević. It is made of the customary bands of brick and stone. The façade is preceded by a portico (an unusual feature), and the central cupola springs from four immense columns. The frescoes inside are the work of two artists, or two groups of artists, one of which is thought to have worked in the time of Vukašin, the other in the reign of Marko Kraljevič. Their subjects include: in the lower half, Christian emperors, biblical kings, angels, and scenes illustrating the Acatist Hymn (in honour of the Virgin, saviour of Byzantium); on the upper level, scenes of the life and Passion of Christ. The church is surrounded by simple conventual buildings and enclosed by sturdy walls, with an imposing gate. The outbuildings include a cellar, where brandy is made, and a very old water mill.

IV BOSNIA-HERCEGOVINA

Bosnia-Hercegovina, although it covers only 51,000km² (20 per cent of Yugoslavia's total area), is a highly diversified region combining Islamic and Christian, Central European and Mediterranean traditions. Because of its splendid scenery, unusual cultural and historical monuments, and outstanding sports facilities (notably the winter-sports centres around Sarajevo, which hosted the 14th Winter Olympic Games in 1984) it is rightly considered an attractive area for visitors.

The name *Bosna* is the first mentioned in the 10C writings of the Byzantine emperor, Constantine Porphyrogenitus, to describe an independent region on an equal footing with Raška (Serbia) and Croatia. The neighbouring region of *Hum* or *Zahumlje*, later Herzegovina, was jointed to Bosnia in the early Middle Ages. Today Bosnia-Hercegovina counts about 4,124,000 inhabitants, 40 per cent of whom are Muslims, 32 per cent Serbs, 18 per cent Croats, 8 per cent 'Yugoslavs', and 2 per cent people of other nationalities. The largest city and the political, economic, and cultural centre of the republic is Sarajevo with a population of 449,000. Other important cities are Banja Luka, Mostar, Tuzla, Zenica, Bihač, Doboj, Jajce, Travnik, and Trebinje.

Considerable areas—around two-and-a-half million hectares—are covered by forest and woodland. Only about 8 per cent of the region is less than 150m above sea level, the average height being 693m. The highest peak is Mt Maglić (2386m). Climatically, Bosnia-Hercegovina is divided into a southern, Mediterranean zone and a northern, continental one. These are separated by he lofty Dinaric Alps, which also divide the region into two watersheds—the Adriatic and the Black Sea. Except for the Neretva, which reaches the coast between Dubrovnik and Split, the largest rivers—the Sana, Una, Bosna, Vrbas, and Drina—belong to the latter. The Trebišnjica, Europe's longest subterranean river, rises again as the Dubrovačka near Dubrovnik. There are a number of mountain lakes (Treskavica, Zelengora) and several artificial lakes (the largest of which are Jablaničko on the River Neretva, Višegradsko on the Drina, and Bilečko on the Trebišnjica).

Of the 3500 species of flora that grow in the region, some—like the Pančić Spruce, a relic of the Tertiary Period—are very rare.

An extremely underdeveloped, agrarian region, Bosnia-Hercegovina has always been a problem area for economic planners. Also, one fourth of the population lost their lives in the Second World War, 130 of the region's 180 industries were destroyed, all 36 mines were dismantled, and the road and rail networks were demolished during the Nazi and Fascist retreats. In the post-war period industrial production has increased about 22 times and the per capita income has quadrupled; yet in 1983 Bosnia-Hercegovina's share in the Yugoslav national income was only around 13 per cent.

27 Zagreb to Sarajevo

ROAD, 426km. Highways N1/E70, N16/E661, N16–N5?E761, N16–2 and and N17–E73.—128km *Bosanska Gradiška.*—49km *Banja Luka.*—77km **Jajce.**—72km *Travnik.*—24km *Kaonik.*—76km **Sarajevo.**

RAILWAY, via Bosanski Novi and Doboj in c 7 hours.

For the traveller arriving from the N, this route provides the first glimpse of Bosnia, an Oriental land of mosques and minarets, men with fezes and women wrapped in complicated, colourful robes. The contrast with Croatia is all the greater because it is unexpected: it comes as a surprise to find the Middle East just across the Sava. The landscape of Bosnia, an unending succession of green mountains and narrow valleys, is also impressive; as is the art, which finds its highest expression in the capital, Sarajevo, the most beautiful Ottoman city in the Balkans.

Zagreb, see Rte 23. The Fraternity and Unity Motorway (N1/E70) cuts swiftly across the Posavina region to (117km) *Okučani junction*. Leave the motorway and turn S on Highway N16.

11km **Bosanska Gradiška** (120m, 7000 inhab.), on the site of the Roman *Servitium*, was held by the Turks from 1537 until 1878, except for three brief intervals (1688–92, 1716–41, and 1789–97). It was one of the more formidable Turkish strongholds in the Balkans; now it is the administrative centre of the *Bosanska Posavina* district and an important port for river traffic on the Sava. The old mills built on rafts in the river are characteristic of the region.

The road touches upon several villages, notably *Laktaši*, with warm (30°C) mineral springs.

49km **Banja Luka** (163m, 130,000 inhab.) is the main industrial and cultural centre of the *Bosanska Krajina*, the northern region of Bosnia traversed by the Vrbas river, on which the town is situated. Originally perhaps a Roman fortification, it was an important stronghold of the medieval kings of Bosnia; in 1528 it fell to the Turks and became the capital of the pashas of Bosnia, who built palaces, baths, and mosques. The new town dates largely from the Austrian period, 1878–1918. Banja Luka was severely damaged by earthquake in 1969 and has been extensively rebuilt. The most noteworthy of the surviving monuments is the *Ferdahija Džamija, a beautiful large mosque built in 1579. At the centre of the inner court the *shadrvan* is surrounded by the *türbe* of the founder (1587), his standard-bearer, and a certain Safi Kuduna (early 17C). To the right of the mosque is the *sahat kula*. On high ground stands the fortress, called the **Kastel**, built in the 16C. To the N, in the Sose Mazara, can be seen another mosque, the **Arnaudija Džamija**, commissioned in 1587 by the Treasurer of Bosnia, Effendi Hausan.

On the outskirts of Banja Luka is another spa, *Gornji Šeher*, with sulphoric waters. **Mt Kozara National Park**, also in the vicinity, can be reached by following the Prijedor road to (54km) *Kozarac*.

Just beyond Banja Luka the road enters the spectacular *Vrbas Gorge, a wild, narrow canyon guarded by ruined castles.

77km **Jajce** (379m, 45,000 inhab.) is a picturesque Oriental town situated amidst the wooded mountains of central Bosnia, at the confluence of the Vrbas and the Pliva.

History. The town stands on a site inhabited in prehistoric times and colonised by the Romans. It is documented for the first time in the 13C, when it was fortified by Htvoje Vukčić Hrvatinić, whose underground sepulchre is referred to locally as the 'catacomb'. Later it became the capital of the Kingdom of Bosnia and witnessed the crowning (1461) and execution of the last king, Stjepan Tomašević. Jajce fell to the Turks in 1463, but was retaken in the same year by the Hungaro-Croat king Matijas Korvin. Being the most important Christian fortress after Belgrade, it held out against the assaults of the Turks until 1528. Thereafter it became a loyal Ottoman city, its inhabitants putting up a fierce resistance against the Austrians in 1878. Jajce also holds a special place in modern Yugoslav history, as the site of the second session of the Antifascist Council of National Liberation (29 November 1943), which laid the foundations of the modern Federal Republic.

The more ancient monuments include the remains of a **Roman Castrum** with a 4C Mythraic Temple, at the W end of the town (adm. 10–1 and 16–18); the cylindrical **Medvjed Tower**, guarding the old (14C) city gate; and a Romanesque bell tower that probably belonged to the destroyed church of St Luke. The main street, the TITO ULICA, leads past more fortifications and a mosque of 1753, the *Sultani Džamija*. In the PLIVSKA KAPLJA, a small square at the E end of the town, stands the **Travnik Gate**, with a Turkish fountain, between the 18C houses of the *Musafir Han*. The **Castle**, a rectangular fortress with imposing corner towers, stands at the centre of a colourful *Turkish quarter; it dates from the 15C. In the ULICA LOLE RIBARA is the *Museum of the Second Session of the Antifascist Council of National Liberation*, with historical documents regarding the formation of the Federal Republic of Yugoslavia. Across from the museum is a viewpoint overlooking the 38m cascade with which the Pliva plunges into the Vrbas.

EXCURSIONS. To the **Plitvice Lakes** (Rte 8), 198km NW by Highway 5, a mountain road. Plenty of time and some careful driving are needed.

5km, left, the *Plivsko jezero*, two small lakes on the Pliva, are famous for their old wooden water-mills.

Beyond the village of *Jezero* the road climbs out of the valley and enters a region of pastureland, with horses, sheep, and cattle.

22km **Mrkonjić Grad** (591m), stands at the crossing of old roads from Dalmatia and Panonia. It preserves a mosque, a seraglio, and some other Turkish buildings.

36km **Ključ** is a large, modern town on the River Sana.

39km **Bosanski Petrovac** (669m) is known for its Oriental rugs. Here a turning (right) winds S to *Drvar*, now Titov Drvar, near which is the cave that served as Marshal Tito's headquarters in the first half of 1944. The road continues across a wild plain.

53km **Bihać** (227m) stands on the border between Bosnia-Hercegovina and Croatia, in a picturesque position on the River Una, overlooked by the remains of a Turkish fortress of the 16C. Also interesting is the *Fetija Džamija* (Victory Mosque), situated in a former Franciscan church, where in 1942 the first session of the Antifascist Council of National Liberation was held (museum).

31km Highway 5 joins Highway 11–13 from Zagreb. Turn left to (12km) **Plitvice**, Rte 8.

Leave Jajce by Highway N16–N5/E761, which follows the Vrbas SE through a narrow gorge. The road passes several old hamlets, notably *Vinac*, with ruins of a Turkish fortress.

35km **Donji Vakuf** (514m, 2000 inhab.) has an ancient stone bridge and a clock tower, monuments characteristic of many Turkish towns. Be careful here to follow the signs for Travnik and Sarajevo.

Highway N16 continues S to *Bugojno* (12km), where it divides into two parts: N16, leading SW to **Split**; and N16–2 SE to *Jablanica* on the Mostar–Sarajevo road, Rte 28.

The road climbs to the Komar pass (with fine views) and then descends the Lašva valley. At the village of *Turbe* some Byzantine and Bosniac ruins have been excavated, but they are of interest only to specialists.

37km **Travnik** (515m, 13,000 inhab.), a busy town at the foot of Mt Vlašić (1943m) was for many centuries the seat of the Bosnian Vezirs. It preserves numerous buildings from the Turkish period, notably the *Hadži Ali Bej* and *Sulejmanija Mosques* (respectively 18C and 19C), a clock tower, a covered market (1757), a fountain, and several tombs. Here also are the home of writer Ivo Andrić (whose *Bridge on the Drina* won the Nobel Prize for literature in 1961), today a *Museum* (adm. 9–12 and 15–19) and an interesting *Natural History Museum* (Trg Republike; same hours).

33km *Kaonik*. The road is joined by Highway N17/E73 from *Zenica* (9km), an important industrial centre situated in a coal-rich region. Zenica is the Roman *Bistua Nova*, and preserves ruins of an early Christian basilica.

N17/E73 continues N to join the main Zagreb-Belgrade road near **Slavonski Brod** (158km). Along this beautiful but tortuous mountain road are:
Maglaj (61km), a picturesque town at the foot of Mt Orzen (917m), overlooked by the ruins of a 16C castle and preserving numerous mosques, notably the *Kuršumli Džamija*.
Doboj (26km), a farming town, at the confluence of the Spreča and the Bosna, overlooked by the imposing ruins of a 13C *Castle* fortified by the Turks, who held it from 1503 until 1687. In the nearby town of **Tešanj** (17km), with a 16C fortress, are the *Ferhadija Mosque* of 1564 with the tomb of the founder (1568); and an Orthodox church with icons and other paintings of the 16–19C.

33km **Visoko**, turning for *Kiseljak* (13km), with cold mineral springs, a favorite excursion point of inhabitants of Sarajevo. Nearby, at *Kreševo*, the local iron handicrafts are interesting.

25km **Ilidža** (490m) is a small spa in pleasant surroundings with some Roman ruins and, near the source of the Bosna river in a park planted with plane-trees, a Turkish Bridge.

8km **SARAJEVO** (531m, 500,000 inhab.), the capital of Bosnia-Hercegovina, is one of the lovelier cities of the Balkans. It lies at the center of a vast, wild highland, along the banks of the small River Miljacka, at the point where the latter flows out of a narrow gorge and into a wide valley. All around are high hills, culminating in Mt Trebević (1620m) on the S and Mt Ozren (1532m) on the N. The town's considerable charm is due in large part to its harmonious mixture of Turkish, Austrian, and modern influences, an authentic mingling of East and West.

Post Office: 8 Obala Vojvode Stepe.

Information: *Turist information center*, 50 Ulica JNA, tel. 25151.

Airport: At Butmir, 12km SW, tel. 41844—*JAT* 4 Ulica Vase Miskina, tel. 517600.

History. The area in which Sarajevo lies was inhabited from prehistoric times by Illyrian tribes; after the Roman conquest and a brief Byzantine interlude it was colonised by the Slavs, who erected a castle, Vrh Bosna, on the hill to the E of the present town. This fell in 1428 to the Turks, from whose seraglio the city takes its name (Sarajevo means 'palace in the fields'). From 1451 to 1553 Sarajevo was the residence de juris of the Turkish Viziers, although in reality it was ruled by native Slavs who had been converted to Islam: the Pasha of Bosnia, in fact, was not allowed to stay more than one night in the city, and the province was administered from Travnik, some 100km away.
Sarajevo's singular political order and its central situation at the crossroads of the main routes through Bosnia made it a prosperous and even luxurious place during the Ottoman period; when in 1878 Bosnia was assigned to Austria by the Treaty of Berlin (1878) the change was unwelcome and met with stern resistance. Hatred of the Austrians increased steadily, fed by South Slav nationalistic fervour. On 28 June 1914, a young Bosnian Serb named Princip, formerly a student at Sarajevo, assassinated the Austrian heir apparent, Archduke Franz Ferdinand, and his wife during a state visit to the Bosnian capital, setting in motion the chain of events that led to the First World War.

The old and new quarters of Sarajevo come together in the large, busy TRG OSLOBODJENJA. The square is planted as a public garden and surrounded by 19C buildings, the most notable of which are the **Orthodox Cathedral** (1872) and the **Umjetnička galerija** (entrance at 38 Ulica JNA, adm. 9–13 and 16–19; closed Sun pm and Mon), containing icons of the 14–19C and modern works by local artists.

From the N side of the square ULICA VASE MISKINA, perhaps the most typically Austrian street of the old town, leads E past (left) the

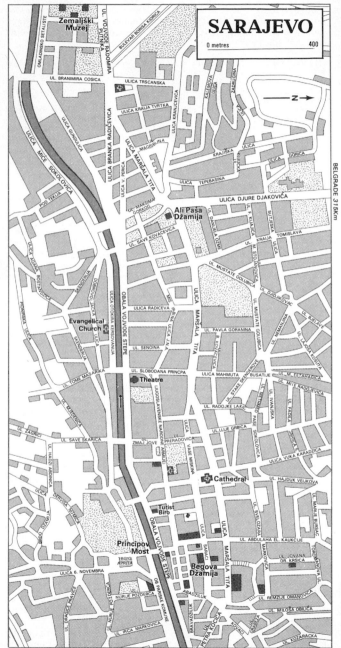

neo-Gothic **Catholic Cathedral**, built in 1889 on the site of a 12C church; and, further on (right) the **Ferhadija džamija**, a mosque erected in 1562 by order of Beg Ferhat. The interior decorations date from the 18C.

At the next corner Ulica Vase Miskina changes its name and its character, becoming ULICA SARAĆI ('Sadlers' Street') and entering a picturesque quarter of Turkish shops. Immediately on the right is the **Gazi Husrevbegov bezistan**, a covered market measuring 106m by 20m, built in 1537–55. Across the street stands the **Sahat-kula**, a clock tower of the 17C, one of the best preserved in Yugoslavia: the characters on the clock-face are in Arabic letters, which is very unusual. Next door is an old *imaret*, a charitable institution that served meals for the poor.

Sarajevo, the old city

The ****Begova džamija**, the finest in Sarajevo, was built in 1531 for the enlightened governor of Bosnia, Gazi Husref. The yard in front of it is planted with trees which shade a *shadrvan* (along one side of the yard are smaller, covered fountains for winter ablutions with warm water); and two *turbehs*, that of the founder (1530) and that of the first administrator of the mosque (1544). The interior, preceded by a graceful portico with domed roof and ogival arches on slim marble columns, has a distinctly mystical air. It combines austere architectural lines with refined decoration (mainly of the 19C); it is crowned by a flattened dome on an octagonal drum, with smaller half-domes all around. On the right is the tall *minbar*; on the end wall, oriented toward Mecca, the *mihrab*. The floor is covered with rose-coloured carpets, all gifts from Arab heads of state.

Across the street from the mosque stands the *Kuršumlija-madrasa**, also founded by Gazi Husref. Built in 1537 in the style of the Muslim schools of Istanbul, it derives its name from the lead plates that cover its roof and many cupolas (*kuršum* means 'lead' in Turkish).

At its E end the Ulica Saraci terminates in a small square before the *Baščaršija Džamija* (1550), which gives its name to a pictureque Turkish neighbourhood of narrow streets and old wooden houses. In accordance with Middle Eastern custom, each street of the crowded, lively **Baščaršija** quarter is devoted to a particular craft or family of crafts: to the N of the mosque, for instance, lies the Kazandžijska ulica, the street of coppersmiths, who still work diligently in dark, cramped shops. Just S of the square stands the **Brusa Bezistan**, a covered market built in 1551 by command of the grand vizier Rustem Paša (a relation of Sultan Suleiman I). Here silks and brocades from Brusa in Asia Minor were once sold; today it is a souvenir market. To the E, in the Halaci, are two buildings once used as warehouses: the Daira, now a restaurant, and the Dubrovačka magaza.

Just on the N side of the Baščarsija is the *Ćekrečki Džamija*, a mosque of 1545; from here OMANOVIĆA ULICA leads to the *Hadži Sinanova tekija**, a former Dervish convent built in 1640 by the wealthy merchant Hadži Sinan and several times restored. It served the rituals of the order of the Kaderi. In the courtyard, Arabic inscriptions of passages from the Koran; against the portico, two rare Turkish 'chronograms', poetic compositions carved in calligraphic characters, of 1709 and 1774.

The **Svrzo House** (6 Kršića ulica, a branch of the Municipal Museum; one ticket gives entrance to both) is an outstanding example of 16C Turkish domestic architecture. Its rooms are furnished much as they used to be and give a good idea of life for the affluent under the old regime. They also show the organisation of a Turkish household with the various divisions between the selamlik and the harem, the receptions room, etc.

In this same part of town is the *Muzej grada Sarajeva** (Municipal Museum of Sarajevo, adm. 9–14, closed Sun), situated in a late 19C Moorish building at 31 Omanovića ulica. The Atrium holds archaeological finds from the Neolithic Age to Roman times, from Sarajevo and its environs. On the ground floor and the floor above are exhibits regarding the Turkish period, mainly costumes, weapons, tools, carpets, Arabic manuscripts, books, and icons ranging from the 15C to the late 19C.

South of the museum, in ULICA MARŠALA TITA, is the old **Orthodox Cathedral**, a tiny 16C building, dedicated to the Holy Archangels, which the Turks allowed to remain active provided it was invisible to the eyes of the faithful. The church was therefore surrounded by a high wall, one side of which still stands. The smoke-darkened interior, with wooden stalls, galleries, and carved iconostasis, possesses an extraordinary atmosphere of peace and spirituality.

In the adjoining Crvena Daira is the **Cathedral Museum**, with 16–18C icons of the Cretan, Russian, and Serbian Schools, illuminated manuscripts, and parts of the antique iconostasis of the cathedral (16–17C).

Across the street stands the **Morića han**, a 16–17C seraglio recently restored as a restaurant. Further on, on the same side, is the former synagogue, established in the 16C but rebuilt several times since, most recently in the 19C. It now houses the *Jewish Museum*, with documents and objects regarding the history of the largely Sephardic

Jewish community in Bosnia. The following tract of Ulica Maršala Tita is lined with fine Secession Style houses constructed around the turn of the century.

There are several other interesting sights at this end of the city. E of the Baščaršija quarter, the **Muzej revolucije** (Museum of the Revolution; adm. 9–13 and 16–18, Sat and Sun 9–13; closed Fri) and **National Library** are housed in the Town Hall, a large ostentatious building in the Spanish-Moorish style. Here Franz Ferdinand received an address of welcome on his last day.

The **Castle** is reached from the Baščaršija by following KOVAČI ULICA, lined with Turkish houses, mostly in wood, with projecting upper floors; the road climbs past some old Turkish cemeteries with curious inscribed stelae surmounted by stone turbans. The castle, built by the Turks in the 15C but much altered in subsequent centuries, is now a barracks. It preserves the original gates and ramparts. The area round and beneath it is a largely Muslim neighbourhood; it has some of the city's more beautiful Turkish houses, in luxuriant gardens. It is especially colourful on market days (Friday and Sunday).

On the left bank of the river is the only other mosque of special note in the old town, the **Careva džamija (Imperial Mosque), built in 1566 by order of Suleiman the Great, on the site of the first Islamic chapel of Sarajevo, established in 1450 but destroyed by fire 30 years later. Across the street is a building which contains Husref Beg's library, with numerous illuminated manuscripts; and a *haman* coeval to the mosque. Behind the mosque stands the old *Konak*, the former palace of the Turkish governors, rebuilt in 1869 and now the seat of the National Assembly of Bosnia-Hercegovina.

Just a few metres W of Careva džamija the Miljacka is crossed by the **Principov most**, a bridge of 1565, rebuilt in 1797. Once called the Latin Bridge because it led to the Catholic quarter, it was given its present name after the assassination of Archduke Franz Ferdinand, which took place near the N end. Here, in the house before which the fact occurred (36 Obala Vojvode Stepe), is the **Muzej Mlade Bosne** (*Young Bosnia Museum*, adm. 9–13, Sun 9–13; closed Sat), devoted to the clandestine movement for Serbian and Bosnian independence. The collection includes some rather macabre items, such as Princip's waistcoat.

Further on, at the corner of OGNJENA ULICA and OBALA VOJVODE STEPE is the *Despić House* (an extension of the Municipal Museum, with the same hours of adm.), an example of 18C domestic architecture, restored and furnished in the late 19C in accordance with the tastes of the time.

The principal sight in the modern town is the **Pašma džamija, built by order of Hadim Ali Paša in the late 16C, the high period of Ottoman architecture. Romantically concealed among the trees in the W part of Ulica Maršala Tita, it is a masterpiece of Muslim architecture. It is preceded by a portico with four columns covered by three small domes; around it is the old Turkish cemetery with a mausoleum. Just beyond, the Executive Committee of the Government of Bosnia-Hercegovina occupies the old palace of the Turkish governor.

The **Zemaljski muzej** (National Museum; adm. Wed, Thurs, Fri 9–13 and 16–19; Tues, Sat and Sun 9–13; closed Mon) occupies a building at 7 Vojvode Putnika, in a garden containing antique architectural fragments, sarcophagi, and Bogomil stelae. Within, the

collections are displayed on two floors. Ground Floor and First Floor
left: Palaeolithic, Neolithic, and Eneolithic finds, Bronze and Iron Age
objects. Ground Floor right and First Floor: Illyrian and Roman
mosaics, inscriptions, altars, sarcophagi, sculpture, and milestones.
First Floor right: Medieval decorative objects in metal from the
9–12C, ceramics, 11–13C reliefs, coins, 14C arms and armour,
tombstones, and sculptural fragments from Bobovac Castle (15C).

EXCURSIONS. To **Mt Trebević**, 1629m. Cableway, in 12 minutes to 1127m,
then by foot to the summit, where there is a broad view over the city and
surrounding hills. At the foot of the mountain extends the gipsy quarter of
Dajanli Osmanbeg, where wooden houses cling on the slopes at impossible
angles, and the streets are little more than dirt paths.

28 Belgrade to Sarajevo and Dubrovnik

ROAD, 612km. Highways N1/E70, 21, 19/E762, 17/E73, and
2/E65.—84km *Šabac*.—53km *Loznica*.—26km *Zvornik*.—47km
Vlasenica.—110km **Sarajevo**.—62km *Konjic*.—22km *Jablanica*.—
52km **Mostar**.—36km *Počitelj*.—26km *Opuzen*.—94km **Dubrovnik**.

RAILWAY from Belgrade to Sarajevo via Ruma, Vinkovci, and Doboj
in c 6 hours; from Sarajevo to **Kardeljevo**, on the Adriatic coast, in c
2½ hours more; from Kardeljevo to **Dubrovnik** by bus in 2–3 hours.

This route, which links the capitals of Serbia and Bosnia with the
chief centre of the Adriatic coast, crosses some of the wilder, more
mountainous countryside in Yugoslavia—which means slow going,
both by road and by rail. There is little to see in the way of
monuments until one reaches the environs of Sarajevo; but from the
Bosnian capital (itself a lovely place, described in Rte 27) to the coast
the region reveals many interesting traces of Turkish occupation.
Indeed, it is here that some of the more famous Turkish monuments
in the Balkans, such as the well-known bridge at Mostar, are to be
found. Also worthy of attention are the Bogomil tombs of Stolac,
vestiges of the brief mystical life of an ancient Christian sect.

Belgrade, see Rte 25. Leave the capital by the Zagreb motorway
(Highway N1/E70). The road passes the airport and proceeds straight
across the Vojvodina plain—55km exit S on Highway N21, which
winds amidst orchards and Hungarian-type villages.

29km **Šabac** (80m, 30,000 inhab.), a market town on the right bank
of the Sava, has remains of a castle built in 1470 by Sultan Mehmet II
and controlled by the Turks until 1867. Beyond, the highway crosses
to the Drina valley, skirting the Mačva plain between the Rivers Sava
and Drina. The villages in this region begin to show typically Bosnian
features.

53km **Loznica** is a leading centre of the textile industry. Just S of the
town is a well-known spa, *Banja Koviljača*.

26km **Zvornik** (144m, 5000 inhab.), lies on the Drina, which here
forms the boundary between Serbia and Bosnia. The town, like so
many others in this area, possesses some remains of a Turkish fortress.

A road on the left winds along the valley of the Drina to *Titova Užice* (129km, Rte
29).

The highway proceeds in a series of tight curves through forested
hills, passing *Drinjača*, on an artificial lake formed by a widening of
the Drina.

47km **Vlasenica**, a village set amidst high mountains and dark
forests, was a centre of partisan resistance in the Second World War.
The Javor Massif (1537m), to the S, is known for its bear and chamois.

A turning on the right leads in c 20km to **Šekovići**, site of *Lovnica Monastery*, a 14C foundation with a 16C church containing interesting frescoes and a coeval iconostasis with paintings by a monk called Longino.

110km **SARAJEVO**, see Rte 27. Just outside the city are the hot mineral springs of *Ilidža*, beyond which the Mostar road, Highway N17/E73, climbs in a series of sharp curves to the Ivan Sedlo Pass (967m), on a spur of *Mt Plesevac* (1605m), the natural boundary between Bosnia and Hercegovina and the watershed between the Adriatic and the Black Sea: to the N springs the Bosna, whose waters, via the Sava and the Danube, flow into the Black Sea; to the S the Neretva, which flows into the Adriatic. As the road descends the W slope of the mountain the climate and vegetation change noticeably.

62km **Konjic** (280m, 3000 inhab.), on the upper Neretva, was once a watering place for caravans directed toward the Adriatic coast. The old stone bridge, built by the Turks in 1682, was destroyed in the Second World War and has been replaced by a modern one. Just W of Konjic extends the *Jablaničko jezero*, a lake, 30km long and 2km wide, formed by a dam at the confluence of the Rama and the Neretva (bathing, boating, fishing on the lake; hunting reserves nearby with the highest concentration of chamois in Europe; mountain climbing and skiing on Mts Čvrsnica and Prenj).

On the other side of Mt Prenj, about 20km from Konjic, lies the small *Boračko jezero*, another good trout-fishing spot somewhat marred by the presence of modern hotels.

22km *Jablanica* (192m, 10,000 inhab.) is a new town surrounded by jagged peaks, culminating in Mt Pločno (2228m). On the Neretva are the remains of a bridge (now a monument) blown up in 1943 by Tito's Partisans to cover their retreat.

From Jablanica a difficult but scenic road twists and turns across the Bosnian hills to **Jajce** (112km, Rte 27). *Prozor* (32km), whose name means 'window', stands at the point where the narrow Rama Valley opens into the uplands. Here the still-visible signs of the last war—burnt-out tanks and slogans painted on walls (*Viva Italia. Viva il Duce. Vinceremo.*)—create an eery sense of timelessness.— The road climbs up to the Makljen Pass, with a simple monument to the Partisans, then descends to the Vrbas valley, passing through *Gornji Vakuf* (24km), *Bugojno* (19km), and *Donji Vakuf* (12km), continuing on through forested valleys to Jajce.

Beyond Jablanica the road and railway twist down the austere Neretva Gorge, a white karst wilderness of unusual beauty, 40km long and up to 1200 deep. Like other parts of Bosnia-Hercegovina, it is inhabited by the *poskok*—a deadly viper (*Vipera ammodites*) also known as the Sand or Longnosed viper and easily recognised by the upright scaly projection on the tip of its snout and the dark zig-zag stripe on silver-grey background on its back. It conveniently warns one of its presence by a loud hiss.

43km **MOSTAR** (59m; 110,000 inhab.), capital of Hercegovina, is a town of Oriental aspect, surely one of the more beautiful Turkish cities of Yugoslavia. It lies on the Neretva, at the centre of a plateau surrounded by high, barren mountains.

Post Office: 24 Moše Pijade.

Information: Hetmostarist, 7 Lacina, tel. 54675; Kujundziluk, tel. 22690.

Airport: 5km S; tel. 907-697; JAT, Braće Fejića 2, tel. 53-248.

History. Mostar was the capital of a Roman province called Andetrium; the present name (*Stari Most*, 'old bridge') appeared around the middle of the 15C, after the Turkish conquest. At that time the city was the splendid capital of the Sandzak of Hercegovina. In 1777 it became the seat of an Orthodox eparchy; in 1878 it passed from the Turks to the Austrians.

Most of the old town with its 17 mosques lies on the left bank of the
Neretva. BRAĆE FEJIĆA ULICA runs N–S parallel to the Neretva. At the
N end, on the right, is the *Roznamedžijina džamija*, a mosque of 1620,
now an art gallery. Further along on the same side, BIŠĆEVIĆA ULICA
leads down to the Neretva. Here are to be seen several fine Turkish
houses, of which the most noteworthy is No. 13, the *Bišćevića House* of
1635, with a modest ethnographical collection. The walls of these older
houses are painted different colours—originally, it is said, to distinguish them in lieu of numbers. The ***Karadjozbegova džamija**, on
the left side of the Braće Fejića ulica, is the most beautiful mosque in
Mostar. It was built in 1557. The façade is preceded by a porch and
fountain (left) for ablutions. The sanctuary, oriented toward Mecca, is
covered by an octagonal dome. The interior is finely painted with
decorative designs and verses from the Koran. The large carpets on the
floor are gifts of noble families; the smaller carpets with the arrow
designs were brought by pilgrims from Mecca.—Adjoining the
mosque are a small cemetery (men are distinguished by a turban or fez
on their tombstone; women by a hat or by a flat top); and the former
Madrasa, or Koran school, of 1570. Across the street is the mausoleum
of Djikić, a poet and national hero.

Mostar, the Stari Most on the Nereteva

*Kugundžiluk** is the name given to the S quarter of the city, almost
entirely made up of 16C Turkish houses (many with interesting cafés).
Here, in the MALA TEPA, stands the *Koski Mehmed Paša džamija*, a
mosque of 1617 with the usual portico and fountain, and a minaret
commanding an excellent *View over the town, the river, and the
surrounding hills.

From the Kujundžiluk the famous *Stari Most (old bridge), designed by the Turkish architect Hajrudin (1566), leads across the Neretva. It is thought to have replaced a Roman bridge and is remarkable in that it crosses the gorge in one span measuring 27m by 20m. The approaches to the bridge are guarded by two fortified towers dating from the 17C, the *Helebija* (where the Turkish garrison stayed) and the *Tara*.

There is a story about its construction. The first span collapsed, and the Sultan, furious, sent for the architect and warned him that, if the next one did not hold, Hajrudin would pay with his head. When at last the bridge was finished the architect was nowhere to be found; certain that it would not stand, he had fled to Bijelo Polje. The townspeople sought him out and bore him to the Sultan, by whom he was duly congratulated. Four centuries later the bridge is still standing.

On the far side of the bridge lie the small *Tabačica džamija*, a 16C mosque; and the Priuječka quarter with its Turkish bazaar, the *Priječka Čaršija*, of 1612. Further along, on the left, the *Kriva ćuprija* (crooked bridge) of 1558 crosses the Radobolja.

MARŠALA TITA ULICA is the main street on the left bank of the Neretva. On the right are the 15C *Hercegusa Tower*, the *Cejvan džamija* of 1552, and the **Muzej** (adm. 9–12, Tues and Fri 16–18; closed Mon), with collections of classical antiquities and medieval artefacts (Bogomil tombstones) and a section devoted to the revolution. Further along, on the same side, are the *Nasuh Aga Vučjaković džamija*, a Muslim sanctuary of 1564, and the **Sahat-kula** of 1664. The *Orthodox Church* of 1833, set back from the street and on higher ground, contains icons, old paintings, and a large painted iconostasis.

EXCURSIONS. To **Blagaj**, 10km SE. This pleasant town lies on the River Buna, in a spectacular setting amongst the karst hills, below the ruined 14C *Castle of Herceg Stefan*, the duke who gave his name to the region of Hercegovina. Just outside the town, near the source of the River Buna (the water bursts forth from a cave at the rate of 43,000 litres/sec.), are the remains of a Dervish monastery and a ruined mosque, both built in the 19C.

36km **Počitelj** is a well-preserved example of a Turkish walled town, with a good Mosque (1563), clock tower, a small han, and the house of the Gavran Kapetanović family.

The Turkish chronicler Evlija Ćelebija, writing in 1664, provides a description of Počitelj that is still accurate. 'The shining mosque was raised by a forebear of our lord Ibrahim-aga. Alongside the town walls, beside the water, his honoured brother built a public kitchen [imaret] which distributes free bread and soup to the inhabitants day and night. On Thursday evenings it distributes spiced meat and savoury and sweet rice. The imaret will remain as long as God wills...In the town there was an elementary religious school [mektab]. Later Lord Ibrahim built a secondary theological school [medresa] and also sent people to build public baths [hamam] and an inn [han]...The houses of the town are built one above the other, facing west towards the river. There are very many walnut trees here. Since the climate is mild fruit grows better here than in other towns.'

Počitelj is the starting point for excursions to (25km) **Stolac** (64m, 2500 inhab.), an attractive village on a rocky bluff, near which lies the **Necropolis of Radimlje** with a fascinating collection of ornamented Bogomils tombs. More of these are to be found near Zvornik and Vlasenica, near Glamoč and Bugojno, and in a roughly triangular concentration between Konjić, Lovreč, and Brotnice.

Near (3km) **Čapljina**, at the hamlet of **Mogorjelo**, are the extensive remains of a 4C fortified Roman villa and two 5C Christian basilicas, with a lapidary collection. **Gabela**, once part of the Republic of Ragusa, has a good medieval square and 16C Turkish fortifications.

11km **Metković** lies near the border of Bosnia-Hercegovina and Croatia.

10km **Opuzen** N17/E73 joins the Adriatic Highway to (94km) **Dubrovnik**, Rte 17.

Stolac, Bogomil tombstones

29   Dubrovnik to Belgrade

ROAD, 424km. Highways N2/E65, N20/E761, and N5–N22/E760.
—31km *Trebinje.*—135km **Foča.**—38km *Goražde.*—40km **Višegrad.**
—75km *Titovo Užice.*—60km *Čačak.*—133km **Belgrade.**

This route follows the ancient caravan trail used by the merchants of Dubrovnik to send their goods overland to Belgrade and Constantinople. Although it is not the usual way to reach the capital from Dubrovnik (the preferred roads go via Sarajevo or Titograd), it is the shortest and certainly the most beautiful. Between Dubrovnik and Foča the road twists and turns through the towering mountains and dense, silent forests of Hercegovina, still one of the least populated regions of Europe. Thereafter it traverses the low hills of northern Serbia to the Sava plain and Belgrade. Careful driving is necessary in the mountain areas.

Dubrovnik, see Rte 22. PUT JUGOSLAVENSKE NARODNE ARMIJE leads eastward from the city centre to the Adriatic Highway.—5km turn left onto N20/E761, which climbs rapidly up the mountains of the coastal range to enter Hercegovina.

26km **Trebinje** (276m, 5000 inhab.), situated on the River Trebišnjica, was a Turkish and Austrian military stronghold. Largely modern in appearance, it preserves several vestiges of the Turkish epoch, namely some old houses, the **Arslanagić Bridge** (1574) on the Trebišnjica, and remnants of defensive walls.

The road climbs to 600m, then descends, touching the W shore of *Bilečko jezero* (lake Bileća), formed by a dam on the Trebišnjica. All around are ruined Turkish fortresses.

30km **Bileća** (476m, 1500 inhab.) is the first of a number of small, impoverished villages which grew up as way stations on the old caravan route. Near here, in 1388, Duke Vlatko Vuković, at the head of an army of King Tvrtko of Bosnia, repelled the first Turkish incursion of the western Balkans.

The road continues to climb amidst harsh, bare mountains.

43km **Gacko** (960m, 1500 inhab.) gives its name to the marshy highland called the Gatačko Polje. In the environs are several Bogomil cemeteries.

A secondary road diverges left for (92km) **Mostar**, Rte 28. Highway 20 winds up the Vrba Valley to the watershed, 1310m, then descends in tight curves to the narrow valley of the Sutjeska.

49km **Tjentište** is a holiday centre known for its hunting, fishing, and mountain climbing. It stands at the N end of the *Sutjeska National Park*, a natural mountain stronghold, which in 1943 was the site of the Partisans' greatest battle with the forces of the Axis. The Peručica, a tributary of the Sutjeska, falls 70m here in a cascade called the *Skakavac*.

The road ascends to another pass (885m), then descends to the valley of the Drina.

23km **Foča** (355m, 7000 inhab.) lies at the confluence of the Drina and the Čehotina. An important trading centre at time of Turks, it still has a distinctly Oriental air. In the old town are several mosques, a han, a clock tower, and an interesting Muslim cemetery. The *Aladža džamija* of 1551 is one of more beautiful monuments of Ottoman architecture in Yugoslavia. The *Muzej*, housed in a former seraglio (11 JNA ulica; adm. 7–13) contains archaeological, historical, and ethnographical material, mainly of local provenance. The fishing in the Drina is excellent (salmon up to 20kg), and the local handicrafts (cutlery, silver filigree) are famous.

A little further on, in the village of *Ustikolina*, is the oldest mosque in Bosnia-Hercegovina, dating from 1464; on the Drina near *Osanića* is another Bogomil cemetery (14–15C).

At (38km) **Goražde** (345m, 3500 inhab.), a modern industrial town, the highway designation changes from N20 to N5.

A mountain road turns W to (29km) **Rogatica**, an important place during Turkish rule, near which archaeologists have discovered one of the largest prehistoric burial grounds in the world (20,000 Bronze Age and Iron Age tombs). Much of the material recovered here is displayed in the National Museum of Sarajevo.

Highway N5 winds N along the Drina, through virgin forest inhabited by bear and eagles. The river is crossed by a magnificent *Bridge 160m long, built in 1571 by the Turkish architect Minar Sinan and celebrated in the novel, *Bridge on the Drina*, by Ivo Andrić (Nobel Prize for literature, 1961). The bridge was built in fulfilment of a vow taken by Vizier Mehmed-Paša Sokolović. According to a local legend, during its construction two infants were walled in the central pier to ensure its safety, but the builder had pity on them and their mother and left spaces between the stones so that she could feed them. In memory of his compassion a thin, milky stream has flowed from these slits for many years; in the past its traces were scraped off and sold as medicinal powder to mothers who could not give milk.

40km **Višegrad** (364m, 5000 inhab.) is an attractive, largely Muslim village surrounded by evergreen forests. From here it is possible to descend the Drina by raft and canoe to Zvornik, in the company of experienced local guides. The full trip takes two days.

Višegrad, the Turkish bridge on the Drina

The road continues through a splendid region of lofty peaks and dark evergreen forests. Before the *Šargan Pass* (980m) Serbia is entered.

75km **Titovo Užice** (411m, 35,000 inhab.) is a large, prosperous town in the valley of the Djetinja, a tributary of the Zapadna Morava. Its strategic importance is underlined by the ruined Turkish citadel of *Užice* which commands the town and the surrounding countryside, and which is believed to stand on the site of a Roman castrum. The town centre is one of the more successful examples of modern urban planning in Yugoslavia. The *Museum of the 1941 Insurrection* occupies a building which was the headquarters of Josip Broz Tito's Popular Army of Liberation in the autumn of 1941. Titovo Užice is famous for its sharp buttery cheese, *kajmak*.

16km N on a mountain road lies the village of *Karan*, where the **Bela Crkva** (White Church), a Serbian Byzantine edifice of 1335, preserves splendid frescoes illustrating the life of the Virgin.

At (24km) *Požega* a turning S leads to (15km) **Arilje**, a village with a lovely, pink church in the Raška style founded by King Dragutin in 1292 and adorned with coeval frescoes of considerable interest. In the narthex, portraits of Kings Dragutin and Milutin, of the latter's wife Katelina, and of Dragutin's sons Urošić and Vladislav; a council of Stefan Nemanja; and members of the Namanjić family (notice that the founder and ruler are almost oblivious of Christ); Sacrifice of Abraham (on the E wall) and Tree of Jesse (on the W wall); in the naos, St. Achilleus (patron saint of the church), Annunciation (on the pillars), Adoration of the Sacrament, and Communion of the Apostles; in the diaconicon, life and miracles of St. Nicholas. Many of the paintings show the naturalistic elements and monumental style typical of the Raška School.

60km **Čačak** (38,000 inhab.), called *Gradac* before the arrival of the Turks, preserves traces of prehistoric and Roman settlements. Once the seat of the powerful Zupani and Rasha families, it was later incorporated into the Kingdom of Serbia. In 1459 it was conquered by the Turks, who transformed the *Bogorodica Gradačka* (Church of the Virgin Mary), erected by Stefan Nemanja's brother Straćimir, into a mosque. The *Municipal Museum* is situated in a house built in 1835 by 'Gospodar' Jovan Obrenović, the brother of Prince Miloš. There is also a Serbian konak with furniture, pictures, costumes, etc.

The Šumadija region around Čačak is famous for its peasant tombstones, called *krajputaši*, which are to be found grouped together in cemeteries, or alone in the fields and on the roadside (the name 'krajputaš' in fact means 'waysider'). Carved in sandstone and often painted in bright blues, reds, greens, and yellows, they almost always bear epitaphs in prose or verse. Krajputaši are also to be found on the Zlatibor massif S of Titovo Užice.

Leave Čačak by the Belgrade road, Highway N22/E760. After a while, the hills gradually melt into the Sava plain.

133km **Belgrade**, see Rte 25.

V MONTENEGRO AND MACEDONIA

As its name suggests, **Montenegro** (Serbo-Croatian *Crna Gora*) is a mountainous land. Of the many towering massifs that extend right down to the coast, Mt Durmitor (2522m), covered with dense beech and pine forests, holds a special place in the hearts of Montenegrins, symbolising their defiance of all invaders.

Montenegro covers an area of 13,812km², 5 per cent of Yugoslavia's total area. It has a population of 584,000, of whom 69 per cent are Montenegrins (accorded a status distinct from that of Serbs only since the Second World War), 13 per cent Muslims, 7 per cent Albanians, 5 per cent 'Yugoslavs', 3 per cent Serbs, 1 per cent Croats, and the rest persons of other nationalities.

Most of the region is mountainous, with harsh, snowy winters, but the southernmost area, along the Adriatic coast and around Lake Skadar, enjoys a mild Mediterranean climate. Crkvice (on Mt Orjen above the Gulf of Kotor) has the highest rainfall in Europe: an annual average of 4500–5000mm.

The rivers of Montenegro flow both into the Adriatic and the Black Seas. Fast, clear mountain streams, they cleave their way through the limestone rock in deep canyons. The canyon of the Tara (1300m) is second in the world in depth and length, and the Piva and Morača gorges (1200m and 1100m respectively) rank among the world's deepest. There are about 30 lakes in Montenegro, most of which are of glacial origin (the best known are Crno on Mt Durmitor, Biogradsko on Mt Bjelasica and Plavsko at the foot of Mt Visitor). Lake Skadar, which Yugoslavia shares with Albania, is the largest lake in the Balkans (391km²).

Flora and fauna are diverse and abundant. About 2800 plant species and sub-species are to be found in Montenegro, and around 80 per cent of the region is covered by forests, meadows, and mountain pastures.

The capital of Montenegro is Titograd (132,000 inhab.), formerly known as Podgorica. Other important towns include Cetinje (the old political and cultural capital), Nikšić, Pljevlja, Bijelo Polje, Ivangrad (formerly Berane), Kotor, Bar, Hercegnovi, and Ulcinj.

Traditionally an impoverished and war-torn land, Montenegro was devastated during the Second World War. The postwar period brought steady modernisation in all fields, and a particularly rapid development of industry, tourism, education, culture, and health services. Then, in 1979, Montenegro suffered a severe earthquake (9° on the Mercalli scale) which took a heavy toll of human lives, wrought widespread destruction, and brought general expansion to a halt. Rebuilding and restoration, carried out in part with international aid, are still underway.

Macedonia is another region of lofty mountains and broad plains, covering 25,713km² (11 per cent of Yugoslavia). It has 1,909,000 inhabitants—67 per cent Macedonians (like the Montenegrins, recognised as a nationality in their own right only since the war), 20 per cent Albanians, 5 per cent Turks, 2 per cent Serbs, 2 per cent Romanies, 2 per cent Muslims, 2 per cent other nationalities. Another one million ethnic Macedonians live abroad, about half of these in neighbouring countries (primarily Bulgaria and Greece) and the remainder mostly in the United States, Canada, and Australia.

The name *Macedonia* initially designated a territory inhabited by Illyrian-Thracian tribes; later it referred to the powerful state of Philip and Alexander of Macedon, and after the Roman conquest of the region in the mid 2C, it survived as a geographical term that was not always clearly defined.

A moderate continental climate prevails, except in the Vardar Valley, where Mediterranean weather is common.

Skopje, the capital and largest city, has a population of 505,000. Other important towns are Bitola (formerly known as Monastir), Prilep, Kumanovo, Tetovo, Titov Veles, Ohrid, Štip, Gostivar, and Kičevo.

In the postwar period Macedonia has experienced substantial changes in its socio-economic structure. In 1984 industry and mining contributed 39 per cent of the social product, agriculture 15 per cent, construction 10 per cent, commerce and tourism 23 per cent, transport and communications 6 per cent. Macedonia contributed 6 per cent of Yugoslavia's GNP for 1983. The region has considerable deposits of iron ore, zinc, chrome, lead, copper, nickel, manganite, gold, silver, and mercury, as well as extensive resources of non-metallic minerals—asbestos, mica, coal, and various kinds of stone, cement marl, quartz, sand, silex, magnesite, etc. In agriculture, Macedonia is notable as the only producer in Yugoslavia of cotton, rice, and early vegetables, and as a large-scale supplier of tobacco (24,000 tons annually), grapes, and various other fruit. Several large irrigation systems have been constructed serving about 20 per cent of the arable land. The most extensive is the Pelagonian Plain around Bitola and Prilep.

30 Dubrovnik to Kotor

ROAD, 97km. Highway N2/E65–E80.—27km *Čilipi.*—23km **Herceg-Novi.**—17km *Kamenari.*—12km *Risan.*—4km **Perast.**—14km **Kotor.** Frequent buses.

This route traverses some of the finest scenery on the Yugoslav coast. The area suffered considerable damage in the earthquake of 1979, and in some places, notably the old town centres, rebuilding is not yet complete. Elsewhere shiny new holiday villages have sprung up all too quickly.

From Dubrovnik to (17km) *Zvekovica,* see Rte 18. Continue straight on through the fertile valley of Konavli, passing (left) the airport of Dubrovnik. Traversing (10km) *Čilipi,* where the inhabitants wear national costume to church on Sunday, you proceed parallel with the coast to the point where the road divides on the boundary between Croatia and Montenegro. The main road branches left and runs high above the shore to Herceg-Novi (see below), whereas a byroad continues straight on to the narrow peninsula of *Prevlaka* (12km) at the mouth of the Boka Kotorska.

The ****Boka Kotorska** (Gulf of Kotor), the grandest natural feature of the Adriatic coast, is a deeply indented and irregularly-shaped fjord surrounded by steep and lofty mountains that rise ever higher towards the interior. The contrast between the intense green of the luxuriant vegetation at sea level and the denuded rock of the mountains is enhanced by the changing colours of the sea, particularly striking effects being gained in winter when the higher mountains are clothed in snow. The abrupt changes in height give the

Boka Kotorska, the Bay of Kotor

region a violent and changeable climate with an unusually heavy rainfall and frequent thunderstorms. A good road encircles the shores of the gulf (see below), but by far the finest impression of its majesty is gained from the water.

By excursion boat to Kotor. The entrance to the gulf lies between Oštri and Mirište points, from which it is a little under 20 miles to Kotor at the far end. On the E side of the fairway is the island of *Mamula*, named for General Lazar Mamula, a former Austrian governor of Dalmatia, who fortified it in 1850. During the First and Second World Wars it was used as a prison camp by the occupying forces. A mile-wide channel leads into the *Bay of Hercegnovi*, with Herceg-Novi itself visible on the far side, whence the narrow strait of *Kumborski tjesnac* (800m) gives access to the broad, triangular and apparently landlocked *Bay of Tivat*, with the town of Tivat directly ahead. As the boat proceeds, with bare limestone mountains descending in folds to the shore on either hand, it becomes apparent that in the NE corner there is an even narrower passage. The mountains part to reveal the channel of *Verige* (300m), whose name, meaning 'chain', has led to a tradition that it was once closed off by this method. Perast is seen framed in the opening ahead before the boat enters the innermost gulf, consisting of the twin bays of Risan and Kotor, which affords the most spectacular marine vistas in Europe outside Norway. The awe-inspiring heights of the Njeguši Mts rise to a climax at Mt Lovćen (1789m) behind Kotor.

In April 1941 Yugoslavs and others compromised by their work for the British were evacuated from the Gulf of Kotor in an RAF flying boat; the British Minister fell into Italian hands, and an attempt at rescue by a British submarine was beaten off by German dive-bombers.

23km **HERCEG-NOVI**, the outermost town (3800 inhab.) of the Boka Kotorska, occupies a position of romantic beauty on precipitous cliffs at the sea's edge. The town is noted for its luxuriant subtropical vegetation and is the leading resort in the Kotor region.

Post office: Njegoševa ul.

Information: *Turističko društvo Savina*, obala 4, tel. 43959.

History. *Herceg-Novi* was founded in 1382 by Stjepan I Tvrtko of Bosnia as a trading post and salt-producing centre. Its strategic position at the mouth of the gulf assured it a stormy history. In the 15C the town came into the possession of Herceg (duke) Stjepan Vukčić Kosači of Zahumlje, from whom it derives its name. The Turks conquered it in 1483, lost it temporarily to a Venetian expedition (aided by Spanish troops) in 1538, but regained it a year later under Khair-ed-din Barbarossa. In 1687 Venice finally drove out the Turks to hold the town until the republic's downfall in 1797. Hereceg-Novi was then disputed between the powers involved in the Napoleonic Wars. To the Austrians (1797–1806) succeeded Russia (1806–07), then France (1807–13), then Britian and Montenegro, both for a few months only, before in 1814 Austria gained firm possession until 1918.

Herceg-Novi comprises the old walled town at the top of the cliffs and the newer district spreading W in the direction of Igalo and down the hillside in a succession of terraces. Fortifications testify to the defensive building of various rulers. **Španjola**, the best-preserved fortress, stands high on a hill overlooking the town. Begun by the Spaniards during their brief occupation (1538), it was completed in its present form by the Turks on their return. The Turks also built the walls on the NE side of the town, including the *Kanli Kula* Bloody Tower), now ruined. In the 17–18C the Venetians completely rebuilt the *Forte Mare* on the seaward side and constructed the *Citadela*. The old town inside the walls has a typical Mediterranean air but is sadly dilapidated, the only building of interest being the Turkish *Sahat-kula* (Clock Tower; 1667), a machicolated tower guarding the main entrance. In the small square that opens inside the gate are the *Gradski Arhiv* (Town Library), with about 25,000 volumes, including a few incunabula and a good collection of works relating to the history of the Adriatic coast; and the *Zavičajni muzej* (Town Museum, adm. 8–11, 15–19). The museum has rooms illustrating the history and ethnography of the region and the National Liberation Struggle, but the most interesting room displays icons of the Boka Kotorska school (mainly 18C), notably by the Dimitrijević-Rafailović family of Risan.

About 1km E of town in a lovely sylvan setting stands the Serbian Orthodox monastery of **Savina**, reached by a minor road through pleasant groves of oak, laurel, and cypress (or by the main road and a downhill walk just before Meljine). The monastery was founded by monks fleeing from Tvrdoš near Trebinje in 1694 and takes its name from St. Sabas (Sava), the most revered saint of the Serbian Orthodox church. Petar I Petrović Njegoš, Prince-Bishop of Montenegro, stayed in Savina while attending school in Herceg-Novi. The larger of the two churches attached to the monastery, harmoniously combining baroque and Byzantine elements, was built by Nikola Foretić of Korčula (1777–79), and contains a good iconostasis by Simo Lazović of Bijelo Polje (1797). The smaller Gothic church was refurbished for monastic use in 1694; the iconostasis dates from various times in the 18C, the Royal Doors being the work of Daskal Dimitrije of Risan (1703), father of the Dimitrijević-Rafailović family of icon painters, while the icon of the Ascension is by his son, Rafailo (1750). The church now houses the TREASURY (adm. 9–12, 4–7), a good collection of work done in the Byzantine tradition set out in showcases round the walls.

The oldest piece is a crystal Cross edged with silver (1219), supposed to have belonged to St. Sava himself. Later works include an unusual silver and enamel Server (petohljebnica) made in Požarevac (1648); a silver model of the original monastery at Tvrdoš (1685); a silver thurible of similar age; two pierced silver lamps and a chalice (17C); a wooden patriarhal Cross with deep relief carvings in miniature (16C); another, bound in silver and enamel (1657); and a silver reliquary of a hand (1759); supposedly of Queen Jelena, wife of Stefan Dušan the Mighty. Vestments and frontals include a beautiful *Brocade embroidered with scenes of the Passion in silver and gold thread (1659), another design made in Russia (18C), a Greek Epitrachelion (14C?), and two 18C omophoria, one of which is embroidered with a Pietà. The LIBRARY in the main building preserves many historical manuscripts, including decrees on parchment by medieval Serbian monarchs (Stefan Dečanski, Uroš, Carica Jelena, Stefan Lazarević, etc.), the Savina krmčija, a nomocanon of the 16C, and a liturgical book (octoechos) dated 1509. Pictures here include portraits of Peter the Great and Catherine the Great of Russia and icons by painters of the Boka Kotorska school (17–18C).

Beyond Herceg-Novi the lower and upper roads join at *Meljine*—Continue along the shore to *Miočevići*, where the highway divides again, the faster road cutting through thickly wooded country higher up the hillside and the lower traversing the villages on the shore.—At (6km) *Baošići* the parish church of Sv. Nikola has an iconostasis by Aleksija Lazović (1805). A plaque indicates the house where Pierre Loti stayed in 1880; the village and the Boka Kotorska are described in his short story, 'Pascale Ivanovic', and in his diary. Beyond *Bijela* (14C frescoes in the Church of Riza Bogorodica), lies (11km) *Kamenari* whence a car ferry across the strait of Verige to Lepetane (5 minutes; comp. Rte 24) affords the fastest route to the S, linking up with the Adriatic Highway via either Tivat or Kotor.

Keeping to the W shore along the road that circles the gulf, you emerge from Verige to a breath-taking view of the inner bays of Risan and Kotor, with bare forbidding mountains rising behind. Out on the right as you turn N are the islands of Gospa od Škrpjela and Sv Djordje (comp. below); Perast is seen across the bay. Just beyond *Kostanjica* the road crosses a bridge over the *Sopt Waterfall*, an unusual feature hereabouts, which gushes from the rock 30m above sea level.

3km **Risan**, the oldest settlement in the Boka Kotorska, at the far end of the bay of Risan, is only a village (1200 inhab.).

Risan (Rhizinion) is linked by legend with the story of Cadmus and Harmonia, who, according to Appian and Euripides, went to reign over Illyria. Historically it was, at any rate, one of the chief towns of the kingdom of Illyria and for a while, under Queen Teuta, its capital. Teuta is thought to have committed suicide here after being defeated by the Romans in 299 BC. In 167 BC the town placed itself under Roman overlordship, subsequently becoming a colonia (Iulium Risinium) attached to the province of Dalmatia. Sacked by the Saracens in 865, the Illyrico-Roman city is said to have been finally destroyed by a landside or an earthquake. In the 10–14C the medieval community was ruled by various local powers and in 1451 passed to the Republic of Ragusa. The Turks occupied it from 1539 to 1687 when it passed to Venice. In Risan the Dimitrijević-Rafailović family of icon-painters was active in the 17–18C. Among many archaeologists to dig here was Sir Arthur Evans (1882–85)*.

Few traces remain of the remote days of Risan's greatness, though archaeological finds have included Greek, Illyrian, and Roman coinage and abundant fragments of Roman temples, statues, sarcophagi, as well as bronze statuettes and a 2C mosaic floor depicting the god Hynos. Some of these, within the foundations of the Illyrico-Roman city, can be seen on the hill of *Carina*, and other Roman remains are said to be visible deep in the water at the edge of the bay. The two fortresses on adjacent hills, Grkavac and Ledenice, were erected by Venice (17–18C) as a defence against the Turks.

Risan is the starting point for excursions to *Mt Orjen* (1893m), the highest mountain on the Adriatic coast, and the mountainous region of *Krivošija*. The inhabitants of Krivošija, now mostly shepherds, are noted for their fierceness and pride and achieved a certain notoriety when they raised two rebellions against Austria (1869–70 and 1881–82) and emigrated en masse to Montenegro rather than submit to military conscription.

Continuing S from Risan, pass almost immediately the Orthodox monastery of *Banja*, founded in the Middle Ages and rebuilt in 1720 after destruction by the Turks. In the treasury is an embroidered epitrachelion made for Župan Stroja Buzescu in Rumania (1606). The Iconostasis is by Petar Rafailović 1775).

4km **Perast** is an attractive Mediterranean township (500 inhab.) with a charming air of faded elegance and wealth. Because of its relatively short period of prosperity, it presents an unusually homogeneous architectural whole, almost entirely baroque in the restrained tradition characteristic of the Adriatic coast. There are few buildings of outstanding merit, but almost none that are ugly or inelegant.

Parestum is first mentioned in 1326 and later in the same century assisted the Venetians to capture its mother city, Kotor, against whom it was in constant rebellion. Both cities passed from Hungary-Croatia to Venice in 1420, and in the 16C Perast emancipated itself from Kotor to become an independent commune. It built up a large merchant fleet and for the next 200 years enjoyed prosperity. With the coming of steam it sank to the status of a large village. Throughout its history Perast was renowned for loyalty to Venice and its sailors enjoyed the distinction of guarding the republic's gonfalon (standard) in time of battle. Its strong maritime tradition began with the foundation of a shipyard as early as 1367 and a nautical school in the 16C and gained European status when Peter the Great of Russia sent 17 young noblemen here in 1698 to train for his embryo navy. Distinquished natives include Matija Zmajević (1680–1713), admiral of Peter the Great's Baltic fleet; the hydrographer, Anton Grubas (18C); and the baroque painter, Tripo Kokolja (1661–1713).

The town, strung out along the narrow strip of land between the mountains and the sea, has no distinct centre. At the N end stands its finest single building, the baroque *Palača Bujović* by G. Fonta (1694), with an open loggia on the ground floor and an immense balcony running the length of the façade above. Once the residence of the Venetian Captain, it now houses the **Zavičajni Muzej** (*Town Museum*, adm. 9.30–12 and 13–6; closed Sat and Sun; undergoing restoration following earthquake damage). Downstairs is a small lapidary collection; on the first floor the many banners include a Venetian gonfalon and the naval banner presented to Admiral Zmajević by Peter the Great. Paintings include portraits of Zmajević and V. Bujović by Tripo Kokolja, and (on the second floor) a self-portrait by Kokolja and icons by the Dimitrijević-Rafailović family of Risan. A balcony on the S side of the museum offers an excellent view over Perast.

Plaques mark the Naval School (*Nautika*) of Captain Marko Martinović just to the N and the house in which Admiral Zmajević was born to the S. Steps mount to the monumental but ruined *Biskupija*, the palace of Abp Andrija Zmajević (1670), with a fine baroque portal and open loggia (view) and damaged wall paintings by Kokolja. Adjoining is the baroque chapel of *Gospa od rozarija* (Our Lady of the Rosaries) where Zmajević lies buried (coat of arms, 15 medallions by

Kokolja), which has an octagonal baroque bell tower of great charm.
Returning to the shore you pass the house of the Cizmai family (coat of
arms) and come to the handsome *Palača Smecchina* (1760) with its
vaulted boathouse; the family chapel of Sv. Marko (1740) is ornamented with a Lion of St. Mark and statues of Christ and SS. Peter and
Paul. Beyond the former *Palača Mazarović* and the *Palača Marković*
(1622), with wrought-iron balustrade, is the small town square with
the former town hall on the NE side. The parish church of **Sv. Nikola**,
founded in the 15C, was rebuilt in its present form in the 17C, when an
ambitious new church was also begun to designs by Giuseppe Beati.
The lofty Bell Tower was completed (1691), the tallest in Montenegro
(55m), and the enormous apse of the unfinished church, abandoned
for lack of funds, stands beside the older building.

In the interior of Sv. Nikola are a baroque font and marble pulpit, the gift of Abp
Zmajević. In the TREASURY (apply to parish priest) are a large Renaissance silver
Cross of Abp Zmajević; a silver tablet depicting the Battle of Perast against the
Turks (1654); a silver-gilt chalice decorated with filigree work (18C), the gift of
Anton Bašić; a large silver censer and a cross of the order of Alexander Nevski,
both presented by Admiral Zmajević. The fine Vestments include the robes of
Abp Zmajević, and *Lace of the 16–19C. An Oriental silk canopy may have come
from the tent of Mehmed-aga Rizvanagić, leader of a Turkish attack on Perast, or
have been taken in the Candian War. The bronze bust of Kikolja in front of the
church is by Vanja Radauš, a Croatian sculptor.

Steps left of the bell tower ascend to the abandoned fortress of *Sv. Križ* (view
over the Boka Kotorska), built by the Venetians c 1600. The neighbouring small
church of *Sv. Ana* has a mural painting by Kokolja.

The main street leads S from the town square parallel with the
water-front and is lined with mansions of former captains and ship
owners. On the right, the *Palača Visković* (1718) has a baroque portal
and loggia and a small private museum (portraits, weapons). Adjacent stands the baroque *Palača Krilović*. Opposite are two similar
mansions, of which the farther one is the large *Palača Balović*. A
second mansion of the Krilović family stands further down on the left,
and at the far end of the street is the complex *Palača Bašić* with a relief
of the Annunciaton (1507) built into the façade. The coast road, built
by the Austrians during the 19C, leads back to the town, affording a
view of the mansions as they originally looked from the sea.

Offshore two small islands can be reached in about 5 minutes by local boat. **Sv.
Djordje** (St. George) a picturesque cypress-clad island, had a Benedictine abbey
as early as the 12C but was plundered by the Turks and suffered heavily in an
earthquake in 1667. The church, reconstructed in 1914, preserves dozens of
memorial slabs engraved with the arms of Perast nobles and sea captains. The
fortifications are mainly French and Austrian.
    The artificial island of **Gospa od Škrpjela** was built in 1452 on an underwater
reef. The manner of construction is commemorated each year on 22 July by the
'Fašinda', when a gaily decorated procession of boats arrives from Perast to
deposit stones around the island to the accompaniment of folk songs (national
dress is now a rare occurrence). The present baroque church of *Gospa od
Škrpjela* (1630) was enlarged in 1720–25 by the addition of an octagonal
presbytery with a cupola. The *Interior, both walls and ceiling, is covered by 68
paintings on wood and canvas by Tripo Kokolja. This, his magnum opus,
accomplished under the direction of Abp Zmajević during the last 15–20 years of
the 17C, makes an overwhelming first impression. Greater famililiarity reveals
that the lower band of paintings around the walls, devoted to scenes from the
Old Testament, is considerably inferior to the four large canvases above (Christ
in the Temple, Descent of the Holy Ghost, Dormition of the Virgin and
Coronation of the Virgin), and these in turn are surpassed by the exuberantly
painted ceiling. A multiplicity of New Testament scenes, interspersed with still
lifes, are divided by a network of moulded and gilt frames and culminate in the
centre in a monumental Ascension of the Virgin. Between the upper and lower
paintings is a band of 2500 little notice plaques. Donated by sailors during the

past three centuries, they are engraved with portraits, realistic scenes of Perast life, heraldic emblems and, above all, ships. The Icon of the Madonna on the high altar is by Lovro Marinov Dobričević of Kotor (15C). A procession similar to the Fašinada is held on 15 August when the icon is taken to Perast for the winter. This commemorates the victory over the Turks in 1654 and one of the boats always contains armed men.

Beyond Perast, drive E along the shore of the Kotorski zaljev, passing through (3km)) *Dražin Vrt*, with the house of Bajo Nikolić-Pivljanin (1672), a celebrated warrior against the Turks, and (2km) *Orahavac*, with 15–16C frescoes in the Orthodox church of Sv. Djordje. Swinging S with the mountains on your left descending almost sheer into the sea, you come to a chain of little villages along the shore, known under the collective name of Dobrota.

2–8km **Dobrota** (1300 inhab.) was an independent settlement in Roman times (*Debratha*) and remained so until 1351, when it was absorbed into Kotor. Four centuries later it was granted the status of an independent commune by Venice (1704) during a period when, like Perast, it prospered as a merchant shipping centre. A number of interesting buildings remain from this period. *Sv. Stasija* (St. Eustace; 1773) in the hamlet of Ljuta is a good example of the so-called Jesuit style, with painted walls and ceiling and a number of paintings, including the Blessed Virgin by Carlo Dolci. In the treasury are trophies captured from the Turks in battle, also vestments and lace, which is a local speciality. The church of *Sv. Matija* (1670), also baroque, farther S at Tomići, contains a Madonna and Child by Giovanni Bellini, St. Nicholas by Pietro Novelli, a 16C silver-gilt reliquary in the shape of a pyramid from Venice, and 17–18C vestments. The shore is lined with baroque mansions erected by former ship owners, especially the Tripković, Ivanović, and Dabinović-Kotkota families (all 18C) of which the largest is the *Palača Milošević* (early 19C). The small 15C church of *Gospa od vrta* (Our Lady of the Garden) contains a contemporary fresco and a painting of Our Lady with St. Dominic by Tripo Kokolja.

1km **KOTOR**, the chief town (5800 inhab.) of the Boka Kotorska, huddles on a narrow spit of land at the foot of Mt Lovćen (1749m), by which it is so overshadowed that the afternoon hours of sunshine are curtailed. Though in its history Kotor follows much the pattern of the Dalmatian cities farther N, its unusual site and greater proximity to the medieval Slavonic states of the interior (and especially the kingdom of Montenegro) have given it a marked individuality. The old quarter is surrounded by a system of CITY WALLS, begun under Byzantium (9–11C) but largely rebuilt in their present form by Venice (15–18C), which is one of the more extensive and complete in Yugoslavia. They climb the steep mountainside behind the town to the Fortress of Sv. Ivan (260m), enclosing an area several times greater than the town itself, with a perimeter of 4.5km and a total extent nearer 6km. They reach a height of just under 20m and a maximum breadth of 10m. Kotor retains its medieval character and is second only to Dubrovnik in the completeness of its preservation. An infinite variety of vistas is afforded by twisting streets and small squares, a typical Eastern Mediterranean feature here developed to a striking degree. Unfortunately the town was seriously damaged in the 1979 earthquake and is only gradually being opened to visitors.

Post office: At Škaljari.
Information: *Turist biro*, Trg Oktobarske Revolucije.
Airport: At Tivat, 11km W.
History. Greek *Acurion* and Roman *Acruvium* were succeeded by the *Decada-*

ron of Byzantium, from which the present name of Kotor (Ital. *Cattaro*) is derived. In 867 the town was ravaged by the Saracens and in 1002 it was sacked by King Samuilo of Macedonia, after which it became part of the Serbian kingdom of Duklja (later Zeta). When Zeta was incorporated into the larger Serbian kingdom of Raška by Stefan Nemanja (1186), Kotor flourished as its chief port. Kotor's status as an independent commune complete with Grand and Lesser Councils of nobles, Senate and coinage dated from Byzantine times, and during its association with Serbia it profited from special trade and political privileges, coming to rival Ragusa as a commercial power and provoking the jealousy of Venice. Raška declined and in 1370 Kotor sought the protection of Hungary-Croatia, but after an attack and temporary occupation by the Venetians under Vittore Pisani (1378) turned to King Tvrtko of Bosnia (1385). In 1391, Kotor attempted to equal its rivals by proclaiming an independent republic, but Turkish advances deprived the city of its hinterland and in 1420 Kotor was forced to seek the protection of Venice. It contrived to prosper despite the establishment of a Turkish *sanjak* on the N shore of the Boka Kotorska (1483), but Turkish sieges in 1539 and 1657, earthquakes in 1563 and 1667, and a plague in 1572 contributed to a steady decline. From 1797 Austria occupied the city, save for brief periods during the Napoleonic Wars under France (1807–13), England (1813) and Montenegro (1813–14), until in 1918 Kotor became part of the newly founded Yugoslavia.

The Kotor sailors' guild (Bokeljska mornarica) is one of the oldest in Europe with an unbroken tradition from AD 809. Natives include Fra Vita, builder of the Serbian monastery church of Dečani; Lovro Marinov Dobričević and Vicko Lovrin, 15C painters; and Andrija Paltašić a pioneer 15C printer.

The following description is provided in the interest of completeness, and in the hope that the more characteristic areas of the town will be accessible by the time of publication.

From the Quay the main entrance to the old town is through the Renaissance *Morska vrata* (Porta Marina, 1555) set in the W wall between the Gradska kafana and the Tržnica (market). On the inner side of the gate is a relief of the Madonna and Child with SS. Bernard and Tryphon (late 15C) and an inscription commemorating a Turkish defeat in 1657. TRG OKTOBARSKE REVOLUCIJE (*Trg oružja*), a spacious L-shaped square with pavement cafés, remains the social centre of the town. The W side of the square is formed by the unfinished *Providurova palata* (Governor's Palace, 16–17C), whose ground floor is occupied by shops. At its N end the *Vijećnica* (Town Hall), built by the French as a theatre (1808) and adapted in 1902, faces the former Venetian Arsenal, whereas a narrow passage between them gives access to the NW corner tower of *Citadela* (1540–1670), and the walk along the top of the N wall (view of the town) beside the river Škurda. Immediately opposite the main gate is the *Gradska kula*, a rectangular tower bearing the arms of Antonio Grimani, the Venetian governor who erected it in 1602. The clock was added in 1810. The obelisk in front was the pillory. Beside the travel office steps mount to the W wall, which is accessible as far as the S gate. The *Lapidary Collection* at the foot of the steps includes the original 12C wheel-window from the cathedral, an inlaid marble Reredos with a relief of St. Tryphon, and a fine pre-Romanesque stone sarcophagus decorated in low relief.

A narrow street leads from the S side of the square between the baroque *Palata Bisanti* (1694; left), with an ornate wellhead in the court, and the *Palata Besuća* (1776), with a superb Venetian Gothic *Portal built into the façade. At the end you emerge into the beautiful little TRG OSLOBODJENJA (Trg brašna), bounded to the E by the *Palata Pima* (late 16C), with baroque façade and court, and to the W by the plain *Palata Vracchien* and *Palata Buća* (16C). Another narrow street leads to the large and irregular cathedral square, TRG POBUNE MORNARA. The small cathedral of **Sv. Tripun** (St. Tryphon), basically

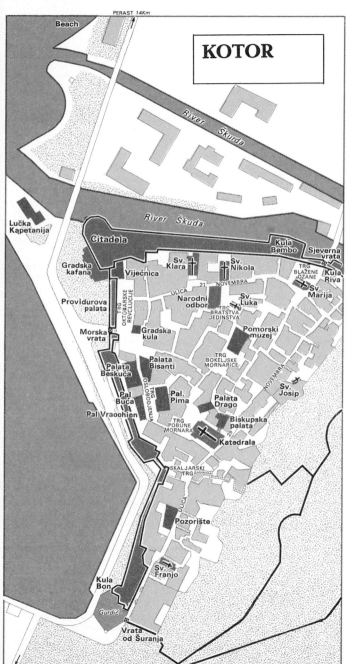

KOTOR

Romanesque in construction, is given a baroque aspect by its projecting W towers, between which a balustrated arch forms a porch.

The first cathedral of Kotor, a rotunda, was erected c 809 under the patronage of Andreacci Saracenis, to house the newly purchased relics of St. Tryphon. This was replaced in 1116 by an aisled basilica with a cupola over the nave and twin towers at the W end, the basis of the present church. After the earthquake of 1667 a completely new W front was constructed and the cupola, removed earlier, was not replaced. Reconstruction and repairs to the remainder were effected with the original materials.

The plain interior is divided into three double bays, massive piers alternating with Roman columns of marble and granite (probably from Risan) with damaged Corinthian columns. The E bays are unrestored. The outstanding feature is the beautiful Gothic *Ciborium* (1362?), with a delicate pyramidal canopy resting on four octagonal columns of red marble, and scenes from the life of St. Tryphon carved on the architrave. The high altar is a copy of an earlier 14C mensa and has a baroque reredos worked in silver-gilt by 17C Venetian smiths. On the wall of the central apse hang three sections of a large polyptych in silver-gilt, the central section by Hans of Basle (1440), the others by local masters. In the S aisle is the Tomb (1532) of Bishop Tripun Bisanti with a full-length effigy.

A door left of the high altar admits to the SACRISTY, into which has been built a fine pre-Romanesque Ciborium (809?) from the first cathedral. Here are kept chalices, monstrances and pastoral crosses. A marble staircase leads to the octagonal RELIQUARIUM above (1652), decorated by Francesco Cabianca of Venice (1704–08). The paintings here include St. Bartholomew by Girolamo da Santacroce, a 15C icon painting on both sides, and the Ecstasy of St. Francis by Tripo Kokolja. In one corner is a small sarcophagus, supposedly the original repository of the relics of St. Tryphon. A baroque marble sarcophagus, by Cabianca, with a kneeling figure of St. Tryphon on the lid, and scenes from his martyrdom depicted in relief on the sides, holds a 17C Venetian casket in silver-gilt containing the saint's relics, a Reliquary of the head (of Gothic workmanship), and a 16C crystal Cross. The remaining reliquaries, about 50 in number, housed in glass cases around the walls, date mainly from the 17–18C. The large Gothic crucifix of wood, said to be the gift of Jelena, consort of Uroš I of Serbia (13C), is probably of much later date. More interesting is a missionary cross used to bless the army of Jan Sobieski before the decisive defeat of the Turks at Vienna in 1683.

A narrow passageway divides the N wall of the cathedral from the Bishop's Palace (numerous coats of arms). Built into the wall is the sarcophagus of the cathedral's first patron, Andreacci Saracenis (died c 850). An excellent Romanesque three-light window, possibly by Fra Vita, is set into the wall of the main apse.

Passing the *Palata Drago* (16C), which has notably Renaissance windows, leave the square by the N side and emerge almost immediately into TRG BOKELJSKE MORNARICE. The baroque *Palata Grgurina* (18C) on the far side houses the **Pomorski Muzej** (adm. 7–19, Sun 9–17), devoted mainly to the history of the Kotar Sailors' Guild (later the Boka Kotorska Navy). Note in particular the armoury, the excellent ship models, and the traditional costumes of the Kotor sailors. The narrow UL. KARAMPANE passes between the museum and the delightful little square of Karampane with a 17C well and the baroque *Palata Lipovac* (18C), to TRG BRATSTVA-JEDINSTVA, bounded on the W side by the 19C *Narodni odbor* (Town Hall). In the centre stands the ancient little church of *Sv. Luka* (1195), Romanesque in conception but with a dome over the nave of Byzantine inspiration. Originally Roman Catholic, it passed to the Orthodox church in 1657 and in 1747 the chapel of Sv. Spiridon was added on the N side. The interior (key from sacristan of Sv. Nikola) contains two iconostases, the smaller of which, in the side chapel, is attributed to Vasilije Rafailović of Risan (18C). The Orthodox *Cathedral of Sv. Nikola* on the N side of the square was designed in the traditional Serbo-Byzantine style by Kiril Iveković (1902–09), and contains a collection of old icons.

UL. 21 NOVEMBRA leads W to *Sv. Antuna*, the much-altered church of the convent of St. Clare (16–17C), with a baroque marble altar by Francesco Cabianca (c 1700), and E past the ruined Venetian Gothic Buća and Drago houses to TRG BLAŽENE OZANE in front of the North Gate. The church of **Sv. Marija** or *Collegiata* (1221), with its alternating courses of pink and white stone, octagonal dome and semicircular apse and blind arcading, successfully fuses Romanesque and Serbo-Byzantine styles of architecture despite the addition of a N aisle (1434) and bell tower (1771). On the exterior can be seen a fine Romanesque two-light window in the apse, a Byzantine arch over the S door and a 17C wooden crucifix hanging beneath a projecting arch on the S wall. Inside are a 14C stone Pietà and a 15C wooden crucifix. The N aisle contains the richly carved sarcophagus of Blažena Ozana (Blessed Osana), a local saint beatified in 1930, with scenes from the saint's life carved in bas-relief by the Croatian sculptor, Antun Augustinčić.

The *Sjeverna vrata* (North Gate), across the square, was erected in 1540 to celebrate the previous year's defeat of Khair-ed-din Barbarossa (inscription). On the W side of the gate is the *Kula Bembo* (1538), from which the walk on the city wall leads to the Citadela (see above); to the E is the handsome *Kula Riva*, best seen from across the bridge over the river Škurda. Riva houses an open-air cinema during the summer months.

Leaving the square by the S side, notice on the left the entrance to the upper system of city walls, with a medallion bearing a stylised Lion of St. Mark (1760) on the archway. Hence a steep path leads up the mountainside to the 15C church of *Gospa od zdravlja* and the fortress of Sv. Ivan (views). Beside the gate a plaque commemorates a former apothecary's shop, one of the earliest in Southern Europe (1326). UL. 29 NOVEMBRA farther E passes the Romanesque chapel of *Sv. Ana* (12C; right) with a variety of medieval sculpture on the S front, and comes to (left) the bell tower and church of *Sv. Josip* (1631), with a baroque high altar and a painting by Angelo Coster. Farther on, the Romanesque door of the disused church of *Sv. Pavle* (1266) faces the street. Pass behind the E end of the cathedral into ŠKALIJARSKI TRG, whence flights of steps on the left lead up to another section of the city walls, with alternative paths to the church of Gospa od zdravlja and fortress of Sv. Ivan.

The quarter S of here, known as **Šuranj**, is the oldest part of Kotor and in spite of neglect amply repays exploration. Gothic and even Romanesque houses still stand and good architectural details abound. UL. 29 NOVEMBRA narrows past the *Narodno pozorište* (National Theatre), adapted from a Venetian military hospital (1769), to reach the ruined *Franciscan Church and Monastery*, a part of whose cloister (17C) can still be visited. A short distance beyond you come to the triple gate of *Vrata od Šuranja*, the inner arch 16C baroque, the middle one Gothic (14C?) and the outer arch 18C, with drawbridge mechanism attached. Beside the gate *Kula Bon* (1473), a round corner tower, affords views of the S part of the town; a walk follows the top of the W wall to the main gate. Below the tower is a large pool formed by a freshwater spring called *Gurdić*, and beyond the bridge the modern suburb of *Škaljari*.

31 Kotor to Ulcinj

ROAD, 113km. Highway N2—4/E752.—18km *Tivat*.—26km **Budva**.—
19km *Petrovac*.—17km *Sutomore*.—9km **Bar**.—24km *Ulcinj*.
Frequent buses.

An alternative route to Budva via Trojica, avoiding Tivat and saving
14km, leaves the Adriatic Highway just outside Kotor. The road is
mountainous for the first few kilometres, offering views back to the
Bay of Kotor and W over the Bay of Tivat, then levels out across the
plain of Grbalj and joins the coast road 12km from Budva.

Leaving Kotor via the suburb of *Škaljari*, leave the more direct road to
Budva on the left. Round the head of the inner bay of Kotor and follow
the W shore to **Prčanj** (900 inhab.), a village that straggles over the
hillside and along the water's edge. Like other places in the Boka
Kotorska, Prčanj has a pronounced nautical tradition and prospered
mainly in the 16–19C. The sailors of Prčanj ran the first regular postal
service on the East Adriatic coast (1625–1806), plying between
Venice, Zadar, Kotor, and Corfù; Captain Ivo Visin of Prčanj became
the first Slav to circumnavigate the globe (1852–59). Sea captains'
sturdy houses testify to its former prosperity, but the pride of the
village is the colossal neo-Renaissance parish church of *Rodjenje
bogorodice* (Birth of Our Lady), erected between 1784 and 1909 to
designs by Bernardino Macaruzzi of Venice. The interior has been
liberally adorned with works of art. A good Italo-Cretan icon forms the
main altarpiece; there are paintings by Palma the Younger, Giovan
Battista Piazzetta, and Antonio Balestra; and three angels sculpted by
G.M. Morlaiter (1746). Works by modern Yugoslav artists include
sculptures of Meštrović and of Rosandić. On a terrace in front of the
church there are busts of Abp Strossmayer and Prince Petar Petrović II
Njegoš by Meštrović.

Continue N from Prčanj along the W shore of the bay of Kotor,
round Rt Gospa at the tip of the Vrmac Peninsula, and enter the
Verige narrows, on the S side of the strait.

7km **Lepetane** is linked by car ferry with Kamenari (see Rte 23) on
the N shore of the Boka Kotorska. Turn SW and S, and follow the shore
of the Bay of Tivat.

7km **Tivat**, the second largest town (3400 inhab.) on the Boka
Kotorska, is sheltered from NE winds by Mt Vrmac. Its pleasant
climate early attracted summer villas of the nobility of Kotor, now
mostly ruined, and sub-tropical vegetation is abundant. Tivat is well
supplied with sandy beaches, to the N around Mt Seljanovo and the
hamlet of Donja Lastva, and to the S around Kalimanj, and has
developed into an attractive little resort.

The luxuriant *Town Park* contains many botanical rarities. In the
centre of the town the small Gothic church of *Sv. Antun* (1373) has the
arms of various Kotor nobles painted on the walls and an inscription
mentioning King Tvrtko I of Bosnia. The remains of the *Palata Buća*
(1548) and a few private chapels survive from their former pleasure
palaces. The church of *Sv. Rok* in Donja Lastva contains an icon of St.
Tryphon by Ilias Moschos, a 17C Greek artist.

In the S corner of the Bay of Tivat are the three small islands of
Prevlaka, Stradioti (or Sv. Marko), and Otok. *Prevlaka* has excavated
remains of a 13C Benedictine Monastery. The 15C Franciscan
Monastery on *Otok* occupies the site of a Benedictine foundation of
the 9–11C (ruined church), the seat (1219–c 1300) of the primate of the
medieval kingdom of Zeta. A road traverses the salt flats of *Soliosko
polje*, which have been in continuous use for 2000 years, to serve the

little known peninsula of Luštica, which descends to the open sea in many deserted sandy beaches. The small bay of *Pržno*, 14km from Tivat, is attracting increasing crowds of tourists. The inhabitants of Luštica are predominantly Orthodox, and the churches, though plain, sometimes have good iconostases. Among the most interesting are those in Sv. Petar (by Daskal Dimitrije; 1704) and Sv. Lazar (Petar Rafailović; 1771), Sv. Andreja and Sv. Nedjelja (both Djordje Rafailović; 1802) at *Zabrdje*. The little church of Sv. Tripun at *Klinci* has 17C wall paintings.

From Tivat a new section of the Adriatic Highway runs past the airport, skirts Soliosko polje and crosses the plain of Grbalj. The shore is hidden and inaccessible behind a range of low hills. Traverse the green Zupa valley to rejoin the coast at (26km) Budva.

   BUDVA (5500 inhab.), with excellent sandy beaches, a tempered climate and an old walled quarter of typically Mediterranean aspect, is the most popular holiday resort in Montenegro. Enjoying particlluar favour with the English, it is rapidly acquiring a modicum of sophistication.

Information: *Turistički savet*, Poštanski Fah 32, tel. 41814; *Montenegro-turist, OOUR* Mogren, tel. 41983.

Airport at Tivat (see above).

Buses from Belgrade, Skopje, Titograd and all the main cities of the Adriatic coast. Also local buses to the Boka Kotorska and to all points on the Montenegrin coast.

History. *Budva*, like Risan, is linked by legend with the name of Cadmus, king of Phoenicia, and was Greek, Illyrian, Roman, and Byzantine by turn. In the 9C the town was sacked by the Saracens and in the 11C joined the medieval Serbian kingdom of Duklja, while preserving its municipal autonomy. A century later Duklja was absorbed into Raška (Serbia) by Stefan Nemanja and in 1371 Budva, by statute, confirmed its status as a self-governing commune similar to the cities of Dalmatia. With the decline of the Nemanjas, however, dynastic quarrels led to the disintegration of Raška and after 50 years of turbulence Budva acceded to Venice in 1443, becoming the most southerly Venetian outpost on the Adriatic coast. Cut off from its hinterlands by the Turks, Budva languished, and the earthquake of 1667 wrought catastrophic damage from which it never recovered, although the city walls were partially repaired in the face of continuing danger from the Turks. With the fall of Venice (1797) Budva passed to Austria, then France (1806), against whom it twice revolted, and back to Austria again until 1918. The town was badly damaged by the earthquake of 1979 and is largely closed to visitors.

The old quarter is girdled with CITY WALLS, one section of which antedates Venetian rule, though the major portion was erected in the 15C and rebuilt in 1639. The stretch facing the sea collapsed in the earthquake. From the *Kopnena vrata* (Land Gate), opposite the Hotel Avala, with the city emblems of Venice and Budva over the doorway, the picturesque main steet leads in a few minutes to the main square. The Catholic cathedral of **Sv. Ivan** in the centre, founded in the 8–9C, has been repeatedly rebuilt and acquired its baroque appearance in the 17C. Among the pictures within are a Madonna (school of Tiepolo), a 16C Venetian painting of SS. Peter and Paul, and a venerable icon with a background of beaten silver. In the Orthodox church of **Sv. Trojica** (Holy Trinity) are paintings by Nicholaos Aspioti of Corfù. Adjoining the church is the open-air cinema, at the rear of which is the 12C church of Santa Maria in Punta. The former *Francisan Monastery* adjacent to the church now contains the **Zavi-čajni Muzej** (Town Museum, adm. 8–11, 14–17), in which are exhibited Phoenician, Greek, and Roman archaeological finds from a

necropolis on the site of the Hotel Avala. The tiny medieval church of
Sv. Sava, where in former times the altars were shared between
Orthodox and Catholic worship, has been adapted as a further section
for the museum. The *Citadela* overlooks the sea on the S side of the
town, affording views E and W of the coast. Hence access may be had
to a walk round the top of the walls.

About 2km N of Budva, beside the road to Cetinje, is *Maine* the village where
Sćepan Mali, the 18C pretender to the Montenegrin throne, first made his
appearance posing as the murdered Tsar Peter III of Russia. The village has two
Orthodox monasteries of which the more interesting is the fortified Podostrog,
now somewhat dilapidated but to be restored. The small basement chapel of Sv.
Gospodja (Our Lady) is completely covered with 17C frescoes, of which those in
the narthex are the easiest to see; the large 18C church beside it contains the
tomb of Vladika Danilo, founder of the Petrović-Njegoš dynasty of Montenegro,
who died here in 1735. Prince Petar II Petrović Njegoš wrote part of his famous
epic poem, 'Gorski vijenac' (The Mountain Wreath), while staying in this
monastery. In the court a fine well-head is decorated with a relief of the royal
arms of Montenegro (two-headed eagle holding a snake in its claws). The
nearby monastery of Podmaine was burt down in 1869, but the surviving church
is decorated with wall paintings by Rafailo Dimitrijević of Risan (1747) and has
an iconostasis by Nicholaos Aspioti. Dositej Obradović (1742–1811), pioneer
Serbian scholar and encyclopaedist, spent several months at this monastery.

The road to Bar traverses a beautiful stretch of coast quite unlike
anything farther N. A ridge of low, green mountains known as
Paštrovske gore in the district of Paštrovići runs parallel with the shore
where long stretches of sand or shingle beaches are interspersed by
craggy headlands and beetling cliffs. The scenery, by comparison
with the remainder of the coast, is both restful and varied.

Leaving Budva, follow the long pebble and shingle beach of
Slavenska plaža, and many striking hotels. On the headland, Rt
Zavala, at the far end of the beach, can be seen the small 15C burial
chapel of Stevan Štiljanović, the last duke of Paštrovići. A mountain
road to Cetinje (33km; comp. Rte 32) swings away to the left. Pass the
sandy beaches of *Bečići, Kamenovo* and *Pržno*, then bear right from
the main road for Sveti Stefan.

10km **Sveti Stefan** is a charming island fishing village that has been
expropriated and converted into a luxury hotel colony, to shoreward
of which is developing an associated holiday resort. The village was
founded in the 15C by the Paštrovići, who maintained their own
autonomous district under Venice, and was fortified in the 16C
against the Turks. A sand-bar joins the village, once an island, to the
mainland and visitors are admitted (fee) to view its narrow crooked
streets and two tiny churches of *Sv. Stefan* (15C) and *Preobraženje*
(The Transfiguration; 1693).

To the N along the shore the *Hotel Miločer*, formerly the summer residence of
the Yugoslav royal family, stands in a beautiful park with Mediterranean and
sub-tropical trees and flowers. Hence a narrow gravel track leads uphill (15
minutes on foot; practicable by car) to the Orthodox Monastery of Praskvica. The
iconostasis of the main church of Sv. Nikola is by Nicholaos Aspioti (1863). A
Gothic chapel (1413) with frescoes survives from an earlier church. The treasury
preserves a 16C copy of the gospels, with engraved silver covers and miniature
reliefs; a silver-gilt chalice presented by Tsar Paul of Russia (18C); and a large
16C icon. A few steps away is the small *Sv. Trojica* (Holy Trinity), the oldest
church in the region (1050 ?). The interior is covered with frescoes (1680–81) by
Radul, the Serbian painter, best in the apse.

The road beyond Sveti Stefan affords excellent retrospective views of
the wide bay of Budva.—At 5km, just off the road (right), is the
Orthodox monastery of *Reževići*, said to have been founded by Czar
Dušan the Mighty of Serbia. The older of its two churches (enlarged in

1714) has 17C frescoes and an iconostasis by Aleksija Lazović (1833). Reževići used to be the seat of the 'Bankada', or Grand Council, of the autonomous district of Paštrovići, elections to which were held at the nearby cove of Drobni pijesak.—At 3km, where the Titograd-Petrovac road crosses the Adriatic Highway, turn right.

1km **Petrovac-na-moru** is a small modern resort (1000 inhab.) set in splendid natural surroundings with dense olive groves almost to the water's edge. Popular with the people of Titograd (only 58km away), Petrovac is laid out with a pleasant promenade and rapidly acquiring the amenities of a pleasure resort. Roman finds have been made in the neighbourhood, of which a 4C mosaic floor (inquire locally for directions) is the most interesting example.

The Adriatic Highway continues SE above the broad sandy beach of *Buljarica*, passing (2km beyond Petrovac) the ruined Orthodox monastery of *Gradište*, with two early churches. Both the larger Gothic church of Sv. Nikola (rebuilt 1620) and the older church of Uspenje (The Assumption) are decorated with good frescoes by Strahinja of Budimlje, a Serbian painter whose Byzantine style is modified by strong Western influences. The church of Sv. Nikola also has an iconostasis by Vasilije Rafailović of Risan (1796).

At the far end of Buljarica bay the road passes a large bentonite quarry and processing plant before striking inland through beautiful hilly country covered with pine woods and olive groves.—14km the spectacular ruins of *Haj-Nehaj* castle, built by the Venetians and later adapted by the Turks, stand on a dizzy spur of rock.

3km **Sutomore**. (Railway station for connections with Bar, Titograd, and Belgrade) is a modern resort village (800 inhab.) strung out along a sand and pebble beach that extends for more than 1.5km. The 12C church of *Sv. Tekla* has twin altars, one for the Catholic rite, the other for Orthodox services. At the SW end of the beach on the headland of Ratac, stand extensive ruins of the ancient Benedictine monastery of *Our Lady of Ratac* (11–13C), including a two-storied burial chapel of early-Christian type.—At 8km a T-junction offers the choice of turning right to Bar or left to Stari Bar.

Bar (1km; Railway station for trains to Titograd and Belgrade. Car ferries several times a week to Dubrovnik, Korčula, Hvar, Split, Zadar, Rab, Rijeka, Bari, Corfù and Igoumenitsa.), at the S end of the wide bay of the same name, is a modern industrial port (2500 inhab.) expanding rapidly to handle the import and export traffic of Serbia and Montenegro.

For the old town turn left, passing (1km) a minor road to Virpazar and take the next road left.—3km. **Stari Bar**, just off the main road, is a little more than a ghost town whose romantic ruins, huddling picturesquely at the foot of Mt Rumija (1594m) give little idea of its former wealth and importance.

After being both a Greek and a Roman colony (*Antibaris*), the town became an important military and trading post under Byzantium and in 1089 was elevated to an archbishopric. In the 12–14C it acknowledged the Nemanja dynasty of Raška and after dynastic squabbles passed to Venice in 1443, by whom it was fortified. In 1571 it was captured by the Turks and remained in their possession until 1878, when it was liberated by Montenegro.

The town is encircled by 15–16C Venetian walls. On the N side can be seen the well-preserved *Aqueduct* (16–17C) that used to bring water to the town. The former *Cathedral* and the church of *Sv. Nikola*, were blown up by explosions of gunpowder in 1881 and 1912. *Sv. Veneranda* and *Sv. Katarina* are both Gothic (14C ?) and an 11–12C Romanesque chapel on the NW side of town has been incorporated into the Venetian Fortress. A large medieval mansion on the W side of town, with traces of frescoes, is thought to have been the *Archbishop's Palace*. The Turks left relatively few marks on the town, in general adapting existing structures, but a large 17C *Haman* bears witness to their long stay.

Beyond Stari Bar the road traverses numerous modern bridges and tunnels, winding among dense and attractive olive groves of great antiquity. There are said to be over half a million trees on the lower slopes of the Rumija mountain range and specimens are estimated to be between 1500 and 2000 years old. Glimpses may be caught of an occasional village mosque, and the peasants in the fields are frequently in national dress, the women in Turkish trousers and vividly embroidered aprons.

24km **ULCINJ** the most southerly (8000 inhab.) town of the Yugoslav coast, is unique on the coast in its Oriental appearance and flavour, though this is fast disappearing. Its popularity as a tourist resort is enhanced by unmatched beaches (with iodine content) and a growing complex of hotels and modern facilities. About three quarters of the population is Albanian.

History. The Greek and Roman colony of *Olcinium* was somewhat to the NW of the present town, but gave its name to the Byzantine settlement which arose on the present site in the 9–10C. In 1181 Ulcinj acknowledged the sovereignty of the Nemanjas of Raška and remained in Serbian hands until 1421, when it transferred its allegiance to Venice. In 1571 it was captured by the Turks and during the 16C became notorious as the seat of the sought-after renegade and pirate, Uluz-Ali, Bey of Algiers. Its fleet was captured and burnt by Turkish forces in 1675, but Ulcinj remained a pirate centre until well into the 18C. In 1878, after a protracted seige, Ulcinj was captured by Montenegro and after brief occupations by Austria (1916–18) and Italy (1918–20) was joined with Yugoslavia.

The town is spread out amphitheatrically over three hills round a sandy bay and harbour. To the E lies the newest hotel and tourist quarter; in the centre the modern section of the town with shops and administrative offices; and in the W is the old fortified citadel, best reached from the beach by taking the ascending path beside the harbour. The massive *Walls*, dating from the 13C but extended and rebuilt by the Venetians and Turks, are imposing on their high cliffs, but are virtually all that is left of the medieval city, for the inside was reduced to rubble by the Montenegrin artillery in 1878. Enter by the *Istočna vrata* (East Gate) and follow the inside perimeter of the walls left to a raised platform, commanding good views W into the cove of Liman. A few steps farther on stone vaults mark the site of the Turkish market, opposite which is the shell of a 14C church and mosque. For religious reasons, the Turks reversed the W door, so that the lintel now forms the threshold and the Gothic capitals can be seen upside down near the ground. The stump of a ruined minaret adjoins the church and to the left is the ruined *Balšićeva kula*, a tower erected by one of the last of the Serbian kings. Following the main street E with houses in a mixture of Venetian and Turkish styles, regain the E gate and footpath.

The central part of the town is grouped around the main street, which runs uphill at right angles to the beach and promenade. On the left is the oldest of seven small mosques, the *Pašina džamija* (Pasha's Mosque, 16C) adjoining which is a small contemporary *haman*. Beyond the 18C Turkish *Sahat-kula* (Clock Tower), at the top of the street is the colourful market place, particularly busy on Tuesdays and Fridays.

Pleasant excursions may be made to the *Velika plaža* (Great Beach), 4km E of town, which extends for an impressive 12km from Rt Djeran to the mouth of the river Bojana (forbidden zone) on the Albanian border. It can be reached on foot from behind the Hotel Galeb (¾ hour); or by road (bus) turning right at the petrol station to cross the edge of Ulcinj plain. Before the beach you come to *Porat Milena*, a narrow canal leading inland to the extensive salt flats of Solila. An interesting feature here are the fishing devices known as *kalimera*, consisting of a net on the end of a long pole that is lowered into the water on a cantilever principle. The Velika plaža, of fine grey sand, slopes gradually to the sea. Although several hotels are projected here, the greater part of the beach remains natural and untouched and it is unwise to stray too close to the Albanian frontier.

A boat trip to the peaceful bay of *Valdinos*, W of the town, affords excellent views of the walls and extensive olive woods for which Ulcinj is noted. The bay itself is deeply indented, with a lovely shingle beach backed by pinewoods; it was here in 1675 that the Ulcinj pirate fleet was waylaid and destroyed.

32   Kotor to Skopje

ROAD, 500km, Highway N2/E65 and secondary roads.—22km *Krstac*.—21km **Cetinje**.—53km *Titograd*.—67km *Kolašin*.—77km *Ivangrad*.—15km *Andrijevica*.—40km *Čakor Pass*.—36km *Peć*.—15km *Dečani*.—58km **Prizren**.—55km *Doganović*.—41km **Skopje**.

This route turns inland from the Adriatic coast to Cetinje, the ancient capital of Montenegro, then crosses the Montenegrin mountains and the fertile plain of Metohija, with its Oriental towns and Serbian Orthodox monasteries, to the modern capital of Macedonia, Skopje. The route is one of the more difficult in the Balkans: the road, which is unpaved for about 50km, presents a formidable challenge even to the most experienced motorist. The mountain scenery is unimaginably dramatic, but the many blind curves above gaping abysses with no guardrail may make it difficult to enjoy. An alternative route, from Ivangrad to Peć via Rožaj, avoids the worst stretch.

Leave Kotor by the Adriatic Highway (N2/E65). Turn left at the road junction in Škaljari and ascend by a steep winding road to the pass and village of (6km) *Trojica* (view of the bays of Tivat and Kotor), where the road for Cetinje and Titograd quits the coast. After about 3km the road begins to climb the side of the mountain in stupendous zigzags, disclosing at every turn a wider vista of the Boka Kotorska.

22km **Krstac** provides a superb **View of the entire gulf.

From Krstac the main road continues downhill to the village of *Njeguši*, birthplace of Petar II, with his former summer residence left of the road. The road now climbs again in a series of zigzags to the pass of *Bukovica* (1500m) and then descends to *Čekanje*, where it is joined by a road from Grahovo and Danilovgrad.

21km **Cetinje** (12,000 inhab.), the former capital of Montenegro, lies on a barren and forbidding plateau (672m) ringed with mountains, and snow-bound at least five months of the year. Although founded in the 15C by Ivan Crnojević, the first ruler of Montenegro, the city today is quite modern and interesting more for the majesty of its surroundings and its historical association than for any architectural merit. The locals look as if they still carry pistols; the atmosphere is Balkan and the Adriatic seems very distant. In the vast Trg Maršala Tita is the former palace of Prince Petar II, the mighty black-bearded prince-bishop, poet, and crack-shot. The low fortified building is called the **Biljarda** (1838) because a billiard table was hauled up for it direct from the sea. It now houses the *Njegoš Museum* and the Ethnographical Museum (adm. 8–13.30). A large relief model of Montenegro is displayed in an annex in the courtyard. Behind the Biljarda is the **Monastery**, founded by Ivan Crnojević in 1484 but destroyed and rebuilt repeatedly over the centuries. In the treasury are good icons, vestments, and a gospel of 1493, one of the first books to be printed in the Cyrillic alphabet. The tiny cruciform chapel contains the sarcophagi of three former Princes of the Njegoš dynasty, Danilo, Mirko, and Petar I. From *Kula tablja*, the ruined tower overlooking the monastery, the heads of executed Turks used to be displayed as a symbol of undying hatred. The modest *Royal Palace* of the later princes of Montenegro, also in Trg Maršala Tita, was last occupied by King Nicholas (died Antibes, 1921). It preserves intact some of the state rooms and houses the **State Museum** (adm. 9–13.40), with collections dealing with local archaeology and history. In the park beside the road for Budva the *Umjet-nička galerija* (Art Gallery) has a selection of works by modern Yugoslav artists.

53km **TITOGRAD** (39m, 85,000 inhab.), the modern capital of Montenegro, was destroyed during the Second World War and rebuilt in the postwar period. Today it is an important administrative and commercial centre, and a university town.

Post Office: 1 Ulica Slobode.

Information: *Turistički Savez Titograda*, 433 Ulica Slobode, tel. 52968.

Airport: at Golubovci, 14km S. *JAT*, 2 Trg Ivana Milutinovića, tel. 44248.

History. The Roman city of *Diocleia*, which grew up at the confluence of the Zeta and Morača rivers, was abandoned in the 7C in favour of a new settlement established at the confluence of the Morača and the Ribnica. The new town, initially called *Ribnica*, was renamed *Podgorica* during the Middle Ages. From the 12C to the 15C it was subject to the kings of Serbia. Under the Turks (1474–1878) it became an important trading post on the road from Bosnia to Scutari. In 1878, at the Congress of Berlin, the city was assigned to Montenegro. It received its present name in 1946.

Where the Ribnica flows into the Morača stand the remains of the **Nemanjin grad**, the medieval castle rebuilt in the 16C by the Turks, who are responsible for the imposing ramparts and cylindrical corner bastions. A few other Turkish edifices survive in the old quarter, called the *Stara Varoš*: these include a 17C clock tower and two mosques, the *Džamija Lukavčevića* and the *Doganjska džamija*. In a park above the Ribnica is the **Archeološka zbirka SRCG**, containing prehistoric, Illyrian, Roman and medieval artefacts found in excavations throughout Montenegro. The **Muzej grada**, or Municipal Museum, next door, has collections dealing with local history, ethnography, etc. The **Prirodnjačka zbirka SRCG** (Natural History Museum of Montenegro), on BRAĆE ZLATIĆANA, also has modest but interesting displays.

EXCURSIONS. To the ruins of **Doclea** (4km N by the Nikšić road, then right at the confluence of the Zeta and Morača). This ancient Roman town, later the capital of the Slavonic principality of Duklja, is thought to have received its name from the Illyrian tribe, Doclaetic. It was destroyed in the late 6C or early 7C. Excavations have brought to light relics of walls, a paved forum, the foundations of a basilica, some columns, baths, and a temple of Diana. Nearby are the remains of two early Christian basilicas, dating from the 5–6C.

To **Medun** (16km NE) built on the site of the Illyrian Meteon, mentioned by Livy. A small village preserving traces of cyclopean walls and medieval and Turkish buildings. The house of writer Marko Miljanović (1833–1919) has been turned into a small museum.

To **Skadarsko jezero** (23km SW by Highway N2/E27). This is the largest lake in the Balkans (370km^2, 222 of which are in Yugoslavia, the rest in Albania); along the W shore are numerous islands dotted with Orthodox churches and convents (in various stages of decay) and, on the islet of Lesendro, vestiges of an Ottoman fortress erected in the 19C.

The road continues through the Morača Valley, here quite fertile thanks to the warm breezes which blow from the Skadarsko jezero. The valley opens up and you immediately come upon the white, domed church of (right) *Morača Monastery, a classic example of the Raška School, founded in 1251. The church of Sv. Bogorodica is a simple but harmonious structure with a narthex, domed naos, and semicircular apse. Most of the fescoes date from the 16C and 17C, and are rather traditional in style. They include, on the W wall, St. George; in the narthex, Genealogy of Christ and Last Judgment (16–17C); in the naos, above the entrance, Dormition of the Virgin (16C); in the diaconicon, Lives of the prophet Elias and of St. Illya: the latter are contemporary with the church and are important to the history of 13C Serbian art. Also noteworthy are the fine 17C iconostasis; and the entrance door, inlaid with ivory tarsia work (17C). The treasure, displayed in the narthex, includes some more good icons and a very early printed book (1493).

67km **Kolašin** (965m 2500 inhab.) is a small, austere town in the valley of the River Tara, surrounded by forested mountains. It is becoming a popular spa, and it is also a good starting point for the ascent of the Bjelasica Range (2137m, among the highest mountains in Montenegro), the slopes of which abound in alpine lakes, springs, and brooks. Much of the area is included in the **Biogradska Gora National Park**, which receives its name from Lake Biogradsko, 1100m above sea level.

77km **IVANGRAD** (664m, 18,000 inhab.) is a modern town whose chief attraction is the modest 12C *Monastery of Djurdjevi Stupovi*, with coeval frescoes.—Highway N2/E65 bears left for (131km) Novi Pazar, Rte. Turn right onto Highway N9, which follows the River Lim.

15km **Andrijevica** (789m, 1500 inhab.), a rather bleak mountain village amidst immense evergreen forests, is a starting point for the ascent of Mt Komovi (2485m). Beyond the town, the road enters a narrow gorge, then winds in a series of sharp curves to (40km) the **Čakor Pass** (1849m), offering magnificent *Views over the surrounding mountains. It then descends in more curves to the valley of the Pećka Bistrica, in the autonomous Kosovo Province, and enters the magnificent **Rugovska Klisura**, the steep walls of which are peppered with swift mountain streams, cascades, and little lakes. The mountains to the S form the Prokletije Range, a natural frontier between Yugoslavia and Albania. The principal peaks are all well over 2000m; beyond stretch the Highlands of Albania, still a most inaccessible and unknown region.

The Rugovska Klisura opens quite suddenly into a broad plain, and Peć comes into view in the distance.

Near the S end of the gorge, set somewhat below the road, lies the **Pećka Patrijaršija** (Patriarchate of Peć), for centuries the headquarters of the Serbian Orthodox church. Some careful driving is needed here, as the turning is easily missed.

The original seat of the Serbian Church was at Žiča (comp. Rte 26B), but this proved to be too near what was then the Hungarian frontier, and in 1253 the patriarchy of Žiča was brought here, to the monastery of Sveta Apostola at Peć, which had been established in the preceding century to subtract the region from the jurisdiction of the Greek patriarch of Ohrid. In 1346 the emperor Dušan granted the patriarchy complete autonomy; it remained here with interruptions until the Turks abolished it in 1766 (although throughout the Turkish era the

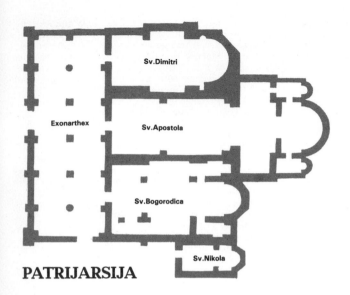

PATRIJARSIJA

monastery remained a centre of national and religious resistance). In 1920, following the expulsion of the Turks, the seat of the Church was moved to the new national capital, Belgrade.

Little remains of the conventual buildings, which were originally quite extensive. However, the churches—of which there are three, joined by a common exonarthex, plus a small chapel—are very well preserved. The simple harmony of their architecture, in conjunction with the awesome beauty of their surroundings, amply repays a visit.

Entrance is gained through the long exonarthex, rebuilt in the 16C, and divided into two aisles. On the somewhat dingy walls are a splendid Last Judgment, a representation of the Calendar with a composition for each day of the year, and portraits of the Nemanjić dynasty. beginning with its founder Stefan Nemanja and ending with Czar Dušan.

The central and oldest church is the *Crkva Sveta Apostola* (church of the Apostles). Built in the 13C to a Latin Cross plan and incorporating parts of a 12C edifice, it is decorated with exceptionally fine frescoes: on the ceiling of the narthex, on two levels, Passion Scenes and more Portraits of Nemanjić Kings (early 14C, retouched 16–17C); in the naos, at the sides of the entrance, fragmentary frescoes of the late 12C–early 14C; and on the ceiling, coeval illustrations of the incarnations of Christ and the Acatist Hymn (invoking the protection of the Virgin Mary against the barbarians). In the cupola and on the arches underneath, Ascension, Descent of the Holy Chost, Doubting of Thomas, Mission of the Apostles, Last Supper, Raising of Lazarus, Prophets and Evangelists, all dating from the mid 13C, and executed by a painter or painters who belonged to same group that worked at Mileševa and Studenica (Rte 26B). In the choir, late 13C frescoes on two levels; Church Fathers and Apostles and, in the dome of the apse, Christ in Judgment. In the transept are more mid-13C frescoes: in the N arm, Transfiguration, Descent into Limbo, and a portrait of Stefan Nemanja; in the S arm, Birth of Christ, Presentation at the Temple, Baptism, and Warrior Saints. In the prothesis, Vision of the prophet Daniel.

The flanking churches of *Sv. Dimitrije* (St. Demetrius, left) and *Sv. Bogorodica* (Our Lady, right) were built in the early 14C; Sv. Dimitrije is the older of the two buildings, by about ten years. The frescoes of the interior, although first painted at the time the church was built, were extensively retouched in the 17C. They include, in the naos, Church Feasts, scenes from the Legend of St. Demetrius, and a Procession of Saints; in the cupola, Ascension, in the apse, Virgin, Communion of Apostles, Adoration of the Mystic Lamb, and Ecumenical Councils and Synods of the Serbian Orthodox Church. The Treasure—including 110 manuscripts from the 12C to the 18C, icons, liturgical objects, vestments, and embroideries—is also displayed in this church. Sv. Bogorodica has a number of remarkable frescoes in the narthex, including 23 portraits of members of the Nemanja dynasty and a beautiful Glykophiloussa (Virgin Nursing); the other paintings (a Calendar and a Last Judgment) date from the 16C. More 14C paintings may be seen in the naos: on the left of the entrance the bishop saint, Arsenije I, founder of the church, offering his plan to the prophet Daniel; above, Dormition of the Virgin. In the prothesis (left), a life of St. Arsenije; in the diaconicon (right), life of St. John the Baptist.

Outside, on the S side of the complex, is the chapel of *Sv. Nikola*, built by the patriarch Danilo, together with the exonarthex, in 1330, and adorned with frescoes illustrating the life of St. Nicholas (1674) and, on a lower level, eminent monks (St. Sava, Danilo, Stefan Nemanja).

3km **Peć** (505m, 60,000 inhab.), situated near the E end of the Rugovo Klisura, at the foot of Mt Koprivnik (2410m), is a market town and industrial centre of some importance, a curious mixture of modern high-rises and old Turkish houses. The population is mainly Albanian (the men wear a characteristic white skull-cap), and the old town is a charming place brimming with artisans' shops and dotted with mosques, minarets, gardens and orchards. Peć owes its fame largely to the ecclesiastical monuments in its environs—the Orthodox Patriarchy, described above, and the Monastery of Dečani, mentioned below—and there is little to see in the town itself, except for an interesting form of domestic architecture called a *kula* ('tower')— a fortified dwelling usually built of stone or brick with small windows and loopholes set high up. The kula is normally surrounded by a high wall; it is to be found throughout Kosovo, to which it came from Albania. One of the finer examples in Peć is the **Jasa Pasha's House** near the women's market (*ženska pijaca*).

15km *Dečani*, a turning on the right leads in 2km to the ****Monastery of Visoki Dečani**, in another forested valley between high mountains. King Stefan Uroš Dečanski founded the monastery in the early 14C, intending the church of Christ Pantokrator as his burial place. The complex, which lies behind a sturdy wall, is entered by an imposing fortified gate. Few of the monastic buildings remain. The church, the work of a Franciscan monk, Vid of Kotor, is influenced by the Romanesque style of Apulia, which is in turn a hybrid of Lombard and Norman motifs. It is a lovely building of pink, white, and grey marble, with a tripartite gabled façade and elegantly carved doors and windows. The richly decorated central portal has columns borne by lions on either side and a relief of Christ between two angels and signs of the Zodiac in the tympanum. Above the door is an ornamented mullioned window. The S door is adorned with a relief showing the Baptism of Christ and an inscription of the architect in Cyrillic lettering—both unusual features for an Orthodox church. On the central apse is a fine mullioned window with carved surround and lions bearing columns. All around the church, the corbels are adorned with beautiful anthropomorphic and zoomorphic heads.

The fourteenth-century Dečani Monastery, built by Francesco Vito from Kotor; detail of the main portal

The interior is entirely covered with frescoes (more than a thousand paintings in all), executed by order of the emperor Dušan between 1335 and 1350. Considered among the greatest masterpieces of Serbian art, they are characterised by fresh colours, lively design, and great attention to detail. The narthex, divided into three bays by octagonal piers with elaborately carved capitals, is dedicated to St. George, and several of the paintings depict his legends. Here also are 365 separate compositions illustrating the Calendar; some excellent portraits of Czar Dušan, his wife Jelena, and their son Uroš; and a Nemanjić family tree with a portrait for every member of the dynasty. The naos is entered by a lovely Romanesque doorway flanked by lions. On the lowest level of the walls, on the piers, and in the arches of the windows are 250 figures of saints; above run cycles representing the life of Christ and the Acts of the Apostles; in the cupola, the Great Feasts of the Church. In the S aisle, the Acatist Hymn; in the N aisle, life of St. Demetrius. On the W wall, stories of St. John the Baptist, the

Liturgy, stories from the Book of Genesis, the legend of Solomon, and episodes from the Book of Daniel; in the centre, the Tree of Jesse, the Last Judgment, and the Dormition of the Virgin. An inscription gives the name of one of the painters of the complex, Srdj Grešni (Serge the Fisherman), of Kotor.

The diaconicon and the prothesis are set apart by two carved and gilt iconostases (18C). The Treasury possesses numerous icons, including *stajaćice* ('standing portraits') of Gabriel the Archangel, the Virgin and Child, St. Nicholas, and St. John the Baptist; a Virgin Pelagonitissa (from Pelegonia, near Bitola); a double icon of the Ascension and the Descent into Limbo, and an image of St. Stefan Dečanski. Also interesting are the collections of 15–16C liturgical objects and vestments; and 150 illuminated manuscripts dating from the 13C to the 19C. The tomb of the founder, covered with an embroidered cloth, lies near the iconostasis and is said to have medicinal properties. Muslims and Christians visit the tomb with similar expectations.

Beyond Dečani the road passes several interesting small towns and villages. The biggest of these is *Djakovica* (23,000 inhab.), near the Albanian border, with several mosques and a strong tradition of craftsmanship (the black pottery, coloured with a mixture of chimney soot and water, is typical).

61km **Prizren** (419m, 54,000 inhab.), extending along both banks of the Prizrenska Bistrica at the foot of the Šar Planina massif (2702m), is a place of brown roofs, white walls, and green gardens.

Post Office: 38 Trg 17 Novembra.

Information: Turist-Kosova, Trg 17 Novembra, tel. 22344.

History. The first to settle on this site were the Romans. Their town, called *Theranda*, became the site of an important crossroads under Byzantium. Annexed to Serbia in the late 12C by Stefan Prvovenčani, from 1331 to 1335 it was a seat of the Nemanjić kings, the remains of whose formidable fortress, the Kaljaja, are clearly visible on the hill SW of the town. Prizren was taken by the Turks in 1455 and reconquered by to Serbia only in 1912.

There are several Turkish monuments in Prizren, notably the 15—16C *Bridge* over the Bistrica, the *Sinan Pašs džamija* (1615), and the 16C *Gazi-Mehmed Pašin Haman* (today an art gallery). Half way up the hill, near the fortress, it is the monastic church of *Sv. Spas* (the Saviour), a small edifice of stone and brick built in 1348 by Czar Dušan. There are also some ruins of a monastery of Michael the Archangel.

By far the most remarkable monument of the city is the church of *Sveta Bogorodica Ljeviška (Our Lady of Ljeviška, adm. summer 7–12 and 14–18; winter 10–12 and 14–16). One of the 42 foundations of King Milutin, it was begun in 1307 over a Byzantine basilica. It is made of alternating bands of brick and stone, with five cupolas, an exonarthex, and a belfry. Under Turkish rule it was transformed into a mosque and the frescoes were covered in plaster, which restorers have only recently finished removing. The paintings, which are among the finest of the 14C, represent, in the exonarthex, the Last Judgment; in the narthex, Nemanjić portraits; in the nave and aisles, more Nemanjić portraits and figures of saints; on the W wall, Dormition of the Virgin; in the cupola, Prophets and Christ Pantokrator; in the central apse, procession of saints and Communion of the Apostles, in the S apse, Virgin, and, on the left, Birth of Christ.

EXCURSIONS. To **Višegrad** (3km S), along the narrow valley of the Bistrica. On a promontory is the upper part of the 14C fortress of Višegrad, now ruined. The lower part of the fortress enclosed the Monastery of Sveti Arhandjela (Holy Archangels), founded by Czar Dušan in 1348 and intended as his burial place. The complex, destroyed by the Turks in the mid 15C, was only recently excavated. Visible today are the foundations and part of the cruciform church of the Archangels, of the oratory of St. Nicholas, and of the monastic buildings set up against the walls of the fortress. The arched bridge that crosses the river gives access, through a tower, to the monastic complex.

Leave Prizren from the E through the beautiful valleys of the Suva and Lepenac rivers, with the high peaks of the Šar Planina to the right, before joining Highway N2/E65 at (55km) *Doganović, whence to* **Skopje**, see Rte 26B.

33 Skopje to Salonika

ROAD, 244km, Highway N1/E75.—54km *Titov Veles.*—31km *Gradsko.*—77km *Gevgelija.*—5km *Bogorojca.*—77km **Salonika**.

RAILWAY, in c 5½ hours, with most trains continuing to Athens.

The main route S from Skopje follows the old caravan route to Greece, through the valley of the River Vardar. Road and railway run parallel for most of the way.

58km **Titov Veles** (156m, 36,000 inhab.), the Greek *Bylazora*, is an agricultural and industrial town rising in terraces on the hills on either side of the River Vardar. Once an important trading centre, it has some interesting Turkish houses and mosques.

N27 diverges E to **Štip** (41km), a Turkish town with remains of a Byzantine fortress and several medieval churches, the most remarkable of which is Sv. Arhandjel, of 1332. The former Pasha's House has been turned into a small museum. 32km further on, near the village of Zletovo, **Lesnovo Monastery** stands on a hill at an altitude of 1000m. It can be reached only by a hard climb (1½ hours), best accomplished with the guidance of a villager. The church, built in 1341 by the despot Oliver, is a beautiful Byzantine edifice with a narthex and two domes, brick-and-stone walls, and geometric inlays on the façade. Within are frescoes of 1349: in the narthex, portraits of Czar Stefan Dušan (stepson of the founder) and his wife, Oliver and his wife and sons, Constantine and Helena; animals, birds, fish, the Calendar, musical instruments; and a group of dancers. In the naos, Oliver holding a model of the church; the death of Sv. Gavrilo Lesnovski (who is buried here), the Life of Christ, and Miracles of St. Michael. The carved iconostasis is among the finest in Macedonia.

At 31km **Gradsko** a minor road diverges S for *Prilep* (54km) and *Bitola* (44km, Rte 34). A few metres further on, on the right, is the entrance to the excavations of ****Stobi**.

An ancient Macedonian town built at the confluence of the Crna Reka and the Vardar, in the first centuries of the Christian era Stobi became the capital of the Roman province of *Macedonia Secunda* and the seat of a bishopric. It flourished until the earthquake of 518, after which it fell into decline. Abandoned in the 14C, it was rediscovered in 1861. Excavations, begun in the 1920s, are still not complete, and work goes on intermittently. Today the walls, fortifications, and most of the area between the two main streets are visible.

The main secular buildings, all palaces, stand in the decumanus inferior. They include the House of Parthenius and House of Perister-ias, both with *piscinae*; and the House of Polyharmos, whose peristyle had colonnades around which elegant guest rooms were arranged. Here also are the town fountain and baths. At the end of the street stands the 2C Greek Theatre, later transformed into an amphitheatre.

Beyond this, near the main square, are remains of several early Christian buildings, namely a 5C cathedral (preserving some columns and mosaics), baptistery (also with mosaics), and bishop's palace. The street ends at a fortified gate in the town walls. Among the other ruins are two small churches and a large number of houses. The Museum, adjoining the entrance to the site, contains a modest but interesting collection of Greek and Roman objects, including small bronzes, pottery and coins, and a statue of a Roman emperor found in the Theatre.

The road continues across one of the hottest valleys in Macedonia, planted with opium poppies and sesame. The latter is used in making a local sweet, *tahan-halva*.

32km **Demir Kapija** stands on the site of the Illyrian *Stenae*; excavations have revealed some Greek and Roman tombs and parts of the Byzantine fortifications. The Demir Kapija Klisura, beyond, was inhabited in the Stone Age.

40km **Gevgelija** (52m, 8,000 inhab.) is located at the centre of a cotton-producing area. A road on the left diverges to (17km) *Novi Dojran*, a resort on the shores of Dojransko ezero (Lake Dojran), on the Greek border.

5km **Bogorojca** Greece is entered and the Vardar becomes the Axios. From here to (77km) **Salonika**, see *Blue Guide Greece*.

34 Skopje to Florina

ROAD, 339km. Highways N26/E65 and N27.—67km *Tetovo*.—136km *Struga*.—14km **Ohrid**.—87km **Bitola**.—16km Niki.—19km **Florina**.

The 'back road' into Greece provides one of the more scenic itineraries in Macedonia, winding through spectacular mountains, touching on two large and beautiful lakes (*Ohridsko ezero* and *Prespansko ezero*), and skirting three national parks (*Mavrovo*, *Galičica*, and *Pelister*). From Niki, the Greek border station, the road continues to (241km) Larissa.

Skopje, see Rte 26B. Follow PARTIZANSKA ULICA W to N26 on the left bank of the Vardar. To the S lie the monasteries of **Matka** and **Andrejaš**, Rte 26B. The road follows the River Fus almost to its source, then descends once more into the broad Vardar valley.

67km **Tetovo** (480m, 29,000 inhab.), formerly known as *Kalkandelen*, spreads over the fertile Pološko Polje, at the foot of the Šar-Planina range (2747m). It is crossed by a swift stream, the Pena. It retains the imprint of centuries of Turkish rule despite the best efforts of modern planners, who have rebuilt the city centre in concrete. Along the road to Ohrid are several of the principal monuments: the *Municipal Museum*, which occupies a former Dervish convent; the *Bridge* on the Vardar; and the famous *Šarena džamija, or Coloured Mosque, of 1495. The last is an unusual building with a tiled roof, no cupola, and a portico painted with floral designs. The walls of the exterior are covered with geometric patterns, and the interior has painted arabesques, views of Istanbul, fountains, gardens, and orchards—all very rare in mosques, where the decoration is generally severe and abstract.

25km **Gostivar** (530m, 14,000 inhab.), another Turkish town, preserves a clock tower and a handsome mosque. Beyond, the road climbs through chestnut and evergreen groves to Vlajnica Pass (1347m), where it enters *Mavrovo National Park, an immense and singularly beautiful forest preserve rising round Lake Mavrovo, 1200m. The inhabitants of the area still dress in colourful costumes. Leave the lake on the left to descend the splendid valley of the Mavrovska, where the trout virtually jump into one's lap. A few kilometres along, on the left, lies the monastery of *Sv. **Jovan Bigorski** (St. John the Baptist), founded in the 11C but rebuilt several times. The present church dates mostly from 18C. It has a beautiful iconostasis carved by the same artists who made the iconostasis in the church of Sv. Spas in Skopje; and fragments of 16C frescoes on the walls. The wooden conventual buildings are typical of 19C Macedonian architecture.

57km **Debar** (649m, 10,000 inhab.), reached by a turning on the right, lies on the Albanian border, which now runs just W of the highway. To the E extends the long, narrow *Ezero Globočica*, an artificial lake on the Crni Drim, which flows into Lake Ohrid. All round the countryside is deserted, except for an occasional peasant or shepherd in colourful Albanian costume.

54km **Struga** (696m, 13,000 inhab.) spreads out on both sides of the Crni Drim, on the N shore of Lake Ohrid. It has a number of fine beaches, and an International Poetry Festival in August. The *Gradski muzej* (Municipal Museum, 69 Ulica D. Durgon) is devoted to local fauna.

6km S of Struga lies the monastey of *Sv. Bogorodica*, now a hotel; here can be seen a small chapel carved in the rock, adorned with 14C frescoes.

The road loops round the N shore of Lake Ohrid. A turning left leads in 7km to the village of *Trebenište*, near which, in 1918, archaeologists discovered an Illyrian necropolis of the 6C BC. Also on the left hånd side of the road are the small monastery of *Sv. Erazmo*, with 14C frescoes; and, further on, remnants of an early Christian basilica also thought to have been dedicated to the missionary saint.

14km **OHRID** (698m, 30,000 inhab.) is the most beautiful city in Macedonia and one of the lovelier places in the Balkans. It lies on the W shore of the immense lake to which it lends its name. The splendour of its artistic treasures is equalled by the charm of its old houses, in stone, white plaster, and dark wood, with Turkish bay windows overlooking quiet, narrow streets.

Post Office: 6 Ulica Boris Kidrič.

Information: Turistiko Društvo Biljana, 2 Partizanska ulica, tel. 22494.

Airport: 10km out of town. *JAT*, 2 Partizanska ulica, tel. 22530.

History. The origin of Ohrid is unknown, although it is certain that its ancient predecessor, *Lychnidos*, was captured by Philip II of Macedonia in the 4C BC, and by the Romans in the 2C BC. The latter built here a splendid city on the *Via Aegnatia* (which ran from Brindisi to Byzantium); in the 4C it became the seat of a bishop. It repelled a siege of Theodoric in 479, but was captured by the Avars and later by the Slavs, only to be taken again by the Byzantines. In the 10C it witnessed a sort of artistic renaissance, under the patronage of the bishop saints Clement and Naum, and of the Bulgaro-Macedonian emperor Samuel (976–1014), who raised it to the status of Orthodox archbishopric. Ohrid was re-taken by the Bulgars in the 13C, by the Serbs in the 14C, and at the turn of the same century by the Turks, who held it until 1912.

Lake Ohrid (*Ohridisko ezero*) is the most beautiful mountain lake of the Balkans. Two-thirds of its area (350km^2) lies in Yugoslavia, the remaining third in Albania. Notwithstanding its altitude (698m) and depth (285m), the lake never freezes; the clïmate on its shores is mild year round. The water is extraordinarily clear, and the shore is lined with lovely shingle beaches. The lake is the home of numerous varieties of fish, including the pink 'salmon trout' (*salmo letnica*).

During the summer Ohrid hosts several cultural events: the *Balkan Folklore Festival* (July); the *Ohrid Summer* (theatre, ballet, music; July–August); and an *International Poetry Festival* (late August).

ULICA BORIS KIDRIČ, leading down to the lake, is flanked by the principal hotels, travel agencies, cafés, etc. It is paralleled by STARA ČARŠIJA ULICA, which divides the old town from the new, and contains the most characteristic old shops. The heart of the old town is reached by SAMUILOVA ULICA, flanked by some of the lovelier 18–19C houses. At the beginning of the street, on the right, is a bastion of the walls erected by the Bulgars in the 10C. Further on, a lane on the left leads to the church of *Sv. Nikola Bolnički* (St. Nicholas of the Hospital), an early 14C foundation with frescoes on the S wall (1334–45) representing Archbishop Nicholas, Czar Dušan. his wife Jelena, and their son Uroš. Within are some remains of 14C pictorial decorations, and, in the gallery, a collection of icons. Across the street is the small 14C church of *Sv. Bogorodica Bolnička* (Our Lady of the Hospital), with a splendid carved and gilt iconostasis by the Debar School artists, and coeval frescoes.

The **Muzej** (62 Samuilova ulica) occupies the *Dom Roveva*, one of the city's more beautiful 19C houses. It includes an ethnographical section (costumes and fishing equipment), an historical section (dealing mainly with the Turkish occupation and the War of Liberation), an archaeological section (with Illyrian, Roman and early Christian antiquities), and a superb collection of 9–14C *icons and Byzantine manuscripts. Across the street is the *Hslosba*, or gallery of modern art.

The ****Cathedral of Sv. Sofija** (adm. 8–14, closed Mon), in the centre of the old town, is a large, three-aisled basilica of brick and stone, erected in 1037–56 over an early Christian basilica (5C). In 1317 the church was given a splendid exonarthex, embellished by a double portico with mullioned windows on the upper level and a number of antique columns below. The interior of the church is adorned with splendid frescoes dating from the 11C to the 14C—strong, yet graceful paintings which foreshadow the works of the early Italian masters. Many of the scenes were lost when the church was transformed into a mosque, under Turkish rule. Of those which remain, the most remarkable are the Last Judgment in the narthex; the Dormition of the Virgin on the W wall of the naos; the story of Jacob's Ladder on the N wall in front of the apse; the Sacrifice of Abraham on the S wall, opposite; and the Virgin and Child and Ascension of Christ, surrounded by angels, in the apse. Here, in the floor, can be seen traces of the early Christian church; the Muslim minbar, or pulpit, has been left as a reminder of the four centuries in which the building was dedicated to Allah.

ULICA KOCO RACIN, on the left, leads up to the small church of *Sv. Jovan Kaneo* (adm. 9–12 and 15–17; closed Mon), in a magnificent position overlooking the lake from a rocky headland. Built in the late 13C in the customary layers of brick and stone, it follows a Greek Cross plan with a central cupola on an octagonal drum. Within are frescoes contemporary with the building, the best of which represent popes and apostles (in the apse) and Christ Pantokrator, angels, saints, and prophets (in the dome). From here a steep path climbs to the **Imaret džamija**, built over the ruined church of *Sv. Pantelejmon*, erected in 893 by St. Clement of Ohrid on the site of an early Christian edifice. Recent excavations have brought to light traces of the church and its fresco decoration, and the tomb of St. Clement (died 916). Nearby is the *Türbe of Sinan Gelebi* (died 1493); and in front of the Imaret are the remains of a large, 5C basilica with mosaic decorations.

Above the town rises the **Fortress**, in all likelihood built by the Byzantines and rebuilt in the late 10C by Czar Samuel. It is one of the larger fortifications in Macedonia, consisting of tall ramparts which run down the hill to the lake, enclosing the old town on the landward side. At the top is the *Gorni Saraj*, or citadel, reached by an imposing gate guarded by two colossal cylindrical towers. The *View extends over the town and the lake to the Albanian shore.

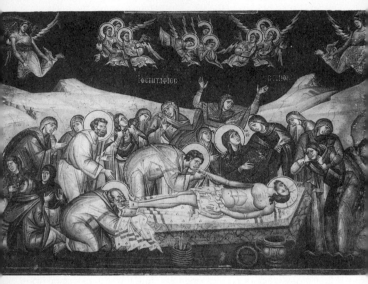

Ohrid, Sv. Kliment: detail of the thirteenth-century frescoes

On a small plateau between the town and the citadel stands the church of ***Sv. Kliment** (adm. 8–12 and 15–18, closed Mon), built in 1295. Originally dedicated to the Virgin, in the 14C, when Sv. Sofija was transformed into a mosque, it became the cathedral of Ohrid, taking the name of St. Clement, whose relics are still preserved here. It is a typically Byzantine church with a single nave and apse, a cupola over the crossing, and a narthex. On the exterior, the masonry forms highly ornamental geometric patterns. Within are frescoes executed in 1295 by the painters Mihajlo and Eutihije, who worked also at Staro Nagoričane and at Sv. Nikita. The paintings illustrate the life of the Virgin, the Old Testament, and the Passion. In the horseshoe-shaped exonarthex, a 19C addition to the church, is displayed a fine collection of icons dating from the 12–14C; those painted on both sides were carried in processions. The chapel of *Sv. Dimitri*, at the rear of the church, preserves some 14C frescoes.

Just behind Sv. Kliment stands the tiny church of *Sv. Konstantin i Jelena*, built in the 14C. The S wall of the building is frescoed with the portraits of the founder (a man named Partenios) and his family, identified by an Old Serbian inscription. Within are late 14C frescoes representing members of the royal family, and a large 15C composition showing the Militancy of Constantine. Not far from here are the church of *Stari Sv. Kliment* (Old St. Clement's); and, nearer the lake, the chapel of *Mali Sveti Vraci* (the Little Healer-Saints), both with 14C frescoes.

EXCURSIONS. To (30km) the **Monastery of Sv. Naum* (adm. 8–12 and 13–18), on the Albanian border. The road passes (14km) the picturesque fishing village of *Peštani*, although most visitors prefer to arrive by boat (departures daily, 90 minutes one way). The monastery, which lies at the S extreme of the lovely Galičica National Park, was established in the 9C by St. Naum. It lies behind a high wall, on a promontory above the lake. The spacious paddock is lined with rustic farm buildings with broad, wooden porches. At the centre stands the church, erected around 900 by the saint himself, who died ten years later and is buried within (his tomb is still much venerated by the peasants). In its present form it dates from the 14C and later. The small, dark interior has a gilt wood iconostasis of 1711, and some undistinguished 19C frescoes.—From here, by footpath or boat one may reach the *Monastery of Sv. Bogorodica Zahumska* (the Virgin of Zaum), on the E shore of the lake, another 14C foundation.

Ohrid, Sv. Naum

From Ohrid to Bitola, Highway 26 winds through more mountainous terrain. The driving is tiring, but the scenery alone makes the trip worthwhile. At (37km) *Resen* a secondary road diverges S to Otesevo, a resort on Lake Prespa.

Prespansko ezero, as it is known in Macedonian, extends over an area of 285km at the point where the Yugoslav, Albanian, and Greek borders meet. It is a wild, lonely place girt by dark forests and lofty peaks. The fishing is reputedly excellent. On the E shore, at Kirbi-novo, a dirt track climbs to the church of **Sv. Djordje* a single-aisled building containing an important group of frescoes (1191) repre-senting the Ascension of Christ, Annunciation, and Virgin and Child with angels in the apse; Feasts of the Church, life of Christ, and life of the Virgin; (on the left St. George, on the right Christ) in the nave; and the Dormition of the Virgin, over the entrance on the W wall. From the steps of the church there is a fine *View over the lake.

36km **Bitola** (618m, 66,000 inhab.), the second-largest city of Macedonia, lies on the plain in ancient times known as *Pelagonia*, at the foot of Mt Pelister (2601m).

History. Bitola is the successor of the ancient *Heraclea Lyncestis*, founded by the Macedonians in the 4C BC. The latter was conquered by Rome, Byzantium, and, in the 8C, by the Bulgars; later it was taken by Czar Dušan and (in 1382) by the Turks, who called it *Monastir*, after the nearby monastery of Bukova. During the 19C and the early 20C it was one of the more important cities of the Balkans. The school established here by Prince Piristi was famous throughout the peninsula, and the Military Academy was the most important of the whole Ottoman Empire˙ (its most distinguished alumnus being Mustafa Kemal, the future Atatürk, father of modern Turkey). The city was taken by the Serbs in 1913, occupied by the Bulgarians during the First World War, and retaken by a Franco-Serbian force in 1918 following a long and bloody battle.

The principal monuments of the city are all located in or around the central MESTNI TRG. They are: the *Hajdar Kaddi džamija*, the *Jeni džamija*, and the *Isak džamija*, all dating from the 16C; the *Bezistan* (Covered Market, 17C); the Sahat Kula (Clock Tower); and the 14C church of *Sv. Dimitrija*, one of the larger ecclesiastical buildings in Yugoslavia, containing a fine old iconostasis and numerous icons.

Nearby, in TITOVA ULICA, is the *Arheološki muzej (Archaeological Museum), almost entirely devoted to finds from Heraclea Lyncestis, with the notable exception of a *house-shaped Neolithic burial urn (2000–1000 BC) and some Bronze Age implements.

At Bitola Highway 26 turns S. 3km out of town along this road lie the ruins of **Heraclea Lyncestis, an ancient Macedonian city founded in the 4C BC by Philip II, father of Alexander the Great. In the Roman age it was an important military base along the Via Aegnatia, linking Brindisi with Byzantium. The seat of a bishop in the 4C, it was destroyed by the Slavs in the 6C. The excavations, begun in 1935, are still under way. They have been brought to light sections of the defensive walls, *Baths*, the portico of the *Forum* (with a number of columns, altars, and statues); a small 5C *Basilica* with a fine mosaic floor depicting plants and animals; another, larger *Basilica* (also of the 5C) with more mosaics; a *Bishop's Palace* with mosaic floors; and, up against the hillside, a *Theatre*. At the highest point of the town lies the *Acropolis* (with remains of a Byzantine fortress); at the entrance to the site is a small collection of recent finds.

13km **Medvitlija** is the last town in Yugoslavia; Greece is entered immediately afterwards at **Niki**, whence to (19km) **Florina**, see *Blue Guide Greece.*

INDEX OF ARTISTS, ARCHITECTS AND CRAFTSMEN

A= Architect
P = Painter
S = Sculptor

INDEX OF ARTISTS

TOPOGRAPHICAL INDEX

NOTES